Encyclopedia of
International Games

Encyclopedia of International Games

DANIEL BELL

McFarland & Company, Inc., Publishers
Jefferson, North Carolina, and London

LIBRARY OF CONGRESS CATALOGUING-IN-PUBLICATION DATA

Bell, Daniel, 1965–
Encyclopedia of international games / Daniel Bell.
p.   cm.
Includes bibliographical references and index.

ISBN 0-7864-1026-4 (illustrated case binding : 50# alkaline paper)

1. Sports—Competitions—Encyclopedias.   2. Sports—
International cooperation—Encyclopedias.   I. Title.
GV721 .B45 2003   796'.03—dc21   2002013826

British Library cataloguing data are available

Cover image ©2003 Digital Vision

Manufactured in the United States of America

*McFarland & Company, Inc., Publishers
Box 611, Jefferson, North Carolina 28640
www.mcfarlandpub.com*

To Mike Johnson: one word can make all the difference

Acknowledgments

A tremendous number of individuals from all over the world have contributed to the compilation of this work, and deserve special recognition and thanks.

Wayne Wilson, Shirley Ito, Bonita Carter and Michael Salmon of the AAF library in Los Angeles have been helpful librarians, researchers and colleagues, and continue to build an extraordinary collection of materials related to sport.

Dave Kelly of the Library of Congress gave a great deal of support, encouragement and assistance in accessing useful materials in Washington, D.C.

Spencer Johnston of the King County Library system also provided much assistance.

Simon Mandl of the Olympic Museum in Lausanne was very helpful in answering early enquiries of the IOC.

I have relied on the work of several researchers and writers, foremost among them David Wallechinsky, Bill Mallon and Wolf Lyberg, who have all done an enormous amount of work in the area of the history of the Olympic Games and other regional games.

Others include Kathryn Therese Dillon for her early work on the South Pacific Games; George Eisen, for his Maccabiah Games study; Lazlo Kutassi, for World University Games research; Cleve Dheenshaw for writing about the Commonwealth Games; Arnd Krüger and James Riordan, experts in the area of worker sport; Joan Scruton, a contemporary of Ludwig Guttman, and historian of the Stoke Mandeville Games and Paralympic Games; Geoffrey Corlett, who has documented the Island Games; Lewis Portelli, historian of the Games of the Small Countries of Europe; and Gary Allison of the 1st Century Project.

All of those mentioned above deserve thanks for preserving the histories of the respective games that they were involved in organizing or studying.

Maire Kennedy of the Dublin Library helped with Tailteann Games materials. Rony Dror was a great help with statistics for regional Maccabi Games.

Several more individuals have offered much support and encouragement along the way. Jeff Grove, Kim Chen, Doug Welch, Catherine Ward, Mike Daly, Atle Naesheim, Wendell Gee, Chris Villani, Mark Hale, Mike Scott, Paul Kiere, Elizabeth O'Halloran, Willie Foster, Scott Somohano, Bruce Tenen, Mark Colborn, Kay Lund, Pierre Millett, Trukie Albarda, Sid Marantz, Bernard Linley, Rob Staakman, George Rugg and Jim Auld.

Finally, I would like to thank one person, Christina Hennessey, without whose help the project would never have been completed. Thanks for checking every line of the manuscript, crafting an index, spurring on more detailed research and encouraging me to continue the project to the very end.

Table of Contents

Preface

This book focuses on international multisport competitions held since 1896 that are based on the model of the modern Olympic Games. "International multisport competitions" are defined as competitions between two or more nations competing in two or more sports in the same location at the same time. The idea of a "games" in this sense is familiar to most. The teams or individuals are usually representatives of national entities but may be regional, local or have some other affiliation such as a school, hospital or police department. The requirement for the purposes of this book is that athletes from different nations come together, not that they be affiliated with national teams.

National games are held in a large number of countries throughout the world, and from time to time some have invited international participants. In most cases, these games have been ignored for the purposes of this book. Organizers of international games find it necessary to hold test events and "pre-games" festivals in order to test their systems for the real events. While these events can be interesting, they are not standardized and I have not attempted to document them in this work.

Tracking the History of International Games

When the decision was made to try to find details of the various international games it was expected that a simple letter to each organizing body would produce the desired information, such as the dates of each games, number of participants, nations, and sports at each games. However, this proved to be very far from the truth. It seems the majority of the games have not kept their own official records of these figures. The next attempt was to write to the various national Olympic committees around the world. This strategy met with mixed success.

In most cases, the games move from city to city and their transient nature contributes to the problem of collecting the history of each games. Generally, there is no central location where data on any particular games is kept. Information produced by one organizing body in one city is rarely sent to the next city or to a central depository, and it was surprisingly difficult to obtain information directly from most of the various umbrella organizations (Commonwealth Games Federation, Pan-American Sports Organization and a host of others) that oversee the games. However, even in the few instances where a games was held in the same location, this does not seem to have made it any easier to track this data.[1]

In every case, the attempt has been made to acquire the "official" figures directly from the custodians or organizers of each games, and priority was given to this information unless it was later proven to be incorrect by other irrefutable sources. When the official governing bodies were unable to provide this information, data was collected from books, magazine articles, the SPORTDISCUS database, newspaper sources, and direct correspondence with hundreds of individuals across the globe. When the project began, the World Wide Web was still in the future. Now it is entrenched as one of our modern communications tools. Information from any of the sources on the Internet was welcomed and in many cases invaluable, while at the same time always subjected to confirmation and verification by other sources. In many cases, the internet provided and continues to provide information where other avenues of inquiry have been silent. Electronic mail offered the opportunity to make quick contact with a large number of sources that would have never been available using conventional communications and research methods.

Attempts to verify data by confirming numbers and dates with other sources many times led, on many occasions, to further confusion, rather than clarification. However, the sources are cited and major discrepancies are noted, when it was difficult to determine what the best figures might be.

Each element of data, the dates, number of participants, nations, and sports, presents its own peculiar difficulties.

Finding the exact dates of the games is important simply because this enables further research. Exact dates became problematic in cases where preliminary sports events actually took place before the opening ceremony, which occurred often. Some sources cite the dates of the opening ceremony; others, the dates of the first event. When available, information on events occurring before the official opening of a games is presented in the data. However, without having complete schedule information for all the games included in this book, the claim can not be made that this issue has been accounted for in every instance. In general, though, the difference in dates is one or two days, and is acceptable for a researcher who wishes to look up the details of any given games in a microfilmed newspaper source.

The participant data, besides one way of indicating how large an event might be, became interesting from the standpoint of the great number of claims that a given games was the "second largest games in the world next to the Olympic Games." Almost every large games—the Pan-American Games, Asian Games, World University Games, Special Olympics and several others—has attempted to make this claim. It turns out that the Olympic Games are not the largest games in terms of number of athletes, an "honor" given the World Masters Games.

Official numbers from the sanctioning bodies were preferred. Numbers from the host city organizing bodies were treated with skepticism, as in many cases the organizing bodies greatly inflate the numbers of participants in an attempt to have the "largest games ever." The more specific numbers were preferred over rounded numbers, and when in doubt, lower, less inflated numbers took precedence.

The second issue related to participation figures is the ratio between male and female participants in a given games. This information is also difficult to track down because the organizers of the various games have not been in the habit of collecting this data at the time it is produced. The issue of male-to-female participation has gained more attention in the last decade, especially since the founding of Atlanta PLUS, an organization dedicated to equal participation for women in the Olympic Games. With this in mind, the attempt was made to capture as much data as possible regarding the male-female ratio, both of the number of participants and the differing numbers of sports for men and women, but in most cases this data is not readily available.

There is an interesting definition in some circles as to the definition of a "participant" in these games. The definition intended in this work is, "athletes that took part in the sporting events in the games." However, more often than not figures are published that include the managers, coaches and attachés that accompany any team to a games. The attempt has been made to use only figures of athletes, but the data are not perfect in this regard. Some games, such as the Socialist Olympics of the 1920s and 1930s, claim as many as 80,000 to 100,000 participants because the games were based on mass gymnastics displays, or mass walking events through cities, as opposed to "competitors" competing in the modern sense.

On the other hand, the definition of participant is sometimes more rigorously applied. While struggling with the difficulty of finding participation figures for each games, I came across an article by Wolf Lyberg in the *Journal of Olympic History* regarding the participation figures for the 1998 Nagano Olympic Winter Games.[2] Mr. Lyberg has an established reputation for providing the IOC with these official participant figures, yet I was surprised to read the following quote: "It is funny that in these technological days, organizers have not yet come up with a program that assures the IOC that only starting[3] athletes have been counted. It is more important that the IOC only pays the sum of 1,200 dollars for each starting athlete. And some of the International Federations—ice hockey as an example—count a player sitting on the bench as a reserve, but not playing, as a starter!" Lyberg goes on to say that he knew his preliminary figure of 2,185 athletes at Nagano was too high because "I had not yet received detailed match reports of the ice hockey games and I was sure that many of the three goaltenders per team never started."

This level of specificity is not always applied to the definition of a participant. It seems as if an athlete could travel all the way to Nagano, eat and sleep in the village, march in the opening ceremonies, mingle with athletes from all over the world, practice with his or her team, dress in the locker room for each game, participate in pregame warm-ups, even stand on the medals stand and receive a medal if the team happened to win, and yet not be counted as an official participant! (The accountants have a different definition.) The intent of de Coubertin's revival was for athletes to take part, not solely in athletic pursuits, but in the complete Olympic experience.

In his book *Fabulous 100 years of the IOC: Facts—figures—and much, much more*, Lyberg devotes ten pages to a quick compilation of some regional games under IOC patronage. He writes, "It has not been easy to 'pick up' the figures which are in compilations, [and] despite almost heroic attempts, I have not managed to dig out all the facts." I agree wholeheartedly. In some cases it borders on nightmarish. (See Appendix 8 for an example.) Simply put, the more "official" sources one seemed to consult, the more disparate answers one was certain to find. The responsibility (not an easy one) is for the games federations themselves to compile accurate and official statistical records.[4]

The Tehran 1974 Asian Games are a random example that happens to be at hand as I write this:

• Information requested directly from the Olympic Council of Asia[5] (presumably the most authoritative source) provided dates, number of nations and number of sports (Tehran, 1974, 25 nations, 16 sports) but no data on male, female or total number of participants.

• Lyberg says the 1974 games had 20 nations and 3010 participants (in this case, he did not give figures for male and female competitors).

• The *Asian Games, Olympic Games, Commonwealth Games Book of Records*, contains a mislabeled matrix (to make matters worse), with sports running top to bottom along the left column, the names of nations running left to right across the top row. However, there are 25 columns for the nations and only 18 are named. According to this source, 2869 athletes participated.

• The book *Asian Games 82, sportsmen souvenir* recounts the history of the games up to 1978 and lists 16 sports and says 19 countries and 2869 athletes participated.

• The history provided on the official Website of the 1998 Asian Games held in Bangkok, Thailand (*www.asiangames.th*), concurs with Lyberg on the number of participants and sports for the 1974 games—3010 athletes and 16 sports—but not the number of countries: 25 to Lyberg's 20.

• For good measure, the brief *Olympic Review* report on the games (Nov.–Dec. 1974, No. 85–86) says "nearly 3000 participants from 25 countries took part in the games."

• Finally, the *Official Report of the 1974 Asian Games* (the source which I unfortunately happened to come upon last) lists 1893 male participants and 432 female participants for a total of 2,325 athletes. However, the report seems to studiously avoid making any mention of the number of nations invited to, entered in, or having participated in the games, other than listing the 26 member nations of the Asian Games Federation.

Determining the number of sports that were held in each games also presented some problems and challenges. Sources presented varying figures and it became a judgment call to choose which figure would be the most accurate. In a few instances, sports that were to be included in pregames information were canceled for various reasons, many times on the eve of the competition. For this reason, some sources will vary in their presentation of the number of sports for a given games. Again, official sources took precedent. At the same time, there were occasions where a sport would be cited as being composed of a certain number of events, and newspaper sources would include data on more than that number of events.

The issue became slightly more clear when I ran across this item in information from the United States Olympic Committee regarding the number of events in each Pan-American Games. "The International Olympic Committee counts the artistic and rhythmic disciplines in gymnastics as one sport (gymnastics); the three disciplines of artistic, hockey and speed roller skating as one sport (roller skating); the aquatic disciplines of diving, swimming, synchronized swimming and water polo as one sport (swimming); and the free-style and Greco-Roman wrestling disciplines as one sport (wrestling). Therefore, the number of sports in each Pan American Games may vary in other reference materials if individual disciplines are counted as sports."[6] For winter games in some tallies, particularly the Olympic Winter Games, Nordic skiing also encompasses ski jumping and the lists reflect this. In other lists and other games, ski jumping has sometimes been considered a separate sport.

The presentation of medals tables in various sources introduced another difficulty. It seems the host country gets to choose the format of the table which would serve to present its performance in the best light. Two methods are used—ranking the nations by most gold medals or by total medals. This can create some interesting juxtapositions. The *Washington Post*, July 4, 1965, listed the top two medal winning nations of the Tenth World Games for the Deaf (held in Washington D.C.) like this:

Nation	Gold	Silver	Bronze	Total
United States	9	21	23	53
Russia	29	15	9	53

The competing nations, whether the games are worldwide or regional, have always had a fascination with medal standings. Regional games can become especially competitive, if not among the athletes, among the journalists for superiority atop the medal standings. Governments tend to use the tables (if they show the country in a positive light) for propaganda purposes. While the medal tables may be informative to look at, it is not certain that they contain any relevance other than perhaps that a certain society, or a segment within that society at a certain time, valued athletic performance above other endeavors.

The 1998 Can-Am Police Fire Games medals table reflects the fact that the number of entries is unlimited and host Canada had the most entrants. The huge number of medals won is a function of two things. First, the competition is broken into age groups, so there are far more medals to hand out than in a true national team event. Second, the various firefighter and police games have traditionally had the greatest number of events, tending to mix their specific fire- and police-related events, and a few more sedentary pursuits such as bridge or darts, with the traditional sports program.

Nation	Gold	Silver	Bronze	Total
Canada	349	288	200	837
United States	133	61	55	249
Puerto Rico	34	14	10	58
Russia	23	6	2	31

Goodwill Games medals tables are skewed for the same reason. The United States and Soviet Union/Russia have always been guaranteed more entrants into the events than the other countries, so the opportunities for medals are greater.

Furthermore, some medals tables, after much research, have been revised. The 1900 through 1908 medal tables from the early Olympic Games have been updated in sources by Mallon and Wallechinsky to reflect the detailed historical work that has been completed in the last several years for those games.[7]

For example, for the 1900 Paris Olympic Games, Wallechinsky's original *Complete Book of the Olympics* lists France as winning 29 gold, 41 silver and 32 bronze medals. In the 1996 edition, this had been revised to 26 gold, 39 silver and 30 bronze medals. By the 2000 edition, the latest research indicated that France had won 18 gold, 27 silver and 21 bronze medals in Paris.

Each medals table needs to be interpreted in light of these factors: whether entries are limited per nation, and who the host nation is.

Many games give awards but do not explicitly keep medals tables. The World Peace Games, the Socialist Olympics, the various scholar-athlete games, the family of corporate games, the Special Olympics and the World Medical Games are some of the games that have decided that medals tables do not fit into the philosophies of participation in their games.

For trivia's sake, this book contains 343 full or partial medals tables (for about 28 percent of the 1220 games included in it) accounting for over 140,000 gold, silver and bronze medals.

Conclusion

This project began out of the attempt to satisfy my curiosity on a few questions regarding the history of a few well-known international competitions. The curiosity grew into the project you see here.

I had the opportunity to compete at the 1987 World University Games in Zagreb, Yugoslavia. While there, the organizers presented the participants with information on the history of those games, and I was surprised to learn these games had been in existence for over 60 years. This piqued my interest, especially when I realized that I did not know when the other international multisport competitions I knew about—the Commonwealth Games, Pan-American Games and Asian Games—had begun. While finding out the answers to these questions, and perusing *Olympic Review*, I came across the mentions of a few other long-established international multisport competitions, such as the South East Asian Games and the Central American and Caribbean Games, and became curious about their histories as well.

In trying to find written information on the histories of these games, I soon discovered that, though the Olympic Games have an almost unending supply of books to refer to, these other games have rarely been covered. This has changed slightly in the last ten years, but in general the number of books covering the regional games, whatever their format, is very limited.

While not intending to set out and write a book, I realized that the information I had gathered might help to fill this vacuum of information if it were to be published.

My hope is that other scholars, researchers, and trained historians will follow up on the information presented here on the phenomenon of the growth of these Olympic-based games, and add some depth to the broad base of information. My sincere appreciation to those scholars who have already in some cases written in depth about these games.

Ongoing Research

Throughout the research for this project, I came across sketchy and perhaps spurious references to over 100 other types of games. In some cases, these turned out to be the same games already covered in this book, being called by different names in different regions or languages. In other cases, I confirmed that these are not sports games—the 1995 World Mining and Energy Games in Australia, for instance, were devoted to events related to the performance of occupational tasks in the mining and drilling professions.

There are several curious references still to explore. For instance, the Korean NOC website in 1998 mentions the sixth China-Japan-Korea Junior Games. The Journalists World Games—begun in 1982—are said to have been held 18 times up to 2001, and I have solid references on the Arab School Games in 1973 and 1998 but no information on other editions of these games. Further research will be reported on the website of the International Games Archive at *www.internationalgames.net*.

Introduction

The Olympic Games are the most well known of the various sports festivals of the ancient world, just as the revived Olympic Games are recognized as the most important international multisport festival of modern times. Nonetheless, during the period of the ancient Olympic Games, 776 B.C. to A.D. 393, there were hundreds of other games held throughout the Greek and Roman world.

H.A. Harris, in his book *Greek Athletes and Athletics*, lists 126 cities of the ancient Greek world that held athletic festivals on an annual, biennial or quadrennial schedule. Some cities held many different festivals during a four-year cycle. Sparta held a total of 12 different games; Athens and Ephesus eight each; Alexandria seven, and Rhodes five. Harris notes that many major cities of the Greek world do not appear on his list, but had stadiums and most likely held games.[8]

Certain games were held in high esteem. The Pythian Games at Delphi, Isthmian Games at Corinth, and Nemean Games at Nemea were three well-known ancient games that together with the Olympic Games were known as the Panhellenic festivals and made a circuit where elite athletes of the day competed. The Olympic and Pythian Games were quadrennial festivals, with the Pythian games held in the intervening even years between the Olympic Games, much like the Olympic and Commonwealth Games alternate today. The Isthmian and Nemean games were both held every second year, with the Isthmian Games taking place in the same years as the Olympic and Pythian Games, and the Nemean Games being held in the odd years between. The Olympic Games had been in existence almost 200 years, beginning in 776 B.C., before the founding of the Pythian and the Isthmian Games, both in 582 B.C., and Nemean Games in 573 B.C.[9]

Ancient games spread as far as Ireland. The Tailteann Games in Ireland predate the ancient Olympic Games, having been held annually from 632 B.C. to A.D. 1169, and, some have argued, may have actually been the inspiration for the Greek Olympic Games.

At the turn of the millennium, there are certain parallels. The Olympic Games are regarded as the pinnacle of international athletic achievement, with dozens of other games either as stepping stones to the Olympics or modeled after them in four year periods. The data in this book includes 1220 instances of over 200 types of games held from 1896 until the end of 2000.[10]

This does not include the many hundreds of national, state, provincial and local games held across the globe each year. Dozens of countries hold, or have held, national games, occasionally inviting participants from neighboring countries. Almost every state in the United States and every province in Canada holds both summer and winter games. Local versions of "Olympic games" are probably too numerous to catalog, and many nations hold national games for disabled, very young, or elderly athletes.

One major difference between ancient and modern games is that in ancient times, games would be based in one city. It was the city that organized the games, in the same stadium, usually at the same time of the year, year after year. The games did not move around, usually because they were associated with religious festivals connected to the city itself. Our modern games, with a few exceptions, move from place to place, making it difficult to track their historic record. One could argue the games are less well known because they move around, only reaching the awareness of certain people in proximity to where the games are held on each occasion. Conversely, the argument could be made that games that stay in one location might be known only in the city where they are held.

Boycotts and violence at the games also have their precedents. Golden, in *Sport and Society in Ancient Greece*, mentions an incident when the Athenian Callipus was caught cheating at the Olympic games by bribing his fellow athletes. The Athenians sent Hyperides, the orator, to argue that Callipus should not have to pay the fine that was imposed as a penalty. Hyperides was turned down and the Athenians decided to boycott the games until it is said, "Apollo, a dutiful son of Zeus, declared that he would not deliver any oracle to them while the debt was outstanding."[11] Golden also mentions the Olympic truce, or ekecheira, which was intended to allow safe passage to Olympia, as opposed to a peace, or eineme, when all wars ceased. This truce was violated in 365 B.C. when the Arcadians invaded Olympia and the sacred temples while the games were going on.[12]

Precursors to the Modern Games

This book focuses on the international multisport competitions held since 1896 that are based on the model of the modern Olympic Games. There were many precursors to the first modern Olympic Games, just as there were mentions of funeral games and athletic events prior to the recording of the first Olympic champion in 776 B.C.

The revival of the Olympic Games was not an original idea by Pierre de Coubertin, the French baron credited with bringing the games back into existence. The idea had been germinating for years, and in some cases, "Olympic Games," mostly local or national in scope, had been in existence in the centuries prior to what is now considered the first modern Olympic Games in Athens in 1896.

Robert Dover's Cotswold Olympicks[13] were begun in 1612 as an annual event held on the Thursday and Friday of Whit Week. The games—which included such events as running, jumping, throwing the javelin, wrestling, horse races, singing, dancing and music—continued on an annual basis for over 239 years, being interrupted only by the English Civil War. They ended in 1852 when it was determined that the events brought crowds that were too large and rowdy into the area.[14]

During the later period of the Cotswold Olympicks, other competitions began to appear. In 1832, Baron de Berenger hosted an Olympic Festival at his Chelsea Stadium in England. In 1838, the baron expanded the idea into the first "Olympic Week," with archery, cricket, rifle shooting, pistol shooting, gymnastics, sailing, rowing, fencing, and, surely a crowd favorite, carousel riding.[15]

Ake Svahn[16] mentions "Olympic Games" competitions in Sweden, near Ramlösa (Helsingborg), held in 1834 and 1836, which included running, gymnastics, wrestling, and pole climbing. The area in Helsingborg still retains place names such as "Race Street," "Fencing Master Street" and "Olympiad Quarter." The competitions were said to have drawn thousands of spectators, while the number of athletes was around 40.

The Much Wenlock Games were a well-known local competition in England begun by William Brookes in 1850 which lasted until 1895. Anthony writes that the most important visitor to see Brookes at the Much Wenlock Games was Pierre de Coubertin.[17]

Rühl and Keuser mention the Shropshire Olympics held in 1860, 1861, 1862 and 1864; the English National Olympic Games held irregularly on six occasions from 1866 until 1883; the Drehberg Olympics held in Germany between 1776 and 1799; and the Palic Olympics in Yugoslavia between 1880 and 1914.

Liverpool, England, hosted its version of an "Olympic Games" in 1862, 1863, 1864 and 1867, with games in 1866 held in Northern Wales. The games were cancelled in 1865 when the Mount Vernon Parade Ground used for the games was sold in parcels. When the Parade Ground closed down, the games were moved to the Zoological Gardens, which at the time, had a seedy reputation. The newspapers reported that the spectators were of high class and refused to go to the Zoological Gardens because of its reputation, and the games did not survive.[18,19]

In France, games, races and contests, which included chariot racing, were held in 1796 at the Festival of the Foundation of the Republic.[20] The "Rondeau Olympic Games" were begun at Rondeau seminary in 1832 and held each leap year on February 29th. The original idea had been instituted when the instructors at the seminary had not prepared lessons for that day in 1832.[21]

In Greece, the Pan-Athenaic Games, or "Zappas Olympics," were held as Greek National Games with mild success in 1859, 1870, 1875 and 1888.

Revival of the Modern Olympic Games

It was against this backdrop that the French Baron Pierre de Coubertin slowly developed his ideas for reviving the Olympic Games. Born on January 1, 1863, de Coubertin had as a young boy witnessed the embarrassing defeat of the French army in the Franco-Prussian war of 1870–71. Through his studies, de Coubertin came to believe that the gymnastics societies of Germany had much to do with the physical fitness of the German people and had made it possible for them to win the war. At the same time, de Coubertin developed an appreciation for the English system of integrating sports and competition into the educational system to help develop bodies as well as minds.

As a wealthy baron, de Coubertin could travel extensively, and he used his trips to the United States, England and Greece to further his knowledge about sporting activities and how they might be used in education and to bring nations together in peace. With the excavation of the ancient Greek site of Olympia, new knowledge came to light about the games of the past which piqued de Coubertin's interest in the Olympic Games. De Coubertin founded the Union des Sports Athlétiques in November 1887 and began to promote athletic exchanges between England and France. He wrote hundreds of articles to promote his budding ideas of international sport. Finally, in June of 1894, he gathered together delegates from 12 nations at the Sorbonne in Paris, ostensibly to discuss issues of professionalism and amateurism in international sports. De Coubertin's real reason for the gathering, however, was to revive the Olympic Games and to establish the International Olympic Committee to accomplish this task. He succeeded, and though he had originally intended the first games to be held in Paris in 1900, it was agreed that Athens should hold the first games in 1896.

The original Olympic Committee consisted of de Coubertin, Dimetrios Vikelas from Greece, Viktor Balck of Sweden, Charles Herbert of England and William Sloan of the United States. It was decided that the presidency of the committee should rotate every four years, and that the games would be held in the country of the current president. The rotation was established as Vikelas, de Coubertin, Sloane, Herbert and Balck, with Vikelas being the first president. The games were held as planned on that rotation, in Athens, Paris, St. Louis, London and Stockholm, but when de Coubertin became IOC president he stayed in that role for the next 30 years.

These events, and the development of the modern Olympic movement, have been written about in great detail, at the expense of all the other games that have been established in the wake of the Olympic revival. This encyclopedia is intended to focus on those other games, and bring to light the histories of the games that, though inspired by the Olympic Games, have always lived in their shadow.

The modern Olympic Games took root slowly and at first did not directly inspire a large number of similar competitions. The year 1900 saw the establishment of the Nordic Games in Stockholm, with IOC member Victor Balck as one of its heads. The games were mostly national in scope but had elite international participation on each occasion.

A decade later, the Academic Olympia were begun in Germany and held between 1911 and 1913 in Germany and Poland. Nineteen eleven also saw athletic events at the Festival of the Empire in London, an early precursor to the Commonwealth Games.

In 1913, the first international games in Asia were established with the Far Eastern Championships (renamed as Far East Championships—a competition held between the Philippines, China and Japan—which lasted until 1934.

With the exception of the Far East Championships, World War I put an end to most international games activity, but games were resumed almost immediately after the end of the war with the well-known Inter-Allied Games held in the brand new Pershing Stadium in Paris.

The decade of the 1920s saw the establishment of some games that would be short-lived and a number that would continue until the present time. In the former category are the International Women's Games (Jeux Olympiques Feminins), first held in 1922 in Paris, the Tailteann Games in Ireland, and the Socialist "workers games," sponsored by both the Red Sport International (which held its first games in Prague in 1921) and the Socialist Worker Sports International (whose first Socialist Olympics games were in Frankfurt in 1925).

Among the games that have continued to this day, the first World Student Games (renamed as World University Games) were held in 1923, the World Games for the Deaf began in Paris in 1924, and the Hapoel Games started in Tel Aviv in 1928.

Up to this time, no regional games had been sponsored by the International Olympic Committee. De Coubertin did try for several years in the late 1920s to establish games in Africa, for Africans, and games were almost ready to begin in Alexandria, Egypt, in 1929 when the colonial powers decided against the idea. However, the IOC was able to help establish games in Central America in 1926. First known as the Central American Games and later the Central American and Caribbean Games, they proudly call themselves "los juegos regionales más antiguos," the oldest regional games.

Though the Great Depression and rumblings of war slowed the development of international sporting events, the 1930s saw the establishment of three competitions that continue to this day: the British Empire Games (now called the Commonwealth Games) for nations of the British Commonwealth, the Maccabiah Games for Jewish athletes, and the Bolivarian Games for the nations in South America which owe their independence from Spain to Simón Bolívar.

During World War II no one was interested in organizing games between nations, but at the conclusion of the war, activities slowly resumed.

Perhaps the most significant games were those established in 1948 in England by Dr. Ludwig Guttman, known as the Stoke Mandeville Wheelchair Games. These first-ever games for disabled athletes would develop into the event we now know as the Paralympic Games. The First Communist World Youth Festival was held in 1947, and FISEC (Fédération Internationale Sportive de l'Enseignement Catholique) established games for Catholic boys in 1948 (and for girls in 1959). FISU, the Fédération International du Sport Universitaire, was established to once again organize games for university students.

The year 1951 was very significant in the growth of international games, with the establishment of the Asian Games, Mediterranean Games and Pan-American Games. The International Olympic Committee showed a commitment to grow by helping to establish regional games for its members. In 1951, the committee proposed several rules for regional games which were eventually ratified in July 1952 at Helsinki. The rules were established so that regional games could "enjoy the sanction, patronage, and support of the International Olympic Committee," and "be permitted to display the Olympic Flag." Regional games organizers had to meet the following (abbreviated) requirements.[22,23]

1. Games must be restricted to amateurs and must not last more than 15 days.

2. Participating countries must have recognized National Olympic Committees, and participants must be a part of national sport federations, which in turn must be part of the International Federations.

3. The games should be confined to athletic sports. No political events must be connected with the games. Specifically, the loudspeaker must be used for sport purposes only and no political speeches were to be permitted.

4. Games must not be held within 12 months before or after an Olympic Games and must not be held more than once every four years in the same region.

5. The ceremonies must not be identical to the Olympic Games.

6. International Federations were in control of the sport arrangements.

7. There must be an international court of appeal.

8. Rules and regulations must be submitted to the IOC for approval.

9. Provision must be made for a representative of the IOC to be present at each set of games.

10. The words "Olympic" and "Olympiad," the five rings, and the Olympic motto, "Citius, Altius, Fortius" must not be used in any manner in connection with regional games. There must be no torch relay, and the Olympic flag could be displayed in only one place in the main stadium.

11. The organizations and facilities should be complete and ready at least a year before the games.

12. Countries eligible to participate in regional games could form themselves into regional sports federations.

Over time, of course, almost every one of these proposals has been overlooked.

New games continued to develop. The Arab Games followed closely behind in 1953. At the end of the decade, the South East Asian Games were established in 1959, and the same year, the Friendship Games in Bangui in Africa were a precursor to the establishment of games for the continent of Africa.

French sports writer Gaston Meyer wrote just after the 1958 Asian Games that the regional games would "sooner or later" serve as elimination events for the Olympic Games. He wrote, "They ought to be considered as such and this should be borne in mind thus facilitating the organization of future Olympics." Today, this does happen in some cases, primarily in team sports where berths to the Olympic Games are earned by winning regional games. It does not occur to perhaps the same extent that Meyer envisioned.[24]

Shortly thereafter, an editorial in the French sports journal *L'Equipe* bemoaned the "Multiplicity of Games" that were being held around the world. Ten was the greatest number held in one year to that point in time. *L'Equipe* was very concerned about games that were held specifically for one race or religion, citing the Arab Games and Maccabiah Games as examples. *L'Equipe* pointed out that, according to the IOC rules at the time, the IOC could only give patronage to games based on a geographical region. Those that qualified were the Central American and Caribbean Games, Pan-American Games, Asian Games and the Mediterranean Games. All other games "do not retain their meaning anymore," the journal said. "They are too expensive for those who take part and whose money is already largely taken to contribute towards their participation in the Olympic Games." To support this argument, *L'Equipe* cited the Pacific Games that had been planned for Honolulu, Hawaii, but had not been held.

In addition to financial considerations, the Pan-Arab Games "did nothing to create a fraternal bond between the Moroccans and Egyptians," and the Mediterranean Games were "fairly endangered today by the racial, political and alas, religious opposition among the countries bordering the sea, which sport, rising above all religions and causes for arguments, should bring together."[25]

Other games showed the state of the globe in the early sixties. The cold war was reflected in games organized by the SCFA, the Sports Committee of Friendly Armies, for athletes from armies friendly with the Warsaw Pact. The Maccabiah Games began to regionalize with the establishment of the European Maccabi Games in 1959, and the Pan-American Maccabi Games in 1964.

The South Pacific Games in 1963 advanced the goal of the IOC to establish games for every region. The Micronesian Games were first held in the region in 1969, but it took 21 years before they were held for the second time, in 1990.

Opportunities for disabled athletes increased with the Pan-American Wheelchair Games in 1967 and the Special Olympics in 1968.

One of the very first games events for children began in 1968 with the establishment of the International School Children's Games.

The decade of the 1970s saw the establishment of a great variety of games, mostly regional in nature, with more games for school and university students, and more games for the disabled. The Arctic Winter Games were first held in 1970. Students from various regions now had the opportunity to compete in the Central American and Caribbean University Games (1972), the All-Africa University Games (1974), the ISF Gymnasiade (1974) and the Arab School Games. The FESPIC, Far East and South Pacific Games for the Disabled (1975), Winter Paralympics (1976), Winter Special Olympics (1977) and World Transplant Games (1978) added to the international schedule for disabled athletes. The IOC continued its regionalization with the South American Games in 1978 and the Indian Ocean Islands

Games in 1979. The 1970s also saw a new category as groups began to organize games based on occupation. The International Law Enforcement Games were begun in 1974, and a regional version, which came to be known as the Can-Am Police Fire Games, began in 1977. The World Medical Games for those in the medical profession began in 1978.

In the 1980s, the IOC established games for its smallest regions, including the South Pacific Mini Games in 1981, the South Asian Federation Games in 1984 and the Games of the Small Countries of Europe in 1985. The World Games were established in 1981 for sports that had not yet been accepted as Olympic sports by the IOC. Disabled sport grew with the addition of the European Special Olympics (1981), the Défi Sportif held annually in Montreal since 1984, the European Heart/Lung Transplant Games (1986) and the Robin Hood Games (1989).

The following table lists the games established from 1980 to the present time, showing the large diversity in regionality and in games for disabled athletes, youth, and masters athletes.

Year	Games	Year	Games
1981	World Games	1986	Honda Masters Games
1981	European Special Olympics	1987	Huntsman World Senior Games
1981	South Pacific Mini Games	1987	Australian Masters Games
1982	Gay Games	1987	International Firefighters Winter Games
1982	JCC Maccabi Games		
1982	Pacific School Games	1987	Peace Arch Games
1982	East African Military Games	1988	World Corporate Games
1982	Alps-Adriatic Winter Youth Games	1989	Francophone Games
1982	Windsor Classic Indoor Games	1989	Robin Hood Games
1982	Journalists World Games	1990	Winter Pan-American Games
1983	World Peace Games / Jeux Mondiaux de le Paix	1990	Firefighters World Games
		1990	North American Indigenous Games
1983	Asia Pacific Games for the Deaf		
1984	South Asian Federation Games	1990	World Equestrian Games
1984	Alps-Adriatic Summer Youth Games	1991	European Youth Olympic Days
		1991	Arafura Games
1984	Défi Sportif	1991	Winter World Corporate Games
1985	Games of the Small Countries of Europe	1992	Euro Games
		1993	East Asian Games
1985	World Police and Fire Games	1993	Winter European Youth Olympic Days
1985	CARIFTA Games		
1985	Island Games	1993	World Scholar Athlete Games
1985	World Masters Games	1993	Baltic Sea Games
1986	Goodwill Games	1993	World Dwarf Games
1986	Asian Winter Games	1993	World Ex-Service Wheelchair and Amputee Games
1986	European Heart/Lung Transplant Games		
		1993	Muslim Women's Games
1986	International Police Winter Games	1993	UK & Ireland Corporate Games

1993	Australian Corporate Games		1996	Stockholm Summer Games
1994	Winter World Transplant Games		1996	International Electrical Engineering Students Sports Games
1994	Australian Universities Games			
1994	African Francophone Games for the Handicapped		1997	Pan-American Games for the Blind
1994	Winter International School Children's Games		1997	Winter X Games
			1997	World Nature Games
1994	Muslim Student Games		1997	West Asian Games
1995	Winter Games for the Disabled		1997	Victorian Corporate Games
1995	X Games		1998	World Youth Games
1995	Pacific Ocean Games		1998	IBSA World Championships for the Blind
1995	Central Asian Games			
1995	Irelands' Scholar Athlete Games		1998	Renaissance Games
1995	Ataturk Dam International Sports Festival		1998	Pan-American Medical Games
			1998	Asian Sports Festival
1995	Military World Games		1998	Asia Pacific Masters Games
1996	Special Olympics West African Games		1998	Special Olympics Mediterranean Games
1996	Centennial Youth Games		1998	Southern Cross Games
1996	CUCSA Games		1998	Australasian Public Sector Games
1996	World Air Games		1999	Pan-Armenian Games
1996	Special Olympics Asia-Pacific Games		1999	Arab Games for the Handicapped
			1999	Islands Corporate Games
1996	World Wheelchair Games		1999	Gravity Games
1996	Special Olympics Small Nations Games		2000	Middle East/Mediterranean Scholar Athlete Games
1996	Special Olympics Gulf Games		2000	Winter Goodwill Games
1996	International Senior Games		2000	Great Outdoor Games
1996	Winter Australian Corporate Games		2000	Winter Gravity Games
			2000	SkyGames
1996	Eastern European Transplant Games		2000	Commonwealth Youth Games
			2000	Pan-American Games for Patients with Asthma
1996	Gorge Games			

The Olympic Name

This list reflects the fact that de Coubertin and the International Olympic Committee jealously guarded the use of the term Olympic. There could be no other Olympic Games.[26] The IOC has, since its beginnings, held steadfast in its opinion that the word Olympic be used for the Olympic Games alone (and more recently the IOC-sponsored European Youth Olympic Days), the Special Olympics being the one outside group granted an exception.

The Far East Championships were first called the "First Asian Olympic Games." The name was changed for all subsequent events.

When Alice Milliat, the founder of the Fédération Sportive Féminine International (FSFI), wanted to establish events for women in 1922, she called her games the Jeux Olympiques Féminins (International Women's Games). Pierre de Coubertin and the International Amateur Athletic Association (IAAF) took notice and a compromise was agreed to. The FSFI would drop the use of the word Olympic and the IOC would admit women into its games.

In 1923, Frenchman Jean Petitjean was promoting his first games for university students as the University Olympic Games. De Coubertin again protested and convinced him to change the name. The International University Games were established, and are now known around the globe as the World University Games, World Student Games, or Universiade. More recently, in 1987, the Huntsman World Senior Games were inaugurated as the World Senior Olympics, but were made to change their name to the World Senior Games the following year. Various Police and Fire Olympics have been asked to refrain from using the word Olympic to describe their events. The USOC took the first Gay Games organizers to court to restrict their use of the word Olympic.

The Special Olympics were begun by Eunice Kennedy Shriver in 1968, and the use of the word Olympic by her organization was addressed by the USOC in 1971. At that time, the USOC gave its approval for the Special Olympics to be the exception to the rule and the only organization outside the Olympic movement with permission to use the word Olympic. This permission was expanded in 1988 when the IOC recognized and endorsed the Special Olympics movement.

Mission Statements

The Baron de Coubertin, over 100 years ago, had hoped that bringing together the youth of the world on the playing fields would further the cause of peace throughout the world. However, the games have not always been peaceful, and there have been many examples of their bringing strife and discord, rather than friendship and peace.

The following mission statements show the lofty goals of many of these games, echoing the Olympic Games in their call for peace. The reality as seen throughout this work is that these games, while perhaps forging many hundreds of thousands of friendships on a personal level, have never risen to the level of actually influencing world peace.

The mission of the **Olympic Games** from the Olympic charter:

—to promote the development of those physical and moral qualities which are the basis of sport,

—to educate young people through sport in a spirit of better understanding between each other and of friendship, thereby helping to build a better and more peaceful world,

—to spread Olympic principles throughout the world, thereby creating international goodwill,

—to bring together the athletes of the world in the great four yearly sports festival, the Olympic Games.

The **Paralympic Games** base their charter on the Olympic Charter with these modifications.

The second principle reads:

—to provide the opportunity for persons with a disability to engage in a high level of competitive sport.

The fourth principle substitutes Paralympic for the Olympic Games.

The **Asian Games** mission is similar. "Help develop the moral and physical qualities of the Youth of Asia by fair competition in amateur sports, friendship, international respect and goodwill."

The very lofty mission statement of the **World Peace Games** reads:

… the World Peace Games Represent:

—One step in a vast movement in favor of sports activities for everyone to fight against the damage done to our civilizations;

—a means given to the men and peoples of the world to be able to express themselves in joy, friendship, fraternity and altruism.

—a privileged place to exchange ideas, thoughts, advice, and to exchange philosophical, religious and political conceptions between men, the international sports movement and civilizations.

—a new facet of humanism in the service of sports, man and peace.

Institute for International Sport (which sponsors the **World Scholar-Athlete Games**, and numerous continental scholar-athlete games) endeavors to:

—help develop future world leaders.

—promote and improve relations among nations.

—promote ethical behavior and sportsmanship.

—encourage individual growth.

The **World Masters Games** continues the theme for older athletes:

—To promote and encourage individuals of any age from all over the world to practice sports and to participate in the World Masters Games with the awareness that competitive sports can continue through life.

—To establish, every four years, an international multisport festival for mature people of any age, condition or standard called the "World Masters Games."

—To promote, through the World Masters Games, friendship and understanding among mature sports people, regardless of age, gender, race, religion or sports status.

Some mission statements have less to do with world issues and more about uplifting those within certain communities.

Special Olympics:

to provide year-round sports training and athletic competition in a variety of sports for children and adults with mental retardation in order to create continuing opportunities for them to develop physical fitness, demonstrate courage, experience the joy of achievement, be included in the community, build skills and make friends.

World Transplant Games:

—encourage the public concept of organ donation.

—encourage people with a potentially fatal disease to live life to the fullest.

—give thanks to organ donor families.

—encourage further research in organ transplantation.

Some are quite simple and possibly achievable. The mission of the **International School Children's Games** is "to enable children and youth from different countries to get together, make friends, and understand one another in annual sports activities on the level of cities."

Themes

Some of the games, besides having mission statements, have attached themes to certain editions of the games. This seems to be a recent and not yet pervasive practice.

One dated example fits with the pattern of most of the other themes, that of emphasizing peace. The Socialist Olympics of 1925 in Frankfurt were held under the slogan, "No More War."

"Friendship, Unity, Progress" (Beijing, 1990), "Asian Harmony" (Hiroshima, 1994) and "Friendship beyond Frontiers" (Bangkok, 1998) have been the themes of the past three Asian Games. The Asian Winter Games themes continue the trend. "Unity, Friendship, Development and Progress" was the theme in Harbin, China, in 1996. Kangwon, 1999 used the slogan, "Asia, Shining brightly through everlasting friendship."

Peace and togetherness is a recurring notion in World University Games themes such as "All in the same boat" (Sheffield, 1991), "Together, One World" (Buffalo, 1993) and "The Youth of the World for a World of Peace" (Zagreb, 1987). The world is still waiting for this to come true.

Games Per Decade

The international games movement has grown rapidly in the past two decades. While 1220 games originated between 1896 and the end of the year 2000,[27] as many games have taken place since 1988 as took place from 1896 to 1987.

1896–1899	1	1960–1969	85
1900–1909	9	1970–1979	139
1910–1919	14	1980–1989	239
1920–1929	41	1900–1999	496
1930–1939	59	2000	57
1940–1949	14		
1950–1959	66		1220

Using this set of data, the midpoint (618th games between 1896 and 2000) occurred in 1988.

Games Per Year

1896	1	1922	4	1946	2	1965	9	1984	19
1900	1	1923	3	1947	2	1966	10	1985	28
1901	1	1924	7	1948	3	1967	10	1986	25
1903	1	1925	3	1949	6	1968	7	1987	35
1904	1	1926	4	1950	5	1969	11	1988	25
1905	1	1927	3	1951	10	1970	13	1989	38
1906	1	1928	10	1952	4	1971	11	1990	38
1908	1	1929	2	1953	8	1972	9	1991	40
1909	2	1930	8	1954	5	1973	14	1992	28
1910	1	1931	6	1955	7	1974	13	1993	48
1911	3	1932	7	1956	6	1975	19	1994	41
1912	1	1933	4	1957	7	1976	12	1995	54
1913	3	1934	6	1958	5	1977	15	1996	50
1914	1	1935	9	1959	9	1978	16	1997	68
1915	1	1936	3	1960	6	1979	17	1998	62
1917	2	1937	6	1961	10	1980	11	1999	68
1919	2	1938	6	1962	8	1981	15	2000	57
1920	1	1939	4	1963	9	1982	22		
1921	4	1940	1	1964	5	1983	21		

Count Per Continent

Continent	Number
Europe	518
North America	345
Asia	143
Oceania	99
Africa	63
South America	52

THE GAMES

Aalborg Youth Games

Marius Andersen, the mayor of Aalborg, a city in northern Denmark, first proposed the idea for a youth games to be held there. The first took place in 1975 with participants from about 15 cities. The games are held every four years, and are open to youth between the ages of 12 and 16 from the sister cities and twin towns of Aalborg.

Year	Host City	Host Nation	Dates
1975	Aalborg	Denmark	NA
1979	Aalborg	Denmark	NA
1983	Aalborg	Denmark	NA
1987	Aalborg	Denmark	NA
1991	Aalborg	Denmark	NA
1995	Aalborg	Denmark	NA
1999	Aalborg	Denmark	July 26–30

1999   Aalborg   Denmark   July 26–30

Cities and Nations: Almer, Holland; Antibes, Germany; Edinburgh, Scotland; Fredrikstad, Norway; Fuglefjord, Faeroe Islands; Galway, Ireland; Gdynia, Poland; Haifa, Israel; Husavik, Iceland; Karlskogga, Sweden; Lancaster, England; Pushkin, Russia; Racine, USA; Rapperswil, Switzerland; Rendsurg, Germany; Riga, Latvia; Riihimaki, Finland; Scoresbysund, Greenland; Solvang, USA; Tulcea, Romania; Varna, Bulgaria; Vilnius, Lithuania; Wismar, Germany

Sports: Athletics, Badminton, Table Tennis, Archery, Bowling, Wrestling, Cricket, Cycling, Soccer, Fencing, Golf, Gymnastics, Handball, Judo, Kayaking, Karate, Orienteering, Sports-riding, Rowing, Rugby, Yachting, Shooting, Sports-dancing, Swimming, Swimming handicapped, Tennis, Diving, Volleyball

Academic Olympia

The "Academic Olympia" were a series of short-lived competitions for university students held between the years 1909 and 1913. All were held in Germany, but the originating idea was born at the Universal Peace Conference in Rome in November 1891, when Hodgson Pratt, the president of the International University Alliance, put forth a proposal for International Student Conferences. University students from Europe and America would gather in various capital cities around the world and participate in competitions in poetry, art, the sciences, and sports. The recommendation was passed unanimously, but no immediate conferences were organized.

In 1909, the first Academic Olympia was held in Leipzig, Germany. German and Austrian universities organized these games to coincide with the celebration of the 500th anniversary of Leipzig University. One year later, in commemoration of the 100th anniversary of Friedrich-Wilhelms-University (the University of Berlin), the second Academic Olympia was held. These first two events were one-day affairs.

On July 8–10, 1911, the third Academic Olympia was held in Dresden, in conjunction with the Hygiebe Fair. Later the same summer, Breslau hosted the next Olympia, also as part of the 100th anniversary of the university.

A fourth competition had been scheduled for Rome in September 1911, to celebrate the 50th anniversary of the unification of Italy. Nine universities were invited and 11 sports were on the program, but the competition was canceled because of poor weather.

The fifth and final Olympia was held in Leipzig in 1913, coinciding with the dedication of the monument "The Multi-Nation's Fight Against Napoleon."

Little is known of the actual sporting events. The games were mainly German student championships with international participation primarily from Austria and students at European universities.[28,29]

Year	Host City	Host Nation	Dates
1909	Leipzig	Germany	July 11
1910	Berlin	Germany	July 3
1911	Dresden	Germany	July 8–10
1911	Breslau	Germany	Aug. 1–3
1913	Leipzig	Germany	Oct. 18–19

African Games

The African Games, after suffering through numerous economic and organizational difficulties throughout their history, have finally been established as one of the world's largest international games.

Two early attempts by Pierre de Coubertin to organize games for the African continent occurred in the 1920s. In April 1923 at the IOC session in Rome, a very specific plan was drawn up that would establish a regional games in Africa, which was to be held every other year.[30] Algiers, Algeria, was chosen to host the first edition of the games in 1925, but the games were not held. They were rescheduled for 1929 in Alexandria, Egypt. The city had completed preparations and was weeks away from opening the games in 1929 when the colonial powers stepped in to cancel them, fearing they would promote African unity and foment revolt.

It was not until 30 years later, after regional games were held in Africa (such as the West African Games and French-backed Community/Friendship Games or Jeux de l'Amitié), that Africa was ready to accept the challenge of a continental games.

On April 12, 1963, the organizers of the various regional games in Africa met in Dakar, Senegal, and awarded the first African Games to Brazzaville in the Republic of the Congo. The aim was to provide "a genuine means of fostering friendship, unity and brotherhood among African nations."[31] South Africa and Rhodesia were specifically excluded from this gathering and would not be included in the games due to their apartheid policies.

Though the games were to foster brotherhood and unity, they opened under a tight ring of security. The Congo-Brazzaville army patrolled every road leading into the city with armored cars, stopping anyone that was not identified as part of the games. The precautions were to secure against "malcontents" or "counter-revolutionaries" who might want to disrupt the games.[32]

On the athletic fields, the 1965 Brazzaville gathering was successful, giving Africa its first glimpse of emerging African stars such as Kenyans Kip Keino, Naftali Temu, and Wilson Kiprugut, Mamo Wolde of Ethiopia, and Tunisia's Mohammed Gammoudi. All would win Olympic medals between 1964 and 1972. Abebe Bikila, the Ethiopian winner of the 1960 and 1964 Olympic marathons, was invited to the games as a guest of honor. He did not compete in Brazzaville as the marathon event was not on the program.[33]

IOC president Avery Brundage was present and met with the organizers to discuss ways in which the International Olympic Committee could help the African nations firmly establish the games.

During the games, an article by Tanzania's President Julius Nyerere was published in the journal *African Unity* which called for one government for all of Africa. "National sovereignty must be surrendered by the nation-states in favor of an all–African government," said Nyerere while proposing a central representative government responsible for things such as foreign affairs, citizenship, economic development, defense, currency, education, police and communications.[34] The African games were supposed to help symbolize this new African unity.

The Kenyan team would experience a bit of culture shock in Brazzaville. While strolling through the market one day during the games, they saw a monkey being slaughtered for meat. Many of the Kenyan team had suffered stomach ailments throughout the games, and whether this was the reason or not the Kenyan team refused to eat meat for the rest of their stay in the games village.[35]

Five commemorative postage stamps were produced for the games, showing cyclists, runners and the games emblem.

Despite the proposal by Nyerere and the work by Brundage, the general development of African sport and of the African games did not proceed smoothly. During meetings in Brazzaville, Bamako in Mali was awarded the next edition of the games, which were to be held in 1969. A coup in 1968 caused them to be canceled, and they were then scheduled for Lagos, Nigeria, in 1971. They were postponed once again, and finally held in January 1973.

A five-hour-long opening ceremony presided over by Nigerian general Yakubu Gowon opened the games, with new IOC president Lord Killanin and former IOC president Avery Brundage in attendance. The games torch was relayed from Brazzaville to Lagos. Sports leaders from the African nations met during the games to establish an Institute for the Development of Sport and Physical Education which was intended to be used to convince the national governments to provide more resources for sports and sports facilities across the continent.[36] Once again security was heavy, mostly in response to the tragedy of the 1972 Munich Olympic Games a few short months before.

During the Lagos games, Ben Jipcho of Kenya tied the world record in the steeplechase running 8:20.8. Kip Keino was surprised in the 1500 meters by a young Tanzanian named Filbert Bayi, who ran 3:37.18 to set a new African Games record. Ethiopia's Miruts Yifter triumphed in the 10,000 meters. Bayi would set world records in the 1500 meters and mile run in the following two years; Yifter would win two gold medals in the 1980 Olympics. Ghana's Alice Annum, a finalist in the 100 and 200 meters in the Munich Olympics, won those events in Lagos with African record times of 11.72 and 22.03 seconds. Munich Olympic gold medalist and 400 meter hurdles world record holder John Aki-Bua of Uganda won his specialty in a games record of 48.49 seconds.

The journalists at the games, most of them members of the Union des Journalistes Sportifs Africains, sent a letter of protest to the Nigerian organizers complaining that they were not being given access to the information and results necessary to properly cover the games. The organizers were chastised for an error they provided to entrants in the cycling events prior to the games. They omitted the zeros from the "100 kilometers for teams" cycling race. Two sprinters from Mauritius showed up thinking they were entered in a 1 kilometer event on a velodrome only to find out Nigeria didn't have a velodrome. The ambitious Mauritians decided not to waste their travel and entered the longer event. However, they did not have enough members for the 100 kilometer team event and had to enter the still longer 170 kilometer individual road race!

Algiers, Algeria, hosted the 1978 games. After beating Libya 1-0, the Egyptian soccer team was attacked by the Libyan football players and by spectators armed with clubs and metal bars. The violence was shown on live television and Egypt's Prime Minister Mamduh Salem ordered all Egyptian athletes home immediately.

The issue of apartheid in South Africa and Rhodesia had not been solved and once again these nations were excluded from the games.

Kenya's Henry Rono, having already set four distance-running world records in 1978, would win the 3000 meter steeplechase and 10,000 meter runs in Algiers. Two weeks later in Edmonton, Canada, Rono would win the steeplechase and 5,000 meter runs at the Commonwealth Games. Boycotts would keep Rono out of the 1976 and 1980 Olympics. Filbert Bayi, also a victim of the 1976 African Olympic boycott, would retain his African Games 1500 meters title setting another record with a time of 3:36.21.

Two Tunisian swimmers dominated the pool. Ali Gharbi won nine gold medals for the men; Miryem Mizouni, nine gold in women's swimming events.

Once again, hopes were high that the games could be organized on a quadrennial schedule, and the 1982 games were awarded to Nairobi, Kenya. However, in December 1980, the Kenyans informed the Supreme Council for Sport in Africa (SCSA) that they would not be able to hold the games on time. Pressure was put on the SCSA to move the games to Tunis, Tunisia, but the SCSA stood firm behind Nairobi. Unfortunately, severe economic difficulties in Kenya and throughout Africa postponed the games again. China stepped in with money and technical assistance to help build Kasarani Stadium, the main venue for the games. They were rescheduled for 1985, then 1986. At the end of 1984, the Kenyans admitted they would still not be ready for the games and proposed dates for August 1987. In February 1985, they informed the SCSA that they had pulled out of hosting the games, but President Daniel Arap Moi convinced his compatriots they could hold the games and two weeks later the games were on again.

Kip Keino and Kenyan Paralympian Japheth Musyoki started out the fourth African Games torch run on July 4, 1987, in Kasarani Stadium; the torch was carried throughout Kenya before returning for the start of the games on August 1. John Ngugi, Kenya's world champion cross-country star, lit the cauldron during the opening ceremonies in which the games were opened by President Moi. Kenya's Voice of Kenya television station invested some 300 million Kenyan shillings on new broadcast equipment for the games.

Besides China's assistance, funding for the games was provided by outside sponsorship, including companies such as Boeing and Coca-Cola, a national lottery, and fees charged to the visiting delegations—$20 per day for each athlete, $30 a day for officials. The SCSA had decreed that there would be no alcohol or tobacco advertising inside games venues.

The Nigerian basketball team was disqualified from the games two weeks before the opening ceremonies and replaced with the Ivory Coast team when it was learned that the Nigerians, as organizers of the qualifying tournament, had failed to inform the team from Ivory Coast when and where the qualifying tournament would be held.

Morocco boycotted the games, pulling out of activities involving the Organization of African Unity over its dispute with Western Sahara.[37] An open-air market surrounding the main stadium gave many small entrepreneurs hopes that they would gain financially from the games. Unfortunately, many did not even make back the fees they paid for stalls as most of the games events were held far away from the main stadium.

Problems with facilities, typical for events of this kind, were prevalent at the games. Kenya's basketball coach, George Namake, complained loudly of the danger of the new Nyayo National Stadium gymnasium which left only two meters of space for the players to slow down before they hit a wall under the basket. Namake wanted the venue reconfigured before the games. Organizers instead placed large cushions on the walls for safety. The artificial turf for the field hockey venue did not arrive and could not be installed until the day before the games. A power failure at Nyayo National Stadium during the games due to a truck crushing an electrical line postponed a football match to the next day.

On the field, events went mostly as expected. Kenyans excelled in athletics and boxing and lost a tight football final to the Egyptian team. Egypt, selected to be the games' next host, won the overall medal count with 31 golds; Tunisia finished second with 28, and Nigeria edged Kenya for third with 23 to 22. During football games, supporters from all sides attempted to use the common tactic of spells and African magic to influence the outcome of games.

In 1991, Cairo, Egypt, hosted the games hoping to impress the IOC and convince them that an African city was ready to hold the Olympic Games. The games did not run as smoothly as expected. A stampede by spectators at the opening ceremonies prevented some dignitaries from getting inside the stadium. The Egyptians had spent some US $250 million for facilities for the games, and gave away most of the tickets for free to fill the stands. Once the games began, the Egyptians were accused on numerous occasions of biased officiating, and computer systems did not work as well as expected.

Numerous star track athletes skipped the games, preferring instead to earn money on the lucrative European track tour. Two star athletes who did show up were Kenya's Moses Kiptanui who won the steeplechase and Namibia's Frank Fredericks who won the 200 meters. Kenya's Susan Sirma won both the women's 1500 and 3000 meter runs.

The medals for the diving events were struck from the records after the completion of the competition when it was ruled that not enough nations had participated in order to make it an official competition.

Egypt again won the most gold medals, 90; Algeria captured 49, with Nigeria winning 43.

The games of 1995 in Harare, Zimbabwe, saw the inclusion of South Africa in the games for the first time after the end of South Africa's longstanding apartheid policies, but the games were marred by protests, drug scandals, poor organization, and a lack of interest from the spectators. The opening ceremonies had only 6,000 in attendance in a stadium that seats 76,000.

South African hammer thrower Rumne Koprivchin, won the gold medal but had only been given his South African citizenship in May, less than the six months required for eligibility in the games, and was disqualified. The Egyptian team also protested that the South African women's gymnastics team's uniforms were too revealing. Women's diving and netball were demoted to demonstration sports when not enough nations showed up to compete.

Sportsmanship was lacking at the games. Nigeria and Egypt, and Algeria and Guinea brawled on the football field. The Zimbabwean security forces used police dogs to assist in escorting the football referee from the field after angry Nigerians confronted him after the match with Egypt. Muhammad Ali, a guest of honor at the games, witnessed fighting both in and outside the boxing ring when fighters from Nigeria and fans from Egypt brawled, throwing chairs across the arena. Nigerians and Algerians tussled during the volleyball competition. Controversy raged over unfair judging in tae kwon do, and the women's handball teams from Zimbabwe and Egypt fought off-court. The Egyptians made ugly allegations that the boxers from South Africa had AIDS, an accusation that was retracted by a letter of apology in an Egyptian newspaper. At the end of the games, it was clear relations were strained. A Nigerian official said, "In general, North Africans don't want to accept defeat and always think they are superior to black Africa."

South Africa's participation changed the complexion of the games. It became an instant rival with perennial winner Egypt, and this was given as one reason for the contentious nature of the games. South Africa won 26 gold medals in the swimming pool alone.

South African pole vaulter Okkert Brits, the heavy favorite, suffered the unfortunate mishap of having his vaulting poles lost in transit to the games. The organizers postponed the pole vault event a number of days to recover the equipment and allow Brits to compete and win the gold medal.

South Africa's Karen Botha lost her bronze medal in the long jump after failing a drug test. Other drug suspensions included Ghana's long jumper Andrew Osuwu, who lost a silver medal, Nigeria's sprinter Paul Egonye, who was responsible for his team being disqualified in the 4 × 100 meter relay, and Egyptian wrestler Mohy Abdel, who was stripped of his medal in the 100 kg class.

Maria Mutola of Mozambique won the women's 800 meters. Ethiopia's Kutre Dulecha won the 1500 meters, while Kenya's Rose Cheruiyot and Sally Barsosio won the 5,000 and 10,000 meter runs.

Kenyans continued to excel in the men's distance-running events with Josephat Machuka winning both the 5,000 and 10,000 meter runs and Bernard Barmasai the steeplechase.

As had occurred in the games of 1991, many big-name stars, mostly in the world of athletics, skipped the games. Noureddine Morceli, Moses Kiptanui, Hassiba Boulmerka, Samuel Matete, Frankie Fredericks, and Haile Gebreselassie were the main no-shows.

The games of Harare were the largest African Games to date with 46 nations and 6,000 participants. IOC president Juan Antonio Samaranch warned the African Olympic Committees not to attempt to copy the Olympic Games, but in the future to present the games on a scale that Africa could manage.

The seventh African Games were held in Johannesburg, South Africa in 1999. Morocco did not participate as it was not a current member of the Organization for African Unity (OAU). Work on the games village in the township of Alexandra proceeded right up until the opening of the games. Brendon Dedekind, a captain of South Africa's swim team, commented on the situation at the village. "Sure there might be a few growing pains, but I've been really impressed. We've got warm beds to sleep in and the transport is good...." There are two sides to every coin, and you can either look at the positive or negative side. When we leave here there will be hundreds of houses for the people of Alex. Whoever thought of this [the village] deserves a pat on the back." Other athletes complained about long lines for food and transportation, dusty streets and bad communication between athletes and officials, but gave top marks to the security efforts.

Outside the village, several labor groups, including the telecommunications and electricity providers picketed. Police and the military had to escort busses carrying athletes through large crowds of chanting strikers.

Juan Antonio Samaranch and 250 dignitaries from Africa and around the world were present at the opening ceremonies in Johannesburg Stadium. Less than 15,000 spectators showed up to watch the dancing, African parables and Zulu warriors, despite pleas by South Africa's sports minister, Ngconde Balfour. Many could not afford the cost of tickets at 60 rand and stayed home. Samaranch, expressed satisfaction with South Africa's organization telling them "this shows that you can organize big events."

In conjunction with the games, Johannesburg staged the SuperSport Extravaganza, the biggest sporting trade show in Africa, and an international seminar for sports journalists. The South Africans hosted about 25,000 visitors including 6,000 athletes and 3,000 officials from throughout the continent.

Johannesburg, which had lost to Athens in the bidding for the 2004 Olympic Games, was hoping to impress FIFA in order to land the 2006 World Cup. Overall, the games were a success, with hosts South Africa outdistancing Nigeria and Egypt in the medals race.

Typical problems at the games included 600 children contracting food poisoning after being fed boxed lunches at the practice session for the opening ceremonies, and striking laborers demonstrating outside games venues, displaying placards which read "No Wages, No All Africa Games." Computer glitches slowed the flow of results and information to journalists. Women's field hockey was demoted to a nonmedal event after the Nigerian team dropped out of the tournament. A melee at the finish of the basketball game between Angola and Egypt forced police to escort the Egyptian team from the court. Haile Gebreselassie, the world record holder in the 5,000 and 10,000 meter runs, opted out of the games for health reasons, depriving the games' organizers of one of their biggest drawing cards.

Olympic stars Maria Mutola (athletics, 800m), Penny Heyns (swimming), Geta Wami (athletics, 10,000 m) all starred in the women's events. South African pole vaulter Okkert Brits won his second African Games gold medal. Assefa Mezgebu of Ethiopia won the men's 10,000 meters. Cameroon beat Zambia 4-3 on penalty kicks to win the football finale.

Drug testing and gender testing caused several controversies. The International Weightlifting Federation (IWF) carried out gender tests on all female lifters. The tests had been phased out in most events as unnecessary, with the IWF the one federation that found them of value.

Nigerian lightweight boxer Osiobe Eneuvwedia was the first competitor expelled from the games after testing positive for the banned steroid 19-Norandosterone. Nigerian officials claimed the substances entered his system when he was hospitalized earlier that year. Jesus Kibunde of the Democratic Republic of was promoted to the gold medal bout but his opponent, Ben Rabah of Tunisia, came down with the flu, so Kibunde won the gold medal after losing his semifinal and not having to throw a single punch in the final.

Nigeria was scheduled to host the games of 2003.

Year	Host City	Host Nation	Dates	Nations	Athletes	Sports
1965	Brazzaville	Congo, Rep. of	July 18–25	28	3000	10
1973	Lagos	Nigeria	January 7–18	37	1500	11
1978	Algiers	Algeria	July 13–28	45	3000	12
1987	Nairobi	Kenya	August 1–12	44	4000	14
1991	Cairo	Egypt	Sept. 20–Oct. 1	42	3000	17
1995	Harare	Zimbabwe	Sept. 13–23	49	6000	19
1999	Johannesburg	South Africa	Sept. 10–19	53	NA	19

1965   Brazzaville   Congo, Rep. of   July 18–25

Nations: Algeria, Cameroon, Chad, Congo Brazzaville, Congo Leopoldville, Ethiopia, Gabon, Ghana, Ivory Coast, Kenya, Madagascar, Niger, Nigeria, Senegal, Tanzania, Togo, Tunisia, Uganda, United Arab Republic, Upper Volta, Zambia (7 more)

Sports: Athletics, Basketball, Boxing, Cycling, Soccer, Handball, Judo, Swimming, Tennis, Volleyball

Sports for Women: Athletics, Basketball

Venues: Stade Omnisports (Athletics, Basketball, Football), Centre Bacongo (Basketball), College Jahouvey (Basketball), Stade Eboue (Football), Lycee Savorgnan (Judo)

MEDALS

Nation	Gold	Silver	Bronze	Total
United Arab Republic	17	10	3	30
Nigeria	9	6	4	19
Kenya	8	11	4	23
Senegal	6	3	7	16
Ivory Coast	5	2	5	12
Algeria	2	3	6	11
Ghana	2	3	6	11
Tunisia	1	5	6	12
Cameroon	1	2	2	5
Congo Brazzaville	1	2	2	5
Madagascar	0	2	4	6
Uganda	0	1	4	5
Upper Volta	0	1	1	2
Chad	0	0	3	3
Gabon	0	0	3	3
Togo	0	0	2	2
Congo Leopoldville	0	0	1	1
Tanzania	0	0	1	1
Niger	0	0	1	1
Ethiopia	0	0	1	1
Zambia	0	0	1	1

1973   Lagos   Nigeria   January 7–18

Nations: Algeria, Cameroon, Congo Brazzaville, Dahomey, Egypt, Ethiopia, Gambia, Ghana, Guinea, Ivory Coast, Kenya, Madagascar, Mali, Morocco, Niger, Nigeria,

Senegal, Somalia, Sudan, Swaziland, Tanzania, Togo, Tunisia, Uganda, Zambia (13 more)

Sports: Athletics, Basketball, Boxing, Cycling, Soccer, Handball, Judo, Swimming, Table Tennis, Tennis, Volleyball

Sports for Women: Athletics, Basketball, Swimming

MEDALS

Nation	Gold	Silver	Bronze	Total
Egypt	25	16	15	56
Nigeria	18	25	20	63
Kenya	9	9	18	36
Uganda	8	6	6	20
Ghana	7	7	13	27
Tunisia	4	6	3	13
Algeria	4	5	13	22
Ethiopia	4	3	6	13
Senegal	4	2	6	12
Ivory Coast	2	0	4	6
Morocco	1	3	3	7
Sudan	1	1	1	3
Guinea	1	1	0	2
Mali	1	1	0	2
Tanzania	1	1	0	2
Zambia	1	0	6	7
Somalia	1	0	0	1
Madagascar	0	2	3	5
Cameroon	0	1	3	4
Congo Brazzaville	0	1	3	4
Gambia	0	1	0	1
Niger	0	1	0	1
Dahomey	0	0	1	1
Swaziland	0	0	1	1
Togo	0	0	1	1

1978   Algiers   Algeria   July 13–28

Nations: Algeria, Cameroon, Chad, Egypt, Ethiopia, Gabon, Ghana, Ivory Coast, Kenya, Libya, Mali, Morocco, Nigeria, Senegal, Sudan, Swaziland, Tanzania, Togo, Tunisia, Uganda, Upper Volta, Zambia (23 more)

Sports: Athletics, Basketball, Boxing, Cycling, Soccer, Handball, Judo, Swimming, Table Tennis, Tennis, Volleyball, Wrestling

Sports for Women: Athletics, Basketball, Swimming, Table Tennis, Tennis, Volleyball

MEDALS

Nation	Gold	Silver	Bronze	Total
Tunisia	29	14	20	63
Nigeria	18	10	15	43
Algeria	16	19	23	58
Kenya	11	8	8	27
Morocco	7	8	11	26

Nation	Gold	Silver	Bronze	Total
Egypt	6	24	15	45
Ghana	4	4	7	15
Libya	4	3	5	12
Senegal	4	2	4	10
Uganda	3	6	5	14
Ivory Coast	2	3	4	9
Zambia	2	0	2	4
Sudan	2	0	0	2
Mali	1	1	0	2
Chad	1	0	0	1
Swaziland	1	0	0	1
Cameroon	0	4	4	8
Togo	0	1	4	5
Ethiopia	0	1	2	3
Upper Volta	0	1	1	2
Tanzania	0	1	1	2
Gabon	0	0	1	1

1987   Nairobi   Kenya   August 1–12

Nations: Algeria, Angola, Burundi, Cameroon, Chad, Congo, Egypt, Ethiopia, Ghana, Ivory Coast, Kenya, Madagascar, Malawi, Mauritius, Mozambique, Nigeria, Rwanda, Senegal, Seychelles, Tanzania, Tunisia, Uganda, Zaire, Zambia, Zimbabwe (19 more)

Sports: Athletics, Basketball, Boxing, Cycling, Soccer, Handball, Field Hockey, Judo, Swimming, Table Tennis, Tennis, Volleyball, Weightlifting, Wrestling (freestyle and Greco-Roman), (rugby demonstration)

Sports for Women: Athletics, Basketball, Handball, Swimming, Table Tennis, Tennis, Volleyball

Venues: Moi International Sports Centre (athletics), Nyayo National Stadium (basketball, handball, swimming), Kenyatta International Conference Centre (boxing), Nairobi roads (cycling), Nyayo and Moi stadiums (football), City Park Stadium (hockey), Bomas of Kenya (judo, volleyball), Premier Club (table tennis), Nairobi Club and Parklands Club (tennis), Charter Hall (weightlifting), City Hall (wrestling)

MEDALS

Nation	Gold	Silver	Bronze	Total
Egypt	31	22	20	73
Tunisia	28	26	22	76
Nigeria	23	16	21	60
Kenya	22	25	16	63
Algeria	13	23	23	59
Senegal	7	2	12	21
Ethiopia	3	5	4	12
Ghana	3	3	1	7
Uganda	3	2	4	9
Zimbabwe	2	5	6	13
Madagascar	2	4	2	8
Cameroon	1	1	7	9

Nation	Gold	Silver	Bronze	Total
Ivory Coast	1	1	2	4
Zaire	1	1	0	2
Mauritius	1	1	0	2
Tanzania	0	2	5	7
Congo	0	2	0	2
Rwanda	0	1	0	1
Zambia	0	0	3	3
Seychelles	0	0	2	2
Chad	0	0	1	1
Angola	0	0	1	1
Mozambique	0	0	1	1
Burundi	0	0	1	1
Malawi	0	0	1	1

1991   Cairo   Egypt   September 20–October 1

Nations: Algeria, Angola, Botswana, Burkina Faso, Cameroon, Central African Republic, Congo, Egypt, Ethiopia, Gabon, Ghana, Ivory Coast, Kenya, Lesotho, Libya, Madagascar, Mauritius, Mozambique, Namibia, Nigeria, Senegal, Seychelles, Sierra Leone, Swaziland, Tanzania, Tunisia, Uganda, Zaire, Zambia, Zimbabwe (12 more)

Sports: Athletics, Basketball, Boxing, Cycling, Soccer, Gymnastics, Handball, Field Hockey, Judo, Karate, Swimming, Table Tennis, Tae Kwon Do, Tennis, Volleyball, Weightlifting, Wrestling, (diving demoted to an exhibition sport for lack of entries)

Sports for Women: Athletics, Basketball, Gymnastics, Handball, Swimming, Table Tennis, Tennis, Volleyball

Venues: National Stadium (athletics), Alexandria Indoor Hall (basketball), Army Force Sport Hall (boxing), Ismalia (cycling), Arab Contractors Stadium (soccer), Alexandria Stadium (soccer), Police Academy in Abassa (gymnastics), New Hall 1 and 2, Cairo (handball, volleyball), Hockey Courts in Cairo (hockey), El Zohor Hall (judo and karate), Shooting Club in the Pyramids Area (shooting), Swimming Complex in Cairo (swimming), Federation Hall in Zamalek Club (table tennis), Balloon Hall in Military College (Tae Kwon Do), Tennis Complex in Cairo Stadium (tennis), New Hall 3 in Cairo (weightlifting), New Hall 4 in Cairo (wrestling)

MEDALS

Nation	Gold	Silver	Bronze	Total
Egypt	90	53	52	195
Nigeria	43	51	43	137
Algeria	49	36	34	119
Kenya	13	17	18	48
Zimbabwe	8	3	13	24
Tunisia	6	4	10	20
Ivory Coast	4	5	3	12
Ethiopia	4	3	5	12
Namibia	4	2	6	12
Senegal	3	4	11	18
Ghana	2	4	6	12
Angola	2	3	5	10
Mozambique	2	0	0	2

Nation	Gold	Silver	Bronze	Total
Mauritius	1	5	6	12
Cameroon	1	4	10	15
Tanzania	1	3	1	5
Uganda	1	1	2	4
Gabon	1	0	3	4
Zambia	1	0	3	4
Lesotho	0	3	3	6
Madagascar	0	2	9	11
Libya	0	1	5	6
Seychelles	0	1	2	3
Central African Rep.	0	1	0	1
Sierra Leone	0	1	0	1
Burkina Faso	0	0	2	2
Zaire	0	0	2	2
Botswana	0	0	1	1
Congo	0	0	1	1
Swaziland	0	0	1	1

1995   Harare   Zimbabwe   September 13–23

Nations: Algeria, Angola, Benin, Botswana, Burkina Faso, Burundi, Cameroon, Cape Verde, Central African Republic, Chad, Comoros, Congo, Djibouti, Egypt, Equatorial Guinea, Ethiopia, Gabon, Gambia, Ghana, Guinea, Guinea Bissau, Ivory Coast, Kenya, Lesotho, Libya, Madagascar, Malawi, Mali, Mauritania, Mauritius, Morocco, Mozambique, Namibia, Nigeria, Rwanda, Sao Tome & Principe, Senegal, Seychelles, Sierra Leone, South Africa, Sudan, Swaziland, Tanzania, Togo, Tunisia, Uganda, Zaire, Zambia, Zimbabwe

Sports: Athletics, Basketball, Boxing, Cycling, Field Hockey, Gymnastics, Handball, Judo, Karate, Swimming, Table Tennis, Tae Kwon Do, Tennis, Weightlifting, Wrestling, Volleyball, (demonstration sports rugby and netball)

Shooting and diving were demoted to demonstration status for lack of entries, diving for the second time in a row.

Sports for Women: Athletics, Basketball, Gymnastics, Handball, Swimming, Table Tennis, Tennis, Volleyball, (diving and netball were to be included but were reduced to demonstration sports due to a lack of entries)

Venues: In Harare—National Sports Stadium (athletics, football, hockey), Zanu PF Hall (judo); other venues: Rufero Stadium, Sodart Hall, City Sports Centre, Games Village, University of Zimbabwe.

In Bulawayo—Barbourfields stadium, Bulawayo roads (cycling), ZITE Trade Centre (women's volleyball), Ascot Hockey Stadium (hockey).

In Chitungwiza—Chitungwiza Community Hall (swimming)

MEDALS

Nation	Gold	Silver	Bronze	Total
South Africa	64	51	39	154
Egypt	61	43	50	154
Nigeria	36	31	40	107
Algeria	15	16	26	57
Kenya	12	11	17	40

Nation	Gold	Silver	Bronze	Total
Tunisia	9	11	19	39
Zimbabwe	6	6	23	35
Cameroon	3	13	10	26
Mauritius	3	6	9	18
Senegal	5	4	6	15
Ethiopia	1	5	6	12
Madagascar	2	2	5	9
Gabon	2	0	6	8
Ghana	1	4	2	7
Namibia	0	4	3	7
Ivory Coast	0	4	2	6
Zambia	0	2	2	4
Mozambique	1	2	0	3
Lesotho	0	1	2	3
Seychelles	0	1	2	3
Angola	0	0	3	3
Swaziland	0	0	3	3
Sierra Leone	1	1	0	2
Tanzania	1	0	1	2
Uganda	0	0	2	2
Burundi	1	0	0	1
Burkina Faso	0	1	0	1
Central African Rep.	0	1	0	1
Guinea	0	1	0	1
Libya	0	1	0	1
Mali	0	1	0	1
Botswana	0	0	1	1
Congo	0	0	1	1

1999   Johannesburg   South Africa   September 10–19

Nations (partial): Algeria, Angola, Botswana, Cameroon, Cape Verde, Central African Republic, DR Congo, Egypt, Ethiopia, Gabon, Ghana, Ivory Coast, Kenya, Lesotho, Madagascar, Malawi, Mali, Mauritius, Namibia, Niger, Nigeria, Senegal, Seychelles, South Africa, Togo, Tunisia, Uganda, Zimbabwe

Sports: Athletics, Baseball, Basketball, Boxing, Cycling, Football, Gymnastics, Handball, Hockey, Judo, Karate, Netball, Swimming, Table Tennis, Tae Kwon do, Tennis, Volleyball, Weightlifting, Wrestling

Venues: Elkah Stadium, Ellis Park Aquatic Centre, Ellis Park Tennis Centre, Expo Auditorium, Expo Centre Hall 6 (a), Expo Centre Hall 6 (b), Expo Centre Hall 7, Expo Centre Hall 8, Expo Centre Rand Show Road, Johannesburg Stadium, Wits University Old Mutual Sports Hall, Orlando Stadium, Pimville Indoor Hall, R554 (Alberton) Swartkoppies Road, Rand Stadium, Randburg Astro Stadium, Randburg Indoor Sports Hall, Randburg Precinct, Vista University, Wembly Indoor Hall

	MEDALS			
Nation	Gold	Silver	Bronze	Total
South Africa	61	55	37	153
Nigeria	48	18	25	91
Egypt	46	54	32	132

Nation	Gold	Silver	Bronze	Total
Tunisia	16	16	19	51
Algeria	11	17	27	55
Kenya	7	7	12	26
Senegal	4	6	5	15
Ethiopia	4	1	2	7
Cameroon	3	10	17	30
Lesotho	3	1	1	5
Angola	3	0	1	4
Ghana	2	1	4	7
Zimbabwe	1	9	11	21
Mauritius	1	5	9	15
Madagascar	1	3	5	9
Gabon	1	3	4	8
Botswana	1	2	1	4
Ivory Coast	1	1	4	6
Seychelles	0	1	6	7
Niger	0	1	2	3
Mali	0	0	2	2
Namibia	0	0	2	2
Cape Verde	0	0	2	2
Malawi	0	0	1	1
Uganda	0	0	1	1
DR Congo	0	0	1	1
Central Afr. Rep.	0	0	1	1
Togo	0	0	0	0

African Francophone Games for the Handicapped (JAPHAF Games)

The African Francophone Games for the Handicapped are better known under their French title, Jeux de l'Avenir des personnes handicapées d'Afrique francophone, which produces the acronym JAPHAF.

The games were begun in response to the Barcelona Paralympics where only one French-speaking African nation was represented.

The games are open to several categories of handicap: physical, visual, mental, and those with hearing difficulties. Sports include archery, African traditional wrestling, basketball, handball, table tennis, wheelchair races, weightlifting, and volleyball.

Eligible nations are Benin, Burkina Faso, Cameroon, Chad, Côte d'Ivoire, Congo Brazzaville, Congo RDC, Gabon, Mali, Mauritania, Niger, Central African Republic, Senegal and Togo. Athletes from Belgium, Switzerland and France have been invited to participate in these games on occasion.

The 2002 games were scheduled to be held in Lomé, Togo.

Year	Host City	Host Nation	Dates	Nations	Athletes	Sports
1994	Ouagadougou	Burkina Faso		6	NA	NA
1996	Cotonou	Benin		7	NA	NA
1998	Dakar	Senegal	April 23–30	NA	NA	NA
2000	Abidjan	Ivory Coast	April 11–15	NA	NA	NA

All-Africa University Games

University Games for students from the continent of Africa have been held on at least two occasions: in Accra, Ghana, in 1974 and Nairobi, Kenya, in 1978, under the guidance of the Federation of African University Sport, FASU (Fédération du Africaine Sport Universitaire).

The 1978 games were originally awarded to Uganda, which bowed out one year before the event. Kenya stepped in at the last minute to replace Uganda.

Kenya's President, Daniel Arap Moi, opened the games with a speech asking the participants and nations "to increase contact and understanding among themselves." The future development of Africa depended on how much Africans could cooperate with one another, Moi said.

Disorganization marked the games. Dr. Sam Ongeri, who was appointed president of the event one month before it was scheduled to begin, left for a visit to West Germany just after it began, leaving his duties to a second in command. Participants complained that there were no announcers in stadiums, no translators for French-speaking athletes, and a lack of equipment and officials. Volleyball referees delayed a game over compensation, refusing to officiate. Organizers promised 60 shillings per day and the referees went back to work. The handball tournament saw rough play, bickering over the rules, and confusion over venues. Basketball and volleyball saw disputes over the eligibility of players from Ivory Coast and Madagascar, other nations claiming the athletes were not university students.

Kenya's world-class runners were the stars of the games, including Samson Kimombwa, former 10,000 meters world record holder.

Egypt won 24 gold, 26 silver and 14 bronze medals, Nigeria 13 gold, 9 silver and 10 bronze, and Kenya 10 gold, 3 silver and 11 bronze.

The third games were to be in Zambia, but no evidence exists that they took place.

Year	Host City	Host Nation	Dates	Nations	Athletes	Sports
1974	Accra	Ghana		NA	NA	NA
1978	Nairobi	Kenya	Dec. 29–Jan. 7	NA	NA	NA

1978   Nairobi   Kenya   December 29–January 7

Nations: Algeria, Angola, Central African Republic, Egypt, Ethiopia, Ghana, Ivory Coast, Kenya, Lesotho, Madagascar, Malagasy Republic, Nigeria, Rwanda, Senegal, Togo, Tunisia, Uganda, Zambia

Sports: Athletics, Basketball, Field Hockey, Football, Handball, Judo, Swimming, Table Tennis, Tennis, Volleyball

Venues: City Park Stadium (Athletics, Opening Ceremonies) Barclays Bank Sports Club, Utalii College, YMCA, Kenyatta University College (Basketball, Handball)

Alps-Adriatic Summer Youth Games

The Alps-Adriatic Summer Youth Games, for the youth of Austria, Italy, Germany, Hungary and Yugoslavia were first held in 1982 in Auronzo, Italy. The first games were winter games, with the first summer games being held in Graz, Austria, in 1984. The games have alternated each year since then, with winter games in the odd years, summer games in the even years.

Year	Host City	Host Nation	Dates
1984	Graz	Austria	
1986	Pula	Yugoslavia	
1988	Trento	Italy	
1990	Linz	Austria	June 26–29
1992	Zalaegerszeg	Hungary	June 23–26
1994	Burghausen	Germany	June 21–24
1996	Siofok (1,024 participants)	Hungary	June 24–27
1998	Venice	Italy	
2000	Friuli-Venezia-Giulia	Italy	

Alps-Adriatic Winter Youth Games

Year	Host City	Host Nation	Dates
1982	Auronzo	Italy	March 28–30
1985	Villach	Austria	
1987	Piancavallo	Italy	
1989	Kranjska Gora	Yugoslavia	
1991	Carinthia	Austria	Feb. 25–27
1993	Bormio	Italy	Jan. 26–29
1995	Biasca/Ticino	Switzerland	Jan. 24–27
1997	Styria	Austria	

Arab Games

The Arab Games have been held on nine occasions since General Mohamed Naguib, the President of Egypt, declared the first Arab Games open on July 26, 1953, in the historic Alexandria Stadium, in Alexandria on the Egyptian Mediterranean coast. The opening ceremonies were highlighted by speeches by Abdel Khalek Hassoun, the Secretary General of the Arab League, Salah Salem, a major in the Egyptian Army, Dr. Abbas Amer, Egypt's Minister of Social Affairs, and President Naguib. Each speaker stressed the theme of Arab cooperation and unity. President Naguib hoped the "games would be a step towards cooperation in other affairs," and Major Salem urged the Arab nations to work together to fight ignorance, poverty and disease.[38] Despite the general desire to organize athletic contests to bring the nations of the Arab region closer together, the history of the games has been clouded by political discord.

The opening ceremony in Alexandria continued well into the evening with two hours of dancing and exercise displays. All of the participants in the first games were male; 657 athletes from nine nations.[39] Women were not permitted to participate in the games until 1985.

Ten sports—athletics, basketball, boxing, fencing, football, gymnastics, shooting, swimming, weightlifting and wrestling—were on the schedule of the first games. Egypt dominated on the playing fields, and the Egyptian State Broadcasting network broadcast results daily in English and French from 11:30 P.M. until midnight.

Spectator interest in the games was mixed. Alexandria Stadium, with a capacity of 30,000, saw crowds of 15,000 for the football final, while only 4,000 showed up for the final day of athletics. Some found other ways to enjoy the games. The Association of Foreigners in Alexandria hosted a garden party with games, dancing, orchestras, bands and gambling in Antoniades Garden.

The closing ceremony was as spectacular as the opening ceremony. The competing teams, which had marched into the opening ceremonies as separate nations, marched into this as one. Egyptian schoolchildren presented a routine depicting the history of farming in Egypt, while cavalry troops, police dogs, and motorcycle riders also gave demonstrations.[40]

The 1957 games were opened in Beirut by Lebanon's President Camille Chamoun in front of 60,000 spectators at the newly constructed Cité Sportive Camille Chamoun. The new sports complex was built at a cost of one million British pounds and named for the President's wife. The venue would also be used for the 1959 Mediterranean Games and Beirut would, for a short time, contemplate using the facilities in a bid for a future Olympic Games. It was the first modern stadium of its kind in the Arab world, with floodlights, loudspeakers, a banked 500 meter cycling track surrounding the 400 meter running track, an attached swimming pool, tennis courts and a basketball arena.

Many people rushed the gates and got into the opening ceremony free, leaving some dignitaries outside who could not get in or did not want to risk the crowds.[41] Colorful dancing, marching and sports displays formed the body of the opening ceremony. Doves were released to fly away but many preferred to land on the fresh grass in the stadium. A few were reported to have been snatched up by young boys to be taken home for supper. A massive traffic jam lasted well into the night after the ceremonies' conclusion.

Ten nations and 1,325 athletes attended the games.[42] Egypt, which overwhelmed the other delegations at the first games, did not send a team to Beirut. The reason was said to be internal squabbling surrounding some of Egypt's athletes who had disobeyed orders and traveled to Moscow to participate in the World Youth Festival earlier that year.[43]

The Lebanese finished on top of the medals table with 31 golds to Tunisia's 24. Iraq and Morocco tied with 13 golds.

King Hassan II of Morocco opened the 1961 games in Casablanca, but without teams from Iraq, Algeria or Tunisia. The Iraqis boycotted the games, protesting the participation of a team from Kuwait, which Iraq at the time was claiming as a part of its territory. Algeria's nonparticipation was due to a three-year-old situation involving a number of its football players who had broken their contracts with teams in France in 1958 to return to Algeria and join the Algerian National Liberation Front. FIFA had banned those players from taking part in any tournament and threatened to ban anyone who played against them. The Algerian Provisional Government sidestepped the question by pulling its teams completely out of the games, but sent a flagbearer as a gesture of goodwill. Tunisia also sent a flagbearer, but no athletes, to the opening ceremonies, citing the Bizerte crisis as the reason for not fielding a team.[44] The Egyptians returned with a strong team, but only seven other nations attended: Jordan, Kuwait, Lebanon, Libya, Morocco, Oman, and Sudan, making this the lowest number of nations participating in the games' history.[45]

Moroccan sprinter Moubarak Bouchaib was the star of the games winning the 100 and 200 meters in world-class times of 10.2 and 21.2 seconds.[46]

The games returned to Egypt in 1965 when Cairo welcomed them. The home team dominated by winning 71 gold medals. The remaining nine teams won just 20 gold medals, with Iraq winning five of its eight golds in wrestling.

The games had been held every four years, but it would be eleven long years before the opening of the next games in Damascus, Syria. The games were scheduled to be held in Tripoli, Libya, in 1969, but a change in government delayed preparations and the games were eventually canceled. Sudan offered to hold them in Khartoum in 1971, but instead Syria was tasked with organizing them in 1974. The Israel-Arab war in October 1973 interrupted those plans. It was not until October 1976 that Syria was ready for the games.[47]

Eleven nations—Bahrain, Jordan, Kuwait, Libya, Mauritania, Morocco, Saudi Arabia, South Yemen, Sudan, Syria, and United Arab Emirates—participated in the fifth Arab Games in Syria. Lebanon and Egypt, usually strong supporters of the games, did not participate.

The Arab nations intended to hold the sixth Arab Games in 1980, but problems relating to the ongoing Israeli-Palestinian conflict led to the games postponement to 1982. Devastation from the war caused the games to be rescheduled to 1985 and moved to Casablanca.

Prior to the Casablanca games, the Council of Arabian Ministers of Youth and Sports met in January 1984 in Algiers and were insistent upon the need to hold the Arab games on a regular four-year basis. At that time, the council chose Iraq to host the 1989 games, Jordan was to be the 1993 host, and Tunisia would put on the games in 1997.[48] None of these games ever took place, and discussion is sparse on the reasons.

The seventh games, held in Casablanca, were very significant as the first Arab games to allow the participation of women. Eighteen sports were on the schedule for men. The eight sports for women were athletics, basketball, gymnastics, handball, swimming, table tennis, tennis and volleyball. Venues in Rabat, Mohamedia and Settat, were used to supplement those in Casablanca.

Pope John Paul II was invited to Morocco by King Hassan and addressed the athletes on common values between the Catholics and Muslims. Egypt was under sanctions by the Arab League for signing a peace treaty with Israel and did not participate in the 1985 Arab Games. The Arab League in 1979 had moved its headquarters to Tunis, from Cairo. In 1987 the sanctions were lifted, and in 1990 the Arab League headquarters were moved back to Cairo.

Said Aouita, Morocco's star distance runner, made an attempt at a world record in the 1500 meters in Casablanca. Aouita had rousing support from his compatriots but fell six seconds shy of the record. Morocco won 57 gold medals, Tunisia 40, and Iraq 20.

In 1992, the games returned to Damascus, Syria, with some events held in the cities of Latakia, Aleppo and Hama. Two thousand five hundred athletes from 17 nations took part.[49] Iraq was banned from the games for its invasion of Kuwait, but Kuwait participated, keeping intact its record as the only country to attend every edition of the Arab Games. Iraqi athletes traveled to the Syrian border and demonstrated against their exclusion from the games.

Hassiba Boulmerka, the Algerian woman who had won the Olympic 1500 meter gold medal earlier that summer in Barcelona, was unchallenged in winning the Arab Games 1500 meter title. Ghada Shoua emerged as Syria's finest female athlete. Four years later, she would win the heptathlon gold medal at the 1996 Atlanta Olympics.

Syria continued the tradition of the host nation rising to the top of the medals table. Egypt, Algeria and Morocco followed.

The next games were to be held in Beirut in 1996, but much work needed to be

completed, including a rebuilding of the Cité Sportive stadium which had been destroyed in the war with Israel.

The first order of business in renewing the stadium in July 1993 was to evict some 700 non–Lebanese Bedouin and Gypsy squatters who had been living in and around the structure for over ten years. Police supervised the removal of the squatters and demolished the huts they had been living in. The rebuilding project was funded with assistance from several Arab states.[50]

Continued conflicts with Israel hampered Beirut's recovery and slowed the renovation of the stadium. When it became clear that the venues would not be ready in 1996, the games were postponed to 1997.

The question of Iraqi participation had not been resolved in the intervening years since the Damascus games. Lebanon refused to give the Iraqis visas when Saudi Arabia, Kuwait, Oman, Bahrain, the United Arab Emirates and Qatar threatened to boycott the games if Iraq was allowed to participate. The Iraqis, incensed, stated that the Arab League had invited them to the games and noted that even the United States had not tried to prevent Iraqi participation in the 1996 Atlanta Olympic Games.[51] The Lebanese held their position. The Iraqi National Olympic Committee, headed by Saddam Hussein's oldest son, tried to force the issue and sent 95 Iraqi athletes to the Lebanese border where the Lebanese refused to let them cross. The Iraqis waited at the border for two days before returning home.

Twenty-one sports were on the schedule with women eligible to compete in 14 of those disciplines. When the games began, failed drug tests, the first to be reported at the Arab Games, were an almost daily occurrence. In the end, 12 athletes were sanctioned: five from Egypt, two each from Saudi Arabia and Syria, and one each from Algeria, Tunisia and Kuwait.

The football final turned into a fiasco when Syrian fans rioted at the end of a 1-0 loss to Jordan. The fans destroyed seats in the stadium, and threw trash and bottles onto the field while the Syrian football players fought with Lebanese photographers.[52]

Eighteen-year-old Baya Rahouli of Algeria was one star of the games, winning the women's 100 meters, 100 meter hurdles, long jump and triple jump. Rania Elwani won nine swimming gold medals for the Egyptian women's swim team. Egypt returned to prominence atop the medals table with 97 golds. Runner-up Algeria had 43 golds.

The postponement of the Arab games to 1997 occurred soon after the Mediterranean Games organizers shifted the timing of their event to the year after rather than the year before the Olympic Games. This meant that for the first time, the Arab Games and Mediterranean Games were held in the same year, perhaps leading to future scheduling conflicts. A minor conflict in 1997 arose when some of the Arab Games entrants waited past the entry deadline to name their teams because they were waiting for results from their athletes' participation in the Mediterranean Games. Because of this, the Arab Sports Confederation moved the games—to be held in 2001 in Amman, Jordan—to 1999, averting further conflicts for the time being.

The 1999 Arab Games had an additional title, the Al Hussein tournament, in memory of Jordan's late King Hussein, who died earlier in the year. Jordan's royal family was very visible at the games. H.R.H. Princess Haya competed in the equestrian events, and was Jordan's flag-bearer at the opening ceremony. The new King, Abdullah II, was greeted enthusiastically at the games' opening ceremonies, and also showed up dressed in a Jordanian football jersey (number 99), to cheer for the home team at several of Jordan's football matches, including the final match in which Jordan defeated

Iraq. The football final took place on Queen Rania's 29th birthday, with the spectators singing "Happy Birthday" to the Queen during halftime. Jordan's football coach, Mohamed Awad, presented his gold medal to the Queen as a birthday present.

Kuwait, angry that Iraq was invited by Jordan to the Arab Games in Amman in August, confirmed its intent to boycott the event and sent only a diplomatic representative to the opening ceremony. Kuwait, ironically the only Arab nation to have participated in all eight previous pan–Arab games, was protesting Iraq's participation, hoping to bring attention to claims that Iraq was still holding many prisoners of war from the 1990 invasion of Kuwait.

Kuwait first voiced its intention to boycott these games in September 1998. Iraq had been banned from previous Arab Games, and their attempt to enter Syria for the 1997 games was unsuccessful, leaving Iraqi athletes stranded at the border.

Jordanian sports minister Mohammed Khair Mamsar resigned over his failure to convince the Kuwaitis to participate in the games.

Three days after the opening ceremony, Sheikh Ahmad al-Fahd al-Sabah, president of the Kuwaiti Olympic Committee, resigned from his position as a representative of the Arab Sports Federation citing interference from the Arab League in Arab sports matters as the reason.

Saudi Arabia's Prince Faisal Fahd—an IOC member and president of the Arab Sports Confederation, the organizing body for the games—died of a heart attack during the event. The Saudi Arabians insisted that the games not be disrupted, though the Prince was remembered in a moment of silence before each event began, flags were flown at half-mast for three days, and the nonsporting festivities associated with the games were suspended.

The Arab Games athletics events were held early. The organizers reached a compromise and allowed all four days of athletics to go ahead before the official opening ceremonies on August 15, in order to allow the athletes time to make it to Seville, Spain, in time for the World Athletics Championships. Jordan's Nada Kawar won the women's shot put and discus titles, while Tunisia's Ali Hkaimi won both the 800 and 1500 meters.

The basketball competition also began early in order to allow the tournament to finish in time for Lebanon and Syria to go the Asian Basketball Championships later in the month.

Soccer riots marred the closing week of the games. Libyan players attacked the Palestinian team after their game in the locker room, and fans rioted in the stadium and in the streets outside, ransacking vendors' stands and smashing car windows. A second riot occurred during the semifinal soccer match between Iraq and Libya. With the Libyan team down 3-1, Libyan fans began rioting, shooting fireworks onto the field, and ripping the brand-new plastic seats out of the King Abdullah stadium and hurling them onto the field. Over 50 people were taken to the hospital with minor injuries. The Arab Games Organizing Committee called an emergency meeting to discuss the issue.

The soccer field was not the only venue where sportsmanship was lacking. During the men's basketball match between Jordan and Syria, the Jordanian fans, upset that Jordan was behind, began to hurl water bottles onto the court. Jordan's Princess Haya, in a highly publicized event, grabbed a microphone from the scorers' table and spoke to the crowd, restoring order.

At least five bodybuilders were suspended and lost medals for drug offenses. Two Moroccan women athletes became the first to fail doping tests at the games. Siham

Hanifi, winner of the 200 meters and a member of the Moroccan 4 × 100 meter relay team, and Karima Shaheen, bronze medalist in the discus, both tested positive for the steroid nandrolone.

A controversy occurred over the eligibility of a number of Qatar's weightlifters to participate. Syria and Bulgaria claimed they were citizens of Bulgaria, Lebanon and Pakistan. The Qataris denied the accusations, claiming that all members of the Qatari weightlifting team had the four years' citizenship required to participate in the games. After several days in which the weightlifting events were suspended, it was determined that one of the Qatari weightlifters had in fact represented Bulgaria, under a different name, and the entire Qatari weightlifting team was disqualified from the competition.

Another controversy over eligibility centered around Lebanese gymnast Laila Sarkis-Khoury who resided in the U.S. and held an American passport. After several countries protested, her father was called upon to present papers verifying her Lebanese citizenship. Sarkis-Khoury went on to win the individual all-around gold medal.

Iraq was not allowed to bring its horses to the games for the equestrian events because the animals did not meet strict international health requirements. Jordan offered to let the Iraqi team use a number of its horses, but the Iraqis declined.

Rania Alwani, Egypt's fastest female swimmer, trained at Southern Methodist University in the United States, won eleven gold medals. Alwani, the holder of multiple Arab swimming records, had won nine gold and two silver medals at the 1997 Arab Games in Beirut.

The closing ceremonies for the games were subdued, organizers canceling all festivities due to the death of Prince Fahd. Algeria was presented with the Arab Games flag and asked to host the 2003 event.

The hosts for the Arab and Mediterranean Games have been loosely intertwined. Alexandria holds the distinction of being the first host for both games, the Mediterranean Games having been inaugurated in 1951. Beirut held the Mediterranean Games in 1959, two years after its first Arab Games, and Casablanca hosted the Arab Games in 1985, two years after it had hosted the Mediterranean Games. Latakia, Syria, hosted the 1987 Mediterranean Games, and the same venues were used for portions of the 1992 Arab Games. Having the opportunity to use the existing facilities and infrastructure may have helped to justify the costs for some these cities.

Year	Host City	Host Nation	Dates	Nations	Athletes	Sports
1953	Alexandria	Egypt	July 26–August 10	9	657	10
1957	Beirut	Lebanon	October 13–27	10	1325	14
1961	Casablanca	Morocco	August 24–Sept 8	8	NA	11
1965	Cairo	Egypt	September 2–14	9	NA	14
1976	Damascus	Syria	October 6–21	11	2500	14
1985	Casablanca	Morocco	August 2–16	20	2000	18
1992	Damascus	Syria	September 4–18	17	2500	17
1997	Beirut	Lebanon	July 13–27	20	2200	21
1999	Amman	Jordan	August 15–31	22	4600	29

1953   Alexandria   Egypt   July 26–August 10

Nations: Egypt, Indonesia, Iran, Iraq, Jordan, Kuwait, Lebanon, Syria, Palestine
Sports: Athletics, Fencing, Gymnastics, Swimming, Wrestling, Basketball, Boxing, Soccer, Shooting, Weightlifting

Venues: Athletics (Alexandria Stadium), Gymnastics (Small Hall), Swimming (Alexandria SC Swimming Pool), Wrestling (Tram SC), Fencing (Alexandria Fencing Club)

1957   Beirut   Lebanon   October 13–27

Nations: Algeria, Iraq, Kuwait, Jordan, Lebanon, Libya, Morocco, Saudi Arabia, Syria, Tunisia
Sports: Athletics, Basketball, Boxing, Cycling, Diving, Fencing, Football, Gymnastics, Shooting, Swimming, Volleyball, Water Polo, Weightlifting, Wrestling
Venues: Cité Sportive Camille Chamoun

MEDALS

Nation	Gold	Silver	Bronze	Total
Lebanon	31	35	19	85
Tunisia	24	13	6	43
Syria	7	13	11	31
Morocco	13	10	6	29
Iraq	13	10	6	29
Jordan	1	3	1	5
Kuwait	0	0	1	1
Libya	0	0	1	1

1961   Casablanca   Morocco   August 24–September 8

Nations: Egypt, Jordan, Kuwait, Lebanon, Libya, Morocco, Oman, Sudan
Sports: Athletics, Basketball, Boxing, Cycling, Football, Gymnastics, Swimming, Tennis, Water Polo, Weightlifting, Wrestling

1965   Cairo   Egypt   September 2–14

Nations: Egypt, Iraq, Kuwait, Lebanon, Libya, Morocco, Palestine, Sudan, Syria
Sports: Athletics, Basketball, Boxing, Cycling, Football, Gymnastics, Handball, Shooting, Swimming, Tennis, Volleyball, Water Polo, Weightlifting, Wrestling

MEDALS

Nation	Gold	Silver	Bronze	Total
United Arab Rep.	71	37	19	127
Iraq	9	18	11	38
Morocco	8	3	3	14
Lebanon	1	11	17	29
Sudan	1	7	3	11
Syria	1	6	25	32
Libya	0	5	3	8
Algeria	0	3	2	5
Palestine	0	1	2	3
Jordan	0	0	3	3

1976   Damascus   Syria   September 4–18

Nations: Bahrain, Jordan, Kuwait, Mauritania, Morocco, Palestine, Saudi Arabia, South Yemen, Sudan, Syria, United Arab Emirates

1985   Casablanca   Morocco   August 2–16

Nations: Algeria, Bahrain, Djibouti, Egypt, Iraq, Jordan, Kuwait, Libya, Mauritania, Morocco, Oman, Palestine, Qatar, Saudi Arabia, Somalia, South Yemen, Sudan, Syria, Tunisia, United Arab Emirates

Sports: Athletics, Basketball, Boxing, Cycling, Equestrian, Football, Golf, Gymnastics, Handball, Judo, Sailing, Swimming, Table Tennis, Tennis, Volleyball, Water Polo, Weightlifting, Wrestling

Sports for Women: Athletics, Basketball, Gymnastics, Handball, Swimming, Table Tennis, Tennis, Volleyball

MEDALS

Nation	Gold	Silver	Bronze	Total
Morocco	57	38	32	127
Algeria	15	40	42	97
Tunisia	40	24	26	90
Iraq	20	20	15	55
Syria	9	11	29	49
Kuwait	0	3	16	19
Libya	6	5	1	12
Lebanon	2	2	3	7
Qatar	2	2	2	6
Bahrain	4	1	0	5
Somalia	0	4	1	5
Saudi Arabia	1	0	3	4
Yemen	1	0	1	2
Sudan	1	1	0	2
Djibouti	0	1	0	1
Jordan	1	0	0	1
Palestine	0	1	0	1

1992   Damascus   Syria   September 4–18

Nations: Algeria, Bahrain, Egypt, Jordan, Kuwait, Lebanon, Mauritania, Morocco, Oman, Palestine, Qatar, Saudi Arabia, Sudan, Syria, Tunisia, United Arab Emirates, Yemen

1997   Beirut   Lebanon   July 13–27

Nations: Algeria, Bahrain, Djibouti, Egypt, Iraq, Jordan, Kuwait, Lebanon, Libya, Mauritania, Morocco, Oman, Palestine, Qatar, Saudi Arabia, Sudan, Syria, Tunisia, United Arab Emirates, Yemen

Sports: Athletics, Basketball, Boxing, Cycling, Equestrian, Fencing, Football, Golf, Judo, Karate, Kick Boxing, Shooting, Swimming, Table Tennis, Tae Kwon Do, Tennis, Volleyball, Weightlifting, Wrestling (Freestyle, Greco-Roman), Yachting

Sports for Women: Athletics, Basketball, Cycling, Equestrian, Fencing, Golf, Judo, Karate, Swimming, Table Tennis, Tae Kwon Do, Tennis, Volleyball, Yachting

MEDALS

Nation	Gold	Silver	Bronze	Total
Egypt	97	55	40	192
Algeria	42	43	44	129

Nation	Gold	Silver	Bronze	Total
Morocco	19	14	14	47
Syria	16	29	36	81
Tunisia	9	12	27	48
Qatar	8	6	2	16
Lebanon	7	16	51	74
Jordan	7	10	21	38
Saudi Arabia	1	10	20	31
Kuwait	1	13	1	15
Oman	0	1	2	3
Sudan	0	1	1	2
Libya	0	1	1	2
Emirates (?)	0	1	0	1
Yemen	0	1	4	5
Palestine	0	0	1	1
Bahrain	0	0	1	1

1999   Amman   Jordan   August 15–31

Nations: Algeria, Bahrain, Comoros, Djibouti, Egypt, Iraq, Jordan, Lebanon, Libya, Morocco, Oman, Palestine, Qatar, Saudi Arabia, Somalia, Sudan, Syria, Tunisia, United Arab Emirates, Yemen (Kuwait was represented at the opening ceremony, but sent no athletes), (Iran, Mauritania?)

Sports: Athletics, Badminton, Basketball, Body Building, Boxing, Bridge, Chess, Cycling, Football, Greco-Roman Wrestling, Equestrian Endurance Race, Fencing, Fin Swimming, Freestyle Wrestling, Gymnastics, Handball, Judo, Karate, Kick Boxing, Shooting, Show Jumping, Squash, Swimming, Surfing, Table Tennis, Tae Kwon Do, Tennis, Volleyball, Weightlifting

MEDALS

Nation	Gold	Silver	Bronze	Total
Egypt	105	79	79	263
Tunisia	40	40	57	137
Algeria	34	31	35	100
Syria	33	38	57	128
Morocco	30	41	42	113
Jordan	26	33	71	130
Saudi Arabia	14	17	16	47
Qatar	12	9	23	44
UAE	8	9	17	34
Iraq	8	7	30	45
Lebanon	7	13	22	42
Oman	4	5	7	16
Yemen	1	0	4	5
Bahrain	0	2	4	6
Palestine	0	1	9	10
Libya	0	0	14	14
Sudan	0	0	1	1

Arab Games for the Handicapped

The first ever Arab Games for the Handicapped (or Arab Paralympics) were held in Amman, Jordan, September 9–20, 1999, under the patronage of King Abdullah II and Queen Rania. The games followed the 1999 Arab Games held in Amman.

Prince Ra'd Ben Zeid, president of the higher Organizing Committee, sent out an open invitation to all Jordanians to attend the games saying there would be no entrance fees to the sports venues.

The inaugural games for disabled athletes in the Arab region came about after the Jordanian delegation returned from the 1996 Atlanta Paralympic Games and wanted to hold a regional competition. The games are open to athletes with physical, mental, sight and hearing disabilities. In the inaugural games, 700 athletes from Jordan, United Arab Emirates, Bahrain, Tunisia, Algeria, Palestine, Qatar, Lebanon, Libya, Egypt, Morocco, Syria, Saudi Arabia, Sudan, Iraq, and Yemen took part. Kuwait did not participate. While not officially stating a boycott of the games, Kuwait had boycotted the 1999 Arab Games in protest over Iraq's participation.

Jordanian television covered the games for five hours daily. Athletics, wheelchair basketball, weightlifting, target ball, table tennis and football were included. Thirteen of the 16 nations won medals. Egypt topped the table and won the wheelchair basketball gold, beating Morocco 64-46. Saudi Arabia beat Jordan 2-1 in the football final.

The next Arab Games for the Handicapped were scheduled to be held in Algeria, after the Arab Games in 2003.

Year	Host City	Host Nation	Dates	Nations	Athletes	Sports
1999	Amman	Jordan	Sept. 9–20	16	700	6

Nations: Algeria, Bahrain, Egypt, Jordan, Iraq, Lebanon, Libya, Morocco, Palestine, Qatar, Saudi Arabia, Sudan, Syria, Tunisia, United Arab Emirates, Yemen

Sports: Athletics, Football, Table Tennis, Target Ball, Weightlifting, Wheelchair Basketball

Arab School Games

The Arab School Games have been held on 12 occasions, but little has been recorded of their history. The 12th edition was held in Casablanca, Morocco, with the school-age youth of 12 Arab nations competing in athletics, basketball and football. The United Arab Emirates won the football tournament, with Libya taking second and Saudi Arabia third. Kuwait won the gold in basketball, defeating Morocco in the championship game.

Beirut, Lebanon held the fifth edition of the games in 1973.

1973	Beirut	Lebanon	
1998	Casablanca	Morocco	Sept. 5–15

1998   Casablanca   Morocco   September 5–15

Nations: Algeria, Egypt, Tunisia, Saudi Arabia, Libya, United Arab Emirates, Lebanon, Kuwait, Jordan, Morocco, Yemen, Sudan

Sports: Athletics, Basketball, Football

Arafura Games

The city of Darwin, Australia, began the Arafura Sports Festival in 1991 with 2,000 athletes from eight nations. The event has been held every two years since that time during the month of May. After the third games in 1995, the name was changed to the Arafura Games. The Arafura Sea, lying north of Darwin and between Australia, Indonesia and Papua New Guinea, gives the event its name.

The games were begun to stimulate tourism in northern Australia, to give developing athletes from this secluded region a chance to participate in international competition as a stepping stone to other international games, and to help promote friendship throughout the region.

Athletes compete as part of a nation or region, and only one team from each designated region may participate. For ceremonial purposes, national flags and anthems are used. The Arafura rules state that the games are open to athletes from "any district of any neighboring country within the parameters of the Tropics of Cancer and Capricorn, notwithstanding from time to time [that] the organizing committee may invite, at its discretion, representatives from outside the nominated areas."[53]

The games have a perpetual mascot, "Rocky" the rock wallaby, who greets the arriving teams at the airport and makes sure everyone has a good time in Darwin during the games.

The Malaysian swimmer, 14-year-old Lim Keng Liat Lim, won nine gold medals in swimming in 1995, swimming times faster than those at Australian Championships.[54]

The games have doubled in size with over 4,000 athletes from 24 nations participating in 1997. While no formal "village" is set up, a games "bed bank" is arranged to provide for the housing needs of the participants and other visitors.

With all of Darwin's international games experience, it entertained thoughts of bidding for the 2006 Commonwealth Games, but Melbourne was chosen as the representative from Australia in the bidding.

The 1999 Arafura Games were held May 22–29 in Darwin. Australia won 203 gold, 204 silver and 201 bronze medals. The rest of the field—19 nations—won 153 gold, 136 silver and 134 bronze.

Year	Host City	Host Nation	Dates	Nations	Athletes	Sports
1991	Darwin	Australia	May 18–25	8	1428	19
1993	Darwin	Australia	April 24–May 1	16	2358	23
1995	Darwin	Australia	May 6–13	17	2578	24
1997	Darwin	Australia	May 10–May 17	24	4200	26
1999	Darwin	Australia	May 22–29	20	3100	25

1995   Darwin   Australia   May 6–13

Nations: Australia, Brunei, Fiji, Hong Kong, Japan, Macau, Malaysia, Nauru, New Zealand, Northern Marianas, Papua New Guinea, Philippines, Singapore, Tahiti, Thailand, Tonga, United States

1997   Darwin   Australia   May 10–17

Nations: Australia, Brunei, China, Chinese Taipei, Fiji, Hong Kong, Indonesia, Japan, Macau, Malaysia, Nauru, New Zealand, Northern Marianas, Papua New Guinea,

(Pacific Oceania), Philippines, Singapore, South Africa, Tahiti, Thailand, United States, Vietnam (two more)

Sports: Athletics, Australian Football, Badminton, Baseball, Basketball, Boxing, Clay Target Shooting, Cricket, Golf, Gymnastics, Field Hockey, Lawn Bowls, Netball, Pistol Shooting, Rugby Union, Sepak Takraw, Soccer, Softball, Squash, Swimming, Table Tennis, Tenpin Bowling, Touch, Triathlon, Volleyball, Water Polo. Futsal (Canceled)

Venues: Marrara Sports Complex (Athletics, Australian Football, Shooting, Cricket, Field Hockey, Sepak Takraw, Volleyball), Marrara Indoor Stadium (Basketball), Darwin Golf Club (Golf), Parap Netball Courts (Netball), Squash World (Squash), Casuarina Swimming Pool (Swimming, Water Polo), Gardens Tennis Complex (Tennis), Fannie Bay Racecourse (Touch), Lake Alexander (Triathlon)

MEDALS

Nation	Gold	Silver	Bronze	Total
Australia	136	131	142	409
Malaysia	36	33	34	103
Indonesia	28	20	16	64
Chinese Taipei	26	14	11	51
Hong Kong	11	11	13	35
Papua New Guinea	10	16	19	45
Fiji	10	6	5	21
Vietnam	9	14	2	25
Philippines	6	4	3	13
China	6	2	8	16
Thailand	5	4	1	10
United States	4	7	9	20
Brunei	3	7	10	20
Northern Marianas	3	4	2	9
New Zealand	3	4	0	7
Pacific Oceania	2	2	0	4
Tahiti	1	1	4	6
Japan	0	3	3	6
South Africa	0	3	3	6
Macau	0	2	3	5
Singapore	0	1	4	5
Nauru	0	0	1	1

1999   Darwin   Australia   May 22–29

Nations (partial): Australia, Brunei, Cambodia, China, Chinese Taipei, Indonesia, Japan, Macau, Malaysia, New Zealand, Papua New Guinea, Philippines, Samoa, Singapore, Sri Lanka, Tahiti, Thailand, Vietnam

Sports: Athletics, Australian Football, Badminton, Basketball, Boxing, Cricket, Football (women), Golf, Gymnastics, Field Hockey, Lawn Bowls, Netball, Pistol Shooting, Rugby Union, Sailing, Sepak Takraw, Softball, Squash, Swimming, Table Tennis, Tennis, Tenpin Bowling, Triathlon, Volleyball, Water Polo

Venues: Marrara Sports Complex (Athletics, Cricket, Field Hockey, Football, Rugby, Volleyball), Marrara Indoor Stadium (Volleyball), Darwin Golf Club (Golf), Darwin Squash Center (Squash), Casuarina Swimming Pool (Swimming, Water Polo),

Gardens Tennis Complex (Tennis), Lake Alexander (Triathlon), Football Park (Australian Rules Football), Spectrum Stadium (Basketball), Foskey Pavilion (Gymnastics), Nightcliff Bowls Club (Lawn Bowls, Ten Pin Bowling), Micket Creek International Shooting Center (Shooting), Darwin Sailing Club (Sailing), The Tank, Darwin High School (Sepak Takraw), The Showgrounds (Softball)

MEDALS

Nation	Gold	Silver	Bronze	Total
Australia	203	204	201	608
Malaysia	55	49	44	148
Philippines	26	22	26	74
Chinese Taipei	18	17	9	44
Papua New Guinea	18	13	11	42
New Zealand	11	3	11	25
Vietnam	6	3	5	14
China	6	2	0	8
Macau	5	3	3	11
Singapore	4	3	3	10
Indonesia	3	6	5	14
Sri Lanka	1	4	7	12
Thailand	0	5	8	13
Cambodia	0	2	0	2
Tahiti	0	2	0	2
Japan	0	1	1	2
Brunei	0	1	0	1
Samoa	0	0	1	1

Arctic Winter Games

The small, spirited Arctic Winter Games were begun to fill the need for the sparsely populated territories of the far north to compete in games with others in similar circumstances in terms of training, facilities and number of competitive opportunities.

The idea was born during the first ever Canada Winter Games held in Quebec City, Quebec, in 1967. Stuart Hodgson, the commissioner of the Northwest Territories, and James Smith, the commissioner of the Yukon Territory, saw their teams outmatched and outnumbered by the teams from the larger Canadian provinces.

The two commissioners discussed creating a competition between the similarly sized regions of the north and approached the governor of Alaska, Walter Hickel, with the idea. Between these three the idea grew into the Arctic Winter Games Corporation which they formed in January, 1968. The corporation sets the rules for the games, selects the host cities from the games bids, and oversees the organizational work of the host cities. The games have been held every two years since their inception in 1970.

The first edition of the games was held in Yellowknife, Northwest Territories, Canada, with Canada's Prime Minister Pierre Trudeau presiding over the opening ceremonies. The Alaskan delegation, perhaps not recognizing the significance of the moment, failed to send any official of rank or importance to the games, which was said to have offended the hosts.

Over the years, Greenland, Northern Quebec, Northern Alberta, two Russian provinces, Tyumen and Magadan, have all participated in the games. The games' constitution opens the event to any peoples north of 60 degrees, but so far the Scandinavian countries have yet to participate. Reflecting the distances and diverse cultures that make up the games, one participant was heard to say, "I didn't know English could be spoken in so many different languages."

The games include the modern sports of skiing, hockey, ice skating, wrestling, volleyball and basketball, and on some occasions snowshoeing and dog mushing. The Arctic Winter Games provide events for people of all ages, from children and teenagers to adults.

The most unique sporting aspect of the Arctic Winter Games is the inclusion of traditional arctic games from the Inuit and Dene peoples, such as the finger pull, snowsnake, stick pull, pole push, one-foot-high kick and two-foot-high kick. Each game or event is a test of strength or a skill used for survival. The snowsnake is a 4½ foot spear made of spruce, thrown underhand to slide along a snow trough ten feet wide with one foot high sides. The event simulates the Inuit peoples method of hunting ptarmigan. In the stick pull, a test of strength, the object is simply to pull a straight round stick out of the opponent's hand, with no twisting or jerking, or shifting of the hand grip. The pole push consists of two teams of four individuals using a 20-foot pole five to six inches in diameter. The object is to push the other team completely out of a 30-foot circle. The teams must both push at all times, and can not pull or let go of the pole. The knuckle hop event tests how far one can travel on just the knuckles. The one-foot- and two-foot-high kicks, kicking an object suspended in the air, test the leaping ability, and were once used as a form of signaling while hunting on the arctic ice. "Airplane" is a test of strength where the contestant extends the arms perpendicular to the body and teammates carry the person inches off the ground as far as they can hold the "airplane" position.

From the beginning, native dancing and cultural exhibitions have been a very important part of the games, and have served to revive the traditions of the native peoples of the north.

Medals given in the games are gold, silver and bronze ulus, a type of seal skinning knife used by the Inuit peoples. The "Ulu News" is published daily for the athletes at the games.

Besides ulus for individual performances, the Hodgson Trophy, donated by and named after the cofounder of the games, has been awarded since 1978 to the team which shows the best team spirit and fair play. Carved from a three-foot-tall Narwhal tusk, and decorated with other soapstone carvings, the beautiful and fragile trophy used to be handed over to each team to take home. Now it stays in Yellowknife and a picture of the trophy is given to the winning team. The team from the Yukon won the trophy the first six times it was awarded, from 1978 to 1988. Since that time the winners, have been Alaska (1990), Northwest Territories (1992), Greenland (1994), Northwest Territories (1996), and in 1998, Yukon.

The 1970 games were an instant hit. Almost half Yellowknife's population of 6,500 showed up at the closing ceremony to cheer the victory of the Northwest Territories team and send well wishes to Whitehorse, where the 1972 games would be held.

In 1972, delegations from Northern Quebec, Greenland and the Soviet Union observed from the sidelines. A few Greenlanders participated in exhibition events, turning in performances that would have won gold ulus in downhill skiing and table tennis.[55] A mountain-climbing exhibition successfully conquered an unnamed peak 150 miles north of Whitehorse and gave the peak the name Mt. Ulu.

Anchorage welcomed the 1974 games, with the teams parading in colorful parkas and hats along E street in Anchorage to an outside opening ceremony in front of the railroad depot. Parachutists dropped in on the ceremonies as the Canadian Air Force band played the national anthems of Canada and the United States. A torch was carried from the ceremony to city hall where it burned for the duration of the games.[56] Native dancers performed dances that reportedly had not been seen in public for over 60 years.

The team uniforms caused a stir at the games, especially the distinctive parkas each team wore at the opening ceremonies. Alaska wore blue and gold parkas and hats to match the state flag. Black and gold were favored by the Yukon Territory. The Arctic Quebec team wore brilliant white parkas with matching toques and mukluks. The Northwest Territories wore blue parkas with polar bear designs and wolf fur trim. Pin trading very quickly became a popular Arctic Winter Games "sport."

Despite the admitted superb organization and facilities of the third games, they drew criticism from one newspaper reporter from Yellowknife who felt that Anchorage was far too large a city to hold the games, the venues were much too far apart, and that "there are too many officials and too many social functions. The attention is being taken away from the athletes."[57] Many athletes said they were overwhelmed by the size of Anchorage and that the barracks-style "village" at Camp Carroll, Fort Richardson, lacked privacy.

In keeping with the times, if not the temperatures, three streakers burst through the gymnasium during the closing ceremonies, clad in nothing more than boots and wool caps.

The small-town feeling would return to the games in 1976 when Schefferville, a mining community in northern Quebec with a population of just 5,000, hosted the games. The games had to be scaled back drastically to fit the size of the town. Unfortunately, they were the last for northern Quebec for over a decade as the expense of travel to that region was too high for most.

In 1978, Hay River and Pine Point, two towns 60 miles apart in the Northwest Territories, hosted the games. A special train was set up to provide transport back and forth, the first ever scheduled passenger rail transportation in the Northwest Territories. Hay River, a town of 4,000, did not have a stadium but solved the problem by stacking empty railroad cargo containers on top of one another with a building at either end along one city block in "downtown" Hay River. The temporary structure quickly came to be known as "Container Stadium" and served as the venue for the opening and closing ceremonies.

Men's adult hockey was banned from the games because of rough play in previous years. The snowshoe biathlon was added as a new sport. Alaskan shooter Joe Nava retired after these games, in his words to give other shooters a chance to win. Nava won 13 of the 14 gold ulus awarded in shooting at the first five games.

The games returned to Whitehorse for their tenth anniversary in 1980. The opening ceremony was held at the S.S. *Klondike*, a riverboat in the Yukon River.

Classrooms were turned into a games "village." Games organizers issued sleeping bags to all 900 athletes which they were allowed to keep at the conclusion of the event. A quick round of food poisoning hit the games village. About 60 athletes became ill but most recovered within a day.

The Alaska men's basketball team lost its very first game in the history of the Arctic Winter Games, but recovered to take the gold ulu.

Fairbanks, Alaska, opened the 1982 games in "Alaskaland," a theme park recreating the history of Alaska. The city spent $7 million dollars refurbishing the Big Dipper Ice Arena and used Fort Wainwright as the athletes village. Eighteen native dance troupes performed during the games. The games had become so popular by this time that in the Yukon Territory, one in every 27 residents tried out for them; in the Northwest Territories, one in every 45 did.[58]

The 1984 games returned to Yellowknife, their first home. A cold snap just before the start had temperatures at 45 degrees below zero. Conditions, though, warmed up just in time for the opening ceremonies. The ceremonies were so popular the fire marshal had to turn people away from Yellowknife Community Arena. The Canadian Broadcasting Company (CBC) televised the games for the first time, employing a crew of 55 people.

Winter triathlon—combining cross country skiing, snowshoeing and speedskating—made its games debut. Men's adult basketball was dropped because of Alaska's domination of past competitions, and men's senior hockey was reinstated with rules to prevent unnecessary roughness.

The Northwest Territories finished first in the overall medal count, bumping Alaska out of its usual top spot.

Northern Quebec and Northern Alberta returned to the games in Whitehorse in 1986. Alaska's Birgitta Kyttle, at 18 years of age, won the women's figure skating gold ulu, to add to her collection of two gold and two silver ulus from the previous four games. Alaska again won the team ulu count.

In Yellowknife in 1990, Greenland and a team from Magadan, Siberia, were welcomed to the games as official participants. Opening ceremonies were broadcast live by the CBC.

The hosts unveiled a mascot for the games—"Knifee," a six-foot-tall knife, colored yellow.

Dog sledding was added as a medal sport in the games, but only for the children's-age divisions, and for short races of 10 km with teams of three or four dogs.

One of the rare controversies of the games occurred when news leaked out that AIDS prevention brochures and condoms were to be given out in the athletes' information packet. The public outrage was so great, especially given that the games included younger-age divisions, that the volunteers were made to take the condoms out of the bags.

At the 1992 games, Brian Randazzo, one of the Arctic Winter Games' true superstars, won the one-foot-high kick for the fourth time in a row, and a total of five gold ulus in the arctic sports events.

Georgia Gustafson could also qualify as an Arctic Games superstar. From 1984 to 1992, she won 14 gold ulus, 2 silver and 2 bronze in the snowshoeing events.

In 1994, for only the second time, the games were held outside the original participating entities when Slave Lake in Northern Alberta hosted them.

Chugiak-Eagle River, Alaska, broke the participation records in 1996 when 1600 participants came to the games.

Yellowknife hosted the 1998 games, the fourth time the small Northwest Territories capital city had staged them. The Russians brought a hockey team for the first time.

The Arctic Winter Games held in Whitehorse in 2000 welcomed a new member, Nunavut. Nunavut, an Inuit word meaning "our land," is the name given to the eastern portion of the Northwest Territories which the Canadian government separated in April 1999 and restored to the Inuit so that they could govern their own lands.

In 2002, Nunavut and Greenland were scheduled to cohost the Arctic Winter Games.

Year	Host City	Host Nation	Dates	Nations	Athletes	Sports
1970	Yellowknife	Canada	March 8–14	2	500	11
1972	Whitehorse	Canada	March 5–11	2	900	12
1974	Anchorage	USA	March 3–9	2	958	17
1976	Shefferville	Canada	March 21–27	2	NA	NA
1978	Hay River/Pine Point	Canada	March 19–25	2	700	14
1980	Whitehorse	Canada	March 16–22	2	900	15
1982	Fairbanks	USA	March 14–20	2	900	15
1984	Yellowknife	Canada	March 18–24	2	NA	13
1986	Whitehorse	Canada	March 16–21	2	1000	17
1988	Fairbanks	USA	March 13–19	2	NA	NA
1990	Yellowknife	Canada	March 11–17	2	NA	NA
1992	Whitehorse	Canada	March 15–21	2	1000	NA
1994	Slave Lake	Canada	March 6–12	2	NA	NA
1996	Chugiak-Eagle River	USA	March 3–10	4	1600	19
1998	Yellowknife	Canada	March 15–22	4	NA	19
2000	Whitehorse	Canada	March 5–11	4	NA	18

1970   Yellowknife   Canada   March 8–14

MEDALS

Nation	Gold	Silver	Bronze	Total
Alaska	28	18	22	68
NW Territories	35	18	10	63
Yukon	7	24	20	51

Sports: Alpine Skiing, Badminton, Basketball, Boxing, Cross-Country Skiing, Curling, Figure Skating, Hockey, Shooting, Table Tennis, Volleyball

1972   Whitehorse   Canada   March 5–11

MEDALS

Nation	Gold	Silver	Bronze	Total
Alaska	49	43	27	119
Yukon	25	31	24	80
NW Territories	25	20	34	79
Arctic Quebec	1	2	0	3

Sports: Alpine Skiing, Badminton, Basketball, Cross-Country Skiing, Curling, Figure Skating, Hockey, Judo, Shooting, Table Tennis, Wrestling, Volleyball

1974   Anchorage   USA   March 3–9

MEDALS

Nation	Gold	Silver	Bronze	Total
Alaska	73	33	35	141
NW Territories	32	47	57	136
Yukon	21	40	26	87
Arctic Quebec	2	2	2	6

Sports: Arctic sports, Archery, Basketball, Badminton, Biathlon, Boxing, Cross Country Skiing, Curling, Figure Skating, Gymnastics, Judo, Hockey, Shooting, Snowshoeing, Table Tennis, Volleyball, Wrestling

1978   Hay River/Pine Point   Canada   March 19–25

Nation	MEDALS			
	Gold	Silver	Bronze	Total
Alaska	158	58	76	292
NW Territories	66	88	90	244
Yukon	40	113	66	219

Sports: Arctic Sports, Badminton, Basketball, Cross-Country Skiing, Curling, Figure Skating, Hockey, Judo, Shooting, Snowshoeing, Snowshoe Biathlon, Table Tennis, Volleyball, Wrestling

1980   Whitehorse   Canada   March 16–22

Nation	MEDALS			
	Gold	Silver	Bronze	Total
Alaska	64	44	38	146
Yukon	38	45	27	110
NW Territories	12	22	12	46

Sports: Arctic Sports, Badminton, Basketball, Cross Country Skiing, Curling, Figure Skating, Gymnastics, Hockey, Judo, Indoor Soccer, Snowshoeing, Snowshoe Biathlon, Table Tennis, Volleyball, Wrestling

1982   Fairbanks   USA   March 14–20

Nation	MEDALS			
	Gold	Silver	Bronze	Total
Alaska	61	47	41	149
Yukon	38	49	32	119
NW Territories	19	21	41	81

Sports: Arctic Sports, Badminton, Basketball, Cross-Country Skiing, Figure Skating, Gymnastics, Hockey, Judo, Indoor Soccer, Shooting, Snowshoeing, Snowshoe Biathlon, Table Tennis, Volleyball

1984   Yellowknife   Canada   March 18–24

Nation	MEDALS			
	Gold	Silver	Bronze	Total
NW Territories	42	33	27	102
Alaska	39	41	23	103
Yukon	23	30	43	96

1986   *Whitehorse   Canada   March 16–21*

MEDALS

Nation	Gold	Silver	Bronze	Total
Alaska	63	39	37	139
NW Territories	33	38	48	119
Yukon	30	43	31	104
Alberta North	0	2	1	3
Arctic Quebec	0	0	1	1

1990   *Yellowknife   Canada   March 11–17*

MEDALS

Nation	Gold	Silver	Bronze	Total
Alaska	63	46	27	136
NW Territories	36	40	41	117
Yukon	19	34	27	80
Alberta	13	6	6	25
Greenland	12	7	2	21

1992   *Whitehorse   Canada   March 15–21*

MEDALS

Nation	Gold	Silver	Bronze	Total
Alaska	72	39	42	153
Yukon	29	42	26	97
NW Territories	25	33	35	93
Alberta	12	18	18	48
Greenland	6	8	5	19
Russia	0	1	0	1

1996   *Chugiak-Eagle River   USA   March 3–10*

Sports: Arctic Sports, Badminton, Cross Country Skiing, Curling, Dog Mushing, Figure Skating, Hockey, Indoor Soccer, Snowshoe Biathlon, Showshoeing, Table Tennis, Volleyball, Basketball, Dene Games, Silhouette Shooting, Short Track Speed Skating, Wrestling, Gymnastics, Ski Biathlon

1998   *Yellowknife   Canada   March 15–22*

Sports: Arctic Sport, Badminton, Cross Country Skiing, Curling, Dog Mushing, Figure Skating, Hockey, Soccer, Snowshoe Biathlon, Showshoeing, Table Tennis, Volleyball, Basketball, Dene Games, Silhouette Shooting, Speed Skating, Wrestling, Gymnastics, Ski Biathlon

MEDALS

Nation	Gold	Silver	Bronze	Total
Alaska	69	58	57	184
Northwest Territories	56	69	65	190
Alberta	33	33	35	101
Yukon	26	26	28	80
Tyumen	25	13	6	44
Greenland	7	13	13	33
Magadan	7	8	10	25

2000   Whitehorse   Canada   March 5–11

Sports: Alpine Skiing, Arctic Sports & Dene Games, Badminton, Basketball, Ski Biathlon, Cross Country-Skiing, Curling, Dog Mushing, Figure Skating, Gymnastics, Hockey, Indoor Soccer, Snowboarding, Snowshoe Biathlon, Snowshoeing, Speed Skating, Volleyball, Wrestling

MEDALS

Nation	Gold	Silver	Bronze	Total
Alaska	62	72	51	185
Northwest Territories	47	32	35	114
Alberta North	37	25	24	86
Yukon	22	32	44	98
Greenland	17	14	13	44
Nunavut	8	11	16	35
Chukotka	6	7	8	21
Magadan	3	5	5	13
Nunavik-Quebec	1	3	7	11

Asia Pacific Games for the Deaf

The Asia Pacific Games for the Deaf developed from the Asia Pacific Deaf Football Championships, first held in Taipei, Taiwan, and sometimes known as the Far Eastern International Deaf Football Championships. The games were then known as the Asia Pacific Deaf Football Championships until 1992 when badminton was added to the program and the name changed to the Asia Pacific Games for the Deaf.

The fifth Asia Pacific Games for the Deaf were held in Kuala Lumpur, Malaysia, in 1996 and set a record for participation, with 700 athletes in four sports. The next games were scheduled to be held in Taipei, Taiwan, November 1–12, 2000.

Year	Host City	Host Nation	Dates	Nations	Athletes	Sports
1983	Taipei	Taiwan	July	4	100	1
1984	Hong Kong	Hong Kong	September	6	160	1
1986	Kyoto	Japan	August	6	165	1
1988	Melbourne	Australia	February	8	220	1
1992	Seoul	South Korea	August	10	400	2
1996	Kuala Lumpur	Malaysia	March	17	700	4
2000	Taipei	Taiwan	November 1–12	25	1000	8

Asia Pacific Masters Games

The inaugural Asia Pacific Masters Games were held from October 31 to November 8, 1998, on the Gold Coast, Australia. The games were very successful, drawing 9500 athletes from 40 nations.

The entry age for most events begins at 30. Participants pay their own transportation and accommodations, like in most masters games. Social activities are arranged along with the sporting events.

The Gold Coast has indicated that it intends to host the games at two-year intervals at least until 2008.

Year	Host City	Host Nation	Dates	Nations	Athletes	Sports
1998	Gold Coast	Australia	Oct. 25–Nov. 5	40	9500	33
2000	Gold Coast	Australia	Oct. 31–Nov. 8	NA	NA	NA

1998   Gold Coast   Australia

Sports: Archery, Athletics, Badminton, Baseball, Basketball, Canoeing, Cricket, Cycling, Dancesport, Dragon Boats, Futsal, Golf, Hockey, Indoor Cricket, Judo, Lawn Bowls, Netball, Polocrosse, Rowing, Rugby League, Rugby Union, Sailing, Shooting, Softball, Surfing, Surf Lifesaving, Swimming, Tae Kwon Do, Tennis, Ten Pin, Touch, Volleyball

Asian Games

International competition between Asian countries has its origins in the Far East Championships which began in 1913, continued every two years until 1927, and were held twice more in 1930 and 1934. The games rotated between China, Japan and the Philippines and included athletics, swimming, tennis, basketball, football and baseball. The games dissolved in 1934 over the issue of the inclusion of Manchukuo, a disputed region between Japan and China.

It was not until the world had begun to recover from the effects of World War II that the idea for an all-Asian competition was revived. Indian Prime Minister Jawaharlal Nehru proposed the idea to other Asian nations in 1947. The Indian Olympic Committee, led by G.D. Sondhi, continued the discussions with Asian neighbors at the 1948 Olympic Games and the first competitions were planned for 1950. Delays slowed the preparations and the first "Asiad" or Asian Games was held in Delhi, India, in 1951. Since 1954, the Asian Games have been held regularly every four years on the even years between the Olympic Summer Games.

Eleven nations paraded into National Stadium in March 1951 for the first Asian Games. China and Vietnam were not invited as their governments were not recognized by India. Pakistan boycotted the first games—it had become independent from India in 1947, and tensions still ran high over the disputed region of Kashmir. A short five-mile relay brought the first games torch from New Delhi's Red Fort to National Stadium where the flame was lit by India's Dalip Singh, a participant in the 1924 Olympic Games. N.C. Kok of Singapore won four swimming gold medals. Pinto of India won the 100 meters in 10.8, the 200 meters in 22.0.

China refused to attend the games of 1954, in Manila, Philippines, when the Taiwanese were allowed to participate, sparking the beginning of a long feud between mainland China and its disputed province. Atsuku Nambu, daughter of 1932 Olympic triple jump champion Chuhei Nambu, led the Japanese team, winning the 100 meters and scoring points in the relays and other events.

Japan, hoping to host the 1964 Olympic Games, built for the 1958 Asian Games what was said to be one of the most modern and beautiful stadiums of its time in the world. The stadium in Tokyo included restaurants, a hotel, movie theater and exhibition hall built underneath the grandstands, modern electric lighting, a gigantic electronic scoreboard, and an automatic sprinkler system.

Gun restrictions in Japan were so tight, that even starting pistols were restricted. After rejecting an idea to station police officers next to every starter with a gun, the Japanese Diet (parliament) gave special approval for the officials to use starting guns.[59]

The games were televised by both the commercial networks and Japan's government television stations. Accredited for the games were 3,320 print, photography, and television personnel to cover 1,422 athletes from 20 nations.

The torch for the games was lit in Manila's Rizal Stadium, and carried by a Japanese navy plane to southern Japan where it was relayed on foot to Tokyo. Japan's 1928 Olympic triple jump champion, Mikio Oda, was given the honor of carrying the torch into the stadium and lighting the Asian Games flame.

China again refused to compete when Taiwan was invited. The North Koreans wanted to send a separate team from South Korea but were not allowed as they were not members of the Asian Games Federation and were expected to be part of a unified Korean team.[60]

Japan completely overwhelmed the visiting nations, winning 67 gold medals. The Philippines and Korea were tied for a distant second in the gold medal count with eight apiece. C.K. Yang, who won four medals for Taiwan, including the decathlon gold, would go on to compete for the University of California at Los Angeles with Rafer Johnson, and finish second to Johnson in the 1960 Olympic decathlon in Rome.

The Japanese spent over $40 million on their new stadium alone, and though the games were a financial loss, they were grateful to be able to restore some of the international goodwill that had been lost in the region during the preceding decade of war.[61]

Mainland China, though, the day after the games, broke off sporting relations with Japan over the issue of the participation of Taiwan.[62]

The games of 1962 were awarded to Jakarta, Indonesia, by a narrow 22-20 vote of the Asian Games Federation and amid pessimism that Indonesia's complete lack of facilities and experience in organizing events of this kind would doom the games. Indonesia first appealed to the United States for economic assistance for the games, but the U.S. was noncommittal. President Sukarno then turned to the USSR, which responded immediately with guarantees for money to build a 100,000-seat sports stadium, swimming pools and arenas. The Japanese gave Indonesia a loan to build a new modern international hotel, and the U.S. finally assisted with money for a new highway that would be used extensively for the games.

The political tensions between mainland China and Taiwan resurfaced as a theme of these games in 1962 as did the issue of Israel's participation. Indonesia, having no diplomatic relations with either Taiwan or Israel, refused visas to both countries, excluding them from entering the country for the games. China, one month before the games were to begin, placed a great amount of diplomatic pressure on Indonesia to influence the decision concerning Taiwan. The Taiwanese protested and attempted to gain the support of other countries in a boycott if Taiwan was not invited. During the week prior the games, with all the nations except Taiwan and Israel in Jakarta, and the Indonesian government unwilling to budge, India's G.D. Sondhi, one of the original founders of the Asian Games, attempted to avoid the official problem by having them called the Jakarta Games and not the Asian Games. Both sides were deadlocked and the federation could not decide what to do after four days of meetings. It was decided to go ahead with the opening ceremony and resume the discussions two days later. Sohndi called a meeting of the Asian Games executive committee, not the full federation, and on August 26, two days after the opening ceremony, issued a statement to the press that the games would not be recognized as the Asian Games but instead would be called the Jakarta Games. The International Federations for basketball and weightlifting immediately pulled their sanction for those events and the competitions in those sports were canceled.

Two days later, the federation met again and reversed the decision. It insisted that the games had full sanction and set up a committee to look into the issues with Taiwan and Israel.

A riot at the end of the games chased Sondhi out of the city and back to India.[63] India went on to win the football final on the last day, and were booed loudly by the Indonesian spectators.

In February 1963, Sondhi used his influence as part of the executive committee of the International Olympic Committee to have sanctions placed against Indonesia, which led to Indonesia establishing the "Games of the New Emerging Forces" (GANEFO) in protest.

In 1966 in Bangkok, Thailand, disorganization typified the games. One spectator was trampled to death in a stampede when fans stormed the opening ceremonies. Both Taiwan and Israel were invited back. Japan, Korea and Thailand were the top medal-winning countries.

Korea had been chosen to host the sixth edition of the Asian Games in 1970 but continuing domestic problems forced the Koreans to decline and Bangkok stepped in to save the games. The same three nations as in 1966—Japan, Korea and Thailand—won the most medals.

In 1974 in Tehran, the Asian Games were especially controversial when the issue of the two Chinas reappeared. In an odd twist, the international governing bodies of swimming (FINA) and athletics (IAAF) each ruled differently on the issue. IAAF said the Taiwanese could compete, FINA voted against their inclusion, and in the end Taiwan did not participate.

After many protests against Israel's participation, the Asian Football Federation voted to eliminate Israel from future competitions. Israel's participation in other events was also protested, the Arab nations, North Korea, Pakistan and China refusing to participate with Israel in tennis, fencing, basketball and football. Adding to the rancor of the games, there were accusations of professionalism against six boxers from Thailand, and two drug suspensions handed out against weightlifters from North Korea and Japan.

In 1978, Bangkok, Thailand, once again stepped in to rescue the games after Islamabad, Pakistan, could not fulfill its responsibilities as host. Israel was expelled entirely from the Asian Games Federation and Bangladesh, Lebanon, Saudi Arabia, United Arab Emirates and Qatar were accepted as new members of the federation.

Japan continued its tradition of winning the most medals in the games, totaling 64 gold, 52 silver and 44 bronze medals.

In 1982 in New Delhi, police arrested more than 700 people three days before the games opened, fearful that Akali Sikh activists might try to disrupt the event. Ten thousand extra police were on hand for security during the games which ended without a major incident.

For the first time, Japan was not atop the medals table when the flame was extinguished. China had outscored the Japanese, with 61 gold medals to Japan's 57 golds.

The games were organized up to this point by the AGF, the Asian Games Federation. In December 1982, the OCA, the Olympic Council of Asia, was formed to take over the organization of the games.

The North Koreans threatened to disrupt the 1986 Asian Games in Seoul, South Korea. Five days before games opened, a large bomb exploded killing five and injuring 36 at Seoul's Kimpo airport causing an increase in security. Five schools and universities were shut down to curb student demonstrations during the games.

In Seoul, Japanese Prime Minister Yasuhiro Nakasone attended the opening ceremonies and was repeatedly asked to apologize for Japan's past mistreatment of Korea.

Li Ning, the Chinese gymnast, and Indian sprinter P.T Usha were the male and female stars of the games, each winning four gold medals. Murobushi Shgenobu of Japan set a record by winning the hammer throw for the fifth consecutive time at the Asian games.

Japan slipped to third in the team medals race. South Korea was second, just one gold behind China.

The controversies continued at the 1990 Asian Games in Beijing which opened September 22, a month after Iraq's invasion of Kuwait. The invasion led to Iraq's banishment from these games. During the invasion of Kuwait on August 2, 1990, Sheikh Fahad Al-Ahmad al-Sabah, the president of the Olympic Council of Asia, and member of the International Olympic Committee from Kuwait, was murdered.

Corporate sponsorship was not what the Chinese had hoped for, as international businesses shied away from sponsoring the games after the June 1989 Tiananmen Square crackdown.

China won 183 gold medals in Beijing, to South Korea's 54.

The 1994 games in Hiroshima, Japan, the first ever held in a noncapital city, were controversial again for the Chinese. Though they had been accused for some time of using illegal drugs, the Chinese had not been caught. However, by the end of the games, 11 Chinese had been suspended for performance-enhancing drugs.

South Korea had proposed that a unified North and South Korean team compete at these games. North Korea rejected the offer, though, due to the political tensions that surrounded its decision to withdraw from the Nuclear Non-Proliferation Treaty and its refusal to allow inspections of two of its nuclear sites by the International Atomic Energy Agency.

In 1994 the Sheikh Fahad Cup was inaugurated to memorialize the slain former president of the OCA. It was awarded to the top medal-winning nation, in this case China.

The 1998 Asian Games were awarded to Bangkok, Thailand, the fourth time since 1966 that the games were to be held in Thailand's capital.

The Olympic Council of Asia contemplated moving the games in January 1995 after frustrating progress reports were heard about their preparations. The Thai organizers convinced the OCA that preparations were going well but worries continued until the end of 1997, with the OCA making frequent checks on the organizing committee's progress.

Thailand, in the end, succeeded in pulling off a magnificent Asian Games in Bangkok, overcoming both the economic and organizational difficulties that had plagued the organizing committee almost since its inception. Chai-Yo, the smiling elephant mascot, welcomed some 6000 athletes from 43 nations to the opening ceremonies. By the time Thailand's Crown Prince Maha Vajiralongkorn declared the games closed on the final day, Thai newspapers had praised them saying that they had succeeded beyond all expectations. IOC president Samaranch, a guest at the opening ceremonies, had also given high marks to the games.

During the games, an Asian Games youth camp was held with 150 participants from 23 countries between the ages of 15 and 22. The camp's mission was to encourage international friendship and its emphasis was on environmental conservation. A pen pal program across Asia was also begun in conjunction with the games to allow children to communicate with youth from other nations about the event.

The host country took advantage of its hometown status to win 24 gold, 26 silver and 40 bronze medals, far surpassing its previous best of 12 gold medals when it hosted the games of 1966. The Chinese, though having won the most gold medals with 129, were disappointed with their overall performance which was far below their records of the previous two games. The Japanese, in third place, were also disappointed. They had won medals in 20 sports when they hosted the 1994 games in Hiroshima; this time they medaled in only 11 sports and suffered an especially crushing 13-1 baseball loss to a team of South Korean professionals. The Japanese did regain the top position as the region's swimming power, overcoming the Chinese and gaining a measure of revenge for the games of 1994 which were marred by Chinese drug use.

The games had a number of stellar athletes. Japan's Naoko Takahashi was the women's outstanding competitor, winning the marathon in an astounding time of 2:21.47, the second fastest time ever run, and more remarkable for the stifling hot weather and the tiny 12-person field for the race. The course later came under strong scrutiny and was thought to be far short of the regulation marathon distance. Qatar's distance star Mohammed Suleiman won the 1500 and 5000 meter runs to bring his career total to five Asian Games gold medals. Chinese women weightlifters set world records on every day of competition. Twin brothers Shunsuke and Shusuke Ito won the gold and silver medals in the 100 meter freestyle for the Japanese. Japan's athletics sprint sensation Koji Ito won the award, and U.S. $100,000 prize, as the outstanding male competitor of the games. Ito won the 100 and 200 meter dashes and was part of the winning Japanese 4x100 relay team. Ito's 10.00 time in the 100 meters was an Asian record, and he just missed becoming the first Asian athlete to run a sub–10 second 100 meters.

Monetary awards by various nations to their athletes were a visible part of the games.

Host Thailand far exceeded its own expectations, winning twice as many gold medals as it had predicted. The Thais budgeted $1 million for rewards to athletes but gave out almost $1.1 million for the 90 medals won. China, though winning the greatest number of golds gave out the least amount as it valued each gold at just $480.

| Nation | Money offered per medal (U.S. $) | | | Medals Won | | | Total $ Awarded |
	Gold	Silver	Bronze	Gold	Silver	Bronze	
Thailand	27,500	8,300	5,500	24	26	40	$1,095,800
Singapore	154,000	77,000	38,5000	2	3	9	$885,500
Hong Kong	64,120			5			$320,600
South Korea	2,300			65			$149,500
Malaysia	21,050			5			$105,250
China	480			129			$61,920
Kuwait	New Car			4			4 Cars

The games were not without the usual carping and minor political sniveling, though they tried to live up to the motto "Friendship Beyond Frontiers."

Saudi Arabia and Afghanistan withdrew before the games began, Afghanistan citing economic difficulties and protesting the amounts the Thai were charging to stay in the village. The Saudi Arabians withdrew in part because the Muslim holy month of Ramadan began during the last week of the games. Iraq was not present for the third games in a row, still banned for its aggressions against Kuwait in 1990.

The Chinese Embassy protested when Taiwanese flags were found flying in various locations around Bangkok. Because of the political disputes between China and Taiwan, it was agreed before the games that only the flag of the National Olympic Committee of Taiwan could be flown. North Korea insisted that it march before South Korea during the opening ceremonies; however, the hosts said that the Thai alphabet would be used, which meant that the South Korean delegation would march into the stadium fourth or fifth while North Korea would be approximately 35th. The teams were also separated in the village as much as possible.

The North Koreans were challenged to prove the ages of their female gymnasts who some nations thought were under the required 16 years. After inspecting their passports, the OCA allowed them to continue the competition.

Both tae kwon do and billiards had embarrassing displays of rancor and unsportsmanship. China, South Korea, Taiwan and the Thai hosts all protested decisions of the judges in the tae kwon do competition, with sit-ins, and near riots in the stands. Police were called in to restore order on more than one occasion. Pakistani and Indian billiards players got into heated discussions over proper behavior during their match play and the Chinese reported that a few of their table tennis players had been approached and offered bribes to throw their matches; all of them refused.

When India's Jyotirmoy Sikhdar won India's very first gold medal of the games the hosts mistakenly began to play the Chinese national anthem, the anthem heard most often at the games. After Indians in the crowd began to boo, the hosts realized their mistake and apologized. The Indian anthem was then played, and later in the day played again as a further apology.

An Asian Games rule that does not allow any nation to collect all three medals in one event caused a row when South Korea protested after taking the first three places in the individual dressage event of the equestrian competition. The bronze medal was awarded to the fourth place Japanese rider. South Korea lost two other medals under the same rule.

Drug suspensions caused other medals to come under dispute. Fakruddin Taher of the United Arab Emirates was disqualified for illegal drug use after winning the silver medal in the 60 kilo class in karate. The OCA ruled that the two bronze medal winners (there is no bronze medal bout and two medals are awarded) would both be given silver medals and the fifth and sixth place winners moved up and were awarded bronze medals.

Drug issues were fortunately not as big a topic at these games as they had been at Hiroshima four years before. Only four athletes failed tests at the games, although a few failed tests prior to the games and were removed from their nations' teams.

The Asian nations used the occasion of the games to discuss Asian solidarity in the World Cup of football. Football's governing body, FIFA, had decided to reduce the number of qualifying positions for the Asian region, from an automatic three nations, plus one playoff slot, to only two nations. This would mean only two of the 43 Asian nations would be participants in the 2002 World Cup to be cohosted by Korea and Japan. If Korea and Japan were to go along with a proposed boycott, this would put them in the most curious position of boycotting a tournament they would be hosting and organizing.

While there were no major health problems for athletes, two coaches from visiting teams died during the games, both of heart attacks. Rizvi Fulile Zain, Sri Lanka's swimming manager, died December 14, and Evgeny Godlevsky, a 63-year-old Uzbeki track coach, died on the final day of the games.

All in all, the games were regarded as a rousing success, with the minor incidents par for the course in most any large international games.

Busan, Korea, is well on its way with preparations for the 2002 Asian Games.

Year	Host City	Host Nation	Dates	Nations	Athletes	Sports
1951	New Delhi	India	March 4–15	11	489	6
1954	Manila	Philippines	May 1–9	18	970	8
1958	Tokyo	Japan	May 24–June 1	20	1422	13
1962	Jakarta	Indonesia	August 24–Sept. 4	16	1545	13
1966	Bangkok	Thailand	December 9–20	18	1945	14
1970	Bangkok	Thailand	December 9–20	18	1752	13
1974	Tehran	Iran	September 1–16	25	2363	16
1978	Bangkok	Thailand	December 9–20	25	2879	19
1982	New Delhi	India	November 19–Dec. 4	33	3345	21
1986	Seoul	South Korea	September 20–Oct. 5	36	3420	25
1990	Beijing	China	September 21–Oct. 5	36	4655	29
1994	Hiroshima	Japan	October 2–16	42	6078	35
1998	Bangkok	Thailand	December 6–20	43	6000	36

1951   New Delhi   India   March 4–15

Nations: Afghanistan, Burma, Ceylon, India, Indonesia, Iran, Japan, Nepal, Philippines, Singapore, Thailand

Sports: Athletics, Swimming, Basketball, Cycling, Football, Weightlifting

MEDALS

Nation	Gold	Silver	Bronze	Total
Japan	24	20	15	59
India	16	16	21	53
Iran	8	7	1	16
Singapore	4	7	2	13
Philippines	4	6	7	17
Ceylon	0	1	0	1
Indonesia	0	0	5	5

1954   Manila   Philippines   May 1–9

Nations: Afghanistan, Burma, Cambodia, Ceylon, Hong Kong, India, Indonesia, Israel, Japan, Korea, Malaysia, North Borneo, Pakistan, Philippines, Singapore, Taiwan, Thailand, Vietnam

Sports: Athletics, Basketball, Boxing, Football, Shooting, Swimming, Weightlifting, Wrestling

MEDALS

Nation	Gold	Silver	Bronze	Total
Japan	39	36	24	99
Philippines	14	14	17	45
South Korea	8	6	5	19
Pakistan	5	6	2	13
India	5	4	8	17
China	2	4	7	13
Burma	2	0	2	4
Israel[64]	2	1	1	4
Singapore	1	4	4	9
Ceylon	0	1	1	2
Afghanistan	0	1	0	1
Indonesia	0	0	3	3
Hong Kong	0	0	1	1

1958   Tokyo   Japan   May 24–June 1

Nations: Afghanistan, Burma, Cambodia, Hong Kong, India, Indonesia, Iran, Israel, Japan, Korea, Malaysia, Nepal, North Borneo, Pakistan, Philippines, Singapore, Ceylon, Taiwan, Thailand, Vietnam

Sports: Athletics, Basketball, Boxing, Cycling, Football, Field Hockey, Shooting, Swimming, Table Tennis, Tennis, Volleyball, Weightlifting, Wrestling

MEDALS

Nation	Gold	Silver	Bronze	Total
Japan	67	41	30	138
Philippines	8	19	22	49
South Korea	8	7	12	27
Iran	7	14	11	32
Taiwan	6	11	17	34
Pakistan	6	11	9	26
India	5	4	4	13
Vietnam	2	0	4	6
Burma	1	2	1	4
Singapore	1	1	1	3
Thailand	0	1	3	4
Hong Kong	0	1	1	2
Indonesia	0	0	6	6
Malaysia	0	0	3	3
Israel	0	0	2	2
Ceylon	0	0	1	1

1962   Jakarta   Indonesia   August 24–September 4

Nations: Afghanistan, Burma, Brunei, Cambodia, Ceylon, Hong Kong, India, Indonesia, Japan, Korea, Malaysia, Pakistan, Philippines, Singapore, Thailand, Vietnam

Sports: Archery, Athletics, Badminton, Basketball, Boxing, Cycling, Football, Field Hockey, Shooting, Swimming, Table Tennis, Tennis, Volleyball, Weightlifting, Wrestling

Venues: Basketball Hall (Basketball), Senajan Tennis Stadium (Tennis), Ikada Stadium (Football), Senajan Hockey Stadium (Field Hockey), Tjibibur Shooting Range (Shooting), Senajan Volleyball Courts (Volleyball), Ikada Sportshall (Weightlifting, Wrestling), Persidja Football Stadium (Archery)

MEDALS

Nation	Gold	Silver	Bronze	Total
Japan	71	56	22	149
Indonesia	11	12	25	48
India	10	13	10	33
Pakistan	8	11	9	28
Philippines	7	6	22	35
South Korea	4	6	11	21
Thailand	2	5	5	12
Malaysia	2	4	8	14
Burma	2	1	5	8
Singapore	1	0	2	3
Ceylon	0	2	2	4
Hong Kong	0	2	0	2
North Korea	0	1	0	1
Afghanistan	0	0	1	1
Cambodia	0	0	1	1
Vietnam	0	0	1	1

1966   Bangkok   Thailand   December 9–20

Nations: Afghanistan, Burma, Ceylon, Hong Kong, India, Indonesia, Iran, Israel, Japan, Korea, Malaysia, Nepal, Pakistan, Philippines, Singapore, Taiwan, Thailand, Vietnam

Sports: Athletics, Badminton, Basketball, Boxing, Cycling, Football, Field Hockey, Shooting, Swimming, Table Tennis, Tennis, Volleyball, Weightlifting, Wrestling

MEDALS

Nation	Gold	Silver	Bronze	Total
Japan	77	48	24	149
Korea	12	18	18	48
Thailand	12	13	9	34
Malaysia	7	5	7	19
India	7	3	11	21
Iran	6	8	16	30
Taiwan	5	4	8	17
Indonesia	4	5	9	18
Israel	3	5	3	11

Nation	Gold	Silver	Bronze	Total
Philippines	2	15	22	39
Pakistan	2	4	2	8
Burma	1	0	5	6
Singapore	0	5	7	12
Vietnam	0	1	1	2
Ceylon	0	0	5	5
Hong Kong	0	0	1	1
North Korea	0	0	1	1

1970   Bangkok   Thailand   December 9–20

Nations: Burma, Cambodia, Ceylon, Hong Kong, India, Indonesia, Iran, Israel, Japan, Korea, Malaysia, Nepal, Pakistan, Philippines, Singapore, Taiwan, Thailand, Vietnam

Sports: Athletics, Badminton, Basketball, Boxing, Cycling, Fencing, Football, Gymnastics, Shooting, Swimming, Volleyball, Weightlifting, Wrestling, Yachting

MEDALS

Nation	Gold	Silver	Bronze	Total
Japan	73	48	24	145
Korea	18	13	30	61
Thailand	9	17	14	40
Iran	9	7	8	24
India	6	9	10	25
Israel	6	6	5	17
Malaysia	5	1	7	13
Burma	3	2	7	12
Indonesia	2	5	12	19
Ceylon	2	2	0	4
Philippines	1	9	11	21
Taiwan	1	5	12	18
Pakistan	1	2	7	10
Singapore	0	6	9	15
Cambodia	0	2	3	5
Vietnam	0	0	2	2

1974   Tehran   Iran   September 1–16

Nations: Afghanistan, Bahrain, Burma, Cambodia, China, Hong Kong, India, Indonesia, Iran, Iraq, Israel, Japan, Korea, Kuwait, Malaysia, Mongolia, Nepal, North Korea, Pakistan, Philippines, Singapore, Sri Lanka, Thailand, Vietnam

Sports: Athletics, Badminton, Basketball, Boxing, Cycling, Fencing, Football, Gymnastics, Field Hockey, Shooting, Swimming, Table Tennis, Tennis, Volleyball, Weightlifting, Wrestling

Sports for Women: Athletics, Badminton, Fencing, Gymnastics, Swimming, Table Tennis, Tennis, Volleyball

Venues: Aryamehr Sports Centre (includes Aryamehr Stadium, Sports Hall) (Gymnastics and wrestling), Swimming Hall, Velodrome, Hockey Fields, Shooting Range, five other Sports Halls (Basketball, Tennis, Fencing, Weightlifting, Volleyball),

Imperial Country Club (Tennis, Trap and Skeet Shooting), Mohammad Reza Shah Hall (Boxing), Persepolis Stadium (Football), Anjadieh Sports Centre (Football, Badminton)

MEDALS

Nation	Gold	Silver	Bronze	Total
Japan	62	47	45	154
China	31	44	26	101
Iran	27	16	13	56
South Korea	15	23	15	53
North Korea	13	10	14	37
Israel	7	3	5	15
India	4	12	11	27
Thailand	4	2	8	14
Indonesia	3	4	4	11
Mongolia	2	5	7	14
Pakistan	2	0	9	11
Sri Lanka	2	0	0	2
Singapore	1	3	7	11
Iraq	1	0	3	4
Philippines	0	2	11	13
Malaysia	0	1	4	5
Burma	0	1	2	3
Kuwait	0	1	0	1
Afghanistan	0	0	1	1

1978   Bangkok   Thailand   December 9–20

Nations: Bangladesh, Brunei, Burma, China, Hong Kong, India, Indonesia, Iraq, Japan, Korea, Kuwait, Lebanon, Malaysia, Mongolia, Nepal, North Korea, Pakistan, Philippines, Qatar, Saudi Arabia, Singapore, Sri Lanka, Syria, Thailand, United Arab Emirates

Sports: Archery, Athletics, Badminton, Basketball, Bowling, Boxing, Cycling, Fencing, Football, Gymnastics, Hockey, Shooting, Swimming, Table Tennis, Tennis, Volleyball, Weightlifting, Wrestling, Yachting

MEDALS

Nation	Gold	Silver	Bronze	Total
Japan	64	52	44	160
China	46	47	49	142
South Korea	15	19	23	57
North Korea	13	14	13	40
India	11	10	7	28
Thailand	8	9	17	34
Indonesia	8	7	17	32
Pakistan	4	5	8	17
Iraq	2	5	5	12
Mongolia	2	2	5	9
Singapore	2	1	3	6
Philippines	1	1	4	6
Malaysia	1	1	3	5

Nation	Gold	Silver	Bronze	Total
Lebanon	1	1	0	2
Syria	1	0	0	1
Burma	0	3	3	6
Hong Kong	0	1	1	2
Sri Lanka	0	0	2	2
Kuwait	0	0	1	1

1982   New Delhi   India   November 19–December 4

Nations: Afghanistan, Bangladesh, Brunei, Burma, China, Hong Kong, India, Indonesia, Iran, Iraq, Japan, Korea, Kuwait, Laos, Lebanon, Malaysia, Maldives, Mongolia, Nepal, North Korea, Oman, Pakistan, Philippines, Qatar, Saudi Arabia, Singapore, Sri Lanka, Syria, Thailand, United Arab Emirates, Vietnam, Yemen (Sanaa), Yemen (Aden)

Sports: Archery, Athletics, Badminton, Basketball, Boxing, Cycling, Equestrian, Football, Golf, Gymnastics, Handball, Hockey, Rowing, Shooting, Swimming, Table Tennis, Tennis, Volleyball, Weightlifting, Wrestling, Yachting

Venues: Nehru Stadium (Opening Ceremony, Athletics, Closing Ceremony), Delhi University Grounds (Archery, Handball), Indoor Stadium (Badminton, Gymnastics, Volleyball), NDMC Indoor Stadium (Basketball), Pragati Maidan Hall (Boxing), Velodrome Rajghat (Cycling), Hrbaksh Stadium (Equestrian), Ambedkar Stadium and DDCA Grounds (Football, Wrestling), Delhi Golf Club (Golf), National Stadium (Hockey-Men), Shivaji Stadium (Hockey-Women), Ramgarh Lake, Jaipur (Rowing), Shooting Range, Tughlaqabad (Shooting), Talkatora Gardens (Swimming), Hauz Khas Stadium (Tennis), Asian Games Village (Weightlifting), Bombay (Yachting)

MEDALS

Nation	Gold	Silver	Bronze	Total
China	61	51	41	153
Japan	57	52	44	153
South Korea	28	28	40	96
North Korea	17	19	20	56
India	13	19	25	57
Indonesia	4	4	7	15
Iran	4	4	4	12
Pakistan	3	3	5	11
Mongolia	3	3	1	7
Philippines	2	3	9	14
Iraq	2	3	4	9
Thailand	1	5	4	10
Kuwait	1	3	3	7
Malaysia	1	0	3	4
Singapore	1	0	2	3
Syria	0	1	1	2
Lebanon	0	1	0	1
Bahrain	0	0	1	1
Hong Kong	0	0	1	1
Qatar	0	0	1	1
Saudi Arabia	0	0	1	1
Vietnam	0	0	1	1

1986   Seoul   South Korea   September 20–October 5

Nations: Bahrain, Bangladesh, Bhutan, China, Hong Kong, India, Indonesia, Iran, Iraq, Japan, Jordan, Kuwait, Lebanon, Malaysia, Maldives, Nepal, Oman, Pakistan, Philippines, Qatar, Saudi Arabia, Singapore, South Korea, Sri Lanka, Thailand, United Arab Emirates, Yemen Arab Republic

Sports: Archery, Athletics, Badminton, Basketball, Bowling, Boxing, Cycling, Fencing, Football, Golf, Gymnastics, Hockey, Judo, Rowing, Shooting, Swimming, Table Tennis, Tennis, Volleyball, Weightlifting, Wrestling

MEDALS

Nation	Gold	Silver	Bronze	Total
China	94	82	46	222
South Korea	93	55	76	224
Japan	58	76	77	211
Iran	6	6	10	22
India	5	9	23	37
Philippines	4	5	9	18
Thailand	3	10	13	26
Pakistan	2	3	4	9
Indonesia	1	5	14	20
Hong Kong	1	1	3	5
Qatar	1	0	3	4
Lebanon	1	0	1	2
Bahrain	1	0	1	2
Malaysia	0	5	5	10
Iraq	0	5	2	7
Jordan	0	3	1	4
Kuwait	0	1	8	9
Singapore	0	1	4	5
Saudi Arabia	0	1	0	1
Nepal	0	0	8	8
Bangladesh	0	0	1	1
Oman	0	0	1	1
Yemen Arab Republic	0	0	0	0
Maldives	0	0	0	0
Sri Lanka	0	0	0	0
United Arab Emirates	0	0	0	0
Bhutan	0	0	0	0

1990   Beijing   China   September 21–October 5

Nations: Afghanistan, Bahrain, Bangladesh, Bhutan, Brunei, Burma, Cambodia, China, Chinese Taipei, Hong Kong, India, Indonesia, Iran, Japan, Jordan, Kuwait, Laos, Lebanon, Macau, Malaysia, Mongolia, Nepal, Oman, Pakistan, Palestine, Peoples Democratic Republic of Korea, Philippines, Qatar, Saudi Arabia, Singapore, South Korea, Sri Lanka, Syria, Thailand, United Arab Emirates, Vietnam, Yemen

Sports: Archery, Athletics, Badminton, Basketball, Boxing, Canoeing, Cycling, Diving, Fencing, Football, Golf, Gymnastics, Handball, Field Hockey, Judo, Kabbadi, Rowing, Sepak Takraw, Shooting, Softball, Swimming, Table Tennis, Tennis, Volleyball, Water Polo, Weightlifting, Wrestling, Wushu, Yachting (Baseball, Squash—demonstration sports)

Venues: University Gymnasium (Basketball), Yuetan Gymnasium (Judo), Haidian Gymnasium (Wushu), Beijing Physical Culture Institute Gymnasium (Boxing), Xiannongtan Gymnasium (Badminton), Chaoyang Gymnasium (Volleyball), Tiantan Tennis Center, Shijingshan Gymnasium (wrestling), Muxiyan Gymnasium (Sports Acrobatics), Ditan Gymnasium (Weightlifting), Changping Velodrome (cycling), Xiannongtan Stadium (Football), Beijiao Natatorium (Swimming, Diving), Workers Stadium (Opening Ceremonies, Athletics, Football, Closing Ceremonies)

1994   Hiroshima   Japan   October 2–16

Sports: Archery, Athletics, Badminton, Baseball, Basketball, Bowling, Boxing, Canoeing, Cycling, Equestrian, Fencing, Football, Golf, Gymnastics, Handball, Hockey, Judo, Kabaddi, Karatedo, Modern Pentathlon, Rowing, Sepak Takraw, Shooting, Softball, Soft Tennis, Tennis, Swimming, Table Tennis, Tae Kwon Do, Tennis, Volleyball, Weightlifting, Wrestling, Wushu, Yachting

Venues: Main Stadium, Hiroshima Regional Park (Opening and Closing Ceremonies, Athletics, Football), Hiroshima Prefectural Sports Center (Gymnastics, Volleyball), Hiroshima City Indoor Swimming Pool (Swimming), Hiroshima City Higashi Ward Sports Center (Handball) Hiroshima City Asakita Ward Sports Center (Table Tennis), Hiroshima City Saeki Ward Sports Center (Sepak Takraw, Weightlifting), Gymnasium, Higashi-Hiroshima Sports Park (Wrestling) Track and Field Stadium, Miyoshi Sports Park (Football) Athletics Stadium, Bingo Regional Sports Park (Football)

MEDALS				
Nation	*Gold*	*Silver*	*Bronze*	*Total*
China	137	92	60	289
Korea	63	53	63	179
Japan	59	68	80	207
Kazahkstan	25	26	26	77
Uzbekistan	10	11	19	40
Iran	9	9	8	26
Chinese Taipei	7	12	24	43
India	4	3	15	22
Malaysia	4	2	13	19
Qatar	4	1	5	10
Indonesia	3	12	11	26
Syria	3	3	1	7
Philippines	3	2	8	13
Kuwait	3	1	5	9
Thailand	1	11	13	25
Saudi Arabia	1	3	5	9
Turkmenistan	1	3	3	7
Mongolia	1	2	6	9
Vietnam	1	2	0	3
Singapore	1	1	5	7
Hong Kong	0	5	7	12
Pakistan	0	4	6	10
Kyrgyzstan	0	4	5	9
Jordan	0	2	2	4

Nation	Gold	Silver	Bronze	Total
United Arab Republic	0	1	3	4
Sri Lanka	0	1	1	2
Macau	0	1	1	2
Bangladesh	0	1	0	1
Tajikistan	0	0	2	2
Brunei	0	0	2	2
Myanmar	0	0	2	2
Nepal	0	0	2	2

1998   Bangkok   Thailand   December 6–20

Venues: The Hua Mark Sports Center—Rajamangala National Stadium (Opening, Closing Ceremonies, Football Athletics), Indoor Stadium (Sepak Takraw), Velodrome (Cycling), Shooting Range (Shooting), Clay Target Shooting Range (Clay Target Shooting), the Bangkok Land Sports Complex (Boxing Ringside, Gymnastics Ringside, Weightlifting Ringside, Volleyball, Billiards & Snooker, Rugby Football, Tennis, Swimming), Rangsit Sports Complex, Thammasat University, Rangsit Campus—Main Stadium, Aquatic Center, Gymnasiums, (Badminton, Handball, Karatedo, Tae Kwon Do, Wushu, Basketball, Wrestling, Judo, Table Tennis, Fencing and Sepak Takraw), Main Stadium, Chiang Mai (Football), Nakhon Sawan Main Stadium (Football), Songkla Main Stadium (Football), Si Sa Ket Main Stadium (Football), Surat Thani Main Stadium (Football), Trang Main Stadium (Football), Suphachalasai Stadium (Football), Din Dang Stadium (Football), Suphan Buri Football Stadium (Football), Thupataemee Stadium (Football), Queen Siritkit Stadium (Baseball, Hockey), Koayai Rimtam Resort (Cycling), Srinakharinwirot University (Handball, Softball, Kabaddi), Kasetsart University (Hockey), Map Prachan Reservoir Chon Buri (Canoeing, Rowing), Fort Adhisorn Riding Club (Equestrian), Ambassador Sport Center (Squash), Ao-Dongtarn Jomtien Beach (Yachting), PS Bowling Bangkapi (Bowling), Alpine Golf and Sports Club (Golf), Royal Thai Army Stadium (Rugby), Suwannawong Gym Hat Yai (Sepak Takraw), Municipal Stadium Trang (Sepak Takraw).

Asian Sports Festival

The Asian Sports Festival, sponsored by the General Association of Asian Sports Federations (GAASF) and the National Sports Association of the Peoples Republic of China, was held in Shenyang, China, to showcase non–Olympic sports in Asia, and to promote the city of Shenyang as a growing international city where sports businesses might be established. An International Sports Film Festival and Sports Culture Exhibition were held in conjunction with the games.

Year	Host City	Host Nation	Dates	Nations	Athletes	Sports
1998	Shenyang	China	August 29–Sept. 6	37	NA	14

Sports: Aerobics, Billiards, Body Building, Bowling, Bridge, Cycling, Dragon Boat Racing, Gateball, Roller Skating, Skateboard, Sports Dancing, Tae Kwon Do, Taijiquan, Water-Related games

Venues: Shenyang Central Stadium (Opening Ceremony), Zhongshan Park

(Skateboarding, Roller-Skating), Beiling Park (Skateboarding, Roller-Skating), Hunhe Amusement Park (Dragon Boat Racing), Huishan Tourist Resort (Water Recreation Games), Second Ring Road Shenyang (Bicycle Race), Lianong Industrial Exhibition Center (Aerobics, Closing Ceremony), Locomotive Gymnasium (Sports Dancing)

Asian Winter Games

Participation in winter sports across Asia has never been at the level of that of the summer sports, due in a large part to geography. In 1986, however, seven nations—China, Hong Kong, India, Japan, Mongolia, North Korea and South Korea—gathered in Sapporo, Japan, site of the 1972 Winter Olympic Games, for the first Asian Winter Games. The host nation won the vast majority of the medals, 29 golds, far surpassing runner-up China's four wins.

India had been chosen to host the second Asian Winter Games but had to remove itself as host in 1989. Japan stepped in and offered its established facilities, and the second edition of the games was held in 1990 once again in Sapporo.[65] One of the most popular winter sports, figure skating, was dropped from the games when the dates conflicted with the world figure skating championships held in Halifax, Canada. The games, using the established facilities, were a windfall for the Japanese Olympic Committee, and turned a profit of some U.S. $420,000. Japan doubled runner-up China's gold medal output 18 to nine.

Sheikh Fahad Al-Ahmad Al-Sabah of Kuwait, the president of the Olympic Council of Asia, presided over both the first and second games. Tragically, the Sheikh would be murdered later that year in the Iraqi invasion of his homeland.

The third edition of the games in 1996 also ran into difficulties with organization. North Korea had been awarded the original games, but withdrew its sponsorship. The bidding process reopened with two candidates: Harbin, China, and Kangwon, South Korea. The delegates of the Olympic Council of Asia, in the general assembly of November 1993, awarded the 1996 games to Harbin, and decided to award the following games, to be held in 1999, to Kangwon.

For the Harbin games, numerous new facilities were constructed and highways to the airport and ski area were upgraded, funded by a special lottery set up for the games. The Yabuli Ski area was renovated, a new gondola ski lift system installed, and a new ski jumping facility constructed. The opening ceremony and speed-skating events were held at the brand new Harbin skating center.

The torch-lighting ceremony for the games was unique, featuring a convex lens made of ice to produce the flame.[66] Wang Xiuli, world champion speed skater, began the torch ceremony, which was held in front of Beijing's Temple of Heaven, next to Tiannamen Square. From the main torch, 31 identical torches were lit to symbolize the 31 provinces, regions and autonomous regions in China, these torches were paraded around Tiananmen Square and then the main torch was flown to Harbin. The torch run within Harbin for the games was short—five days and 30 kilometers—but went throughout the city.

Chinese athletes scored 15 gold medals. Kazakhstan, participating in the games for the first time, won 14 golds. Japan and South Korea each finished with eight golds.

A financial slowdown in Asia hampered the preparations for the 1999 games, but the Koreans finished just in time. The theme was "Asia shining brightly through everlasting friendship." There was a torch relay, throughout the province of 943 kilometers.

Kuwait, after practicing for just one month, participated in ice hockey, but was beaten 35-0 by China and 44-1 by Japan. The goal was the first ever scored in ice hockey by any Arab nation in an international games.

The 2003 Asian Winter Games are scheduled to be held in Aomori, Japan.

Year	Host City	Host Nation	Dates	Nations	Athletes	Sports
1986	Sapporo	Japan	March 1–8	7	295	7
1990	Sapporo	Japan	March 9–14	9	310	6
1996	Harbin	China	Feb. 4–11	16	494	9
1999	Kangwon	South Korea	Jan. 30–Feb. 6	19	522	7

1986   Sapporo   Japan   March 1–8

Nations: China, Hong Kong, India, Japan, South Korea, North Korea, Mongolia
Sports: Figure Skating, Speed Skating, Short-Track Speed Skating, Ice Hockey, Alpine Skiing, Cross-Country Skiing, Biathlon (90 m ski jump as demonstration)

MEDALS

Nation	Gold	Silver	Bronze	Total
Japan	29	23	6	58
China	4	5	12	21
South Korea	1	5	12	18
North Korea	1	2	5	7

1990   Sapporo   Japan   March 9–14

Nations: China, India, Iran, Japan, Korea, North Korea, Taiwan, Mongolia, Philippines
Sports: Speed Skating, Short-Track Speed Skating, Ice Hockey, Alpine Skiing, Cross-Country Skiing, Biathlon (115 m ski jump as demonstration)

MEDALS

Nation	Gold	Silver	Bronze	Total
Japan	18	16	13	47
China	9	9	8	26
South Korea	6	7	8	21
North Korea	0	1	4	5
Mongolia	0	0	1	1

1996   Harbin   China   February 4–11

Nations: China, Chinese Taipei, Hong Kong, India, Iran, Japan, Kazakhstan, South Korea, Kuwait, Kyrgyzstan, Lebanon, Tajikistan, Thailand, Mongolia, Pakistan, Uzbekistan
Sports: Cross-Country Skiing, Biathlon, Freestyle, Ice Hockey, Speed Skating, Short Track, Figure Skating, Alpine Skiing, Ski Jump
Venues: Feichi Ice Hockey Hall (Opening Ceremony, Ice Hockey, Closing Ceremony), Harbin Skating Center (Speed Skating, Short-Track Speed Skating, Figure Skating), Yabuli Ski Area (Downhill, Cross-country, Freestyle, Ski-jumping, Biathlon)

| | MEDALS | | | |
Nation	Gold	Silver	Bronze	Total
China	15	7	15	37
Kazakhstan	14	9	8	31
Japan	8	14	10	32
South Korea	8	10	8	26
Uzbekistan	0	1	1	2

1999   Kangwon   South Korea   January 30–Feb. 6

Sports: Alpine Skiing, Biathlon, Cross-Country Skiing, Ice Hockey, Speed Skating, Short-Track Speed Skating, Figure Skating

Ataturk Dam International Sports Festival

The Ataturk Dam International Sports Festival is sponsored by the Turkish Olympic Committee, the Turkish government authority for the Ataturk Dam, and the Turkish government department responsible for youth and sports.

The festival's goals are to promote Olympism among youth, economic development, and tourism to the area.

The sports festival consists of water sports: sailing, rowing, canoeing, swimming, diving and underwater sports.

In 1999, athletes from Bulgaria, Israel and Romania joined their Turkish hosts at the games.

Year	Host City	Host Nation	Dates	Nations	Athletes	Sports
1995	Ataturk Dam	Turkey	October 6–7	NA	NA	NA
1996	Ataturk Dam	Turkey	October 4–5	NA	NA	NA
1997	Ataturk Dam	Turkey	October 3–4	NA	NA	NA
1998	Ataturk Dam	Turkey	October 9–10	NA	NA	NA
1999	Ataturk Dam	Turkey	September 24–25	4	396	5
2000	Ataturk Dam	Turkey		NA	NA	NA

Australasian Public Sector Games

The Australasian Public Sector Games began in 1998 as part of Australia's Active for Life program to promote health in the workplace. To be eligible to participate one must be employed in a government service, the Australian Defense Force, police or fire service, a public school or university, or public health or any organization providing services to the public sector.

The 2000 edition of the games had 3,500 participants in 18 sports.

Year	Host City	Host Nation	Dates	Nations	Athletes	Sports
1998	Melbourne	Australia	April 15–19	NA	3200	18
2000	Melbourne	Australia	April 26–30	NA	3500	18

2000   Melbourne   Australia   April 26–30

Sports: Athletics, Badminton, Basketball, Cycling, Duathlon, Football, Golf, Indoor Cricket, Lawn Bowls, Netball, Road Run/walk, Softball, Squash, Swimming, Table Tennis, Tennis, Touch, Volleyball

Australian Masters Games

One of the first regional masters games, the Australian Masters Games have been successful at drawing international participation since their inception in 1987.

Thirty nations, the record to date, participated in the 1993 games in Perth. Participants must be at least 30 years of age to compete in most events.

The 2001 Australian Masters Games were to be held in Newcastle and the Hunter Valley, in New South Wales, Australia, in October.

Year	Host City	Host Nation	Dates	Nations	Athletes	Sports
1987	Hobant	Australia	Nov. 28–Dec. 12	8	3600	40
1989	Adelaide	Australia		4	NA	40
1991	Brisbane	Australia	Oct. 8–20	17	NA	40
1993	Perth	Australia	April 20–May 2	30	NA	40
1995	Melbourne	Australia	Oct.	25	8000	45
1997	Canberra	Australia	Oct. 23–31	27	8811	32
1999	Adelaide	Australia	Sept. 25–Oct. 3	NA	NA	NA

1997   Canberra   Australia   October 23–31

Nations: Australia, Bangladesh, Brazil, Brunei, Bulgaria, Canada, Chile, Croatia, England, Fiji, Germany, Guam, Hong Kong, India, Indonesia, Italy, Japan, Lithuania, New Zealand, Pakistan, Papua New Guinea, Russia, Singapore, South Africa, Sri Lanka, Ukraine, United States

Sports: Archery, Athletics, Badminton, Baseball, Basketball, Canoeing, Croquet, Cycling, Equestrian (Carriage Driving, Combined training, Dressage, Eventing, Polocrosse, Showjumping, Western Performance), Futsal, Golf, Field Hockey, Ice Hockey, Indoor Cricket, Indoor Rowing, Lawn Bowls, Netball, Rowing, Rugby Union, Sailing, Shooting, Soccer, Softball, Squash, Swimming, Table Tennis, Tennis, Tenpin Bowling, Touch, Triathlon and Duathlon, Volleyball, Water Polo

Australian Universities Games

The Australian Universities Games are an interesting example of a national games which has from time to time welcomed international participation. The games are sponsored by the Australian University Sports Federation (AUSF) and are open to university students whose universities are affiliated with the AUSF or who have been invited to compete by the AUSF.

Australian university teams must qualify to participate in the games by competing against each other in smaller conference games throughout Australia.

In 1996, New Zealand, South Africa and Singapore were invited to compete. In 1998, participants from ten overseas countries took part in the games.

Year	Host City	Host Nation	Dates	Nations	Athletes	Sports
1994	Wollongong	Australia	Sept. 25–30	NA	NA	NA
1995	Darwin	Australia	Sept. 24–30	NA	NA	NA
1996	Canberra	Australia	Sept. 29–Oct. 4	4	5500	21
1997	Bundoora	Australia	Sept. 28–Oct. 3	NA	NA	24
1998	Melbourne	Australia	Sept. 28–Oct. 3	11	6000	23
1999	Perth	Australia	Sept. 26–Oct. 1	NA	NA	NA
2000	Ballarat	Australia	October 2–6	NA	NA	NA

Baltic Games

The Baltic Games were held in Malmö, Sweden, in connection with the Baltic Exhibition from June 5th to August 9th, 1914. Four nations—Denmark, Finland, Germany, and Russia—were invited to join host Sweden in the events.

Eighteen sports were on the schedule, but the sailing competitions were canceled due to the beginning of World War I.[67]

Year	Host City	Host Nation	Dates	Nations	Athletes	Sports
1914	Malmö	Sweden	June 5–Aug. 14	5	NA	17

Nations: Denmark, Finland, Germany, Russia, Sweden
Sports: Athletics, Canoeing, Cycling, Equestrian, Fencing, Football, Golf, Gymnastics, Modern Pentathlon, Rowing, Swimming, Shooting, Sailing (cancelled), Tennis, Tug of War, Walking, Weightlifting, Wrestling

Baltic Sea Games

In November 1988, Estonia invited representatives of the nations surrounding the Baltic Sea to meetings in Moscow to initiate discussions on the idea of a games for the region. In April 1989, at the first Sports Conference of the Baltic Sea Countries, Tallinn, Estonia, was chosen to be the first host of the Baltic Sea Games, to be held in the summer of 1993.

The main goal of the games is "to promote by means of sport the mutual understanding and friendship among the young peoples of the Baltic Sea countries."[68]

Ten nations surrounding the Baltic are eligible to compete: Denmark, Estonia, Finland, Germany, Latvia, Lithuania, Norway, Poland, Russia and Sweden. All the eligible nations and 1,177 athletes participated in the inaugural games. Lithuania came out on top of the medals race, edging Russia by one gold, 39 to 38.

The second Baltic Sea Games were held from June 25 to July 6, 1997. Participation more than doubled with 2,550 athletes in 26 sports. Many cities across Lithuania were used in order to provide enough facilities for the games. Vilnius was the main venue, while other events were held in the cities of Klaipëda, Trakai, Diauliai, Kaunas, Panevëpys, and Elektrënai. Lithuania again garnered the most gold medals with 62. Belarus, a neighbor of Lithuania but not bordering the Baltic Sea, was invited to the 1997 games and finished second with 58 gold medals, ahead of Russia's third place total of 43.

The 2001 games are scheduled to be held in Riga, Latvia.

Year	Host City	Host Nation	Dates	Nations	Athletes	Sports
1993	Tallinn	Estonia	June 22–July 3	10	1177	14
1997	Vilnius	Lithuania	June 25–July 6	11	2550	26

1993   Tallin   Estonia   June 22–July 3

Nations: Denmark, Estonia, Finland, Germany, Latvia, Lithuania, Norway, Poland, Russia, Sweden

Sports: Athletics, Basketball, Canoeing, Cycling, Fencing, Greco-Roman Wrestling, Handball, Gymnastics, Judo, Orienteering, Shooting, Sport Dance, Swimming, Volleyball

MEDALS

Nation	Gold	Silver	Bronze	Total
Lithuania	39	29	27	95
Russia	38	32	20	90
Poland	23	3	6	32
Latvia	17	31	32	80
Estonia	16	30	35	81
Finland	16	12	26	54
Germany	11	20	8	39
Sweden	9	11	17	37
Norway	1	2	0	3
Denmark	0	1	1	2

1997   Vilnius   Lithuania   June 25–July 6

Nations: Belarus, Denmark, Estonia, Finland, Germany, Latvia, Lithuania, Norway, Poland, Russia, Sweden

Sports: Athletics, Badminton, Basketball, Boxing, Canoeing, Cycling Track, Cycling Road, Darts, Fencing, Freestyle Wrestling, Greco-Roman Wrestling, Gymnastics, Handball, Ice Hockey, Judo, Modern Pentathlon, Orienteering, Rowing, Rugby, Sambo, Shooting (Rifle and Pistol), Trap and Skeet Shooting, Sport Dance, Swimming, Weightlifting, Yachting

MEDALS

Nation	Gold	Silver	Bronze	Total
Lithuania	62	65	51	178
Belarus	58	37	27	122
Russia	43	40	46	129
Poland	30	26	38	94
Latvia	9	11	34	54
Germany	7	3	4	14
Estonia	6	16	23	45
Sweden	5	8	7	20
Finland	1	10	7	18
Norway	0	0	0	0
Denmark	0	0	0	0

Bolivarian Games

Six nations—Venezuela, Peru, Panama, Ecuador, Colombia and Bolivia—have celebrated the Bolivarian Games since 1938, in honor of the man who gained their independence from Spain, Simón Bolívar. Colombian Alberto Nariño Cheyne of Bogota first proposed the idea and received the International Olympic Committee's approval for the regional games in Berlin in 1936.[69] ODEBO, the Organization Depontivo Bolivariano, is responsible for organizing the games.

The inaugural games in 1938 were timed to commemorate the 400-year anniversary of the founding of the city of Bogota, Colombia.

World War II disrupted plans for a second games which were originally scheduled for 1945. Postwar difficulties postponed the games in Lima, Peru, to December 1946–January 1947.

In 1951, runners carried a torch from Santa Marta, Colombia, where Simón Bolívar died, to the opening of the games in Caracas, the city of Bolívar's birth.[70] Caracas was chosen as the games' host during meetings at the 1948 London Olympic Games, but preparations did not start in earnest until one year before the event. The organizers pushed to complete the stadiums and swimming pool the week before the games began in December 1951.

At the conclusion of the 1951 games, the next were awarded to La Paz, Bolivia, and were to be held in 1955, with Ecuador and Panama named as alternative sites. The suggestion was made that any events requiring "physical exertion" be held at sea level, rather than the extreme altitude of La Paz.[71] In the end, none of these sites was used. Bolivia gave up the games, citing no specific reason, then Ecuador's internal problems did not allow it to organize the event. The next games were not held until 1961 in Barranquilla, Colombia.

Organizational difficulties postponed the fifth games in Ecuador from August to November of 1965. The football tournament, by far the most popular event in the Bolivarian games, turned ugly for a short time during the Venezuela-Ecuador final match when a Venezuelan player began to take out his frustrations by kicking other players rather than the ball. The secretary of the Venezuelan soccer federation angrily entered the field to help stop the incident.

In keeping with the history of the Bolivarian Games, the sixth games in Maracaibo, which were originally planned for September-October 1969, were opened in August 1970.

The next games in Panama City, Panama, in 1973 returned to the scheduled time of the year after the Olympic Games, and the Bolivarian Games have been able to hold to this four-year cycle since that time.

In 1977, the games were held in La Paz, Bolivia, and still have the distinction of being the international games held at the highest altitude (3500 meters above sea level). The Bolivarians claimed at the end of the games that "the altitude of La Paz did not have the slightest influence on athletes' performances,"[72] presumably a reference to the endurance events which are generally negatively affected by altitude. La Paz expanded the capacity of its main stadium from 20,000 to 56,000 to accommodate the games.

Venezuela overwhelmed the competition at the 1985 games in Cuenca, Ecuador, with 102 gold medals. Colombia finished with 58 golds, Ecuador and Peru with 26, Panama 12, and Bolivia one.[73]

The 1997 games in Arequipa, Peru, were severely criticized for their lack of organization.[74,75] Ambato, Ecuador was the scheduled host for the 2001 Bolivarian Games.

Year	Host City	Host Nation	Dates	Nations[76]	Athletes	Sports
1938	Bogota	Colombia	August 6–21[77]	6	NA	NA
1946	Lima	Peru	December 26–Jan. 6	6	NA	NA
1951	Caracas	Venezuela	December 5–21	6	796	21
1961	Barranquilla	Colombia	December 3–16	6	NA	NA
1965	Quito, Guayaquil	Ecuador	Nov. 20–Dec. 5	6	NA	16
1970	Maracaibo	Venezuela	August 22–Sept. 6	6	1351	18
1973	Panama City	Panama	Feb. 17–March 3	6	NA	17
1977	La Paz	Bolivia	October 15–29	6	1600	17
1981	Barquisimeto	Venezuela	December 4–14	6	NA	NA
1985	Cuenca	Ecuador	November 9–18	6	2000	18
1989	Maracaibo	Venezuela	January 15–25	6	NA	NA
1993	Cochabamba	Bolivia	April 24–May 2	6	NA	NA
1997	Arequipa	Peru	October 17–26	6	1565	21

1938   Bogota   Colombia   August 6–21

Nations: Bolivia, Colombia, Ecuador, Panama, Peru, Venezuela

1946   Lima   Peru   December 26–January 6

Nations: Bolivia, Colombia, Ecuador, Panama, Peru, Venezuela

1951   Caracas   Venezuela   December 5–21

Nations: Bolivia, Colombia, Ecuador, Panama, Peru, Venezuela
Sports: Athletics, Basketball, Baseball, Billiards, Boxing, Chess, Cycling, Equestrian, Fencing, Football, Gymnastics, Golf, Pentathlon, Shooting, Skeet Shooting, Swimming and Diving, Table Tennis, Tennis, Volleyball, Weightlifting, Wrestling
Venues: Estadio Olimpico

1961   Barranquilla   Colombia   December 3–16

Nations: Bolivia, Colombia, Ecuador, Panama, Peru, Venezuela

1965   Quito, Guayaquil   Ecuador   November 20–December 5

Nations: Bolivia, Colombia, Ecuador, Panama, Peru, Venezuela
Sports: Athletics, Basketball, Boxing, Chess, Cycling, Fencing, Football, Gymnastics, Judo, Lawn Tennis, Shooting, Swimming, Table Tennis, Weightlifting, Wrestling, Yachting
Venues: Estadio Olimpico Atahualpa (Athletics, Opening Ceremony), Coliseo Cubierto Guayacil (Judo, Table Tennis), Bahia de Salinas (Yachting), Estadio Yeyo Uraga (Baseball), Piscina Olimpica (Swimming), Coliseo Huancavilca (Wrestling), Poligono Vicente Pin Moreno (Shooting)

MEDALS

Nation	Gold	Silver	Bronze	Total
Venezuela	62	52	38	152
Colombia	30	19	22	71
Peru	23	34	24	81
Ecuador	18	23	43	84
Panama	7	13	8	28
Bolivia	4	2	3	9

1970 Maracaibo Venezuela August 22–September 6

Nations: Bolivia, Colombia, Ecuador, Panama, Peru, Venezuela

1973 Panama City Panama February 17–March 3

Sports: Athletics, Basketball, Baseball, Bowling, Boxing, Cycling, Fencing, Football, Gymnastics, Judo, Swimming and Diving, Shooting, Softball, Volleyball, Water Polo, Weightlifting, Wrestling
Venues: Estadio Revolucion (Athletics, Football), Gimnasio Nuevo Panama (Basketball), Estadio Juan D. Arosemena (Baseball), Gimnasio Neco de la Guardia (Boxing), Veledromo Neuva Generacion (Cycling), Gimnasio de Betania (Fencing), Colegio La Salle (Gymnastics), Gimnasio San Miguelito (Judo, Weightlifting, Wrestling), Piscina Patria (Swimming and Diving), Piscina Adan Gordon (Water Polo), Estadio Santa Rita (Softball), Poligono El Renacer (Shooting), Gimnasio Jose Dolores Moscoto (Volleyball), Club Bolerama (Bowling)

1977 La Paz Bolivia October 15–29

Nations: Bolivia, Colombia, Ecuador, Panama, Peru, Venezuela
Sports: Athletics, Basketball, Boxing, Cycling, Equestrian, Fencing, Soccer, Gymnastics, Judo, Swimming (Diving), Tennis, Volleyball, Water Polo, Shooting, Weightlifting, Wrestling (exhibitions of Bowling, Golf, Mountaineering)
Sports for Women: Athletics, Basketball, Equestrian, Fencing, Gymnastics, Swimming, Tennis, Volleyball, Bowling
Venues: Estadio Olimpico La Paz (Equestrian, Athletics, Football), Sucre Tennis Club (Tennis), Gimnasio Clun Japones (Judo), Gimnasio Escuela Naval (Wrestling), Colisea Ciudad de La Paz (Basketball, Volleyball), Camcha de la YMCA (Basketball), Instituto Americanos (Boxing, Volleyball), Camcha Colegio Mariscal Baraun (Volleyball), Estadio Simón Bolívar (Football), Estadio Lastra (Football) Ave Arce (Bowling, Exhibition), Cancha Colegio Loreto (Basketball), Piscina Olimpica (Swimming), Piscina Obrajes (Swimming), Pista Colegio Militar (Athletics), Club los Sargentos (Equestrian), Gimnasio Colegia Militar (Gymnastics, Judo, Wrestling), Picadero Colegio Militar (Equestrian), Poligono de Tiro (Shooting), Velódromo Olimpico (Cycling), Club de Tenis La Paz (Tennis), Gimnasio Colegio Saint Andrews (Fencing), Club de Caza y Pesca (Skeet), Mallasilla Golf Club (Golf exhibition), Cine Teatro Tesla (Weightlifting)

1981 Barquisimeto Venezuela December 4–14

Nations: Bolivia, Colombia, Ecuador, Panama, Peru, Venezuela

1985   Cuenca   Ecuador   November 9–18

Nations: Bolivia, Colombia, Ecuador, Panama, Peru, Venezuela
Sports: Athletics, Basketball, Baseball, Boxing, Cycling, Equestrian, Football, Gymnastics, Judo, Tae Kwon Do, Tennis, Table Tennis, Shooting, Swimming, Volleyball, Weightlifting, Wrestling, Yachting
Sports for Women: Athletics, Basketball, Equestrian, Gymnastics, Judo, Swimming, Tennis, Table Tennis, Shooting, Volleyball
Venues: Estadio Municipal Alejandro Serrano Aguilar (Athletics, Football), Coliseo Ciudad de Cuenca (Basketball), Estadio Yeyo Uraga in Guayacil (Baseball), Coliseo Manuel J. Calle (Boxing), Velódromo de Totoracocha (Cycling), Batallion General Davalos (Gymnastics), Colisea Rafael Borja (Weightlifting), Piscina Olimpica (Swimming), Coliseo Benigno Malo (Tae Kwon Do), Cuenca Tenis y Golf Club (Tennis), Coliseo Tecnico Salesiano (Table Tennis), Colisea Universidad de Cuenca (Judo), Poligonos de Totracocha y Ucubamba (Shooting), Coliseo Manuela Garaicoa (Volleyball), Bahia de Salinas (Yachting)

MEDALS

Nation	Gold	Silver	Bronze	Total
Venezuela	102	85	45	232
Colombia	58	61	63	182
Ecuador	26	42	54	122
Peru	26	22	54	102
Panama	12	14	22	48
Bolivia	1	2	10	13

1989   Maracaibo   Venezuela   January 15–25

Nations: Bolivia, Colombia, Ecuador, Panama, Peru, Venezuela

1993   Cochabamba   Bolivia   April 24–May 2

Nations: Bolivia, Colombia, Ecuador, Panama, Peru, Venezuela

1997   Arequipa   Peru   October 17–26

Nations: Bolivia, Colombia, Ecuador, Panama, Peru, Venezuela
Sports: Athletics, Basketball, Beach Volleyball, Bowling, Boxing, Cycling, Equestrian, Fencing, Football, Gymnastics, Judo, Tae Kwon Do, Shooting, Swimming, Softball, Table Tennis, Tennis, Volleyball, Weightlifting, Wrestling, Mountain Climbing (exhibition)

Britain's Festival of Sport

To mark the 100-year anniversary of Britain's Great Exhibition of 1851, the British declared 1951 to be the Festival of Britain Year. In conjunction with the Festival was "Britain's Festival of Sport."

These "games" stretch the definition of a modern international games somewhat. Most games at present have rules limiting the length to around 16 days or less. Britain's

Festival of Sport went from May 12 to at least August 11, with sports and games played around the country. In this sense, they are more like the very first Olympic Games which stretched on for several months.[78]

Several tournaments were held throughout the duration of the festival. Football was the greatest attraction with 150 games, both international and club, played in May. The games made history when Argentina played England, and became the first South American team ever to play in England.

Women participated in field hockey, lacrosse and netball.

1951   London   England   May 5–September 8

Nations: Argentina, Australia, Austria, Belgium, Denmark, England, Finland, France, Germany, India, Ireland, Luxembourg, Malta, Portugal, Norway, Scotland, Sweden, Switzerland, South Africa, Turkey, United States, Wales, Yugoslavia[79]

Sports: Athletics, Field Hockey, Football, Lacrosse, Motor-Boating, Netball, Tennis[80]

British Commonwealth Paraplegic Games

The British Commonwealth Paraplegic Games[81] were a direct outgrowth of the 1960 games in Rome that were to become known as the first Paralympics. Australian neurosurgeon George Bedbrook was the head of the Australian team at the 1960 Paralympics. Bedbrook suggested to other representatives of the Commonwealth that a similar event be associated with the Commonwealth Games to be held in Perth in 1962. About ten nations and 100 athletes took part in the competitions, and the Commonwealth Paraplegic Games Council was formed to develop further events for disabled athletes from the Commonwealth countries.

The games were held again four years later in conjunction with the Kingston Commonwealth games in 1966, and with the participation of some of the Caribbean nations the number of athletes participating doubled to about 200.

Edinburgh hosted the third games in 1970. More athletes were said to have attended, but exact numbers were not reported. The athletes used many of the venues of the able-bodied games held in Edinburgh in 1970.

The final games were held as part of the 1974 Christchurch, New Zealand, Commonwealth Games. The growth in participation had been slow, but more importantly, Canada, which had not shown much enthusiasm for the games since the beginning, had not agreed to host or promote them for 1978 in conjunction with the Commonwealth Games in Edmonton.[82]

Bedbrook and the Commonwealth Paraplegic Games Council turned their efforts towards the development of regional games for disabled athletes. Bedbrook founded the Far East and South Pacific Games for the Disabled, also known as the FESPIC Games.

In 1994, when the Commonwealth Games returned to Victoria, Canada, the games included a limited number of events for disabled athletes in swimming, athletics and lawn bowls. A substantial number of nations were entered, including Australia, Canada, Cyprus, England, Hong Kong, Kenya, Malawi, Mauritius, New Zealand, Northern Ireland, Scotland, Singapore, Wales and Zimbabwe.

In September 1997, the Commonwealth Games Federation unanimously approved a proposal that would bring disabled athletes back into the Commonwealth Games as full team members in full medal status events. [83] The games of 2006 would be required to present a minimum of one sport with one event for men and women, and a maximum of two sports and four events in each sport. The sports would be chosen from athletics, swimming, lawn bowls, weightlifting and table tennis. A consideration was made by the subcommission studying the matter to hold a full Commonwealth Games for disabled athletes, but it was eventually decided that the Commonwealth Games did not have sufficient resources to accomplish this.

Year	Host City	Host Nation	Dates	Nations	Athletes	Sports
1962	Perth	Australia		10	100	NA
1966	Kingston	Jamaica		NA	200	NA
1970	Edinburgh	Scotland		NA	NA	NA
1974	Christchurch	New Zealand		NA	NA	NA

Can-Am Police-Fire Games

The Can-Am Police-Fire Games were first held in 1977 when the Police and Fire competitions of Washington, Oregon, and Western Canada were combined into one. The organizers felt that the games would be better served if the resources of the three regions were pooled.

The games were known as the Northwest Police and Fire Olympics from 1980 until 1983, and the Northwest Police-Fire Athletic Federation Games until 1995, when the name was officially changed to the Can-Am Police-Fire Games.

The participants of the Can-Am Police-Fire Games are all sworn federal, provincial, state, county and municipal police officers (male and female, active and retired) and firefighters. Police reservists with two years' service in their department are also eligible to participate.

The games are generally held on an annual basis. Exceptions were made in the years 1989 and 1997 when the World Police and Fire Games were held close by in Vancouver and Calgary.

In 1998 the games changed significantly when athletes from Puerto Rico and Russia, the first nations outside the U.S. and Canada, took part for the first time. The athletes paraded down Winnipeg's main street as part of the opening ceremonies. For the first time, a torch run was part of the games, beginning at Peace Arch park on the Canada-US border of Washington and British Columbia and being relayed to Winnipeg. Besides the athletic events, the games include social gatherings, police and fire seminars, training sessions, and an exposition of the latest police and fire equipment.

As the games have grown, they have spread further away geographically from their Pacific Northwest United States roots. The 1998 Games were held in Regina, Saskatchewan, and the 2000 games were held in Milwaukee, Wisconsin.

Like their world counterpart, the World Police and Fire Games, these games have events related to the working environment of both police and firefighting professions, such as auto extrication, fire attack, muster, narcotics dog, police service dog, SWAT, Toughest Cop Alive and Toughest Firefighter Alive.

The Milwaukee games continued to push the definition of "sporting event" with a "Cook-Off" sport, with competition in appetizer, dessert and entrée. The Milwaukee games are also the only known games to offer paintball as a sport.

The World Police and Fire Games returned to the United States, to Indianapolis, Indiana, in the year 2001, so no Can-Am games were scheduled for that year.

One winter edition of the games was held in 1989 at Mt. Bachelor, Oregon, but participation was not sufficient to convince the organizers to organize a second winter games.

Year	Host City	Host Nation	Dates*	Nations	Athletes	Sports
1977	Spokane	USA		NA	250	NA
1978	Seattle	USA		NA	350	NA
1979	Ellensburg	USA		2	550	NA
1980	Spokane	USA		2	1000	NA
1981	Bellevue	USA		2	1000	NA
1982	New Westminster	Canada		2	850	NA
1983	Edmonton	Canada		2	700	NA
1984	Seattle	USA		2	630	NA
1985	Calgary	Canada		2	800	NA
1986	Ellensburg	USA		2	450	NA
1987	Salem	USA		2	800	NA
1988	Moscow-Pullman	USA		2	800	NA
1989	Mt. Bachelor (winter)	USA	winter	NA	50	NA
1990	Boise	USA		2	520	NA
1991	Tri-Cities (Kennewick)	USA		2	525	NA
1992	Walla Walla	USA		2	1000	NA
1993	Calgary	Canada		2	1000	NA
1994	Portland	USA		2	1200	NA
1995	Bellingham	USA		2	1200	NA
1996	Tri-Cities (Kennewick)	USA	June 24–30	2	800	43
1998	Regina	Canada	June 22–28	4	NA	46
2000	Milwaukee	USA	July 2–10	3	NA	44

*games traditionally start the 3rd week in June

1996   Tri-Cities (Kennewick)   USA   June 24–30

Sports: Archery, Arm Wrestling, Basketball (3-man), Basketball (5-man), Bass Fishing, Biathlon, Bowling, Canine, Cross Country, Cycling, Darts, Duathlon, Golf, Half-marathon, Karate, Horseshoes, Motorcycle Rodeo, Mountain Bike, Muster, Paintball, Pistol Shooting, Pocket Billiards, Powerlifting, Racquetball, Rifle (Small Bore), Rifle (Large Bore), Skeet, Sporting Clays, Slow Pitch Softball, Swat Competition, Swimming, Table Tennis, Tennis, 10 km Run, Toughest Competitor, Toughest Firefighter, Track & Field, Trap Shoot, Triathlon, Tug of War, Volleyball (2-man), Volleyball (4-man), Water Skiing

1998   Regina   Canada   June 22–28

Nations: Canada, Puerto Rico, Russia, United States
Sports: Angling, Archery, Athletics, Arm Wrestling, Badminton, Basketball, Bench Press, Biathlon, Billiards, Bowling, Canine, Cross Country, Curling, Cycling, Darts, Extrication, Golf, Hockey, Horseshoes, Karate, Motorcycle Rodeo, Mountain Biking,

Paintball, Pistol Shooting, Powerlifting, Racquetball, Rifle, Running Road Racing, Rugby, Skeet Shooting, Soccer, Softball (Slow Pitch), Softball (Fast Pitch), Sporting Clays, SWAT, Swimming, Toughest Cop Alive, Toughest Firefighter Alive, Tennis, Table Tennis, Trap Shooting, Triathlon, Beach Volleyball, Court Volleyball, Water Skiing, Wrestling. (Official figures list 47 sports. Decathlon was listed separately from Athletics.)

Venues: Qu'Appelle Lakes (Angling), Regina Wildlife Federation (Archery, Sporting Clays), Exhibition Auditorium (Arm Wrestling, Bench Press, Powerlifting), Regina High School (Badminton), Miller High School, Leboldus High School, Riffell High School (Basketball), RCMP Training Academy (Biathlon, Cycling Criterium, Karate, Pistol Shooting, Rifle Small Bore, Toughest Cop Alive), the Crooked Cue (Billiards), Golden Mile Bowling (5-Pin Bowling), Glencairn Bowling (10-Pin Bowling), Regina Exhibition Park (Canine, Motorcycle Rodeo), Douglas Park (Cross Country Running, Athletics), Caledonian Curling Club (Curling), Highway No. 11 & Pasqua St. (Cycling Time Trials), Chamberlain Triangle (Cycling Road Race), Army, Navy & Air Force Veterans Club (Darts), No. 2 Fire Hall (Extrication, Toughest Firefighter Alive), Murray, Tor Hill, Avonlea Golf Courses (Golf), Twin Arenas, NW Leisure Center (Hockey), Kiwanis Park (Horseshoes), Wascana Trails (Mountain Biking, Dual Slalom, Cross Country), Paintball Paradise (Paintball), Racquet Courts North (Racquetball), Burdec range (Rifle, Large Bore), Douglas Park (Road Races, 5 km, 10 km, 21 km), Regina Rugby Club (Rugby), Regina Gun Club (Skeet, Trap Shooting), Realtor's Park (Soccer), Maxwell's Amusements (Softball—Slow Pitch), Kaplan Field (Softball—Fast Pitch), RPS Emergency Training Site (SWAT), Lawson Aquatic Center (Swimming), Regina Beach (Swimming—Open Water, Triathlon), Lakeshore Tennis Club (Tennis), O'Neil High School (Table Tennis), University of Regina (Court Volleyball, Beach Volleyball), Wascana Lake (Water Skiing), Riffel High School (Wrestling)

MEDALS

Nation	Gold	Silver	Bronze	Total
Canada	349	288	200	837*
United States	133	61	55	249
Puerto Rico	34	14	10	58
Russia	23	6	2	31

*This is the largest recorded number of total medals won by one "Nation" at a games. The significance of this number is fairly minute, however, as only four nations were represented, unlimited numbers of entries were permitted, the games have a very large number of events, the games have age categories, and finally the top medal-winning nation was the host.

2000   Milwaukee   USA   July 2–10

Nations: Canada, Puerto Rico, United States
Sports: Angling, Archery, Athletics, Auto Extrication, Basketball, Beach Volleyball, Bench Press, Biathlon, Body Building, Bowling, Cook-Off, Cross-Country, Cycling, Darts, Fire Attack, Flag Football, Football, Golf, Horseshoes, Martial Arts, Mountain Bike, Muster, Narcotics Dog, Paintball, Pistol, Pocket Billiards, Police Service Dog, Powerlifting, Racquetball, Rifle, Running, SWAT, Skeet, Softball, Swimming, Toughest Cop Alive, Toughest Firefighter Alive, Table Tennis, Tennis, Trap Shooting, Triathlon, Tug of War, Wrestling, Wrist Wrestling.

Canterbury Centennial Games

Christchurch, New Zealand, hosted a Canterbury Centennial Games from December 25, 1950, to January 5, 1951 (one of the rare instances of a games spanning over a New Year[84]). The games were part of the centennial celebrations of the founding of the Canterbury Association in New Zealand.[85]

Athletes from Australia, Canada, Great Britain, Fiji, Jamaica, the Netherlands, Sweden and the United States joined the New Zealanders in five sports.

Roger Bannister won the mile in 4:09.9 but the crowd was said to be disappointed when he finished sixth and last in the 800 meters the following day. The athletics events were unique in that there were both English and metric distance races on the track. On the schedule were races at 100, 220, 440, 880 yards and the mile and two mile, and separate races at 100, 200, 400, 800, 1500 and 5000 meters. Jamaica's Arthur Wint won the 440 yards, 400 meters and 880 yard events.

Australia beat the University of California eight in the rowing final. Cycling events were held for both amateur and professional cyclists.

Australian Shirley Strickland, a bronze medalist in the 100 meters at the 1948 London Olympics, won the 100 yards, 220 yards, 200 meters and 80 meter hurdles. Her compatriot Marjorie Jackson won the 75 yards and 100 meter races and finished second to Strickland in the 200 meters. Jackson would go on to win both the 100 and 200 meters at the 1952 Helsinki Olympic games.

Year	Host City	Host Nation	Dates	Nations	Athletes	Sports
1950	Christchurch	New Zealand	Dec. 25, 1950– Jan. 5, 1951	9	NA	5

Nations: Australia, Canada, Great Britain, Fiji, Jamaica, Netherlands, New Zealand, Sweden, United States
Sports: Athletics, Boxing, Cycling, Rowing, Swimming
Sports for Women: Athletics, Swimming

CARIFTA[86] Games

The CARIFTA Games began as a track and field (athletics) only meet in 1972 for the nations who were members of the Caribbean Free Trade Agreement, and were held annually under that name until 1984. The games were first presented as a multisport competition in 1985 and, in addition to athletics, included boxing, cycling, shooting, swimming, lawn tennis, and table tennis. Traditionally, the games are held on three days over the Easter weekend.

Austin Sealy, the president of the National Olympic Committee of Barbados, founded the event. Today the athlete selected as the best performer in the athletics competition in the games is awarded the Austin Sealy Trophy. The stated mission of the games has always been to unify the Caribbean region.

The games are for junior-aged athletes in two divisions: under 20 and under 17. Many of the stars of the Caribbean athletics world, such as Bert Cameron, Michelle Freeman, Obadele Thompson and Kareem Street-Thompson, had their first chance at international competition in the CARIFTA Games.

In 1993, the games events were spread out among a few countries. Barbados hosted the swimming events, Guyana the boxing competitions, and Martinique the athletics.

In 1994, the Queens Baton, the Commonwealth's counterpart to the Olympic torch, made a stop in Bridgetown, Barbados, for the opening of the CARIFTA Games. The Queens Baton had already been to Africa, India and Asia on its way to the opening ceremonies of the 1994 Commonwealth Games in Victoria, Canada, later that summer.[87]

In 1998, the games were scaled back, with Trinidad and Tobago hosting only the track and field events.

Year	Host City	Host Nation	Dates	Nations	Athletes	Sports
1985	Bridgetown	Barbados	April 6–9	23	700	7
1986	Basse-Terre	Guadeloupe	March 29–31	21	NA	NA
1987	Port of Spain	Trinidad	April 18–20	NA	NA	NA
1988	Kingston	Jamaica	April 7–9	NA	NA	NA
1989	Bridgetown	Barbados	August 19–22	26	2000	8
1990	Kingston	Jamaica	March 19–21	NA	NA	NA
1991	Port of Spain	Trinidad	March 30–April 1	NA	NA	NA
1992	Nassau	Bahamas	April 18–20	NA	NA	NA
1993	Fort de France	Martinique	April 9–11	NA	NA	NA

The events of 1993 were spread out among a few countries: athletics in Martinique, swimming in Barbados, and boxing in Guyana.[88]

Year	Host City	Host Nation	Dates	Nations	Athletes	Sports
1994	Bridgetown	Barbados	April 2–4	19	NA	NA
1995	George Town	Cayman Islands	April 15–17	NA	NA	NA
1996	Kingston	Jamaica	April 6–8	NA	NA	NA
1997	Nassau	Bahamas	March 29–31	NA	NA	NA
1998	Port of Spain	Trinidad and Tobago	April 11–13	NA	NA	1
1999		Martinique		NA	NA	NA
2000	St. George	Grenada		NA	NA	NA

1985   Bridgetown   Barbados   April 6–9

Nations: Anguilla, Antigua-Barbuda, Bahamas, Barbados, Bermuda, British Virgin Islands, Cayman Islands, Dominica, Grenada, Guyana, French Guiana, Jamaica, Guadeloupe, Martinique, Montserrat, Netherlands Antilles, St. Kitts and Nevis, St. Lucia, St. Vincent, Suriname, Trinidad and Tobago, Turks and Caicos Islands, U.S. Virgin Islands
Sports: Athletics, Tennis, Table Tennis, Boxing, Cycling, Shooting, Swimming
Sports for Women: Athletics, Shooting, Swimming, Table Tennis, Tennis

1989   Bridgetown   Barbados   August 19–22

Sports: Athletics, Badminton, Basketball, Boxing, Cycling, Swimming, Tennis, Table Tennis
Venues: National Stadium (Opening Ceremonies, Athletics, Cycling), YMCA (Basketball), Barbados Community College (Basketball, Badminton, Table Tennis), Steel Shed (Boxing), Garrison Secondary School (Boxing), Wildey Aquatic Center (Swimming)

1994   Bridgetown   Barbados   April 2–4

Nations: Antigua and Barbuda, Aruba, Bahamas, Barbados, Bermuda, British Virgin Isles, Cayenne, Cayman Islands, Dominica, Grenada, Guadeloupe, Guyana, Jamaica, Martinique, St. Kitts and Nevis, St. Lucia, St. Vincent and Grenadines, Trinidad and Tobago, U.S. Virgin Islands

MEDALS

Nation	Gold	Silver	Bronze	Total
Jamaica	28	23	18	69
Bahamas	7	8	8	23
Trinidad and Tobago	7	4	5	16
Barbados	6	7	6	19
Guadeloupe	5	6	1	12
Martinique	2	5	0	7
Bermuda	2	0	3	5
Grenada	1	1	2	4
Cayman Islands	0	1	2	3
Guyana	0	1	1	2
Cayenne	0	1	1	2
St. Kitts & Nevis	0	1	0	1
St. Lucia	0	0	1	1
Antigua and Barbuda	0	0	0	0
Aruba	0	0	0	0
British Virgin Isles	0	0	0	0
Dominica	0	0	0	0
St. Vincent and Grenadines	0	0	0	0
U.S. Virgin Islands	0	0	0	0

1998   Port of Spain   Trinidad and Tobago   April 11–13

Sports: Athletics only

Centennial Youth Games

Under the motto "Friendship Beyond all Bounds," the Danish Sports Confederation celebrated 100 years of existence by sponsoring a Centennial Youth Games in Aalborg, Denmark, in 1996. Sports and social and cultural activities were included in the celebration which opened on August 4, the day the 1996 Atlanta Olympic Games ended. The games were open to all athletes between the ages of 12 and 18 who paid the 600 Danish kroner fee and brought a chaperone with them to Aalborg.

Although the games were a one-time celebration, Aalborg has hosted the Aalborg Youth Games on a quadrennial schedule since 1975. This is a games for youth between the ages of 12 and 16 from the sister cities of Aalborg.

Year	Host City	Host Nation	Dates	Nations	Athletes	Sports
1996	Aalborg	Denmark	August 4–11	36	4000	24

Nations: Azerbaijan, Austria, Belarus, Belgium, Czech Republic, Denmark, England, Estonia, Faroe Islands, Finland, Germany, Gibraltar, Greece, Greenland, Iceland, Ireland, Israel, Italy, Latvia, Luxembourg, Macedonia, Netherlands, Norway, Poland, Portugal, Russia, Scotland, Slovakia, Sweden, Switzerland, Taiwan, Turkey, Ukraine, Zimbabwe

Sports: Archery, Athletics, Badminton, Basketball, Bowling, Cycling, Diving, Equestrian, Fencing, Football, Golf, Handball, Judo, Rowing, Rugby, Shooting, Sports Dancing, Swimming (as well as handicapped events), Table Tennis, Tennis, Volleyball, Weightlifting, Wrestling

Central African Games

Financial and organizational difficulties have made games in certain regions difficult to sustain. Central Africa is one such region.

Brazzaville in the Republic of the Congo in 1972 organized a "Central African Cup," a precursor to the Central African Games, with Cameroon, Chad, Central African Republic and Gabon attending. Men competed in athletics, boxing, basketball, cycling, football, handball and volleyball, while women had four events: athletics, basketball, handball and volleyball.

The first games with the title Central African Games were held in Libreville, Gabon, in 1976, scheduled just prior to the Montreal Olympic Games with the hope of giving the athletes a final test before Canada. The test ended up being the high point of the season for many athletes after the African boycott of the Montreal games.

Competition was intense, especially on the basketball court. *La Semaine* wondered whether it was basketball or boxing. "It's not the place for babies, or invalids," the paper reported.[89] The Central African Republic won the gold, Cameroon the silver, Congo the bronze.

Luanda, Angola, hosted the second edition of the Central African Games in 1981, so far the only international games to be held in Angola.

The third Central African Games opened under rainy skies in 1987 in Brazzaville. The games were held in April and for some sports were the qualifying competitions for the African Games to be held later that year in August in Nairobi. These have been the last Central African Games to be held to date.

Year	Host City	Host Nation	Dates	Nations	Athletes	Sports
1976	Libreville	Gabon	June 30–July 10	11	1312	8
1981	Luanda	Angola	Aug. 20–Sept 2	10	1200	8
1987	Brazzaville	Congo, Rep. of	April 18–30	11	1044	5

1976 Libreville Gabon June 30–July 10

Nations: Angola, Burundi, Cameroon, Central African Republic, Congo, Chad, Gabon, Rwanda, Sao Tome and Principe, Zaire (one more)

Sports: Athletics, Basketball, Boxing, Cycling, Football, Handball, Judo, Volleyball

1981 Luanda Angola August 20–September 2

Sports: Athletics, Basketball, Boxing, Cycling, Football, Handball, Judo Volleyball

1987   Brazzaville   Congo, Rep. of   April 18–30

Nations: Angola, Burundi, Cameroon, Central African Republic, Chad, Congo, Equatorial Guinea, Gabon, Rwanda, Sao Tome and Principe, Zaire
Sports: Athletics, Basketball, Football, Handball, Volleyball
Sports for Women: Athletics, Basketball, Handball, Volleyball
Venues: Stade de la Révolution (Athletics, Football, Handball), Stade de la Démocratisation du sport à Ouenzé (Basketball, Handball), Centre Sportif de Universitaire de Makélékélé (Basketball, Volleyball), Caserne des Sapeurs Pompiers (Volleyball), Stade d'Ornano (Basketball, Handball)

MEDALS

Nation	Gold	Silver	Bronze	Total
Cameroon	11	12	6	29
Burundi	7	4	4	15
Gabon	5	5	6	16
Congo	4	8	7	19
Rwanda	4	4	3	11
Angola	3	3	8	14
Zaire	2	0	1	3
Sao Tome and Principe	0	0	1	1

Central American and Caribbean Games

The Central American and Caribbean Games, held since 1926, are the oldest continuous regional games. The first two editions of the games were called the Central American Games. In 1934 the full title, Central American and Caribbean Games, was adopted.

On July 4, 1924, at the 1924 Paris Olympic Games, representatives from Mexico, Cuba, Colombia, and Venezuela met to establish a gathering to be known as the Central American Games to be held in 1926 and continue on every four years. The goal of the representatives was to create a games in which athletes could "participate in a competition for the sole pleasure of taking part in it, and for the physical, mental, social and moral benefits that result from such participation."[90]

The Central American and Caribbean Games' flame, a tradition from the very first event, is lit from the Aztec flame from Mount Estrella outside Mexico City before each games.

The first edition of the games in 1926 was a small gathering of three nations. The Cubans and Guatemalans visited Mexico City and 271 athletes participated in seven sports. Guatemala's president died on the eve of the event and the Guatemalans had to overcome great difficulties, but still managed to send a team.

The second Central American Games in 1930 in Havana, Cuba, started out on a high note when the U.S. Ambassador to Cuba, Harry F. Guggenheim, insisted that Puerto Rico be included. A last-minute effort was needed to pull together a team of four athletes, and money was raised by donations from Puerto Rican citizens to fly them by plane, a rarity at that time, to Havana. Women competed in the games for the first time, in tennis.

It was a controversial games, where athletes complained about bad food, poor housing conditions and unfair officiating. The greatest controversy was in the swimming competition which was postponed for two weeks after a black swimmer from Panama was excluded by the Havana Yacht club where the events were first scheduled to be held. The events were eventually resumed at the Y.M.C.A., but not before Panamanian President Pablo Aroseman sent a cable to the Panamanian delegation calling them home.

By the third games in 1935, the name had been changed to the Central American and Caribbean Games to reflect the participation of the Caribbean nations. San Salvador, El Salvador, was given the honor of hosting the next edition. The games were held early in 1935, having been postponed one year due to a tornado[91] that hit El Salvador in 1934.

The fourth games were held in Panama City, Panama, from February 4–24, 1938. Jamaica participated for the first time, becoming the first English-speaking nation to join in the games. The games were disrupted by protests and complaints about safety of the athletes. Unruly crowds led to the cancelation of both the men's and women's basketball final games because the safety of the visiting teams could not be guaranteed.

World War II then took its toll, canceling the 1942 edition of the games, but they were revived in 1946 in Barranquilla, Columbia, with the next games held in 1950 in Guatemala City, Guatemala. The 1954 games were scheduled to be held in Panama City but Panama had to forego them. Mexico City took over to host the event.

The eighth edition of the Central American and Caribbean Games were postponed one year due to political unrest in the host country, Venezuela. When they were finally held in 1959, the Cuban revolution prevented that country from attending.

Jamaica became the first English-speaking nation to host these games in 1962 in Kingston, and athletes from the Bahamas and Barbados competed for the first time. The games were hosted for an economical U.S. $213,220.00.

The 1966 games in San Juan, Puerto Rico, are significant for "the battle of Cerro Pelado." Many factions wanted to ban Cuba from the games for political reasons after Castro's rise to power, but Don German Rieckehoff, president of the Organizing Committee, stood alone in his insistence that Cuba be allowed to compete. While the argument raged, the Cubans' boat, the "Cerro Pelado," was not allowed into Puerto Rican waters. Under intense pressure, Rieckehoff stood firm and finally convinced the governor of Puerto Rico to change his mind. The governor told Rieckehoff that he would allow the Cubans into the country, but that they would have to leave their boat and be picked up and brought to shore on a ship of Puerto Rican ownership. This is precisely what happened and Cuba participated in the games.

On the athletic fields, the pole vaulting Cruz brothers of Puerto Rico won gold (Rolando) and silver (Ruben). This was not the first or the second, but the third time they had accomplished this feat. They had also won gold and silver at Caracas in 1959, and at Kingston in 1962.

Mexico, up to that point in time, had been the dominant sports nation, finishing atop the medals standings in nine of the previous ten games (except for Havana 1930). In Panama City in 1970, the time had come for the Cubans to take over and become the dominant athletic nation in the region. The Cubans won nearly every team sport: baseball, football, water polo, men's volleyball and women's basketball. In the other two team sports, men's basketball and women's volleyball, they earned the bronze. The Cubans completely dominated in gymnastics, winning all 14 gold medals plus 12 silver and 12 bronze. They captured all 12 gold medals in women's athletics, 15 of 20 gold medals in men's athletics, every gold medal in wrestling and had similarly impressive performances in boxing, fencing and judo. In all, Cuba won 99 gold, 60 silver and 51 bronze medals. All the other countries combined won just 82 gold medals.

Santo Domingo, Dominican Republic, was chosen to host the 1974 games, but only after the iron-fisted dictator Trujillo had been assassinated and civil war ceased. Numerous new facilities were built for these games. The Cubans once again dominated on the playing fields, winning 101 of the 163 gold medals awarded. Cuba's 400 and 800 meter runner Alberto Juantorena emerged onto the international stage for the first time.

Medellín, Colombia's "City of Flowers," hosted the 13th Central American and Caribbean Games in 1978. Cuba, continuing to prove its athletic prowess, dominated as it had in the previous two editions, winning 120 of the 188 gold medals, including full sweeps of all the medals awarded in gymnastics, judo and fencing. In wrestling, the Cubans won nine of the ten categories, and in weightlifting they won 29 of the 30 medals awarded.

Alberto Juantorena, at 6500 foot altitude, ran the 400 meters in 44.27 seconds, just .01 off his best time from the 1976 Montreal Olympics. He also won the 800 meters with a time of 1:47.2.

Mayaguez, Puerto Rico, was originally selected to the host the next edition of the games in 1982, but they were switched to Havana, Cuba, when Puerto Rico could not keep its commitment.

About 200 Puerto Ricans went to Cuba to watch the games. However, U.S. President Ronald Reagan, on April 19, 1982, had banned travel to Cuba by U.S. citizens. Violators technically faced up to ten years in prison and a $10,000 fine.

Completing a spectacular career, Alberto Juantorena won the 800 meters and was treated like a head of state in his native country.

The 16th games were scheduled to be held in Guatemala, until the Guatemalan government pulled its financial support early in 1990. Mexico fortunately stepped in and hastily organized the games for later that year, the second time it had rescued them.

Carlos Salinas de Gortari, President of Mexico, opened the 16th edition of the Games on the anniversary of Mexico's revolution. IOC president Juan Antonio Samaranch was present to view the opening ceremonies.

The 17th edition was held a bit early in November 1993 in Ponce, Puerto Rico. Forty-five Cubans defected over the course of the games.

The 18th edition, held in August 1998 in Maracaibo, Venezuela, broke records for participation, with 1827 female and 3487 male athletes attending, for a total of 5314.

The Cuban team once again outdistanced all others combined, winning 191 gold medals. The rest of the teams won a combined 188 gold.

Mexico lost two gold medals when Nancy Contreras, a cyclist, and Erendira Villegas, a swimmer, both failed drug tests. Two Venezuelan athletes also failed drug tests: Tahyani Villaroel, a swimming silver, and José Ramón Jiminez, a weightlifting bronze.

The games ended the evening of August 22 with ceremonies in José Encarnacion Romero stadium, and the games flag was passed on to El Salvador, scheduled to host the next games in the year 2002.

Year	Host City	Host Nation	Dates	Nations	Athletes	Sports
1926	Mexico City	Mexico	October 12–Nov 2	3	271	7
1930	Havana	Cuba	March 15–April 5	9	596	10
1935	San Salvador	El Salvador	March 16–April 5	9	741	14
1938	Panama City	Panama	February 5–24	10	1216	18
1946	Barranquilla	Columbia	December 8–28	13	1540	19
1950	Guatemala City	Guatemala	February 8–March 12	14	1390	19
1954	Mexico City	Mexico	March 6–20	12	1321	19
1959	Caracas	Venezuela	January 6–18	12	1150	17
1962	Kingston	Jamaica	August 14–26	15	1559	16
1966	San Juan	Puerto Rico	June 11–25	18	1689	17
1970	Panama City	Panama	Feb. 27–March 14	20	2095	16
1974	Santo Domingo	Dominican Republic	Feb. 27–Mar 13	23	2052	18
1978	Medellín	Colombia	July 7–22	21	2605	19
1982	Havana	Cuba	August 7–18	22	2799	21
1986	Santiago de Los Caballeros	Dominican Republic	June 24–July 5	26	2963	25
1990	Mexico City	Mexico	Nov. 20–December 4	29	4224	30
1993	Ponce, San Juan	Puerto Rico	November 19–30	31	3570	30
1998	Maracaibo	Venezuela	August 8–22	31	5314	32

1926   *Mexico City   Mexico   October 12–November 2*

Nations: Mexico, Cuba, Guatemala
Sports: Athletics, Baseball, Basketball, Fencing, Shooting, Swimming, Tennis

MEDALS

Nation	Gold	Silver	Bronze	Total
Mexico	25	24	18	67
Cuba	14	15	15	44
Guatemala	0	0	3	3

1930   *Havana   Cuba   March 15–April 5*

Nations: Costa Rica, Cuba, El Salvador, Guatemala, Honduras, Jamaica, Mexico, Panama, Puerto Rico
Sports: Athletics, Baseball, Basketball, Diving, Fencing, Football, Shooting, Swimming, Tennis, Volleyball

MEDALS

Nation	Gold	Silver	Bronze	Total
Cuba	28	19	21	68
Mexico	12	18	10	40
Panama	4	1	5	10
Puerto Rico	0	3	0	3
Honduras	0	1	1	2
Costa Rica	0	1	1	2
Jamaica	0	1	0	1
Guatemala	0	0	2	2
El Salvador	0	0	2	2

1935   San Salvador   El Salvador   March 16–April 5

Nations: Costa Rica, Cuba, El Salvador, Guatemala, Honduras, Mexico, Nicaragua, Panama, Puerto Rico

Sports: Athletics, Baseball, Basketball, Boxing, Diving, Equestrian, Football, Fencing, Golf, Shooting, Swimming, Tennis, Volleyball, Wrestling

MEDALS

Nation	Gold	Silver	Bronze	Total
Mexico	37	20	21	78
Cuba	31	30	24	85
Puerto Rico	5	5	5	15
El Salvador	4	4	10	18
Guatemala	1	10	8	19
Panama	1	5	2	8
Costa Rica	0	1	0	1
Nicaragua	0	1	0	1

1938   Panama City   Panama   February 5–24

Nations: Colombia, Costa Rica, Cuba, El Salvador, Jamaica, Mexico, Nicaragua, Panama, Puerto Rico, Venezuela

Sports: Athletics, Baseball, Basketball, Boxing, Cycling, Diving, Equestrian, Fencing, Football, Golf, Shooting, Swimming, Tennis, Volleyball, Water Polo, Weightlifting, Wrestling

MEDALS

Nation	Gold	Silver	Bronze	Total
Mexico	24	32	16	72
Panama	24	22	20	66
Cuba	24	17	19	60
Puerto Rico	16	11	11	38
Jamaica	9	5	8	22
Venezuela	3	2	6	11
El Salvador	0	5	8	13
Costa Rica	0	2	1	3
Colombia	0	0	2	2
Nicaragua	0	0	1	1

1946   Barranquilla   Columbia   December 8–28

Nations: Colombia, Costa Rica, Cuba, Dominican Republic, El Salvador, Guatemala, Jamaica, Mexico, Netherlands Antilles, Panama, Puerto Rico, Trinidad and Tobago, Venezuela

Sports: Athletics, Baseball, Basketball, Boxing, Cycling, Diving, Fencing, Football, Golf, Gymnastics, Shooting, Softball, Swimming, Tennis, Volleyball, Water Polo, Weightlifting, Wrestling (Frontenis)

MEDALS

Nation	Gold	Silver	Bronze	Total
Cuba	29	26	23	78
Mexico	26	22	28	76

Nation	Gold	Silver	Bronze	Total
Panama	13	17	10	40
Puerto Rico	9	8	7	24
Jamaica	6	11	9	26
Colombia	5	8	3	16
Trinidad and Tobago	4	3	5	12
Dominican Republic	4	2	1	7
Venezuela	3	3	5	11
Netherlands Antilles	3	1	2	6
Guatemala	2	3	3	8
Costa Rica	2	0	1	3
El Salvador	1	3	3	7

1950   Guatemala City   Guatemala   February 8–March 12

Nations: Colombia, Costa Rica, Cuba, Dominican Republic, El Salvador, Guatemala, Haiti, Jamaica, Mexico, Netherlands Antilles, Panama, Puerto Rico, Trinidad and Tobago, Venezuela

Sports: Athletics, Baseball, Shooting, Boxing, Cycling, Diving, Equestrian, Fencing, Football, Golf, Gymnastics, Lawn Bowls, Shooting, Swimming, Tennis, Volleyball, Water Polo, Weightlifting, Wrestling

MEDALS

Nation	Gold	Silver	Bronze	Total
Mexico	43	24	26	93
Cuba	24	27	28	79
Puerto Rico	12	2	10	24
Jamaica	10	10	3	23
Guatemala	9	25	25	59
Panama	8	9	10	27
Netherlands Antilles	3	2	1	6
Colombia	2	4	4	10
El Salvador	2	4	3	9
Trinidad and Tobago	1	2	1	4
Nicaragua	1	0	1	2
Haiti	0	1	0	1
Honduras	0	0	2	2
Costa Rica	0	0	1	1

1954   Mexico City   Mexico   March 6–20

Nations: Colombia, Cuba, Dominican Republic, El Salvador, Guatemala, Jamaica, Mexico, Netherlands Antilles, Panama, Puerto Rico, Venezuela

Sports: Athletics, Baseball, Shooting, Boxing, Cycling, Diving, Equestrian, Fencing, Football, Golf, Gymnastics, Shooting, Swimming, Tennis, Volleyball, Water Polo, Weightlifting, Wrestling

MEDALS

Nation	Gold	Silver	Bronze	Total
Mexico	47	42	35	124
Cuba	29	19	20	68

Nation	Gold	Silver	Bronze	Total
Venezuela	14	18	21	53
Colombia	8	6	9	23
Panama	7	7	8	22
Puerto Rico	6	9	9	24
Jamaica	5	10	4	19
Guatemala	3	8	11	22
El Salvador	2	1	2	5
Netherlands Antilles	1	1	0	2
Dominican Republic	0	1	1	2

1959   Caracas   Venezuela   January 6–18

Nations: Colombia, Costa Rica, El Salvador, Guatemala, Guyana, Jamaica, Mexico, Netherlands Antilles, Nicaragua, Panama, Puerto Rico, Venezuela

Sports: Athletics, Baseball, Basketball, Boxing, Cycling, Diving, Equestrian, Fencing, Football, Gymnastics, Shooting, Swimming, Tennis, Volleyball, Water Polo, Weightlifting, Wrestling

MEDALS

Nation	Gold	Silver	Bronze	Total
Mexico	53	37	42	132
Venezuela	35	31	34	100
Puerto Rico	9	19	8	36
Panama	7	6	11	24
Colombia	6	10	4	20
Netherlands Antilles	4	5	3	12
Guyana	2	1	1	4
Guatemala	1	5	7	13
El Salvador	1	3	5	9
Jamaica	1	2	1	4
Nicaragua	0	0	2	2
Costa Rica	0	0	1	1

1962   Kingston   Jamaica   August 14–26

Nations: Bahamas, Barbados, Colombia, Cuba, Dominican Republic, El Salvador, Guatemala, Guyana, Jamaica, Mexico, Netherlands Antilles, Panama, Puerto Rico, Trinidad and Tobago, Venezuela

Sports: Athletics, Baseball, Basketball, Boxing, Cycling, Diving, Fencing, Football, Sailing, Shooting, Swimming, Tennis, Volleyball, Water Polo, Weightlifting, Wrestling

MEDALS

Nation	Gold	Silver	Bronze	Total
Mexico	37	25	27	89
Venezuela	15	27	15	57
Cuba	12	11	13	36
Puerto Rico	11	14	13	38
Colombia	10	4	11	25

Nation	Gold	Silver	Bronze	Total
Jamaica	8	7	8	23
Trinidad and Tobago	4	4	7	15
Netherlands Antilles	4	3	2	9
Bahamas	4	1	1	6
Panama	3	7	4	14
Dominican Republic	2	1	2	5
Guyana	1	3	2	6
Guatemala	1	2	2	5
El Salvador	0	2	3	5
Barbados	0	1	2	3

1966   San Juan   Puerto Rico   June 11–25

Nations: Bahamas, Barbados, Colombia, Cuba, Dominican Republic, El Salvador, Guatemala, Guyana, Jamaica, Mexico, Netherlands Antilles, Nicaragua, Panama, Puerto Rico, Trinidad and Tobago, U.S. Virgin Islands, Venezuela, (one more)

Sports: Athletics, Baseball, Basketball, Boxing, Cycling, Diving, Fencing, Football, Judo, Sailing, Shooting, Swimming, Tennis, Volleyball, Water Polo, Weightlifting, Wrestling

MEDALS

Nation	Gold	Silver	Bronze	Total
Mexico	38	23	22	83
Cuba	35	19	24	78
Puerto Rico	27	27	29	83
Venezuela	10	23	21	54
Colombia	10	12	12	34
Jamaica	7	7	8	22
Trinidad and Tobago	7	7	4	18
Panama	1	4	4	9
Guatemala	1	2	3	6
Barbados	1	1	2	4
Bahamas	1	0	0	1
Netherlands Antilles	0	5	1	6
U.S. Virgin Islands	0	4	1	5
Dominican Republic	0	1	2	3
Guyana	0	1	1	2
Nicaragua	0	1	0	1
El Salvador	0	0	2	2

1970   Panama City   Panama   February 27–March 14

Nations: Bahamas, Belize, Colombia, Cuba, Dominican Republic, Guatemala, Guyana, Jamaica, Mexico, Netherlands Antilles, Nicaragua, Panama, Puerto Rico, Suriname, Trinidad and Tobago, U.S. Virgin Islands, Venezuela, (three more)

Sports: Athletics, Baseball, Basketball, Boxing, Cycling, Diving, Fencing, Football, Gymnastics, Judo, Shooting, Swimming, Volleyball, Water Polo, Weightlifting, Wrestling

MEDALS

Nation	Gold	Silver	Bronze	Total
Cuba	98	61	51	210
Mexico	38	46	40	124
Colombia	15	9	13	37
Puerto Rico	13	18	25	56
Venezuela	6	16	18	40
Panama	5	17	19	41
Netherlands Antilles	5	6	10	21
Trinidad and Tobago	1	2	3	6
Jamaica	1	0	1	2
Guyana	0	2	4	6
Guatemala	0	2	4	6
Dominican Republic	0	2	1	3
Nicaragua	0	1	4	5
U.S. Virgin Islands	0	0	1	1
Bahamas	0	0	1	1

1974   Santo Domingo
Dominican Republic   February 27–March 13

Nations: Bahamas, Barbados, Belize, Bermuda, Colombia, Costa Rica, Cuba, Dominican Republic, El Salvador, Guatemala, Guyana, Haiti, Honduras, Jamaica, Mexico, Netherlands Antilles, Panama, Puerto Rico, Suriname, Trinidad and Tobago, U.S. Virgin Islands, Venezuela, (1 more)

Sports: Athletics, Baseball, Basketball, Boxing, Cycling, Diving, Football, Gymnastics, Judo, Sailing, Shooting, Softball, Swimming, Tennis, Volleyball, Water Polo, Weightlifting, Wrestling

MEDALS

Nation	Gold	Silver	Bronze	Total
Cuba	101	55	35	191
Mexico	26	30	26	82
Venezuela	14	16	25	55
Puerto Rico	9	24	36	69
Colombia	9	17	18	44
Costa Rica	3	3	2	8
Jamaica	2	3	2	7
Netherlands Antilles	2	0	5	7
Panama	1	12	11	24
Dominican Republic	1	5	14	20
Barbados	1	2	1	4
U.S. Virgin Islands	1	0	1	2
Belize	1	0	0	1
Trinidad and Tobago	0	2	3	5
El Salvador	0	2	1	3
Bahamas	0	1	0	1
Haiti	0	0	1	1
Bermuda	0	0	1	1
Guatemala	0	0	1	1

Nation	Gold	Silver	Bronze	Total
Suriname	0	0	1	1
Guyana	0	0	1	1

1978   Medellín   Colombia   July 7–22

Nations: Bahamas, Barbados, Bermuda, Colombia, Costa Rica, Cuba, Dominican Republic, El Salvador, Guatemala, Jamaica, Mexico, Netherlands Antilles, Nicaragua, Panama, Puerto Rico, Suriname, Trinidad and Tobago, U.S. Virgin Islands, Venezuela, (two more)

Sports: Athletics, Baseball, Basketball, Boxing, Cycling, Diving, Fencing, Football, Gymnastics, Judo, Softball, Swimming, Shooting, Synchronized Swimming, Tennis, Volleyball, Water Polo, Weightlifting, Wrestling

Venues: Atanasio Girardot Stadium, Bello Municipal Park, Envigado Municipal Park

MEDALS

Nation	Gold	Silver	Bronze	Total
Cuba	120	44	18	182
Mexico	25	48	43	116
Puerto Rico	13	15	33	61
Colombia	8	24	36	68
Jamaica	6	6	5	17
Venezuela	5	23	29	57
Dominican Republic	3	8	16	27
Costa Rica	2	4	3	9
Bahamas	2	0	2	4
Trinidad and Tobago	1	5	2	8
Netherlands Antilles	1	1	2	4
U.S. Virgin Islands	1	1	1	3
Bermuda	1	0	1	2
Panama	0	6	5	11
Nicaragua	0	1	2	3
Barbados	0	1	0	1
Suriname	0	1	0	1
Guatemala	0	0	6	6
El Salvador	0	0	2	2

1982   Havana   Cuba   August 7–18

Nations: Bahamas, Barbados, Bermuda, Belize, Costa Rica, Cuba, Dominican Republic, Granada, Guatemala, Guyana, Haiti, Jamaica, Mexico, Netherlands Antilles, Nicaragua, Panama, Puerto Rico, Suriname, Trinidad and Tobago, U.S. Virgin Islands, Venezuela, (one more)

Sports: Archery, Athletics, Basketball, Baseball, Boxing, Cycling, Diving, Fencing, Football, Gymnastics, Field Hockey, Judo, Sailing, Shooting, Softball, Swimming, Synchronized Swimming, Table Tennis, Tennis, Volleyball, Water Polo, Weightlifting, Wrestling

Venues: Pedro Marrero (Athletics), Coliseo Ciudad Deportiva (Basketball), Latinoamericano Ciudad Deportivo (Baseball), P. Carrasco (Boxing), Ciudad Deportiva

(Boxing), Autopista Habana del Este (Cycling), Ciudad Deportiva (Diving, Swimming), CVD Jesus Menendez (Synchronized Swimming), CVD Parque Marti (Fencing), C. Armada, CVD S. Jose La Polar, P. Marrero (Football), Valdes Daussa (Gymnastics), CVD Eduardo Saborit (Field Hockey), Mariposa ISCF (Judo, Wrestling), CVD A. Maceo, Santiago de Cuba (Weightlifting), CVD Cerro (Water Polo), CSO J.A. Echeverria, CSO J.A. Mella (Softball, Tennis), CVD Luyano (Tennis), CVD Garcia More (Table Tennis), Campo Tiro Enrique Borbonet (Shooting), Parque Lenin (Archery), Litoral Habanero (Sailing), Ataneo A. Mestre Gimnasium, Universitario S. de Cuba (Volleyball)

MEDALS

Nation	Gold	Silver	Bronze	Total
Cuba	173	71	38	282
Mexico	29	55	47	131
Venezuela	19	39	54	112
Puerto Rico	7	43	54	104
Dominican Republic	4	8	22	34
Jamaica	4	3	6	13
Costa Rica	3	1	4	8
U.S. Virgin Islands	2	5	4	11
Bahamas	2	3	4	9
Guatemala	2	1	6	9
Trinidad and Tobago	1	2	6	9
Guyana	1	0	1	2
Haiti	1	0	0	1
Panama	0	11	9	20
Nicaragua	0	3	5	8
Belize	0	1	0	1
Netherlands Antilles	0	0	3	3
Barbados	0	0	2	2
Bermuda	0	0	2	2
Granada	0	0	2	2
Suriname	0	0	1	1

1986   Santiago de los Caballeros
Dominican Republic   June 24–July 5

Nations: Antigua, Bahamas, Barbados, Belize, Cayman Islands, Colombia, Costa Rica, Cuba, Dominican Republic, Guatemala, Guyana, Haiti, Honduras, Jamaica, Mexico, Netherlands Antilles, Panama, Puerto Rico, Suriname, Trinidad and Tobago, U.S. Virgin Islands, Venezuela, (three more)

Sports: Archery, Athletics, Basketball, Baseball, Boxing, Cycling, Diving, Fencing, Football, Gymnastics, Field Hockey, Judo, Rowing, Sailing, Shooting, Softball, Swimming, Synchronized Swimming, Table Tennis, Tennis, Volleyball, Water Polo, Weightlifting, Wrestling

MEDALS

Nation	Gold	Silver	Bronze	Total
Cuba	174	81	44	299
Mexico	40	49	44	133

Nation	Gold	Silver	Bronze	Total
Venezuela	18	42	60	120
Puerto Rico	13	29	51	93
Costa Rica	11	0	3	14
Colombia	10	22	37	69
Dominican Republic	9	34	27	70
Trinidad and Tobago	3	6	7	16
Jamaica	2	8	7	17
Guatemala	2	4	9	15
Bahamas	2	4	4	10
Panama	1	5	11	17
U.S. Virgin Islands	1	1	2	4
Guyana	1	1	1	3
Suriname	1	0	0	1
Netherlands Antilles	0	1	4	5
Belize	0	1	0	1
Honduras	0	1	0	1
Barbados	0	0	5	5
Haiti	0	0	1	1

1990   Mexico City   Mexico   November 20–December 4

Nations: Antigua, Bahamas, Barbados, Bermuda, Colombia, Costa Rica, Cuba, Dominican Republic, El Salvador, Granada, Guatemala, Guyana, Haiti, Honduras, Jamaica, Mexico, Netherlands Antilles, Nicaragua, Panama, Puerto Rico, Suriname, Trinidad and Tobago, U.S. Virgin Islands, Venezuela, (five more)

Sports: Archery, Athletics, Badminton, Basketball, Baseball, Boxing, Canoeing, Cycling, Diving, Fencing, Football, Gymnastics, Field Hockey, Judo, Racquetball, Rowing, Sailing, Shooting, Softball, Swimming, Synchronized Swimming, Table Tennis, Tae Kwon Do, Tennis, Volleyball, Water Polo, Weightlifting, Wrestling

MEDALS

Nation	Gold	Silver	Bronze	Total
Cuba	180	90	51	321
Mexico	112	99	84	295
Puerto Rico	21	47	40	108
Colombia	18	29	39	86
Venezuela	14	42	72	128
Dominican Republic	5	11	29	45
Jamaica	4	4	5	13
Guatemala	2	5	25	32
Costa Rica	1	7	11	19
Panama	1	2	10	13
Suriname	1	1	1	3
Trinidad and Tobago	0	5	8	13
Nicaragua	0	4	6	10
Honduras	0	4	2	6
Antigua	0	2	1	3
Bermuda	0	1	5	6
U.S. Virgin Islands	0	1	3	4
El Salvador	0	1	3	4

Nation	Gold	Silver	Bronze	Total
Guyana	0	1	2	3
Barbados	0	1	0	1
Granada	0	0	1	1
Netherlands Antilles	0	0	1	1
Haiti	0	0	1	1
Bahamas	0	0	1	1

1998   Maracaibo   Venezuela   August 8–22

Nations: Antigua, Bahamas, Barbados, Belize, Bermuda, British Virgin Islands, Cayman Islands, Colombia, Costa Rica, Cuba, Dominica, Dominican Republic, El Salvador, Granada, Guatemala, Guyana, Haiti, Honduras, Jamaica, Mexico, Netherlands Antilles, Nicaragua, Panama, Puerto Rico, St. Kitts and Nevis, St. Vincent and the Grenadines, St. Lucia, Suriname, Trinidad and Tobago, U.S. Virgin Islands, Venezuela

Sports: Archery, Athletics, Baseball, Basketball, Beach Volleyball, Bowling, Boxing, Cycling, Diving, Equestrian, Fencing, Field Hockey, Gymnastics, Judo, Karate, Racquetball, Rhythmic Gymnastics, Rowing, Sailing, Shooting, Soccer, Softball, Swimming, Synchronized Swimming, Table Tennis, Tae Kwon Do, Tennis, Triathlon, Volleyball, Water Polo, Weightlifting, Wrestling

Venues: Polideportivo Complex, Jose Encarnacion Romero Olympic Stadium (Athletics, Cycling, Soccer) Luis Aparicio the Great Baseball Stadium (Baseball), Belisario Aponte Indoor Gymnasium, Polideportivo Complex Swimming Pool, Cotarerra Gymnasium (Boxing), Dome of Cabimas (Volleyball, Basketball), La Victoria Gymnasium (Gymnastics, Table Tennis, Fencing), Cabimas Polygon (Shooting)

MEDALS

Nation	Gold	Silver	Bronze	Total
Cuba	191	74	69	334
Mexico	61	87	71	219
Venezuela	56	68	67	191
Colombia	19	42	51	112
Puerto Rico	11	21	48	80
Dominican Republic	7	20	44	71
Suriname	7	1	0	8
Jamaica	6	13	10	29
El Salvador	4	11	21	36
Guatemala	3	11	22	36
Panama	3	6	4	13
Netherlands Antilles	3	2	5	10
Costa Rica	2	3	5	10
Bahamas	2	2	4	8
Barbados	2	2	4	8
Trinidad and Tobago	1	8	5	14
U.S. Virgin Islands	1	1	0	2
Nicaragua	0	2	6	8
Honduras	0	1	5	6

Nation	Gold	Silver	Bronze	Total
Haiti	0	0	3	3
Aruba	0	0	1	1
Guyana	0	0	1	1

Central American and Caribbean University Games[92,93]

Richard McGehee mentions that these regional university games grew from eight nations and four sports in 1972 to 16 nations and seven sports in 1990. The games are administered by the Organización Deportiva Universitaria Centroamericana y del Caribe (ODUCC) which was established in 1970.

The eighth games were held in Guadalajara, Mexico, in July 1997, and the ninth in San Germán, Puerto Rico, in the summer of 2000 with 900 athletes in eight sports.[94]

As of 2000, the ODUCC members were: Barbados, Colombia, Costa Rica, Cuba, Dominican Republic, El Salvador, Guatemala, Haiti, Honduras, Jamaica, Mexico, Nicaragua, Panama, Puerto Rico, Suriname, Venezuela and the Virgin Islands, with Ecuador an associate member.

Year	Host City	Host Nation	Dates	Nations	Athletes	Sports
1972	San Juan	Puerto Rico		8	NA	4
1975	Mexico City	Mexico		NA	NA	NA
1977	Santo Domingo	Dominican Republic		NA	NA	NA
1982	Barquisimeto	Venezuela		NA	NA	NA
1986	Havana	Cuba		NA	NA	NA
1990	Guatemala City	Guatemala		16	NA	7
7th	Unknown					
1997	Guadalajara	Mexico				
2000	San Germán	Puerto Rico	July 30–Aug. 5	14	900	8

2000　San Germán　Puerto Rico　July 30–Aug. 5

Sports: Athletics, Baseball, Basketball, Football, Judo, Table Tennis, Volleyball, Weightlifting

Central American Games

The first competition known as the Central American Games was an event held in 1921 as part of the centennial celebrations of Guatemala. Three other nations, El Salvador, Costa Rica, and Honduras, joined the host country in athletics, baseball, soccer, tennis, tug of war and swimming. The games were to have been continued, with El Salvador the chosen host for 1923, but they were never held because of the region's political unrest.[95]

In 1972, Carlos Manuel Arana Osorio of the Guatemalan Olympic Committee invited the National Olympic Committees from the Central American region to a special meeting to discuss forming a competition that would be smaller in size than the

Pan-American Games or the Central American and Caribbean Games. ORDECA, the Organización Deportiva Centro Americana, was formed at this meeting.[96] The executive secretary of the Guatemalan Olympic Committee, Ingrid Keller, was tireless in her efforts to see the games for the region established, and was rewarded when they were sanctioned by the IOC late in 1972. Costa Rica, El Salvador, Guatemala, Honduras, Nicaragua and Panama were the original founding nations, with Belize admitted in 1990.

The first games were held in Guatemala City, Guatemala, in 1973 with 966 athletes competing. The star of the games was Costa Rica's Maria del Milagro París, who won 12 gold and one silver medal in swimming.

Only five nations participated in the 1977 games, Honduras opting to stay home. Sixteen million dollars were spent on upgrading facilities in San Salvador, El Salvador. The Flor Blanca stadium, built for the 1935 Central American and Caribbean Games, was reconstructed and enlarged to hold 60,000 spectators. Shortages of steel and cement meant that the new indoor sports center was not finished in time, and the events to be held there had to be switched to other venues. Panama won 68 gold medals, El Salvador was second with 45, and Costa Rica third with 43. The individual star again was Maria del Milagro París, this time winning ten gold and two silver medals.

Managua, Nicaragua, was to hold the 1981 edition of the games, but political strife surrounding the Sandinista Revolution forced their cancelation. It was not until 1986 that a city again stepped in to host the games, and it was Guatemala City. Panama was not able to send a team to these games due to its own political upheavals.

In 1990, the participation figures had grown to 1,635 athletes, from the seven nations. Honduras spent a considerable amount of money upgrading its sports facilities for these games. Panama sent just two athletes, as the games were staged shortly after U.S. troops entered Panama.

The 1994 games were held in San Salvador, El Salvador, after Nicaragua was forced to abandon plans for hosting them. Swimmer Claudia Fortin of Honduras won five gold, five silver, and one bronze medal in the pool.

San Pedro Sula, Honduras, hosted the sixth games in December 1997, with a record 3,080 athletes from the seven Central American nations participating in 28 sports.

Guatemala City, Guatemala, was scheduled to host the 2001 games.

Year	Host City	Host Nation	Dates	Nations	Athletes	Sports
1973	Guatemala City	Guatemala	November 24–Dec 1	5	966	16
1977	San Salvador	El Salvador	November 25–Dec 4	5	1296	19
1986	Guatemala City	Guatemala	January 4–	4	1320	24
1990	Tegucigalpa	Honduras	January 5–14	7	1635	23
1994	San Salvador	El Salvador	January 14–23	7	2657	NA
1997	San Pedro Sula	Honduras	December 5–14	7	3080	28

1921   Guatemala City   Guatemala

Nations: Costa Rica, El Salvador, Guatemala, Honduras
Sports: Athletics, Baseball, Soccer, Tennis, Tug of War, Swimming*

1973   Guatemala City   Guatemala   November 24–December 1

Nations: Costa Rica, El Salvador, Guatemala, Nicaragua, Panama
Sports: Athletics, Basketball, Boxing, Cycling, Equestrian, Fencing, Football, Judo, Wrestling, Swimming, Weightlifting, Shooting, Softball, Table Tennis, Volleyball

1977   San Salvador   El Salvador   November 25–December 4

Nations: Costa Rica, El Salvador, Guatemala, Nicaragua, Panama
Sports: Athletics, Baseball, Basketball, Boxing, Cycling, Equestrian, Fencing, Football, Gymnastics, Judo, Wrestling, Swimming, Weightlifting, Softball, Table Tennis, Volleyball, Water Polo, Shooting
Venues: Flor Blanca National Stadium (Athletics and Football), National Gymnasium (Basketball), National Pelote Park (Baseball), Champagnat del Liceo Salvadoreno Gymnasium (Boxing and Weightlifting), National Velodrome (Cycling), Izalco Jockey Club (Equestrian Sports), Central American Pavilion of the International Fair (Fencing and Gymnastics), Choi Gymnasium (Judo)

| | MEDALS | | | |
Nation	Gold	Silver	Bronze	Total
Panama	68	47	43	158
El Salvador	45	57	44	146
Costa Rica	43	36	47	126
Guatemala	35	46	33	114
Nicaragua	9	12	24	45

Honduras did not compete.

1986   Guatemala City   Guatemala   January 4–?

Nations: Costa Rica, El Salvador, Guatemala, Nicaragua
Sports: Athletics, Badminton, Baseball, Basketball, Boxing, Chess, Cycling, Equestrian, Fencing, Football, Gymnastics, Judo, Lawn Bowls, Rowing, Sailing, Shooting, Swimming, Softball, Table Tennis, Volleyball, Water Polo, Weightlifting, Wrestling

1990   Tegucigalpa   Honduras   January 5–14

Nations: Belize, Costa Rica, El Salvador, Guatemala, Honduras, Nicaragua, Panama
Sports: Athletics, Baseball, Basketball, Boxing, Chess, Cycling, Equestrian, Fencing, Football, Gymnastics, Judo, Lawn Bowling, Racquetball, Softball, Swimming, Tae Kwon Do, Tennis, Shooting, Volleyball, Water Polo, Weightlifting, Wrestling, (exhibition–Bodybuilding)

1994   San Salvador   El Salvador   January 14–23

Nations: Belize, Costa Rica, El Salvador, Guatemala, Honduras, Nicaragua, Panama

1997   San Pedro Sula   Honduras   December 5–14

Nations: Belize, Costa Rica, Guatemala, El Salvador, Honduras, Nicaragua, Panama
Sports: Athletics, Baseball, Basketball, Bodybuilding, Boxing, Chess, Cycling, Equestrian, Fencing, Football, Gymnastics, Judo, Karate, Lawn Bowling, Racquetball, Softball, Swimming, Tae Kwon Do, Table Tennis, Tennis, Shooting, Triathlon, Volleyball, Water Polo, Weightlifting, Wrestling, (exhibition—Rowing, Beach Volleyball)

Central Asian Games

The Central Asian Games, which emerged out of the breakup of the Soviet Union, give athletes from the former Soviet republics of Kazakhstan, Kyrgyzstan, Tajikistan, Turkmenistan and Uzbekistan a chance to display their skills in international competition.

International Olympic Committee President Juan Antonio Samaranch attended the opening ceremonies of both editions of the Central Asian Games, in Tashkent, Uzbekistan, in 1995 and Alma-Ata, Kazakhstan, in 1997, to show the support of the IOC for this fledgling competition.[97]

James Riordan, in his book *Sport in Soviet Society*, mentions that "The first Central Asian Olympics" were held in Tashkent in 1920 as part of the Soviet Spartakiads. Most of the sports played were the national equestrian events and wrestling of Uzbekistan, but the games marked the first time the Russians, Uzbeks, Kazakhs, and Turkmenian and Kirghiz peoples had competed together in any sports event of this kind.[98]

Year	Host City	Host Nation	Dates	Nations	Athletes	Sports
1995	Tashkent	Uzbekistan	September 2–9	5	NA	12
1997	Alma-Ata	Kazakhstan	September 13–20	5	NA	14
1999	Bishkek	Kyrgyzstan	October 2–7	NA	NA	NA

1995   Tashkent   Uzbekistan   September 2–9

Nations: Kazakhstan, Kyrgyzstan, Tajikistan, Turkmenistan, Uzbekistan
Sports: Traditional Central Asian Wrestling, Freestyle Wrestling, Athletics, Swimming, Basketball, Volleyball, Fencing, Shooting, Cycling, Weightlifting, Boxing, Tennis

Commonwealth Games

The suggestion for a Commonwealth "Olympics" was proposed as early as 1891 when J. Astley Cooper proposed the formation of a "Pan-Britannic" sports contest. The idea was ahead of its time and no meetings were ever arranged.[99]

In 1911, in conjunction with the British "Festival of the Empire," in London, Britain, Canada, South Africa and Australasia (Australia and New Zealand) held sporting events. On September 27, 1924, the Canadian Amateur Athletic Union passed a proposal to begin a British Empire Games.

The Canadian contingent, largely due to the efforts of one man, Bobby Robinson, willed the first games into existence despite a general hesitation on the part of many of the invitees. Some thought that the effort to institute the British Empire Games was an attempt to overshadow the Olympic Games. It was not until the city of Hamilton, Ontario, offered to pay for much of the travel costs of the teams that the idea was finally accepted.

Eleven nations took part in the first games: Australia, Bermuda, British Guiana, Canada, England, Northern Ireland, Newfoundland, New Zealand, Scotland, South Africa and Wales.

Since their establishment, the Commonwealth Games have undergone a number of name changes. They began as the British Empire Games in 1930, and from 1954 to

1966 were known as the British Empire and Commonwealth Games. The name was changed to the British Commonwealth Games in 1970, and finally in 1990 the word British was dropped altogether and the games are now simply called the Commonwealth Games.

The Commonwealth Games are unique for their use of the Queen's Baton, which carries the Queen's message, rather than a torch relay. The tradition of the Queen's Baton and Message began at the 1958 games in Cardiff, Wales. Each country designs its own baton, of which there is only one (unlike the various torch relays in which numerous torches are made and the flame is sometimes passed from torch to torch). The Queens Baton is usually quite ornate, made with silver, gold and sometimes gemstones from the host country. The relay throughout the years has become longer and more elaborate. The first ever Queen's Message Relay in 1958 began at Buckingham Palace and was taken north through England, into Wales, down the west coast and back to Cardiff. Roger Bannister, Chris Chataway and Peter Driver, all champions from the 1954 games, started the relay off from Buckingham Palace. The most recent relays have been extended world tours, with stops in most every Commonwealth country before arriving at the games.

The Queen's Message is usually a simple greeting and welcome. The 1958 message read:

> To all athletes assembled at Cardiff for the Sixth British Empire and Commonwealth Games I send a warm welcome and my very best wishes.
>
> I am delighted that so many Commonwealth countries have sent teams to Wales for these Games. The number is larger than ever and more than three times as great as for the first meeting in Hamilton in 1930.
>
> It is welcome proof of the increasing value which is being placed today on physical strength and skill as an essential factor in the development of the whole man; healthy in mind and body.
>
> It also gives me the greatest personal pleasure to know that so many members of the Commonwealth family are meeting in friendly rivalry and competition.
>
> I hope that many lasting friendships will grow from this great meeting of athletes and spectators and that you will all go home with a better understanding of the value of our Commonwealth of nations.
>
> I am greatly looking forward to being with you at the end of next week.
>
>   Elizabeth R.[100]

The 1930 games in Hamilton were judged a success and the next games were to be held in Johannesburg, South Africa, in 1934. Foreshadowing much of the history that was to occur in South African sport for the next 50 years, there were protests against South Africa's racial policies and the 1934 games were switched to London.

The 1938 games in Sydney, Australia, were held in February, the winter season for the teams from the northern hemisphere. These teams traveled long distances by ship, doing what little training they could on board. The timing suited the home team just fine, and the Australians won a total of 65 medals to Canada's 44 and England's 39.

At the 1938 games, the selection committee chose the French-Canadian city of Montreal for the next event. World War II interfered and by the time the war was over the committee had selected New Zealand for the 1950 games, and Auckland was named the host city. These games were well-run, well-attended and ended up with a profit.

The 1954 games in Vancouver, Canada are best known for the "Miracle Mile" matchup between Roger Bannister of England and John Landy of Australia, the first mile race ever in which two runners ran under four minutes.

Cardiff, Wales, was chosen for the 1958 games. The Welsh were very proud to have been awarded the event and did their job well. It would be the last games for 28 years in which athletes from South Africa participated. A number of demonstrations against the all-white South African team took place in London and Cardiff. South Africa withdrew from the Commonwealth in 1961 and would not be allowed to return to the Commonwealth Games until the 1994 games in Victoria, Canada.

The athletes' village in Perth, Australia, for the 1962 games was considered to be the best ever at that time. The government of Western Australia held a design competition and built 150 homes from the winning entry. The homes were used by the athletes during the games then sold at public auction afterward. The Perth games were the hottest on record with temperatures reaching 105 degrees during the opening ceremonies.

During the meetings of the Commonwealth Games Federation in 1962, a proposal was made, with the thought of reducing travel costs for the Commonwealth teams, to hold future Commonwealth Games during the Olympic years, a few weeks before the Olympics in a Commonwealth city close to where the Olympics were to be held. This proposal was voted down.

Kingston, Jamaica, hosted the 1966 games, the first games to be held outside Canada, Great Britain, Australia and New Zealand. There was much uncertainty as to whether or not Jamaica could organize the games successfully. The Jamaicans could not provide television broadcasting facilities so the foreign broadcasters had to bring their own equipment and technicians. Radio Jamaica hired three former Olympic stars, Harold Abrahams, Jesse Owens, and Johnny Weissmuller, as commentators for the games.

Kip Keino, the emerging Kenyan star, won the one- and three-mile runs, both in Commonwealth record times. Fifteen new swimming world records were set in a very fast Kingston pool.

The Commonwealth Games are frequently called the "Family Games" and the 1970 version at Edinburgh was just that. Three husband and wife pairs all from England won medals. The Paynes, Howard and Rosemary, won the men's hammer throw and women's discus respectively. It was Howard's third consecutive hammer gold medal. Sheila Sherwood won the women's long jump while her husband, John, won the men's 400 meter hurdles. In badminton, Sue Whetnall won a gold while her husband, Peter, won a silver. Two Scottish brothers continued the family theme. On the first day of competition, Laughlin Stewart delighted the home crowd by winning a magnificent 10,000 meter race to beat the Olympic champion, Naftali Temu of Kenya, and the world record–holder, Ron Clarke of Australia. On the last day, Laughlin's younger brother, Ian, not to be outdone, beat Kip Keino in the 5000 meters. The events at the Edinburgh games were measured in meters rather than yards for the first time.

Sylvia Potts of New Zealand was the central figure in the most dramatic story of the games. Leading a close 1500 meter race, in the final stretch her tired legs buckled and she tumbled to the track a mere two steps from the finish line. The rest of the field swept past her to take the medals and Potts ended up ninth. When the games went to Christchurch four years later, Potts was chosen to carry the Queen's Baton in the opening ceremony.

Twenty years after Landy and Bannister had tangled over one mile, New Zealand's

John Walker and Tanzania's Filbert Bayi ran a race just as brilliant in the 1974 Christchurch, New Zealand, games, both breaking the 1,500 meter world record. Bayi won that day in 3:32.2 with Walker second in 3:32.5. Kenya's Ben Jipcho finished third in 3:33.2. It was Jipcho's third medal of the games; he had already won the steeple-chase and 5000 meters.

The games' security was the tightest ever. The massacre at the 1972 Munich Olympics had changed the nature of security measures at international games forever. The citizens of Christchurch made up for the heightened tension with their hospital-ity, inviting journalists and TV reporters home to dinner. When the Ugandan bicy-cling team showed up without bicycles, assuming the organizers would provide them, the people of Christchurch came through and found some bikes for the Ugandans to ride.

Edmonton, Canada, hosted the 1978 games and was able to build its Common-wealth Stadium for $20 million, considerably less than the estimated $1 billion that the city of Montreal would end up paying for its 1976 Olympic Stadium.

South Africa was not present at the Edmonton games, but its presence was still felt. It was only two years after the majority of African nations had boycotted the 1976 Olympic Games over the New Zealand rugby tour of South Africa, and one year after the Gleneagles Agreement was signed which prohibited any sporting contacts with South Africa by other Commonwealth nations. Nigeria, still not happy with the lack of progress over the issue of apartheid, pulled out of the 1978 Edmonton Games over the issue and organizers were afraid that other African nations would consider another boycott. No other African nation followed Nigeria's lead, however.

Nineteen-year-old Gidemas Shahanga of Tanzania won the marathon. This was an impressive feat, considering it was only two weeks after his seventh-place finish in the marathon at the third African Games in Algiers, Algeria.

Kenya's Henry Rono, denied the opportunity to compete in the Montreal and Moscow Olympic Games due to boycotts, won both the 5000 meters and the 3000 meter steeplechase.

In 1982, Australia hosted the games once again, this time in Brisbane. An African boycott of the games was averted when the Commonwealth secretariat in May 1982 strongly condemned the 1981 tour of New Zealand by a South African rugby team and reaffirmed the Gleneagles agreement.

Brisbane welcomed the athletes with Waltzing Matilda, a huge hollow kangaroo, leading the opening ceremonies parade. Once on the field, the kangaroo's pouch opened up and schoolchildren poured onto the field. Australia's Raelene Boyle was chosen to carry the Queen's Baton, and also won the women's 400 meters, her sev-enth Commonwealth Games gold medal of a long and distinguished career.

Near the end of the games, about 200 aborigines and their supporters were arrested as they tried to gain entry to the stadium to stage a protest for land rights. Several days of protests had culminated in a demonstration at the stadium and demands for the removal of Queensland's premier, Johannes Bjelke-Petersen, whom they considered to be racist.

When the games returned to Edinburgh in 1986, the question of South Africa had still not been solved. When a New Zealand rugby team decided to tour South Africa, the majority of the African and Caribbean nations moved to boycott the Edinburgh games. Thirty-two nations stayed home while only 26 took part. Distance runner Zola Budd and swimmer Annette Crowley, both South Africans intending to compete for

Britain, were excluded from the games in an effort to try and appease the boycotting nations, to no avail.

Daley Thompson won his third straight Commonwealth decathlon, though he got into difficulties with the organizers and sponsors for scratching the word Guinness from his competition number, saying he was protesting the promotion of alcohol.

In 1990 at the Auckland games, the African nations threatened to boycott yet again in protest at another British rugby and cricket tour to South Africa. Anver Versi, of the news magazine *New African*, had made strong arguments against a boycott. He wrote, "anyone who has followed [the] international press will know that African victories in the World Championships and the Olympics have done more to raise the status of Africans in the eyes of the world than all the speechifying and politicking that goes on every day." In the end, African nations went to Auckland and were successful.

The year 1990 saw the first drug scandal at a Commonwealth Games. An Indian weightlifter, Subratakumar Paul, was the first to test positive. Members of the Welsh team then voiced very strong opinions to the press that athletes testing positive should never be allowed to compete again. Two days later, two Welsh lifters tested positive.

Peter Elliot won the 1500 meter race in which New Zealand star John Walker fell and finished last. Elliot insisted that Walker, the former world record-holder and Olympic champion, who had first competed in the 1974 games, accompany him on a lap of honor. Sebastian Coe also ended his international career in Auckland.

South Africa was welcomed back into the Commonwealth Games in 1994 in Victoria, Canada, after the apartheid government had been dismantled and the South Africans agreed to let anyone compete on a Commonwealth Games team. Hezekiah Sepeng became the first black South African to win a medal in the Commonwealth Games by taking the 800 meter silver. Two years later at the Atlanta Olympic Games he would repeat the performance, winning the silver and becoming the first black South African to win an Olympic medal.

Horace Dove-Edwin from the small African nation of Sierra Leone, ran extremely well throughout the rounds of the 100 meters, eventually finishing second to the great Linford Christie of England in the final. An extremely joyous and emotional victory lap by Dove-Edwin followed. The Sierra Leonese team had become the darlings of Victoria when it was discovered that they had stayed in the village and watched the opening ceremonies on television because they felt they didn't have the proper attire to march.

The citizens of Victoria made sure the team had the uniforms to march in the closing ceremony. It all came crashing down two days later when it was announced that Dove-Edwin had not passed his postrace drug test. Considering it was for the very same drug Ben Johnson had been found using in Seoul, the Canadians were not amused.

Disabled athletes, who had had a smaller version of the Commonwealth Games from 1962 to 1974, were included in the Victoria games with events in swimming, athletics and lawn bowls.

In 1998, the Commonwealth Games were held in Kuala Lumpur, Malaysia, the first time they had been staged outside an English-speaking country. In the months leading up to the games the organizers had to overcome a weak Asian economy, a water shortage, and smoke from forest fires which had raged out of control in neighboring Indonesia. Numerous times the games were rumored to be on the verge of being moved or canceled but the Malaysian government, though forced to slash the games budget, held firm and fulfilled their commitment.

The Queen's Baton was carried to the stadium on an elephant and presented to Prince Edward by Malaysia's first ever Commonwealth medal winner, Koh Eng Tong, a bronze medalist in weightlifting from the 1954 games. The Scots wore their traditional kilts in the opening parade, despite being warned of mosquitoes. The Singaporeans were booed, reflecting the cold relations between themselves and the hosts.

There were new team sports added to the games including cricket, rugby, netball, and men's and women's field hockey. Team sports up to this time had not been included in the games to emphasize that they were between individuals and not nations.

Prize money was discussed at the meeting of the Commonwealth Games Federation, but was voted down. The federation was upset with IAAF President Primo Nebiolo, who refused to switch the dates of the IAAF World Cup so as not to conflict with the Commonwealth Games. Numerous athletes chose the prize money of the World Cup over the medals of the Commonwealth Games, and the event in Kuala Lumpur lost some of its star attractions.

The games' medical chief, Dr. Geoffrey Haigh, announced that any athlete testing positive for marijuana at the games would be given the news privately in order to give them a chance to leave the country quietly. Games organizers wanted to ensure that athletes did not run afoul of Malaysia's strict drug laws which were severe and could include the death penalty, particularly for trafficking in illegal substances.

When the games began and the athletes took center stage, Judy Oakes of England won the shot put gold, and at 40 years of age she became the oldest woman to win a gold medal at the Commonwealth Games. This continued an amazing streak of medals in six straight games. Oakes won the bronze in 1978, gold in 1982, silver in 1986 and 1990, and gold in 1994.

The Kenyans dominated the distance events as expected. In the 5000 meters, Daniel Komen, Thomas Nyariki and Richard Limo swept the medals. In the steeplechase, John Kosgei won gold, Bernard Barmasai, the world record-holder, won the silver, and Kipkurui Misoi the bronze. Simon Maina won the 10,000 meter run, Laban Rotich the 1500, and Japheth Kimutai the 800 meters, and South African Hezekiel Sepeng finished second in the 800 for the second games in a row. Ato Boldon of Trinidad beat Frankie Fredericks of Namibia 9.88 to 9.96 in the 100 meters.

Marcus Stephen, from tiny Nauru, swept the 62 kg weightlifting division for the second games in a row to bring his personal Commonwealth gold medal total and his nation's to seven.

Australia won 80 gold medals, and England and Canada were second and third with 36 and 30 gold medals. Malaysia performed well as hosts and its athletes won ten gold medals.

At the closing ceremonies, several thousand volunteers were kept outside the stadium after being promised they could attend. A near riot broke out before police were able to control the situation, but few of the volunteers were able to see any of the ceremonies.

Manchester, England, is busily preparing to host the 2002 Commonwealth Games.

Year	Host City	Host Nation	Dates	Nations	Athletes	Sports
1930	Hamilton	Canada	August 16–23	11	400	6
1934	London	England	August 4–11	16	500	6
1938	Sydney	Australia	February 5–12	15	590	7
1950	Auckland	New Zealand	February 4–11	12	590	9
1954	Vancouver	Canada	July 30–August 7	24	789*	9

Year	Host City	Host Nation	Dates	Nations	Athletes	Sports
1958	Cardiff	Wales	July 18–26	35	1358*	9
1962	Perth	Australia	November 21– Dec. 1	35	1041	9
1966	Kingston	Jamaica	August 4–13	34	1316*	10
1970	Edinburgh	Scotland	July 16–25	42	1744*	10
1974	Christchurch	New Zealand	January 24– February 2	38	1276	9
1978	Edmonton	Canada	August 3–12	45	1475	10
1982	Brisbane	Australia	Sept. 30–October 9	46	2150	10
1986	Edinburgh	Scotland	July 24–August 2	26	2123*	10
1990	Auckland	New Zealand	Jan. 24–February 3	54	2896*	10
1994	Victoria	Canada	August 18–28	63	2557	10
1998	Kuala Lumpur	Malaysia	September 10–20	70	4100	15

*Figures with an asterisk are from the Commonwealth Institute and are figures for both athletes and officials. Other figures are from Dheenshaw with the exception of 1994 and 1998.

The following nations lists are not complete.

1930 Hamilton Canada August 16–23

Nations: Australia, Bermuda, British Guiana, Canada, England, Northern Ireland, Newfoundland, New Zealand, Scotland, South Africa, Wales
Sports: Athletics, Boxing, Lawn Bowling, Rowing, Swimming, Wrestling
Sports for Women: Swimming
Venues: Hamilton Civic Stadium, Prince of Wales School (Athletes' Village—Men), Royal Connaught Hotel (Village Women)

MEDALS

Nation	Gold	Silver	Bronze	Total
England	23	13.5	12	48.5
Canada	19	22	15.5	56.5
South Africa	6	4	7.5	17.5
Australia	2	4	1	7
New Zealand	2	2.5	1	5.5
Scotland	2	1	4.5	7.5
Wales	0	2	1	3
Ireland	0	1	0	1
British Guiana	0	1	0	1
Newfoundland	0	0	0.5	0.5

1934 London England August 4–11

Nations: Australia, Bermuda, British Guiana, Canada, England, Hong Kong, India, Jamaica, Northern Ireland, Newfoundland, New Zealand, Rhodesia, Scotland, South Africa, Trinidad, Wales
Sports: Athletics, Boxing, Cycling, Lawn Bowling, Swimming, Wrestling
Sports for Women: Athletics, Swimming
Venues: White City Stadium (Opening Ceremonies, Athletics), Empire Pool at Wembley Stadium (Swimming), Manchester Athletic Club Fallowfield Grounds in Manchester (Cycling)

MEDALS

Nation	Gold	Silver	Bronze	Total
England	29	19	20.5	68.5
Canada	14	25	9	48
Australia	8	4	2	14
South Africa	7	10	5	22
Scotland	5	3	15	23
New Zealand	1	0	2.5	3.5
British Guiana	1	0	0	1
Wales	0	3	3	6
Northern Ireland	0	1	2	3
Jamaica	0	1	1	2
Rhodesia	0	0	2	2
India	0	0	1	1

1938   Sydney   Australia   February 5–12

Nations: Australia, Bermuda, British Guiana, Canada, Ceylon, England, Fiji, India, Northern Ireland, New Zealand, Rhodesia, Scotland, South Africa, Trinidad, Wales

Sports: Athletics, Boxing, Cycling, Lawn Bowling, Rowing, Swimming, Wrestling
Sports for Women: Athletics, Swimming
Venues: Sydney Cricket Ground (Opening Ceremonies, Athletics), North Sydney Olympic Pool (Swimming), Henson Park (Cycling)

MEDALS

Nation	Gold	Silver	Bronze	Total
Australia	24	19	22	65
Canada	13	16	15	44
England	15	14	10	39
South Africa	10	10	6	26
New Zealand	5	7	12	24
Scotland	0	2	3	5
Wales	2	1	0	3
Rhodesia	0	0	2	2
Ceylon	1	0	0	1
British Guiana	0	1	0	1

1950   Auckland   New Zealand   February 4–11

Nations: Australia, Canada, Ceylon, England, Fiji, Malaysia, New Zealand, Nigeria, Rhodesia, Scotland, South Africa, Wales

Sports: Athletics, Boxing, Cycling, Fencing, Lawn Bowling, Rowing, Swimming, Weightlifting, Wrestling
Sports for Women: Athletics, Fencing, Swimming
Venues: Eden Park (Opening Ceremonies, Athletics), Western Springs Stadium (Cycling, Closing Ceremonies), Newmarket Olympic Pool (Swimming), Ardmore Park Teachers' Training Camp (Village), Lake Karapiro (Rowing)

MEDALS

Nation	Gold	Silver	Bronze	Total
Australia	24	27	19	80
New Zealand	10	22	21	53
England	19	16	13	48
Canada	8	9	14	31
South Africa	8	4	7	19
Scotland	5	2	3	10
Fiji	1	2	2	5
Malaysia	2	1	1	4
Ceylon	1	2	1	4
Nigeria	0	1	0	1
Rhodesia	0	1	0	1
Wales	0	1	0	1

1954   Vancouver   Canada   July 30–August 7

Nations: Australia, Barbados, British Guiana, Canada, England, Hong Kong, Jamaica, N. Ireland, N. Rhodesia, New Zealand, Nigeria, Pakistan, S. Rhodesia, Scotland, South Africa, Trinidad, Uganda, Wales

Sports: Athletics, Boxing, Cycling, Fencing, Lawn Bowling, Rowing, Swimming, Weightlifting, Wrestling

Sports for Women: Athletics, Fencing, Swimming

Venues: Empire Stadium (Opening Ceremonies, Athletics), University of British Columbia Empire Pool (Swimming), Pacific National Exhibition Forum (Boxing), Exhibition Gardens (Weightlifting), Empire Oval—China Creek Park (Cycling), Lord Byng High School (Fencing), Vedder Canal (Rowing), Kerrisdale Arena (Wrestling)

MEDALS

Nation	Gold	Silver	Bronze	Total
England	23	24	20	67
Australia	20	11	17	48
South Africa	16	7	12	35
Canada	9	20	14	43
New Zealand	7	6	6	19
Scotland	6	2	5	13
N. Rhodesia	1	5	4	10
Nigeria	1	3	3	7
Wales	1	1	5	7
Pakistan	1	3	2	6
Trinidad	2	2	0	4
S. Rhodesia	2	1	0	3
N. Ireland	2	1	0	3
Jamaica	1	0	0	1
Hong Kong	0	1	0	1
Uganda	0	1	0	1
Barbados	0	1	0	1
British Guiana	0	0	1	1

1958   Cardiff   Wales   July 18–26

Nations: Australia, Bahamas, Barbados, British Guiana, Canada, England, Ghana, India, Isle of Man, Jamaica, Kenya, Malaysia, New Zealand, Nigeria, Northern Ireland, Pakistan, Rhodesia, Scotland, Singapore, South Africa, Trinidad and Tobago, Uganda, Wales

Sports: Athletics, Boxing, Cycling, Fencing, Lawn Bowling, Rowing, Swimming, Weightlifting, Wrestling

Sports for Women: Athletics, Fencing, Swimming

Venues: Cardiff Arms Park (Opening Ceremonies, Athletics), Empire Pool (Swimming), Sophia Gardens Pavilion (Boxing, Wrestling, Lawn Bowls), Maindy Stadium (Cycling), Guest Keen Sports Club (Lawn Bowls), Cae'r Castell School (Fencing), Lake Padarn (Rowing), Memorial Hall in Barry (Weightlifting)

MEDALS

Nation	Gold	Silver	Bronze	Total
England	29	22	29	80
Australia	27	22	17	66
South Africa	13	10	8	31
Canada	1	10	16	27
New Zealand	4	6	9	19
Scotland	5	5	3	13
Wales	1	3	7	11
Pakistan	3	5	2	10
Jamaica	4	2	1	7
Northern Ireland	1	1	3	5
India	2	1	0	3
Rhodesia	0	0	3	3
Singapore	2	0	0	2
Bahamas	1	1	0	2
Barbados	1	1	0	2
Malaysia	0	2	0	2
Nigeria	0	1	1	2
Kenya	0	0	2	2
Uganda	0	1	0	1
Isle of Man	0	0	1	1
Trinidad and Tobago	0	0	1	1
British Guiana	0	1	0	1
Ghana	0	0	1	1

1962   Perth   Australia   November 21–December 1

Nations: Australia, Bahamas, Barbados, British Guiana, Canada, England, Fiji, Ghana, Jamaica, Jersey, Kenya, Malaya, New Zealand, Northern Ireland, Pakistan, Papua New Guinea, Rhodesia, Scotland, Singapore, Trinidad and Tobago, Uganda, Wales

Sports: Athletics, Boxing, Cycling, Fencing, Lawn Bowling, Rowing, Swimming, Weightlifting, Wrestling

Sports for Women: Athletics, Fencing, Swimming

Venues: Perry Lakes Stadium (Opening Ceremonies, Athletics) Canning River

(Rowing) Beatty Park Pool (Swimming), Lake Monger Velodrome (Perth) (Cycling), Victoria Drill Hall (Fencing)

MEDALS

Nation	Gold	Silver	Bronze	Total
Australia	38	36	31	105
England	29	22	27	78
New Zealand	10	12	10	32
Canada	4	12	15	31
Scotland	4	7	3	14
Pakistan	8	1	0	9
Ghana	3	5	1	9
Rhodesia	0	2	5	7
Uganda	1	1	4	6
Wales	0	2	4	6
Jamaica	3	1	1	5
Kenya	2	2	1	5
Fiji	0	0	2	2
Trinidad and Tobago	0	0	2	2
Singapore	2	0	0	2
Northern Ireland	0	0	1	1
Papua New Guinea	0	0	1	1
Barbados	0	0	1	1
British Guiana	0	0	1	1
Jersey	0	0	1	1
Malaya	0	0	1	1
Bahamas	0	1	0	1

1966   Kingston   Jamaica   August 4–13

Nations: Australia, Bahamas, Barbados, Bermuda, Canada, England, Ghana, Guyana, India, Isle of Man, Jamaica, Kenya, Malaysia, New Zealand, Nigeria, Northern Ireland, Pakistan, Papua New Guinea, Scotland, Trinidad and Tobago, Uganda, Wales

Sports: Athletics, Badminton, Boxing, Cycling, Fencing, Lawn Bowling, Shooting, Swimming, Weightlifting, Wrestling

Sports for Women: Athletics, Badminton, Fencing, Shooting, Swimming

Venues: National Stadium (Opening Ceremonies, Athletics, Cycling), Stadium Pool (Swimming), Convention Hall (Wrestling), Kingston Arena (Badminton), Sabina Park (Boxing), Ward Theatre (Weightlifting)

MEDALS

Nation	Gold	Silver	Bronze	Total
England	33	24	23	80
Australia	23	28	22	73
Canada	14	20	23	57
New Zealand	8	5	3	16
Ghana	5	2	2	9
Trinidad and Tobago	5	2	2	9
Pakistan	4	1	4	9

Nation	Gold	Silver	Bronze	Total
Kenya	4	1	3	8
India	3	4	3	10
Nigeria	3	4	3	10
Wales	3	2	2	7
Malaysia	2	2	1	5
Scotland	1	4	4	9
Northern Ireland	1	3	3	7
Isle of Man	1	0	0	1
Jamaica	0	4	8	12
Bahamas	0	1	0	1
Bermuda	0	1	0	1
Guyana	0	1	0	1
Papua New Guinea	0	1	0	1
Uganda	0	0	3	3
Barbados	0	0	1	1

1970   Edinburgh   Scotland   July 16–25

Nations: Australia, Barbados, Canada, England, Fiji, Gambia, Ghana, Guyana, Hong Kong, India, Isle of Man, Jamaica, Kenya, Malawi, Malaysia, New Zealand, Nigeria, Northern Ireland, Pakistan, Scotland, Singapore, St. Vincent, Tanzania, Trinidad and Tobago, Uganda, Wales, Zambia

Sports: Athletics, Badminton, Boxing, Cycling, Fencing, Lawn Bowling, Shooting, Swimming, Weightlifting, Wrestling

Sports for Women: Athletics, Badminton, Fencing, Swimming

Venues: Meadowbank Stadium (Opening Ceremonies, Athletics), Meadowbank Centre (Badminton, Fencing), Balgreen (Lawn Bowls), Holyrood Park (Athletes' Village, Cycling Road Race), Murrayfield Ice Rink (Boxing), Meadowbank Sports Center Hall No. 1 (Wrestling), Royal Commonwealth Pool (Swimming), Leith Town Hall (Weightlifting), Meadowbank Velodrome (Cycling)

MEDALS

Nation	Gold	Silver	Bronze	Total
England	27	25	32	84
Australia	36	24	22	82
Canada	18	24	24	66
Scotland	6	8	11	25
Kenya	5	3	6	14
New Zealand	2	6	6	14
India	5	3	4	12
Wales	2	6	4	12
Pakistan	4	3	3	10
Northern Ireland	3	1	5	9
Trinidad and Tobago	0	4	3	7
Jamaica	4	2	1	7
Uganda	3	3	1	7
Ghana	2	3	2	7
Zambia	0	2	2	4
Malaysia	1	1	1	3

Nation	Gold	Silver	Bronze	Total
Nigeria	2	0	0	2
Singapore	0	1	1	2
Fiji	0	0	1	1
St. Vincent	0	0	1	1
Malawi	0	0	1	1
Isle of Man	0	0	1	1
Gambia	0	0	1	1
Tanzania	0	1	0	1
Barbados	0	1	0	1
Hong Kong	1	0	0	1
Guyana	0	0	1	1

1974   *Christchurch   New Zealand   January 24–February 2*

Nations: Australia, Canada, England, Ghana, India, Jamaica, Kenya, Lesotho, Malaysia, New Zealand, Nigeria, Northern Ireland, Scotland, Singapore, St. Vincent, Swaziland, Tanzania, Trinidad and Tobago, Uganda, Wales, Western Samoa, Zambia

Sports: Athletics, Badminton, Boxing, Cycling, Lawn Bowling, Shooting, Swimming, Weightlifting, Wrestling

Sports for Women: Athletics, Badminton, Shooting, Swimming

Venues: Ilam University (Games Village), QE II Park Stadium (Athletics, Opening Ceremonies), Town Hall (Wrestling), Canterbury Court (Boxing), Woolston Working Men's Club (Lawn Bowling), Denton Park Velodrome (Cycling), QE II Park Commonwealth Games Pool (Swimming), James Hay Theatre—Christchurch New Town Hall (Weightlifting), Burnett Range (Shooting)

MEDALS

Nation	Gold	Silver	Bronze	Total
Australia	29	29	25	83
England	28	31	22	81
Canada	25	18	18	61
New Zealand	9	8	18	35
Kenya	7	2	9	18
Scotland	3	5	10	18
India	4	8	3	15
Wales	1	5	4	10
Nigeria	3	3	4	10
Ghana	1	3	5	9
Uganda	2	4	3	9
Northern Ireland	3	1	2	6
Malaysia	1	0	3	4
Zambia	1	1	1	3
Jamaica	2	1	0	3
Tanzania	1	0	1	2
Trinidad and Tobago	0	1	1	2
Western Samoa	0	1	1	2
Singapore	0	0	1	1
Lesotho	0	0	1	1
St. Vincent	1	0	0	1
Swaziland	0	0	1	1

1978   Edmonton   Canada   August 3–12

Nations: Australia, Canada, England, Ghana, Guyana, Hong Kong, India, Isle of Man, Jamaica, Kenya, Malaysia, New Zealand, Northern Ireland, Papua New Guinea, Scotland, Tanzania, Trinidad and Tobago, Wales, Western Samoa, Zambia

Sports: Athletics, Badminton, Boxing, Cycling, Gymnastics, Lawn Bowling, Shooting, Swimming, Weightlifting, Wrestling

Sports for Women: Athletics, Badminton, Gymnastics, Shooting, Swimming

Venues: Commonwealth Stadium (Opening Ceremonies, Athletics), Kinsmen Aquatics Centre (Swimming), Edmonton Gardens (Boxing), Edmonton Jubilee Auditorium (Weightlifting), Strathcona Ranges (Shooting), University of Alberta Varsity Arena (Badminton), Argyll Velodrome (Cycling), Northlands Coliseum (Gymnastics), Coronation Park (Lawn Bowls), University of Alberta Gymnasium (Wrestling)

MEDALS

Nation	Gold	Silver	Bronze	Total
Canada	45	31	33	109
England	27	29	31	87
Australia	24	33	27	84
Kenya	7	6	5	18
New Zealand	5	5	10	20
India	5	4	6	15
Scotland	3	6	5	14
Jamaica	2	2	3	7
Wales	2	1	5	8
Northern Ireland	2	1	2	5
Hong Kong	2	0	0	2
Malaysia	1	2	1	4
Guyana	1	1	1	3
Ghana	1	1	1	3
Tanzania	1	1	0	2
Trinidad and Tobago	0	2	2	4
Zambia	0	2	2	4
Papua New Guinea	0	1	0	1
Western Samoa	0	0	3	3
Isle of Man	0	0	1	1

1982   Brisbane   Australia   September 30–October 9

Nations: Australia, Bahamas, Bermuda, Canada, England, Fiji, Guernsey, Hong Kong, India, Jamaica, Kenya, Malaysia, New Zealand, Nigeria, Northern Ireland, Scotland, Singapore, Swaziland, Tanzania, Uganda, Wales, Zambia, Zimbabwe

Sports: Archery, Athletics, Badminton, Boxing, Cycling, Lawn Bowling, Shooting, Swimming, Weightlifting, Wrestling

Sports for Women: Archery, Athletics, Badminton, Lawn Bowls, Shooting, Swimming

Venues: QE II Stadium (Opening ceremonies, Athletics), Sleeman Sports Complex (Swimming, Badminton, Cycling, Weightlifting), Brisbane City Hall (Wrestling), Moorooka Club (Lawn Bowls), Festival Hall (Boxing), Murarrie Recreation Reserve (Archery), Belmont Range (Shooting), Griffith University (Athletes Village)

MEDALS

Nation	Gold	Silver	Bronze	Total
Australia	39	39	29	107
England	38	38	32	108
Canada	26	23	33	82
Scotland	8	6	12	26
New Zealand	5	8	13	26
India	5	8	3	16
Nigeria	5	0	8	13
Kenya	4	2	4	10
Wales	4	4	1	9
Bahamas	2	2	2	6
Jamaica	2	1	1	4
Tanzania	1	2	2	5
Malaysia	1	0	1	2
Fiji	1	0	0	1
Hong Kong	1	0	0	1
Zimbabwe	1	0	0	1
Northern Ireland	0	3	3	6
Zambia	0	1	5	6
Uganda	0	3	0	3
Guernsey	0	1	1	2
Bermuda	0	0	1	1
Singapore	0	0	1	1
Swaziland	0	0	1	1

1986   Edinburgh   Scotland   July 24–August 2

Nations: Australia, Botswana, Canada, Cayman Islands, Cook Islands, England, Falkland Islands, Fiji, Gibraltar, Guernsey, Hong Kong, Isle of Man, Jersey, Lesotho, Malawi, Maldives, Malta, New Zealand, Norfolk Islands, Northern Ireland, Scotland, Singapore, Swaziland, Wales, Western Samoa, Vanuatu

Sports: Athletics, Badminton, Boxing, Cycling, Lawn Bowling, Rowing, Shooting, Swimming, Weightlifting, Wrestling

Sports for Women: Athletics, Badminton, Lawn Bowls, Rowing, Shooting, Swimming

Venues: Meadowbank Sports Complex (Badminton), Ingliston Centre (Boxing), Strathclyde Park, Glasgow (Rowing), Balgreen (Lawn Bowls), Royal Commonwealth Pool (Swimming), Playhouse Theatre (Wrestling, Weightlifting)

MEDALS

Nation	Gold	Silver	Bronze	Total
England	52	42	49	143
Canada	51	34	30	115
Australia	40	46	33	119
New Zealand	8	16	14	38
Wales	6	5	12	23
Scotland	3	12	18	33
Northern Ireland	2	4	9	15
Isle of Man	1	0	0	1

Nation	Gold	Silver	Bronze	Total
Guernsey	0	2	0	2
Swaziland	0	1	0	1
Hong Kong	0	0	2	2
Malawi	0	0	2	2
Botswana	0	0	1	1
Jersey	0	0	1	1
Singapore	0	0	1	1

1990   Auckland   New Zealand   January 24–February 3

Nations: Australia, Bahamas, Bangladesh, Bermuda, Canada, Cyprus, England, Ghana, Guernsey, Guyana, Hong Kong, India, Jamaica, Jersey, Kenya, Malaysia, Malta, Nauru, New Zealand, Nigeria, Northern Ireland, Papua New Guinea, Scotland, Tanzania, Uganda, Wales, Western Samoa, Zambia, Zimbabwe

Sports: Athletics, Badminton, Boxing, Cycling, Gymnastics, Judo, Lawn Bowling, Shooting, Swimming, Weightlifting

Sports for Women: Athletics, Badminton, Cycling, Gymnastics, Judo, Lawn Bowls, Shooting, Swimming

Venues: Glen Innes (Games Village), Aotea Centre (Weightlifting), Mount Smart Stadium (Athletics), Henderson Pool (Swimming), Pakuranga (Lawn Bowls), Badminton Hall (Badminton), Logan Campbell Theatre (Boxing), Manukau Velodrome (Cycling), ASB Stadium (Gymnastics)

MEDALS

Nation	Gold	Silver	Bronze	Total
Australia	52	54	56	162
England	47	40	42	129
Canada	35	41	37	113
New Zealand	17	14	27	58
India	13	8	11	32
Wales	10	3	12	25
Kenya	6	9	3	18
Nigeria	5	13	7	25
Scotland	5	7	10	22
Malaysia	2	2	0	4
Jamaica	2	0	2	4
Uganda	2	0	2	4
Northern Ireland	1	3	5	9
Nauru	1	2	0	3
Hong Kong	1	1	3	5
Cyprus	1	1	0	2
Bangladesh	1	0	1	2
Jersey	1	0	1	2
Bermuda	1	0	0	1
Guernsey	1	0	0	1
Papua New Guinea	1	0	0	1
Zimbabwe	0	2	1	3
Ghana	0	2	0	2
Tanzania	0	1	2	3

Nation	Gold	Silver	Bronze	Total
Zambia	0	0	3	3
Bahamas	0	0	2	2
Western Samoa	0	0	2	2
Guyana	0	0	1	1
Malta	0	0	1	1

1994   Victoria   Canada   August 18–28

Nations: Australia, Bermuda, Botswana, Canada, Cyprus, England, Ghana, Guernsey, Hong Kong, India, Jamaica, Kenya, Malaysia, Namibia, Nauru, New Zealand, Nigeria, Norfolk Island, Northern Ireland, Pakistan, Papua New Guinea, Scotland, Seychelles, South Africa, Sri Lanka, Tanzania, Tonga, Trinidad and Tobago, Uganda, Wales, Western Samoa, Zambia, Zimbabwe

Sports: Athletics, Badminton, Boxing, Cycling, Gymnastics, Lawn Bowls, Shooting, Swimming, Weightlifting, Wrestling, (Lacrosse—demo)

Venues: Centennial Stadium (Opening Ceremonies, Closing Ceremonies, Athletics), Juan de Fuca Recreation Centre (Cycling, Wrestling, Lawn Bowling), Esquimalt's Archie Browning Sports Centre (Boxing), Memorial Arena (Gymnastics), Royal Theatre (Weightlifting), Royal Athletic Park (Lacrosse), McKinnon Gymnasium, University of Victoria (Badminton), Saanich Commonwealth Place (Swimming, Synchronized Swimming, Diving), Pat Bay Highway (Cycling Road Race), Heal's Range (Shooting)

MEDALS

Nation	Gold	Silver	Bronze	Total
Australia	87	52	43	182
Canada	40	42	46	128
England	31	45	49	125
Nigeria	11	13	13	37
Kenya	7	4	8	19
India	6	11	7	24
Scotland	6	3	11	20
New Zealand	5	16	20	41
Wales	5	8	6	19
Northern Ireland	5	2	3	10
Nauru	3	0	0	3
South Africa	2	4	5	11
Jamaica	2	4	2	8
Malaysia	2	3	2	7
Cyprus	2	1	2	5
Sri Lanka	1	2	0	3
Zambia	1	1	2	4
Namibia	1	0	1	2
Zimbabwe	0	3	3	6
Papua New Guinea	0	1	0	1
Western Samoa	0	1	0	1
Hong Kong	0	0	4	4
Pakistan	0	0	3	3
Trinidad and Tobago	0	0	2	2

Nation	Gold	Silver	Bronze	Total
Uganda	0	0	2	2
Bermuda	0	0	1	1
Botswana	0	0	1	1
Ghana	0	0	1	1
Guernsey	0	0	1	1
Norfolk Island	0	0	1	1
Seychelles	0	0	1	1
Tanzania	0	0	1	1
Tonga	0	0	1	1

1998   Kuala Lumpur   Malaysia   September 10–20

Nations: Antigua and Barbuda, Australia, Bahamas, Bangladesh, Barbados, Belize, Bermuda, Botswana, British Virgin Islands, Brunei, Cameroon, Canada, Cayman Islands, Cook Islands, Cyprus, Dominica, England, Falkland Islands, Fiji, Ghana, Gibraltar, Grenada, Guernsey, Guyana, India, Isle of Man, Jamaica, Jersey, Kenya, Kiribati, Lesotho, Malawi, Malaysia, Maldives, Malta, Mauritius, Montserrat, Mozambique, Namibia, Nauru, New Zealand, Norfolk Island, Northern Ireland, Pakistan, Papua New Guinea, Samoa, Scotland, Seychelles, Sierra Leone, Singapore, Solomon Islands, South Africa, Sri Lanka, St. Helena, St. Kitts and Nevis, St. Lucia, St. Vincent and the Grenadines, Swaziland, Tanzania, The Gambia, Tonga, Trinidad and Tobago, Turks and Caicos, Tuvalu, Uganda, Vanuatu, Wales, Zambia, Zimbabwe

Sports: Athletics, Badminton, Boxing, Cricket, Cycling, Field Hockey, Gymnastics, Lawn Bowls, Netball, Rugby, Shooting, Squash, Swimming, Tenpin Bowling, Weightlifting

Venues: National Sports Complex Bukit Jalil (Athletics, Aquatics, Gymnastics, Field Hockey, Squash), Kuala Lumpur Badminton Stadium (Badminton), Kuala Lumpur Velodrome (Cycling), Lake Titiwanga (Athletics, Walking), Lawn Bowls Complex Bukit Kana (Lawn Bowls), Netball Stadium Bukit Kana (Netball), Shah Alma (Cycling Road Race), Shah Alma Indoor Stadium (Boxing), P.J. Stadium (Rugby), PKNS, Royal Slander Club, Rubber Research Institute, Club Amman, TNB Sports Grounds, Royal Military Club, Slander Turf Club (Cricket), The Mines (Weightlifting), Langkaui International Shooting Range (Shooting)

MEDALS

Nation	Gold	Silver	Bronze	Total
Australia	80	61	58	199
Great Britain	36	47	53	136
Canada	30	31	38	99
Malaysia	10	14	12	36
South Africa	9	11	14	34
New Zealand	8	7	20	35
Kenya	8	5	4	17
India	7	10	8	25
Jamaica	4	2	0	6
Wales	3	4	8	15
Scotland	3	2	7	12
Nauru	3	0	0	3

Nation	Gold	Silver	Bronze	Total
Northern Ireland	2	1	2	5
Zimbabwe	2	0	3	5
Ghana	1	1	3	5
Cyprus	1	1	1	3
Mauritius	1	1	1	3
Tanzania	1	1	1	3
Trinidad and Tobago	1	1	1	3
Bahamas	1	1	0	2
Mozambique	1	1	0	2
Barbados	1	0	2	3
Lesotho	1	0	0	1
Cameroon	0	3	3	6
Namibia	0	2	1	3
Seychelles	0	2	0	2
Sri Lanka	0	1	1	2
Bermuda	0	1	0	1
Fiji	0	1	0	1
Isle of Man	0	1	0	1
Pakistan	0	1	0	1
Papua New Guinea	0	0	1	1
Uganda	0	0	1	1
Zambia	0	0	1	1

Commonwealth Youth Games

The Commonwealth Youth Games were the idea of Louise Martin, chair of the Commonwealth Games Council for Scotland. The first were held in Edinburgh in August 2000, when 597 athletes under the age of 18 from 15 Commonwealth nations participated in eight sports.

To help promote the games within Scotland, the Commonwealth Games Council had a team of youths produce a newsletter which was circulated to all Scotland's high schools. Spectators under 18 were allowed in for free.

The opening ceremonies were held in Edinburgh Castle, under the eyes of the games' patron, the Lord Provost of Edinburgh, Eric Milligan, and Prince Edward, the Earl of Wessex. Athletes paraded behind their national flags and the games flame was lit from a torch made of glass.

Australia topped the final medal table with 37 golds and 87 in total. England finished right behind with 36 golds, but had 96 total medals. Leading individuals were Australian swimmers Joshua Krogh with six gold and one bronze and Jodie Henry with five golds.

The day after the competitions were concluded, the Edinburgh hosts arranged for a cultural day for the competitors and a tour around Edinburgh.

The Commonwealth Games Federation intends to hold the games again in 2004. Four unnamed Australian cities were in the running to host these second Commonwealth Youth Games.

Year	Host City	Host Nation	Dates	Nations	Athletes	Sports
2000	Edinburgh	Scotland	August 10–14	15	597	8

Nations: Australia, Barbados, Canada, England, India, Isle of Man, Jersey, Nauru, New Zealand, Northern Ireland, Malaysia, Scotland, South Africa, Wales, Zimbabwe
Sports: Athletics, Fencing, Field Hockey, Gymnastics, Squash, Swimming, Tennis, Weightlifting
Venues: Craiglockhart Tennis Centre, Heriot-Watt University (Fencing and Squash), Meadowbank Stadium (Athletics), Meadowbank Sports Centre (Gymnastics), Meadowmill Sports Centre, East Lothian (Weightlifting), Peffermill National Hockey Centre, Royal Commonwealth Pool (Swimming), Heriot-Watt University (Riccarton Campus) (Games Village)

Community/Friendship Games

With the development of the Commonwealth Games, many of the African nations associated with the Commonwealth began to participate in the international sports movement. The French then moved to create a competition that would give the French-speaking African nations an arena in which to compete. The result was the precursor to the African Games known as the Community Games or the Friendship Games, Jeux de l'Amitié.

The very first Community Games were held in Tananarive (Antananarivo), Madagascar in April 1960. Abdou Seye won a gold medal in those games while running for Senegal. His bronze medal in the 1960 Rome Olympic Games was credited to France, as many colonies having no National Olympic Committees of their own were obliged to compete for a nation that did.

Abidjan, Ivory Coast, hosted the Jeux de l'Amitié the following year,[101] with 13 nations competing. Less than a year and a half later, the games were hosted in Dakar, with 25 nations in attendance, almost double the previous games' number. The Dakar games were the first to have events open to women. [102]

The influence of these games helped to establish the first African Games in Brazzaville in 1965.

Year	Host City	Host Nation	Dates	Nations	Athletes	Sports
1960	Antananarivo	Madagascar	April 13–19	14	800	8
1961	Abidjan	Ivory Coast	December 24–30	13	1070	9
1963	Dakar	Senegal	April 11–21	25	1617	10

1960   Antananarivo   Madagascar   April 13–19

Nations: Cameroon, Central African Republic, Chad, Congo, Côte d'Ivoire, Dahomey, France, Gabon, Guadeloupe, Madagascar, Mali, Martinique, Niger, Reunion

1961   Abidjan   Ivory Coast   December 24–30

Nations: Ivory Coast, France, Gabon, Nigeria, Comoros, Senegal, Cameroon, Congo, Dahomey, Madagascar, Mauritania, Upper Volta, Chad, Réunion
Sports: Football, Athletics, Handball, Volleyball, Swimming, Basketball, Boxing, Cycling, Judo
Sports for Women: Athletics, Basketball, Swimming, Volleyball

1963 Dakar Senegal April 11–21

Nations: France and its territories, French-speaking countries, and Liberia, Nigeria, Gambia, Ghana, Sierra Leone and three Mediterranean nations

Sports: Athletics, Basketball, Boxing, Cycling, Football, Handball, Judo, Swimming, Tennis, Volleyball

CUCSA Games

The African Student Games Zone VI, also known as the Confederation of University and College Sports Associations (CUCSA) Games, are held annually.

University or college students from Angola, Botswana, Lesotho, Malawi, Mozambique, Namibia, South Africa, Swaziland, Zambia and Zimbabwe are eligible for the games. South Africa was first allowed to participate in the seventh games held in 1996. No information is available on the first six editions of the games.

Unfortunately, the most recent games have been troubled by disorganization and lack of fair play. A fuel shortage during the 1999 Games in Lusaka, Zambia, led to transportation cutbacks. Some teams had to walk back and forth between stadiums and the games village.[103]

The 2000 games in Maputo, Mozambique were so chaotic that discussions were held on whether or not the games would continue.[104] Poor planning, changes in schedules, lack of sportsmanship, lack of an appeals process for disputes and arguments over eligibility, led one CUCSA executive board member, Aaron Ngiambi of Zambia, to say that the games should be nullified due to unfairness.

When Mozambique's newspaper reported that most of Mozambique's basketball team were not university students, the other teams began to demand identification. Before the Namibia-Mozambique football match, the Namibians asked to see student identification for the players from Mozambique. The team from Mozambique said they would have ID at halftime. When the identification did not come through Namibia forfeited the rest of the match. Mozambican officials claimed that they kept the entire team's student IDs at their offices to avoid the documents getting lost but forced the other countries to produce their IDs with every match played.

To make matters worse, participants claimed that the hosts failed to provide athletes with nutritious food, serving the same meals day after day.

The mood did not improve after the games. The Namibian team was detained at the Mozambique border for three hours while on their way home.[105] Eight students were found to have stolen bedding and other items from the athletes' village where they had stayed in Maputo. After an investigation, the Namibian authorities banned all eight students from participating in the next CUCSA games and from representing Namibia for 12 months. In addition, two other Namibian students were banned for fighting during the soccer matches. The Namibian sports authorities apologized to the nation over what had become a minor international incident.

CUCSA organizers decided to skip a year and hold the next CUCSA games in 2002 in Swaziland.

Year	Host City	Host Nation	Dates	Nations	Athletes	Sports
1996	Zomba	Malawi	Sept. 16–21	10	NA	7
1997	Harare	Zimbabwe		NA	NA	NA

Year	Host City	Host Nation	Dates	Nations	Athletes	Sports
1998	Johannesburg	South Africa	July 20–25	10	NA	11
1999	Lusaka	Zambia	June 13–20	NA	NA	NA
2000	Maputo	Mozambique	July 16–23	10	NA	NA

1996   Zomba   Malawi   September 16–21

Sports: Athletics, Basketball, Football, Netball, Squash, Tennis, Volleyball
Nations: Angola, Botswana, Lesotho, Malawi, Mozambique, Namibia, South Africa, Swaziland, Zambia, Zimbabwe

1998   Johannesburg   South Africa   July 20–25

Sports: Athletics, Basketball, Chess, Darts, Football, Netball, Rugby, Softball, Squash, Table Tennis, Volleyball
Nations: Angola, Botswana, Lesotho, Malawi, Mozambique, Namibia, South Africa, Swaziland, Zambia, Zimbabwe

2000   Maputo   Mozambique   July 16–23

Nations: Angola, Botswana, Lesotho, Malawi, Mozambique, Namibia, South Africa, Swaziland, Zambia, Zimbabwe

Défi Sportif

Défi Sportif or "Sports Challenge" is a competition for disabled athletes held annually in the spring in Montreal, Canada. Events are scheduled for athletes with five types of disability: hearing, visual, intellectual, physical and mental illness.

The games started modestly in 1984 as a local event sponsored by the Regional Association for the Recreation of Disabled Persons of the Island of Montreal, with the simple mission to promote sports and recreation for disabled persons.

The first games with athletes from outside Canada was in 1988 when a team of French swimmers came to participate. In 1991, teams from the United States joined in the wheelchair rugby competitions, and teams from Switzerland and Sweden followed in 1994 and 1996. The 1997 competition saw participants from Algeria, France, Nigeria, Sweden, Switzerland, and United States as well as host Canada.

The games are televised throughout the province of Quebec and are sponsored by over 90 organizations in the community. An annual benefit concert also helps fund the games.

Sports events in the games include athletics, basketball, boccia, cosom hockey, goalball, wheelchair road racing, rugby, soccer, swimming, tandem cycling, tennis and volleyball.

Canadian wheelchair racers and Paralympians Jeff Adams and Chantal Peticlerc have been frequent competitors at the games.

The 2000 Défi Sportif had nine nations, 16 sports and 1700 participants—all the most in the games' history. Belgium, Canada, France, Germany, Great Britain, Hungary, Japan, Switzerland and the United States were represented at the 2000 games.

Year	Host City	Host Nation	Dates	Nations	Athletes	Sports
1988	Montreal	Canada	May 3–8	NA	NA	NA
1989	Montreal	Canada	May 2–7	NA	NA	NA

Year	Host City	Host Nation	Dates	Nations	Athletes	Sports
1990	Montreal	Canada	May 1–6	NA	NA	NA
1991	Montreal	Canada	April 26–May 5	NA	NA	NA
1992	Montreal	Canada	April 27–May 3	NA	NA	NA
1993	Montreal	Canada	April 30–May 9	NA	NA	NA
1994	Montreal	Canada	April 27–May 1	NA	NA	NA
1995	Montreal	Canada	April 26–30	NA	NA	NA
1996	Montreal	Canada	April 24–28	4	1100	NA
1997	Montreal	Canada	April 30–May 4	7	1186	12
1998	Montreal	Canada	May 1–3	NA	NA	NA
1999	Montreal	Canada	April 29–May 2	NA	NA	NA
2000	Montreal	Canada	April 26–30	9	1700	16

1996   Montreal   Canada   April 24–28

Nations: Canada, France, Switzerland, United States

1997   Montreal   Canada   April 30–May 4

Nations: Algeria, Canada, France, Nigeria, Sweden, Switzerland, United States
Sports: Athletics, Basketball, Boccia, Cosom Hockey, Cycling (Tandem), Football, Goalball, 10km Road Race Wheelchair, Rugby, Swimming, Wheelchair Tennis, Volleyball (exhibition—Badminton, Rhythmic Gymnastics, Intercrosse)
Venues: Complexe Sportif Claude-Robillard (Athletics, Cosom Hockey, Basketball, Boccia, Badminton, Rhythmic Gymnastics, Swimming, Volleyball), College de Rosemont (Rugby, Goalball, Tandem Cycling, Running Road Race), College de Maisonneuve (Basketball), Tennis Club St. Laurent (Tennis)

2000   Montreal   Canada   April 26–30

Nations: Belgium, Canada, France, Germany, Great Britain, Hungary, Japan, Switzerland, United States
Sports: Athletics, Badminton, Basketball, Boccia, Cosom Hockey, Cycling, Fencing, Football, Handcycling, Rhythmic Gymnastics, Swimming, Tandem Cycling, Tennis, Volleyball, Wheelchair Racing, Wheelchair Rugby

Dutch Commonwealth Games

The Dutch Commonwealth Games or Koninkrijkspelen were held annually from 1966 to 1975 when Suriname gained its independence from the Netherlands and stopped participating in the event. From 1966 to 1974, Aruba, Curaçao, Netherlands and Suriname were the participating nations. The games were revived in 1995 on a biennial basis, with the Netherlands, Curaçao and Aruba as participants.

Year	Host City	Host Nation	Dates	Nations	Athletes	Sports
1966	Parimaribo	Suriname	August 7–	4	NA	NA
1967	Willemstad	Curaçao	Aug. 13–21	4	NA	NA
1968	Utrecht	Netherlands	Aug 5–11	4	NA	NA
1969	Parimaribo	Suriname	July 25–Aug. 2	4	NA	NA

Year	Host City	Host Nation	Dates	Nations	Athletes	Sports
1970	Oranjestad	Aruba	July 31–Aug. 9	4	NA	NA
1971	Utrecht	Netherlands	July 31	4	NA	NA
1972	Willemstad	Curaçao	July 21–30	4	NA	NA
1973	Parimaribo	Suriname	Aug. 8	4	NA	NA
1974	Zandvoort	Netherlands	Aug. 10–17	4	NA	NA
1975	Parimaribo	Suriname	Aug. 1–6	4	NA	NA
1995	Oranjestad	Aruba	July 16–21	3	NA	NA
1997	Willemstad	Curaçao	July 26–Aug. 1	3	NA	NA
1999	St. Maarten	Netherlands Antilles	July 24–30	3	NA	NA

East African Military Games

There has been at least one East African Military Games, which was held in 1982 in Lusaka, Zambia, to coincide with the opening of the CISM (Conseil Internationale du Sport Militaire) regional offices in Lusaka.

Five nations (Botswana, Tanzania, Uganda, Zambia, Zimbabwe) with about 200 athletes, all men, competed in three sports, basketball, boxing and football. Kenya and Mozambique were also invited to the games but were not able to attend.

Host Zambia won nearly all the gold medals, winning the basketball and football tournaments and nine of ten gold medals in boxing.

Year	Host City	Host Nation	Dates	Nations	Athletes	Sports
1982	Lusaka	Zambia	Oct. 13–18	5	200	3

Nations: Botswana, Tanzania, Uganda, Zambia, Zimbabwe
Sports: Basketball, Boxing, Football
Venues: Zambia State Insurance Corporation sports complex (Basketball), Independence Stadium (Football), Woodlands Stadium (Boxing)

East African University Games

The *East African Medical Journal* (focusing on sports injuries) reported that the seventh East African University Games were held in Kampala, Uganda, in 1970, and that 528 athletes (423 male and 105 female) from six universities in east and central Africa and Malagasy took part. The games comprised 13 sports, according to the journal.[106]

In 1999, the Kenyan press mentioned that the East African University Games were to be held in Njoro, Kenya, in December that year.[107]

Nothing has been uncovered of games in east Africa before or between these two mentions.

Year	Host City	Host Nation	Dates	Nations	Athletes	Sports
1970	Kampala	Uganda	Dec. 7–12	NA	528	13
1999	Njoro	Kenya	Dec.	NA	NA	NA

1970 Kampala Uganda Dec. 7–12

Sports: Athletics, Badminton, Basketball, Boxing, Cricket, Field Hockey, Football, Rugby, Squash, Swimming, Tennis, Table Tennis, Volleyball

East Asian Games

The East Asian Games were established by the East Asian National Olympic Committees (EANOC) in January 1992 in meetings in Beijing, China, and are governed by the EAGA, the East Asian Games Association. China, Chinese Taipei, Guam, Hong Kong, Japan, Kazakhstan, Macau, Mongolia, North Korea and South Korea form the current membership.

Shanghai, China, hosted the first East Asian Games in May 1993. Along with the sporting events, Shanghai organized exhibitions in sports photography, sports art and sports philately. A games highlight was Julio Iglesias performing at the closing ceremony.

Under the theme "Unity, Peace, New East Asia," the second East Asian Games were held May 10–19, 1997, in Pusan, South Korea. Nine nations (North Korea being the only member absent) competed for 168 gold medals in 14 sports.

After overcoming opposition from Japan and Hong Kong, Australia has been invited to participate in the East Asian Games. Japan argued that Australia was not part of the traditional region of the games, while Hong Kong objected that Australia was simply too strong a sporting power. The Australians responded by saying that both Australia and the East Asian nations would benefit from sharing expertise in the sports they were strong in.

The 2001 games were scheduled to be held in Osaka, Japan. Macau has been chosen as the host for the 2005 games.

Year	Host City	Host Nation	Dates	Nations	Athletes	Sports
1993	Shanghai	China	May 9–18	8	NA	12
1997	Pusan	South Korea	May 10–19	9	1700	14

1993 Shanghai China May 9–18

Nations: China, Chinese Taipei, Hong Kong, Japan, Macau, Mongolia, North Korea, South Korea

Sports: Athletics, Badminton, Basketball, Bowling, Boxing, Football, Gymnastics, Judo, Rowing, Swimming, Weightlifting, Wushu

MEDALS

Nation	Gold	Silver	Bronze	Total
China	105	74	34	213
Japan	25	37	55	117
Korea	23	28	40	91

(only top three available)

1997 Pusan South Korea May 10–19

Nations: China, Chinese Taipei, Guam, Hong Kong, Japan, Kazakhstan, Korea, Macau, Mongolia

Sports: Athletics, Badminton, Basketball, Boxing, Football, Gymnastics, Judo, Rowing, Soft Tennis, Swimming, Tae Kwon Do, Weightlifting, Wrestling, Wushu (demonstration sport—Bowling)

Sports for Women: Athletics, Badminton, Basketball, Gymnastics, Judo, Rowing, Soft Tennis, Swimming, Wushu (demo—Bowling)

Venues: Kuduk Stadium (Opening and Closing Ceremonies, Football, Athletics), Changwon Stadium (Football), Ulsan Stadium (Football), Kuduk Gymnasium (Basketball), Sajik Swimming Pool (Swimming), KBS Pusan Hall (Boxing), Gymnasium of National Fisheries, University of Pusan (Judo), Gymnasium of Kyungnam High School (Wrestling), Gymnasium of Pusan Commercial High School (Tae Kwon Do)

MEDALS

Nation	Gold	Silver	Bronze	Total
China	62	59	64	185
Japan	47	53	53	153
Korea	45	38	51	134

(only top three available)

Eastern European Transplant Games

The first Eastern European Transplant Games were held in Tiszaujvaros, Hungary, August 5–14, 1996. One hundred and forty athletes from eight nations took part in the games, competing in angling, athletics, badminton, swimming and table tennis.

Year	Host City	Host Nation	Dates	Nations	Athletes	Sports
1996	Tiszaujvaros	Hungary	Aug. 5–14	8	140	5

Nations: Bulgaria, Hungary, Lithuania, Poland, Russia, Romania, Slovakia, Ukraine

Sports: Angling, Athletics, Badminton, Swimming, Table Tennis

Euro Games

A European version of the Gay Games, the Euro Games are held annually with the exception of the years the Gay Games are held. The 1999 Euro Games were awarded to Manchester, England, but withdrawn when support for the event did not materialize. The games were rescheduled for the year 2000 in Zurich.

Year	Host City	Host Nation	Dates	Nations	Athletes	Sports
1992	The Hague	Netherlands		NA	300	NA
1993	The Hague	Netherlands		NA	300	NA
1995	Frankfurt	Germany	April 14–17	NA	1800	16
1996	Berlin	Germany	May 16–19	NA	3000	NA
1997	Paris	France	June 20–23	NA	NA	11
2000	Zurich	Switzerland		NA	NA	NA

1995   Frankfurt   Germany   April 14–17

Sports: Badminton, Basketball, Bowling, Cheerleader Contest, Soccer, Athletics, Handball, Martial Arts (Judo, Karate), Chess, Swimming, Squash, Ballroom Dancing, Tennis, Table Tennis, Triathlon, Volleyball

1997   Paris   France   June 20–23

Sports: Badminton, Basketball, Bowling, Football, Handball, Martial Arts, Pétanque, Road Running, Swimming, Tennis, Volleyball

European Heart/Lung Transplant Games

The European Heart/Lung Transplant Games are held under the jurisdiction of the European Heart Transplant Federation (EHTF). EHTF's goals are:

—to promote the donation of organs among the population by means of events of all kinds likely to demonstrate the quality of life regained by transplantees, especially through sporting events and social activities.

—to promote the exchange of information among the member associations, with the view to ensuring that they are informed of the most recent developments in the treatment and rehabilitation of transplantees.

—to promote the exchange of information on national laws and regulations and thereby encourage improvement in the European Community legislation.

In 1988, the Dutch National Heart Transplant Association invited a few other nations to Gorsel for a friendly sports gathering. The same groups got together again in France and England in the next two years. The games returned to the Netherlands in 1992 and had some 200 participants from ten nations.

The group began discussing more formal ways to organize the games, including forming a games federation. In July 1994 at the fifth games in Helsinki, the European Heart Transplant Federation (EHTF) was founded. Representatives from 15 nations signed the founding documents: Austria, Belgium, Finland, France, Germany, Great Britain, Ireland, Israel, Italy, Netherlands, Norway, Russia, Spain, Sweden and Switzerland.

The games have maintained their biennial schedule having been held in Lausanne, Switzerland, in 1996, Bad Oeynhausen, Germany, in 1998 and Sandefjord, Norway, in 2000.

The games generally comprise competitions in athletics, badminton, cycling, golf, swimming, table-tennis, tennis and volleyball.

Year	Host City	Host Nation	Dates	Nations	Athletes	Sports
1988	Gorsel	Netherlands		NA	NA	NA
1990	Paris	France		NA	NA	NA
1991	London	England		NA	NA	NA
1992	Enschede	Netherlands		10	200	NA
1994	Helsinki	Finland		NA	NA	NA
1996	Lausanne	Switzerland	July 18–22	17	218	NA
1998	Bad Oeynhausen	Germany		NA	NA	NA
2000	Sandefjord	Norway	June 25–July 3	NA	NA	NA

European Maccabi Games

The European Maccabi Games are regional games for Jewish athletes. Though European in name, the games have had participation from the United States, Australia, and Canada. Israel has also participated on each occasion.

The games are under the jurisdiction of the European Maccabi Federation which was founded in Switzerland in 1948 to foster Jewish sports, culture, education and leadership. The European Maccabi Games are their federation's largest undertaking.

The games in Glasgow, Scotland, had events for both senior- and junior (under 17)-aged athletes.

Year	Host City	Host Nation	Dates	Nations	Athletes	Sports
1959	Copenhagen	Denmark	August 16–19	13	400	10
1963	Lyon	France	June 1–3	11	400	9
1974	Copenhagen	Denmark	August 8–11	9	NA	6
1979	Leicester	England	August 3–10	13	500	8
1983	Antwerp	Belgium	July 8–15	18	700	9
1987	Copenhagen	Denmark	March 10–17	21	446	10
1991	Marseille	France	July 10–17	24	928	9
1995	Amsterdam	Netherlands	July 7–14	25	1300	10
1999	Glasgow	Scotland	July 25–30	28	1500	12

1959   Copenhagen   Denmark   August 16–19

Nations: Austria, Belgium, Denmark, Great Britain, Finland, France, Holland, Italy, Ireland, Israel, Norway, Sweden, Switzerland
Sports: Athletics, Fencing, Football, Handball, Swimming, Table Tennis, Tennis, Water Polo, Weightlifting, Wrestling

1963   Lyon   France   June 1–3

Nations: Austria, Belgium, Denmark, Great Britain, Finland, France, Holland, Italy, Ireland, Israel, Switzerland
Sports: Athletics, Basketball, Football, Handball, Judo, Swimming, Table Tennis, Tennis, Water Polo

1974   Copenhagen   Denmark   August 8–11

Nations: Austria, Denmark, Finland, Germany, Great Britain, Holland, Israel, Sweden, United States
Sports: Basketball, Football, Handball, Table Tennis, Tennis, Ten-Pin Bowling

1979   Leicester   England   August 3–10

Nations: Austria, Belgium, Denmark, Finland, France, Germany, Great Britain, Holland, Italy, Israel, Spain, Sweden, Switzerland
Sports: Badminton, Basketball, Football, Handball, Table Tennis, Tennis, Ten-Pin Bowling, Volleyball

1983   Antwerp   Belgium   July 8–15

Nations: Australia, Austria, Belgium, Denmark, Finland, France, Germany, Gibraltar, Great Britain, Greece, Holland, Ireland, Italy, Israel, Norway, Sweden, Switzerland, United States

Sports: Basketball, Bowling, Football, Karate, Mini-Football, Squash, Table Tennis, Tennis, Volleyball

1987   Copenhagen   Denmark   March 10–17

Nations: Australia, Austria, Belgium, Canada, Denmark, Finland, France, Germany, Gibraltar, Great Britain, Greece, Holland, Ireland, Italy, Israel, Norway, Spain, Sweden, Switzerland, United States, Yugoslavia

Sports: Bridge, Football, Karate, Mini-Football, Shooting, Squash, Table Tennis, Tennis, Ten-Pin Bowling, Volleyball

1991   Marseille   France   July 10–17

Nations: Austria, Belgium, Bulgaria, Czechoslovakia, Denmark, Finland, France, Germany, Great Britain, Greece, Holland, Hungary, Ireland, Israel, Italy, Norway, Poland, Portugal, Soviet Union, Spain, Sweden, Switzerland, Turkey, Yugoslavia

Sports: Basketball, Football, Karate, Mini-Football, Squash, Table Tennis, Tennis, Ten-Pin Bowling, Volleyball

1995   Amsterdam   Netherlands   July 7–14

Nations: Austria, Belgium, Bulgaria, Czech Republic, Denmark, Finland, France, Germany, Gibraltar, Great Britain, Holland, Hungary, Israel, Italy, Latvia, Lithuania, Norway, Russia, Romania, Scotland, Spain, Sweden, Switzerland, Turkey, United States

Sports: Basketball, Bridge, Football, Karate, Mini-Football, Squash, Table Tennis, Tennis, Ten-Pin Bowling, Volleyball

1999   Glasgow   Scotland   July 25–30

Nations: Austria, Belarus, Belgium, Croatia, Czech Republic, Denmark, Finland, France, Georgia, Germany, Gibraltar, Great Britain, Holland, Hungary, Israel, Italy, Lithuania, Norway, Poland, Russia, Scotland, Slovakia, Spain, Sweden, Switzerland, Turkey, Ukraine, United States

Sports: Basketball, Bowling, Bridge, Chess, Football, Golf, Karate, Mini-Football, Squash, Table Tennis, Tennis, Volleyball

European Special Olympics

In 1981, the first regional European Special Olympic Games were held in Brussels, Belgium.

The 1990 games in Scotland saw the first team from Russia to participate in an international Special Olympics event.

A Special Olympics Europe-Eurasia office was opened in Brussels in 1997 to take over the organization of Special Olympics activities across Europe including the planning of the 2000 European Special Olympics and regional events such as the Mediterranean Special Olympic Games.

Year	Host City	Host Nation	Dates	Nations	Athletes	Sports
1981	Brussels	Belgium	May	NA	2000	NA
1985	Dublin	Ireland	July 4–7	NA	NA	NA
1990	Strathclyde	Scotland	July 20–27	30	2400	NA
1992	Barcelona	Spain	Sept. 9–13	30	3700	13
1994	Granollers	Spain	NA	NA	NA	NA
1996	Athens	Greece	May 19–25	36	NA	NA
2000	Groningen	Netherlands	May 26–June 4	NA	NA	NA

European Youth Olympic Days

Young European athletes from ages 12 to 18 have had the opportunity every other year since 1991 to compete in an Olympics of their own, the summer European Youth Olympic Days. The EYOD charter expressly states that the games are to uphold the Olympic atmosphere with "no kind of demonstration or political, religious or racial propaganda." Winter games have been held in 1993, 1995, 1997, and 1999 (more information is available in the appendices.)

Brussels, Belgium, hosted the first summer games in 1991, which were held in conjunction with the celebrations of both the 60th birthday and the 40th year of the reign of Badouin, King of Belgium.

Valkenswaard, the Netherlands, hosted the second edition of the summer games in 1993 when the event torch was in the shape of a large tulip. Young athletes from 43 nations participated, with Russia and Spain both earning nine gold medals, and Italy eight.

The British university town of Bath was the venue for the summer games in 1995. An Olympic torch was run from Greece, traveling through 16 European nations before arriving at the games. Princess Anne assisted as president of the Oorganizing Committee and guest of honor at the opening ceremony. Forty-six nations participated with the British leading the medals table with 41, 24 of which were gold.

International Olympic Committee President Juan Antonio Samaranch was present at the Lisbon University Students' Stadium in Lisbon, Portugal, for the opening ceremonies of the fourth summer games in 1997 with 2,500 athletes from 47 nations in attendance. Yachting was included on the schedule for the first time. Samaranch and several European Olympic Committee members showed their support of the young athletes at the Esbjerg, Denmark, opening ceremony in the summer of 1999. Russia held on to its position at the top of youth sport in Europe by winning 19 gold medals.

Year	Host City	Host Nation	Dates	Nations	Athletes	Sports
1991	Brussels	Belgium	July 12–21	33	2084	NA
1993	Valkenswaard	Netherlands	July 3–9	43	1850	10
1995	Bath	England	July 9–14	47	2000	10
1997	Lisbon	Portugal	July 18–24	47	2500	10
1999	Esbjerg	Denmark	July 10–16	48	2324	11

1993   Valkenswaard   Netherlands   July 3–9

Nations: Albania, Andorra, Armenia, Austria, Azerbaijan, Belarus, Belgium, Bosnia and Herzegovina, Bulgaria, Croatia, Cyprus, Czech Republic, Denmark, Estonia,

Finland, France, Georgia, Germany, Great Britain, Greece, Hungary, Iceland, Ireland, Italy, Latvia, Liechtenstein, Lithuania, Luxembourg, Malta, Moldova, Netherlands, Norway, Poland, Portugal, Romania, Russia, San Marino, Slovakia, Slovenia, Spain, Sweden, Switzerland, Turkey, Ukraine (Pregames reports listed these 44 nations. Postgames reports mentioned 43 nations without saying which nation was missing)

Sports: Athletics, Basketball, Cycling, Field Hockey, Football, Gymnastics, Judo, Swimming, Tennis, Volleyball (boys did not participate in Field Hockey, Gymnastics or Volleyball)

Sports for Girls: Athletics, Gymnastics, Field Hockey, Judo, Swimming, Tennis, Volleyball

Medals

Nation	Gold	Silver	Bronze	Total
Russia	9	10	6	25
Spain	9	6	5	20
Italy	8	5	8	21
Netherlands	6	6	5	17
Romania	6	4	7	17
Great Britain	5	7	9	21
Ukraine	5	5	7	17
France	5	2	4	11
Hungary	4	3	3	10
Germany	4	3	2	9
Poland	3	2	3	8
Belgium	3	1	3	7
Czech Republic	2	2	3	7
Croatia	2	1	1	4
Bulgaria	1	2	3	6
Greece	1	2	2	5
Azerbaijan	1	2	1	4
Sweden	1	1	3	5
Ireland	1	1	1	3
Slovakia	1	1	0	2
Cyprus	1	0	0	1
Estonia	1	0	0	1
Belarus	0	2	3	5
Slovenia	0	2	3	5
Portugal	0	2	1	3
Denmark	0	2	0	2
Georgia	0	1	1	2
Switzerland	0	1	1	2
Moldova	0	0	1	1

1995   Bath   England   July 9–14

Sports: Athletics, Gymnastics, Judo, Field Hockey, Swimming, Volleyball (4 more)

1997   Lisbon   Portugal   July 18–24

Nations: Andorra, Armenia, Austria, Azerbaijan, Belarus, Belgium, Bosnia-Herzegovina, Bulgaria, Croatia, Cyprus, Czech Republic, Denmark, Estonia, Finland, France,

Georgia, Germany, Great Britain, Greece, Hungary, Iceland, Ireland, Israel, Italy, Latvia, Liechtenstein, Lithuania, Luxembourg, Macedonia, Malta, Moldova, Monaco, Netherlands, Norway, Poland, Portugal, Romania, Russia, San Marino, Slovakia, Slovenia, Spain, Sweden, Switzerland, Turkey, Ukraine, Yugoslavia

Sports: Athletics, Basketball, Cycling, Football, Handball, Gymnastics, Judo, Swimming, Volleyball, Yachting

MEDALS

Nation	Gold	Silver	Bronze	Total
Russia	18	13	11	42
Ukraine	11	5	6	22
Great Britain	10	2	11	23
Germany	6	4	9	19
France	4	10	7	21
Italy	4	6	6	16
Romania	3	5	4	12
Austria	3	1	3	7
Finland	3	1	2	6
Sweden	2	4	3	9
Spain	2	2	3	7
Denmark	2	2	0	4
Belgium	2	1	8	11
Ireland	2	1	1	4
Iceland	2	1	1	4
Hungary	2	1	0	3
Slovakia	2	0	0	2
Belarus	1	4	2	7
Netherlands	1	2	5	8
Greece	1	2	3	6
Czech Republic	1	2	1	4
Georgia	1	1	1	3
Yugoslavia	1	0	1	2
Cyprus	1	0	0	1
Turkey	0	3	1	4
Switzerland	0	3	1	4
Slovenia	0	2	2	4
Lithuania	0	2	1	3
Poland	0	1	3	4
Portugal	0	1	2	3
Israel	0	1	1	2
Armenia	0	1	0	1
Norway	0	1	0	1
Bulgaria	0	0	1	1
Croatia	0	0	1	1

1999   Esbjerg   Denmark   July 10–16

Sports: Athletics, Badminton, Basketball, Cycling, Football, Judo, Swimming, Tennis

Sports for Girls: Athletics, Badminton, Gymnastics, Handball, Judo, Swimming, Tennis, Volleyball

	MEDALS			
Nation	*Gold*	*Silver*	*Bronze*	*Total*
Russia	19	12	4	35
France	9	5	7	21
Great Britain	7	9	5	21
Hungary	5	3	2	10
Germany	4	4	10	18
Poland	3	4	8	15
Ukraine	3	4	5	12
Denmark	3	3	1	7
Croatia	3	2	2	7
Sweden	3	1	6	10
Israel	3	0	3	6
Italy	2	6	6	14
Slovakia	2	4	4	10
Netherlands	2	1	8	11
Spain	2	1	3	6
Luxembourg	2	0	0	2
Georgia	1	3	3	7
Czech Republic	1	2	1	4
Yugoslavia	1	2	0	3
Belgium	1	1	2	4
Norway	1	1	1	3
Switzerland	1	1	1	3
Turkey	1	1	1	3
Portugal	1	1	0	2
Austria	1	1	0	2
Lithuania	1	0	5	6
Armenia	1	0	0	1
Romania	0	4	2	6
Finland	0	4	1	5
Belarus	0	3	2	5
Estonia	0	3	1	4
Greece	0	3	0	3
Moldova	0	2	1	3
Azerbaijan	0	0	4	4
Slovenia	0	0	1	1
Cyprus	0	0	1	1
Latvia	0	0	1	1

Far East and South Pacific Games for the Disabled

George Bedbrook, the Australian doctor who was instrumental in beginning the British Paraplegic Commonwealth Games, was also an important individual in the establishment of the FESPIC games, or Far East and South Pacific Games for the Disabled. Dr. Bedbrook turned his attention to games for the Asian and Pacific region when interest in similar events for the Commonwealth subsided.

The FESPIC games now include events in four classes: paraplegics and quadriplegics (governed by the International Stoke Mandeville Wheelchair Sports Federation [ISMWSF]), those with cerebral palsy (governed by the Cerebral Palsy–International Sports and Recreation Association [CP-ISRA]), the blind (governed by the International Blind Sports Association [IBSA]), and amputees (governed by the International Sports Organization for the Disabled [ISOD]).

The FESPIC region is diverse, stretching from Pakistan to New Zealand, with populous nations such as India and China competing alongside the tiny islands of the Pacific.

The 1999 games, with the theme "Equality in our World," were held in January 1999 in Bangkok, Thailand, using the same facilities as the Asian Games staged in Bangkok the previous month in 1988.

Year	Host City	Host Nation	Dates	Nations	Athletes	Sports
1975	Oita & Beppu	Japan	June 1–3	18	973	8
1977	Parramatta	Australia	November 20–26	16	430	11
1982	Sha Tin	Hong Kong	October 31–Nov 7	23	744	10
1986	Surakarta	Indonesia	August 31–Sept 7	19	834	12
1989	Kobe	Japan	September 15–20	41	1646	13
1994	Beijing	China	September 4–10	42	2081	14
1999	Bangkok	Thailand	January 10–16	34	2389	15

1975   Oita & Beppu   Japan   June 1–3

Sports: Archery, Athletics, Dartchery, Fencing, Swimming, Table Tennis, Weightlifting, Wheelchair Basketball

1977   Parramatta   Australia   November 20–26

Sports: Archery, Athletics, Dartchery, Fencing, Lawn Bowls, Shooting, Snooker, Swimming, Table Tennis, Weightlifting, Wheelchair Basketball

1982   Sha Tin   Hong Kong   October 31–November 7

Sports: Archery, Athletics, Carpetball, Fencing, Lawn Bowls, Shooting, Swimming, Table Tennis, Weightlifting, Wheelchair Basketball

1986   Surakarta   Indonesia   August 31–September 7

Sports: Archery, Athletics, Badminton, Fencing, Football, Lawn Bowls, Sitting Volleyball, Shooting, Swimming, Table Tennis, Weightlifting, Wheelchair Basketball

1989   Kobe   Japan   September 15–20

Sports: Archery, Athletics, Badminton, Fencing, Football, Judo, Lawn Bowls, Shooting, Swimming, Table Tennis, Weightlifting, Wheelchair Basketball, Wheelchair Tennis

1994   Beijing   China   September 4–10

Sports: Archery, Athletics, Badminton, Boccia, Fencing, Goal Ball, Judo, Sitting Volleyball, Shooting, Swimming, Table Tennis, Weightlifting, Wheelchair Basketball, Wheelchair Tennis

1999   Bangkok   Thailand   January 10–16

Sports: Archery, Athletics, Badminton, Wheelchair Basketball, Boccia, Fencing, Football, Goalball, Judo, Powerlifting, Shooting, Swimming, Table Tennis, Wheelchair Tennis, Sitting and Standing Volleyball

Far East Championships

The precursor to the present Asian Games was the Far East Championships, a successful competition early in the 20th century which rotated between China, Japan and the Philippines, with these three nations the only competitors for most of the games.

Elwood Brown, an American missionary in the Philippines with the Young Men's Christian Association (YMCA), was instrumental in the founding of the games. In 1911, Brown founded the Philippine Amateur Athletic Foundation and this group quickly planned sports competitions to be held in conjunction with the Manila Carnival of 1913.

The original games were called the "First Oriental Olympic Games" but the name was quickly changed to the Far East Championships in 1915.[108]

Distance and the expense of travel kept the games small. India, Java, Thailand, Malaya and Ceylon were invited to the games in 1921 but all declined for reasons of cost and distance.

Java, Thailand and French Indo-China were invited once again but did not accept. The games were held on a biennial basis until 1927 when the decision was made to hold them quadrennially, in the even years between the Olympic Games.

The last games on this schedule were in 1934. A political dispute over the inclusion of the disputed territory of Manchukuo (Manchuria) in the games broke up the Far Eastern Athletic Association.[109] China pulled out of discussions over the issue and Japan threatened to boycott, but the games went ahead. After the 1934 edition concluded, however, the Far East Athletic Association was disbanded.

A games was discussed for Tokyo in 1938, but war on the horizon silenced the plans for it.

Meanwhile, G.D. Sondhi of India was planning the First Western Asiatic Games in Delhi and Patalia in March 1934. Athletics, swimming and field hockey were on the schedule. India, Afghanistan, Ceylon and Palestine participated in the games. The second Western Asiatic Games had been awarded to Tel Aviv in Palestine for 1938, but they were never organized due to the war.

The Asian Games were to be revived in 1951; the West Asian Games in 1997.

Year	Host City	Host Nation	Dates	Nations	Athletes	Sports
1913	Manila	Philippines	Feb. 3–7	3	NA	7
1915	Shanghai	China	May 15–21	3	NA	8
1917	Tokyo	Japan	May 8–12	3	NA	8
1919	Manila	Philippines	May 12–16	3	NA	7
1921	Shanghai	China	May 30–Jun 3	3	NA	7
1923	Osaka	Japan	May 21–25	3	NA	7
1925	Manila	Philippines	May 17–22	3	NA	7
1927	Shanghai	China	August 28–31	3	NA	7

Year	Host City	Host Nation	Dates	Nations	Athletes	Sports
1930	Tokyo	Japan	May 24–27	3	NA	7
1934	Manila	Philippines	May 16–20	4	NA	7

1913   Manila   Philippines   February 3–7

Nations: China, Japan, Philippines
Sports: Athletics, Swimming and Diving, Tennis, Basketball, Volleyball, Football, Baseball

1915   Shanghai   China   May 15–21

Nations: China, Japan, Philippines
Sports: Athletics, Cycling, Swimming and Diving, Tennis, Basketball, Volleyball, Football, Baseball

1917   Tokyo   Japan   May 8–12

Nations: China, Japan, Philippines
Sports: Athletics, Swimming and Diving, Tennis, Basketball, Volleyball, Football, Baseball

1919   Manila   Philippines   May 12–16

Nations: China, Japan, Philippines
Sports: Athletics, Swimming and Diving, Tennis, Basketball, Volleyball, Football, Baseball

1921   Shanghai   China   May 30–June 3

Nations: China, Japan, Philippines
Sports: Athletics, Swimming and Diving, Tennis, Basketball, Volleyball, Football, Baseball

1923   Osaka   Japan   May 21–25

Nations: China, Japan, Philippines
Sports: Athletics, Swimming and Diving, Tennis, Basketball, Volleyball, Football, Baseball

1925   Manila   Philippines   May 17–22

Nations: China, Japan, Philippines
Sports: Athletics, Swimming and Diving, Tennis, Basketball, Volleyball, Football, Baseball

1927   Shanghai   China   August 28–31

Nations: China, Japan, Philippines
Sports: Athletics, Swimming and Diving, Tennis, Basketball, Volleyball, Football, Baseball

1930   Tokyo   Japan   May 24–27

Nations: China, Japan, Philippines
Sports: Athletics, Swimming and Diving, Tennis, Basketball, Volleyball, Football, Baseball

1934   Manila   Philippines   May 16–20

Nations: China, Japan, Philippines, Dutch East Indies
Sports: Athletics, Swimming and Diving, Tennis, Basketball, Volleyball, Football, Baseball

Festival of the Empire Sports Meeting

The Festival of the Empire celebrating the coronation of King George V in 1911 was the occasion for the first gathering of Commonwealth nations in a multisport event. Great Britain, Canada, Australasia and South Africa competed in athletics, boxing, swimming, and wrestling and the King served as patron of the games.

In a toast to the "overseas athletes" at a dinner the night before the athletics competitions were to begin, Lord Desborough stated, "wherever the great ideals of athletics are carried out they not only tended to the cementing of friendships between individuals but between nations."

The schedule was limited, with five athletics events on June 24: 100 yards, 220 yards, 880 yards, mile, and 120 yard hurdles. Boxing contests for heavyweights and wrestling for middleweights were held on June 29. Two swimming races, of 100 yards and one mile, were held on July 1.

Canada won the challenge cup, called the Empire Trophy, for winning the team events in athletics.

Year	Host City	Host Nation	Dates	Nations	Athletes	Sports
1911	London	England	June 24–July 1	4	NA	4

Nations: Australasia, Canada, Great Britain, South Africa
Sports: Athletics, Boxing, Swimming, Wrestling

Firefighters World Games

The Firefighters World Games are open to all full-time, volunteer, industrial and military firefighters, emergency medical services personnel, and rescue specialty teams. A unique aspect of the games is that competition is open to spouses in some events.

Held every other year since 1990, the Firefighters World Games are one of the largest multisport competitions in terms of the number of events held. The 1996 games in Edmonton, Alberta, listed 57 sports and events open for competition. Athletes compete in age groups starting from 18–30, then continuing in five year increments to the age of 60. Edmonton's competition drew 2,143 athletes from 25 nations.

In addition to the more standard sporting events, the Firefighters World Games include specialty events based upon the work skills of firefighters, such as the bucket brigade, confined space rescue, fire truck rodeo, high-angle rescue, hose laying, vehicle extrication as well as the toughest firefighter alive competition combining the hose, obstacle course and ladder events, and, in 1996, a 24-story tower run in full firefighter's gear complete with air tanks.

The 2000 games were held in Mantes-Yvelines, France.

Year	Host City	Host Nation	Dates	Nations	Athletes	Sports
1990	Auckland	New Zealand	April 22–29	17	1800	34
1992	Las Vegas	USA	May 16–22	22	4000	45
1994	Perth	Australia	March 20–26	17	1814	48
1996	Edmonton	Canada	July 28–August 3	25	2143	57
1998	Durban	South Africa	May 17–23	26	1765	55
2000	Mantes-Yvelines	France	July 6–13	NA	NA	NA

1990   Auckland   New Zealand   April 22–29

Nations: Australia, Belgium, Bermuda, Canada, England, Finland, France, Hong Kong, Netherlands, New Zealand, Nigeria, Solomon Islands, Sweden, Switzerland, Trinidad and Tobago, USA, Western Samoa

Sports: Arm Wrestling, Badminton, Basketball, Bucket Brigade, Canoeing, Cross Country, Cycling, Darts, Golf, Horseshoes, Indoor Cricket, Lawn Bowls, Marathon and Half-marathon, Pool/Eight Ball, Power Lifting, Rowing, Rugby Sevens, Sailing, Skeet and Trench Shooting, Snooker, Soccer, Softball Fastpitch, Squash, Swimming, Table Tennis, Tennis, Ten-Pin Bowling, Touch Football, Toughest Firefighter Alive, Track and Field, Triathlon, Tug of War, Volleyball, Windsurfing

Venues: Prince Arthur Hotel, Auckland City (Arm Wrestling), College Rifles, Remuera (Badminton, Squash, Touch Football), YMCA Stadium, Auckland City (Basketball), Motat, Western Springs (Bucket Brigade, Horseshoes, Tug of War), Lake Pupuke, Takapuna (Canoeing, Rowing, Windsurfing), Ellerslie Racecourse, Ellerslie (Cross Country), Metropolitan Auckland (Cycling), Auckland Working Men's Club (Darts), Pupuke Golf Club, North Shore (Golf), Royal Oak Indoor Sports Centre (Indoor Cricket), Balmoral Bowling Club (Lawn Bowls), Auckland Waterfront (Marathon and Half-marathon), Howick Club Inc., Howick (Billiards, Eight Ball), Weight Lifting Assoc., Epsom (Powerlifting), Carlton Rugby Club, Epsom (Rugby Sevens), Auckland Harbour (Sailing), Waitemata Gun Club, Kumeu (Skeet and Trench Shooting), Onehunga Working Men's Club (Snooker), Ngataringa Bay Sports Complex (Soccer), Rosedale Park, Albany (Softball—Fastpitch) Henderson Swimming Complex (Swimming), Table Tennis Club, Epsom (Table Tennis), ASB Tennis Centre, Parnell (Tennis), Manukau Superstrike, Manukau Central (Ten-Pin Bowling), Fire Service Regional Training Centre, Mt. Wellington (Toughest Firefighter Alive), Mt. Smart Stadium, Penrose (Athletics), Long Bay Regional Park (Triathlon), ASB Stadium, Kohimarama (Volleyball)

1992   Las Vegas   USA   May 16–22

Nations: Argentina, Austria, Australia, Belgium, Brazil, Canada, Chile, Estonia, Finland, France, Germany, Hong Kong, Korea, Latvia, Lithuania, Netherlands, New Zealand, Sweden, Taiwan, Uzbekistan, United Kingdom, USA

Sports: Archery, Arm Wrestling, Badminton, Basketball (Team), Basketball

3-on-3, Billiards, Body Building, Bowling—Ten-Pin, Bucket Brigade, Canoeing, Cross Country, Cycling, Darts, Flag Football, Golf, Handball, Horseshoes, Judo, Karate, Lawn Bowls (carpet), Marathon, Over the Line, Poker, Powerlifting, Rugby Sevens, Racquet Ball, Sailing, Skeet Shooting, Soccer, Softball—Slowpitch, Softball—Fastpitch, Squash, Swimming, Table Tennis, Tennis, Toughest Firefighter Alive, Track and Field, Trap Shooting, Triathlon, Tug of War, Volleyball (Team), Volleyball—2 man, Water Skiing, Windsurfing, Wrestling

Venues: Mountain Springs (Archery), Sahara Hotel (Arm Wrestling, Bodybuilding, Judo, Karate, Poker, Powerlifting, Wrestling), Bonanza High School (Badminton), University of Nevada, Las Vegas (Basketball—Team, Handball, Racquetball, Swimming, Tennis, Track and Field, Volleyball), Las Vegas High School (Basketball 3-on-3), Family Billiards (Billiards), Sante Fe Hotel & Casino (Bowling—Ten-Pin), Wet & Wild Amusement Park (Bucket Brigade), Sunset Park (Canoeing, Over the Line), Floyd Lamb Park (Cross Country, Marathon), Red Rock Canyon (Cycling), Duffy's Tavern (Darts), Silver Bowl Park (Flag Football, Rugby Sevens, Soccer), Mesquite Golf Course, Black Mountain Golf Course, Angel Park Golf Course (Golf), Jaycee Park (Horseshoes), Hacienda Hotel & Casino (Lawn Bowls—Carpet), Lake Mead (Sailing, Windsurfing), Nellis Rod & Gun Club (Skeet Shooting), Las Vegas Softball Complex (Softball—Fast Pitch, Slow Pitch), Green Valley Athletic Club (Squash), Cashman Field Expo Area, (Table Tennis), Clark County Training Centre (Toughest Firefighter Alive), Las Vegas Gun Club (Trap Shooting), Boulder Beach, Lake Mead (Triathlon), Freedom Park (Tug of War), Ed Fountain Park (Volleyball, 2-Man), Newberry Lake, California (Water Skiing)

1994   Perth   Australia   March 20–26

Nations: Australia, Belgium, Canada, Czech Republic, Estonia, Finland, France, Germany, Great Britain, Hong Kong, Ireland, Japan, Latvia, Netherlands, New Zealand, Russia, South Africa, Sweden, Switzerland, Taipei, USA

Sports: Angling, Archery, Arm Wrestling, Badminton, Basketball 5-on-5, Basketball 3-on-3, Body Building, Bowling—Ten-Pin, Bucket Brigade, Canoeing, Cross Country, Cycling, Darts, Dragon-Boat Racing, Eight Ball, Flag Football, Golf, Grid Iron, Horseshoes, Indoor Cricket, Judo, Karate, Lawn Bowls, Marathon and Half-marathon, Poker, Powerlifting, Rugby Sevens, Sailing, Skeet Shooting, Soccer, Softball—Slowpitch, Softball—Fastpitch, Squash, Surfing, Swimming, Table Tennis, Tennis, Touch Football, Toughest Firefighter Alive, Track and Field, Trap Shooting, Triathlon, Tug of War, Volleyball (Team), Volleyball—2 man (beach), Water Skiing, Windsurfing, Wrestling

Venues: Hillarys Boat Harbour, Hillarys (Angling), Whiteman Park Shooting Complex (Archery), Langley Park (Arm Wrestling, Flag Football, Football [Grid-Iron], Rugby Sevens, Touch Football), Belmont "Oasis" Leisure Centre (Badminton, Basketball 5-on-5, Basketball 3-on-3, Swimming), Sheraton Perth Hotel (Body Building, Darts, Eight Ball), Morley Bowl, Morley (Ten-Pin Bowling), Matilda Bay Reserve, Crawley (Bucket Brigade, Dragon-Boat Racing, Horseshoes, Triathlon, Tug of War), Canning Bridge Rowing Course (Canoeing), Hale Reserve, West Perth (Cross Country), Midvale Speed Dome (Criterium and Track) Perry Lakes, Floreat (Road Race), Langley Park (Cycling, Roller Sprint), The Vines Resort, Mt. Lawley Golf Club, Yokine Golf Club (Golf), Alexander Park Indoor Sports Centre (Indoor Cricket), Perth Fire

Station Gymnasium (Judo, Karate, Wrestling), Thornlie Bowling Club, Thornlie (Lawn Bowls), McCallum Park, South Perth (Marathon and Half-marathon), Superdrome, Mt. Claremont (Poker, Powerlifting), South of Perth Yacht Club, Applecross (Sailing), Whiteman Park Shooting Complex (Skeet Shooting, Trap Shooting), Miles Park, Cloverdale (Soccer), Mirrabooka Softball Stadium (Softball, Fast Pitch, Slow Pitch), Kenwick Squash Centre, Kenwick (Squash), Triggs Beach (Surfing), W.A. Table Tennis Assoc., Belmont (Table Tennis), Belmont Tennis Club, Belmont (Tennis), Perry Lakes Stadium, Floreat (Track and Field), Loftus Recreational Centre, Leederville (Volleyball—Team), City Beach (Volleyball 2-Man, Beach), Burswood River Front (Water Skiing), Nedlands Yacht Club, Nedlands (Windsurfing)

MEDALS (no other figures available)

Nation	Total
Australia	628
New Zealand	266
United States	127
Great Britain	102
Sweden	77
Hong Kong	76
Canada	54
South Africa	33
Japan	19
France	17
Finland	13
Czech Republic	10
Netherlands	8
Switzerland	7
Germany	6
Belgium	4
Estonia	4
Ireland	1
Latvia	0
Russia	0

1996   Edmonton   Canada   July 28–August 3

Nations: Australia, Austria, Belgium, Brazil, Canada, Czech Republic, Estonia, Finland, France, Germany, Hong Kong, Ireland, Italy, Japan, Latvia, Netherlands, New Zealand, Norway, Scotland, South Africa, South Korea, Sweden, Switzerland, United States, Wales

Events: Advanced Life Support, Archery, Arm Wrestling, Badminton, Basketball (5-on-5) Basketball (3-on-3), Body Building, Bowling, Bucket Brigade, Canoeing (Voyageur Canoe), Confined Space Rescue, Cycling, Darts, Fastball, Fire Truck Rodeo, Flag Football, Golf, Half-marathon, Handball, High Angle Rescue, Horseshoes, Hose Laying, Ice Hockey, Judo, Karate, Lawn Bowls, Mountain Bike, Orienteering, Over the Line, Pocket Billiards, Poker, Powerlifting, Racquetball, Rugby Sevens, Sailing, Skeet, Slo-Pitch, Soccer, Squash, Swimming, Table Tennis, Toughest Firefighter Alive, Track and Field, Trap, Triathlon, Tug of War, Vehicle Extraction, Volleyball (6 person), Beach Volleyball (2 Person), Walleyball, Waterskiing, Wrestling (Windsurfing, Rodeo, Curling and Kayak Polo were all canceled)

Venues: Northlands Agricom (Firefighters Events), Royal Glenora (Badminton, Handball, Racquetball, Squash, Table Tennis, Tennis), University of Alberta (Basketball 5-on-5, 3-on-3, Half-marathon, Judo, Volleyball, Wrestling, Closing Ceremony), Kinsmen Sports Centre (Swimming, Walleyball, Soccer), Strathcona Archery Club (Archery), Edmonton Centre (Arm Wrestling, Body Building, Cycling—Roller Sprint, Darts, Karate, Poker, Powerlifting), Gateway Lanes (Ten-Pin Bowling), North Saskatchewan River, Grierson Hill Park (Voyageur Canoe), Hawrelak Park (Cross Country, Cycling Prologue), Argyll Velodrome (Track Cycling), Mink Lake (Cycling Road Race), Legislative Grounds (Cycling Criterium), William Lede Park (Fast-pitch Softball, Slow-pitch Softball, Over the Line) Norwesters Rugby Club, Edmonton Research Park (Rugby Sevens, Flag Football), Raven Crest, The Ranch, Goose Hummock (Golf), Edmonton Horseshoe Centre (Horseshoes), Clairview and Castledowns Twin Rinks (Ice Hockey) Commonwealth Lawn Bowls (Lawn Bowls), Terwilliger Park (Cycling—Mountain Bike, Orienteering), Nicholby's (Billiards), Lake Wabamun (Sailing), Strathcona Gun Club (Skeet Shooting, Trap Shooting), Kinsman Park (Soccer), Rice Howard Way/Sunlife Building (Toughest Firefighter Alive), Strathcona Athletic Field (Athletics), Miquelon Lake (Triathlon), Grierson Hill Park (Tug of War), Edmonton Research Park (Beach Volleyball), Knox Landing (Water Skiing)

MEDALS

Nation	Gold	Silver	Bronze	Total
Canada	122	122	100	344
Australia	121	87	45	253
United States	109	81	52	242
New Zealand	67	67	58	192
England	42	65	49	156
France	39	39	16	94
Sweden	33	29	21	83
Hong Kong	30	35	28	93
Netherlands	28	14	26	68
Finland	24	8	2	34
Brazil	21	15	17	53
Czech Republic	13	7	0	20
Japan	10	11	4	25
Austria	10	1	5	16
Italy	8	2	6	16
Belgium	6	10	11	27
South Africa	4	7	7	18
Germany	3	6	12	21
Norway	3	0	0	3
Latvia	2	0	2	4
South Korea	1	5	1	7
Scotland	1	2	1	4
Switzerland	1	0	0	1
Estonia	0	1	0	1
Wales	0	0	1	1

1998   Durban   South Africa   May 17–23

Nations: Australia, Austria, Belgium, Bermuda, Brazil, Canada, Czech Republic, England, Estonia, France, Finland, Germany, Hong Kong, Italy, Ireland, Northern Ireland, Japan, Latvia, Netherlands, New Zealand, Norway, Scotland, South Africa, South Korea, Sweden, United States

Events: Angling, Archery, Arm Wrestling, Athletics, Badminton, Basketball, Body Building, Ten-Pin Bowling, Canoeing, Cross Country, Cycling, Darts, Eight Ball, Football, Golf, Indoor Cricket, Judo, Karate, Marathon, Half-marathon, Power Lifting, Sailing, Skeet, Soccer, Softball, Squash, Surfing, Swimming, Table Tennis, Tennis, Touch Rugby, Toughest Firefighter Alive, TM Trap, Triathlon, Tug of War, Volleyball, Water Skiing, Windsurfing, Wrestling (web site lists these 39 as "some" of the events)

Venues: Durban Exhibition Centre (Advanced Life Support, Arm Wrestling, Body Building, Darts, High-Angle Rescue, Cycling—Roller Sprint, Judo, Karate, Poker, Powerlifting, Vehicle Extrication, Wrestling), Nagle Dam (Angling—Fresh Water, Canoeing), Off Durban Coast (Angling—Deep Sea), Durban Coastline (Angling—Surf), Kings Park Archery Club (Archery), Natal Badminton Hall (Badminton), Natal Technicon (Basketball 5-on-5, 3-on-3), Disc Entertainment Centre (Bowling, Ten-Pin), Durban Beachfront (Bucket Brigade, Horseshoes, Hoselaying, Volleyball, 2-Man, Beach), University of Natal (Cross Country), Kings Park (Cycling Road Time Trial), Kings Park Track (Cycling Criterium), Cyril Geohegan Cycle Stadium (Track Cycling), Kings Park (Cycling Road Race), Umhlanga (Mountain Biking), Disaster Management Centre (Disaster Challenge), Durban Harbour (Dragon-Boat Racing, Sailing, Windsurfing), Durban Bazaar (Billiards—Eight Ball), Durban Country Club (Golf), Kings Park Athletic Stadium (Half-marathon, Marathon, Track and Field), Durban Ice Rink (Ice Hockey), Umlilo Congella Bowls Club (Lawn Bowls), Kings Park Rugby Stadium (Rugby Sevens, Touch Rugby), Boulder Hill Gun Club, Ashburton (Skeet Shooting, Trap Shooting), Kings Park Soccer Stadium (Soccer), Queensmead (Softball, Fastpitch, Slow-pitch), Westville Country Club (Squash), North Beach (Surfing), Kings Park Swimming Pool (Swimming, Water Polo), Natal Table Tennis Hall (Table Tennis), Westridge Park Tennis Stadium (Tennis), Durban Lower Marine Parade (Toughest Firefighter Alive), Durban-Westville University (Volleyball—Team), Thornlie Dam (Water Skiing)

MEDALS*

Nation	Gold	Silver	Bronze	Total
South Africa	89	81	84	254
France	73	62	38	173
England	60	38	34	132
Australia	56	41	30	127
Netherlands	43	24	20	87
Brazil	41	31	44	116
Hong Kong	31	38	26	95
Sweden	31	32	21	84
United States	28	18	6	52
Finland	19	6	4	29
Canada	14	11	7	32
Italy	14	10	7	31
Germany	5	5	3	13
New Zealand	4	2	8	14
Belgium	3	7	3	13
Scotland	3	1	0	4

Nation	Gold	Silver	Bronze	Total
Czech Republic	2	1	1	4
Bermuda	1	3	2	6
Austria	1	2	4	7
South Korea	1	1	1	3
Ireland	1	0	0	1
Latvia	0	2	1	3
Norway	0	1	3	4
Estonia	0	1	1	2
Northern Ireland	0	0	2	2
Japan	0	0	1	1

*United Nations medals not included in medal count (all nations present won medals). U.N. teams were mixed teams.

FISEC Games

The FISEC Games (Fédération Internationale Sportive de l'Enseignement Catholique) have been contested on an annual basis since 1948. The games are for Catholic school students between 14 and 17 years of age. They were for boys only from 1948 to 1959, and then separate games were organized for girls. The two games were joined into one in 1980.

Year	Host City	Host Nation	Dates
1987	Genk	Belgium	
1988	Louvain	Belgium	
1989	Burgos	Spain	
1990	Liverpool	England	
1991	Maastricht	Netherlands	
1992	Milan	Italy	
1996	Somerset/London	Great Britain	
1997	Valletta	Malta	
1998	Gran Canaria	Spain	July 22–28
1999	Lisbon	Portugal	July 21–27
2000	Nantes	France	July 19–25

Note: Full list now available at www.internationalgames.net

Francophone Games

The Conférence des Ministres de la Jeunesse et des Sports (CONFEJES) for French-speaking nations was created in 1969 by participants with a common desire to establish a policy to promote and protect youth. For the first two decades of its existence, the CONFEJES focused on training group leaders and instructors.

In September 1987, the heads of state and government for several French-speaking nations met in Quebec City, Canada, for a summit. One result of the meeting was the establishment of the Francophone Games, an event exclusively for the French-speaking nations, and CONFEJES was given the responsibility of organizing them.

The inaugural games were held in Morocco in the summer of 1989 with 30 nations participating. They include a very strong cultural component with medals given for performances in the arts, singing and French music. Canada sends three separate teams to the Francophone Games: two from Quebec and New Brunswick, where French is widely spoken, and a team composed of the rest of Canada. This created some interesting moments during postevent television interviews in Morocco when some of the less fluent French-speaking Canadian athletes had assistants whispering answers to them in French from just outside the range of the cameras.

The second games were held in Paris, France, in 1994, a year after they were originally scheduled. The games were not given much attention by the media, the Paris paper *Le Monde* devoting one day to preview articles on July 1, four days before the games opened, then ignoring them until they ended on July 13.

Antananarivo, Madagascar, was selected as the host for the 1997 games. One of the poorest cities in the world, Antananarivo did its utmost to clean its streets and paint its buildings to present its best side for the games. Despite these efforts, the athletes from other nations had trouble with the conditions—they said the village was very unsanitary, with rodents in the rooms, and there was no heat.

Madagascar has more French passport holders than any other African nation even though the French language was banned from the country during the first reign of Admiral Didier Ratsiraka between the years 1975 and 1991. Ratsiraka was exiled in Paris and regained the presidency of Madagascar in February 1997. It was suggested that the games were awarded to Madagascar in order to help France enhance its image there and in other parts of Africa.[110]

There was controversy in Canada over its part in funding the games, when claims were made by some English speakers that the country was spending more money on its teams for the 1997 Francophone Games than it had on those for the 1996 Atlanta Olympic Games. Bonnie Brown, a member of Canada's Parliament, responded to the charges by stating that while it was true that Canada and France, as two of the stronger nations economically, were providing direct financial support to Madagascar for the games, Canada had spent over 40 times more supporting athletes for the Olympic Games than athletes for the Francophone Games.[111] Given the limited number of sports in the Francophone Games, it is not likely that more money would be spent on teams for those games.

The 1997 Francophone Games included six sports: athletics, basketball, boxing, football, judo, and lawn tennis. The cultural competitions included sculpture, song, traditional dance, storytelling, literature, painting and photography.

Canadian athletes had run-ins, one dangerous, one humorous, with the animal kingdom at the games. Canadian boxer Isaac Mitchell was bitten in the hand by a rodent while asleep in his room at the games village and had to receive treatment to prevent rabies. Runner Vicki Lynch Pounds was competing in the 800 meter event when an iguana wandered out of the grass onto the track. Pounds leapt the reptile, but a runner in the pack reportedly tripped, fell over the animal, and didn't finish the race.

The next games were scheduled for 2001 in Ottawa, Canada, which outbid Beirut, Lebanon, to host these games.[112]

Early in 1998, Quebec was threatening to boycott the 2001 games if it was not given a part in their organization. The Canadian federal government and the provincial governments of Ontario, Quebec and New Brunswick have been listed as official government partners in the games.

Year	Host City	Host Nation	Dates	Nations	Athletes	Sports
1989	Rabat, Casablanca	Morocco	July 8–22	30	NA	4
1994	Paris	France	July 5–13	28[113]	NA	7
1997	Antananarivo	Madagascar	August 27–Sept. 6	49	2000	6

1989   Rabat   Casablanca   Morocco   July 8–22

Sports: Athletics, Judo, Basketball, Football

MEDALS

Nation	Gold	Silver	Bronze	Total
France	32	23	19	74
Canada	22	18	27	67
Morocco	6	7	6	19
Senegal	3	3	4	10
Belgium	1	1	4	6
Djibouti	1	1	1	3
Egypt	1	1	1	3
Rwanda	1	1	0	2
Madagascar	1	1	0	2
Ivory Coast	1	0	3	4
Switzerland	1	0	1	2
Tunisia	0	2	2	4
Luxembourg	0	1	0	1
Congo	0	0	1	1
Gabon	0	0	1	1
Mauritius	0	0	1	1

1994   Paris   France   July 5–13

Nations: Belgium, Burkina Faso, Burundi, Cameroon, Canada New Brunswick, Canada Quebec, Canada, Central Africa, Congo, Côte d'Ivoire, Djibouti, Dominica, Egypt, France, Gabon, Guinea, Lebanon, Luxembourg, Madagascar, Mali, Mauritius, Morocco, Romania, Senegal, Switzerland, Togo, Tunisia, Vietnam (15 more)
Sports: Athletics, Basketball, Football, Handball, Judo, Table Tennis, Wrestling
Sports for Women: Athletics, Handball, Judo, Table Tennis
Arts: Contemporary Dance, Painting, Sculpture, Singing, Storytelling, Television Production, Traditional Dance

MEDALS

Nation	Gold	Silver	Bronze	Total
France	28	28	24	80
Romania	16	3	5	24
Canada	14	11	14	39
Canada Quebec	8	4	16	28
Morocco	6	11	7	24
Tunisia	4	7	2	13
Egypt	2	5	4	11
Switzerland	2	1	5	8
Senegal	2	1	3	6

Nation	Gold	Silver	Bronze	Total
Belgium	1	3	6	10
Madagascar	1	2	3	6
Burkina Faso	1	1	1	3
Togo	1	0	1	2
Lebanon	1	0	0	1
Guinea	1	0	0	1
Cote d'Ivoire	0	3	3	6
Congo	0	3	2	5
Cameroon	0	1	2	3
Canada New Brunswick	0	1	2	3
Central Africa	0	1	0	1
Gabon	0	1	0	1
Dominique	0	1	0	1
Mali	0	1	0	1
Mauritius	0	0	2	2
Luxembourg	0	0	2	2
Vietnam	0	0	1	1
Burundi	0	0	1	1
Djibouti	0	0	1	1

1997   Antananarivo   Madagascar   August 27–September 6

Nations: Belgium, Benin, Burkina Faso, Burundi, Cameroon, Canada New Brunswick, Canada Quebec, Canada, Cape Verde, Central Africa, Chad, (Communaute Francaise de Belgique), Comoros, Congo, France, Gabon, Guinea, Haiti, Lebanon, Luxembourg, Madagascar, Mali, Mauritius, Moldova, Monaco, Niger, Romania, Rwanda, Senegal, Seychelles, Sao Tome and Principe, Togo, Tunisia, Vietnam[114]

Sports: Athletics, Basketball, Boxing, Judo, Football, Tennis
Sports for Men: Athletics, Boxing, Football, Judo, Lawn Tennis
Sports for Women: Athletics, Basketball
Arts: Sculpture, Photography, Painting, Tale, Traditional Dance, Literature, Song
Venues: Stade d'Athlétisme d'Alorobia (Athletics, Football), Stade de Mahamasina (Opening Ceremonies, Football, Closing Ceremonies), Palais des Sports de Mahamasina (Basketball, Boxing), ACSA (Tennis), Stade d'Ankorondrano (Judo), Gymnase de Mahamasina (Boxing)

MEDALS

Nation	Gold	Silver	Bronze	Total
France	20	17	9	46
Madagascar	11	4	10	25
Canada	7	11	10	28
Belgium	4	2	4	10
Tunisia	3	3	4	10
Romania	3	1	2	6
Cameroon	2	3	8	13
Senegal	2	1	5	8
Ivory Coast	2	1	4	7
Mauritius	1	6	6	13

Nation	Gold	Silver	Bronze	Total
Canada Quebec	1	2	4	7
Gabon	1	1	5	7
Burundi	1	1	1	3
Burkina Faso	0	1	2	3
Seychelles	0	1	2	3
Lebanon	0	1	1	2
Luxembourg	0	1	0	1
Canada New Brunswick	0	0	2	2
Cape Verde	0	0	1	1
Central African Republic	0	0	1	1
Morocco	0	0	1	1

Friendship Games 84

The 1980 Olympic boycott had ramifications beyond the return boycott of 1984. The Soviet Bloc nations assembled for competitions in a number of cities the week after the 1984 Los Angeles Olympic Games (August 16–30, 1984). The competitions do not fit the strict criteria for an international games held in one location at one time; nevertheless, they were grouped together by the organizers under the name Friendship Games 84. Ted Turner, of Turner Broadcasting, was approached by the Soviets and asked to televise the games on his networks, but declined.[115] Two years later, he was back in Moscow, creating and televising the inaugural Goodwill Games.

Pravda commented, "The Friendship 84 competitions in Moscow will yet again not only demonstrate sporting achievements but also that socialist society provides more favorable facilities for the human being's all-round physical and spiritual development."[116]

Moscow hosted the opening ceremonies and athletics (for men), swimming, cycling and rowing. The other sports were spread out in the following cities and nations:

• Prague, Czechoslovakia (Women's Athletics)

• Havana, Cuba (Boxing)

• Warsaw, Poland (Judo)

• Katowice, Poland (Tennis)

• Tallinn, Soviet Union (Sailing)

• Olomouc, Czechoslovakia (Gymnastics)[117]

Much was made of the comparison of athletic achievements between the Friendship Games 84 and the Los Angeles Olympic Games in the press reports from both the East and West, especially in athletics, swimming and cycling where performances could be objectively measured. In men's athletics, the Friendship Games 84 had better performances in eight of the 24 events. In women's events, the Friendship Games 84 had better marks in 12 of the 17 events.[118] Official results were full of comments such as "the scores of the current competitions are higher than those of the champions of the Los Angeles Games."[119]

Between 40 and 45 nations took part in the games, with the Soviet Union and

East Germany winning the vast majority of medals in nearly every event. Cubans dominated the boxing competitions held in Havana.

Year	Host City	Host Nation	Dates
1984	Moscow	Soviet Union	August 16–30

Nations: 45

Sports: Athletics, Basketball, Boxing, Cycling, Field Hockey, Gymnastics, Judo, Rowing, Sailing, Shooting, Swimming, Tennis.[120]

Venues: Moscow, Soviet Union (Athletics, Swimming, Cycling, Rowing), Prague, Czechoslovakia (Women's Athletics), Havana, Cuba (Boxing), Warsaw, Poland (Judo), Katowice, Poland (Tennis), Tallin, Soviet Union (Sailing), Olomouc, Czechoslovakia (Gymnastics)

Games of the New Emerging Forces (GANEFO)

The Games of the New Emerging Forces, or GANEFO Games, were founded in response to the International Olympic Committee's sanctions imposed on Indonesia after a very political Asian Games in 1962.

In May 1958, the Asian Games Council (by a vote of 22–20) awarded the fourth Asian Games to Jakarta, Indonesia. At the time, Indonesia had no facilities and there were doubts whether or not venues could be readied in four years. The Indonesians appealed to the United States government for monetary assistance but did not receive an answer. An appeal to the Soviet Union for help won an immediate response. The Soviets granted 50 million rubles in credit in order to build the facilities necessary for the games. The Japanese loaned money for the building of the Hotel Jakarta, which would become the main hotel for games dignitaries. The United States finally came to Indonesia's assistance with the building of a highway from the main harbor to the sports complex, but never acknowledged this contribution as aid specifically for the Asian Games.

The facilities were completed in time, but it was rumored that the Indonesian government would not be granting visas to visitors from either Israel or Taiwan. The Asian Games Federation executive committee in April 1962 called a meeting to look into the matter and toured the Asian Games village. The flags of both Israel and Taiwan were displayed along with the other nations' and this consoled the delegates for a time, who assumed that the visa issue would be resolved.

However, in July 1962, the Indonesian ambassador to China delivered a letter to his government from China. In the letter, the Chinese stated that they were strongly against Taiwan's participation in the 1962 Asian Games. At the same time, the Taiwanese government was lobbying for a boycott of the games if they were not included.

Three days before the games were to begin, Guru Dutt Sondhi of India, one of the founders of the Asian Games, stated that because Taiwan and Israel had not been granted visas, the Asian Games Committee should remove its sanction from the games. No consensus was reached and the games opened on August 24, 1962. Two days later, a decision was reached in a meeting called by Sondhi but without the presence of the president of the Asian Games Federation, Indonesian Sultan Hamnegku Buwono IX. A press release was issued by Sondhi stating that the games were not to be officially known as the fourth Asian Games, but the "Jakarta Games." The international basketball and weightlifting federations immediately withdrew their sanction and those events were canceled.

Two days later the decision regarding the naming of the games was reversed in another meeting of the Asian Games Federation, and Sondhi was literally run out of town by an angry mob, escaping on a plane back to India.

In February 1963, Sondhi used his position as a member of the IOC's executive board to have Indonesia suspended indefinitely from the IOC. The IOC stated that it would rescind the suspension for "the scandalous occurrence at the Fourth Asian Games," only if Indonesia promised no further political discrimination.

Indonesia responded by going ahead with plans for the GANEFO Games, an idea that had originally been proposed by Indonesian President Sukarno in a speech in November 1962 in Tokyo.

In November 1963, 3,000 athletes from 48 nations participated in the first GANEFO Games. The soccer final was decided by a coin toss after the United Arab Republic (UAR) and North Korea had fought to the end of regulation time and a 30-minute overtime period to a 1–1 tie. The crowd of 110,000 booed and jeered each member of the UAR's winning team as he received his medal. The Indonesian crowd had booed the Indian soccer team in a similar fashion at the previous year's Asian Games in Indonesia.

North Korea's Shin Keum Dan won the 800 meters in a time of 1:59.1, the first time under two minutes for a woman, but the International Amateur Athletic Federation (IAAF) never ratified the time as a world record.

The hope had been to establish a quadrennial competition, with the 1967 games to be held in Cairo, Egypt, or Peking as an alternate site, but neither chose to go forward with the games. Rapidly shifting political alliances moved once again, and after a coup in Indonesia the government established business relationships with Taiwan while relationships with mainland China cooled. All of these factors contributed to the cancelation of the second games.

In September 1965, a smaller group called the Asian-GANEFO was formed. This brief chapter in athletic history ended in December 1966 at the conclusion of the first such games in Phnom Penh, Cambodia, in which 15 nations participated.

1963   *Jakarta   Indonesia   November 10–22*

Nations: Afghanistan, Albania, Algeria, Argentine, Arab Palestine, Belgium, Bolivia, Brazil, Bulgaria, Burma, Cambodia, Ceylon, Chile, China (Peoples Republic), Cuba, Czechoslovakia, Dominican Republic, Finland, France, East Germany, Guinea, Hungary, Indonesia, Iraq, Italy, Japan, North Korea, Laos, Lebanon, Mali, Morocco, Mexico, Netherlands, Nigeria, Pakistan, Philippines, Poland, Romania, Saudi Arabia, Somalia, Syria, Thailand, Tunisia, United Arab Republic, USSR, Uruguay, North Vietnam, Yugoslavia

	MEDALS			
Nation	*Gold*	*Silver*	*Bronze*	*Total*
China	68	58	45	171
Soviet Union	27	21	9	57
United Arab Republic	22	18	12	52

Nation	Gold	Silver	Bronze	Total
Indonesia	21	25	35	81
North Korea	13	15	24	52
Argentina	5	0	4	9
Japan	4	10	14	28

(incomplete)

One Asian-GANEFO was held:

1966   Phnom Penh   Cambodia   November 25–December 6

Nations: Arab Palestine, Cambodia, Ceylon, China, Indonesia, Iraq, North Korea, Laos, Lebanon, Mongolia, Pakistan, Saudi Arabia, Syria, North Vietnam, Yemen

Games of the Small Countries of Europe

The regionalization of the Olympic movement took a further step in May 1981 at the meetings of the general assembly of the Association of European National Olympic Committees in Athens when a proposal came from the Maltese delegation to create a games for nations with populations of less than one million people. The idea languished until the 1984 Los Angeles Olympic Games when delegates from Andorra, Cyprus, Iceland, Liechtenstein, Luxembourg, Malta, Monaco and San Marino met and decided that San Marino would be the host for the first "Games of the Small Countries of Europe" in May 1985.

The International Olympic Committee has added its financial support to each edition of the games, and paid the travel costs for the visiting nations for the very first games. It was IOC President Samaranch who suggested that the games be held on a biennial basis rather than the more customary quadrennial schedule.

The games give these very small nations a chance to host, compete fully in and win medals in international competition. Iceland, for instance, has so far won the most medals in these games, over 30 gold medals on a number of occasions. At the Olympic Games, however, Iceland has won one silver and one bronze medal, but no gold. Both of those medals came in the summer and not the winter games.

Cyprus has always finished well in the small countries games, has won a smattering of medals in the Commonwealth and Mediterranean Games, but not an Olympic medal as of 2000. The medals won in the Commonwealth and Mediterranean games have all been after 1987, so it looks like the games of the small countries have had a positive effect on the development of sports in Cyprus.

Luxembourg has won one gold medal in the Olympic Games, Josy Barthel's stunning victory in the 1500 meters in Helsinki in 1952, but has won 88 gold medals in the first six editions of the small nations games.

Liechtenstein, San Marino, Malta, Monaco and Andorra have all had similar results. At the same time, the medals tables of the competition between these small nations sometimes look similar to the tables at larger games with two or three nations dominating and the nations at the bottom winning one or two (sometimes zero) gold medals. Andorra from 1985 to 1995 won a total of five gold medals. The games, like all of the games for smaller regions (e.g., Island Games, Micronesian Games), allow the very smallest of nations and principalities to share in the Olympic experience, and provide competitive opportunities for athletes to develop. Many of the national records for these nations have been set in these competitions. The Games of the Small Countries of Europe are the only games that Iceland, Liechtenstein, Malta and San Marino have ever hosted.

The first games in 1985 lived up to their name by being small not only in the size of the nations but in the number of participants as well. Two hundred and sixty athletes marched into Serravalle Stadium in San Marino on May 23, 1985, for the opening ceremony. The first games comprised seven sports: athletics, basketball, cycling, judo, shooting, swimming and weightlifting. The Italian National Olympic Committee came to the assistance of the Olympic committee of San Marino to help organize the event.

Iceland won 21 gold medals, and 32 medals in total. Cyprus won 15 gold. Luxembourg won fewer gold medals, 11, but the most total medals, 52.

The second edition of the games were opened by Prince Rainier, Prince Albert and Princess Caroline of Monaco in 1989. The swimmers from Iceland again stole the show winning 21 of Iceland's total of 27 gold medals. B. Olafsdottir of Iceland won four individual races.

Cyprus hosted the third games and after President George Vassiliou declared them open, Cyprus was able to use its home advantage to win 26 gold medals to 21 for Iceland. Iceland's E. Edvardson won two more individual gold medals in men's swimming, to bring his all-time total to nine for the first three editions of the games.

At the fourth games in Andorra la Vella, the capital of Andorra, Iceland with its powerful women's swimmers came back to tie Cyprus with 24 gold medals. Iceland won a few more bronze and silver to take the top spot. Luxembourg was close behind with 22 gold.

Malta's women's doubles tennis team of Helen Asciak and Carol Curmi won the title for the third games in a row.

One benefit of the games is that they are a catalyst to upgrade the sporting infrastructure of the host nations. For the 1993 games, Malta constructed a new athletics facility, shooting ranges and a swimming complex.

The new athletics field was covered with a large blue carpet to symbolize the Mediterranean Sea, the same carpet used at the opening ceremony of the 1992 Barcelona Olympic Games. The torch for the games was lit at the temples of Gjantija and relayed around Malta and carried into the stadium on horseback, by Maltese polo player Salvu Darmanin. The torch was then handed to Carmel Busuttil, Malta's national soccer captain, who lit the games flame.

Iceland's swimmers led the way again with Bryndis Olafdottir winning seven gold medals on the women's side. Cyprus, normally the dominant nation in the athletics events, held true to form by winning 18 gold medals on the track.

The next games were held in 1995 in Luxembourg, with the opening ceremonies and athletic events staged in Josy Barthel Stadium, Iceland won with 33 gold medals, Cyprus came in second with 22 gold, and Luxembourg was nudged into third with 20 gold.

Iceland may not have done itself any favors by choosing "Snowie the Snowman" as the mascot for the 1997 games in Reykjavik, the first international games ever held in Iceland. The games were moved to the first week of June from their traditional mid-May dates and the hosts assured participants of mild Icelandic summer weather and sunlight almost 24 hours a day. Unfortunately, unseasonably bad weather struck the week of the games. The opening ceremonies were shrouded in fog, high winds post-poned some of the events during the week, and even a few snow flurries fell. The closing ceremonies were moved inside to the Laugardalshöll arena to get out of the cold.

At the opening ceremony, the games torch was brought into Laugardulur Stadium on a white Icelandic horse, much as it had arrived in 1993 in Malta. Prince Henri of Denmark, Princess Nora of Liechtenstein and IOC President Juan Antonio Samaranch were all guests of Iceland's President Ólafur Ragnar Grímmson, who opened the games.

In one of the few politically charged moments of these games, the team from Cyprus almost left for home during the middle of the event when it was discovered that the flag of the Turkish Cypriots instead of the flag of Cyprus had been used in the program for the gymnastics events. After a formal apology, the team from Cyprus decided to stay.

Iceland won 33 gold medals, 32 silver and 31 bronze. Cyprus finished with 29 gold medals; Luxembourg with 24 gold.

In a spirited basketball competition, San Marino lost to Malta 69–67, and Monaco 67–65, then came back in the fifth-place contest to beat Andorra 108–106 in a triple overtime thriller.

Liechtenstein hosted the 1999 edition, the last of the nations to stage the Games of the Small Countries of Europe. This was the first ever international games Liechtenstein had hosted.

The games have begun a second round of nations with San Marino the scheduled host for the 2001 event.

Year	Host City	Host Nation	Dates	Nations	Athletes	Sports
1985	San Marino	San Marino	May 23–26	8	260	7
1987	Monte Carlo	Monaco	May 14–17	8	600	8
1989	Nicosia	Cyprus	May 17–20	8	NA	9
1991	Andorra la Vella	Andorra	May 21–25	8	650	8
1993	Valletta	Malta	May 25–29	8	NA	9
1995	Luxembourg	Luxembourg	May 29–June 3	8	697	9
1997	Reykjavik	Iceland	June 3–7	8	765	10
1999	Vaduz	Leichtenstein	May 24–29	8	NA	9

1985   San Marino   San Marino   May 23–26

Nations: Andorra, Cyprus, Iceland, Liechtenstein, Luxembourg, Malta, Monaco, San Marino

Sports: Athletics, Basketball, Cycling, Judo, Swimming, Shooting, Weightlifting

Sports for Women: Athletics, Swimming

Venues: Serraville Sports Center (Athletics, Weightlifting, Judo), Serraville Sports Center Indoor Basketball Court (Basketball), Fonnte dell 'Ovo Road (Cycling), Tavolucci Swimming Pool (Swimming), Murata Stand (Clay Shooting), Ex Mesa Serraville (Target Shooting)

MEDALS

Nation	Gold	Silver	Bronze	Total
Iceland	21	7	4	32
Cyprus	15	8	9	32
Luxembourg	11	23	18	52

Nation	Gold	Silver	Bronze	Total
San Marino	2	11	11	24
Malta	0	0	1	1
Monaco	0	0	2	2
Andorra	0	0	4	4
Liechtenstein	0	0	4	4

1987   Monte Carlo   Monaco   May 14–17

Nations: Andorra, Cyprus, Iceland, Liechtenstein, Luxembourg, Malta, Monaco, San Marino
Sports: Athletics, Basketball, Judo, Shooting, Swimming, Tennis, Volleyball, Weightlifting
Sports for Women: Athletics, Swimming, Tennis
Venues: Stade Louis II (Athletics), Stade Omnisports (Opening Ceremonies)

MEDALS

Nation	Gold	Silver	Bronze	Total
Iceland	27	14	7	48
Luxembourg	15	26	21	62
Cyprus	13	17	16	46
Monaco	6	3	11	20
Liechtenstein	3	1	6	10
Malta	1	1	4	6
San Marino	1	5	5	11
Andorra	0	0	1	1

1989   Nicosia   Cyprus   May 17–20

Nations: Andorra, Cyprus, Iceland, Liechtenstein, Luxembourg, Malta, Monaco, San Marino
Sports: Athletics, Basketball, Cycling, Judo, Shooting, Swimming, Tennis, Volleyball, Yachting
Sports for Women: Athletics, Basketball, Swimming, Tennis, Volleyball
Venues: Makarion Stadium (Opening Ceremonies)

MEDALS

Nation	Gold	Silver	Bronze	Total
Cyprus	26	25	28	79
Iceland	21	20	9	50
Luxembourg	12	16	18	46
Liechtenstein	5	2	7	14
Monaco	5	7	9	21
Andorra	3	1	4	8
San Marino	2	4	2	8
Malta	1	1	3	5

1991   Andorra la Vella   Andorra   May 21–25

Nations: Andorra, Cyprus, Iceland, Liechtenstein, Luxembourg, Malta, Monaco, San Marino

Sports: Athletics, Basketball, Cycling, Judo, Shooting, Swimming, Tennis, Volleyball

Sports for Women: Athletics, Basketball, Swimming, Tennis, Volleyball

Venues: Els Serradels Swimming Complex (Swimming)

MEDALS

Nation	Gold	Silver	Bronze	Total
Iceland	24	17	18	59
Cyprus	24	14	20	58
Luxembourg	22	21	15	58
Monaco	8	13	13	34
Malta	1	2	4	7
San Marino	1	2	3	6
Andorra	0	5	8	13
Liechtenstein	0	3	3	6

1993   Valletta   Malta   May 25–29

Nations: Andorra, Cyprus, Iceland, Liechtenstein, Luxembourg, Malta, Monaco, San Marino

Sports: Athletics, Swimming, Basketball, Cycling, Judo, Shooting, Tennis, Volleyball, Yachting

Sports for Women: Athletics, Basketball, Judo, Swimming, Tennis, Volleyball

Venues: Ta' Qali National Stadium (Opening Ceremonies), University of Malta Sports Complex, Msida (Swimming), Matthew Micallef St. John Track, Marsa (Athletics), Ta' Qaki Pavilion (Basketball), Mosta/Ghajn Tuffieha Circuit (Cycling), Gozo Sports Pavilion (Judo), Bidnija Ranges (Shooting), Marsa Sports Club (Tennis), Corradino Pavilion (Volleyball—Men), De la Salle College (Volleyball—Women)

MEDALS

Nation	Gold	Silver	Bronze	Total
Iceland	36	17	15	68
Cyprus	26	23	22	71
Luxembourg	8	14	10	32
Monaco	7	11	11	29
Malta	4	7	20	31
Liechtenstein	4	2	7	13
San Marino	2	6	5	13
Andorra	0	6	10	16

1995   Luxembourg   Luxembourg   May 29–June 3

Nations: Andorra, Cyprus, Iceland, Liechtenstein, Luxembourg, Malta, Monaco, San Marino

Sports: Athletics, Basketball, Cycling, Judo, Shooting, Swimming, Table Tennis, Tennis, Volleyball

Sports for Women: Athletics, Basketball, Judo, Shooting, Swimming, Table Tennis, Tennis, Volleyball

Venues: Stade Josy Barthel (Opening, Closing Ceremonies, Athletics), Piscine Olympique Luxembourg-Kirchberg (Swimming), Hall Omnisports Stade Josy Barthel

(Judo, Table Tennis), Hall Omnisports Hamm (Shooting), Institute National de Sports Luxembourg-Fetschenhof (Basketball), Hall Omni Bonnevoie (Volleyball—Women), Patinoire de Kockelscheuer (Volleyball—Men) Cessange (Cycling—road)

Nation	MEDALS Gold	Silver	Bronze	Total
Iceland	33	17	28	78
Cyprus	22	25	22	69
Luxembourg	20	26	12	58
Liechtenstein	5	2	1	8
Monaco	3	4	17	24
Andorra	2	5	8	15
San Marino	2	5	2	9
Malta	1	4	7	12

1997   Reykjavik   Iceland   June 3–7

Nations: Andorra, Cyprus, Iceland, Liechtenstein, Luxembourg, Malta, Monaco, San Marino
Sports: Athletics, Basketball, Gymnastics, Judo, Sailing, Shooting, Swimming, Table Tennis, Tennis, Volleyball
Sports for Women: Athletics, Basketball, Gymnastics, Table Tennis, Judo, Sailing, Shooting, Swimming, Tennis, Volleyball
Venues: Laugurdalur Sports Centre, Reykjavik City Stadium (Athletics), Reykjavik City Swimming Pool (Swimming), Nautholsvik (Sailing), Austerberg Hall (Volleyball, Judo), Tennis Hall (Tennis)

1999   Vaduz   Liechtenstein   May 24–29

Nations: Andorra, Cyprus, Iceland, Liechtenstein, Luxembourg, Malta, Monaco, San Marino

Nation	MEDALS Gold	Silver	Bronze	Total
Iceland	29	20	24	73
Luxembourg	20	16	19	55
Cyprus	14	13	15	42
San Marino	6	5	7	18
Andorra	5	12	11	28
Monaco	5	9	6	20
Malta	4	8	8	20
Liechtenstein	3	3	2	8

Gay Games

The Gay Games were founded by Dr. Tom Waddell, a 1968 Olympic decathlete from the United States. The games are intended to provide gay athletes a forum to compete, but are open to all athletes.

In 1980, Dr. Waddell saw a gay men's bowling tournament on television and the idea for a gay Olympics was born. A U.S. Gay Olympic Committee was formed with plans to sponsor the "Gay Olympic Games." However, the committee was forced to change its name to San Francisco Arts and Athletics (SFAA) and the name of the games to the Gay Games after the United States Olympic Committee obtained a restraining order in August 1982 to prohibit the use of the word "Olympic" to describe the competition. In a lawsuit after the games, a California court affirmed the right of the USOC to use the word exclusively, based on the Amateur Sports Act of 1978. In March 1987, the US Supreme Court upheld the decision.

San Francisco had considered bidding for the 1996 Olympic Games but dropped the idea when gay activists lobbied to keep the city out of the running in protest of the actions of the USOC.

The first Gay Games in San Francisco in 1982 had 1,300 participants from 12 countries. Tina Turner sang at the opening ceremony in Kezar Stadium. A torch run was held from Stonewall in New York City to San Francisco.

The 1986 games were also held in San Francisco and more than doubled in size, with 3400 participants. One year later, Dr. Waddell died of AIDS.

The SFAA met in the summer of 1989 and voted to change its name to the more international Federation of Gay Games.

The 1990 games in Vancouver, Canada, had over 7,000 athletes. Bruce Hayes, a swimming gold medalist for the U.S. in the 1984 Olympic Games won seven gold medals. A cultural festival and nightly dance added to the social festivities of the games.

In March 1994, the U.S. Justice Department waived the rules for the time period of the games allowing persons infected with HIV to enter the country. This action sparked protests prior to the 1994 New York Games by groups opposed to what was seen as promotion of the gay lifestyle.

New York City Mayor Rudolph Giuliani, who had several run-ins with gay-rights advocates early in his term as mayor, was to open the games at Columbia University Stadium.

The 1994 games in New York City were held to coincide with the "Stonewall 25" celebrations, to commemorate the anniversary of the Stonewall uprising, and a festival of films, theater, dance and music. Lesbian wrestling and gay pairs figure skating were two of the new events added to the schedule. Bruce Hayes returned and won six gold medals in the swimming events to add to his seven gold from Vancouver, and set three masters world records. The majority of the competitors in the games focus not on world records or winning but on the personal satisfaction of participation.

The triathlon event was canceled after a mix-up in which precautionary ambulances failed to show up before the start of the event. Athletes, organizers and the mayor's office were upset at the oversight, which prompted an immediate investigation by the mayor.

In 1998, the Gay Games were held in Europe for the first time with Amsterdam, Netherlands, as the host. Just prior to the opening, the games' executive director, Marc Janssens, was fired when it was discovered he had wrongfully authorized spending over $1 million more than the allowed budget. Rather than cancel the games, the Amsterdam City Council stepped in to make up the deficit.

The ice-skating competition was held under protest after the International Skating Union (ISU) refused to sanction the event. ISU stated that any skater participating in the Gay Games would be banned from other sanctioned ice-skating competitions.

Another controversy arose over the inclusion of transsexual athletes in the Gay Games.

Transsexuals were not allowed to compete unless they could provide evidence of "completed gender transition," stating that a man in the process of becoming a woman would still have superior physical capacities. Others protested that rules involving transsexual participation were counter to the spirit of the games' ideals of equality and privacy.

The final controversy of the games was caused by Sue Emerson, the British Gay Games organizer, who said that there were widespread instances of participants deliberately entering into lower categories of skill in their sport in order to win medals, and that organizers were considering forgoing medals all together at the Sydney games in 2002, except for medals of participation.

Year	Host City	Host Nation	Dates	Nations	Athletes	Sports
1982	San Francisco	USA	August 28–Sept. 5	12	1300	14
1986	San Francisco	USA	August 7–18	17	3400	17
1990	Vancouver	Canada	August 4–11	29	7400	29
1994	New York	USA	June 18–25	44	10864	31
1998	Amsterdam	Netherlands	August 1–8	61	14403	29

1994   New York   USA   June 18–25

Sports: Aerobics, Athletics, Badminton, Basketball, Biathlon, Billiards, Bowling, Cycling, Diving, Figure Skating, Flag Football, Football, Golf, Ice Hockey, Inline Skating, Judo, Marathon, Martial Arts, Physique, Powerlifting, Racquetball, Softball, Sports Climbing, Squash, Swimming, Table Tennis, Tennis, Volleyball, Water Polo, Wrestling

Venues: Pelham Bay Golf Course (Golf), Hudson Lanes (Bowling), Flushing Meadow (Tennis, Soccer), Lehman College (Basketball), Ashpalt Green (Swimming, Diving), Randalls Island (Softball), Carmine Recreation (Martial Arts), Lost Battalion Hall (Table Tennis), Queens College (Volleyball), Amsterdam Billiards (Billiards), Hotel Pennsylvania (Physique, Aerobics), Prospect Park (Flag Football, Cycling), Hunter College (Racquetball), Downing Stadium (Athletics), Abe Stark Arena (Figure Skating, Ice Dancing, Ice Hockey), Riverside Park (Cycling), Ringwood State Park (Cycling), Inner Wall, New Paltz (Sport Climbing), New York Sports Club (Squash), Queens College (Badminton), Central Park (Softball, Soccer)

1998   Amsterdam   Netherlands   August 1–8

Sports: Badminton, Basketball, Billiards, Bowling, Body Building, Dancing, Bridge, Chess, Cycling, Ice Hockey, Judo, Karate, Marathon, Martial Arts, Rowing, Squash, Softball, Soccer, Sports Climbing, Swimming, Table Tennis, Tennis, Athletics, Triathlon, Volleyball, Water Polo, Weightlifting, Windsurfing, Wrestling, (Diving as demonstration sport; Figure Skating canceled)

Goodwill Games

The Goodwill Games were founded by Ted Turner of Turner Broadcasting as a competition that would bring the United States and the Soviet Union back together on the playing fields after the boycotts of the 1980 and 1984 Olympic Games. The games have been a success in the athletic arena but have lost millions of dollars on each of the occasions they have been held, which always brings a new round of discussions as to whether or not they will survive. After each games, Turner has pledged to go on, stating that the games have always had the greater purpose of promoting international goodwill over making a financial profit.

Soviet leader Mikhail Gorbachev presided over the opening ceremonies of the first games in Moscow in 1986, in an environment that was heavy with Cold War tensions. The U.S. Defense Department prohibited 12 athletes, all military personnel, from traveling to Moscow as part of the U.S. team, citing regulations that prohibit "any activity determined to be political in nature or intended to benefit selectively or profit any agency or commercial concern." The Soviet Union played politics by refusing to allow Israel and South Korea to send teams to the games. Even Howard Cosell, the late sports announcer, denounced the games and Ted Turner for meddling in the political affairs of the U.S. and Soviet Union, protesting in the press "I don't want Ted Turner to be my Secretary of State."

Twelve years later, at the 1998 event, Turner was asked to recall some of his favorite memories of prior games. He mentioned the first games' opening ceremonies and the "Soviet Union clearly sending a message to everyone in the United States and the world global television audience, that they wanted peace and they wanted this [the Cold War] to end. And the American team wanted the same thing. When those games were over, the cold war was over. It just took a little while for everyone to realize it."[121]

During the 1986 games, history was made in women's basketball when the U.S. team beat the Soviets ending a streak by the Soviet women's basketball team of 152 straight victories in international competition since 1958. Ben Johnson would defeat Carl Lewis in the 100 meters for his first major international win. The games were the first international event to have competition in motoball, or motorcycle polo.

Perhaps the most moving moment of the games from the standpoint of international relations was when 1986 world figure-skating champion Debi Thomas of the U.S. paired up with skater Vladimir Potin for an ice-dancing routine, the first time two skaters from different countries had performed together in an international competition.

The 10th World Basketball Championships held in Madrid, Spain, were carried on Turner's television station and considered to be the Goodwill Games basketball tournament as well. The United States won their first ever men's world championship, downing the Soviets 87–85 in the final.

Seattle was quietly named the host of the second Goodwill Games for 1990, chosen over 11 other American cities including Atlanta, home of Turner's media empire. Seattle, reticent at first, slowly warmed to the games by renovating Husky Stadium, building a new aquatic center, and lining up corporate and government support.

In 1990, in keeping with the Goodwill Games' theme "Uniting the World's Best," the athletes did not march in the opening ceremonies as separate nations but as one large contingent. Reba McEntire and Seattle-born saxophonist Kenny G added their music to the ceremony.

Cultural exchanges were a large part of the Goodwill experience with some 1,000 Soviet citizens able to visit the U.S. and stay with host families in Seattle. Soviet cosmonauts visited schoolchildren in Seattle. A Goodwill Arts Festival was organized and the Moscow Circus paid a visit.

At the conclusion of the Seattle games, the next edition was awarded to Leningrad, Soviet Union. By 1994, many things had changed. Leningrad had reverted to its former name of St. Petersburg and the Soviet Union was no longer intact.

Some things, however, had not changed. Ice skating was delayed one day because the ice wasn't ready. Swimming was also delayed a day when the pool, nicknamed the "Black Lagoon" by the swimmers, had no chlorine or filtration. The Swedish swimmers pulled out of the swim competition. Ironically, it was a Swedish company that had renovated the pool.

Attendance was not good at the events. It was reported that most of the 70,000 spectators at the opening ceremonies in Kirov Stadium had received free tickets from the organizers.

The city of St. Petersburg was left better off after the games. Some 300 miles of roads were repaved, computer equipment was donated after the event, and 70 new buses used for Goodwill Games transportation were added to the St. Petersburg fleet.

The concept of the Goodwill Games is different from that of many international competitions, focusing on elite performance rather than participation. By limiting the number of athletes invited to participate to what the Goodwill Games committees consider the best eight athletes in the world in each event, the chore of organizing the games becomes simpler. The sport federations choose the best Russian and American athlete and the next six best in the world based on world rankings. There are no heats, only finals.

The Goodwill Games have actually diminished in size over their brief existence. Approximately 3,000 athletes and 79 countries took part in the inaugural event in Moscow. Fifty-four nations and 2,312 athletes competed in Seattle. Fifty-six nations and 2,000 athletes went to St. Petersburg in 1994.

Jackie Joyner Kersee retained her title as the only person to win a heptathlon competition at a Goodwill Games, having won in Moscow, Seattle and St. Petersburg before conquering a strong New York field.

"Goodwill" in New York was not as expansive as it may have been between some of the Iranian exiles and the Iranian wrestling team which showed up to grapple against the USA. Iranian fans wearing T-shirts bearing the image of the leader of the National Council of Resistance in Iran, caused a 20-minute delay when the Iranian team walked out in midmatch demanding that all of the protesters be removed from the arena. Only a few of the most vociferous protesters were escorted from the stands, with officials explaining to the Iranian team that protests of this type are allowed in a free society. After Iranian team captain Mohammad Talaie returned to the ring waving an Iranian flag, the match resumed.

One Cuban, cyclist Ivan Dominguez, was thought to have defected from the games.

While ticket sales were not as brisk as they could have been, the games did not lose as much money as the first editions. Some athletes came out well ahead, with this edition of the Goodwill Games offering substantial prize money to the athletes. Michael Johnson won $40,000 for his 400 meters victory, and an extra $3,000 for having the fastest time in the world. More big money came when Johnson anchored the U.S. team to a world record in the 4 × 400 meters relay to pick up another $5,000 dollars for the win and split $100,000 with his teammates. All told, Johnson made $73,000 for his week's work. Mihaela Melinte picked up a $50,000 dollar bonus for her world record in the hammer throw. South African swimmer Penny Heyns picked up a bonus of $10,000 for setting a world record in the 50 meter breaststroke en route to winning the 100 meter event. Goodwill Games officials noted that the $50,000 dollar bonus was specifically for events on the regular schedule. The 50-meter event was not on the schedule and though officials were not obliged to pay any bonus at all, they gave Heyns $10,000 dollars as a reward for her record.

Seventeen-year-old gymnast Sang Lan of China ended her career after she fell while practicing her vault. The accident left her paralyzed. Her parents were granted emergency visas to be with their daughter who had lived and trained 700 miles from home for six years and had rarely seen her mother and father. Sang was cheered by a visit from film star Leonardo DiCaprio, who visited the fallen gymnast in her hospital room after she voiced her wish to hospital staff to see him. Sang remained in New York for months after the games for rehabilitation.

Moses Kiptanui, Kenya's three-time world champion and former world record-holder, failed to finish the steeplechase when he pulled out of the race with a possible career-threatening achilles injury. He missed a season of running but recovered and returned to competition in 2000.

There was much speculation that the Goodwill Games may be on their last go-around, but Ted Turner and Time Warner have decided to forge ahead with a fifth edition. They have stated that the value of the games and the goodwill they have spread throughout the world, and the fact that they helped bring an end to the Cold War, are reasons enough for them to continue. Brisbane, Australia, was named as the host of the 2001 Goodwill Games. The event was moved to 2001 in order not to conflict with other events such as the World Cup and Winter Olympic Games. Brisbane beat out other cities from around the world including Hong Kong, Shanghai, and Guangzhou, China, Osaka, Japan, Rio de Janeiro, Brazil, and Buenos Aires, Argentina.

In addition to the summer event, a Winter Goodwill Games has been established. The first edition was held in Lake Placid, USA, in 2000.

Year	Host City	Host Nation	Dates	Nations	Athletes	Sports
1986	Moscow	Soviet Union	July 5–20	79	3000	18
1990	Seattle	USA	July 20–August 5	54	2312	21
1994	St. Petersburg	Russia	July 23–August 7	56	2000	24
1998	New York	USA	July 19–August 2	60	1300	15

1986   Moscow   Soviet Union   July 5–20

Nations: (partial list) Algeria, Angola, Argentina, Australia, Botswana, Brazil, Bulgaria, Canada, China, Colombia, Costa Rica, Czechoslovakia, Denmark, East Germany, Ethiopia, Finland, France, Great Britain, Greece, Hungary, Iceland, Israel, Italy, Ivory Coast, Jamaica, Japan, Kenya, Kuwait, Malaysia, Mexico, Mongolia, Netherlands, New Zealand, Nigeria, North Korea, Norway, Panama, Peru, Poland, Portugal, Puerto Rico, Romania, Senegal, South Korea, Soviet Union, Spain, Sweden, Switzerland, Syria, Tanzania, Turkey, United States, Uruguay, Venezuela, West Germany

Sports: Athletics, Basketball, Boxing, Cycling, Diving, Gymnastics, Handball, Judo, Modern Pentathlon, Motoball, Rowing, Swimming, Tennis, Volleyball, Water Polo, Weightlifting, Wrestling, Yachting

Sports for Women: Athletics, Basketball, Cycling, Diving, Gymnastics, Handball, Modern Pentathlon, Rowing, Swimming, Tennis, Volleyball, Yachting

	MEDALS			
Nation	Gold	Silver	Bronze	Total
Soviet Union	118	80	43	241
United States	42	49	51	142
East Germany	7	11	10	28

Nation	Gold	Silver	Bronze	Total
Romania	6	6	6	18
Bulgaria	4	7	20	31
Poland	2	3	6	11
Canada	2	0	2	4
Japan	1	0	3	4
Australia	1	0	2	3
Great Britain	1	0	1	2
Portugal	1	0	1	2
Ethiopia	1	0	0	1
Switzerland	1	0	0	1
Czechoslovakia	0	9	1	10
China	0	4	5	9
France	0	2	2	4
Mongolia	0	1	5	6
Hungary	0	1	5	6
Venezuela	0	1	2	3
West Germany	0	1	1	2
Turkey	0	1	1	2
Finland	0	1	0	1
Nigeria	0	1	0	1
North Korea	0	0	6	6
Italy	0	0	5	5
Brazil	0	0	2	2
Norway	0	0	1	1
Colombia	0	0	1	1
Ivory Coast	0	0	1	1
Kenya	0	0	1	1
Kuwait	0	0	1	1
Netherlands	0	0	1	1
Peru	0	0	0	0

1990   Seattle   USA   July 20–August 5

Nations: Australia, Bahamas, Brazil, Bulgaria, Canada, China, Cuba, Colombia, Czechoslovakia, Denmark, Djibouti, East Germany, Egypt, Ethiopia, France, Great Britain, Hungary, Iceland, Ireland, Italy, Ivory Coast, Jamaica, Japan, Kenya, Korea, Mexico, Mongolia, Morocco, Netherlands, New Zealand, Niger, Nigeria, Norway, Oman, Peru, Poland, Puerto Rico, Portugal, Romania, Somalia, South Korea, Soviet Union, Spain, Suriname, Sweden, Switzerland, Taiwan, Tanzania, Turkey, United States, Venezuela, Virgin Islands, West Germany, Yugoslavia

Sports: Athletics, Baseball, Basketball, Boxing, Cycling, Diving, Figure Skating, Gymnastics, Handball, Ice Hockey, Judo, Modern Pentathlon, Rowing, Rhythmic Gymnastics, Swimming, Synchronized Swimming, Volleyball, Water Polo, Weightlifting, Wrestling (men did not compete in Rhythmic Gymnastics or Synchronized Swimming)

Sports for Women: Athletics, Basketball, Cycling, Diving, Figure Skating, Gymnastics, Judo, Modern Pentathlon, Rowing, Rhythmic Gymnastics, Swimming, Synchronized Swimming, Volleyball

Venues: Husky Stadium (Opening Ceremonies, Athletics), Cheney Stadium (Baseball), Seattle Coliseum (Basketball), Seattle Center Arena (Boxing), Marymoor Park

Velodrome (Cycling), Tacoma Dome (Figure Skating, Gymnastics, Ice Hockey), Seattle University (Judo), King County Fairgrounds, (Modern Pentathlon), Montlake Cut (Rowing), Spokane (Rhythmic Gymnastics), King County Aquatics Center (Swimming, Diving, Synchronized Swimming, Water Polo), University of Washington, Edmundson Pavilion (Volleyball—Men), Spokane (Volleyball—Women, Weightlifting, Wrestling)

MEDALS

Nation	Gold	Silver	Bronze	Total
Soviet Union	66	68	54	188
United States	60	53	48	161
East Germany	11	8	24	43
Bulgaria	8	7	9	24
China	6	7	3	16
Cuba	6	4	3	13
West Germany	4	3	8	15
Canada	4	1	6	11
Poland	4	1	0	5
South Korea	3	2	2	7
Spain	3	2	2	7
Romania	2	4	2	8
Japan	2	3	10	15
Italy	2	2	1	5
Yugoslavia	2	1	0	3
Netherlands	1	1	5	7
Hungary	1	1	5	7
Jamaica	1	1	2	4
Denmark	1	1	1	3
Mongolia	1	1	0	2
Surinam	1	0	0	1
Morocco	1	0	0	1
Mexico	1	0	0	1
Czechoslovakia	1	0	0	1
Australia	0	4	3	7
Great Britain	0	2	2	4
Turkey	0	2	1	3
Ethiopia	0	2	0	2
New Zealand	0	2	0	2
Brazil	0	1	6	7
Kenya	0	1	1	2
Bahamas	0	1	0	1
Virgin Islands	0	0	1	1
France	0	0	1	1
Ireland	0	0	1	1
Sweden	0	0	1	1

1994   St. Petersburg   Russia   July 23–August 7

Nations: Algeria, Armenia, Australia, Austria, Belarus, Belgium, Brazil, Bulgaria, Canada, China, Costa Rica, Cuba, Denmark, Egypt, Estonia, Finland, France, Georgia, Germany, Great Britain, Hungary, Iran, Ireland, Italy, Jamaica, Japan, Kazakhstan, Kenya, Latvia, Mexico, Moldova, Morocco, Mozambique, Namibia, Netherlands, New

Zealand, Nigeria, Norway, Poland, Portugal, Puerto Rico, Romania, Russia, Slovakia, Slovenia, Somalia, South Korea, Spain, Sweden, Syria, Turkey, Ukraine, United States, Uzbekistan, Virgin Islands, Zambia

Sports: Archery, Athletics, Basketball, Beach Volleyball, Boxing, Canoeing, Cycling, Diving, Figure Skating, Football, Gymnastics, Handball, Kayaking, Rowing, Short-Track Speed Skating, Swimming, Synchronized Swimming, Tae Kwon Do, Triathlon, Volleyball, Water Polo, Wrestling (3 more)

MEDALS

Nation	Gold	Silver	Bronze	Total
Russia	68	50	53	171
United States	37	39	43	119
China	12	9	6	27
South Korea	10	5	0	15
Cuba	9	9	6	24
Ukraine	8	5	12	25
Norway	4	0	0	4
Belarus	3	6	14	23
Great Britain	3	5	3	11
Canada	3	4	5	12
France	3	3	6	12
Germany	2	7	13	22
Italy	2	1	4	7
Spain	2	1	4	7
Kenya	2	1	3	6
Poland	1	3	2	6
Romania	1	3	0	4
Japan	1	2	4	7
Turkey	1	2	3	6
Sweden	1	2	2	5
Denmark	1	1	1	3
Costa Rica	1	1	0	2
Ireland	1	1	0	2
Belgium	1	0	4	5
Puerto Rico	1	0	1	2
Georgia	1	0	0	1
Virgin Islands	1	0	0	1
Slovenia	1	0	0	1
New Zealand	1	0	0	1
Mozambique	1	0	0	1
Mexico	1	0	0	1
Algeria	1	0	0	1
Morocco	1	0	0	1
Armenia	0	3	0	3
Nigeria	0	2	0	2
Latvia	0	2	0	2
Australia	0	1	3	4
Finland	0	1	2	3
Zambia	0	1	0	1
Somalia	0	1	0	1
Portugal	0	1	0	1

Nation	Gold	Silver	Bronze	Total
Namibia	0	1	0	1
Iran	0	1	0	1
Estonia	0	1	0	1
Brazil	0	1	0	1
Austria	0	1	0	1
Uzbekistan	0	0	4	4
Netherlands	0	0	2	2
Jamaica	0	0	2	2
Moldova	0	0	2	2
Hungary	0	0	2	2
Slovakia	0	0	2	2
Bulgaria	0	0	2	2
Syria	0	0	1	1
Egypt	0	0	1	1
Kazakhstan	0	0	1	1

1998   New York   USA   July 19–August 2

Nations: (partial list) Algeria, Argentina, Armenia, Australia, Bahamas, Belarus, Brazil, Bulgaria, Canada, China, Cuba, Czech Republic, Ecuador, France, Germany, Great Britain, Greece, Hungary, Iceland, Iran, Italy, Jamaica, Japan, Kazakhstan, Kenya, Lithuania, Mexico, Morocco, Mozambique, Nigeria, Norway, Poland, Romania, Russia, Trinidad and Tobago, Turkey, Ukraine, United States, Uzbekistan, World All Stars

Sports: Athletics, Basketball, Beach Volleyball, Boxing, Cycling, Diving, Figure Skating, Gymnastics, Rhythmic Gymnastics, Soccer, Swimming, Synchronized Swimming, Triathlon, Water Polo, Wrestling

Venues: World Financial Center, Battery Park (Opening Ceremonies, Closing Ceremonies), Nassau County Mitchell Athletic Complex (Athletics, Soccer), Madison Square Garden (Basketball), The Theater at Madison Square Garden (Boxing, Wrestling), Wagner College Stadium (Cycling), Nassau County Goodwill Games Swimming and Diving Center (Swimming, Diving, Synchronized Swimming, Water Polo), Nassau Veterans Memorial Coliseum (Figure Skating, Gymnastics, Rhythmic Gymnastics), New York City (Triathlon), Wollman Rink in Central Park (Beach Volleyball)

MEDALS				
Nation	Gold	Silver	Bronze	Total
United States	41	49	42	132
Russia	35	29	30	94
Cuba	8	5	4	17
China	7	7	6	20
Kenya	5	4	4	13
Germany	3	3	10	16
Australia	2	6	2	10
Belarus	2	5	2	9
Jamaica	2	2	5	9
Iran	2	1	1	4
Brazil	2	0	1	3
Kazakhstan	2	0	1	3
Great Britain	2	0	0	2

Nation	Gold	Silver	Bronze	Total
Ukraine	1	6	3	10
Romania	1	3	5	9
Trinidad and Tobago	1	1	0	2
Czech Republic	1	0	1	2
Italy	1	0	1	2
Uzbekistan	1	0	1	2
Nigeria	1	0	0	1
Algeria	1	0	0	1
Mozambique	1	0	0	1
Bulgaria	0	2	2	4
France	0	2	1	3
Mexico	0	2	0	2
Turkey	0	1	5	6
Morocco	0	1	1	2
Poland	0	1	1	2
Argentina	0	1	1	2
Bahamas	0	1	0	1
Canada	0	1	0	1
World All Stars	0	1	0	1
Japan	0	0	2	2
Ecuador	0	0	1	1
Greece	0	0	1	1
Hungary	0	0	1	1
Iceland	0	0	1	1
Lithuania	0	0	1	1
Armenia	0	0	1	1
Norway	0	0	1	1

Gorge Games

The Gorge Games were conceived and founded by Peggy Lalor, an outdoor adventure sports enthusiast, in the fall of 1995 to celebrate the outdoor recreational environment of the Columbia River in the state of Oregon. They began in 1996.

Climbing, kayaking, kite sports, mountain biking, off-road triathlon, outrigger canoe, 49 sailing, trail running and windsurfing are the types of events usually included in the games.

The Gorge Games quickly grew from a small privately organized event in 1996 to an event with corporate sponsorship and national and international television exposure. The 1999 games, though, were canceled at the last minute due to difficulties with gaining adequate sponsorship.

The first three games had minimal international participation, with the occasional competitor from Canada and Japan.

The organizers intend to hold the games on an annual basis as long as the sponsors and the community support them.

Year	Host City	Host Nation	Dates
1996	Hood River	USA	July
1997	Hood River	USA	July 11–19

Year	Host City	Host Nation	Dates
1998	Hood River	USA	July 11–18
2000	Hood River	USA	July 8–15

Gravity Games

The Gravity Games, U.S. television network NBC's response to ESPN's X Games, were first held in the summer of 1999 in Providence, Rhode Island.

The second edition of the games was also held in Providence in July 2000, but was not televised until October and November of that year.

The games feature the standard extreme sports such as aggressive in-line, bike (dirt, street, vert), motocross, skateboarding (downhill, street, vert), street luge and wakeboarding.

Year	Host City	Host Nation	Dates	Nations	Athletes	Sports
1999	Providence	USA	Sept. 5–12	NA	NA	6
2000	Providence	USA	July 15–23	14	250	8

1999   Providence   USA   September 5–12

Sports: Aggressive In-line, Bike (Dirt, Street, Vert), Motocross, Skateboarding (Downhill, Street, Vert), Street Luge and Wakeboarding.

2000   Providence   USA   July 15–23

Sports: Bike (Dirt, Street, Vert), Aggressive In-line (Street, Vert), Freestyle Motocross, Skateboarding (Street, Vert)

Hapoel Games

The Hapoel Sports Association (Hapoel meaning "the worker" in Hebrew) is the worker's sport organization of Israel. The organization is affiliated with the Histadrut, or the General Federation of Labor in Israel, and the CSIT (Confédération Sportive Internationale du Travail), the International Workers Sport Federation.

Mass sport is one of the main goals of the Hapoel organization, and Hapoel sponsors many mass marches, swims and hikes throughout Israel on an annual basis, as well as tournaments in over 30 sports. The Hapoel Games have been held from 1928, with the last edition in 1995. The games have had a lack of support in recent years and the 1999 edition was not staged.

Athletes from around the world without restriction were invited to compete in the Hapoel games, though the first four editions of the games in 1928, 1930, 1932 and 1935 were national in scope. Over the years, more than 70 nations have sent delegations. The main events generally center around Tel Aviv's Ramat Gan stadium, but events are spread out across the nation.

The 1975 games were a chance for the Germans to show their support for the sport movement in Israel, after the tragic events of the 1972 Munich Olympic Games. Eighty

West German athletes were accompanied to Israel by West German Olympic Committee president Willi Daume and five members of the German Bundestag.

The Israeli government has shown its support for the games. Presidents and prime ministers have been usual guests of honor at the opening and closing ceremonies.

Apartheid in South Africa was an issue in the games. In 1979, Uri Zimri, the head of Hapoel international relations, said "Hapoel has never invited South Africa to the Hapoel Games," although newspaper reports in 1961 did list South Africa as a participant for that year. In 1987, games organizers reaffirmed their stand by not inviting South Africa.[122]

While the games encourage mass sport, over the years many elite athletes have participated in the games including athletics stars Kip Keino of Kenya, Miruts Yifter of Ethiopia and John Aki-Bua of Uganda, American pole vaulter Don Bragg, former 100 meters world record-holder Charles Greene, Romanian women's high jump Olympic Champion Iolanda Balas, and Italian 200 meter world record-holder Pietro Mennea.

The Hapoel organization has evolved in its attitudes towards mass sport. The motto of the organization has been changed from "Thousands and Champions" to "Champions and Thousands." Ukrainian pole vault world champion Sergei Bubka was invited to the 1995 games and paid $75,000 for his participation. This was seemingly in opposition to the role of the Hapoel, which is to promote the worker and not the elite.

Year	Host City	Host Nation	Dates	Nations	Athletes	Sports
1928	Tel Aviv	Israel	Sept. 29–30	1	780	NA
1930	Tel Aviv	Israel	October 10–12	1	1200	NA
1932	Tel Aviv	Israel	October 21–25	1	2500	NA
1935	Tel Aviv	Israel	April 18–21	1	10000	2
1952	Tel Aviv	Israel	April 14–18	NA	NA	NA
1956	Tel Aviv	Israel	May 10–17	5	NA	NA
1961	Tel Aviv	Israel	May 1–6	33	NA	15
1966	Tel Aviv	Israel	May 1–7	25	1500	13
1971	Tel Aviv	Israel	April 29–May 5	25	1500	NA
1975	Tel Aviv	Israel	May 1–9	21	1700	18
1979	Tel Aviv	Israel	May 1–8	NA	NA	NA
1983	Tel Aviv	Israel	May 1–7	NA	6700	NA
1987	Tel Aviv	Israel	May 4–11	NA	NA	NA
1991	Tel Aviv	Israel	May 6–13	36	6700	NA
1995	Tel Aviv	Israel	June 11–15	NA	NA	22

1956   Tel Aviv   Israel   May 10–17

Nations: Israel, Austria, Belgium, Britain, Switzerland

1961   Tel Aviv   Israel   May 1–6

Nations: Austria, Belgium, Burma, Congo-Brazzaville, Cyprus, Denmark, Ethiopia, Finland, France, Ghana, Great Britain, Holland, Italy, Ivory Coast, Japan, Kenya, Israel, Liberia, Malagasy, Nepal, Nigeria, Norway, Philippines, Portugal, Senegal, South Africa, Sweden, Switzerland, Togo, Turkey, Uganda, United States, Yugoslavia

Sports: Athletics, Basketball, Boxing, Cycling, Football, Gymnastics, Handball, Shooting, Swimming, Table Tennis, Tennis, Volleyball, Weightlifting, Wrestling, Yachting

MEDALS

Nation	Gold	Silver	Bronze	Total
Israel	35	49	35	119
Great Britain	14	7	7	28
Yugoslavia	13	2	2	17
Sweden	9	5	2	16
Finland	7	4	4	15
United States	6	1	0	7
Switzerland	4	4	4	12
France	4	4	2	10
Nigeria	3	2	1	6
Ghana	2	1	1	4
Austria	2	12	14	28
Belgium	2	4	4	10
Turkey	2	1	4	7
Uganda	2	0	0	2
Burma	2	3	0	5
Japan	1	4	0	5
Denmark	1	2	0	3
Senegal	1	1	1	3
Ivory Coast	1	1	0	2
Kenya	1	1	0	2
Norway	1	1	0	2
Ethiopia	0	0	1	1
Malagasy Republic	0	1	0	1
Holland	0	0	5	5
Philippines	0	0	1	1

1966   Tel Aviv   Israel   May 1–7

Nations: Austria, Belgium, Chad, Congo-Brazzaville, Czechoslovakia, Ghana, Great Britain, Holland, Hungary, Israel, Ivory Coast, Malagasy Republic, Nigeria, Poland, Romania, Senegal, Soviet Union, Sweden, Switzerland, United States, Yugoslavia (four more)

Sports: Athletics, Basketball, Cycling, Gymnastics, Handball, Sailing, Shooting, Swimming, Table Tennis, Tennis, Water Polo, Weightlifting, Volleyball (and Folklore contests)

Venues: Ramat Gan Stadium (Athletics), Galit Pool (Swimming), Yad Eliyahu (Basketball), Haifa, Beersheba, Kfar Saba (Volleyball), Givatayim, Herzliya (Handball), Hebrew University in Jerusalem (Gymnastics), Mitchell Hall in Jerusalem (Wrestling), Beit Hapoel, Petah Tikva (Table Tennis), Hapoel Courts, North Tel Aviv (Tennis), Ramat Gan Range (Shooting), Rokach Road, Tel Aviv (Cycling)

1971   Tel Aviv   Israel   April 29–May 5

Nations: Austria, Denmark, Kenya, Israel, Ethiopia, Sweden, Great Britain, Holland, United States, Uganda, Ivory Coast, West Germany, Korea, Yugoslavia, Singapore, Italy, Belgium (eight more)

Sports: Athletics, Basketball, Chess, Cycling, Fencing, Football, Handball, Shooting, Swimming, Table Tennis, Tennis, Volleyball, Water Polo, Weightlifting, Yachting

1995   Tel Aviv   Israel   June 11–15

Sports: Archery, Athletics, Badminton, Basketball, Canoeing, Chess, Fencing, Football, Gymnastics, Handball, Judo, Karate, Shooting, Swimming, Synchronized Swimming, Table Tennis, Tennis, Triathlon, Weightlifting, Wrestling, Yachting, Water Polo

Honda Masters Games

The Honda Masters Games, begun in 1986, were the first ever multisport masters competition held in Australia and the second in the world after the World Masters Games. The games, with age groups from 30 and over, are open to international participation but are largely regional. They are a biennial event held in Alice Springs. The first games had about 1000 participants; the current editions draw between 4000 and 5000.

Australian sports heroines Dawn Fraser and Evonne Goolagong-Cawley were present at the 2000 games' opening ceremony. Fraser competed in every games from 1986 to 1998 in swimming.

Alice Springs Mayor Fran Erlich joined in the 2000 games, winning a silver in the 50 meter freestyle, one place ahead of her sister and main rival Marie.

The 2000 games saw the first disabled competitors in lawn bowls, who competed against able-bodied players.

The spirit of the games, especially among the older competitors, is plainly evident. Margaret Russell, 86, of North Queensland, also known as "Super Gran," took up the hammer throw and won gold with a new games record of 8.24 m. Margaret had been throwing the hammer for four months. "Basically I don't mind having a go at anything that is on offer," she said. "I'm still learning in a lot of events but I am improving all the time. Back when I was growing up my parents were all work, work, work and there wasn't much time for sport."

Eighty-three-year-old Lionel Merrett, also a hammer thrower, won gold in his division and said, "I am only new to all of this and will get better as we go."

Year	Host City	Host Nation	Dates	Nations	Athletes	Sports
1986	Alice Springs	Australia	NA	NA	1000	21
1988	Alice Springs	Australia	N A	NA	NA	NA
1990	Alice Springs	Australia	NA	NA	NA	NA
1992	Alice Springs	Australia	Oct. 17–25	NA	NA	NA
1994	Alice Springs	Australia	NA	NA	NA	NA
1996	Alice Springs	Australia	Oct. 19–27	NA	NA	29
1998	Alice Springs	Australia	Oct. 17–24	NA	NA	26
2000	Alice Springs	Australia	Oct. 21–28	NA	NA	26

1998   Alice Springs   Australia   October 17–24

Sports: Athletics, Badminton, Baseball, Basketball, Cricket, Cycling, Darts, Eightball, Equestrian, Gliding, Golf, Hockey, Lawn Bowls, Motorcycling, Netball, Rugby

Union, Shooting, Softball, Squash, Swimming, Table Tennis, Tennis, Tenpin Bowling, Touch, Triathlon/Duathlon, Volleyball

2000   Alice Springs   Australia   October 21–28

Sports: Athletics (Road and Cross Country, Track and Field), Badminton, Baseball, Basketball, Cricket, Cycling, Darts, Eightball, Equestrian (includes Polocrosse), Gliding, Golf, Hockey, Lawn Bowls, Motorcycling, Netball, Rugby Union, Shooting (Clay Target, Full Bore, Pistol, Sporting), Softball, Squash, Swimming, Table Tennis, Tennis, Ten-pin Bowling, Touch, Triathlon/Duathlon, Volleyball

Huntsman World Senior Games

The Huntsman World Senior Games, named after their principal sponsor, Jon Huntsman, occur annually in St. George, Utah. Athletes 50 years of age and over are eligible to compete in five-year age divisions, up to 85-plus years of age.

The first games, founded in 1987 by John H. Morgan, were called the World Senior Olympics. The name was changed due to pressure from the U.S. and International Olympic committees, which reserve the use of the word Olympic to describe their sports events.

Five hundred athletes participated in the first games. In 1996, 3,600 athletes from 15 nations gathered. Celebrity guests in 1996 included former major-league baseball player Harmon Killebrew and American track stars Al Joyner, Florence Griffith-Joyner, Jackie Joyner-Kersee and her coach-husband, Bob Kersee. Jackie Joyner-Kersee was the games' final torchbearer for the opening ceremony.

The competitions are divided into two weeks scheduled annually in the middle of October. Each week has its own opening ceremony and opening dinner. The athletes and visitors are responsible for their own housing arrangements in local hotels.

Along with sporting events, games festivities include dinners, social events, guest speakers, free health screening, and optional tours to the Grand Canyon and to Bryce Canyon and Zion National Parks. Over 2,000 volunteers from the city of St. George work each year to make the games a success.

Year	Host City	Host Nation	Dates	Nations	Athletes	Sports
1987	St. George	USA	October 10–23	NA	500	NA
1988	St. George	USA	October 8–21*	NA	NA	NA
1989	St. George	USA	October 14–27*	NA	NA	NA
1990	St. George	USA	October 13–26*	4	1000	NA
1991	St. George	USA	October 14–25	NA	1500	NA
1992	St. George	USA	October 13–24	NA	2500	NA
1993	St. George	USA	October 11–22	NA	NA	NA
1994	St. George	USA	October 10–23	10	3000	NA
1995	St. George	USA	October 17–29	NA	NA	15
1996	St. George	USA	October 12–25	15	3600	16
1997	St. George	USA	October 13–24	15	4000	17
1998	St. George	USA	October 12–24	29	4500	17
1999	St. George	USA	October 11–22	13	NA	18
2000	St. George	USA	October 9–21	12	NA	NA

*estimated dates from newspaper references

*1990   St. George   USA   October 13–26**

Nations: USA, Canada, Mexico, Germany

1995   St. George   USA   October 17–29

Sports: Basketball Free Throw/3 Point, Basketball, Bowling, Cycling, Duathlon, Golf, Horseshoes, Racquetball, Road Race, Soccer, Softball, Swimming, Table Tennis, Tennis, Track and Field, Volleyball

1996   St. George   USA   October 12–25

Nations: Australia, Azerbaijan, Bermuda, Brazil, Canada, England, Germany, Ireland, Japan, Latvia, Mexico, Philippines, Russia, Spain, United States
Sports: Basketball Free Throw/3 Point, Basketball, Bowling, Cycling, Golf, Horseshoes, Racquetball, Road Race, Soccer, Softball, Swimming, Table Tennis, Tennis, Track and Field, Triathlon, Volleyball

1997   St. George   USA   October 13–24

Nations: Belarus, Bermuda, Brazil, Bulgaria, Canada, Germany, Ireland, Japan, Latvia, Russia, Scotland, Switzerland, Ukraine, United States (one more)
Sports: Basketball Free Throw/3 Point, Basketball (5-on-5, 3-on-3), Bowling, Bridge, Cycling, Golf, Horseshoes, Mountain Biking, Racquetball, Road Race, Soccer, Softball, Swimming, Table Tennis, Tennis, Track and Field, Volleyball

1998   St. George   USA   October 12–24

Nations: Armenia, Australia, Bermuda, Brazil, Canada, Germany, Great Britain, Isle of Man, Ireland, Kenya, Mexico, New Zealand, Norway, Philippines, Russia, Spain, Ukraine, United States, Venezuela (10 more)
Sports: Athletics, Basketball, Bowling, Bridge, Tennis, Cycling, Golf, Horseshoes, Mountain Biking, Racquetball, Road Racing, Softball, Swimming, Table Tennis, Basketball Free Throw and 3–Point Shooting, Triathlon, Volleyball (also Social Tennis, Social Golf)
Venues: Dane Hansen Stadium (Opening Ceremonies), Snow Canyon Softball Complex (Softball), Sand Hollow Aquatic Center, Bluff Creek Park (Cycling—Criterium)

1999   St. George   USA   October 11–22

Nations: Brazil, Canada, England, Germany, Ireland, Japan, Latvia, Malaysia, Mexico, Norway, Russia, Spain, United States
Sports: Athletics, Bridge, Basketball, Basketball Free Throw and 3–Point Shooting, Bowling, Cycling, Golf, Horseshoes, Mountain Biking, Racquetball, Road Racing, Softball, Square Dancing, Swimming, Table Tennis, Tennis, Triathlon, Volleyball

2000   St. George   USA   October 9–21

Nations: Bermuda, Brazil, Bulgaria, Canada, France, Germany, Malaysia, Mexico, Russia, Slovakia, Ukraine, United States

Sports: Athletics, Basketball, Bowling, Bridge, Cycling, Golf, Horseshoes, Lawn Bowling, Mountain Biking, Racquetball, Road Races, Softball, Square Dancing, Swimming, Table Tennis, Tennis, Triathlon, Volleyball

IBSA World Championships for the Blind

IBSA (International Blind Sports Association) World Championships for the Blind in Madrid in 1998 were the first ever interdisciplinary games sponsored by IBSA. The Spanish Federation for Blind Sports hosted the games with 750 blind athletes competing in athletics, swimming, goalball and judo. Prince Felipe de Borbon de Asturias was the guest of honor at the opening ceremony in Madrid's Rayo Vallecano Stadium; IOC President Samaranch also attended.

The sports are adapted slightly for blind participants. Goalball is a form of indoor soccer in which bells are placed inside a ball to provide aural cues for the players. Swimmers are assisted by coaches who tap on their heads or shoulders to signal a turn, or to prevent an injury at the finish. Runners are paired with a guide and are given signals by the tapping of elbows or by pulling on a short tether attached to an arm. Field event athletes, such as long jumpers and triple jumpers, are assisted with verbal instructions.

Year	Host City	Host Nation	Dates	Nations	Athletes	Sports
1998	Madrid	Spain	July 17–26	72	750	4

1998   Madrid   Spain   July 17–26

Nations: Algeria, Australia, Austria, Belarus, Belgium, Brazil, Canada, China, Croatia, Cuba, Denmark, Dominican Republic, Estonia, Finland, France, Germany, Great Britain, Ireland, Israel, Italy, Japan, Kenya, Lithuania, Mexico, New Zealand, Norway, Panama, Poland, Portugal, Russia, Slovakia, South Africa, Spain, Sweden, Taiwan, Thailand, Tunisia, Ukraine, United States (33 more)

Sports: Athletics, Goalball, Judo, Swimming

Venues: Instalaciones del Consejo Superior de Deportes (Athletics, Goalball, Judo), Centro Natación "M-86" (swimming)

MEDALS

Nation	Gold	Silver	Bronze	Total
Spain	29	30	22	81
Canada	12	6	6	24
Great Britain	10	10	9	29
Germany	9	7	5	21
Cuba	8	3	2	13
Australia	6	7	5	18
China	6	1	5	12
United States	5	8	15	28
Portugal	5	2	5	12
Belarus	5	9	3	17
Ukraine	4	2	9	15
Mexico	4	0	1	5

Nation	Gold	Silver	Bronze	Total
Tunisia	4	0	0	4
Russia	4	6	8	18
Italy	3	3	4	10
Norway	2	0	3	5
Poland	2	6	6	14
Japan	2	4	3	9
Denmark	2	2	2	6
Austria	1	2	0	3
Finland	1	2	0	3
Estonia	1	1	2	4
Israel	1	1	1	3
Ireland	1	1	0	2
Panama	1	1	0	2
Slovakia	1	0	0	1
Lithuania	1	2	6	9
France	1	5	5	11
Algeria	0	3	2	5
Brazil	0	0	1	1
Taiwan	0	0	2	2
Belgium	0	0	4	4
Sweden	0	1	0	1
Kenya	0	1	0	1
Dominican Republic	0	1	1	2
South Africa	0	1	2	3
New Zealand	0	2	1	3
Croatia	0	0	1	1
Thailand	0	2	1	3

Indian Ocean Island Games

In July 1974, the National Olympic Committees of Réunion, Mauritius, Seychelles and Sri Lanka met to discuss plans for the formation of a regional competition for the island nations of the Indian Ocean.

The original games in 1979 were awarded to Réunion as the initiator of the games. The games are intended to be held every four years, but have been held irregularly since the first event.

The games returned to their birthplace, Réunion, in 1998 and were opened by Jean Daubigny, the Prefect of Réunion, and Ram Ruhee, the IOC member from Mauritius.

Year	Host City	Host Nation	Dates	Nations	Athletes	Sports
1979	St. Denis	Réunion	August 25–Sept. 2	5	680	13
1985	Port Louis	Mauritius	August 24–Sept. 1	5	NA	13
1990	Antananarivo	Madagascar	August 24–Sept. 2	NA	NA	NA
1993	Victoria	Seychelles		7	1200	13
1998	St. Denis	Réunion		6	NA	NA

1979   St. Denis   Réunion   August 25–September 2

Nations: Maldives, Comoros Islands, Seychelles, Reunion, Mauritius

Sports: Athletics, Badminton, Basketball, Boxing, Cycling, Football, Rugby, Sailing, Swimming, Tennis, Table Tennis, Volleyball, Weightlifting

1985   Port Louis   Mauritius   August 24–September 1

Nations: Maldives, Comoros Islands, Seychelles, Reunion, Mauritius

1993   Victoria   Seychelles

Nations: Madagascar, Maldives, Comoros Islands, Seychelles, Reunion, Mauritius, Sri Lanka
Sports: Athletics, Badminton, Basketball, Boxing, Cycling, Football, Judo, Swimming, Tennis, Table Tennis, Volleyball, Weightlifting, Yachting

Inter-Allied Games

"Were you a soldier in the great war?" Men who answered yes to this question were eligible to participate in the Inter-Allied Games held in Paris from June 22 to July 6, 1919.[123]

On January 9, 1919, less than two months after the end of World War I, General John Pershing sent letters of invitation to 29 of the allied nations and territories inviting them to compete in the Inter-Allied Games later that year. Eighteen nations eventually accepted the invitation. The games were held with the assistance of the YMCA (Young Men's Christian Association) and its energetic representative Elwood Brown.[124]

A vast amount of work had to be done to prepare for the games in a very short time. Colombes Stadium was considered for the main games venue, the same stadium used for the 1900 Olympic Games in Paris. However, the American organizers felt that it wouldn't be fair to the competitors of other nations to have the competitions in a facility that the Americans had just finished using for their AEF (American Expeditionary Forces) finals, and it was decided to construct a stadium that would be a neutral venue for all.

The area chosen, near the Bois de Vincennes just outside Paris, had most recently been used for training soldiers. One of the first tasks was to fill in the trenches and remove the barbed wire to prepare for construction.

The YMCA was to pay for the construction of the stadium. The Parisian contracting firm of Buisson and Giffard designed the facility, a private contractor was to construct the concrete stadium, and French military engineers were to finish the track and field. The stadium designs were approved on February 24 and construction began on April 11. On May 1, French workers went on strike. American soldiers were brought in to complete the stadium. Working three eight-hour shifts per day, 3,300 soldiers were put to work mixing and pouring cement for the stadium that would encircle a 500-meter track, and seat 25,000 spectators. The French engineers completed the track surface, rolling and watering layers of cinders, and finished their task two weeks before the games.

Repairs to existing roads from Paris to the stadium were completed and new access roads around the stadium were built. A large parking facility was created to handle the spectators' vehicles.

A commission was set up to determine the sports to be included in the games. Some suggested events that would be related to the activities of war, such as a bayonet competition and hand-grenade throwing. The bayonet competition, it was decided, would be a difficult event to judge, and it was discarded, as were events in diving and walking and for the very same reason. The hand-grenade throw was the only military type of event included on the program.

The decorations committee made plans to have the flags of all the participating nations liberally placed around the stadium. Some nations' flags were readily available and could be purchased in Paris. Other nations' flags were in short supply or, in the cases of Czecho-Slovakia and Hedjaz, two hardly recognized nations, their flag designs were not even known. Once the designs were discovered, 16 French seamstresses were put to the task of sewing new flags for a number of weeks before the games.

The games organizers were far ahead of their time in a number of areas. A sophisticated motor pool was set up which very satisfactorily handled the transportation needs of the competitors, officials, and spectators throughout the games.

The publicity department of the games was well organized into four sections: press, printing and advertising, information service, and historical. The press section composed articles and press releases prior to the games and made them available to the press of all of the Allied countries involved. News was also transmitted via radio through this department. Behind the stadium, telegraphs, telephones, typewriters and motorcycle couriers were available for the general press throughout the games.

The printing and advertising section published over 100,000 posters and post cards, and all of the tickets for the games, as well as rule books and maps for spectators. A daily program was prepared for each day of the games which listed the contestants for the day's events as well as the results from the previous day. The department would begin after the day's events were over and, working through the night, would produce 20,000 copies of the programs by the next morning.

The information service section staffed 41 information booths throughout Paris for the duration of the games. Seventy-five noncommissioned French Army officers who spoke English were assigned to this task, after a ten-day training program just prior to the games.

The historical section compiled the final report of the games and published the extensive history book. The history book was so extensive, in fact, that today we probably know as much about these games as any other of the era.

On the field, as expected, the American soldiers ran away with the majority of events. Charlie Paddock, who was to win the Olympic Games 100 meters the following year, won the 100 and 200 meters at the Inter-Allied games, equaling the 200 meter world record of 21⅗ seconds in the process.

Year	Host City	Host Nation	Dates	Nations	Athletes	Sports
1919	Paris	France	June 22–July 6	18	1500	19

Nations: Australia, Belgium, Czecho-Slovakia, Serbia, Hedjaz, United States, France, Italy, Canada, Great Britain, New Zealand, Portugal, Romania, Greece (possibly Brazil and three more)

Sports: American Football, Athletics, Baseball, Basketball, Boxing, Cross Country, Equestrian, Fencing, Golf, Hand-Grenade Throwing, Rowing, Rugby, Shooting, Soccer, Swimming, Tennis, Tug of War, Water Polo, Wrestling

Venues: Pershing Stadium, Mare de St. James (swimming), Racing Club and Stade Français (Tennis), Colombes Stadium (Rugby), La Boulie Golf Links (Golf)

International Electrical Engineering Students Sports Games

In the summer of 1996, a small group of electrical engineering students from Croatia, Slovakia and Slovenia gathered in Zagreb, Croatia, for the International Electrical Engineering Students Sports Games.

There is no evidence that the games have been organized a second time.

Year	Host City	Host Nation	Dates	Nations	Athletes	Sports
1996	Zagreb	Croatia	July 16–18	3	100	4

Nations: Croatia, Slovakia, Slovenia
Sports: Basketball, Cross Country, Football, Volleyball

International Firefighters Winter Games

The annual International Firefighters Winter Games are advertised as a week of skiing and snowboard racing, and fun and camaraderie with firefighters from all over the world. Fundraising events at the games go to support charitable organizations.

Year	Host City	Host Nation	Dates	Nations	Athletes	Sports
1987	North Lake Tahoe**	USA	March 1–5*	NA	NA	NA
1988	North Lake Tahoe**	USA	March 6–10*	NA	NA	NA
1989	North Lake Tahoe**	USA	March 5–9*	NA	NA	NA
1990	North Lake Tahoe**	USA	March 4–8*	NA	NA	NA
1991	North Lake Tahoe**	USA	March 3–7*	NA	NA	NA
1992	North Lake Tahoe**	USA	March 1–5*	NA	NA	NA
1993	North Lake Tahoe**	USA	March 7–11*	NA	NA	NA
1994	North Lake Tahoe**	USA	March 6–10*	NA	NA	NA
1995	North Lake Tahoe**	USA	March 5–9*	NA	NA	NA
1996	North Lake Tahoe**	USA	March 3–7*	NA	NA	NA
1997	South Lake Tahoe	USA	March 2–6*	NA	NA	NA
1998	South Lake Tahoe	USA	March 1–5	NA	NA	2
1999	North Lake Tahoe	USA	Feb. 28–March 4	NA	NA	2
2000	North Lake Tahoe	USA	Feb. 27–March 2	NA	NA	2

*No specific dates given by the organizers.

**Organizers' information indicates that the games have been at several different ski resorts in North Lake Tahoe and twice in the South Lake Tahoe area.

1998   South Lake Tahoe   USA   March 1–5

Sports: Skiing, Snowboarding

> *1999   North Lake Tahoe   USA   February 28–March 4*

Sports: Skiing, Snowboarding

> *2000   North Lake Tahoe   USA   February 27–March 2*

Sports: Skiing, Snowboarding

International Law Enforcement Games

The International Law Enforcement Games grew out of the establishment of the United States National Law Enforcement Games in 1971 by a group of police officers in California led by Duke Nyhus. In 1974, the games became an international event and the name was changed to the International Law Enforcement Games.

Held primarily in the United States, the games' board decided in 1988 to attempt to award the event to a city outside the United States on every other occasion, but so far this has only happened three times.

Events in the games range from the triathlon and "Toughest Cop Alive" to the more sedentary darts and snooker.

Year	Host City	Host Nation	Dates	Nations	Athletes	Sports
1974	San Francisco	USA		NA	NA	NA
1976	Jacksonville	USA		NA	NA	NA
1978	San Diego	USA		NA	NA	NA
1980	Nassau, NY	USA		NA	NA	NA
1982	Austin	USA		NA	NA	NA
1984	Phoenix	USA		NA	NA	NA
1986	Columbus	USA		NA	NA	NA
1988	Sydney	Australia		NA	NA	NA
1990	Calgary	Canada		NA	NA	NA
1992	Washington, DC	USA	August	NA	NA	NA
1994	Birmingham	USA		NA	NA	NA
1996	Salt Lake City	USA	August 3–10	20	4000	35
1998	Dubai	United Arab Emirates	Nov. 6–12	NA	NA	29
2000	Cocoa Beach	USA		17	5600	40

1998   Dubai   United Arab Emirates   November 6–12

Sports: Arm Wrestling, Athletics, Basketball, Bench Press, Billiards, Bowling, Chess, Cross Country, Cycling Road—Country, Darts, Golf, Judo, Karate, Road Running (Half-Marathon, 10 km), Pistol—combat, Powerlifting, Practical Shooting, Rifle, Snooker, Soccer 5–a-side, Squash, Swimming, Table Tennis, Tennis, Toughest Cop Alive, Trap and Skeet, Triathlon, Tug of War, Volleyball

2000   Cocoa Beach   United States

Nations: Australia, Austria, Bulgaria, Canada, Czech Republic, England, France, Germany, Holland, Hong Kong, Hungary, Italy, Kazakhstan, Latvia, Russia, Sweden, Switzerland, United States

Sports: 3–Point Contest, Arm Wrestling, Athletics, Basketball, Bass Tourney, Bench Press, Billiards, Bowling, Chess, Cross Country, Cycling, Darts, Flag Football, Golf, Horseshoes, Judo, Kata & Karate, Mounted Police, Mountain Bike, Pistol, Police Motorcycle, Powerlifting, Practical Shooting, Racquetball, Rifle, Running (Half-Marathon, 10K), Shotgun, Skeet (Trap & Clays), Soccer, Softball, Sport-a-thon, Swimming, Table Tennis, Tennis, Toughest Cop Alive, Triathlon, Tug-of-War, Volleyball, Wrestling

International Police Winter Games

Police officers from around the world are invited to participate in the annual International Police Winter Games. Eleven of the 13 editions of these very small games have been held at Heavenly Valley in the Lake Tahoe area, while Blackcomb Mountain in Canada hosted the 1990 and 1999 events. The 1998 games were held in Innsbruck, Austria, the first time the games were held in Europe.

According to games organizers, each event has averaged around 290 participants over the years, with athletes from Australia, Austria, Canada, England, Japan and New Zealand joining the perennial U.S. hosts.

Downhill skiing, cross-country skiing and hockey have been included in the games.

Year	Host City	Host Nation	Dates	Nations[125]	Athletes	Sports
1986	South Lake Tahoe	USA	March 2–6*[126]	NA	130	NA
1987	South Lake Tahoe	USA	March 1–5*	NA	NA	NA
1988	South Lake Tahoe	USA	March 6–10*	NA	NA	NA
1989	South Lake Tahoe	USA	March 5–9*	NA	389	NA
1990	Blackcomb/Whistler	Canada	March 4–8*	NA	120	NA
1991	South Lake Tahoe	USA	March 3–7*	NA	NA	NA
1992	South Lake Tahoe	USA	March 1–5*	NA	NA	NA
1993	South Lake Tahoe	USA	March 7–11*	NA	NA	NA
1994	South Lake Tahoe	USA	March 6–10*	NA	NA	NA
1995	South Lake Tahoe	USA	March 5–9*	NA	NA	NA
1996	South Lake Tahoe	USA	March 3–7*	NA	NA	NA
1997	North Lake Tahoe	USA	March 2–6*	6	NA	4
1998	Innsbruck	Austria	March 1–5	12	NA	3
1999	Blackcomb/Whistler	Canada	March 7–12	NA	NA	4
2000	Lake Tahoe	USA	March	7	NA	3

1997   North Lake Tahoe   USA   March 2–6

Nations: Australia, Austria, Canada, England, New Zealand, United States
Sports: Alpine Skiing, Biathlon, Hockey, Nordic Skiing

1998   Innsbruck   Austria   March 1–5

Nations: Austria, Canada, Czech Republic, Germany, Great Britain, Hungary, Italy, Lithuania, Luxembourg, Sweden, Switzerland, United States
Sports: Alpine Skiing (Downhill, Slalom, Giant Slalom, Super Giant Slalom, Dual Slalom), Hockey, Nordic Skiing

1999   Blackcomb/Whistler   Canada   March 7–12

Sports: Alpine Skiing, Biathlon, Hockey, Nordic Skiing

2000   Lake Tahoe   USA   March

Nations: Australia, Austria, Canada, Germany, Italy, Romania, United States
Sports: Alpine Skiing, Hockey, Nordic Skiing

International School Children's Games

The International School Children's Games, sponsored by the International Schoolsport Federation (ISF), have been primarily a European tradition, and are unique in that the participating entities are cities rather than nations. School groups from various cities gather for these small games that present a limited schedule of events and are relatively short in duration, which keeps the costs affordable and organization manageable.

The games rules allow for more than one edition to be staged in any one year. Each city can bring a team of 40 participants, and the teams pay their own travel costs while the host city provides accommodations.

The games were founded by Metod Klemenc, a Yugoslavian school teacher with the simple goal of bringing school-age children from different nations together to better understand one another. The very first games in Celje, Yugoslavia, were a simple one day athletics meet with children from Yugoslavia, Czechoslovakia, Slovenia, Switzerland and Austria. The 1994 games were the first games with children from the United States, when a school from Flint, Michigan participated.

After 25 years of summer games, the International School Children's Games movement initiated its first winter games, which are to be held every two years rather than on the annual schedule on which the summer games are held.

The 2000 games in Hamilton, Ontario, Canada, were the largest ever, with 28 nations attending.

Year	Host City	Host Nation	Dates	Nations	Athletes	Sports
1968	Celje	Yugoslavia	June 5	5	NA	1
1970	Udine	Italy	June 20–21	5	NA	2
1972	Graz	Austria	June 30–July 1	7	NA	3
1974	Murska Sobota	Yugoslavia	May 19	3	NA	2
1974	Darmstadt	West Germany	August 22–25	7	NA	3
1976	Murska Sobota	Yugoslavia	May 20–23	5	NA	2
1976	Geneva	Switzerland	June 11–13	10	NA	3
1978	Ravne na Koroskem	Yugoslavia	September 22–24	6	NA	3
1980	Lausanne	Switzerland	September 26–29	6	NA	3
1982	Darmstadt	West Germany	June 11–13	10	NA	3
1983	Troyes	France	June 17–19	6	NA	3
1983	Murska Sobota	Yugoslavia	September 23	4	NA	3
1984	Geneva	Switzerland	June 15–17	11	NA	4
1985	Granollers	Spain	September 7–9	7	NA	4
1986	Lausanne	Switzerland	June 5–8	6	NA	4

Year	Host City	Host Nation	Dates	Nations	Athletes	Sports
1987	Graz	Austria	June 23	15	NA	3
1988	Szombathely	Hungary	June 24–25	15	NA	4
1989	Andorra	Andorra	June 2–4	12	NA	4
1990	Uhzgorod	Ukraine	June 30–July 3	16	NA	4
1991	Bratislava	Slovakia	May 31–June 2	8	NA	3
1992	Geneva	Switzerland	June 18–21	12	NA	3
1993	Darmstadt	Germany	July 17–18	17	NA	4
1994	Hamilton	Canada	June 15–19	23	NA	3
1994	Slovenj Gradec	Slovenia	September 24	5	NA	3
1995	Celje	Slovenia	June 11	5	NA	3
1996	Sopron	Hungary	June 26–30	11	NA	3
1997	Sparta	Greece	June 11–15	18	NA	3
1998	Logroño	Spain	June 10–14	21	NA	3
1999	Medias	Romania	June 9–13	13	NA	3
1999	Csky Krumlov	Czech Republic	September 24–26	6	NA	3
1999	Velenje	Slovenia	September 27–29	5	NA	3
2000	Hamilton	Canada	July 1–8	28	NA	7

1968   Celje   Yugoslavia   June 5

Nations: Yugoslavia, Czechoslovakia, Austria, Switzerland, Italy
Sports: Athletics

1970   Udine   Italy   June 20–21

Nations: Yugoslavia, Austria, Switzerland, Italy, Germany
Sports: Athletics, Swimming

1972   Graz   Austria   June 30–July 1

Nations: Yugoslavia, Hungary, England, Germany, Austria, Switzerland, Norway, Italy
Sports: Athletics, Swimming, Tennis

1974   Murska Sobota   Yugoslavia   May 19

Nations: Yugoslavia, Austria, Hungary
Sports: Athletics, Table Tennis

1974   Darmstadt   West Germany   August 22–25

Nations: Yugoslavia, England, West Germany, Austria, Switzerland, Norway, France
Sports: Athletics, Swimming, Handball

1976   Murska Sobota   Yugoslavia   May 20–23

Nations: Yugoslavia, West Germany, Austria, Italy, Hungary
Sports: Basketball, Table Tennis

1976   Geneva   Switzerland   June 11–13

Nations: Yugoslavia, West Germany, Austria, Italy, Hungary, Belgium, England, Czechoslovakia, France, Poland
Sports: Athletics, Swimming, Table Tennis

1978   Ravne na Koroskem   Yugoslavia   September 22–24

Nations: Yugoslavia, West Germany, Switzerland, Austria, Italy, Hungary
Sports: Athletics, Swimming, Table Tennis

1980   Lausanne   Switzerland   September 26–29

Nations: Yugoslavia, England, West Germany, Austria, France, Switzerland
Sports: Athletics, Swimming, Orienteering

1982   Darmstadt   West Germany   June 11–13

Nations: Yugoslavia, Netherlands, England, West Germany, Switzerland, Austria, Spain, Hungary, Norway, France
Sports: Athletics, Swimming, Table Tennis

1983   Troyes   France   June 17–19

Nations: Yugoslavia, Netherlands, West Germany, Switzerland, France, Spain
Sports: Athletics, Swimming, Judo

1983   Murska Sobota   Yugoslavia   September 23

Nations: Yugoslavia, Hungary, Austria, Italy
Sports: Athletics, Table Tennis, Orienteering

1984   Geneva   Switzerland   June 15–17

Nations: Yugoslavia, Switzerland, West Germany, Hungary, Austria, Spain, France, Belgium, Monaco, Russia, Israel
Sports: Athletics, Swimming, Table Tennis, Tennis

1985   Granollers   Spain   September 7–9

Nations: Andorra, West Germany, Switzerland, Spain, Austria, Monaco, France
Sports: Athletics, Swimming, Handball, Basketball

1986   Lausanne   Switzerland   June 5–8

Nations: Andorra, Switzerland, Spain, Monaco, France, Italy
Sports: Athletics, Swimming, Mini Volleyball, Triathlon

1987   Graz   Austria   June 23

Nations: Andorra, Spain, Czechoslovakia, Turkey, England, West Germany, Switzerland, Austria, Luxembourg, Yugoslavia, Monaco, France, Hungary, Italy, Norway
Sports: Swimming, Tennis, Table Tennis

1988   Szombathely   Hungary   June 24–25

Nations: Andorra, Czechoslovakia, Yugoslavia, West Germany, Switzerland, Austria, Russia, Finland, Monaco, France, Bulgaria, Hungary, Ukraine
Sports: Athletics, Swimming, Table Tennis, Tennis

1989   Andorra   Andorra   June 2–4

Nations: Andorra, Czechoslovakia, West Germany, Switzerland, Spain, Austria, Yugoslavia, Monaco, France, San Marino, Hungary, Ukraine
Sports: Athletics, Swimming, Judo, Tennis

1990   Uzhgorod   Ukraine   June 30–July 3

Nations: Andorra, Czechoslovakia, Yugoslavia, Italy, Germany, Switzerland, Spain, Austria, Israel, Canada, Monaco, Soviet Union, France, Romania, Ukraine
Sports: Athletics, Swimming, Table Tennis, Tennis

1991   Bratislava   Slovakia   May 31–June 2

Nations: Andorra, Slovakia, Germany, Switzerland, Austria, Slovenia, Monaco, Hungary, Ukraine
Sports: Athletics, Swimming, Tennis

1992   Geneva   Switzerland   June 18–21

Nations: Andorra, Slovakia, Slovenia, Italy, Germany, Israel, Switzerland, Canada, Monaco, Hungary, Austria, France, Ukraine
Sports: Athletics, Swimming, Tennis

1993   Darmstadt   Germany   July 17–18

Nations: Netherlands, Andorra, Slovakia, Italy, Turkey, Slovenia, England, Germany, Austria, Canada, Latvia, Spain, Poland, Switzerland, Hungary, France, Ukraine
Sports: Athletics, Swimming, Table Tennis, Mixed Volleyball

1994   Hamilton   Canada   June 15–19

Nations: Aboriginal Team Ontario Canada, Netherlands, Andorra, China, Slovakia, Italy, Slovenia, England, Germany, Canada, United States, Switzerland, Latvia, Peru, Spain, India, Monaco, Poland, Korea, Hungary, Greece, France, Ukraine
Sports: Athletics, Swimming, Tennis

1994   Slovenj Gradec   Slovenia   September 24

Nations: Slovenia, Czech Republic, Italy, Hungary, Austria
Sports: Athletics, Volleyball (girls), Handball (boys)

1995   Celje   Slovenia   June 11

Nations: Slovenia, Austria, Germany, Croatia, Hungary
Sports: Athletics, Handball, Tennis

1996   Sopron   Hungary   June 26–30

Nations: Netherlands, Italy, Slovenia, Germany, Canada, Switzerland, Romania, Hungary, Greece, Ukraine, Austria
Sports: Athletics, Swimming, Tennis

1997   Sparta   Greece   June 11–15

Nations: Andorra, Netherlands, Slovakia, Italy, Slovenia, England, Germany, Canada, South Africa, Greece, Switzerland, Spain, Romania, Cyprus, Bulgaria, Hungary, Austria
Sports: Athletics, Swimming, Cycling

1998   Logroño   Spain   June 10–14

Nations: Andorra, Austria, Canada, Chile, China, France, Germany, Great Britain, Greece, Hungary, Italy, Netherlands, Poland, Portugal, Romania, Slovakia, Slovenia, Switzerland, Spain, Turkey, Ukraine
Sports: Athletics, Tennis, Swimming

1999   Csky Krumlov   Czech Republic   September 24–26

Nations: Austria, Croatia, Czech Republic, Germany, Slovakia, Slovenia
Sports: Athletics, Badminton, Volleyball

1999   Velenje   Slovenia   September 27–29

Nations: Germany, Poland, Romania, Slovakia, Slovenia
Sports: Athletics, Beach Volleyball, Swimming

1999   Medias   Romania   June 9–13

Nations: Andorra, Canada, Germany, Great Britain, Greece, Hungary, Italy, Netherlands, Romania, Slovakia, Slovenia, Spain, Switzerland
Sports: Athletics, Basketball, Tennis

2000   Hamilton   Canada   July 1–8

Nations: Albania, Andorra, Austria, Canada, Cameroon, Czech Republic, England, Germany, Greece, Israel, Hungary, Italy, Jamaica, Japan, Korea, Latvia, Luxembourg, Mexico, Monaco, Netherlands, Poland, Romania, Scotland, Slovenia, Slovakia, Spain, Switzerland, United States
Sports: Athletics, Baseball, Basketball, Gymnastics, Swimming, Soccer, Volleyball

International Senior Games

Six hundred competitors over the age of 50 from eight nations participated in the inaugural International Senior Games in Bermuda. The organizers had hoped for as many as 3,500 participants in the games which had 18 sports on the schedule. Despite efforts to increase interest in the event, the next games, scheduled for 1998, were canceled.

The Institute for International Sport has taken over the games' organization, renamed the games the World Senior Games, and intends to hold them in Rhode Island in 2000.

Year	Host City	Host Nation	Dates	Nations	Athletes	Sports
1996	Hamilton	Bermuda	April	8	600	18

International Women's Games

The International Women's Games were begun by Alice Milliat, the founder of the Fédération Sportive Féminine Internationale (FSFI), in direct response to the lack of events for women in the Olympic Games. The first two editions of the International Women's Games, or Jeux Olympiques Féminins, were limited to athletics events, yet were successful meetings that showed that women could participate and compete in sports events.

Pershing Stadium in Paris was the venue for the first games, a one-day track meet on August 20, 1922, which drew a crowd of 20,000. The longest event was a 1000 meter run.

The International Olympic Committee and International Amateur Athletic Federation (IAAF) took offense at the use of the word Olympic for these competitions. In meetings with Milliat, they agreed to include events for women in the Olympic Games of 1928 in Amsterdam; in return the FSFI would forego the use of the word Olympic for its events.

Göteborg, Sweden, hosted the second meeting in August 1926. The schedule was extended to three days of athletics, though no other sports were included. Participation numbers were still limited—only 92 women—but they were international, with 15 nations represented.

The events for women in the 1928 Olympic Games did not go as well as intended in the eyes of the IOC. In the 800 meter run, a few women finished the race and collapsed, which did not sit well with the expectations for women at the time, though men had been collapsing in athletic events for ages. The IOC then changed its mind, voting in 1929 not to include women's events in the Olympic Games. In 1930, the IOC reversed the decision again and decided to include women's events in the 1932 games.

The FSFI continued on undeterred. The 1930 games were held in Prague, Czechoslovakia, with three new sports included on the schedule: basketball, team handball, and the Czech game "hazena." Two hundred and fourteen women participated in these games.

Women's athletics were included in the 1932 and 1936 Olympic Games and in the 1934 International Women's Games held in London in 1934. Handball was dropped from the 1934 program, which left athletics and basketball.

The final games in 1938 in Vienna were considered to be only European championships, and the FSFI was disbanded shortly thereafter. World War II also interrupted the games.

In 1948 when the Olympic Games resumed after the war, women's events were solidly on the Olympic program.

Year	Host City	Host Nation	Dates	Nations	Athletes	Sports
1922	Paris	France	August 20	NA	NA	1
1926	Götenburg	Sweden	August 27–29	15	92	1
1930	Prague	Czechoslovakia	September	NA	214	4
1934	London	England	August	NA	NA	2
1938	Vienna	Austria	NA	NA	NA	NA

1922   Paris   France   August 20

Sports: Athletics

1926   Götenburg   Sweden   August 27–29

Sports: Athletics

1930   Prague   Czechoslovakia   September

Sports: Athletics, Handball, Basketball, Hazena
Venues: Letna Stadium

1934   London   England   August

Sports: Athletics, Basketball
Venues: White City Stadium

Irelands' Scholar Athlete Games

The Irelands' Scholar Athlete Games are a regional games sponsored by the Institute for International Sport. The first edition of the games in 1995 were named the Belfast Scholar Athlete Games. The intent of the games is to mix both athletics and academic events, with special emphasis on the Catholic-Protestant interactions in Northern Ireland.

Year	Host City	Host Nation	Dates	Nations	Athletes	Sports
1995	Jordanstown	Northern Ireland		3	120	NA
1996	Jordanstown	Northern Ireland	Aug. 10–17	3	400	NA
1998	Jordanstown	Northern Ireland	Aug. 14–22	NA	NA	8
2000	Limerick	Ireland	Aug. 11–19	NA	NA	NA
2000	Jordanstown	Northern Ireland	Aug. 4–14	NA	NA	NA

ISF Gymnasiade

Since 1974, the International Schoolsport Federation (ISF) has sponsored a "Gymnasiade" for young athletes between the ages of 13 and 17. The participants must be students; however, students from full- or part-time sports schools are not eligible.

The first ISF Gymnasiade was held in Wiesbaden, West Germany. Until 1990, the event was held every two years, but since then, has been on a four-year schedule.

The gymnasiades are limited to a few sports, generally athletics, swimming and artistic and rhythmic gymnastics.

Team sizes are also limited, to keep the event within a reasonable scale. The rules for the 1998 games allowed for teams of 36 boys and 26 girls in athletics, 12 boys and 12 girls in swimming, six boys and six girls for artistic gymnastics, and nine girls for rhythmic gymnastics.

The delegations pay their own transportation and housing costs which further decreases the costs to the hosts.

The International Schoolsport Federation is a member of the General Association of International Sports Federations (GAISF), is recognized by the International Olympic Committee, and also sponsors student championships in sports such as basketball, football, handball and volleyball.

Year	Host City	Host Nation	Dates[127]	Nations	Athletes	Sports
1974	Wiesbaden	West Germany	June 7–8	NA	NA	NA
1976	Orléans	France	June 26	NA	NA	NA
1978	Izmir	Turkey	July 22–23	NA	NA	NA
1980	Turin	Italy	June 6–7	NA	NA	NA
1982	Lille	France	June 4–6	NA	NA	NA
1984	Florence	Italy	June 7–9	NA	NA	NA
1986	Nice	France	June 4–6	NA	NA	NA
1988	Barcelona	Spain	July 6–8	NA	NA	NA
1990	Brugge	Belgium	May 24–27	NA	NA	NA
1994	Nicosia	Cyprus	May 17–20	NA	NA	NA
1998	Shanghai	China	October 12–19	NA	NA	4*

*Traditionally four sports per games

1998   Shanghai   China   October 12–19

Sports: Athletics, Gymnastics, Rhythmic Gymnastics, Swimming

Island Games[128]

The initial suggestion for the Island Games was put forth by the Isle of Man Sports Council in 1982. The council proposed the games as part of the Isle of Man's 1985 "Year of Sport," as a way to increase tourism and to allow equitable competition between small island nations and regions.

Geoffrey Corlett was named director of the Year of Sport, which included 12 full months of athletics events, of which the first interisland games was to be the centerpiece.

Invitations were first sent out to the islands that had traditional Scandinavian connections with the Isle of Man. Orkney, Shetland, Gotland, Iceland, Frøya and Hitra were the first islands to agree to send teams to the games. From the original invitations, word of mouth brought interest from other islands such as Åland and the Isle of Wight which were gladly accepted as entrants. Other islands such as the Falkland Islands, the Isle of Capri in Italy, and Prince Edward Island were invited to the first games, but could not accept the initial invitation. In total, 15 islands came to the first games in 1985, assisted by the Isle of Man which offered free accommodations for up to 50 people from each visiting contingent.

Athletics, badminton, cycling, shooting, swimming and volleyball are the obligatory sports of the games. Each organizing committee then rounds out its full schedule with sports of its own choosing.

The athletics clubs on the Isle of Man had hoped to be able to have an all-weather track installed for the athletics events at the games. Funding was not available and the events took place on a grass track at Queen Elizabeth II School, which worked well for the first games. The Isle of Man won the most medals with Guernsey, Isle of Wight, Jersey, Orkney, and Åland following.

After the conclusion of the first games in July 1985, the team representatives met and decided to form the Island Games Association. What had begun on the invitation from the Isle of Man now became the responsibility of all of the islands participating, and the next games were awarded to the island of Guernsey in the English Channel.

For the 1987 games, the government of Guernsey granted the games association free use of the already established sports facilities and a grant of 25,000 British pounds to stage the games, which were applauded for their organization, festive opening and closing ceremonies, and hearty sports competition.

The third games, in 1989, in the town of Tórshavn in the Faroe Islands, a self-governing territory of Denmark, were the most challenging to date in terms of organization. Unlike the first two venues, the Faroe Islands needed to build facilities and provide living space for the visiting athletes. The events were spread out among several of the Faroe Islands, and some athletes were given lodging in private homes. The opening ceremonies were held in Gundadalur Stadium in Tórshavn, and then the athletes traveled to various islands where their events would be held. This created a unique situation in the ceremonies: it was decided that there would be four simultaneous closing ceremonies, in Klaksvik, Toftir, Tvoroyi and Tórshavn. The Swedish island of Åland was officially represented at each ceremony as the host for the next games.

A number of interesting traditions have grown up around the games in their short existence. In 1991, the hosts from Åland instituted what has become known as the water ceremony. Each island was invited to bring a bottle of water from its shores to pour into a communal fountain especially made for the ceremony which would be turned on for the duration of the games. This popular ritual has been included in each opening ceremony ever since.

The Island Games Association has also made it a tradition to present to each organizing committee a tree which is planted in a suitable location and marked with a bronze plaque to commemorate the games.

Eighteen nations were present at the opening ceremonies in Åland. Eighteen sky-divers were to drop into the stadium, each with a flag of a participating nation. Everyone shared a laugh when only 16 flags made it to the stadium—one parachutist landed in a street; another in a garden. The Isle of Man's hold on the trophy for the "best overall performance" in the games was broken as host Åland topped the standings.

The 1993 games were awarded to the Isle of Wight, with Princess Anne opening the event on the grounds of Carisbrooke Castle. Participation in the games by this time had grown to 2000 athletes and the sports venues were spread across ten towns on the island. Windsurfing was added to the schedule; ironically, for games for countries surrounded by water, it was the first event to be held on the water. Triathlon and netball were demonstration events.

The next games, the "Sunshine Games" in Gibraltar in 1995, were once again scheduled to be opened by Princess Anne but she could not attend. Prince Andrew happened to be visiting Gibraltar and graciously complied when he was asked to fill in. Gibraltar, not an island in the geographical sense, was enough of an island in other ways that the Island Games accepted it as a member in 1987.

The island of Jersey hosted the seventh edition of the games in 1997 and for the fourth time in a row topped the medals table, winning a games record 75 gold medals.

The Swedish island of Gotland hosted the 1999 games, with most events in Visby, swimming in Hemse, golf in Stanga and Västergarn, table tennis in Slite, shooting in Lokrume, and sailing in Fårosünd. Gotland finished on top of the medals stand for the first time ever with 37 golds. Guernsey was second with 27 golds, and previous four-time champion Jersey third with 24 golds.

While other games have laid claim to the name the "Friendly Games," the Island Games have shown, with their organization and demeanor, to truly be one of the friendliest games of all.

Year	Host City	Host Nation	Dates	Nations	Athletes	Sports
1985	Douglas	Isle of Man	July 18–24	15	700	7
1987	St. Peter Port	Guernsey	September 10–17	18	1000	9
1989	Tórshavn	Faroe Islands	July 5–13	15	1000	11
1991	Mariehamn	Åland	June 23–29	18	1500	13
1993	Sandown	Isle of Wight	July 3–10	19	2000	14
1995	Gibraltar	Gibraltar	July 15–22	18	1200	14
1997	St. Helier	Jersey	June 28–July 5	20	1658	14
1999	Visby	Gotland	June 26–July 2	22	1900	14

1985   Douglas   Isle of Man   July 18–24

Nations: Åland, Faroe Islands, Froya, Gotland, Guernsey, Hitra, Iceland, Isle of Man, Isle of Wight, Jersey, Malta, Orkney, Shetland, St. Helena, Ynes Mon

Sports: Athletics, Badminton, Cycling, Football, Shooting, Swimming, Volleyball

Venues: QEII School, Peel (Athletics), Palace Lido (Football), Aquadrome (Swimming), Summerland (Badminton, Volleyball), TT Grandstand, Castletown and Port St. Mary (Cycling), Blue Point (Skeet Shooting), West Nappin, Jurby (English Match .22 Shooting), Raggatt Quarry, Patrick (Free Pistol), Ballagick, Santon (Automatic Ball Trap Shooting), Youth & Community Center, Onchan (Air Pistol and Air Rifle)

MEDALS

Nation	Gold	Silver	Bronze	Total
Isle of Man	25	19	24	68
Guernsey	13	8	16	37
Isle of Wight	8	9	9	26
Jersey	8	12	2	22
Orkney	3	6	6	15
Åland	8	2	4	14
Gotland	3	8	2	13
Iceland	3	1	3	7
Shetland	0	0	4	4
Froya	1	1	2	4
Alderney	1	2	1	4

Nation	Gold	Silver	Bronze	Total
Faroe Islands	0	2	1	3
Ynes Mon	0	1	1	2
St Helena	0	0	1	1
Malta	0	1	0	1

1987   St. Peter Port   Guernsey   September 10–17

Nations: Åland, Alderney, Faroe Islands, Froya, Gibraltar, Gotland, Guernsey, Hitra, Iceland, Isle of Man, Isle of Wight, Jersey, Malta, Orkney, Sark, Shetland, St. Helena, Ynes Mon

Sports: Archery, Athletics, Badminton, Bowling, Cycling, Shooting, Swimming, Table Tennis, Volleyball

Venues: King George V Playing Fields (Archery), Osmond Prialx Memorial Playing Fields (Athletics), Guernsey Badminton Association Hall (Badminton), Guernsey Bowls Stadium (Indoor Bowls), Cobo United Air Rifle Club, Fort Le Marchant, Hogue Patris, Portinfer, Vale Castle (Shooting), Beau Sejour Pool (Swimming), Beau Sejour, Sarnia Hall (Table Tennis), Beau Sejour, Sir John Loveridge Hall (Volleyball)

MEDALS

Nation	Gold	Silver	Bronze	Total
Isle of Man	26	30	23	79
Guernsey	17	19	28	64
Jersey	23	20	16	59
Gotland	15	7	5	27
Åland	7	9	9	25
Isle of Wight	3	4	10	17
Malta	6	1	2	9
Faroe Islands	1	2	5	8
Gibraltar	2	3	3	8
Ynes Mon	0	3	3	6
Iceland	2	2	2	6
Shetland	1	0	3	4
Orkney	1	1	2	4
Sark	0	1	0	1

1989   Tórshavn   Faroe Islands   July 5–13

Nations: Åland, Faroe Islands, Froya, Gibraltar, Gotland, Greenland, Guernsey, Hitra, Iceland, Isle of Man, Isle of Wight, Jersey, Orkney, Shetland, St. Helena, Ynes Mon

Sports: Archery, Athletics, Badminton, Cycling, Football, Gymnastics, Judo, Shooting, Swimming, Table Tennis, Volleyball

Venues: Tórshavn Badmintonhollin (Badminton), Tvoroyi Itrottarhollin (Table Tennis), Tórshavn Itrottarhollin a Nabb (Gymnastics), Klaksvik, Ki-Hollin and Fuglafjordur Itrottarhollin (Volleyball), Vagur, Klaksvik, Fuglafjordur, Gota (Football), Tórshavn Laeraraskulin (Archery), Tórshavn Gundadakshollin (Judo), Tórshavn I Sandvikum (Clay-Shooting), Toftir Stadion (Athletics), Tórshavn Svimjihollin (Swimming), Selatrad–Toftir (Marathon)

MEDALS

Nation	Gold	Silver	Bronze	Total
Isle of Man	34	28	23	85
Guernsey	9	12	16	37
Iceland	14	12	8	34
Faroe Islands	13	5	10	28
Gotland	11	9	6	26
Åland	5	11	9	25
Isle of Wight	8	8	6	22
Jersey	5	8	7	20
Orkney	4	3	4	11
Gibraltar	1	1	6	8
Greenland	0	1	3	4
Shetland	0	3	1	4
Ynes Mon	0	3	0	3

1991   Mariehamn   Åland   June 23–29

Nations: Åland, Faroe Islands, Froya, Gibraltar, Gotland, Greenland, Guernsey, Hitra, Iceland, Isle of Man, Isle of Wight, Jersey, Orkney, Prince Edward Island, Saaremaa, Shetland, St. Helena, Ynes Mon

Sports: Archery, Athletics, Badminton, Cycling, Football, Golf, Gymnastics, Judo, Shooting, Swimming, Table Tennis, Tennis, Volleyball

Venues: Backeberg (Archery), Idrotts Parken (Athletics, Tennis), Bollhalla (Badminton), Kantarellen, Vikingavallen, Kermesse, Sjalvstyrelse Garden (Cycling), Hammarvallen, Idrotts Parken, Vikingavallen, Markusbole (Football), Kastelholm (Golf), Idrottsgarden (Golf), Idrottsgarden (Judo), Bredmorange in Lemland (Shooting), Idrottsgarden (Swimming), Godbyhallen (Table Tennis), Vikinghallen, Idrottsgarden (Volleyball)

MEDALS

Nation	Gold	Silver	Bronze	Total
Jersey	20	16	33	69
Åland	23	24	12	59
Isle of Man	20	15	18	53
Gotland	19	11	14	44
Guernsey	13	13	16	42
Faroe Islands	6	10	11	27
Isle of Wight	2	10	10	22
Iceland	9	5	8	22
Saaremaa	8	7	3	18
Greenland	2	1	6	9
Gibraltar	2	4	2	8
Orkney	2	5	1	8
Ynes Mon	0	2	1	3
Prince Edward Island	1	1	0	2
Shetland	0	1	1	2

1993   Sandown   Isle of Wight   July 3–10

Nations: Åland, Faroe Islands, Froya, Gibraltar, Gotland, Greenland, Guernsey, Hitra, Iceland, Isle of Man, Isle of Wight, Jersey, Orkney, Prince Edward Island, Saaremaa, Shetland, St. Helena, Ynes Mon

Sports: Archery, Athletics, Badminton, Cycling, Football, Golf, Gymnastics, Judo, Shooting, Swimming, Table Tennis, Tennis, Volleyball, Windsurfing

MEDALS

Nation	Gold	Silver	Bronze	Total
Jersey	31	29	33.3	93.3
Isle of Wight	26	23	18	67
Isle of Man	15	22	21.5	58.5
Guernsey	17	17	18	52
Iceland	17	19	9.7	45.7
Gotland	18.5	17.5	9	45
Åland	17	13	14.5	44.5
Faroe Islands	5	5	13	23
Saaremaa	3	5	4.5	12.5
Gibraltar	5.5	0.5	6	12
Orkney	0	2	2	4
Ynes Mon	0	2	2	4
Shetland	0	0	2	2
Greenland	0	1	0.5	1.5
Falkland Islands	0	0	1	1
Prince Edward Island	0	0	1	1

1995   Gibraltar   Gibraltar   July 15–22

Nations: Åland, Faroe Islands, Froya, Gibraltar, Gotland, Greenland, Guernsey, Iceland, Isle of Man, Isle of Wight, Jersey, Orkney, Saaremaa, Shetland, St. Helena, Ynes Mon

Sports: Archery, Athletics, Badminton, Cycling, Football, Gymnastics, Judo, Sailing, Shooting, Swimming, Table Tennis, Tennis, Volleyball, Windsurfing

MEDALS

Nation	Gold	Silver	Bronze	Total
Jersey	37	30	32	99
Guernsey	23	27	26	76
Isle of Man	24	16	21	61
Gotland	10	17	13	40
Isle of Wight	16	6	18	40
Faroe Islands	10	14	15	39
Åland	8	12	14	34
Gibraltar	5	7	10	22
Saaremaa	8	10	3	21
Iceland	5	6	9	20
Ynes Mon	0	3	8	11
Orkney	2	3	2	7
Shetland	0	1	2	3
Greenland	2	0	0	2

1997   St. Helier   Jersey   June 28–July 5

Sports: Archery, Athletics, Badminton, Cycling, Football, Golf, Gymnastics, Sailing, Shooting, Swimming, Table Tennis, Tennis, Volleyball, Windsurfing

MEDALS

Nation	Gold	Silver	Bronze	Total
Jersey	75	47	48	170
Isle of Wight	22	14	14	50
Åland	20	13	8	41
Guernsey	18	39	38	95
Gotland	14	9	16	39
Isle of Man	13	26	20	59
Saaremaa	8	7	8	23
Faroe Islands	5	10	22	37
Shetland	3	5	6	14
Orkney	3	1	3	7
Ynes Mon	2	3	9	14
Gibraltar	2	1	2	5
Greenland	2	1	1	4
Falkland Islands	0	2	5	7
Alderney	0	1	0	1
Iceland	0	0	1	1

1999   Visby   Gotland   June 26–July 2

Nations: Åland, Alderney, Cayman Islands, Falklands, Froya, Faeroe Islands, Gibraltar, Gotland, Greenland, Guernsey, Hitra, Isle of Man, Isle of Wight, Jersey, Orkney, Prince Edward Island, Rhodes, Saaremaa, Sark, Shetland, St. Helena, Ynes Mon

Sports: Archery, Athletics, Badminton, Basketball, Cycling, Football, Golf, Sailing, Shooting (Blackpowder, Clay Target, Pistol, Rifle), Swimming, Table Tennis, Ten-Pin Bowling, Tennis, Volleyball

MEDALS

Nation	Gold	Silver	Bronze	Total
Gotland	37	27	29	93
Guernsey	27	27	31	85
Jersey	24	30	29	83
Isle of Man	16	18	21	55
Isle of Wight	13	17	10	40
Cayman Islands	11	2	9	22
Åland	9	8	7	24
Rhodes	8	9	4	21
Faroe Islands	7	12	9	28
Shetland	6	3	8	17
Saaremaa	4	6	10	20
Greenland	4	1	2	7
Yves Mon	2	1	3	6
Gibraltar	1	5	3	9
Falkland Islands	1	2	3	6
Orkney	0	1	1	2
St. Helena	0	0	1	1
Alderney	0	0	1	1

Islands Corporate Games

The Islands Corporate Games are a regional games of the World Corporate Games family of events. Anyone is eligible to participate in the games, from any region.

The Island Corporate Games were first held in 1999, and the intention was to hold them on an annual basis thereafter.

Year	Host City	Host Nation	Dates
1999	St. Helier	Jersey	Oct. 8–10

JCC Maccabi Games

The Maccabi Games movement began in 1932 with the establishment of the Maccabiah Games and expanded into regional games with the European Maccabi Games in 1959 and the Pan-American Maccabi Games in 1964. That regionalization continued with the establishment of the North American Maccabi Youth Games in 1982. The "North American" was dropped from the name in the early nineties and "Youth" was dropped a few years later, and the games now go by the name JCC (Jewish Community Centers) Maccabi Games.

Teams are based upon cities from around the U.S., and Canada, with delegations from Mexico also participating on an annual basis. Israel has a standing invitation to the games, and through the years there have been consistent entries from Australia and Britain as well occasional participation from Colombia, Costa Rica, Venezuela, Lithuania and the former Soviet Union.

With the exception of 1983, when no event was held, the games were staged annually in a single city from 1982 to 1990. In 1991, due to concerns over the growing size of the event and the desire to include more participants, the games were split up into regions, with games being held in as many as six cities. All of the games incorporate essentially the same events; the purpose is not to break the events up but to give more athletes a chance to compete in them.

The games are meant to strengthen Jewish bonds, and so participants must be Jewish.[129]

A new program instituted for the 1998 Games is the Day of Caring/Day of Sharing, where the athletes take part in a day of community service.

Year	Host City	Host Nation	Dates	Nations	Athletes	Sports
1982	Memphis	USA	August	NA	300	NA
1984	Detroit	USA	August	NA	1000	NA
1985	Columbus OH	USA	August	NA	400	NA
1986	Toronto	Canada	August	NA	2000	NA
1987	Miami	USA	August	NA	400	NA
1988	Chicago	USA	August 18–25	NA	2100	NA
1989	Pittsburgh	USA	Aug	NA	500	NA
1990	Detroit	USA	August 19–26	NA	2200	NA
1991	Wayne	USA	August	NA	NA	NA
1991	Omaha	USA	August	NA	NA	NA
1991	Cleveland	USA	August	NA	NA	NA
1992	Baltimore	USA	August 23–29	NA	2500	NA

Year	Host City	Host Nation	Dates	Nations	Athletes	Sports
1993	Sarasota	USA	August 15–19	NA	400	NA
1993	St. Louis	USA	August 15–19	NA	700	NA
1993	Pittsburgh	USA	August 22–26	NA	800	NA
1993	Boston	USA	August 22–26	NA	1000	NA
1994	Cleveland	USA	August 14–19	NA	2600	NA
1995	Los Angeles	USA	August 13–17	NA	1000	NA
1995	Columbus OH	USA	August 13–17	NA	600	NA
1995	Houston	USA	August 13–17	NA	800	NA
1995	Orlando	USA	August 13–17	NA	500	NA
1995	Long Island	USA	August 20–24	NA	1200	NA
1996	St. Louis	USA	August 11–16	NA	1200	NA
1996	Wayne	USA	August 18–23	NA	2500	NA
1997	Milwaukee	USA	August 10–15	NA	700	10
1997	Pittsburgh	USA	August 17–22	NA	800	10
1997	Sarasota	USA	August 10–15	3	600	7
1997	Kansas City	USA	August 10–15	NA	800	11
1997	Hartford	USA	August 17–22	3	900	11
1997	Seattle	USA	August 17–22	4	1000	10
1998	Charlotte	USA	August 9–14	NA	800	NA
1998	Detroit	USA	August 16–23	NA	3000	NA
1999	Columbus	USA	August 8–13	NA	NA	NA
1999	Houston	USA	August 8–13	4	NA	12
1999	Rochester	USA	August 15–20	NA	NA	NA
1999	Cherry Hill	USA	August 15–20	4	1300	6
2000	Tucson	USA	August 3–9	NA	NA	NA
2000	Boca Raton	USA	August 6–11	NA	NA	NA
2000	Richmond	USA	August 13–18	NA	NA	NA
2000	Cincinnati	USA	August 13–18	NA	NA	NA
2000	Staten Island	USA	August 20–25	NA	NA	NA

1997   Sarasota   USA   August 10–15

Nations: Canada, Mexico, United States

1997   Hartford   USA   August 17–22

Nations: Canada, Israel, United States

1997   Seattle   USA   August 17–22

Nations: Canada, Israel, Mexico, United States
Sports: Athletics, Baseball, Basketball, Bowling, Chess, Football, Softball, Swimming, Table Tennis

1999   Cherry Hill, NJ   USA   August 15–20

Sports: Baseball, Basketball, Football, Softball, Swimming, Tennis

1999   Houston   USA   August 8–13

Nations: Great Britain, Israel, Mexico, United States

Sports: Athletics, Baseball, Basketball, Bowling, Chess, Dance, Football, Golf, Gymnastics, Racquetball, Swimming, Table Tennis

Journalists World Games

The Journalists World Games were first held in Nice, France in 1982, and were sponsored by the Union des Journalistes Sportifs.

Athletics, cycling, football, swimming and volleyball were on the schedule with the journalists competing in three age groups: under 35, 35 to 45, and over 45. A professional media card is required to compete in the games.

The games are *said* to be held annually, but it seems that the journalists must only play in the games and not write about them, as their history seems to be unrecorded to date.

Year	Host City	Host Nation	Dates	Nations	Athletes	Sports
1982	Nice	France	June 1–6	NA	NA	NA
1998	Athens	Greece		NA	NA	NA
1999	Estrie	Canada	Sept. 24–Oct. 3	NA	NA	NA
2000	Liège	Belgium		NA	NA	NA

Latin American Games

The Latin American Games (also called the South American Olympics) were organized in Rio de Janeiro with the support of the International Olympic Committee.

Teams from Argentina, Chile and Uruguay joined the Brazilians in athletics and football. Despite plans for a second edition, no further games were held.

Year	Host City	Host Nation	Dates	Nations	Athletes	Sports
1922	Rio de Janeiro	Brazil		4	NA	2

Maccabiade Winter Games

The idea for a Winter Maccabiah games first emerged very close to the time of the first summer Maccabiah Games in the early 1930s. The first winter Maccabiade was organized in Zakopane, Poland, in 1933. A number of nations were invited, and Italy and Hungary were banned from participating by their governments. Within Poland, certain elements protested the gathering of Jewish athletes. The newspaper *Nei Warzawa* stated "it is a bad omen for the Polish people that Jews are permitted to invite their brothers from all over the world for the demonstration of Jewish physical strength in Maccabi uniform.[130]

Weather wreaked havoc with the games schedule. Rain forced cancelation of the speed- and figure-skating events, an avalanche wiped out the ski jump, and the overall organization of the games was not up to international standards.

The Maccabi organization decided to go ahead with another edition of the games, which were awarded to Czechoslovakia and to be held in 1935. The Czech government at the time was perhaps the most accepting of the Jewish people of any of the Eastern European states.[131] Members of the Maccabi in Germany and in Poland joined the Czech Maccabi Organizing Committee and the second edition of the games ran much more smoothly. The cooperation was not without cost. The German government harassed Maccabi Germany and let the organizing body of the games know that they would not be providing visas to the German participants. The Czech government responded that they would boycott the 1936 Berlin Olympic Games and the German government relented and provided the visas. Thereafter, the German press responded by ignoring the games completely.

Once again weather caused the cancelation of a good portion of the events. Rain made the skating rink unusable, the speed- and figure-skating events were canceled, and the ice hockey tournament abandoned after one game.

Cultural events, ballet recitals, and movies about Palestine provided entertainment and education in the evenings.

Host City	Host Nation	Year
Zakopane	Poland	1933
Banská-Bystrica	Czechoslovakia	1935

Zakopane   Poland   1933

Sports: Bobsled, Ice Hockey, Nordic Skiing. (Speed Skating and Figure Skating both canceled due to the weather. The Ski Jump was wiped out by an avalanche.) No explicit mention of Alpine Skiing.

Banská-Bystrica   Czechoslovakia   1935

Sports: Alpine Skiing, Bobsled, Figure Skating, Ice Hockey, Military Ski Patrol, Nordic Skiing, Speed Skating

Maccabiah Games

The Maccabiah Games are open to the Jewish people from nations around the world. The games take their name from the valiant Jewish leader Judah Maccabaeus who defeated the Syrians and restored the Jewish rites in the temple in Jerusalem in 165 B.C.

The inspiration for the games grew out of the establishment of the gymnastics clubs at the turn of the 20th century, which were in turn established in response to the anti–Semitic policies which kept the Jews from joining other clubs. These clubs spread quickly throughout Europe, and in 1911 Jewish journalist Fritz Abraham first expressed the idea of holding a "Jewish Olympics." World war interrupted the progress towards this goal, but in 1921 the Maccabi World Union was created and its chairman, Dr. Gustav Spiegler, revived the idea in an article written in 1924. The Jewish Olympiad was to offer athletic competitions for the body and have contests in the sciences and humanities to give attention to Jewish achievements in these disciplines. The same article introduced the idea of Jewish athletes competing as a team in the Olympic Games rather than for many different countries as had been the practice.

Various attempt to organize the games throughout the 1920s (and the European Maccabi Games in Vienna in 1925) failed, but Josef Yekutieli, an active member of

Maccabi Eretz Israel, doggedly continued to push the idea. Finally at the annual congress of the Maccabi World Union in Czechoslovakia in June 1929, Yekutieli gave a convincing speech which inspired the delegates to vote to hold the first games in 1932.

The first Maccabiah Games were held in the midst of a worldwide depression. The occasion called for the construction of Israel's first major sports stadium which was completed just before the games began on March 28, 1932. The Palestinian government allowed an unlimited quota of athletes to enter the country for the event. Railroad fares were reduced 50 percent inside the country for those attending the games.

Three hundred and ninety athletes from 18 nations competed, similar in size and scope to the very first Olympic Games 36 years before. One hundred and twenty carrier pigeons, ten for each of the lost tribes of Israel, were released in order to symbolically carry news of the first games around the world. Women competed in athletics, swimming, fencing and gymnastics.

The second Maccabiah, in 1935, was held under heightening world tensions. The Palestinian police banned the scheduled parade of athletes through Tel Aviv one day before the opening of the games, fearing it would lead to disorder. German athletes had been ordered by their government not to travel to Israel to compete, but 134 did so, refusing to carry the German flag in the opening ceremonies.

Reporters queried the president of the United States Maccabi Association before their departure to the games about a possible boycott of the 1936 Berlin Olympics. The official stance of the organization was to leave the decision to the individual athletes.

This edition of the Maccabiah Games came to be known as the "Aliyah Maccabiah" or the Maccabiah of Immigration. The year 1935 was a period of very strict immigration and many of the 1350 athletes remained behind to live in Palestine.

The 1938 Maccabiah Games were canceled, as were the 1938 Western Asiatic Games which were also scheduled to be held in Tel Aviv. One reason was due to the rising political conflicts worldwide, but another reason was in response to the immigration that took place after the 1935 games. The Mandate authorities felt that another games might lead to a fresh surge of immigration.

World War II put an end to the games for over a decade, but in 1950 they were revived and a new 50,000-seat stadium was constructed at Ramat Gan. These games were the first to take place in the modern state of Israel, which was formally recognized in 1948. Some 800 athletes from 20 nations participated.

The size of the games remained relatively the same in 1953: 890 athletes from 22 nations participated. A new tradition, the games' torch, was begun. The torch was lit in Modi'im, the birthplace of Judah Maccabaeus, and carried to the Maccabiah Stadium.

In 1957, several "Iron Curtain" countries stayed away from the games due to Israel's Sinai campaign in the year before. Two Olympic gold medal winners, gymnast Agnes Keleti from Hungary and race-walker Henry Laskau from the United States gave winning performances. It was proposed at these games that the athletes be housed in a permanent village for all subsequent games.

The International Olympic Committee recognized the Maccabiah Games as an official "Regional Sports Event" at the 1961 games and the Maccabi World Union was given official recognition by the International Olympic Committee. Part of the opening ceremony was a march past of 180 Israeli soldiers, each carrying an Uzi machine gun. Yosef Lahav of the Haifa Maccabi Club was the final torchbearer. The idea of a games village was made a reality in 1961 when over 1,000 athletes from 27 nations stayed in the newly constructed complex.

Dick Savitt, the 1952 Wimbledon champion, competed in the 1961 games' tennis tournament, winning the doubles championship. American Mike Hermann was voted the best athlete at the games, winning the decathlon with a new games record, and the long jump and pole vault.

Ramat Gan Stadium was upgraded for the 1965 games with 5,000 more seats and floodlights for night competition. The torchbearer for the games was Debra Turner-Marcus, the first female torchbearer, three years before the Olympic Games had a woman carry the torch. A new basketball arena was also constructed. Fifteen-year-old American swimmer Mark Spitz was the star of the games, winning three gold medals.

Four years later, in 1969, a new swimming pool was built in Yad Eliahu. All Maccabiah athletes participated in a pilgrimage to Jerusalem's Western Wall. The Israeli basketball team surprised the Americans, winning 74–70.

Tal Brody, the American-born Israeli basketball star, was given the honor of carrying the torch in the opening ceremony of the 1973 games. The Israeli team beat the Americans for the second time in a row. The games were dedicated to the 11 Israeli athletes who were murdered during the 1972 Munich Olympic Games less than one year before.

Twenty-five swimming records were broken at the tenth Maccabiah games in 1977, including all but one of Mark Spitz's records. The games were expanded to include other events such as chess and bridge, as well as seminars on health, medicine and the history of Jewish sport. Esther Roth, an Olympic sprinter for Israel, won three gold medals on the track.

The 1981 edition of the Maccabiah Games was dedicated to the memory of Pierre Gildesgame, president of the Maccabi World Union and International Maccabiah Games Committee, who had been killed in a car accident the previous year. Three thousand four hundred and fifty athletes from 33 countries participated.

Mark Spitz carried the Maccabiah torch into the stadium for the 1985 opening ceremonies. A record 3,639 athletes from 37 countries took part. A junior Maccabiah competition was begun to encourage younger athletes to participate, and several events were held for athletes 50 and over.

In 1989, Jews from South Africa were banned from competition due to South Africa's continuing racist policies. This caused much consternation among some who felt that Jews banning other Jews from competition was equally unjust. A team from the Soviet Union competed for the very first time in the games.

Five thousand and sixty-one participants from 48 countries, both record figures, competed in 32 sports in the 1993 games. Croatia, Cuba, the Czech Republic, Estonia, Latvia, Lithuania, Romania and Slovakia all competed for the first time. Bulgaria and Poland competed in the games, their first participation since 1938.

Tragedy struck the 1997 games during the opening ceremonies when a small temporary footbridge, meant to carry athletes over the Yarkon River to the entrance of the stadium for the parade, collapsed. The Australian delegation, one of the first in line, took the brunt of the disaster, with scores of injuries and two deaths from the fall. Two other athletes died in the weeks after from complications from the polluted river.

The games ceremony went on without the athletes, with dancing, a tribute to 100 years of Zionism, and fireworks: it was a decision that was loudly criticized. U.S. gymnastics champion Kerri Strug carried the games torch into the stadium, handing it to Israeli basketball star Mickey Berkowitz. Finally, at the end of the ceremony, the stadium announcer informed the audience of the tragedy, and explained why the athletes had not been included in the ceremony. When the gravity of the situation was finally realized, the games were postponed by one day.

Two investigations were begun immediately by the Israeli police and the ministry of education. However, in December 1997, Maccabi Australia delegates to the Maccabi World Union resigned in protest over the fact that an independent inquiry into the bridge collapse had not been initiated and that the Maccabi World Union had taken no responsibility in the matter.

Later that month, five Israelis were charged with negligent manslaughter, including the builders, designers and materials providers for the bridge, and Yoral Eyal, the head of the Maccabiah Games Organizing Committee. The bridge had been built without a permit and was not up to Israeli building regulations. The Israeli government shortly thereafter paid the first $100,000 (USD) installment of a previously agreed-to $500,000 loan to the victims families.

The matter has yet to reach a resolution, with the Maccabi Australia leaders still calling for an inquiry by Israel's Knesset. In January 1999, Debbie Marcus, the torchbearer of the 1965 games, and three other Maccabiah champions returned their medals and trophies from the games in protest, demanding again that the Maccabi World Union take responsibility for the accident and that MWU president Ronald Bakalarz step down.

In the 1990s, the very purpose of the Maccabiah Games was questioned. Whereas the games used to provide Jewish athletes their main opportunity for international competition, Jewish athletes are now able to compete in most (but not all) international events. The Maccabiah Games have also adapted, and now hold events for masters age groups and for physically disabled athletes. The best Jewish athletes in modern times have not made the Maccabiah Games a major event on their schedules, but the event retains cultural significance for its participants, giving many of them the opportunity to visit Israel for the first time.

Year	Host City	Host Nation	Dates	Nations	Athletes	Sports
1932	Tel Aviv	Israel	March 29–April 6	18	390	16
1935	Tel Aviv	Israel	April 2–10	28	1350	18
1950	Tel Aviv	Israel	September 28–Oct. 9	20	800	17
1953	Tel Aviv	Israel	September 20–29	22	890	19
1957	Tel Aviv	Israel	September 15–24	20	980	19
1961	Tel Aviv	Israel	August 29–Sept 5	27	1000	20
1965	Tel Aviv	Israel	August 23–31	25	1200	22
1969	Tel Aviv	Israel	July 28–August 6	27	1456	22
1973	Tel Aviv	Israel	July 9–19	26	1499	23
1977	Tel Aviv	Israel	July 12–21	34	2694	28
1981	Tel Aviv	Israel	July 6–16	33	3450	32
1985	Tel Aviv	Israel	July 15–25	37	3639	30
1989	Tel Aviv	Israel	July 3–13	46	4417	32
1993	Tel Aviv	Israel	July 5–15	48	5061	32
1997	Tel Aviv	Israel	July 14–25	53	5500	30

1932   Tel Aviv   Israel   March 29–April 6

Sports: Athletics, Basketball, Boxing, Diving, Equestrian, Fencing, Field Hockey, Football, Gymnastics, Handball, Motorcycling, Swimming, Table Tennis, Tennis, Wrestling, Water Polo

Nations: Austria, Bulgaria, Czechoslovakia, Denmark, Egypt, Germany, Great Britain, Greece, Israel, Latvia, Lithuania, Morocco, Poland, Romania, Switzerland, Syria, United States, Yugoslavia

1935   Tel Aviv   Israel   April 2–10

Nations: Austria, Belgium, Bulgaria, Czechoslovakia, Danzig, Denmark, Egypt, Estonia, France, Germany, Great Britain, Greece, Hungary, Israel, Italy, Latvia, Libya, Lithuania, Morocco, Netherlands, Poland, Romania, South Africa, Switzerland, Syria, Turkey, United States, Yugoslavia
Sports: Athletics, Boxing, Cycling, Diving, Fencing, Field Hockey, Football, Gymnastics, Judo, Rowing, Shooting, Swimming, Table Tennis, Tennis, Weightlifting, Wrestling, Water Polo, Volleyball

1950   Tel Aviv   Israel   September 28–October 9

Nations: Argentina, Australia, Austria, Belgium, Canada, Denmark, Finland, France, Germany, Great Britain, Ireland, India, Israel, Libya, Netherlands, South Africa, Sweden, Switzerland, Turkey, United States
Sports: Athletics, Basketball, Boxing, Cycling, Diving, Fencing, Field Hockey, Football, Gymnastics, Handball, Judo, Swimming, Tennis, Weightlifting, Wrestling, Water Polo, Volleyball

1953   Tel Aviv   Israel   September 20–29

Nations: Argentina, Australia, Austria, Belgium, Brazil, Canada, Chile, Denmark, Finland, France, Germany, Great Britain, Italy, Ireland, India, Israel, Netherlands, Rhodesia, South Africa, Switzerland, Turkey, United States
Sports: Athletics, Basketball, Boxing, Cycling, Diving, Fencing, Football, Gymnastics, Handball, Judo, Lawn Bowls, Shooting, Table Tennis, Swimming, Tennis, Weightlifting, Wrestling, Water Polo, Volleyball

1957   Tel Aviv   Israel   September 15–24

Nations: Argentina, Australia, Austria, Belgium, Brazil, Canada, Chile, Denmark, Finland, France, Great Britain, Ireland, India, Israel, Mexico, Netherlands, Rhodesia, South Africa, Switzerland, United States
Sports: Athletics, Basketball, Boxing, Cycling, Diving, Fencing, Football, Gymnastics, Handball, Judo, Lawn Bowls, Shooting, Table Tennis, Swimming, Tennis, Weightlifting, Wrestling, Water Polo, Volleyball

1961   Tel Aviv   Israel   August 29–September 5

Nations: Argentina, Australia, Austria, Belgium, Brazil, Canada, Columbia, Congo, Chile, Denmark, Finland, France, Great Britain, Guatemala, Ireland, India, Israel, Italy, Mexico, Netherlands, Rhodesia, South Africa, Switzerland, Sweden, Turkey, United States, Uruguay
Sports: Athletics, Basketball, Boxing, Cycling, Diving, Fencing, Football, Gymnastics, Handball, Judo, Lawn Bowls, Shooting, Table Tennis, Rowing, Swimming, Tennis, Weightlifting, Wrestling, Water Polo, Volleyball

MEDALS

Nation	Gold	Silver	Bronze	Total
United States	58	29	24	111
Israel	28.5	47	38	113.5
South Africa	11	14	9	34
Britain	10	6	17	33
Netherlands	7	9	0	16
Australia	6	5.5	6	17.5
Canada	5	5	5	15
Italy	3	5	6	14
France	2.5	2	1	5.5
Rhodesia	1	3	0	4
Denmark	1	1.5	0	2.5
India	1	0	0	1
Argentina	0	4	1	5
Brazil	0	0	1	1
Chile	0	0	1	1
Sweden	0	0	1	1
Uruguay	0	0	1	1

1965   Tel Aviv   Israel   August 23–31

Nations: Argentina, Australia, Austria, Belgium, Brazil, Canada, Chile, Denmark, Finland, France, Great Britain, Iran, Ireland, India, Israel, Italy, Mexico, Netherlands, Peru, Rhodesia, South Africa, Switzerland, Sweden, United States, Venezuela

Sports: Athletics, Basketball, Boxing, Clay Pigeon, Cycling, Diving, Fencing, Football, Golf, Gymnastics, Handball, Judo, Lawn Bowls, Rowing, Shooting, Swimming, Table Tennis, Tennis, Volleyball, Weightlifting, Wrestling, Water Polo

MEDALS

Nation	Gold	Silver	Bronze	Total
United States	73	46	32	151
Israel	41	60	42	143
Great Britain	22	11	20	53
South Africa	14	11	9	34
Holland	6	7	7	20
Australia	2	6	8	16
Italy	3	4	4	11
Mexico	4	3	2	9
Canada	1	5	3	9
Argentina	2	4	2	8
Rhodesia	1	3	0	4
Brazil	1	0	1	2
France	0	4	2	6
Iran	1	0	0	1
Denmark	1	0	0	1
Belgium	0	1	1	2
Finland	0	0	2	2
Switzerland	0	1	0	1
Austria	0	0	1	1
India	0	0	1	1

1969   Tel Aviv   Israel   July 28–August 6

Nations: Argentina, Australia, Austria, Belgium, Brazil, Canada, Chile, Denmark, Finland, France, Germany, Great Britain, Greece, Ireland, Israel, Italy, Mexico, Netherlands, Peru, Rhodesia, South Africa, Switzerland, Sweden, Turkey, United States, Uruguay, Venezuela

Sports: Athletics, Basketball, Boxing, Clay Pigeon, Cycling, Diving, Fencing, Football, Golf, Gymnastics, Handball, Judo, Lawn Bowls, Rowing, Shooting, Table Tennis, Swimming, Tennis, Weightlifting, Wrestling, Water Polo, Volleyball

1973   Tel Aviv   Israel   July 9–19

Nations: Argentina, Australia, Austria, Belgium, Brazil, Canada, Chile, Costa Rica, Denmark, Finland, France, Germany, Great Britain, Greece, Ireland, Israel, Italy, Mexico, Netherlands, Peru, Rhodesia, South Africa, Spain, Switzerland, Sweden, United States

Sports: Athletics, Basketball, Boxing, Clay Pigeon, Cycling, Diving, Fencing, Football, Golf, Gymnastics, Handball, Judo, Lawn Bowls, Shooting, Squash, Table Tennis, Rowing, Swimming, Tennis, Weightlifting, Wrestling, Water Polo, Volleyball

1977   Tel Aviv   Israel   July 12–21

Nations: Argentina, Australia, Austria, Belgium, Bolivia, Brazil, Canada, Chile, Costa Rica, Denmark, Ecuador, Finland, France, Germany, Great Britain, Greece, India, Ireland, Israel, Italy, Jamaica, Japan, Mexico, Netherlands, Norway, Peru, South Africa, Spain, Switzerland, Sweden, United States, Uruguay, Venezuela, Virgin Islands

Sports: Athletics, Badminton, Basketball, Boxing, Bridge, Chess, Clay Pigeon, Cricket, Diving, Fencing, Football, Golf, Gymnastics, Handball, Judo, Karate, Lawn Bowls, Mini-football, Rowing, Shooting, Squash, Swimming, Table Tennis, Tennis, Volleyball, Weightlifting, Wrestling, Water Polo

1981   Tel Aviv   Israel   July 6–16

Nations: Argentina, Australia, Austria, Belgium, Bermuda, Bolivia, Brazil, Canada, Chile, Costa Rica, Denmark, Ecuador, Finland, France, Germany, Great Britain, Greece, India, Ireland, Israel, Italy, Mexico, Netherlands, New Zealand, Peru, Puerto Rico, South Africa, Spain, Switzerland, Sweden, United States, Uruguay, Venezuela

Sports: Athletics, Badminton, Basketball, Boxing, Bridge, Chess, Clay Pigeon, Cricket, Diving, Fencing, Field Hockey, Football, Golf, Gymnastics, Handball, Judo, Karate, Lawn Bowls, Mini-football, Shooting, Softball, Squash, Table Tennis, Rowing, Rugby Union, Sailing, Swimming, Tennis, Weightlifting, Wrestling, Water Polo, Volleyball

1985   Tel Aviv   Israel   July 15–25

Nations: Argentina, Australia, Austria, Belgium, Bermuda, Brazil, Canada, Chile, Colombia, Denmark, Ecuador, Finland, France, Germany, Gibraltar, Great Britain, Guam, India, Israel, Italy, Japan, Mexico, Netherlands, Norway, Panama, Peru, Puerto Rico, South Africa, Switzerland, Sweden, United States, Uruguay, Venezuela, Virgin Islands, Yugoslavia, Zaire, Zimbabwe

Sports: Athletics, Badminton, Basketball, Clay Pigeon, Cricket, Diving, Fencing, Field Hockey, Football, Golf, Gymnastics, Handball, Judo, Karate, Lawn Bowls, Mini-football, Rhythmic Gymnastics, Shooting, Softball, Squash, Table Tennis, Rowing, Rugby Union, Sailing, Swimming, Tennis, Weightlifting, Wrestling, Water Polo, Volleyball

1989   Tel Aviv   Israel   July 3–13

Nations: Argentina, Australia, Austria, Belgium, Bermuda, Bolivia, Brazil, Canada, Chile, Colombia, Costa Rica, Denmark, Ecuador, Finland, France, Germany, Gibraltar, Great Britain, Greece, Guatemala, Hungary, Hong Kong, India, Ireland, Israel, Italy, Japan, Korea (South), Lithuania, Mexico, Netherlands, New Zealand, Norway, Panama, Peru, Puerto Rico, Singapore, South Africa, Spain, Switzerland, Sweden, United States, Uruguay, Venezuela, Yugoslavia, Zaire

Sports: Athletics, Badminton, Basketball, Bridge, Chess, Clay Pigeon, Cricket, Diving, Fencing, Field Hockey, Football, Golf, Gymnastics, Handball, Judo, Karate, Lawn Bowls, Mini-football, Shooting, Softball, Squash, Table Tennis, Rowing, Rugby Union, Sailing, Swimming, Tennis, Ten-pin Bowling, Weightlifting, Wrestling, Water Polo, Volleyball

1997   Tel Aviv   Israel   July 14–25

Sports: Athletics, Badminton, Basketball, Beach Volleyball, Bridge, Clay Pigeon, Fencing, Field Hockey, Football, Golf, Gymnastics, Half-marathon, Ice Hockey, Judo, Karate, Rowing, Rugby, Sailing, Shooting, Softball, Squash, Swimming, Table Tennis, Tennis, Ten-pin Bowling, Triathlon, Volleyball, Water Polo, Weightlifting, Wrestling

Sports for Juniors: Athletics, Basketball, Football, Swimming, Tennis

Sports for Masters: Athletics, Golf, Squash, Swimming, Tennis, Triathlon

Sports for Physically Disabled: Half-marathon, Swimming, Tennis

Mediterranean Games

The nations eligible for the Mediterranean Games are the countries surrounding the Mediterranean Sea, making for an interesting mix of African, Arab and European participants. Israel has been the only country excluded for fear that the Arab nations would not participate if it were to compete. Ten nations competed in the first games in 1951; 21 in 1997. Each Mediterranean Games host city has, to this point, been situated on the Mediterranean coast. No inland city has yet been chosen to host the games.

The Comité International des Jeux Méditerranéens, CIJM, was not established until 1961, ten years after the first games were held. Mohamed Taher Pasha, a tireless Egyptian sportsman, is credited with being the father of the Mediterranean Games, and led them through their early years of development.

Ten nations and 734 athletes, all men, competed at the first games held in Alexandria, Egypt. (A proposal that women be included was not made until 1959, and women did not participate until 1967.) Alain Mimoun, born in Algeria but competing for France, won the 5,000 and 10,000 meter runs. Mimoun would win three Olympic silver medals in 1952 and 1956, finishing second to Czechoslovakian great Emil Zatopek on each occasion before finally winning the 1956 Olympic marathon.

In 1955 in Barcelona, a young banker named Juan Antonio Samaranch, 25 years from taking over the head of the International Olympic Committee, helped to organize the games in his hometown. Water from the Mediterranean Sea was used in the games relay. An amphora filled at Ampurias was carried to Barcelona and poured into a fountain during the opening ceremony.

Alain Mimoun again won the 5000 and 10,000 meter runs in Montjuic Stadium and Joaquim Blume of Spain won six gold medals in gymnastics.

In August 1955, a Mr. Glovinski of Israel lodged a complaint with IOC President Avery Brundage that Israel had been discriminated against because it had not received and invitation to the games in Barcelona. The Spanish organizers claimed that they were only obligated to send out invitations to the nations that had participated in the first games in Alexandria. Brundage, in a statement incongruent with several of his other statements and the rules passed by the IOC relating to regional games, said, "The I.O.C. considers that it would be going beyond its power, were it to interfere in the internal affairs of the regional games' organization."[132]

A report in the IOC Bulletin on the Barcelona Games ironically stated, "I can affirm that at the Mediterranean Games, the important thing was not to win but to have the honor to participate in them." These words were written by the young banker Samaranch.[133] At discussions over the issue in 1959, another Spanish representative, J. A. Elalo-Osano stated that the issue of Israel's participation in the Mediterranean Games was not discrimination on Spain's part. He gave the example of Spain inviting Israel to the World University Games held in 1955 in San Sebastian, a month after the Mediterranean Games in Barcelona.[134]

The Israel issue is an unbroken thread in the early history of the Mediterranean Games. The 1959 edition had been awarded to Lebanon but its relations with Israel were on very shaky ground. In August 1958, the IAAF passed a resolution stating that all nations in a region affiliated with the federation must be invited to any regional games in the area. However, the writer in the IOC Bulletin proposed that the Lebanese organizers change the name of the games to the "Lebanon Games," "Beirut Games," or the "Tri-Continental Games." This would have the effect of rendering the IAAF resolution moot, as the games would not fall under the title of an official regional games and the Lebanese could then invite, or not invite, any nation they desired.[135]

In 1959 at the games in Beirut, a proposal to allow European nations that did not border the Mediterranean to participate was voted down. The United Arab Republic, a team composed of Syria and Egypt, beat out France for the total team medals title.

IOC reports vaguely mention a political protest at the games which "marred the proceedings." "The police in charge applied severe measures to maintain order," one says. The report congratulates the organizers for their police force which was "capable of handling the situation most efficiently and energetically ... with bludgeons and guns!"[136]

The case of Israel was brought up again at IOC meetings with the International Federations in February and June 1963. At the February meeting, the IOC passed several motions declaring that it and international federations were completely opposed to any interference in sport on political, racial or religious grounds, and specifically any interference of the passage of participants between countries. They also decided that area games should not be granted to nations that did not allow the free entry of all athletes.[137]

Under rules adopted by the CIJM, nations had to apply to participate at least two years before the games. This was said to be the reason that Israel (and Libya and Albania) was excluded. At the meeting in June, however, the issue was still not resolved. Mr. State, the representative from the International Weightlifting Federation, pointed out that Israel had been applying for membership in the games for the past eight years. Another rule was mentioned, that 75 percent of the member countries must vote to allow another country into the games. Given the makeup of the Mediterranean region, this would make it impossible for Israel to be admitted into the games. Mr. State stated flatly, "this is discrimination" and gave that discrimination as reason enough for weightlifting to pull its sanction and events from the games.

IOC President Avery Brundage stated that the IOC had nothing to do with these games and could exert no pressure either way on the matter, because the Mediterranean Games had not asked the IOC for patronage and the IOC had not given it. Therefore, the argument went, the IOC could not become involved in the internal matters of the Mediterranean Games. Brundage did suggest, however, that the name of the games might be changed to the Neapolitan Games. He went on to suggest that perhaps the regional games had served their purpose and had been surpassed by the various world championships and other events.[138]

At the festivities in 1963, Avery Brundage, the CIJM president from Lebanon, Gabriel Gemayel, and Antonio Segni, the Italian President, opened the games in Naples, Italy. Italy went to the top spot in the overall medals table with 69 medals to runner-up France's 30.

Drug testing was introduced to the games in 1967 in Tunis, Tunisia, and women participated in the games for the first time. Al Menzah Stadium, the main venue in Tunis, was built by the Bulgarians. Tunisia's Mohammed Gammoudi, a medallist in three Olympic Games, including 1968 where he won the 5,000 meters gold, took both the 5,000 and 10,000 meter Mediterranean Games titles for the second time in a row.

The first item of business in 1971 at the games in Izmir, Turkey, was to say farewell to the founder of the event, Mohammed Taher Pasha, who had died the year before at the age of 91. France's Guy Drut raced to a gold medal for France in the 110 meter hurdles. Five years later, he would win the same event at the 1976 Montreal Olympic Games. France overall had its worst showing ever, winning just seven gold medals and slipping to seventh position. Yugoslavia, on the other hand, had its best games ever, finishing second with 27 gold medals to Italy's 51 golds. Abdon Pamich, an Italian walker, won his third gold medal in three Mediterranean Games.

Algeria hosted the seventh edition of the games in Algiers in 1975. Italy, with stars such as diver Klaus Dibiasi, high jumper Sara Simeoni, and sprinter Pietro Mennea, came to Algiers and won the medals race while France climbed back to second among its Mediterranean rivals. Lord Killanin, the Irish President of the IOC, gave high marks to the facilities in Algiers.

Split, Yugoslavia, which had lost out to Algiers in the bid for the 1975 games, was chosen over Casablanca as host for the 1979 games. Casablanca was awarded the 1983 games instead.

Yugoslavia made good use of the home advantage to win the gold medals race at the 1979 games. The city of Split served as the main venue, but events were held in other towns in the region within 50 miles of Split; namely, Sibenik, Trogir, Sinj, Makarska, Zadar and Supetar. Pietro Mennea, fresh from his world record in the 200 meters at the World University Games in Mexico City, won the 100 and 200 meter dashes.

Juan Antonio Samaranch, now president of the International Olympic Committee, and Moroccan Prince Heretier Sidi Mohamed opened the games of 1983 in Casablanca. Moroccan distance star Said Aouita made the Prince and all Moroccans proud by winning the 800 and 1500 meter runs. Aouita would go on to win the 5000 meters at the 1984 Los Angeles Olympics and the 1987 World Championships.

Aouita repeated his double gold-medal performance at the 1987 games in Latakia, Syria, this time winning the 1500 and 5000 meter runs.

The Soviet Union lent its assistance by training the 25,000 school-aged children who took part in the opening ceremonies in Latakia in the Al-Assad sports complex, named for the Syrian president and built especially for the games. The European Broadcasting Union televised the games throughout Europe.

In Latakia, President Hafez Assad used the opening ceremonies to issue a plea for peace and to denounce nuclear weapons. The games were centered around Latakia with events also held in Aleppo and Damascus.

Bassel Assad, the son of President Assad, won the equestrian gold medal at the games and gave a speech in favor of peace at the closing ceremonies.

The emergence of North African women athletes marked the Athens games of 1991. Hassiba Boulmerka of Algeria won both the 1500 and 800 meter runs in Athens, despite protests from factions within her country that said that to run with legs uncovered was a serious offense against Islamic law. Boulmerka would win the 1500 meters at the 1992 Olympic Games in Barcelona as well as the World Championships in 1991 and 1995.

In 1993, the CIJM voted to change the schedule so that the games are held the year after rather than the year before the Olympics. At the 1993 games, events took place in over 20 cities across the Languedoc-Rousillon region of France, with every town taking its turn to host an event or two. Reflecting the breakup of Yugoslavia, the CIJM accepted applications for membership from Bosnia-Herzegovina, Croatia and Slovenia, as well as from San Marino. Events for the disabled were held for the first time, including the 1500 meter wheelchair track event and 100 meters swimming for both men and women. World champion and world record-holder Noureddine Morceli from Algeria easily won the 1500 meters, but his compatriot Hassiba Boulmerka, who began waving to the crowd down the finishing straight, celebrating a presumed second straight Mediterranean Games 1500 meter victory, was caught just a half-step before the finish line by Frédérique Quentin of France.

Bari, Italy, was chosen over Tunis, Tunisia, and Valencia, Spain, for the right to hold the 1997 Mediterranean Games. Tunis was in turn chosen to host the 2001 games.

Year	Host City	Host Nation	Dates	Nations	Athletes	Sports
1951	Alexandria	Egypt	October 5–20	10	734	13
1955	Barcelona	Spain	July 16–25	9	900	19
1959	Beirut	Lebanon	October 11–26	13	1000	14
1963	Naples	Italy	September 21–29	13	NA	17
1967	Tunis	Tunisia	September 8–17	12	NA	14
1971	Izmir	Turkey	October 6–17	14	NA	18
1975	Algiers	Algeria	August 23–Sept. 6	15	2000	18
1979	Split	Yugoslavia	September 15–29	15	2500	24
1983	Casablanca	Morocco	September 3–17	16	1700	20
1987	Latakia	Syria	September 11–25	18	NA	18
1991	Athens	Greece	June 28–July 12	18	NA	23
1993	Languedoc-Rousillon	France	June 16–27	20	3000	26
1997	Bari	Italy	June 13–27	21	NA	27

1951   Alexandria   Egypt   October 5–20

Nations: Egypt, France, Greece, Italy, Lebanon, Malta, Spain, Syria, Turkey, Yugoslavia
Sports: Athletics, Basketball, Boxing, Diving, Fencing, Football, Gymnastics, Rowing, Swimming, Water Polo, Weightlifting, Wrestling

MEDALS

Nation	Gold	Silver	Bronze	Total
Italy	28	22	12	62
France	26	13	5	44
Egypt	20	26	19	65
Turkey	10	3	7	20
Greece	4	9	8	21
Yugoslavia	3	5	7	15
Spain	1	4	4	9
Lebanon	0	5	14	19
Syria	0	3	10	13

1955   Barcelona   Spain   July 16–25

Nations: Egypt, France, Greece, Italy, Lebanon, Monaco, Spain, Syria, Turkey
Sports: Athletics, Basketball, Boxing, Cycling, Diving, Equestrian, Fencing, Field Hockey, Football, Gymnastics, Roller Hockey, Rowing, Rugby, Sailing, Shooting, Swimming, Water Polo, Weightlifting, Wrestling

MEDALS

Nation	Gold	Silver	Bronze	Total
France	41	35	34	110
Italy	36	33	24	93
Egypt	13	21	25	59
Spain	12	16	19	47
Turkey	9	3	3	15
Greece	1	7	9	17
Lebanon	1	2	4	7
Syria	0	0	2	2

1959   Beirut   Lebanon   October 11–26

Nations: France, Greece, Italy, Lebanon, Malta, Monaco, Morocco, Spain, Tunisia, Turkey, United Arab Republic, Yugoslavia
Sports: Athletics, Basketball, Boxing, Cycling, Diving, Fencing, Football, Gymnastics, Shooting, Swimming, Water Polo, Weightlifting, Wrestling, Volleyball

MEDALS

Nation	Gold	Silver	Bronze	Total
France	26	27	16	69
United Arab Republic	23	21	30	74
Turkey	13	8	1	22
Italy	12	5	4	21
Yugoslavia	11	9	8	28

Nation	Gold	Silver	Bronze	Total
Greece	8	9	13	30
Spain	5	12	12	29
Lebanon	3	10	17	30
Tunisia	3	2	1	6
Morocco	2	3	2	7

1963   Naples   Italy   September 21–29

Nations: France, Greece, Italy, Lebanon, Malta, Morocco, Spain, Tunisia, Turkey, United Arab Republic, Yugoslavia

Sports: Athletics, Basketball, Boxing, Cycling, Diving, Fencing, Football, Gymnastics, Field Hockey, Rowing, Sailing, Shooting, Swimming, Tennis, Water Polo, Weightlifting, Wrestling, Volleyball

MEDALS

Nation	Gold	Silver	Bronze	Total
Italy	32	21	16	69
Turkey	10	3	4	17
France	8	14	8	30
Yugoslavia	6	8	8	22
Egypt	5	13	9	27
Spain	4	4	12	20
Syria	0	1	3	4
Tunisia	0	1	1	2
Morocco	0	0	7	7
Greece	0	0	5	5
Lebanon	0	0	1	1
Monaco	0	0	1	1

1967   Tunis   Tunisia   September 8–17

Nations: Egypt, France, Greece, Italy, Lebanon, Malta, Monaco, Morocco, Spain, Syria, Tunisia, Turkey, Yugoslavia

Sports: Athletics, Basketball, Boxing, Cycling, Fencing, Football, Gymnastics, Handball, Swimming, Tennis, Water Polo, Weightlifting, Wrestling, Volleyball

MEDALS

Nation	Gold	Silver	Bronze	Total
Italy	35	26	22	83
Yugoslavia	15	16	5	36
Spain	10	14	27	51
Turkey	9	9	6	24
France	7	4	4	15
Tunisia	5	9	11	25
Greece	5	6	12	23
Morocco	1	1	3	5
Algeria	0	0	3	3
Libya	0	0	2	2
Lebanon	0	0	1	1

1971   Izmir   Turkey   October 6–17

Nations: Algeria, France, Greece, Italy, Lebanon, Malta, Libya, Morocco, Spain, Tunisia, Turkey, Yugoslavia

Sports: Athletics, Basketball, Boxing, Cycling, Diving, Fencing, Football, Gymnastics, Judo, Sailing, Shooting, Swimming, Tennis, Water Polo, Weightlifting, Wrestling, Volleyball

MEDALS

Nation	Gold	Silver	Bronze	Total
Italy	51	38	30	119
Yugoslavia	27	25	26	78
Spain	18	25	24	67
Turkey	18	12	15	45
Greece	8	8	24	40
Egypt	7	10	12	29
France	7	9	7	23
Tunisia	3	6	2	11
Syria	0	2	6	8
Morocco	0	2	6	8
Libya	0	0	1	1
Algeria	0	0	1	1

1975   Algiers   Algeria   August 23–September 6

Nations: Algeria, Egypt, France, Greece, Italy, Libya, Malta, Monaco, Morocco, Spain, Syria, Tunisia, Turkey, Yugoslavia

Sports: Athletics, Basketball, Boxing, Cycling, Diving, Fencing, Football, Gymnastics, Handball, Judo, Sailing, Shooting, Swimming, Tennis, Water Polo, Weightlifting, Wrestling, Volleyball

MEDALS

Nation	Gold	Silver	Bronze	Total
Italy	51	40	36	127
France	31	25	23	79
Yugoslavia	24	17	23	64
Spain	14	27	29	70
Turkey	12	11	8	31
Greece	9	12	16	37
Egypt	6	12	15	33
Algeria	4	7	9	20
Syria	3	2	11	16
Tunisia	3	2	2	7
Lebanon	3	0	1	4
Morocco	0	4	4	8
Libya	0	1	2	3

1979   Split   Yugoslavia   September 15–29

Nations: Algeria, Egypt, France, Greece, Italy, Lebanon, Libya, Malta, Monaco, Morocco, Spain, Syria, Tunisia, Turkey, Yugoslavia

Sports: Athletics, Basketball, Boxing, Canoeing, Cycling, Diving, Equestrian, Fencing, Football, Gymnastics, Handball, Field Hockey, Judo, Rowing, Rugby, Sailing, Shooting, Swimming, Table Tennis, Tennis, Water Polo, Weightlifting, Wrestling, Volleyball

MEDALS

Nation	Gold	Silver	Bronze	Total
Yugoslavia	56	38	33	127
France	55	40	34	129
Italy	49	63	47	159
Spain	16	20	32	68
Greece	7	10	13	30
Turkey	5	5	14	24
Egypt	3	9	10	22
Algeria	1	5	10	16
Tunisia	1	2	9	12
Lebanon	1	1	0	2
Syria	1	0	0	1
Morocco	0	2	3	5

1983   Casablanca   Morocco   September 3–17

Nations: Algeria, Egypt, France, Greece, Italy, Lebanon, Malta, Monaco, Morocco, Spain, Syria, Tunisia, Turkey, Yugoslavia

Sports: Athletics, Basketball, Boxing, Cycling, Diving, Fencing, Football, Golf, Gymnastics, Handball, Judo, Modern Pentathlon, Rugby, Swimming, Table Tennis, Tennis, Water Polo, Weightlifting, Wrestling, Volleyball

MEDALS

Nation	Gold	Silver	Bronze	Total
Italy	53	43	46	142
France	32	39	26	97
Spain	17	20	27	64
Yugoslavia	16	18	19	53
Greece	11	10	13	34
Turkey	12	5	14	31
Egypt	1	9	12	22
Morocco	8	5	7	20
Algeria	4	3	7	14
Tunisia	4	1	4	9
Syria	0	3	2	5
Lebanon	1	2	0	3

1987   Latakia   Syria   September 11–25

Nations: Algeria, Egypt, France, Greece, Italy, Lebanon, Libya, Malta, Monaco, Morocco, Spain, Syria, Tunisia, Turkey, Yugoslavia (three more)

Sports: Athletics, Basketball, Boxing, Cycling, Diving, Equestrian, Football, Gymnastics, Handball, Judo, Shooting, Swimming, Table Tennis, Tennis, Water Polo, Weightlifting, Wrestling, Volleyball

MEDALS

Nation	Gold	Silver	Bronze	Total
Italy	69	45	38	152
Spain	15	21	33	69
France	16	30	22	68
Yugoslavia	17	19	17	53
Turkey	8	9	22	39
Greece	7	14	16	37
Syria	9	6	12	27
Morocco	9	8	3	20
Egypt	4	4	6	14
Algeria	5	3	4	12
Tunisia	2	4	5	11
Albania	3	1	4	8
Cyprus	2	0	0	2
San Marino	0	1	0	1
Lebanon	0	1	0	1

1991   Athens   Greece   June 28–July 12

Nations: Albania, Algeria, Cyprus, Egypt, France, Greece, Italy, Lebanon, Libya, Malta, Monaco, Morocco, San Marino, Spain, Syria, Tunisia, Turkey, Yugoslavia

Sports: Athletics, Basketball, Boxing, Canoeing, Cycling, Diving, Equestrian, Fencing, Football, Golf, Gymnastics, Handball, Judo, Rowing, Sailing, Shooting, Swimming, Table Tennis, Tennis, Water Polo, Weightlifting, Wrestling, Volleyball

MEDALS

Nation	Gold	Silver	Bronze	Total
Italy	67	49	52	168
France	48	57	34	139
Spain	22	39	49	110
Greece	9	21	30	60
Turkey	23	11	12	46
Yugoslavia	16	13	9	38
Egypt	8	10	17	35
Morocco	5	5	10	20
Algeria	9	3	5	17
Syria	4	2	5	11
Albania	0	4	4	8
Tunisia	1	0	5	6
Cyprus	1	2	1	4
Lebanon	1	1	1	3

1993   Languedoc-Rousillon   France   June 16–27

Nations: Albania, Algeria, Bosnia, Cyprus, Egypt, France, Greece, Italy, Lebanon, Monaco, Morocco, Spain, Syria, Tunisia, Turkey, Yugoslavia (four more)

Sports: Archery, Athletics, Basketball, Boxing, Canoeing, Cycling, Diving, Equestrian, Fencing, Football, Golf, Gymnastics, Handball, Judo, Karate, Rowing, Rugby, Sailing, Shooting, Swimming, Table Tennis, Tennis, Water Polo, Weightlifting, Wrestling, Volleyball (Disabled Athletics, Swimming)

MEDALS

Nation	Gold	Silver	Bronze	Total
France	84	54	57	195
Italy	38	45	43	126
Turkey	34	20	10	64
Greece	17	25	24	66
Spain	14	41	33	88
Croatia	9	6	19	34
Morocco	7	7	13	27
Algeria	5	6	11	22
Slovenia	5	6	8	19
Egypt	4	9	16	29
Syria	4	2	5	11
Bosnia	2	0	1	3
Tunisia	1	1	8	10
Albania	0	2	0	2
Cyprus	0	1	2	3
San Marino	0	1	0	1
Malta	0	0	1	1

1997   Bari   Italy   June 13–27

MEDALS

Nation	Gold	Silver	Bronze	Total
Italy	73	62	57	192
France	56	45	46	147
Turkey	28	14	21	63
Spain	20	32	47	99
Greece	19	22	20	61
Algeria	7	7	8	22
Croatia	5	16	10	31
Slovenia	5	8	10	23
Yugoslavia	5	4	13	22
Morocco	5	4	9	18
Egypt	3	6	10	19
Tunisia	2	3	9	14
Syria	2	1	2	5
Malta	0	1	1	2
San Marino	0	1	0	1

Micronesian Games

The Micronesian Games were first held in 1969 in Saipan, the capital of the Northern Marianas. Seven small island nations—Palau, the Marshall Islands, Yap, Chuuk (formerly Truk), Pohnpei (formerly Ponape), Kosrae (formerly Kusiae) and the host Northern Marianas—made up the first Micronesian Games.

Men and women participated in athletics, swimming and volleyball, while men also competed in basketball, baseball, canoeing, tennis and table tennis. A very special event, the Micronesian All-Around, was created to showcase skills that were considered essential for survival in the South Pacific including coconut tree climbing, coconut husking, coconut throwing, spear throwing, swimming, and diving.

A second games scheduled to be held in 1972 never took place. However, two decades later the games were revived. The same seven island nations, with the addition of Guam, returned to Saipan in 1990 for the second games, which saw 875 athletes compete in the same sports as in the 1969 games. Palau edged Guam in the overall medals race with 29 golds to 22. Many individual athletes had a chance to shine. Swimmers Anneka Sakovitch of the Northern Marianas and Cindy Friesz of the Marshall Islands each won five gold medals.

At the conclusion of the games, the Micronesian Games Council was formed to oversee the development of future events and Guam was chosen as the host for the next edition which was to be held in 1994.

Nauru joined the 1994 games in Agana, Guam, which had nearly 2,000 athletes participating in the opening ceremonies at George Washington High School. The number of sports also increased. Softball, basketball, canoeing, tennis and table tennis were added to the schedule for women. Added to the men's competition were softball, weightlifting and spearfishing. In addition, beach volleyball, golf, bodybuilding, powerlifting, tae kwon do, women's weightlifting and water polo were demonstration sports.

The 1998 games were held in Koror, Palau, with the Republic of Kiribati the newest nation to join in. Palau spent some five million dollars to prepare facilities and athletes for the games, which were recognized as the most organized and professionally run Micronesian Games to date. The work paid off as Palau won a total of 118 medals to Guam's 81. Tiny Nauru, led by its weightlifting team, won a total of 38 gold medals, the most of any team. Marcus Stephen, Nauru's weightlifting star, broke three Oceania and Commonwealth records at the games. Nauru decided in 1994 that it was too small a nation to have a comprehensive sports program and that it would pour most of its efforts into developing a world-class weightlifting team, a goal which it is coming close to achieving.

Drug testing was introduced at the 1998 games. One of the substances mentioned as banned was betelnut, which was not allowed during competition or in the games village.

Palau, Guam and the Northern Marianas are not yet members of the International Olympic Committee due to rules that state that each member must be a fully independent nation. Guam and the Northern Marianas are both territories of the United States and residents of the those territories would at this time compete for the U.S. in the Olympic Games if qualified. All three are working on becoming IOC members on their own.

The 2002 Micronesian Games have been awarded to Pohnpei.

Year	Host City	Host Nation	Dates	Nations	Athletes	Sports
1969	Saipan	Northern Marianas	July 4–12	7	NA	9
1990	Saipan	Northern Marianas		8	875	9
1994	Agana	Guam	March 26–April 2	9	1500	13
1998	Koror	Palau	August 1–9	10	1900	13

1969   Saipan   Northern Marianas   July 4–12

Nations: Marianas, Palau, Marshall Islands, Yap, Truk,* Ponape,** Kusaie*** (*now Chuuk, **now Pohnpei, ***now Kosrae)

Sports: Athletics, Baseball, Basketball, Canoe Racing, Micronesian All-Around, Swimming, Table Tennis, Tennis, Volleyball
Sports for Women: Athletics, Swimming, Volleyball

MEDALS

Nation	Gold	Silver	Bronze	Total
Palau	26	21	12	59
Ponape/Kusaie	17	16	10	43
Marshalls	4	1	3	8
Truk	2	6	12	20
Marianas	2	4	6	12
Yap	0	1	8	9

1990   Saipan   Northern Marianas

Nations: Chuuk, Guam, Marshall Islands, Northern Marianas, Kosrae, Palau, Pohnpei, Yap
Sports: Athletics, Baseball, Basketball, Canoe Racing, Micronesian All-Around, Swimming, Table Tennis, Tennis, Volleyball

MEDALS

Nation	Gold	Silver	Bronze	Total
Palau	29	11	15	55
Guam	22	20	13	55
Pohnpei	12	11	9	32
CNMI	9	17	12	38
Marshalls	7	5	7	19
Chuuk	1	6	8	15
Kosrae	0	0	1	1

1994   Agana   Guam   March 26–April 2

Nations: Chuuk, Guam, Marshall Islands, Nauru, Northern Marianas, Kosrae, Palau, Pohnpei, Yap
Sports: Athletics, Baseball, Basketball, Micronesian-All Around (coconut tree climbing, coconut husking, spearing coconuts, swimming, diving for objects), Outrigger Canoes, Softball, Swimming, Tennis, Underwater Spearfishing, Wrestling, Weightlifting, Volleyball
Sports for Women: Athletics, Basketball, Canoe Racing, Table Tennis, Tennis, Softball, Swimming, Volleyball

MEDALS

Nation	Gold	Silver	Bronze	Total
Guam	56	26	29	111
Palau	17	30	22	69
Marshalls	16	13	18	47
CNMI	14	34	30	78
Nauru	9	4	4	17
Pohnpei	6	13	6	25
Kosrae	0	1	3	4
Chuuk	0	1	3	4

1998   Koror   Palau   August 1–9

Nations: Chuuk (FSM), Guam, Kiribati, Kosrae (FSM), Nauru, Northern Marianas, Marshall Islands, Palau, Pohnpei (FSM), Yap (FSM) [FSM = Federated States of Micronesia]

Sports: Athletics, Baseball, Basketball, Micronesian All-Around, Outrigger Canoes, Swimming, Softball (Fast-pitch, Slow-pitch), Table Tennis, Tennis, Underwater Spearfishing, Volleyball, Weightlifting, Wrestling

	MEDALS			
Nation	*Gold*	*Silver*	*Bronze*	*Total*
Nauru	38	3	10	51
Northern Marianas	36	27	15	78
Guam	35	27	19	81
Palau	31	58	29	118
Marshall Islands	5	7	21	33
Yap	5	4	8	17
Kosrae	4	5	11	20
Chuuk	3	7	7	17
Pohnpei	0	8	13	21
Kiribati	0	8	7	15

Middle East/Mediterranean Scholar Athlete Games

The Institute for International Sport sponsored the first Middle East/Mediterranean Scholar Athlete Games in the summer of 2000 at Tel Aviv University.

The games were modeled on the World Scholar Athlete Games where the athletes were placed on teams with youth from other countries. In addition to sports, events included art, dance, theater and writing/poetry.

Shimon Peres, Nobel Peace Prize winner and Prime Minister of Israel (1986–88), addressed the games participants on the topic of ending violence and border fighting in the Middle East.

Year	*Host City*	*Host Nation*	*Dates*	*Nations*	*Athletes*	*Sports*
2000	Tel Aviv	Israel	June 24–July 3	10	300	7

Nations: Cyprus, Greece, Ireland, Israel, Jordan, Palestine, South Africa, Switzerland, United States, Turkey

Sports: Athletics, Basketball, Chess, Football, Swimming, Tennis, Volleyball

Military World Games

The Conseil International du Sport Militaire, CISM, has held military world championships in numerous sports since its foundation in 1948, but had not formed a multisport competition until 1995.

The proposal for the first games came in 1990, the same year that the Warsaw Pact military sports organization (SCFA—Sports Committee of Friendly Armies) disbanded and the participating nations became part of the CISM. With the combining of the two organizations, the International Olympic Committee gave official recognition to the CISM in 1994.

The first Military World Games were held in Rome in 1995. Four thousand athletes from the militaries of 86 nations competed in 17 sports, including special military and naval pentathlons. All branches of the military, army, navy, air force and special forces were invited to compete.

Harrison Dillard, a four-time Olympic gold medallist, who also won four events in the military athletic meet in Frankfurt, Germany, after World War II, was a guest of honor at the games.

The game's motto was "Friendship through Sport," and the charter of the games states that "any political or religious action during the games, in particular the dissemination of propaganda, documents, pictures, brochures, reviews etc. is strictly forbidden." The Libyan football team violated the games rules by wearing T-shirts and warm-ups with anti–U.S. slogans and by protesting the United Nations Security Council's sanctions against Libya. After being warned by the organizing committee to stop wearing the shirts or go home, the Libyans left the games, but not until a confrontation in downtown Rome between an American and Libyan ended with the Libyan being tossed into a fountain.[139]

One Iranian Major, after his competition in the shooting events, contacted Iranian opposition groups in Rome and they helped him defect.

The home Italians put together a star football team but were shocked to lose 2–1 to unheralded Cyprus.

Thomas Hellreigel, the German ironman triathlete, won his specialty in Rome, while in the Olympic Stadium, world championship and Olympic finalists Artur Bagach (shot put—Russia) and Igor Kovac (triple jump—Slovakia) won their events.

The Russian military team finished ahead of all other teams with 62 gold, 28 silver and 37 bronze medals.

By 1998, the 50th anniversary of the founding of the CISM, the organization had 115 members and had scheduled a second Military World Games to be held in Mar del Plata, Argentina. Organizational difficulties in 1998 forced CISM to choose an alternate host. Zagreb, Croatia, ironically, close to the armed conflict in Yugoslavia, was chosen for the 1999 games. CISM was hoping to bring the militaries together in peaceful pursuits.

The Croatian military sportsmen and women were very successful on their home fields, the men beating the U.S. for the gold medal in basketball and Greece for the water polo title. The women beat North Korea for the volleyball championship. The Croatian men also won silver in handball and bronze in volleyball.

Egypt overcame a first-round loss 5–0 to Ukraine in football to win the gold 5–4 over Greece in a tie-breaker penalty shootout.

Several military world records were set at the games. On the track, Belarus' Natalia Duhnova won in the women's 800 meters with 2:00.84, and Russia's Irina Rosikhina ran 52.46 in the women's 400m. Germany's Thomas Goller recorded 48.75 for the 400 meter hurdles and Stanislavs Olijars of Latvia broke the military world record in the 110 meter hurdles with a time of 13.31 seconds. In the field, Maurizio Marian (Italy) and Michael Stolle (Germany) shared a pole vault record of 5.70 meters (18' 8½"), while Andriy Skvaruk of Ukraine threw the hammer 79.76 meters (26' 8"). Nadine Klienert broke the shot put record with a throw of 19.12 meters (62' 8¾"). Several records were set in swimming. Two Italian swimmers scored double world records. Lorenzo Vismar swam 22.06 in the 50 meter freestyle and 49.56 in the 100 meter freestyle. Emilijano Brambilla swam the 400 meter freestyle in 3:50.92 and the 1500 meter freestyle in 15:27.58.

Russia dominated the competition with 46 gold, 35 silver and 31 bronze medals. China followed with 30 gold, 22 silver and 16 bronze. Italy finished third with 72 medals: 20 gold, 26 silver and 26 bronze. The United States was seventh with eight gold, ten silver and eight bronze.

Year	Host City	Host Nation	Dates	Nations	Athletes	Sports
1995	Rome	Italy	September 6–15	86	4000	17
1999	Zagreb	Croatia	Aug. 8–17	78		22

1995   Rome   Italy   September 6–15

Sports: Athletics, Basketball, Boxing, Cycling, Equestrian, Fencing, Judo, Military Pentathlon, Modern Pentathlon, Parachuting, Shooting, Football, Swimming, Triathlon, Volleyball, Wrestling, Naval Pentathlon

Venues: Stadio Olimpico (Athletics), S. Severa, Cecchignola, Piscina delle Ros (Military Pentathlon), Tor di Quinto, Riano (Modern Pentathlon), Sabaudia in Latina (Naval Pentathlon), Anzio (sailing), Guidonia (Parachuting), S. Severa, Tor di Quinto (Shooting), Stadio dei Marmi (Marathon), Laquila, Sulmona (Cycling), Tor di Quinto, Montelibretti (Equestrian), Foro Italico (Swimming), Trevignano (Triathlon), Ariccia (Boxing), Viterbo (Fencing), Ostia (Judo, Wrestling), Viterbo, Montefiascione (Basketball), Flaminio, Manziana, Formello, Genzano, Pomezia, Valmontone, Stadio Olimpico (Football).

1999   Zagreb   Croatia   August 8–17

Sports: Athletics, Basketball, Boxing, Cycling, Diving, Fencing, Football, Handball, Judo, Kayaking, Lifesaving, Military Pentathlon, Naval Pentathlon, Rowing, Orienteering, Shooting, Swimming, Tae Kwon Do, Triathlon, Water Polo, Wrestling, Volleyball

Venues: Maksimir Stadium (Opening Ceremonies, Football), Galgovo Stadium (Football), Stadium Sisak (Football), Vrapèanski Potok (Shooting), Luèko Airport (Parachuting), Officers' School Jastrebars (Military Pentathlon), Jarun SRC (Naval Pentathlon), Delnice, Kraljev, Vrh, Ponikve (Orienteering), Mladost Stadium (Athletics), Jarun SRC (Triathlon, Rowing, Canoeing), Sutinska Vela (Judo), Pesèenica Sports Hall (Wrestling), Dom Sportova Sports Hall (Boxing, Handball), Zagreb Fair (Fencing), Karlovac Sports Hall (Tae Kwon Do), Mladost SRC, Salata SRC (Swimming, Rescuing, Diving, Water Polo), Kutija Sibica (Handball) Drazen Petroviç Sports Hall (Volleyball), Mladost Volleyball Center (Volleyball), Kres Sports Hall, Trhsko (Volleyball)

Muslim Student Games

The first Muslim Student Games were held in Tehran, Iran, in July 1994 with 910 athletes from eight Muslim nations.

Following the rules of Islamic law, and the example of the Muslim Women's Games and Iranian National Games, the women's competitions in basketball, table tennis, and volleyball were held in completely segregated arenas.

The games are organized to provide opportunities for Muslim students to learn more about their own culture and civilization, and the Muslim cultures of other nations.

In March 1995, the Sports and Physical Education Federation of International Muslim College Students was formed to oversee the sports events between Muslim college students of different nations.

Year	Host City	Host Nation	Dates	Nations	Athletes	Sports
1994	Tehran	Iran	July 21–28	8	910	5

Nations: Azerbaijan, Indonesia, Iran, Kazakhstan, Kyrgyzstan, Pakistan, Tajikistan, Turkmenistan
Sports: Basketball, Football, Volleyball, Wrestling
Sports for Women: Basketball, Table Tennis, Volleyball

Muslim Women's Games

The Muslim Women's Games, or Islamic Countries' Women's Sports Solidarity Games, were founded by Faezeh Hashemi, the vice president of the Iranian Olympic committee and daughter of Iranian President Hashemi Rafsanjani. The games, which reflect a clash between the different ideas of feminism in the west and strict Muslim beliefs, were begun in an attempt to find some middle ground between the two views.

At the 1992 Barcelona Olympics, 35 nations, many of them Muslim, had no women participants. The group Atlanta PLUS was formed in response to this to influence the International Olympic Committee to ban from the Olympics nations which did not allow women to compete. Terming this "gender apartheid," Atlanta PLUS petitioned the IOC to live up to the Olympic Charter which discourages any form of discrimination. Atlanta PLUS wrote, "This is neither a cultural/religious issue nor a women's only issue," but instead an issue of women's rights and human rights.

The distinctly different Muslim response was that the discrimination came from the governing bodies of world sport who created environments in which Muslim women could not compete while retaining their Muslim values. In his speech at the opening of the first games, President Rafsanjani stated that "the problem lies in the current manner of the practice of sports in the world and regional competitions. We value all those who have a respect for purity and continence and for restrictions thereby applied by our religion on women as well as men in view of fatwa [an Islamic legal opinion] and the realities of creation."

The first games were held in Tehran, Iran, February 13–19, 1993. Iran paid the expenses of ten teams to travel there. Four hundred and eighty-three athletes from Azerbaijan, Bahrain, Bangladesh, Iran, Kyrgyzstan, Malaysia, Maldives, Pakistan, Syria, Tajikistan and Turkmenistan marched in the opening ceremony. Ironically, Saudi Arabia and other gulf nations likely to be sympathetic with the format of the women-only games, did not send athletes as no athletic structures were in place in those countries to produce trained women athletes for competition.

In compliance with Islamic law, the female athletes at the opening ceremonies wore full hijab (dress conforming to Muslim law), a new experience for many of the women from less fundamental Muslim regions. Men were permitted as spectators at the opening ceremonies but during competition in athletics, swimming, basketball, badminton, handball, and table tennis, women wore modern sports uniforms and armed guards patrolled outside arenas to prohibit men from entering. Men were allowed to watch shooting, where women competed wearing the full hijab.

The games were administered, coached, and officiated entirely by women. An official film documentary of the games was created during the event, produced entirely by women. When the games were over, the film was shown to women's only audiences throughout Iran.

The second Muslim Women's Games were held in Tehran, December 13–22, 1997. Pakistan was originally asked to host the 1997 games. It did host a small women's only competition in 1996 with 320 athletes from 11 nations as a test competition for the main event, but opposition within Pakistan forced the games to be moved back to Tehran.[140,141]

Year	Host City	Host Nation	Dates	Nations	Athletes	Sports
1993	Tehran	Iran	February 13–19	11	483	8
1996	Islamabad	Pakistan	November 1–5	11	320	6
1997	Tehran	Iran	December 13–22	13	748	13

1993   Tehran   Iran   February 13–19

Nations: Azerbaijan, Bahrain, Bangladesh, Iran, Kyrgyzstan, Malaysia, Maldives, Pakistan, Syria, Tajikistan, Turkmenistan
Sports: Athletics, Badminton, Basketball, Handball, Swimming, Shooting, Table Tennis, Volleyball

1996   Islamabad   Pakistan   November 1–5

Sports: Athletics, Basketball, Handball, Shooting, Swimming, Table Tennis
Nations: Azerbaijan, Bangladesh, Bosnia, Kazakhstan, Kyrgyzstan, Malaysia, Pakistan, Syria, Tajikistan, Turkmenistan, Uzbekistan

1997   Tehran   Iran   December 13–22

Sports: Athletics, Badminton, Basketball, Chess, Equestrian, Gymnastics, Handball, Karate, Squash, Swimming, Shooting, Tennis, Volleyball
Nations: Azerbaijan, Bangladesh, Bosnia, Indonesia, Iran, Jordan, Kazakhstan, Kyrgyzstan, Pakistan, Sudan, Syria, Tajikistan, Turkmenistan

MEDALS

Nation	Gold	Silver	Bronze	Total
Iran	58	55	37	150
Kazakhstan	35	2	9	46
Indonesia	19	13	0	32
Kyrgyzstan	13	10	5	28
Syria	10	29	25	64
Azerbaijan	7	13	32	52
Turkmenistan	6	11	41	58
Pakistan	3	14	9	26

Nation	Gold	Silver	Bronze	Total
Sudan	2	0	0	2
Jordan	1	1	0	2
Bosnia	1	1	0	2
Bangladesh	0	2	1	3
Tajikistan	0	0	0	0

New Zealand Games

The New Zealand Games were a four-day event held one year after the 1974 Christchurch Commonwealth Games, with the New Zealanders hoping to make good use of the facilities created for those games. Despite hopes to continue the event, it was held on only one occasion.

Year	Host City	Host Nation	Dates	Nations	Athletes	Sports
1975	Christchurch	New Zealand	Jan. 23–26	13		5

Nations: Australia, Canada, Finland, Great Britain, Holland, Japan, Kenya, New Zealand, Sweden, Tanzania, United States, USSR, Yugoslavia

Nordic Games

Strong leadership and ideology contributed to the establishment of the Nordic Games in Sweden at the turn of the 20th century. Sweden's Central Association for the Promotion of Sports (CF) had been founded in 1897. In 1899, the group decided to hold the first "Nordic Games" in 1901, a wintertime festival of sports.

The CF consisted of numerous military officers and some of the elite in Swedish society. An especially prominent figure in the history of the games was Viktor Balck, a military officer and one of the original five founding members of the IOC. Balck helped organize the Nordic Games for almost 30 years.

Sweden was going through a period of heightened nationalism and wanted to establish a competition during the winter to display its prowess. Originally, the Swedish Tourist Association helped to promote the first games, with the hope that they would increase tourism.

The games were international, though the vast majority of participants were Swedish. The Swedes did not want the Nordic Games confused with the Olympic Games, and at times the Nordic Games organizers were completely against Swedish participation in the Winter Olympics.

The games were able to survive during the First World War, but circumstances after the war led to the last Nordic Games being organized in 1926.

Two significant changes occurred after the 1926 edition which led to the games' demise. Viktor Balck died in 1928 and much of the organizational impetus died with him. The CF's role in organizing sports was taken over by the Sveriges Riksidrotts-forbund (RF) which placed less emphasis on the organization of the games. A lack of snow contributed to the games' cancellation in 1930. Though editions were planned in 1934 and 1942, the worldwide depression of the 1930s and the growing success of the Winter Olympic Games ended the Nordic Games for good. [142,143]

Year	Host City	Host Nation	Dates	Nations*	Athletes	Sports
1901	Stockholm	Sweden	February 9–17	NA	NA	5
1903	Kristiania (Oslo)	Norway	Jan. 31–Feb. 6	NA	NA	NA
1905	Stockholm	Sweden	February 4–12	NA	NA	7
1909	Stockholm	Sweden	February 6–14	NA	2000	8
1913	Stockholm	Sweden	February 7–16	NA	NA	8
1917	Stockholm	Sweden	February 10–18	NA	NA	6
1922	Stockholm	Sweden	February 4–12	NA	NA	8
1926	Stockholm	Sweden	February 6–14	NA	NA	7

*Nations lists come from data in the results and may not be comprehensive

1901   Stockholm   Sweden   February 9–17

Nations: Austria, Finland, Norway, Sweden
Sports: Bandy, Endurance Riding, Figure Skating, Speed Skating, Nordic Skiing

1905   Stockholm   Sweden   February 4–12

Nations: England, Finland, Sweden
Sports: Bandy, Endurance Riding, Figure Skating, Speed Skating, Nordic Skiing
(Distanslopning pa skidor—155 km?, motorcycles?)

1909   Stockholm   Sweden   February 6–14

Nations: Austria, Denmark, Finland, Germany, Hungary, Norway, Sweden
Sports: Bandy, Combined Event, Endurance Riding, Figure Skating, Speed Skating, Nordic Skiing (Distanslopning pa skidor—155 km?, motorcycles?)

1913   Stockholm   Sweden   February 7–16

Nations: Austria, England, Finland, Germany, Hungary, Norway, Russia, Sweden
Sports: Bandy, Combined Event, Endurance Riding, Figure Skating, Ski Jumping, Speed Skating, Nordic Skiing (Distanslopning pa skidor?)

1917   Stockholm   Sweden   February 10–18

Nations: Denmark, Norway, Sweden
Sports: Bandy, Combined Event, Figure Skating, Ski Jumping, Speed Skating, Nordic Skiing

1922   Stockholm   Sweden   February 4–12

Nations: Austria, Finland, Norway, Sweden
Sports: Bandy, Combined Event, Endurance Riding, Figure Skating, Ice Hockey, Ski Jumping, Speed Skating, Nordic Skiing

1926   Stockholm   Sweden   February 6–14

Nations: Finland, Norway, Sweden

Sports: Bandy, Combined Event, Endurance Riding, Figure Skating, Ice Hockey, Ski Jumping, Speed Skating, Nordic Skiing

North American Indigenous Games

The North American Indigenous Games, open to Native American peoples from across the United States and Canada, have been described by organizers as part sports festival, cultural fair, spiritual revival and family reunion. The mission of the games is to "improve the quality of life for indigenous peoples by supporting self-determined sport and cultural activities which encourage equal access to participation in the social and cultural fabric of the community they reside in and which respects indigenous distinctiveness."[144] The games can be termed international by virtue of the fact that the U.S. and Canada participate, or because of the 400 or more indigenous nations that have participated in the games, but teams enter based on state or provincial boundaries.

The inaugural games held in Edmonton, Canada, in 1990 drew 3,000 athletes in 12 sports. The opening ceremonies were stayed at the University of Alberta Butterdome. During the games, Alwyn Morris, a Mohawk from Canada, who won gold and bronze medals in kayaking at the 1984 Olympic Games in Los Angeles, spoke to the athletes urging them to never give up on their dreams. To the organizers he said, "make sure these games happen again and again. I don't want to be the only native to go to the Olympics."[145]

Billy Mills, part Sioux and winner of the 10,000 meter run for the United States at the 1964 Tokyo Olympic Games, has expressed his support for the games on many occasions, saying "The active participation in sporting and cultural events provides the young aboriginal person of today an opportunity to showcase their hidden talents to themselves, their community and the community at large."[146] The games have one other long-term mission. "Our goal is to one day march a team of native athletes into the Olympic Games," Henry Harper, a 1995 Team Minnesota board member, told the *Minnesota Star-Tribune* newspaper.[147]

The games are primarily aimed at youth from ages 13 to 21, but some events are scheduled for adults. In 1997, about 4500 of the athletes were under 22 years of age, with 500 participants over the age of 21. The sports in the games range from archery and boxing to soccer and volleyball as well as demonstrations of traditional native sports. In 1997, these included war canoe races, lahal and arctic sports.

Each edition of the games includes a cultural festival with displays of Native American music, singing and dancing.

Instead of a games torch, the North American Indigenous Games have a relay called the Sacred Run with a Sacred Lance and Sacred Bundle. The first Sacred Run began at the Sacred Medicine Wheel area in Wyoming, and the Sacred Bundle was carried north 1100 kilometers to Edmonton. The second Sacred Run carried the lance and bundle from Edmonton to Prince Albert, Saskatchewan, the site of the second games in 1993. The 1995 games in Blaine, Minnesota, the largest to date with 8,000 participants, also incorporated the Sacred Run.

The 1997 games were held in Victoria, British Columbia. The natives of the Pacific coast used the opportunity for a traditional tribal journey in oceangoing canoes, which traveled from various parts of the Pacific coast to Victoria and were welcomed in

Victoria's Inner Harbor in a traditional Coast Salish welcoming ceremony. In addition to indigenous peoples from across Canada and the United States, native peoples from Australia, New Zealand and Japan joined in the cultural festivities at the Victoria games.

The 1999 games, which were to be jointly held in Fargo, North Dakota, and Moorhead, Minnesota, were canceled when funding lagged and the event could not be organized. The next games are scheduled to be held in Winnipeg, Canada, in 2002.

Year	Host City	Host Nation	Dates	Nations	Athletes	Sports
1990	Edmonton	Canada	July 1–7	2	3000	12
1993	Prince Albert	Canada	July 18–25	2	4400	8
1995	Blaine	USA	July 31–Aug. 5	2	8000	17
1997	Victoria	Canada	August 3–10	2	5000	21

1990   Edmonton   Canada   July 1–7

Nations: Canada, United States
Sports: Athletics, Basketball, Boxing, Canoeing, Lacrosse, Shooting, Swimming, Softball, Football, Volleyball, Wrestling, (Archery?)

1993   Prince Albert   Canada   July 18–25

Nations: Canada, United States
Sports: Archery, Badminton, Baseball, Golf, Lacrosse, Football, Volleyball, Wrestling

1995   Blaine   USA   July 31–August 5

Nations: Canada, United States

1997   Victoria   Canada   August 3–10

Nations: Canada, United States
Sports: Archery, Athletics, Badminton, Baseball, Basketball, Canoeing, Football, Golf, Lacrosse, Shooting, Softball, Swimming, Tae Kwon Do, Volleyball, Wrestling, (5 demonstration sports—War Canoe Races, Futsal, Lahal, Hoop Dancing, Arctic Sports)
Venues: Saanich Tribal School (Archery), UVIC Centennial Stadium (Athletics), Claremont High (Badminton), Lambrick Park (Baseball), McKinnon Gym, UVIC (Basketball), Stelly's Secondary (Boxing, Wrestling, Tae Kwon Do), Elk Lake (Canoeing), Glen Meadows Golf (Golf), Braefoot Athletic Center (LaCrosse), North Saanich Rod and Gun Club (Rifle Shooting), Work Point Gym (Volleyball), Rotary Park (Softball, Fastball)

Olympic Games

The first modern Olympic Games were held in Athens in 1896, but the groundwork had been laid in the decades before that time.[148]

The revival of the Olympic Games was not an original idea by Pierre de Coubertin, the French Baron credited with bringing the games back into existence. The idea had been germinating for years, and in some cases, "Olympic Games," mostly local or national in scope, had been in existence in the centuries prior to what is now considered the first modern Olympic Games in Athens in 1896.

Robert Dover's Cotswold Olympicks[149] began in 1612 and ended in 1852 when the games became unmanageable.[150] In 1832, Baron de Berenger hosted an Olympic festival at his Chelsea Stadium, in England, and in 1838 expanded the idea into the first "Olympic Week."[151] The Much Wenlock Games were a well-known local competition in England. Begun by William Brookes in 1850, they lasted until 1895. Coubertin observed these games and may have gained some inspiration from them.[152] Several other national Olympic games were held in England, Germany, France and Yugoslavia at varying times and intervals from 1776 until 1914. In Greece, the Pan-Athenaic Games, or "Zappas Olympics," were held as Greek National Games with mild success in 1859, 1870, 1875 and 1888.

De Coubertin spent several years traveling around Europe and to the United States to gather allies for his idea to revive the Olympic Games. He mentioned the idea to the Union des Sports Athlétiques on November 25, 1892, at a meeting in Paris, and finally, in June 1894, invited dozens of interested parties to an international sport conference in Paris, at which Coubertin raised the possibility of the revival of the Olympic Games. There were 79 delegates there, representing 49 organizations from nine countries.

On June 23, 1894, the idea was finally established. The Olympic Games were to be revived. The first IOC president was not de Coubertin, but Dimítrios Vikélas, a Greek, who presided over the IOC until the end of the 1896 games. The presidency was to rotate among members, with the position going to a citizen of the next host country. De Coubertin was named the next president, but the rules were changed and he remained in that role until 1925. Though the first games were in Athens, Pierre de Coubertin spoke of Paris as the city where the Olympics were revived.[153]

From the beginning the games were designed with the high ideal that the youth of the world were to be brought together in peaceful competition. No discrimination would be allowed in race, religion, or political affiliation. The games were to be contests between individuals and not between countries. Immediately the media of the day began tallying up medal and points totals, though the International Olympic Committee, in particular de Coubertin, did not intend medal standings to be recognized. He insisted that the games be awarded to cities, not nations, and later wrote that the "fundamental whim of Olympism is somehow tied up with the Greek notion of the city."[154]

At the Session of the IOC held in Athens during the first Olympic Games, the representative from Germany, Gebhardt, suggested that all nations establish a National Olympic Committee, thus setting the stage for the structure of the IOC and its relationship to the national committees that we know today.

Following 1896, the games were a string of long-drawn-out affairs, spread over several months rather than a span of 15 to 17 days which has been the standard since 1932. The games of Paris in 1900 lasted 131 days; the St. Louis games in 1904, 155 days; and the London games in 1908, 189 days. These games, without Olympic villages and global media coverage, had a very different feel than the games of the late 20th century. Along with the extended schedules, the relatively small size of the games meant that transportation and housing, for both spectators and athletes, were not the issues for organizers that they are today.

Year	Host City	Host Nation	Dates	Days Long
1896	Athens	Greece	April 6–15	10
1900	Paris	France	May 20–Oct. 28	131
1904	St. Louis	USA	July 1–Nov. 23	155
1906*	Athens	Greece	April 22–May 2	11
1908	London	England	April 27–Oct. 31	189
1912	Stockholm	Sweden	May 5–July 22	78
1920	Antwerp	Belgium	April 20–Sept. 12	145
1924	Paris	France	May 4–July 27	84
1928	Amsterdam	Netherlands	May 17–Aug. 12	87
1932	Los Angeles	USA	July 30–Aug. 14	16
1936	Berlin	Germany	Aug. 1–16	16
1948	London	England	July 29–Aug. 14	17
1952	Helsinki	Finland	July 19–Aug. 3	16
1956	Melbourne	Australia	Nov. 22–Dec. 8	17
1960	Rome	Italy	Aug. 25–Sept. 11	16
1964	Tokyo	Japan	Oct. 10–24	15
1968	Mexico City	Mexico	Oct. 12–27	16
1972	Munich	Germany	Aug. 26–Sept. 10	16
1976	Montreal	Canada	July 17–Aug. 1	16
1980	Moscow	Soviet Union	July 19–Aug. 3	16
1984	Los Angeles	USA	July 28–Aug. 12	16
1988	Seoul	South Korea	Sept. 17–Oct. 2	16
1992	Barcelona	Spain	July 25–Aug. 10	17
1996	Atlanta	USA	July 19–Aug. 4	17
2000	Sydney	Australia	Sept. 16–Oct. 1	16

*Not considered official by the IOC

The Paris games were loosely tied to the 1900 Paris World's Fair. Many of the events were called "Championships of the Exposition," and many participants would leave Paris not realizing that they had competed in the Olympic Games. The French and Americans quibbled over competitions scheduled for Sundays, the Americans not wanting to break the Sabbath.

The 1904 Games in St. Louis were also entangled with a major fair, the Louisiana Purchase Exposition. The games were originally awarded to Chicago, but then switched to St. Louis. The St. Louis organizers wanted the games as part of the fair and threatened to hold their own games if Chicago would not give them the event. Chicago backed down and the games were moved to St. Louis.

The Olympic Games were not the only thing to move from Chicago to St. Louis. The Great Ferris Wheel, built by George Washington Ferris for the World's Columbian Exposition in 1893 in Chicago, was also dismantled and sent to St. Louis for use in the 1904 fair.

Because of the distance, the number of nations and athletes competing in 1904 was about half the number that had competed in Paris in 1900.

One of the most truly embarrassing moments in Olympic history was the inclusion of an event given the name "Anthropology Days" by the organizers.[155] These events are usually mentioned mostly in passing in reviews of the 1904 games but a closer look reveals some of the deep prejudices and misunderstandings that were held in some quarters of various western populations at the time.

The events in question took place on August 12 and 13, and were arranged ostensibly to prove or disprove the prowess of certain groups from around the world in response to the "startling rumors and statements that were made in relation to the speed, stamina and strength of each and every particular tribe that was represented at St. Louis...." The games were held in August so that "the many physical directors and gentlemen interested in scientific work could be present and benefit by the demonstrations."

Of course, these "athletes" from among the "tribes" were in St. Louis due not to their athletic prowess but as part of the World's Fair exhibits, and it was quite unfair to compare their performances to the very best performances to date by western-trained athletes, a fact that these "trained anthropologists" conveniently overlooked.

The tribes represented were Pygmy, Bacuba and Zulu from Africa, Moros from the Philippines, Patagonians from South America, Ainu from Japan, Syrians from "Beyrout," Cocopa from Mexico, and Sioux, Pawnee, Chippewa, Cherokee, Crow and Pueblo from North America.

The report from the games criticized the running of these native people. The fastest time for the dash of 11⅕ seconds was mocked as a "time that almost any winner of a schoolboy event would eclipse at will." The winning shot put of 30 ft. 5 in. was described as "a ridiculously poor performance that astonished all who witnessed it." The report continues, "Of course the argument might be made that these savages had not been taught the art of shot-putting. Quite true, but one would think that the life these men have led should enable them to easily have put this shot much further."

The 56 pound weight throw results drew even harsher criticism. The report stated "the savages did not take kindly at all" to the event. The results were compared to the record holder Flanagan, whose throw would have bested the three Ainus from Japan, whom the report mentions were 28, 38 and 57 years of age!

The report is respectful in only one area, the pole climbing event. The winners performance showed "marvelous agility, strength of limb and great endurance," and "the times of all the savages in this event were praiseworthy and worthy of record."

The unnecessarily harsh report concluded, "Lecturers and authors will in the future please omit all references to the natural athletic ability of the savage, unless they can substantiate their alleged feats."

Pierre de Coubertin was incensed when he heard about these events being held in proximity to the games. "As for that outrageous charade it will of course lose its appeal when black men, red men, and yellow men learn to run jump and throw and leave the white men behind them."[156] Nearly 100 years later, the record does stand that athletic prowess is can and does emanate from every corner of the globe.

De Coubertin then realized that holding the games in conjunction with any other large event was a disaster and vowed never to let it happen again.

The Greeks then reasserted their claim that Greece should be the home of the games and to back up that assertion, hosted the 1906 games, known as the Intercalated Games. Much later the games would be declared unofficial by the IOC. At the time, however, they may have saved the still fledgling Olympic revival. De Coubertin was originally against the idea but gave his support when he realized that the Greeks were organizing far better games than had taken place in 1900 and 1904. Going against the pattern of the previous two games, the 1906 games were just 11 days long.

Berlin, Milan and Rome expressed interest in hosting the 1908 games. Rome was chosen, but had to give up the event when Mt. Vesuvius erupted in 1906. London was appointed as the alternate site. The Games were held in a new stadium, Shepherd's Bush, a multievent facility which had a running track, cycling track, football field, swimming pool, and space for wrestling and gymnastics with room for 68,000 spectators.

Politics began to insert themselves into the games. The United States and Great Britain, fierce athletics rivals of the era, argued over rules. Several other countries joined the protests. Flags became an issue when the British did not allow the Irish flag into the stadium, the Russians wouldn't allow the Finns to fly their flag and the British forgot to place the Swedish and American flags above the stadium for the opening ceremonies. Sweden left during the middle of the games over a dispute about wrestling rules.

The Swedes recovered in time to show their hospitality at the 1912 games held in the capital, Stockholm, in a beautiful brand-new stadium that is still in use in the year 2000. Sweden, at the time, did not allow boxing matches, and boxing was dropped from the schedule. In response, the IOC passed a rule limiting the power of future organizing committees.

A marathon runner from Portugal collapsed in Stockholm and died of heat stroke. He was the first athlete to die in the modern Olympic Games.[157]

Jim Thorpe would become the first of many athletes to be penalized for being a professional athlete. After winning the Olympic pentathlon and decathlon championships in 1912, Thorpe had his medals taken away in 1913 when it was revealed that he had played semiprofessional baseball prior to the games.

Berlin was chosen to host the 1916 Olympic Games over bids from Alexandria, Egypt; Amsterdam, Netherlands; Brussels, Belgium; Budapest, Hungary; and Cleveland, United States. However, the games were abandoned due to World War I.

When the Olympic games resumed in 1920, Germany, Austria, Hungary, Bulgaria and Turkey were not invited because of animosities stemming from the war. Antwerp was chosen over Atlanta, Budapest, Cleveland, Havana, Lyon and Philadelphia to host the games.

The 1920 games were spartan, by necessity, with resources scarce from the devastation of the war. De Coubertin insisted the games be held on schedule, however, and the Belgians responded with a well-organized affair.

Spartan conditions caused discomfort for the American team as well. Sent to the games on an army transport ship, the *Matioka*, the athletes (figuring they deserved better accommodations than soldiers, it seems) protested vigorously. What they felt in enthusiasm, they lacked in timing. They revolted while the ship was in the mid–Atlantic, not realizing that no matter how loudly they howled those in charge couldn't change a thing. The "Mutiny of the Matioka" cooled off until the team reached Antwerp, when a second revolt broke out. One athlete, Dan Ahearn, upset with housing arrangements, found his own lodging and was kicked off the team by American officials. Nearly 200 American athletes petitioned for his reinstatement, or they would refuse to compete. American officials then rescinded the suspension.[158]

Finnish athletes won gold, silver and bronze in the javelin throw. This was the first time since the modern revival that athletes from the same nation, other than the United States, had accomplished the feat of taking all three medals in an event.

The Belgian citizens had little money left over to spend on athletics and entertainment, and this meant that the stadiums were less than full during the early days of the games. The Belgian organizers responded by allowing schoolchildren and the public to watch the games for free. The games lost money and the Belgian government picked up the tab.

De Coubertin was looking to expand the games, and the city of Los Angeles (as well as Amsterdam, Barcelona, Prague and Rome) was willing to host them in 1924. However, de Coubertin wanted the games, "the thirtieth anniversary of the Olympic revival," to be held in Paris. Nonetheless, on several occasions he did suggest that Los Angeles host a games for the Americas in 1923 as a way to prepare athletes for the 1924 Olympics. The strategy was that if political troubles arose again in Europe, these games could be postponed to 1924 and become the Olympic Games.[159] No games were held in 1923 or 1924 in Los Angeles, and Paris successfully hosted them in 1924.

In many cases, the games had begun to cause international incidents rather than bring athletes together peaceably. Calls for the end of the Olympic Games began to show up in the press. The boorish behavior of many spectators at the 1924 games was met with a wave of protest. Germany was still not allowed to compete as it remained under sanctions resulting from World War I.

In 1925, Henri Baillet-Latour of Belgium was named the next president of the IOC—a position he would hold until his death in 1942.

Amsterdam was awarded the 1928 games, but de Coubertin wanted Los Angeles to stand by if, due to the financial situation in Europe, Amsterdam could not stage the event. American Olympic Committee member William May Garland politely refused, saying Los Angeles would be ready in 1932.[160]

The 1928 Amsterdam games saw the debut of the Olympic flame which was simply lit over the stadium for the duration of the event. The relay would not begin for another two Olympiads.

Women were allowed to compete in athletics for the first time ever, but when several of the women's 800 meter runners finished the race exhausted, officials once again placed limits on female participation. It would be 1960 before women would be allowed to run further than 200 meters.

The American sprinter Charlie Paddock was accused of professionalism, but was cleared to compete. This decision led George Wightman, one of the vice-presidents of the American Olympic Committee (AOC), to resign in protest.

Another protest occurred when a Major William Kennelly took four athletes to Amsterdam, including former Olympic participants and current world record-holders, all of whom had failed to make the team, and tried to force the AOC to include them. The AOC refused and Kennelly let the matter rest.

In October 1930, the IOC executive board decided to change the rules and have all medals awarded directly after each event, with the medalists on an awards stand. Up to that time, the awards were generally handed out in one ceremony on the last day of the games.

The Great Depression and long travel distances put the games out of reach for many nations in 1932. The local Southern California protest group "Bread not Circuses" expressed its displeasure that money was being spent on the games rather than on necessities.

The games had the very first specially constructed Olympic village, reserved for men. Women were housed in the much more elegant Chapman Park Hotel near downtown Los Angeles. They were fully chaperoned.

Paavo Nurmi was tossed out of the games for professionalism. He had received money for his running in Europe and the United States.

The huge 105,000-seat Los Angeles Memorial Coliseum hosted the opening and closing ceremonies and athletic events. Ten world records were set on the new coliseum track. Cycling events were held on a specially constructed board track in the famous Rose Bowl in Pasadena.

The suitors for the 1936 edition of the games were Alexandria, Barcelona, Berlin, Budapest, Buenos Aires, Cologne, Dublin, Frankfurt, Helsinki, Lausanne, Nuremburg, Rio de Janeiro and Rome. Germany was awarded the games in 1931, two years before Adolf Hitler came to power.

Such was the furor over the treatment of Jews and other minorities in the new Germany that long and heated debates on both sides of the Atlantic brewed for several months before the 1936 Berlin Olympic Games.[161] Many felt a boycott was in order. A notable exception was Avery Brundage, the president of the American Olympic Committee.

The Nazis built a huge stadium and sports complex and decorated Berlin with several thousand Nazi banners and swastikas. The Germans staged the first ever Olympic torch relay, which began in Olympia and traveled through Greece, Bulgaria, Yugoslavia, Hungary, Austria and Czechoslovakia before arriving in Germany.[162]

The games were on a form of television for the first time. A closed-circuit system was set up to broadcast them to theaters in Berlin. Newsreels were used to spread the games to cities throughout Europe, and the Germans used their zeppelins to transport the film.

Albert Speer, Hitler's architect and one of his inner circle during the war, recalled a conversation with Hitler in his book *Inside the Third Reich*. "We walked about the Olympic Games and I pointed out that my athletics field did not have the prescribed Olympic proportions. Without any change of tone, as if it were a matter settled beyond the possibility of discussion, Hitler observed: 'No matter. In 1940 the Olympic Games will take place in Tokyo. But thereafter they will take place in Germany for all time to come, in this stadium. And then we will determine the measurements of the athletic field.'"[163]

The games are best remembered not as a Nazi success, but the opposite. Jesse Owens, a black American, by his performance fully refuted any notion of "Aryan supremacy." Jesse and his long jump rival Luz Long became fast friends and corresponded until the time Long was killed in North Africa during the war. The strength of the friendship prevailed even after that, as Jesse served as best man at the wedding of Karl Long, Luz's son. Oak trees were awarded to the gold medal winners. Many of these trees were planted around the globe in the victors' hometowns and are still alive.[164]

On September 2, 1937, the reviver of the Olympic Games, Pierre de Coubertin, died while on an afternoon walk in Parc de la Grange in Geneva. He is buried in Lausanne, Switzerland, but was granted his wish that his heart be buried in Olympia, Greece.

Tokyo, Japan, was chosen to host the 1940 games out of a field of 13 cities that had bid for them—Alexandria, Athens, Barcelona, Budapest, Buenos Aires, Dublin, Lausanne, London, Montreal, Rio de Janeiro, Rome, and Toronto. This was the most interest ever expressed in hosting the games. Japan, however, entangled in war with China, gave up the games in the summer of 1938. The IOC immediately chose Helsinki as a substitute, but the Soviet Union invasion of that country and the violent upheaval of World War II ended all thoughts of an Olympic Games in 1940.

London was awarded the games of 1944, over Athens, Budapest, Helsinki, Detroit, Lausanne, Montreal and Rome, but this was in essence a symbolic gesture since no one expected the war to stop for a games. In the interim, IOC president Baillet-Latour died in June 1942. Sweden's Sigfrid Edstrom assumed the interim leadership of the IOC but was not elected to the presidency until 1946. When the war did end, the IOC executive board (which hadn't met since June 1939[165]) met in London in August 1945 and again awarded the British capital the games. Lausanne and four U.S. cities—Baltimore, Los Angeles, Minneapolis and Philadelphia—had also been considered.

In the bleak days after the war, with food and fuel being rationed, many in Britain thought that going ahead with the games was foolish. Nonetheless, by the summer of 1948, London responded, not with a lavish games, but with a well-run athletic festival, despite the weather which began with a heat wave and ended with several days of rain.

The Olympic village was not fancy. Men were housed in Uxbridge on an army base; women in dormitories at Southlands College.

The IOC ruled that Israel could not compete in the games as it did not yet have a National Olympic Committee that was recognized by the IOC. In any case, the Arab nations had threatened to boycott if Israel were given permission to compete.

Germany and Japan were also not invited to the games. The Soviet Union did not come to London, but Hungary, Yugoslavia and Poland were the first communist nations to take part in the modern games.

Helsinki finally got its chance to host the games, in 1952, having been selected over Los Angeles, Minneapolis, Amsterdam, Detroit, Chicago, Philadelphia, Athens, Lausanne and Stockholm.

The most significant new entrants in Helsinki were the athletes from the Soviet Union. The Soviet presence was felt before the games, however, when they refused to allow the Finns to bring the Olympic torch from Olympia across a small part of Estonia. The Finns instead took the torch through Sweden and the Arctic circle and brought it south to Helsinki.

When the Soviet Union arrived in Helsinki, they set up their own Olympic village at the Porkalla Naval Base, with room for the Bulgarians, Czechs, Hungarians, Poles and Romanians as well. Before the games, the Soviets sent several athletes home after they were determined to be "politically unreliable."

East Germany asked for permission to compete separately from West Germany but the IOC refused, as the West Germans had the recognized federation.

The IOC allowed both People's Republic of China and Taiwan to enter the games but Taiwan withdrew its entry in protest.

Finland chose one of its greatest Olympians, Paavo Nurmi, to relay the Olympic flame around the stadium, and another, Hannes Kolehmainen, to light the cauldron.

Avery Brundage of the U.S. was elected the new president of the IOC at its meetings in Helsinki.

IOC sessions in June 1955 changed the rules for boxing. There would no longer be a bout for the bronze medal: both semifinal losers would get a bronze.

Melbourne had outpolled Buenos Aires by a single vote for the honor of hosting the 1956 games, leaving Los Angeles, Detroit, Mexico City, Chicago, Minneapolis, Philadelphia, Montreal and San Francisco to bid another day.

As the games headed to the southern hemisphere for the first time, there was internal bickering between the federal and state governments in Australia over who was to pay for what. This meant that preparations lagged so much that IOC president Avery Brundage suggested Rome might be more ready to host the 1956 event. Melbourne recovered and preparations were completed in time.

Very strict horse quarantine laws in Australia meant that the equestrian events were held in Stockholm, Sweden, from June 10 to 17. The rest of the events were held in spring in the southern hemisphere, from November 22 to December 8. Stockholm had been selected over bids from Paris, Rio de Janeiro, Berlin, Los Angeles and Buenos Aires.

The Australians insisted that there be one Olympic village in Melbourne. The Soviet bloc athletes would have to live with the athletes from the rest of the world, or not come to the games at all.

The Netherlands, Spain and Switzerland boycotted the events in Melbourne in 1956 to protest the Soviet invasion of Hungary. The Swiss later changed their minds, but couldn't find transportation in time and ended up missing the Melbourne events. Switzerland kept alive its streak of having athletes compete in every modern Olympic Games because they had competed in the equestrian events in Stockholm.

When Israel attacked Egypt, and Britain and France moved into the Suez Canal area, Egypt, Iraq and Lebanon withdrew from the games.

Finally, when the Australians let the Nationalist Chinese (Republic of China—Taiwan) enter the games, the People's Republic of China pulled out. East and West Germany competed as a combined team on orders from the IOC.

Rome, which had been selected for the 1908 games, finally got its chance 52 years later, chosen over Lausanne, Detroit, Budapest, Brussels, Mexico City and Tokyo to host the 1960 games. Rome was a mixture of new and old in the staging of the events in Rome. Wrestling, for instance, was held in the Basilica of Maxentius.

The Republic of China was forced by the IOC to march under the name Formosa. As its members passed the reviewing stand, the leader of the delegation held up a sign reading "Under protest" and then just as quickly put it away.

The 1960 Olympics were the first to be fully televised. Eurovision gave live broadcasts throughout Europe, and tapes of the games were flown to New York City and broadcast by CBS in the United States.

The issue of apartheid in South Africa and Rhodesia was beginning to become troublesome. Kenya was supposed to host the 1963 IOC session in Nairobi but refused visas to IOC representatives from South Africa and Portugal. The IOC moved the session to Baden-Baden, West Germany.[166]

The 1964 Tokyo games took place in the magnificent stadiums that the Japanese had built for the 1958 Asian Games. Detroit, Vienna and Brussels had also been eyeing the 1964 games.

The games opened with the Olympic flame being lit by Yoshinori Sakai, a young man had been born in Hiroshima on the day the atom bomb was dropped there.

For the first time, South Africa was banned by the IOC for its apartheid policies after the South African Non-Racial Olympic Committee (SAN-ROC) had been formed in January 1963. The goal of SAN-ROC was to publicize the existence of apartheid in South African sport and encourage the IOC to force change in South Africa. The group would eventually be successful in having South Africa expelled from the IOC in 1970.

Indonesia and North Korea withdrew from the games—fallout from an incident at the 1962 Asian Games held in Indonesia. The Indonesians led the leaders from Israel and Taiwan to believe that they would be welcome at the games, then at the last minute refused to give them visas. The IOC later suspended Indonesia from competitions.

Indonesia responded by hosting its own games, the Games of the New Emerging Forces (GANEFO) in 1963. Several sport federations, most notably in athletics and swimming, said they would ban any athletes who competed in the GANEFO games. Indonesia and North Korea withdrew from the 1964 Olympics in protest, but they were the only nations to actually try and enter athletes who had competed in GANEFO and knew that they would be penalized most by the bans.

The North Koreans, in an interesting exchange with IOC president Avery Brundage as they were threatening to withdraw, accused the IOC of discriminating against the six athletes who had competed in GANEFO that they were trying to enter in the Olympic Games. President Brundage said, "You complain that the IOC wants to stop six competitors—at the same time you prevent 174 of your own sportsmen from participating! Who has done the right thing?"[167]

The games village was a converted U.S. military facility. It comprised bungalows and flats which had been built at the end of World War II.[168]

The Tokyo games would be the last of the relatively peaceful games for some time.

Mexico City was awarded the 1968 games with disregard for the over 7000-foot altitude. It won over the bids from Buenos Aires, Detroit and Lyon.

Mexico City's organizers, for several reasons, held three test competitions, or "Little Olympics," in 1965, 1966 and 1967 which included several sports. The 1966 games had some 800 athletes from 27 nations. The events gave the Mexican organizers a chance to practice their organization. These "Little Olympics" were also held in order to give doctors a chance to study the effects of altitude on athletic performance, and to give the athletes a chance to feel the effects as well. The IOC passed regulations after this prohibiting these kinds of events held in host cities before the games.[169]

For the first time a woman was the final torch bearer. Enriqueta Basilio de Sotela carried the torch to the top of the stadium to light the flame.

In February 1968, the IOC held a postal vote and decided to invite South Africa to the games, but in April this was rescinded. Rhodesia, also for reasons of its apartheid policies, was excluded from the 1968 games as well.

Student protests in Mexico City, primarily over the amount of money spent for the games instead of to help the poor in Mexico, were suppressed by the Mexican army. Just ten days before the games, between 200 and 300 students were killed when the army fired on the protesters. There were another 1000 wounded.

Protests inside the arenas, though less violent, gained more attention. Some had been advocating a boycott by blacks over the poor treatment of their race in the United States. Instead, several athletes, in particular Tommie Smith and John Carlos, gave the "black power" salute on the victory stand after winning the gold and bronze medals in the 200 meter dash on the track. The IOC banned the two athletes immediately for using the podium for a political statement.

East Germany was finally given the right to participate separately from West Germany. On May 15, 1970, in Amsterdam, the IOC voted to expel South Africa.

In 1971, the IOC decided to eliminate the term amateur from the Olympic Charter which opened the doors for professional athletes in every sport to compete in the games.

Munich, West Germany, was selected over Montreal, Madrid and Detroit (it was Detroit's eighth try to obtain the games) to stage the 1972 games. Perhaps the saddest days in modern Olympic history occurred at the games in Munich when Arab terrorists entered the Olympic village and overran the Israeli team. Two Israelis were murdered in the village, and another nine killed while on the ground inside helicopters in an attempt by German soldiers to ambush the terrorists and free the hostages at a military airport outside Munich.

The events overshadowed the fine athletic performances of the Olympics and forever changed security measures for organizers of all games.

The IOC had toured Rhodesia in 1971 and decided the nation could be invited to Munich. However, after many African nations had threatened a boycott, the IOC backed down and told Rhodesia to stay away from the games.

Drug testing, which was carried out on a limited basis in 1968, was expanded in 1972. Seven athletes were suspended from the games.

The U.S. basketball team lost for the very first time in the Olympic Games amid a controversy over the clock during the last three seconds of the final game against the Soviet Union. The Soviets were given three chances to inbound the ball. The first two failed; the final one succeeded. The U.S. team refused to attend the award ceremony or accept the silver medals.

In Munich, Lord Killanin of Ireland was elected the new IOC president.

Competition between the Soviet Union and the U.S. heated up outside the arena when both countries wanted to host the 1976 Olympic Games.

In the spring of 2000, newly declassified government papers in the U.S. were made public which spoke of White House plans to help both Denver and Los Angeles obtain the 1976 winter and summer games to coincide with U.S. Bicentennial celebrations.

In December 1969, Moscow unexpectedly announced its candidacy for the 1976 summer games. Los Angeles to that point had been regarded as the strong front-runner.

The declassified papers mention grants for coaches, athletes and facilities for foreign countries (although both the U.S. and Soviet Union had been giving such grants for decades) and that contact be made with U.S. ambassadors abroad to exert pressure that would bring the U.S. cities the votes in the May 1970 IOC elections. U.S. President Richard Nixon ordered Henry A. Kissinger and the State Department to join in an "all-out" effort to capture the Olympic prize.[170]

Nixon also asked that Soviet Ambassador Anatoly Dobrynin be told that "we would support Moscow in 1980 if the Soviets withdrew in 1976."

Nonetheless, the State Department rejected two proposals by the Los Angeles committee. One was that all 72 IOC members be given "pieces of moon rock." The department said moon rocks should be reserved for heads of state. The department also opposed a request that Nixon write to each member of the IOC seeking their vote, because "it can be construed as interference and a violation of one of the fundamental principles of the Olympic movement."

In the end, Vietnam may have been the deciding factor. When the IOC met in Amsterdam on May 12, the first ballot read Moscow 28, Montreal 25 and Los Angeles 17. With Los Angeles out of the running, 16 of the 17 L.A. votes went to Montreal, shocking both the Americans and Soviets.

The U.S. was awarded the 1976 Olympic Winter Games. They went to Denver, but Coloradans had second thoughts and later voted to give up the games. Innsbruck took their place as the 1976 Winter Games host.

After spending enormous amounts of money for the games and suffering a poor economy in the years leading up to them which saw the value of the Canadian dollar plummet, Montreal became the victim of the largest boycott up to that time at the Olympic Games. African athletes were victims as well, when African governments decided to call their athletes home to protest the fact that New Zealand was being allowed to compete at the games. The African nations wanted New Zealand out because its national rugby team had toured South Africa. In the end, 20 African nations plus Guyana and Iraq pulled out of the 1976 games.

At first, Canada refused to allow the Republic of China (Taiwan) team to enter the country as the Canadian government did not recognize Taiwan as a nation. The Canadians relented, but then would not allow the Taiwanese to compete as the Republic of China, insisting that they be called Taiwan. The matter was never sorted out. The IOC backed Canada and the Republic of China went home.

The friendly relations that the Olympic Games were supposed to produce took another bruising when U.S. President Jimmy Carter chose to use the 1980 Moscow games as a political tool to protest the Soviet Union's invasion of Afghanistan. Moscow had been chosen over Los Angeles to host the 1980 Games.

At the 1980 Olympic Winter Games in Lake Placid, Cyrus Vance, the Secretary of State of the United States, upset the IOC members with a speech at the opening of the IOC session in which he tried to convince the IOC to move or cancel the Moscow Games.[171]

During the summer of 1980, several mentions were made of western nations hosting alternative games, but none of those plans were ever completed.

Sixty-five western governments told their athletes to stay away from the games. Several nations went but protested in other forms: not marching in the opening ceremony, marching behind the Olympic flag or the National Olympic Committee flag from their country, or not allowing their anthem to be played at the awards ceremonies.

Juan Antonio Samaranch of Spain was elected IOC president in July 1980 at the 83rd session of the IOC just before the opening of the Moscow games.

In September 1981, the Olympic rings were a topic of discussion at the World Intellectual Property Organization (WIPO) Congress in Nairobi. Twenty-two nations signed an agreement to protect the rings from unauthorized use.[172]

That same month in Baden-Baden, Sebastian Coe addressed the issue of drug use in sport at the Olympic Congress. It was one of the first instances of an athletes voice being represented at an Olympic Congress.[173]

In October 1981, Pirjo Häggman (Finland) and Flor Isava Fonseca (Venezuela) became the first women elected to IOC membership.[174]

After Munich, Montreal and Moscow, very few cities were clamoring to host the Olympic Games. Los Angeles and Tehran were the early bidders for the 1984 games. When Tehran dropped out, Los Angeles was given the games by default.

The 1984 Olympic Games at Los Angeles were to change the Olympic movement substantially and provide the groundwork for it to find better ways to finance the games. Though some decry the "over–commercialization" of the games, they are fewer than those who protest paying for the games with tax dollars.

The 1984 Olympic Games are often criticized as the games which brought commercialism to the Olympics. However, in the "Official Report" of the 1980 Moscow games, the hosts state that there were 222 Soviet enterprises that were named official supplier or official sponsor of the event. Los Angeles had 29 official sponsors and suppliers. The difference was exclusivity. Los Angeles required sponsors to pay more for exclusive sponsorship rights.

The Los Angeles games made a profit of some 240 million dollars of which 60 percent was turned over to the U.S. Olympic Committee and 40 set aside for a foundation to fund youth sports in southern California.

The Soviet Union led a boycott of the 1984 games, claiming that the Americans could not ensure the safety of the Soviet athletes in Los Angeles. Certain fringe groups in Los Angeles had been agitating and sending materials in the mail to the Soviet Olympic Committee and government threatening protests. Most observers felt that the boycott was simply retaliation for the U.S. boycott of the 1980 Olympic Games.

For some time, the IOC attempted to assist in the development of sport in nations that were financially disadvantaged. In March 1983, it decided, under its Olympic Solidarity program, to pay for three athletes and one official to go to the winter games and for six athletes and two officials to go to the summer games, all from countries who needed assistance.

North Korea wanted to host some of the events for the Olympic Games of 1988, which Seoul, South Korea, had been awarded over Nagoya, Japan. After long discussions, the IOC, at the Lausanne session in October 1986, agreed that North Korea could host table tennis and archery. In September 1987, the North Koreans stated that they wanted to host eight events. In the end, North Korea boycotted the games. Cuba and Ethiopia joined the North Koreans in the boycott.

The defining moment of the games was when Canadian sprinter Ben Johnson was found to have violated the IOC drug policies. His performances had been enhanced by steroids.

The 1988 Seoul games were the first to have the Paralympic Games held directly afterward in the same city. They were also the last to have homing pigeons at the opening ceremonies. Several of the birds came to rest on the unlit torch. Later in the ceremony when the torch was set ablaze, no effort was made to shoo the birds away and a worldwide television audience saw several birds incinerated.

Tennis had been a demonstration sport in 1988. In August 1989, the IOC brought it back as a full medal sport and allowed professionals to play. The IOC added, however, that tennis players who competed in South Africa would not be eligible for the Olympics.

In 1990, Kuwaiti IOC member Sheikh Fahad al-Ahmad Al Sabah, who was also president of the Olympic Council of Asia, was killed during Iraq's invasion of Kuwait.

Paris, Barcelona, Brisbane, Belgrade, Birmingham and Amsterdam were all hopefuls for the 1992 Olympic Games, but they were ultimately awarded to Barcelona.

The Barcelona games distinctly reflected the changing political alliances of the globe. The Soviet Union competed as the Unified Team, but this was the last time the athletes would compete together. East and West Germany competed as one. South Africa returned to the games, since African states having voted on October 19, 1991, to accept the nation back. Cuba and North Korea participated after several absences, and Latvia, Lithuania, Estonia, and Croatia competed as independent nations.

War in Yugoslavia and U.N. sanctions against it meant that Yugoslavia was not allowed to send a team to Barcelona. Independent athletes from Serbia-Montenegro were allowed as "Independent Participants." This represented an about-face on the part of the IOC on an issue that it had ruled on once before. During the boycott of 1976, James Gilkes, a sprinter from Guyana, had asked the IOC that he be allowed to compete as an individual, under the IOC flag. The IOC refused, saying that athletes needed to be affiliated with a National Olympic Committee. In 1992, when the IOC allowed athletes from Serbia-Montenegro to compete independently, they had no official national governing body at the time.

In March 1993, both the Czech and Slovak National Olympic Committees were recognized after the "Velvet Divorce" of Czechoslovakia.

Also in 1993, on June 23, "Olympic Day" (the anniversary of the day in 1894 on which it was agreed that the Olympics were to be officially revived), the Olympic Museum opened in Lausanne.

Athens was the sentimental favorite among the candidates for the Centennial Olympic Games of 1996, but it was Atlanta that emerged the winner over Athens, Toronto, Melbourne, Manchester and Belgrade.

The U.S. organizers upset some of their visiting guests with the crass commercial presence surrounding the games, severe transportation problems and computer glitches. In the midst of the games, a bomb in Centennial Olympic Park, the public centerpiece of the games, killed one and injured over a hundred others. A Turkish journalist died of a heart attack while covering the story.

The Atlanta games marked the first time that all National Olympic Committees (a record 197) invited to compete sent athletes.

In November 1998, the IOC began one of its darkest chapters when it was revealed that there were bribes and other inducements being given to IOC members in trade for votes for the bidding cities.

On November 24, the television station KTVX in Salt Lake City reported that the Salt Lake City Organizing Committee paid for the daughter of IOC member René Essomba of Cameroon to go to college in the U.S. Very soon, other allegations of free health care, sham jobs and other gifts to IOC members and their relatives were being mentioned.

In early December, the president of the Salt Lake City Organizing Committee, Frank Joklik, released a list of 13 people who had received financial aid or scholarships from the committee. Shortly after this revelation, IOC President Juan Antonio Samaranch ordered an internal investigation of the Salt Lake City Organizing Committee's payments to IOC members and relatives and placed a ban on IOC members traveling to cities that were bidding for the games. The crisis deepened when Swiss IOC member Marc Hodler stated that bribes had affected the outcome of the voting for every Olympic Games from 1996 to 2002.

Later in December, the U.S. Justice Department, the FBI and a U.S. senate commission, led by former U.S. Senator George Mitchell, began investigations.

In January, the president of the Salt Lake City Organizing Committee, Frank Joklik, and vice-president, Dave Johnson, both resigned. IOC president Samaranch sent letters to 13 IOC members demanding explanations of their purported roles in the scandal and set a special IOC meeting for the middle of March for the IOC to specifically deal with the issues that had arisen from the incident.

In the meantime, there were reports that Sydney had been involved in vote buying and that Nagano's accounting records had all been destroyed, making it impossible to verify whether it had broken spending rules. Nagano had allegedly spent some $22,000 per IOC member—well above the limit set by the IOC.

On the 19th of January 1999, the IOC member from Finland, Pirjo Häggman, became the first IOC member to resign. By the IOC meeting in March, ten members had either resigned or been expelled. Many people were also calling for President Samaranch to resign, including some members of the Mitchell commission in the U.S., but Samaranch had strong support from his fellow IOC members and stayed in office. At the March meetings, the IOC established two commissions—an Ethics

Commission and an IOC 2000 Commission—which were tasked to look into the issues of ethics and reform in the Olympic movement. The IOC 2000 Commission would release its findings in December 1999 with 50 recommendations.

In May 1999, the scandal continued when the Salt Lake City Organizing Committee released a list, known internally as the "Geld Document," which contained information on IOC members and their families, and what they might be interested in or in need of.

The case against Salt Lake Olympic bid leaders Tom Welch and Dave Johnson continued. The two were indicted in July 1999 on several counts of conspiracy and racketeering for their alleged roles in paying $1 million to bring the games to Salt Lake City. Their trial was not scheduled to begin until the summer of 2001.

In December 1999, the IOC met in Lausanne for an Extraordinary Session to discuss and vote on recommendations of the IOC 2000 Commission. The commission made 50 recommendations pertaining to the IOC in several areas including its structure and organization, the IOC's role, and the designation of host cities for the games. The recommendations covered a wide variety of topics including terms of office and age limits for IOC members, representation of athletes on the IOC, gifts, visits to candidate cities (the recommendation was to forbid them), accountability of finances in the Olympic Movement, the role of Olympic Solidarity programs of the IOC, and doping. All of the commission's recommendations were accepted by the members of the IOC.[175,176]

The host city election procedure was substantially changed at the 110th IOC session in December 1999. Cities applying for the games are not considered to be official candidates until applications have been examined and approved by the IOC executive board. The board selects only cities that are adequately equipped to continue forward into the full bid process. Official visits from IOC members to bid cities and visits of members of bid committees to IOC members are no longer allowed.

The Olympic Oath was updated adding a clause concerning doping. The Athlete's Oath now reads, "In the name of all the competitors I promise that we shall take part in these Olympic Games, respecting and abiding by the rules which govern them, committing ourselves to a sport without doping and without drugs, in the true spirit of sportsmanship, for the glory of sport and the honor of our teams."

After dealing with the scandal, the Olympic movement looked towards the Sydney Olympic Games. Sydney had been chosen over Beijing, Berlin, Brasilia, Istanbul and Manchester for the right to hold the 2000 games. Athletes from 199 delegations—nearly every eligible National Olympic Committee in the world—participated in the summer games held from September 15 to October 1, 2000. Afghanistan was not invited to Sydney after the IOC determined that it did not have a legitimate National Olympic Committee. Different factions in the country were fighting to be considered the true NOC. Zaire competed as the Democratic Republic of the Congo, and Western Samoa competed as Samoa. Eritrea, Federated States of Micronesia, and Palau were the three new NOCs represented, bringing the total to 199. One more delegation, called "Individual Olympic Athletes," which comprised athletes from the war-torn region of East Timor, was welcomed to the games but not counted in the tally of NOCs.

The games brought North and South Korea together, for at least one moment, when the two nations reached an agreement to march together in the opening ceremony.

Australia's most notable female Olympic stars—Betty Cuthbert, Shirley Strickland, Raelene Boyle, Dawn Fraser, Shane Gould and Debbie Flintoff-King—carried the torch into Stadium Australia. Cathy Freeman, Australia's world champion 400 meter runner, represented Australia's aboriginal peoples when she lit the flame. Freeman later won the 400 meter gold medal.

Triathlon and tae kwon do were new sports, and women competed in water polo and modern pentathlon for the first time.

In all, 10,651 athletes—6,582 men and 4,069 women—participated in the games. This represented the highest percentage (38 percent) of women participants ever at an Olympic Games.

The bidding field for the 2004 games was crowded: the preliminary list consisted of Athens, Buenos Aires, Cape Town, Istanbul, Lille, Rio de Janeiro, Rome, San Juan, Seville, Stockholm and St. Petersburg, with Athens, Buenos Aires, Cape Town, Rome and Stockholm the finalist cities. With the ultimate selection of Athens, Africa and South America remain the two continents yet to host an Olympic Games. Athens' preparations for the games have come under much criticism for not proceeding at the pace that some outside observers and the IOC would like.

The original ten cities that bid for the 2008 Olympic Games were Bangkok, Beijing, Cairo, Havana, Istanbul, Kuala Lumpur, Osaka, Paris, Seville, and Toronto. The final five candidates were Beijing, Istanbul, Osaka, Paris and Toronto. The host of the 2008 games, as well as a successor for retiring IOC president Samaranch, will be chosen in July 2001 at the IOC meetings in Moscow.

Year	Host City	Host Nation	Dates	Nations	Athletes[177]	Sports
1896	Athens	Greece	April 6–15	13	245	9
1900	Paris	France	May 20–Oct. 28	26	1118	18
1904	St. Louis	USA	July 1–Nov. 23	12	627	12
1906*	Athens	Greece	April 22–May 2	20	847	12
1908	London	England	April 27–Oct. 31	23	2023	17
1912	Stockholm	Sweden	May 5–July 22	28	2490	14
1920	Antwerp	Belgium	April 20–Sept. 12	29	2668	21
1924	Paris	France	May 4–July 27	44	3070	17
1928	Amsterdam	Netherlands	May 17–Aug. 12	46	3014	17
1932	Los Angeles	USA	July 30–Aug. 14	37	1328	16
1936	Berlin	Germany	August 1–16	49	3956	20
1948	London	England	July 29–Aug. 14	59	4064	19
1952	Helsinki	Finland	July 19–Aug. 3	69	4879	19
1956	Melbourne	Australia	Nov. 22–Dec. 8	67	3258	19
1960	Rome	Italy	Aug. 25–Sept. 11	83	5348	19
1964	Tokyo	Japan	October 10–24	93	5081	21
1968	Mexico City	Mexico	October 12–27	112	5423	20
1972	Munich	West Germany	Aug. 26–Sept. 10	122	7173	23
1976	Montreal	Canada	July 17–Aug. 1	92	6024	23
1980	Moscow	Soviet Union	July 19–Aug. 3	81	5217	23
1984	Los Angeles	USA	July 28–Aug. 12	141	6797	23
1988	Seoul	South Korea	Sept. 17–Oct. 2	160	8465	26
1992	Barcelona	Spain	July 25–Aug. 10	172	9370	28
1996	Atlanta	USA	July 19–Aug. 4	197	10310	31
2000	Sydney	Australia	Sept. 15–Oct. 1	199	10651	28

*not considered official by the IOC

1896   Athens   Greece   April 6–15

Nations: Australia, Austria, Chile, Cuba, Denmark, Egypt, France, Germany, Great Britain, Greece, Hungary, Italy, Sweden, Switzerland, United States
Sports: Athletics, Cycling, Fencing, Gymnastics, Shooting, Swimming, Tennis, Weightlifting, Wrestling
Sports for Women: None

MEDALS

Nation	Gold	Silver	Bronze	Total
United States	11	7	2	20
Greece	10	16	19	45
Germany	6	5	2	13
France	5	4	2	11
Great Britain	2	3	3	8
Hungary	2	1	3	6
Austria	2	1	2	5
Australia	2	0	0	2
Denmark	1	2	3	6
Switzerland	1	2	0	3
Combined	1	1	1	3
Egypt	0	1	0	1

1900   Paris   France   May 20–October 28

Nations: Argentina, Australia, Austria, Belgium, Bohemia, Canada, Cuba, Denmark, France, Germany, Great Britain, Greece, Haiti, India, Iran, Italy, Luxembourg, Mexico, Netherlands, Norway, Peru, Romania, Russia, Spain, Sweden, Switzerland, United States
Sports: Archery, Athletics, Cricket, Croquet, Cycling, Equestrian, Fencing, Football, Gymnastics, Polo, Rowing, Rugby, Sailing, Shooting, Swimming, Tennis, Tug of War, Yachting
Sports for Women: Croquet, Equestrian, Golf, Tennis, Yachting

MEDALS

Nation	Gold	Silver	Bronze	Total
United States	21	14	15	50
France	18	27	21	66
Great Britain	12	9	7	28
Switzerland	6	1	1	8
Combined	4	3	5	12
Belgium	3	3	1	7
Germany	3	2	2	7
Italy	3	2	0	5
Australia	2	0	3	5
Cuba	1	1	0	2
Canada	1	0	1	2
Luxembourg	1	0	0	1
Spain	1	0	0	1
Austria	0	3	3	6
Hungary	0	2	2	4
Netherlands	0	1	2	3

Nation	Gold	Silver	Bronze	Total
Norway	0	1	1	2
Bohemia	0	1	1	2
Denmark	0	0	2	2
Sweden	0	0	1	1
Mexico	0	0	1	1

1904   St. Louis   USA   July 1–November 23

Nations: Australia, Austria, Cuba, Canada, France, Germany, Great Britain, Greece, Norway, South Africa, Switzerland, United States
Sports: Athletics, Boxing, Cycling, Diving, Fencing, Football, Gymnastics, Rowing, Swimming, Tennis, Weightlifting, Wrestling
Sports for Women: Tennis

MEDALS

Nation	Gold	Silver	Bronze	Total
United States	67	72	75	214
Germany	4	4	4	12
Canada	4	1	1	6
Cuba	3	0	0	3
Hungary	2	1	1	4
Combined	2	1	0	3
Austria	1	1	1	3
Great Britain	1	1	0	2
Switzerland	1	0	1	2
Greece	1	0	1	2
Ireland	1	0	0	1
France	0	0	0	0

1906*   Athens   Greece   April 22–May 2

Nations: Australia, Austria, Belgium, Bohemia, Canada, Denmark, Egypt, Finland, France, Germany, Great Britain, Greece, Hungary, Italy, Netherlands, Norway, Sweden, Switzerland, Turkey, United States
Sports: Athletics, Cycling, Diving, Fencing, Football, Gymnastics, Rowing, Shooting, Swimming, Tennis, Weightlifting, Wrestling
Sports for Women: Tennis

*not considered official by the IOC

MEDALS

Nation	Gold	Silver	Bronze	Total
France	15	9	16	40
United States	12	6	6	24
Greece	8	13	12	33
Great Britain	8	11	5	24
Italy	7	6	3	16
Germany	4	6	5	15
Switzerland	4	3	1	8
Austria	3	3	3	9

Nation	Gold	Silver	Bronze	Total
Denmark	3	2	1	6
Sweden	2	5	7	14
Hungary	2	5	3	10
Belgium	2	1	3	6
Finland	2	1	1	4
Norway	1	1	0	2
Canada	1	1	0	2
Netherlands	0	1	2	3
Turkey	0	1	1	2
Combined	0	1	0	1
Australia	0	0	3	3
Bohemia	0	0	2	2

1908   London   England   April 27–October 31

Nations: Australasia,[178] Austria, Belgium, Bohemia, Canada, Denmark, Finland, France, Germany, Great Britain, Greece, Iceland, Hungary, Italy, Netherlands, Norway, Russia, South Africa, Sweden, Switzerland, Turkey, United States

Sports: Archery, Athletics, Boxing, Cycling, Diving, Fencing, Figure Skating, Football, Gymnastics, Field Hockey, Rowing, Sailing, Shooting, Swimming, Tennis, Water Polo, Wrestling

Sports for Women: Sailing, Tennis

MEDALS

Nation	Gold	Silver	Bronze	Total
Great Britain	56	51	39	146
United States	23	12	12	47
Sweden	8	6	11	25
France	5	5	9	19
Germany	3	5	5	13
Hungary	3	4	2	9
Canada	3	3	10	16
Norway	2	3	3	8
Italy	2	2	0	4
Belgium	1	5	2	8
Australia	1	2	1	4
Russia	1	2	0	3
Finland	1	1	3	5
South Africa	1	1	0	2
Greece	0	3	1	4
Denmark	0	2	3	5
Bohemia	0	0	2	2
Netherlands	0	0	2	2
New Zealand	0	0	1	1
Austria	0	0	1	1

1912   Stockholm   Sweden   May 5–July 22

Nations: Australasia, Austria, Belgium, Bohemia, Canada, Chile, Denmark, Egypt, Finland, France, Germany, Great Britain, Greece, Hungary, Iceland, Italy, Japan, Luxembourg, Netherlands, Norway, Portugal, Russia, Serbia, South Africa, Sweden, Switzerland, Turkey, United States

Sports: Athletics, Cycling, Diving, Equestrian, Fencing, Football, Gymnastics, Modern Pentathlon, Rowing, Shooting, Swimming, Tennis, Water Polo, Wrestling

Sports for Women: Swimming, Tennis

MEDALS

Nation	Gold	Silver	Bronze	Total
United States	25	18	20	63
Sweden	23	24	17	64
Great Britain	10	15	16	41
Finland	9	8	9	26
France	7	4	3	14
Germany	5	13	7	25
South Africa	4	2	0	6
Norway	3	2	5	10
Hungary	3	2	3	8
Canada	3	2	2	7
Italy	3	1	2	6
Belgium	2	1	3	6
Denmark	1	6	5	12
Australia	1	2	2	5
Greece	1	0	1	2
Combined	1	0	0	1
Russia	0	2	3	5
Austria	0	2	2	4
Netherlands	0	0	3	3
New Zealand	0	0	1	1

1920   Antwerp   Belgium   April 20–September 12

Nations: Argentina, Australia, Belgium, Brazil, Canada, Chile, Czechoslovakia, Denmark, Egypt, Estonia, Finland, France, Great Britain, Greece, India, Italy, Japan, Luxembourg, Monaco, Netherlands, New Zealand, Norway, Portugal, South Africa, Spain, Sweden, Switzerland, United States, Yugoslavia

Sports: Archery, Athletics, Boxing, Cycling, Diving, Equestrian, Fencing, Figure Skating, Football, Gymnastics, Field Hockey, Ice Hockey, Modern Pentathlon, Rowing, Sailing, Shooting, Swimming, Tennis, Water Polo, Weightlifting, Wrestling

Sports for Women: Diving, Figure Skating, Sailing, Swimming, Tennis

MEDALS

Nation	Gold	Silver	Bronze	Total
United States	41	27	27	95
Sweden	19	20	25	64
Finland	15	10	9	34
Great Britain	14	15	13	42
Belgium	13	11	11	35
Norway	13	9	9	31
Italy	13	5	5	23
France	9	19	13	41

Nation	Gold	Silver	Bronze	Total
Netherlands	4	2	5	11
Denmark	3	9	1	13
South Africa	3	4	3	10
Canada	3	3	3	9
Switzerland	2	2	7	11
Estonia	1	2	0	3
Brazil	1	1	1	3
Australia	0	2	1	3
Japan	0	2	0	2
Spain	0	2	0	2
Greece	0	1	0	1
Luxembourg	0	1	0	1
Czechoslovakia	0	0	2	2
New Zealand	0	0	1	1

1924   Paris   France   May 4–July 27

Nations: Argentina, Australia, Austria, Belgium, Brazil, Bulgaria, Canada, Chile, Cuba, Czechoslovakia, Denmark, Ecuador, Egypt, Estonia, Finland, France, Great Britain, Greece, Haiti, Hungary, India, Ireland, Italy, Japan, Latvia, Lithuania, Luxembourg, Mexico, Monaco, Netherlands, New Zealand, Norway, Philippines, Poland, Portugal, Romania, South Africa, Spain, Sweden, Switzerland, Turkey, United States, Uruguay, Yugoslavia

Sports: Athletics, Boxing, Cycling, Diving, Equestrian, Fencing, Football, Gymnastics, Modern Pentathlon, Rowing, Sailing, Shooting, Swimming, Tennis, Water Polo, Weightlifting, Wrestling

Sports for Women: Diving, Fencing, Swimming, Tennis

MEDALS

Nation	Gold	Silver	Bronze	Total
United States	45	27	27	99
Finland	14	13	10	37
France	13	15	10	38
Great Britain	9	13	12	34
Italy	8	3	5	16
Switzerland	7	8	10	25
Norway	5	2	3	10
Sweden	4	13	12	29
Netherlands	4	1	5	10
Belgium	3	7	3	13
Australia	3	1	2	6
Denmark	2	5	2	9
Hungary	2	3	4	9
Yugoslavia	2	0	0	2
Czechoslovakia	1	4	5	10
Argentina	1	3	2	6
Estonia	1	1	4	6
South Africa	1	1	1	3
Uruguay	1	0	0	1

Nation	Gold	Silver	Bronze	Total
Canada	0	3	1	4
Austria	0	3	1	4
Poland	0	1	1	2
Japan	0	0	1	1
Romania	0	0	1	1
New Zealand	0	0	1	1
Portugal	0	0	1	1
Haiti	0	0	1	1

1928   Amsterdam   Netherlands   May 17–August 12

Nations: Argentina, Australia, Austria, Belgium, Bulgaria, Canada, Chile, Cuba, Czechoslovakia, Denmark, Egypt, Estonia, Finland, France, Germany, Great Britain, Greece, Haiti, Hungary, India, Ireland, Italy, Japan, Latvia, Lithuania, Luxembourg, Malta, Mexico, Monaco, Netherlands, New Zealand, Norway, Panama, Philippines, Poland, Portugal, Rhodesia, Romania, South Africa, Spain, Sweden, Switzerland, Turkey, United States, Uruguay, Yugoslavia

Sports: Athletics, Boxing, Cycling, Diving, Equestrian, Fencing, Football, Gymnastics, Field Hockey, Modern Pentathlon, Rowing, Sailing, Shooting, Swimming, Water Polo, Weightlifting, Wrestling

Sports for Women: Athletics, Diving, Fencing, Gymnastics, Sailing, Swimming

MEDALS

Nation	Gold	Silver	Bronze	Total
United States	22	18	16	56
Germany	10	7	14	31
Finland	8	8	9	25
Sweden	7	6	12	25
Italy	7	5	7	19
Switzerland	7	4	4	15
France	6	10	5	21
Netherlands	6	9	4	19
Hungary	4	5	0	9
Canada	4	4	7	15
Great Britain	3	10	7	20
Argentina	3	3	1	7
Denmark	3	1	2	6
Czechoslovakia	2	5	2	9
Japan	2	2	1	5
Estonia	2	1	2	5
Egypt	2	1	1	4
Austria	2	0	1	3
Australia	1	2	1	4
Norway	1	2	1	4
Poland	1	1	3	5
Yugoslavia	1	1	3	5
South Africa	1	0	2	3
India	1	0	0	1
Uruguay	1	0	0	1

Nation	Gold	Silver	Bronze	Total
Spain	1	0	0	1
Ireland	1	0	0	1
New Zealand	1	0	0	1
Belgium	0	1	2	3
Chile	0	1	0	1
Haiti	0	1	0	1
Portugal	0	0	1	1
Philippines	0	0	1	1

1932   Los Angeles   USA   July 30–August 14

Nations: Argentina, Australia, Austria, Belgium, Brazil, Canada, China, Colombia, Czechoslovakia, Denmark, Estonia, Finland, France, Germany, Great Britain, Greece, Haiti, Hungary, India, Ireland, Italy, Japan, Latvia, Mexico, Netherlands, New Zealand, Norway, Philippines, Poland, Portugal, South Africa, Spain, Sweden, Switzerland, United States, Uruguay, Yugoslavia

Sports: Athletics, Boxing, Cycling, Diving, Equestrian, Fencing, Gymnastics, Field Hockey, Modern Pentathlon, Rowing, Sailing, Shooting, Swimming, Water Polo, Weightlifting, Wrestling

Sports for Women: Athletics, Diving, Fencing, Swimming

MEDALS

Nation	Gold	Silver	Bronze	Total
United States	41	32	30	103
Italy	12	12	12	36
France	10	5	4	19
Sweden	9	5	9	23
Japan	7	7	4	18
Hungary	6	4	5	15
Finland	5	8	12	25
Great Britain	4	7	5	16
Germany	3	12	5	20
Australia	3	1	1	5
Argentina	3	1	0	4
Canada	2	5	8	15
Netherlands	2	5	0	7
Poland	2	1	4	7
South Africa	2	0	3	5
Ireland	2	0	0	2
Czechoslovakia	1	2	1	4
Austria	1	1	3	5
India	1	0	0	1
Denmark	0	3	3	6
Mexico	0	2	0	2
Switzerland	0	1	0	1
New Zealand	0	1	0	1
Latvia	0	1	0	1
Philippines	0	0	3	3
Uruguay	0	0	1	1
Spain	0	0	1	1

1936   Berlin   Germany   August 1–16

Nations: Afghanistan, Argentina, Australia, Austria, Belgium, Bermuda, Bolivia, Brazil, Bulgaria, Canada, Chile, China, Colombia, Czechoslovakia, Denmark, Egypt, Estonia, Finland, France, Germany, Great Britain, Greece, Hungary, Iceland, India, Italy, Japan, Latvia, Liechtenstein, Luxembourg, Malta, Mexico, Monaco, Netherlands, New Zealand, Norway, Peru, Philippines, Poland, Portugal, Romania, South Africa, Sweden, Switzerland, Trinidad and Tobago, Turkey, United States, Uruguay, Yugoslavia

Sports: Athletics, Basketball, Boxing, Canoeing, Cycling, Diving, Equestrian, Fencing, Football, Gymnastics, Handball, Field Hockey, Modern Pentathlon, Rowing, Sailing, Shooting, Swimming, Water Polo, Weightlifting, Wrestling

Sports for Women: Athletics, Diving, Fencing, Gymnastics, Swimming

MEDALS

Nation	Gold	Silver	Bronze	Total
Germany	33	26	30	89
United States	24	20	12	56
Hungary	10	1	5	16
Italy	8	9	5	22
Finland	7	6	6	19
France	7	6	6	19
Sweden	6	5	9	20
Japan	6	4	8	18
Netherlands	6	4	7	17
Great Britain	4	7	3	14
Austria	4	6	3	13
Czechoslovakia	3	5	0	8
Argentina	2	2	3	7
Estonia	2	2	3	7
Egypt	2	1	2	5
Switzerland	1	9	5	15
Canada	1	3	5	9
Norway	1	3	2	6
Turkey	1	0	1	2
India	1	0	0	1
New Zealand	1	0	0	1
Poland	0	3	3	6
Denmark	0	2	3	5
Latvia	0	1	1	2
Yugoslavia	0	1	0	1
South Africa	0	1	0	1
Romania	0	1	0	1
Mexico	0	0	3	3
Belgium	0	0	2	2
Portugal	0	0	1	1
Australia	0	0	1	1
Philippines	0	0	1	1

1948   London   England   July 29–August 14

Nations: Afghanistan, Argentina, Australia, Austria, Belgium, Bermuda, Brazil, British Guiana, Burma, Canada, Ceylon, Chile, China, Colombia, Cuba, Czechoslovakia, Denmark, Egypt, Finland, France, Great Britain, Greece, Hungary, Iceland, India, Iran, Iraq, Ireland, Italy, Jamaica, Lebanon, Liechtenstein, Luxembourg, Malta, Mexico, Monaco, Netherlands, New Zealand, Norway, Pakistan, Panama, Peru, Philippines, Poland, Portugal, Puerto Rico, Singapore, South Africa, South Korea, Spain, Sweden, Switzerland, Syria, Trinidad and Tobago, Turkey, United States, Uruguay, Venezuela, Yugoslavia

Sports: Athletics, Basketball, Boxing, Canoeing, Cycling, Diving, Equestrian, Fencing, Football, Gymnastics, Field Hockey, Modern Pentathlon, Rowing, Sailing, Shooting, Swimming, Water Polo, Weightlifting, Wrestling

Sports for Women: Athletics, Canoeing, Diving, Fencing, Gymnastics, Swimming

MEDALS

Nation	Gold	Silver	Bronze	Total
United States	38	27	19	84
Sweden	16	11	17	44
France	10	6	13	29
Hungary	10	5	12	27
Italy	8	12	9	29
Finland	8	7	5	20
Turkey	6	4	2	12
Czechoslovakia	6	2	3	11
Switzerland	5	10	5	20
Denmark	5	7	8	20
Netherlands	5	2	9	16
Great Britain	3	14	6	23
Argentina	3	3	1	7
Australia	2	6	5	13
Belgium	2	2	3	7
Egypt	2	2	1	5
Mexico	2	1	2	5
South Africa	2	1	1	4
Norway	1	3	3	7
Jamaica	1	2	0	3
Austria	1	0	3	4
India	1	0	0	1
Peru	1	0	0	1
Yugoslavia	0	2	0	2
Canada	0	1	2	3
Portugal	0	1	1	2
Uruguay	0	1	1	2
Ceylon	0	1	0	1
Trinidad and Tobago	0	1	0	1
Cuba	0	1	0	1
Spain	0	1	0	1
South Korea	0	0	2	2
Panama	0	0	2	2
Brazil	0	0	1	1

Nation	Gold	Silver	Bronze	Total
Poland	0	0	1	1
Puerto Rico	0	0	1	1
Iran	0	0	1	1

1952   Helsinki   Finland   July 19–August 3

Nations: Argentina, Australia, Austria, Bahamas, Belgium, Bermuda, Brazil, British Guiana, Bulgaria, Burma, Canada, Ceylon, Chile, Cuba, Czechoslovakia, Denmark, Egypt, Finland, France, Germany, Gold Coast, Great Britain, Greece, Guatemala, Hong Kong, Hungary, Iceland, India, Indonesia, Iran, Ireland, Israel, Italy, Jamaica, Japan, Lebanon, Liechtenstein, Luxembourg, Mexico, Monaco, Netherlands Antilles, Netherlands, New Zealand, Nigeria, Norway, Pakistan, Panama, People's Republic of China, Philippines, Poland, Portugal, Puerto Rico, Romania, Saar, Singapore, South Africa, South Korea, Soviet Union, Spain, Sweden, Switzerland, Thailand, Turkey, United States, Uruguay, Venezuela, Vietnam, Yugoslavia

Sports: Athletics, Basketball, Boxing, Canoeing, Cycling, Diving, Equestrian, Fencing, Football, Gymnastics, Field Hockey, Modern Pentathlon, Rowing, Sailing, Shooting, Swimming, Water Polo, Weightlifting, Wrestling

Sports for Women: Athletics, Canoeing, Diving, Equestrian, Fencing, Gymnastics, Swimming

MEDALS

Nation	Gold	Silver	Bronze	Total
United States	40	19	17	76
Soviet Union	22	30	19	71
Hungary	16	10	16	42
Sweden	12	13	10	35
Italy	8	9	4	21
Czechoslovakia	7	3	3	13
France	6	6	6	18
Finland	6	3	13	22
Australia	6	2	3	11
Norway	3	2	0	5
Switzerland	2	6	6	14
South Africa	2	4	4	10
Jamaica	2	3	0	5
Belgium	2	2	0	4
Denmark	2	1	3	6
Turkey	2	0	1	3
Japan	1	6	2	9
Great Britain	1	2	8	11
Argentina	1	2	2	5
Poland	1	2	1	4
Yugoslavia	1	2	0	3
Canada	1	2	0	3
Romania	1	1	2	4
Brazil	1	0	2	3
New Zealand	1	0	2	3
India	1	0	1	2

Nation	Gold	Silver	Bronze	Total
Luxembourg	1	0	0	1
Germany	0	7	17	24
Netherlands	0	5	0	5
Iran	0	3	4	7
Chile	0	2	0	2
Lebanon	0	1	1	2
Austria	0	1	1	2
Ireland	0	1	0	1
Mexico	0	1	0	1
Spain	0	1	0	1
Uruguay	0	0	2	2
Trinidad and Tobago	0	0	2	2
South Korea	0	0	2	2
Egypt	0	0	1	1
Portugal	0	0	1	1
Venezuela	0	0	1	1
Bulgaria	0	0	1	1

1956   Stockholm   Sweden   June 10–17
Melbourne   Australia   November 22–December 8

Nations (Stockholm): Argentina, Australia, Austria, Belgium, Brazil, Bulgaria, Canada, Denmark, Egypt, Finland, France, Germany, Great Britain, Hungary, Ireland, Italy, Japan, Netherlands, Norway, Portugal, Romania, Spain, Sweden, Switzerland, Turkey, United States, USSR, Venezuela

Sport: Equestrian

Nations (Melbourne): Afghanistan, Argentina, Australia, Austria, Bahamas, Belgium, Bermuda, Brazil, British Guiana, Bulgaria, Burma, Cambodia, Canada, Ceylon, Chile, Colombia, Cuba, Czechoslovakia, Denmark, Ethiopia, Fiji, Finland, France, Germany, Great Britain, Greece, Hong Kong, Hungary, Iceland, India, Indonesia, Iran, Ireland, Israel, Italy, Jamaica, Japan, Kenya, Liberia, Luxembourg, Malaya, Mexico, New Zealand, Nigeria, North Borneo, Norway, Pakistan, Peru, Philippines, Poland, Portugal, Puerto Rico, Republic of China, Romania, Singapore, South Africa, South Korea, Soviet Union, Sweden, Thailand, Trinidad and Tobago, Turkey, Uganda, United States, Uruguay, Venezuela, Vietnam, Yugoslavia

Sports: Athletics, Basketball, Boxing, Canoeing, Cycling, Diving, Equestrian, Fencing, Football, Gymnastics, Field Hockey, Modern Pentathlon, Rowing, Sailing, Shooting, Swimming, Water Polo, Weightlifting, Wrestling

Sports for Women: Athletics, Canoeing, Diving, Equestrian, Fencing, Gymnastics, Swimming

MEDALS				
Nation	Gold	Silver	Bronze	Total
Soviet Union	37	29	32	98
United States	32	25	17	74
Australia	13	8	14	35
Hungary	9	10	7	26
Italy	8	8	9	25
Sweden	8	5	6	19

Nation	Gold	Silver	Bronze	Total
Germany	7	13	7	27
Great Britain	6	7	11	24
Romania	5	3	5	13
Japan	4	10	5	19
France	4	4	6	14
Turkey	3	2	2	7
Finland	3	1	11	15
Iran	2	2	1	5
Canada	2	1	3	6
New Zealand	2	0	0	2
Poland	1	4	4	9
Czechoslovakia	1	4	1	6
Bulgaria	1	3	1	5
Denmark	1	2	1	4
Ireland	1	1	3	5
Norway	1	0	2	3
Mexico	1	0	1	2
Brazil	1	0	0	1
India	1	0	0	1
Yugoslavia	0	3	0	3
Chile	0	2	2	4
Belgium	0	2	0	2
South Korea	0	1	1	2
Argentina	0	1	1	2
Iceland	0	1	0	1
Pakistan	0	1	0	1
South Africa	0	0	4	4
Austria	0	0	2	2
Bahamas	0	0	1	1
Uruguay	0	0	1	1
Switzerland	0	0	1	1
Greece	0	0	1	1

1960   Rome   Italy   August 25–September 11

Nations: Afghanistan, Argentina, Australia, Austria, Bahamas, Belgium, Bermuda, Brazil, British Guiana, British West Indies, Bulgaria, Burma, Canada, Ceylon, Chile, Colombia, Cuba, Czechoslovakia, Denmark, Ethiopia, Fiji, Finland, France, Germany, Ghana, Great Britain, Greece, Haiti, Hong Kong, Hungary, Iceland, India, Indonesia, Iran, Iraq, Ireland, Israel, Italy, Japan, Kenya, Lebanon, Liberia, Liechtenstein, Luxembourg, Malaya, Malta, Mexico, Monaco, Morocco, Netherlands Antilles, Netherlands, New Zealand, Nigeria, Norway, Pakistan, Panama, Peru, Philippines, Poland, Portugal, Puerto Rico, Rhodesia, Romania, San Marino, Singapore, South Africa, South Korea, Soviet Union, Spain, Sudan, Sweden, Switzerland, Taiwan, Thailand, Tunisia, Turkey, Uganda, United Arab Republic, United States, Uruguay, Venezuela, Vietnam, Yugoslavia

Sports: Athletics, Basketball, Boxing, Canoeing, Cycling, Diving, Equestrian, Fencing, Football, Gymnastics, Field Hockey, Modern Pentathlon, Rowing, Sailing, Shooting, Swimming, Water Polo, Weightlifting, Wrestling

Sports for Women: Athletics, Canoeing, Diving, Equestrian, Fencing, Gymnastics, Swimming

MEDALS

Nation	Gold	Silver	Bronze	Total
Soviet Union	43	29	31	103
United States	34	21	16	71
Italy	13	10	13	36
Germany	12	19	11	42
Australia	8	8	6	22
Turkey	7	2	0	9
Hungary	6	8	7	21
Japan	4	7	7	18
Poland	4	6	11	21
Czechoslovakia	3	2	3	8
Romania	3	1	6	10
Great Britain	2	6	12	20
Denmark	2	3	1	6
New Zealand	2	0	1	3
Bulgaria	1	3	3	7
Sweden	1	2	3	6
Finland	1	1	3	5
Yugoslavia	1	1	0	2
Austria	1	1	0	2
Pakistan	1	0	1	2
Greece	1	0	0	1
Norway	1	0	0	1
Ethiopia	1	0	0	1
Switzerland	0	3	3	6
France	0	2	3	5
Belgium	0	2	2	4
Iran	0	1	3	4
Netherlands	0	1	2	3
South Africa	0	1	2	3
Egypt	0	1	1	2
Argentina	0	1	1	2
India	0	1	0	1
Taiwan	0	1	0	1
Singapore	0	1	0	1
Portugal	0	1	0	1
Canada	0	1	0	1
Ghana	0	1	0	1
Morocco	0	1	0	1
British West Indies	0	0	2	2
Brazil	0	0	2	2
Venezuela	0	0	1	1
Iraq	0	0	1	1
Mexico	0	0	1	1
Spain	0	0	1	1

1964   Tokyo   Japan   October 10–24

Nations: Afghanistan, Algeria, Argentina, Australia, Austria, Bahamas, Belgium, Bermuda, Bolivia, Brazil, British Guiana, Bulgaria, Burma, Cambodia, Cameroon,

Canada, Ceylon, Chad, Chile, Colombia, Costa Rica, Cuba, Czechoslovakia, Denmark, Dominican Republic, Ethiopia, Finland, France, Germany, Ghana, Great Britain, Greece, Hong Kong, Hungary, Iceland, India, Iran, Iraq, Ireland, Israel, Italy, Ivory Coast, Jamaica, Japan, Kenya, Lebanon, Liberia, Liechtenstein, Luxembourg, Madagascar, Malaysia, Mali, Mexico, Monaco, Mongolia, Morocco, Nepal, Netherlands Antilles, Netherlands, New Zealand, Niger, Nigeria, Northern Rhodesia, Norway, Pakistan, Panama, People's Republic of Congo, Peru, Philippines, Poland, Portugal, Puerto Rico, Rhodesia, Romania, Senegal, South Korea, Soviet Union, Spain, Sweden, Switzerland, Taiwan, Tanganyika, Thailand, Trinidad and Tobago, Tunisia, Turkey, Uganda, United Arab Republic, United States, Uruguay, Venezuela, Vietnam, West Indies, Yugoslavia

Sports: Athletics, Basketball, Boxing, Canoeing, Cycling, Diving, Equestrian, Fencing, Football, Gymnastics, Field Hockey, Judo, Modern Pentathlon, Rowing, Sailing, Shooting, Swimming, Volleyball, Water Polo, Weightlifting, Wrestling

Sports for Women: Athletics, Canoeing, Diving, Equestrian, Fencing, Gymnastics, Swimming, Volleyball

MEDALS

Nation	Gold	Silver	Bronze	Total
United States	36	26	28	90
Soviet Union	30	31	35	96
Japan	16	5	8	29
Germany	10	22	8	40
Italy	10	10	7	27
Hungary	10	7	5	22
Poland	7	6	10	23
Australia	6	2	10	18
Czechoslovakia	5	6	3	14
Great Britain	4	12	2	18
Bulgaria	3	5	2	10
New Zealand	3	0	2	5
Finland	3	0	2	5
Romania	2	4	6	12
Netherlands	2	4	4	10
Turkey	2	3	1	6
Sweden	2	2	4	8
Denmark	2	1	3	6
Yugoslavia	2	1	2	5
Belgium	2	0	1	3
France	1	8	6	15
Switzerland	1	2	1	4
Canada	1	2	1	4
Ethiopia	1	0	0	1
Bahamas	1	0	0	1
India	1	0	0	1
South Korea	0	2	1	3
Trinidad and Tobago	0	1	2	3
Tunisia	0	1	1	2
Argentina	0	1	0	1
Philippines	0	1	0	1
Cuba	0	1	0	1

Nation	Gold	Silver	Bronze	Total
Pakistan	0	1	0	1
Iran	0	0	2	2
Uruguay	0	0	1	1
Brazil	0	0	1	1
Ghana	0	0	1	1
Ireland	0	0	1	1
Kenya	0	0	1	1
Mexico	0	0	1	1
Nigeria	0	0	1	1

1968   Mexico City   Mexico   October 12–27

Nations: Afghanistan, Algeria, Argentina, Australia, Austria, Bahamas, Barbados, Belgium, Bermuda, Bolivia, Brazil, British Honduras, Bulgaria, Burma, Cameroon, Canada, Central African Republic, Ceylon, Chad, Chile, Colombia, Costa Rica, Cuba, Czechoslovakia, Democratic Republic of Congo, Denmark, Dominican Republic, East Germany, Ecuador, El Salvador, Ethiopia, Fiji, Finland, France, Ghana, Great Britain, Greece, Guatemala, Guinea, Guyana, Honduras, Hong Kong, Hungary, Iceland, India, Indonesia, Iran, Iraq, Ireland, Israel, Italy, Ivory Coast, Jamaica, Japan, Kenya, Kuwait, Lebanon, Libya, Liechtenstein, Luxembourg, Madagascar, Malaysia, Mali, Malta, Mexico, Monaco, Mongolia, Morocco, Netherlands Antilles, Netherlands, New Zealand, Nicaragua, Niger, Nigeria, Norway, Pakistan, Panama, Paraguay, Peru, Philippines, Poland, Portugal, Puerto Rico, Romania, San Marino, Senegal, Sierra Leone, Singapore, South Korea, Soviet Union, Spain, Sudan, Surinam, Sweden, Switzerland, Syria, Taiwan, Tanzania, Thailand, Trinidad and Tobago, Tunisia, Turkey, Uganda, United Arab Republic, United States, Uruguay, U.S. Virgin Islands, Venezuela, Vietnam, West Germany, Yugoslavia, Zambia

Sports: Athletics, Basketball, Boxing, Canoeing, Cycling, Diving, Equestrian, Fencing, Football, Gymnastics, Field Hockey, Modern Pentathlon, Rowing, Sailing, Shooting, Swimming, Volleyball, Water Polo, Weightlifting, Wrestling

Sports for Women: Athletics, Canoeing, Diving, Equestrian, Fencing, Gymnastics, Swimming, Volleyball

MEDALS

Nation	Gold	Silver	Bronze	Total
United States	45	28	34	107
Soviet Union	29	32	30	91
Japan	11	7	7	25
Hungary	10	10	12	32
East Germany	9	9	7	25
France	7	3	5	15
Czechoslovakia	7	2	4	13
West Germany	5	11	10	26
Australia	5	7	5	17
Great Britain	5	5	3	13
Poland	5	2	11	18
Romania	4	6	5	15
Italy	3	4	9	16
Kenya	3	4	2	9

Nation	Gold	Silver	Bronze	Total
Mexico	3	3	3	9
Yugoslavia	3	3	2	8
Netherlands	3	3	1	7
Bulgaria	2	4	3	9
Iran	2	1	2	5
Sweden	2	1	1	4
Turkey	2	0	0	2
Denmark	1	4	3	8
Canada	1	3	1	5
Finland	1	2	1	4
Ethiopia	1	1	0	2
Norway	1	1	0	2
New Zealand	1	0	2	3
Tunisia	1	0	1	2
Pakistan	1	0	0	1
Venezuela	1	0	0	1
Cuba	0	4	0	4
Austria	0	2	2	4
Switzerland	0	1	4	5
Mongolia	0	1	3	4
Brazil	0	1	2	3
Belgium	0	1	1	2
South Korea	0	1	1	2
Uganda	0	1	1	2
Jamaica	0	1	0	1
Cameroon	0	1	0	1
Argentina	0	0	2	2
Greece	0	0	1	1
India	0	0	1	1
Taiwan	0	0	1	1

1972   Munich   West Germany   August 26–September 10

Nations: Afghanistan, Albania, Algeria, Argentina, Australia, Austria, Bahamas, Barbados, Belgium, Bermuda, Bolivia, Brazil, British Honduras, Bulgaria, Burma, Cambodia, Cameroon, Canada, Chad, Chile, Colombia, Costa Rica, Cuba, Czechoslovakia, Dahomey, Denmark, Dominican Republic, East Germany, Ecuador, Egypt, El Salvador, Ethiopia, Fiji, Finland, France, Gabon, Ghana, Great Britain, Greece, Guatemala, Guyana, Haiti, Hong Kong, Hungary, Iceland, India, Indonesia, Iran, Ireland, Israel, Italy, Ivory Coast, Jamaica, Japan, Kenya, Kuwait, Lebanon, Lesotho, Liberia, Liechtenstein, Luxembourg, Madagascar, Malawi, Malaysia, Mali, Malta, Mexico, Monaco, Mongolia, Morocco, Nepal, Netherlands Antilles, Netherlands, New Zealand, Nicaragua, Niger, Nigeria, North Korea, Norway, Pakistan, Panama, Paraguay, People's Republic of Congo, Peru, Philippines, Poland, Portugal, Puerto Rico, Romania, San Marino, Saudi Arabia, Senegal, Singapore, Somalia, South Korea, Soviet Union, Spain, Sri Lanka, Sudan, Suriname, Swaziland, Sweden, Switzerland, Syria, Taiwan, Tanzania, Thailand, Togo, Trinidad and Tobago, Tunisia, Turkey, Uganda, United States, Upper Volta, Uruguay, U.S. Virgin Islands, Venezuela, Vietnam, West Germany, Yugoslavia, Zambia

Sports: Archery, Athletics, Basketball, Boxing, Canoeing, Cycling, Diving, Equestrian, Fencing, Football, Gymnastics, Handball, Field Hockey, Judo, Modern Pentathlon, Rowing, Sailing, Shooting, Swimming, Volleyball, Water Polo, Weightlifting, Wrestling

Sports for Women: Archery, Athletics, Canoeing, Diving, Equestrian, Fencing, Gymnastics, Swimming, Volleyball

MEDALS

Nation	Gold	Silver	Bronze	Total
Soviet Union	50	27	22	99
United States	33	31	30	94
East Germany	20	23	23	66
West Germany	13	11	16	40
Japan	13	8	8	29
Australia	8	7	2	17
Poland	7	5	9	21
Hungary	6	13	16	35
Bulgaria	6	10	5	21
Italy	5	3	10	18
Sweden	4	6	6	16
Great Britain	4	5	9	18
Romania	3	6	7	16
Cuba	3	1	4	8
Finland	3	1	4	8
Netherlands	3	1	1	5
France	2	4	7	13
Czechoslovakia	2	4	2	8
Kenya	2	3	4	9
Yugoslavia	2	1	2	5
Norway	2	1	1	4
North Korea	1	1	3	5
New Zealand	1	1	1	3
Uganda	1	1	0	2
Denmark	1	0	0	1
Switzerland	0	3	0	3
Canada	0	2	3	5
Iran	0	2	1	3
Belgium	0	2	0	2
Greece	0	2	0	2
Colombia	0	1	2	3
Austria	0	1	2	3
Mexico	0	1	0	1
Tunisia	0	1	0	1
Turkey	0	1	0	1
Mongolia	0	1	0	1
Lebanon	0	1	0	1
South Korea	0	1	0	1
Argentina	0	1	0	1
Pakistan	0	1	0	1
Ethiopia	0	0	2	2
Brazil	0	0	2	2

Nation	Gold	Silver	Bronze	Total
Spain	0	0	1	1
Ghana	0	0	1	1
India	0	0	1	1
Jamaica	0	0	1	1
Niger	0	0	1	1
Nigeria	0	0	1	1

1976   Montreal   Canada   July 17–August 1

Nations: Andorra, Antigua, Argentina, Australia, Austria, Bahamas, Barbados, Belgium, Bermuda, Bolivia, Brazil, British Honduras, Bulgaria, Cameroon, Canada, Cayman Islands, Chile, Colombia, Costa Rica, Cuba, Czechoslovakia, Denmark, Dominican Republic, East Germany, Ecuador, Egypt, Fiji, Finland, France, Great Britain, Greece, Guatemala, Haiti, Honduras, Hong Kong, Hungary, Iceland, India, Indonesia, Iran, Ireland, Israel, Italy, Ivory Coast, Jamaica, Japan, Kuwait, Lebanon, Liechtenstein, Luxembourg, Malaysia, Mexico, Monaco, Mongolia, Morocco, Nepal, Netherlands Antilles, Netherlands, New Zealand, Nicaragua, North Korea, Norway, Pakistan, Panama, Papua New Guinea, Paraguay, Peru, Philippines, Poland, Portugal, Puerto Rico, Romania, San Marino, Saudi Arabia, Senegal, Singapore, South Korea, Soviet Union, Spain, Sri Lanka, Suriname, Sweden, Switzerland, Thailand, Trinidad and Tobago, Tunisia, Turkey, United States, Uruguay, U.S. Virgin Islands, Venezuela, West Germany, Yugoslavia

Sports: Archery, Athletics, Basketball, Boxing, Canoeing, Cycling, Diving, Equestrian, Fencing, Football, Gymnastics, Handball, Field Hockey, Judo, Modern Pentathlon, Rowing, Sailing, Shooting, Swimming, Volleyball, Water Polo, Weightlifting, Wrestling

Sports for Women: Archery, Athletics, Basketball, Canoeing, Diving, Equestrian, Fencing, Gymnastics, Handball, Rowing, Sailing, Swimming, Volleyball

MEDALS

Nation	Gold	Silver	Bronze	Total
Soviet Union	49	41	35	125
East Germany	40	25	25	90
United States	34	35	25	94
West Germany	10	12	17	39
Japan	9	6	10	25
Poland	7	6	13	26
Bulgaria	6	9	7	22
Cuba	6	4	3	13
Romania	4	9	14	27
Hungary	4	5	13	22
Finland	4	2	0	6
Sweden	4	1	0	5
Great Britain	3	5	5	13
Italy	2	7	4	13
France	2	3	4	9
Yugoslavia	2	3	3	8
Czechoslovakia	2	2	4	8
New Zealand	2	1	1	4

Nation	Gold	Silver	Bronze	Total
South Korea	1	1	4	6
Switzerland	1	1	2	4
Norway	1	1	0	2
Jamaica	1	1	0	2
North Korea	1	1	0	2
Denmark	1	0	2	3
Mexico	1	0	1	2
Trinidad and Tobago	1	0	0	1
Canada	0	5	6	11
Belgium	0	3	3	6
Netherlands	0	2	3	5
Spain	0	2	0	2
Portugal	0	2	0	2
Australia	0	1	4	5
Iran	0	1	1	2
Mongolia	0	1	0	1
Venezuela	0	1	0	1
Brazil	0	0	2	2
Thailand	0	0	1	1
Austria	0	0	1	1
Puerto Rico	0	0	1	1
Bermuda	0	0	1	1
Pakistan	0	0	1	1

1980   Moscow   Soviet Union   July 19–August 3

Nations: Afghanistan, Algeria, Andorra, Angola, Australia, Austria, Belgium, Benin, Botswana, Brazil, Bulgaria, Burma, Cameroon, Colombia, Costa Rica, Cuba, Cyprus, Czechoslovakia, Denmark, Dominican Republic, East Germany, Ecuador, Ethiopia, Finland, France, Great Britain, Greece, Guatemala, Guinea, Guyana, Hungary, Iceland, India, Iraq, Ireland, Italy, Jamaica, Jordan, Kuwait, Laos, Lebanon, Lesotho, Libya, Luxembourg, Madagascar, Mali, Malta, Mexico, Mongolia, Mozambique, Nepal, Netherlands, New Zealand, Nicaragua, Nigeria, North Korea, People's Republic of Congo, Peru, Poland, Portugal, Puerto Rico, Romania, San Marino, Senegal, Seychelles, Sierra Leone, Soviet Union, Spain, Sri Lanka, Sweden, Switzerland, Syria, Tanzania, Trinidad and Tobago, Uganda, Venezuela, Vietnam, Yugoslavia, Zambia, Zimbabwe

Sports: Archery, Athletics, Basketball, Boxing, Canoeing, Cycling, Diving, Equestrian, Fencing, Football, Gymnastics, Handball, Field Hockey, Judo, Modern Pentathlon, Rowing, Sailing, Shooting, Swimming, Volleyball, Water Polo, Weightlifting, Wrestling

Sports for Women: Archery, Athletics, Basketball, Canoeing, Diving, Equestrian, Fencing, Gymnastics, Handball, Field Hockey, Rowing, Sailing, Swimming, Volleyball

MEDALS				
Nation	Gold	Silver	Bronze	Total
Soviet Union	80	69	46	195
East Germany	47	37	42	126
Bulgaria	8	16	17	41

Nation	Gold	Silver	Bronze	Total
Cuba	8	7	5	20
Italy	8	3	4	15
Hungary	7	10	15	32
Romania	6	6	13	25
France	6	5	3	14
Great Britain	5	7	9	21
Poland	3	14	15	32
Sweden	3	3	6	12
Finland	3	1	4	8
Czechoslovakia	2	3	9	14
Yugoslavia	2	3	4	9
Australia	2	2	5	9
Denmark	2	1	2	5
Brazil	2	0	2	4
Ethiopia	2	0	2	4
Switzerland	2	0	0	2
Spain	1	3	2	6
Austria	1	2	1	4
Greece	1	0	2	3
India	1	0	0	1
Belgium	1	0	0	1
Zimbabwe	1	0	0	1
North Korea	0	3	2	5
Mongolia	0	2	2	4
Tanzania	0	2	0	2
Mexico	0	1	3	4
Netherlands	0	1	2	3
Ireland	0	1	1	2
Uganda	0	1	0	1
Venezuela	0	1	0	1
Jamaica	0	0	3	3
Lebanon	0	0	1	1
Guyana	0	0	1	1

1984   Los Angeles   USA   July 28–August 12

Nations: Algeria, Andorra, Antigua, Argentina, Australia, Austria, Bahamas, Bahrain, Bangladesh, Barbados, Belgium, Belize, Benin, Bermuda, Bhutan, Bolivia, Botswana, Brazil, British Virgin Islands, Burma, Cameroon, Canada, Cayman Islands, Central African Republic, Chad, Chile, Chinese Taipei, Colombia, Costa Rica, Cyprus, Denmark, Djibouti, Dominican Republic, Ecuador, Egypt, El Salvador, Equatorial Guinea, Fiji, Finland, France, Gabon, Gambia, Ghana, Great Britain, Greece, Grenada, Guatemala, Guinea, Guyana, Haiti, Honduras, Hong Kong, Iceland, India, Indonesia, Iraq, Ireland, Israel, Italy, Ivory Coast, Jamaica, Japan, Jordan, Kenya, Kuwait, Lebanon, Lesotho, Liberia, Liechtenstein, Luxembourg, Madagascar, Malawi, Malaysia, Mali, Malta, Mauritania, Mauritius, Mexico, Monaco, Morocco, Mozambique, Nepal, Netherlands Antilles, Netherlands, New Zealand, Nicaragua, Niger, Nigeria, Norway, Oman, Pakistan, Panama, Papua New Guinea, Paraguay, People's Republic of China, People's Republic of Congo, Peru, Philippines, Portugal, Puerto Rico, Qatar, Romania, Rwanda, San Marino, Saudi Arabia, Senegal, Seychelles, Sierra Leone, Singapore,

Solomon Islands, Somalia, South Korea, Spain, Sri Lanka, Sudan, Suriname, Swaziland, Sweden, Switzerland, Syria, Tanzania, Thailand, Togo, Tonga, Trinidad and Tobago, Tunisia, Turkey, Uganda, United Arab Emirates, United States, Uruguay, U.S. Virgin Islands, Venezuela, West Germany, Western Samoa, Yemen Arab Republic, Yugoslavia, Zaire, Zambia, Zimbabwe

Sports: Archery, Athletics, Basketball, Boxing, Canoeing, Cycling, Diving, Equestrian, Fencing, Football, Gymnastics, Handball, Field Hockey, Judo, Modern Pentathlon, Rowing, Sailing, Shooting, Swimming, Volleyball, Water Polo, Weightlifting, Wrestling

Sports for Women: Archery, Athletics, Basketball, Canoeing, Cycling, Diving, Equestrian, Fencing, Gymnastics, Handball, Field Hockey, Rowing, Sailing, Shooting, Swimming, Synchronized Swimming, Volleyball

MEDALS

Nation	Gold	Silver	Bronze	Total
United States	83	61	30	174
Romania	20	16	17	53
West Germany	17	19	23	59
China	15	8	9	32
Italy	14	6	12	32
Canada	10	18	16	44
Japan	10	8	14	32
New Zealand	8	1	2	11
Yugoslavia	7	4	7	18
South Korea	6	6	7	19
Great Britain	5	10	22	37
France	5	7	16	28
Netherlands	5	2	6	13
Australia	4	8	12	24
Finland	4	2	6	12
Sweden	2	11	6	19
Mexico	2	3	1	6
Morocco	2	0	0	2
Brazil	1	5	2	8
Spain	1	2	2	5
Belgium	1	1	2	4
Austria	1	1	1	3
Portugal	1	0	2	3
Kenya	1	0	2	3
Pakistan	1	0	0	1
Switzerland	0	4	4	8
Denmark	0	3	3	6
Jamaica	0	1	2	3
Norway	0	1	2	3
Greece	0	1	1	2
Nigeria	0	1	1	2
Puerto Rico	0	1	1	2
Ireland	0	1	0	1
Thailand	0	1	0	1
Syria	0	1	0	1
Ivory Coast	0	1	0	1

Nation	Gold	Silver	Bronze	Total
Egypt	0	1	0	1
Colombia	0	1	0	1
Peru	0	1	0	1
Turkey	0	0	3	3
Venezuela	0	0	3	3
Algeria	0	0	2	2
Zambia	0	0	1	1
Cameroon	0	0	1	1
Dominican Republic	0	0	1	1
Iceland	0	0	1	1
Taiwan	0	0	1	1

1988   Seoul   South Korea   September 17–October 2

Nations: Afghanistan, Algeria, American Samoa, Andorra, Angola, Antigua, Argentina, Australia, Austria, Bahamas, Bahrain, Bangladesh, Barbados, Belgium, Belize, Benin, Bermuda, Bhutan, Bolivia, Botswana, Brazil, British Virgin Islands, Bulgaria, Burkina Faso, Burma, Cameroon, Canada, Cayman Islands, Central African Republic, Chad, Chile, Chinese Taipei, Colombia, Cook Islands, Costa Rica, Cyprus, Czechoslovakia, Denmark, Djibouti, Dominican Republic, East Germany, Ecuador, Egypt, El Salvador, Equatorial Guinea, Fiji, Finland, France, Gabon, Gambia, Ghana, Great Britain, Greece, Grenada, Guam, Guatemala, Guinea, Guyana, Haiti, Honduras, Hong Kong, Hungary, Iceland, India, Indonesia, Iran, Iraq, Ireland, Israel, Italy, Ivory Coast, Jamaica, Japan, Jordan, Kenya, Kuwait, Laos, Lebanon, Lesotho, Liberia, Libya, Liechtenstein, Luxembourg, Malawi, Malaysia, Maldives, Mali, Malta, Mauritania, Mauritius, Mexico, Monaco, Mongolia, Morocco, Mozambique, Nepal, Netherlands Antilles, Netherlands, New Zealand, Niger, Nigeria, Norway, Oman, Pakistan, Panama, Papua New Guinea, Paraguay, People's Republic of China, People's Republic of Congo, Peru, Philippines, Poland, Portugal, Puerto Rico, Qatar, Romania, Rwanda, San Marino, Saudi Arabia, Senegal, Sierra Leone, Singapore, Solomon Islands, Somalia, South Korea, Soviet Union, Spain, Sri Lanka, St. Vincent and the Grenadines, Sudan, Suriname, Swaziland, Sweden, Switzerland, Syria, Tanzania, Thailand, Togo, Tonga, Trinidad and Tobago, Tunisia, Turkey, Uganda, United Arab Emirates, United States, Uruguay, U.S. Virgin Islands, Vanuatu, Venezuela, Vietnam, West Germany, Western Samoa, Yemen Arab Republic, Yemen Democratic Republic, Yugoslavia, Zaire, Zambia, Zimbabwe

Sports: Archery, Athletics, Basketball, Boxing, Canoeing, Cycling, Diving, Equestrian, Fencing, Football, Gymnastics, Handball, Field Hockey, Judo, Modern Pentathlon, Rowing, Sailing, Shooting, Swimming, Table Tennis, Tennis, Volleyball, Water Polo, Weightlifting, Wrestling

Sports for Women: Archery, Athletics, Basketball, Canoeing, Cycling, Diving, Equestrian, Fencing, Gymnastics, Handball, Field Hockey, Rowing, Sailing, Shooting, Swimming, Synchronized Swimming, Table Tennis, Tennis, Volleyball

MEDALS

Nation	Gold	Silver	Bronze	Total
Soviet Union	55	31	46	132
East Germany	37	35	30	102

Nation	Gold	Silver	Bronze	Total
United States	36	31	27	94
South Korea	12	10	11	33
West Germany	11	14	15	40
Hungary	11	6	6	23
Bulgaria	10	12	13	35
Romania	7	11	6	24
France	6	4	6	16
Italy	6	4	4	14
China	5	11	12	28
Great Britain	5	10	9	24
Kenya	5	2	2	9
Japan	4	3	7	14
Australia	3	6	5	14
Yugoslavia	3	4	5	12
Czechoslovakia	3	3	2	8
New Zealand	3	2	8	13
Canada	3	2	5	10
Poland	2	5	9	16
Norway	2	3	0	5
Netherlands	2	2	5	9
Denmark	2	1	1	4
Brazil	1	2	3	6
Finland	1	1	2	4
Spain	1	1	2	4
Turkey	1	1	0	2
Morocco	1	0	2	3
Austria	1	0	0	1
Portugal	1	0	0	1
Surinam	1	0	0	1
Sweden	0	4	7	11
Switzerland	0	2	2	4
Jamaica	0	2	0	2
Argentina	0	1	1	2
Iran	0	1	0	1
Senegal	0	1	0	1
Netherlands Antilles	0	1	0	1
VIR[179] (British Virgin Islands)	0	1	0	1
Indonesia	0	1	0	1
Costa Rica	0	1	0	1
Chile	0	1	0	1
Peru	0	1	0	1
Belgium	0	0	2	2
Mexico	0	0	2	2
Colombia	0	0	1	1
Djibouti	0	0	1	1
Greece	0	0	1	1
Mongolia	0	0	1	1
Pakistan	0	0	1	1
Philippines	0	0	1	1
Thailand	0	0	1	1

1992   Barcelona   Spain   July 25–August 10

Nations: Algeria, American Samoa, Andorra, Angola, Antigua, Argentina, Aruba, Australia, Austria, Bahamas, Bahrain, Bangladesh, Barbados, Belgium, Belize, Benin, Bermuda, Bhutan, Bolivia, Bosnia and Herzegovina, Botswana, Brazil, British Virgin Islands, Bulgaria, Burkina Faso, Cameroon, Canada, Cayman Islands, Central African Republic, Chad, Chile, Chinese Taipei, Colombia, Cook Islands, Costa Rica, Croatia, Cuba, Cyprus, Czechoslovakia, Denmark, Djibouti, Dominican Republic, Ecuador, Egypt, El Salvador, Equatorial Guinea, Estonia, Ethiopia, Fiji, Finland, France, Gabon, Gambia, Germany, Ghana, Great Britain, Greece, Grenada, Guam, Guatemala, Guinea, Guyana, Haiti, Honduras, Hong Kong, Hungary, Iceland, Independent Olympic Participants, India, Indonesia, Iran, Iraq, Ireland, Israel, Italy, Ivory Coast, Jamaica, Japan, Jordan, Kenya, Kuwait, Laos, Latvia, Lebanon, Lesotho, Libya, Liechtenstein, Lithuania, Luxembourg, Madagascar, Malawi, Malaysia, Maldives, Mali, Malta, Mauritania, Mauritius, Mexico, Monaco, Mongolia, Morocco, Mozambique, Myanmar, Namibia, Nepal, Netherlands Antilles, Netherlands, New Zealand, Nicaragua, Niger, Nigeria, North Korea, Norway, Oman, Pakistan, Panama, Papua New Guinea, Paraguay, People's Republic of China, People's Republic of Congo, Peru, Philippines, Poland, Portugal, Puerto Rico, Qatar, Romania, Rwanda, San Marino, Saudi Arabia, Senegal, Seychelles, Sierra Leone, Singapore, Slovenia, Solomon Islands, South Africa, South Korea, Spain, Sri Lanka, St. Vincent and the Grenadines, Sudan, Suriname, Swaziland, Sweden, Switzerland, Syria, Tanzania, Thailand, Togo, Tonga, Trinidad and Tobago, Tunisia, Turkey, Uganda, Unified Team, United Arab Emirates, United States, Uruguay, U.S. Virgin Islands, Vanuatu, Venezuela, Vietnam, Western Samoa, Yemen, Zaire, Zambia, Zimbabwe

Sports: Archery, Athletics, Badminton, Baseball, Basketball, Boxing, Canoeing, Cycling, Diving, Equestrian, Fencing, Football, Gymnastics, Handball, Field Hockey, Judo, Modern Pentathlon, Rowing, Sailing, Shooting, Swimming, Table Tennis, Tennis, Volleyball, Water Polo, Weightlifting, Wrestling

Sports for Women: Archery, Athletics, Badminton, Basketball, Canoeing, Cycling, Diving, Equestrian, Fencing, Gymnastics, Handball, Field Hockey, Judo, Rowing, Sailing, Shooting, Swimming, Synchronized Swimming, Table Tennis, Tennis, Volleyball

MEDALS

Nation	Gold	Silver	Bronze	Total
Soviet Union (unified team)	45	38	28	111
United States	37	34	37	108
Germany	33	21	28	82
China	16	22	16	54
Cuba	14	6	11	31
Spain	13	7	2	22
South Korea	12	5	12	29
Hungary	11	12	7	30
France	8	5	16	29
Australia	7	9	11	27
Italy	6	5	8	19
Canada	6	5	7	18
Great Britain	5	3	12	20

Nation	Gold	Silver	Bronze	Total
Romania	4	6	8	18
Czechoslovakia	4	2	1	7
North Korea	4	0	5	9
Japan	3	8	11	22
Bulgaria	3	7	6	16
Poland	3	6	10	19
Netherlands	2	6	7	15
Kenya	2	4	2	8
Norway	2	4	1	7
Turkey	2	2	2	6
Indonesia	2	2	1	5
Brazil	2	1	0	3
Greece	2	0	0	2
Sweden	1	7	4	12
New Zealand	1	4	5	10
Finland	1	2	2	5
Denmark	1	1	4	6
Morocco	1	1	2	4
Ireland	1	1	0	2
Ethiopia	1	0	2	3
Algeria	1	0	1	2
Estonia	1	0	1	2
Lithuania	1	0	1	2
Switzerland	1	0	0	1
Jamaica	0	3	1	4
Nigeria	0	3	1	4
Latvia	0	2	1	3
South Africa	0	2	0	2
Austria	0	2	0	2
Namibia	0	2	0	2
Belgium	0	1	2	3
Croatia	0	1	2	3
Iran	0	1	2	3
Yugoslavia	0	1	2	3
Israel	0	1	1	2
Taiwan	0	1	0	1
Mexico	0	1	0	1
Peru	0	1	0	1
Mongolia	0	0	2	2
Slovenia	0	0	2	2
Thailand	0	0	1	1
Argentina	0	0	1	1
Bahamas	0	0	1	1
Colombia	0	0	1	1
Ghana	0	0	1	1
Malaysia	0	0	1	1
Pakistan	0	0	1	1
Philippines	0	0	1	1
Puerto Rico	0	0	1	1
Qatar	0	0	1	1
Suriname	0	0	1	1

1996 Atlanta USA July 19–August 4

Nations: Afghanistan, Albania, Algeria, American Samoa, Andorra, Angola, Antigua and Barbuda, Argentina, Armenia, Aruba, Australia, Austria, Azerbaijan, Bahamas, Bahrain, Bangladesh, Barbados, Belarus, Belgium, Belize, Benin, Bermuda, Bhutan, Bolivia, Bosnia and Herzegovina, Botswana, Brazil, British Virgin Islands, Brunei Darusallam, Bulgaria, Burkina Faso, Burundi, Cambodia, Cameroon, Canada, Cape Verde, Cayman Islands, Central African Republic, Chad, Chile, China, Chinese Taipei, Colombia, Comoros, Congo, Cook Islands, Costa Rica, Croatia, Cuba, Cyprus, Czech Republic, Denmark, Djibouti, Dominica, Dominican Republic, Ecuador, Egypt, El Salvador, Equatorial Guinea, Estonia, Ethiopia, Fiji, Finland, France, Gabon, Gambia, Georgia, Germany, Ghana, Great Britain, Greece, Grenada, Guam, Guatemala, Guinea, Guinea-Bissau, Guyana, Haiti, Honduras, Hong Kong, Hungary, Iceland, India, Indonesia, Iran, Iraq, Ireland, Israel, Italy, Ivory Coast, Jamaica, Japan, Jordan, Kazakhstan, Kenya, Kyrgyzstan, Kuwait, Laos, Latvia, Lebanon, Lesotho, Liberia, Libya, Liechtenstein, Lithuania, Luxembourg, Macedonia, Madagascar, Malawi, Malaysia, Maldives, Mali, Malta, Mauritania, Mauritius, Mexico, Moldova, Monaco, Mongolia, Morocco, Mozambique, Myanmar, Namibia, Nauru, Nepal, Netherlands Antilles, Netherlands, New Zealand, Nicaragua, Niger, Nigeria, North Korea, Norway, Oman, Pakistan, Palestine, Panama, Papua New Guinea, Paraguay, Peru, Philippines, Poland, Portugal, Puerto Rico, Qatar, Romania, Russia, Rwanda, San Marino, Sao Tome and Principe, Saudi Arabia, Senegal, Seychelles, Sierra Leone, Singapore, Slovakia, Slovenia, Solomon Islands, Somalia, South Africa, South Korea, Spain, Sri Lanka, St. Kitts and Nevis, St. Lucia, St. Vincent and the Grenadines, Sudan, Suriname, Swaziland, Sweden, Switzerland, Syria, Tajikistan, Tanzania, Thailand, Togo, Tonga, Trinidad and Tobago, Tunisia, Turkey, Turkmenistan, Uganda, Ukraine, United Arab Emirates, United States, Uruguay, Uzbekistan, Vanuatu, Venezuela, Vietnam, Virgin Islands, Western Samoa, Yemen, Yugoslavia, Zaire, Zambia, Zimbabwe

Sports: Archery, Athletics, Badminton, Baseball, Basketball, Boxing, Canoeing, Cycling, Diving, Equestrian, Fencing, Football, Gymnastics, Handball, Field Hockey, Judo, Modern Pentathlon, Rowing, Sailing, Shooting, Swimming, Table Tennis, Tennis, Volleyball, Water Polo, Weightlifting, Wrestling

Sports for Women: Archery, Athletics, Badminton, Basketball, Canoeing, Cycling, Diving, Equestrian, Fencing, Football, Gymnastics, Handball, Field Hockey, Judo, Rowing, Sailing, Shooting, Softball, Swimming, Synchronized Swimming, Table Tennis, Tennis, Volleyball

MEDALS

Nation	Gold	Silver	Bronze	Total
United States	39	25	33	97
Russia	32	28	28	88
China	28	16	15	59
Australia	16	25	17	58
Germany	14	17	26	57
France	13	14	11	38
Italy	13	8	13	34
Netherlands	12	9	4	25
Cuba	11	11	7	29
Great Britain	11	10	7	28

Nation	Gold	Silver	Bronze	Total
Romania	11	6	9	26
South Korea	8	9	11	28
Hungary	8	6	3	17
Poland	6	5	3	14
Japan	5	8	5	18
Bulgaria	5	6	2	13
Greece	4	6	3	13
Sweden	4	5	3	12
Norway	4	3	3	10
Ethiopia	4	1	3	8
Ukraine	3	10	10	23
Kazakhstan	3	4	0	7
Belarus	3	3	11	17
Canada	3	3	8	14
Spain	3	3	5	11
Iran	3	0	1	4
Turkey	3	0	1	4
Czech Republic	2	3	3	8
Kenya	2	3	2	7
Denmark	2	3	1	6
Finland	2	1	1	4
Austria	2	1	0	3
Lithuania	2	0	3	5
Azerbaijan	2	0	1	3
Slovenia	2	0	0	2
Switzerland	1	6	2	9
Indonesia	1	3	2	6
Slovakia	1	3	1	5
Mexico	1	2	3	6
Algeria	1	1	3	5
Uzbekistan	1	1	2	4
Yugoslavia	1	1	1	3
Latvia	1	1	1	3
Bahamas	1	1	0	2
New Zealand	1	0	3	4
Thailand	1	0	2	3
Estonia	1	0	2	3
Croatia	1	0	1	2
Cameroon	1	0	0	1
Colombia	1	0	0	1
Mozambique	1	0	0	1
Brazil	0	6	6	12
Jamaica	0	4	3	7
Nigeria	0	3	0	3
Belgium	0	2	3	5
South Africa	0	2	3	5
Argentina	0	2	2	4
Morocco	0	1	4	5
Chinese Taipei	0	1	4	5
North Korea	0	1	3	4

Nation	Gold	Silver	Bronze	Total
Moldova	0	1	1	2
Saudi Arabia	0	1	1	2
Trinidad and Tobago	0	1	1	2
Uruguay	0	1	0	1
Vietnam	0	1	0	1
Ireland	0	1	0	1
Georgia	0	0	6	6
Portugal	0	0	2	2
Costa Rica	0	0	2	2
Sri Lanka	0	0	1	1
Barbados	0	0	1	1
Chile	0	0	1	1
Iceland	0	0	1	1
India	0	0	1	1
Israel	0	0	1	1
Kuwait	0	0	1	1
Kyrgyzstan	0	0	1	1
Macedonia	0	0	1	1
Qatar	0	0	1	1
Armenia	0	0	1	1

2000   Sydney   Australia   September 15–October 1

Nations: Albania, Algeria, American Samoa, Andorra, Angola, Antigua and Barbuda, Argentina, Armenia, Aruba, Australia, Austria, Azerbaijan, Bahamas, Bahrain, Bangladesh, Barbados, Belarus, Belgium, Belize, Benin, Bermuda, Bhutan, Bolivia, Bosnia and Herzegovina, Botswana, Brazil, British Virgin Islands, Brunei Darusallam, Bulgaria, Burkina Faso, Burundi, Cambodia, Cameroon, Canada, Cape Verde, Cayman Islands, Central African Republic, Chad, Chile, China, Chinese Taipei, Colombia, Comoros, Congo, Cook Islands, Costa Rica, Croatia, Cuba, Cyprus, Czech Republic, Denmark, Democratic Republic of the Congo, Djibouti, Dominica, Dominican Republic, Ecuador, Egypt, El Salvador, Equatorial Guinea, Eritrea, Estonia, Ethiopia, Federated States of Micronesia, Fiji, Finland, France, Gabon, Gambia, Georgia, Germany, Ghana, Great Britain, Greece, Grenada, Guam, Guatemala, Guinea, Guinea-Bissau, Guyana, Haiti, Honduras, Hong Kong, Hungary, Iceland, India, Indonesia, Iran, Iraq, Ireland, Israel, Italy, Ivory Coast, Jamaica, Japan, Jordan, Kazakhstan, Kenya, Kyrgyzstan, Kuwait, Laos, Latvia, Lebanon, Lesotho, Liberia, Libya, Liechtenstein, Lithuania, Luxembourg, Macedonia, Madagascar, Malawi, Malaysia, Maldives, Mali, Malta, Mauritania, Mauritius, Mexico, Moldova, Monaco, Mongolia, Morocco, Mozambique, Myanmar, Namibia, Nauru, Nepal, Netherlands Antilles, Netherlands, New Zealand, Nicaragua, Niger, Nigeria, North Korea, Norway, Oman, Pakistan, Palau, Palestine, Panama, Papua New Guinea, Paraguay, Peru, Philippines, Poland, Portugal, Puerto Rico, Qatar, Romania, Russia, Rwanda, Samoa, San Marino, Sao Tome and Principe, Saudi Arabia, Senegal, Seychelles, Sierra Leone, Singapore, Slovakia, Slovenia, Solomon Islands, Somalia, South Africa, South Korea, Spain, Sri Lanka, St. Kitts and Nevis, St. Lucia, St. Vincent and the Grenadines, Sudan, Suriname, Swaziland, Sweden, Switzerland, Syria, Tajikistan, Tanzania, Thailand, Togo, Tonga, Trinidad and Tobago, Tunisia, Turkey, Turkmenistan, Uganda, Ukraine, United Arab Emirates, United States, Uruguay, Uzbekistan, Vanuatu, Venezuela, Vietnam, Virgin

Islands, Yemen, Yugoslavia, Zambia, Zimbabwe, (and Individual Olympic Athletes, which was not counted as an NOC delegation at Sydney)

Sports: Archery, Athletics, Badminton, Baseball, Basketball, Beach Volleyball, Boxing, Canoe/Kayak, Cycling, Diving, Equestrian, Fencing, Field Hockey, Football, Gymnastics, Judo, Modern Pentathlon, Mountain Bike, Rhythmic Gymnastics, Rowing, Sailing, Shooting, Softball, Swimming, Synchronized Swimming, Table Tennis, Tae Kwon Do, Team Handball, Tennis, Trampoline, Triathlon, Volleyball, Water Polo, Weightlifting, Wrestling

Sports for Women: Archery, Athletics, Badminton, Basketball, Beach Volleyball, Canoe/Kayak, Cycling, Diving, Equestrian, Fencing, Field Hockey, Football, Gymnastics, Judo, Modern Pentathlon, Mountain Bike, Rhythmic Gymnastics, Rowing, Sailing, Shooting, Softball, Swimming, Synchronized Swimming, Table Tennis, Tae Kwon Do, Team Handball, Tennis, Trampoline, Triathlon, Volleyball, Water Polo, Weightlifting

MEDALS

Nation	Gold	Silver	Bronze	Total
United States	39	25	33	97
Russia	32	28	28	88
China	28	16	15	59
Australia	16	25	17	58
Germany	14	17	26	57
France	13	14	11	38
Italy	13	8	13	34
Netherlands	12	9	4	25
Cuba	11	11	7	29
Great Britain	11	10	7	28
Romania	11	6	9	26
South Korea	8	9	11	28
Hungary	8	6	3	17
Poland	6	5	3	14
Japan	5	8	5	18
Bulgaria	5	6	2	13
Greece	4	6	3	13
Sweden	4	5	3	12
Norway	4	3	3	10
Ethiopia	4	1	3	8
Ukraine	3	10	10	23
Kazakhstan	3	4	0	7
Belarus	3	3	11	17
Canada	3	3	8	14
Spain	3	3	5	11
Iran	3	0	1	4
Turkey	3	0	1	4
Czech Republic	2	3	3	8
Kenya	2	3	2	7
Denmark	2	3	1	6
Finland	2	1	1	4
Austria	2	1	0	3
Lithuania	2	0	3	5

Nation	Gold	Silver	Bronze	Total
Azerbaijan	2	0	1	3
Slovenia	2	0	0	2
Switzerland	1	6	2	9
Indonesia	1	3	2	6
Slovakia	1	3	1	5
Mexico	1	2	3	6
Algeria	1	1	3	5
Uzbekistan	1	1	2	4
Yugoslavia	1	1	1	3
Latvia	1	1	1	3
Bahamas	1	1	0	2
New Zealand	1	0	3	4
Thailand	1	0	2	3
Estonia	1	0	2	3
Croatia	1	0	1	2
Cameroon	1	0	0	1
Colombia	1	0	0	1
Mozambique	1	0	0	1
Brazil	0	6	6	12
Jamaica	0	4	3	7
Nigeria	0	3	0	3
Belgium	0	2	3	5
South Africa	0	2	3	5
Argentina	0	2	2	4
Morocco	0	1	4	5
Chinese Taipei	0	1	4	5
North Korea	0	1	3	4
Moldova	0	1	1	2
Saudi Arabia	0	1	1	2
Trinidad and Tobago	0	1	1	2
Uruguay	0	1	0	1
Vietnam	0	1	0	1
Ireland	0	1	0	1
Georgia	0	0	6	6
Portugal	0	0	2	2
Costa Rica	0	0	2	2
Sri Lanka	0	0	1	1
Barbados	0	0	1	1
Chile	0	0	1	1
Iceland	0	0	1	1
India	0	0	1	1
Israel	0	0	1	1
Kuwait	0	0	1	1
Kyrgyzstan	0	0	1	1
Macedonia	0	0	1	1
Qatar	0	0	1	1
Armenia	0	0	1	1

Olympic Winter Games

Year	Host City	Host Nation	Dates	Nations	Athletes	Sports
1924	Chamonix	France	Jan. 25–Feb. 4	16	294	4
1928	St. Moritz	Switzerland	Feb. 11–19	25	495	5
1932	Lake Placid	USA	Feb. 4–15	17	306	5
1936	Garmisch-Partenkirchen	Germany	Feb. 6–16	28	755	5
1948	St. Moritz	Switzerland	Jan. 30–Feb. 8	28	713	7
1952	Oslo	Norway	Feb. 14–25	28	732	6
1956	Cortina D'Ampezzo	Italy	Jan. 26–Feb. 5	30	818	6
1960	Squaw Valley	USA	Feb. 18–28	32	665	6
1964	Innsbruck	Austria	Jan. 29–Feb. 9	36	1186	8
1968	Grenoble	France	Feb. 6–18	37	1293	8
1972	Sapporo	Japan	Feb. 3–13	35	1232	8
1976	Innsbruck	Austria	Feb. 4–15	37	1028	8
1980	Lake Placid	USA	Feb. 14–23	37	1159	8
1984	Sarajevo	Yugoslavia	Feb. 7–19	49	1274	8
1988	Calgary	Canada	Feb. 13–28	57	1423	8
1992	Albertville	France	Feb. 8–23	64	2147	9
1994	Lillehammer	Norway	Feb. 12–25	67	1727	10
1998	Nagano	Japan	Feb. 7–22	72	2176	13

Though the very first Olympic Winter Games were held in 1924, and were recognized as Olympic only after the fact, several winter competitions were held before 1924 that led up to the establishment of the games. Figure skating was part of the 1908 and 1920 summer Olympic Games and ice hockey was also contested in 1920.

Where the first modern international summer games were the Olympic Games, the first modern international winter games were the Nordic Games organized by Sweden. The IOC suggested that Sweden hold a winter games or add winter events to the 1912 Stockholm summer games. The Swedes declined, not wanting to infringe on their Nordic Games.

The Germans supported the idea of winter events and planned to hold them in 1916 but World War I interfered with all Olympic plans for that year.

On May 27, 1925, the IOC changed the Olympic Charter to sanction winter games. The rules established at the time, stated that the country given to host the summer games could also choose to host the winter games as well.[180]

However, it was the year before in Chamonix, France, that the first winter competitions to be considered "Olympic" were held. The games had been called the "International Sports Week" at the time, but the IOC retroactively recognized them as the first Olympic Winter Games

The second winter games were held in 1928 in St. Moritz, Switzerland. Bad weather, rain and warm temperatures disrupted many events. German athletes returned to these games. They had not been allowed to compete in the 1924 games because they were still under sanctions resulting from World War I.

The 1932 games held in Lake Placid were not a financial success due in part to the global depression and the fact that the organizers had splurged on new facilities including a stadium and bobsled run. Only 17 nations were able to send representatives to the games, below the 25 who had participated in St. Moritz.

The U.S. bobsledders came up with a new, and short-lived strategy: heating the sled's runners with a blowtorch before they raced. The practice was outlawed shortly after the games.

Differences in rules made the speed skating events a fiasco. The Americans generally raced in packs with all skaters racing at the same time, while the European rules mandated that skaters skate in pairs and use times to determine the winners. Five-time Olympic champion Clas Thunberg of Finland dropped out of the events in protest and Americans came away with all four gold medals.

The 1936 games in Garmisch-Partenkirchen, Germany, were opened by Adolf Hitler and gave the world a closer glimpse of the direction in which Germany was headed. The facilities were state of the art, and spectators abundant (130,000 stood in the snow to watch the final day of the ski jump) but the signs and symbols of the Nazi regime were everywhere. The ski jump landing area had a Nazi swastika carved into the hill.

The IOC declared that hotel ski instructors were professional athletes and not eligible to compete in the games, which upset the Austrian and Swiss delegations.

For the first time women were allowed to compete in a sport other than figure skating, with alpine skiing events for women added to the schedule. Great Britain upset Canada to win the hockey gold medal, for the first and only time to date. Controversy erupted over the eligibility of several British players who had been born in the British Isles but were living in and had learned to play hockey in Canada.

Sapporo was first awarded the 1940 games, but withdrew due to Japan's conflict with China. The games were moved to St. Moritz, which also withdrew. Garmisch-Partenkirchen was selected to hold the games for the second time in a row, but the war finally brought a halt to all Olympic plans.

Cortina D'Ampezzo, Italy, was selected over Montreal and Oslo for the 1944 games, but the choice was moot with the continuation of the war.

St. Moritz, Switzerland, was able to organize an efficient games in 1948. Neutrality in World War II had proven to be an advantage. Shortages and travel restrictions made it difficult for spectators to visit the games. Even sporting equipment was in short supply in some cases, making it hard on the athletes as well. Japan and Germany were not invited because of war sanctions.

A controversy in hockey ensued when the United States, in a dispute over jurisdiction and control of amateur hockey in the U.S., sent two teams. The USOC and the Amateur Hockey Association of the United States (AHAUS), recognized different teams. The IOC refused to allow either team to compete. The Swiss organizers didn't help matters when they said that the USOC team could march in the opening ceremonies, but the AHAUS team could play in the tournament. The IOC after first refusing to sanction the hockey tournament decided to give its approval, but only if the U.S. team was stricken from the results.

Germany and Japan were both invited back to the Oslo, Norway, games in 1952. Several bobsled teams were aided by the extreme size and weight of their athletes. The bobsled rules were changed after these games with the institution of weight limits.

In 1956, Cortina D'Ampezzo, Italy, finally got its chance to host the games. The event saw several Olympic firsts: the first entry of the Soviet Union in a winter games and the first live television broadcasts of winter events. Giuliana Minuzzi became the first woman to recite the Olympic Oath at an opening ceremony.[181]

The selection of Squaw Valley for the 1960 games caused some controversy, primarily among the European countries which complained about the lack of facilities and the great altitude of the village high in California's Sierra Nevada mountains. Organizers wanted the event specifically to develop the area, and built all the facilities from scratch, except for a bobsled run which they were unable to manage. It was mentioned that the bobsled events could be held in Lake Placid instead, but the IOC preferred that all events be held in one location and so bobsledding was not a part of the 1960 games. South Africa participated in the winter games for the first time, but would be banned for its apartheid policy and not compete again until 1994.

The 1964 Innsbruck, Austria, games were the first in which the Olympic torch was lit in ancient Olympia, Greece. The international popularity of the games continued to grow with a world television audience of over one billion.

Two athletes were killed in practice before the games. Kazimerz Skrzypecki of Poland, who participated in luge, and Ross Milne, a skier from Australia, both died in accidents.

The 1968 games saw seven different Olympic villages scattered throughout the French Alps, with the main venues in Grenoble, France.

Professionalism, particularly among the alpine skiers, was the controversy surrounding these games. Skiers had begun to display sponsors' logos on their equipment and uniforms and the IOC threatened to ban athletes who persisted with such displays. In return, the skiers threatened to boycott the games. A compromise was reached when the skiers agreed to remove any advertising before they were interviewed or had any photographs taken.

Professionalism remained a hot issue for the 1972 games in Sapporo, Japan. Austria's Karl Schranz was expelled from the games for professionalism.

The Canadian ice hockey team boycotted the 1972 games. Canada had asked the IOC for permission to use professional players arguing that the European nation's systems were in essence professional. The IOC refused and Canada declined to send a team to both the 1972 and 1976 winter games.

Denver, Colorado, was chosen to host the 1976 winter games. However, in October 1973, for tax reasons, the citizens of Colorado voted not to permit the games to be held in their state. Tampere, Finland; Mont Blanc, France; Lake Placid, and Innsbruck stepped forward with bids, with Innsbruck eventually chosen.

Despite the fact that Denver had backed out of the 1976 games, Lake Placid, New York, was selected to host the 1980 winter games.

The small upstate New York village had difficulties with transportation throughout the games, frustrating many visitors. The Olympic Village was constructed in Ray Brook, five miles out of town. The facility was built specifically to become a prison (after much protest from the community), and the rooms were said to be windowless, dark and not as festive as an Olympic village could have been.

Lake Placid had the smallest opening ceremonies since the 1956 Cortina games.[182]

The games are best remembered for the American ice hockey gold medal surprise and Eric Heiden winning all five speed-skating events.

The 1984 games were awarded to Sarajevo, Yugoslavia, which hosted a wonderful event. There was no talk of the boycotts that were to take place in the summer games of that year, and little indication of the war that was to engulf the region shortly thereafter.

In July 1992, Zetra Ice Stadium in Sarajevo was destroyed during the Bosnian conflict. The stadium was used as a morgue for some time, and eventually as a staging area for military operations. The military was finally moved out in September 1997, and work began on restoring the facility. It was reopened in 1999.

The IOC agreed to pay the expenses of one male and one female participant from each nation. Egypt, the British Virgin Islands, Monaco, Puerto Rico, and Senegal made their Winter Olympics debuts in 1984.

After bidding for the 1964, 1968 and 1972 Olympic Winter Games, Calgary, Canada, finally landed the prize for 1988 and spent over U.S. $400 million on new facilities, including the Saddledome for hockey, a new speedskating oval at the University of Calgary, and Canada Olympic Park where a new bobsled/luge track and ski jumps were built. Calgary has successfully transformed these into post–Olympic training and competition facilities.

ABC, the American Broadcasting Company, paid $309 million for the television rights to the Calgary games. The network's influence caused the dates of the event to be lengthened.

Massive changes in the global political landscape meant that in 1992, Estonia, Latvia and Lithuania returned to the Albertville Olympic Winter Games as independent nations. Latvia and Estonia had last participated independently in 1936; Lithuania in 1928.

Germany, after unification, competed as one for the first time since 1964. The former Soviet republics, making the transition to freedom, participated as the Unified Team.

The 1994 Lillehammer games are fondly remembered as one of the best-organized and most enthusiastic.

Thousands of Norwegians camped out in tents next to the Nordic skiing courses and cheered for all the athletes.

The Soviet Union was no more. Belarus, Kazakhstan, Ukraine and Uzbekistan all won medals.

South Africa, which had competed in the 1992 Barcelona summer games, returned also to the winter games after an absence of over 30 years.

In 1998, Nagano, high in the Japanese Alps, became the most southerly city to host a winter games.

Ross Rebagliati of Canada became snowboarding's first Olympic gold medalist, and also the first snowboarder to test positive for marijuana use. For a day, he was stripped of his gold medal, but after an appeal in which he argued that the positive test was due to second-hand smoke, the decision was overturned and the medal returned to the Canadian.

Women's ice hockey was added to the games. The United States won the gold in this event over Canada.

Several new expensive facilities were built for the games. Since that time, though, Nagano has not been able to make use of them, and it costs the Japanese several million tax dollars a year to maintain these facilities.[183]

The candidature of Salt Lake City for the 2002 Olympic Winter Games was the catalyst for the darkest chapter in modern Olympic history.

On November 24, 1998, the television station KTVX in Salt Lake City reported irregularities and allegations of scholarship payments, free health care, sham jobs and other gifts to IOC members and their families. The allegations prompted inquiries by the IOC, USOC, FBI, U.S. Senate and Salt Lake City Organizing Committee. These inquiries led to resignations and dismissals of several IOC members and members of the Salt Lake City Organizing Committee including the leader of the bid, Tom Welch, and the vice-president of the organizing committee, Dave Johnson. In December 1999, as a direct result of the scandal (and against the IOC based in Switzerland), the IOC met to vote on a list of 50 recommendations for reform within the IOC and Olympic movement.[184]

The case against Salt Lake Olympic bid leaders Tom Welch and Dave Johnson continued. Their trial took place in the summer of 2001.

The backlash from the scandal was thought to have affected the choice for the city for the 2006 Olympic Winter Games. The supposed front-runner Sion, Switzerland, was outvoted by Turin, Italy. Klagenfurt, Austria, Helsinki, Finland (in a joint bid with Lillehammer, Norway), Poprad-Tarta, Slovakia, and Zakopane, Poland, were also candidates.

1924   Chamonix   France   January 25–February 4

Nations: Austria, Belgium, Canada, Czechoslovakia, Finland, France, Great Britain, Hungary, Italy, Latvia, Norway, Poland, Sweden, Switzerland, United States, Yugoslavia

Sports: Figure Skating, Ice Hockey, Nordic Skiing, Speed Skating
Sports for Women: Figure Skating

MEDALS

Nation	Gold	Silver	Bronze	Total
Norway	4	7	6	17
Finland	4	3	3	10
Austria	2	1	0	3
United States	1	2	1	4
Switzerland	1	0	1	2
Sweden	1	0	0	1
Canada	1	0	0	1
Great Britain	0	1	2	3
France	0	0	1	1
Belgium	0	0	1	1

1928   St. Moritz   Switzerland   February 11–19

Nations: Argentina, Austria, Belgium, Canada, Czechoslovakia, Estonia, Finland, France, Germany, Great Britain, Hungary, Italy, Japan, Latvia, Lithuania, Luxembourg, Mexico, Netherlands, Norway, Poland, Romania, Sweden, Switzerland, United States, Yugoslavia

Sports: Figure Skating, Ice Hockey, Nordic Skiing, Skeleton, Speed Skating
Sports for Women: Figure Skating

MEDALS

Nation	Gold	Silver	Bronze	Total
Norway	6	4	5	15
United States	2	2	2	6
Sweden	2	2	1	5
Finland	2	1	1	4
Canada	1	0	0	1
France	1	0	0	1
Austria	0	3	1	4

Nation	Gold	Silver	Bronze	Total
Belgium	0	0	1	1
Czechoslovakia	0	0	1	1
Germany	0	0	1	1
Great Britain	0	0	1	1
Switzerland	0	0	1	1[185]

1932   Lake Placid   USA   February 4–15

Nations: Austria, Belgium, Canada, Czechoslovakia, Finland, France, Germany, Great Britain, Hungary, Italy, Japan, Norway, Poland, Romania, Sweden, Switzerland, United States

Sports: Bobsled, Figure Skating, Ice Hockey, Nordic Skiing, Speed Skating
Sports for Women: Figure Skating

MEDALS

Nation	Gold	Silver	Bronze	Total
United States	6	4	2	12
Norway	3	4	3	10
Sweden	1	2	0	3
Canada	1	1	5	7
Finland	1	1	1	3
Austria	1	1	0	2
France	1	0	0	1
Switzerland	0	1	0	1
Germany	0	0	2	2
Hungary	0	0	1	1

1936   Garmisch-Partenkirchen   Germany   February 6–16

Nations: Australia, Austria, Belgium, Bulgaria, Canada, Czechoslovakia, Estonia, Finland, France, Germany, Great Britain, Greece, Hungary, Italy, Japan, Latvia, Liechtenstein, Luxembourg, Netherlands, Norway, Poland, Romania, Spain, Sweden, Switzerland, Turkey, United States, Yugoslavia

Sports: Bobsled, Figure Skating, Ice Hockey, Nordic Skiing, Speed Skating
Sports for Women: Figure Skating

MEDALS

Nation	Gold	Silver	Bronze	Total
Norway	7	5	3	15
Germany	3	3	0	6
Sweden	2	2	3	7
Finland	1	2	3	6
Switzerland	1	2	0	3
Austria	1	1	2	4
Great Britain	1	1	1	3
United States	1	0	3	4
Canada	0	1	0	1
Hungary	0	0	1	1
France	0	0	1	1

1948   St. Moritz   Switzerland   January 30–February 8

Nations: Argentina, Austria, Belgium, Bulgaria, Canada, Chile, Czechoslovakia, Denmark, Finland, France, Great Britain, Greece, Hungary, Iceland, Italy, Lebanon, Liechtenstein, Netherlands, Norway, Poland, Romania, South Korea, Spain, Sweden, Switzerland, Turkey, United States, Yugoslavia

Sports: Alpine Skiing, Bobsled, Figure Skating, Ice Hockey, Nordic Skiing, Skeleton, Speed Skating

Sports for Women: Alpine Skiing, Figure Skating

MEDALS

Nation	Gold	Silver	Bronze	Total
Norway	4	3	3	10
Sweden	4	3	3	10
Switzerland	3	4	3	10
United States	3	4	2	9
France	2	1	2	5
Canada	2	0	1	3
Austria	1	3	4	8
Finland	1	3	2	6
Belgium	1	1	0	2
Italy	1	0	0	1
Hungary	0	1	0	1
Czechoslovakia	0	1	0	1
Great Britain	0	0	2	2

1952   Oslo   Norway   February 14–25

Nations: Argentina, Australia, Austria, Belgium, Bulgaria, Canada, Chile, Czechoslovakia, Denmark, Finland, France, Germany, Great Britain, Greece, Hungary, Iceland, Italy, Japan, Lebanon, Netherlands, New Zealand, Norway, Poland, Portugal, Romania, Spain, Sweden, Switzerland, United States, Yugoslavia

Sports: Alpine Skiing, Bobsled, Figure Skating, Ice Hockey, Nordic Skiing, Speed Skating

Sports for Women: Alpine Skiing, Figure Skating, Nordic Skiing

MEDALS

Nation	Gold	Silver	Bronze	Total
Norway	7	3	6	16
United States	4	6	1	11
Finland	3	4	2	9
Germany	3	2	2	7
Austria	2	4	2	8
Canada	1	0	1	2
Italy	1	0	1	2
Great Britain	1	0	0	1
Netherlands	0	3	0	3
Sweden	0	0	4	4
Switzerland	0	0	2	2
Hungary	0	0	1	1
France	0	0	1	1

1956   Cortina D'Ampezzo   Italy   January 26–February 5

Nations: Australia, Austria, Belgium, Bolivia, Bulgaria, Canada, Chile, Czechoslovakia, Finland, France, Germany, Great Britain, Greece, Hungary, Iceland, Iran, Italy, Japan, Lebanon, Liechtenstein, Netherlands, Norway, Poland, Romania, South Korea, Soviet Union, Spain, Sweden, Switzerland, Turkey, United States, Yugoslavia

Sports: Alpine Skiing, Bobsled, Figure Skating, Ice Hockey, Nordic Skiing, Speed Skating

Sports for Women: Alpine Skiing, Figure Skating, Nordic Skiing

MEDALS

Nation	Gold	Silver	Bronze	Total
Soviet Union	7	3	6	16
Austria	4	3	4	11
Finland	3	3	1	7
Switzerland	3	2	1	6
Sweden	2	4	4	10
United States	2	3	2	7
Norway	2	1	1	4
Italy	1	2	0	3
Germany	1	0	0	1
Canada	0	1	2	3
Japan	0	1	0	1
Hungary	0	0	1	1
Poland	0	0	1	1
East Germany	0	0	1	1

1960   Squaw Valley   USA   February 18–28

Nations: Argentina, Australia, Austria, Bulgaria, Canada, Chile, Czechoslovakia, Denmark, Finland, France, Germany, Great Britain, Hungary, Iceland, Italy, Japan, Lebanon, Liechtenstein, Netherlands, New Zealand, North Korea, Norway, Poland, South Africa, South Korea, Soviet Union, Spain, Sweden, Switzerland, Turkey, United States

Sports: Alpine Skiing, Biathlon, Figure Skating, Ice Hockey, Nordic Skiing, Speed Skating

Sports for Women: Alpine Skiing, Figure Skating, Nordic Skiing, Speed Skating

MEDALS

Nation	Gold	Silver	Bronze	Total
Soviet Union	7	5	9	21
Germany	4	3	1	8
United States	3	4	3	10
Norway	3	3	0	6
Sweden	3	2	2	7
Finland	2	3	3	8
Canada	2	1	1	4
Switzerland	2	0	0	2
Austria	1	2	3	6

Nation	Gold	Silver	Bronze	Total
France	1	0	2	3
Poland	0	1	1	2
Netherlands	0	1	1	2
Czechoslovakia	0	1	0	1
Italy	0	0	1	1[186]

1964   Innsbruck   Austria   January 29–February 9

Nations: Argentina, Australia, Austria, Belgium, Bulgaria, Canada, Chile, Czechoslovakia, Denmark, Finland, France, Germany, Great Britain, Greece, Hungary, Iceland, India, Iran, Italy, Japan, Lebanon, Liechtenstein, Mongolia, Netherlands, Norway, Poland, Romania, South Korea, Soviet Union, Spain, Sweden, Switzerland, Turkey, United States, Yugoslavia

Sports: Alpine Skiing, Biathlon, Bobsled, Figure Skating, Ice Hockey, Luge, Nordic Skiing, Speed Skating

Sports for Women: Alpine Skiing, Figure Skating, Luge, Nordic Skiing, Speed Skating

MEDALS

Nation	Gold	Silver	Bronze	Total
Soviet Union	11	8	6	25
Austria	4	5	3	12
Norway	3	6	6	15
Finland	3	4	3	10
France	3	4	0	7
Sweden	3	3	1	7
Germany	3	2	3	8
United States	1	2	3	6
Netherlands	1	1	0	2
Canada	1	0	2	3
Great Britain	1	0	0	1
Italy	0	1	3	4
North Korea	0	1	0	1
Czechoslovakia	0	0	1	1

1968   Grenoble   France   February 6–18

Nations: Argentina, Australia, Austria, Bulgaria, Canada, Chile, Czechoslovakia, Denmark, East Germany, Finland, France, Great Britain, Greece, Hungary, Iceland, India, Iran, Italy, Japan, Lebanon, Liechtenstein, Monaco, Morocco, Netherlands, New Zealand, North Korea, Norway, Poland, Romania, Soviet Union, Spain, Sweden, Switzerland, Turkey, United States, West Germany, Yugoslavia

Sports: Alpine Skiing, Biathlon, Bobsled, Figure Skating, Ice Hockey, Luge, Nordic Skiing, Speed Skating

Sports for Women: Alpine Skiing, Figure Skating, Luge, Nordic Skiing, Speed Skating

MEDALS

Nation	Gold	Silver	Bronze	Total
Norway	6	6	2	14
Soviet Union	5	5	3	13
France	4	3	2	9
Italy	4	0	0	4
Austria	3	4	4	11
Netherlands	3	3	3	9
Sweden	3	2	3	8
West Germany	2	2	3	7
United States	1	5	1	7
Finland	1	2	2	5
East Germany	1	2	2	5
Czechoslovakia	1	2	1	4
Canada	1	1	1	3
Switzerland	0	2	4	6
Romania	0	0	1	1

1972   Sapporo   Japan   February 3–13

Nations: Argentina, Australia, Austria, Belgium, Bulgaria, Canada, Czechoslovakia, East Germany, Finland, France, Great Britain, Greece, Hungary, Iran, Italy, Japan, Lebanon, Liechtenstein, Mongolia, Netherlands, New Zealand, Norway, Philippines, Poland, Romania, South Korea, Soviet Union, Spain, Sweden, Switzerland, Taiwan, United States, West Germany, Yugoslavia

Sports: Alpine Skiing, Biathlon, Bobsled, Figure Skating, Ice Hockey, Luge, Nordic Skiing, Speed Skating

Sports for Women: Alpine Skiing, Figure Skating, Luge, Nordic Skiing, Speed Skating

MEDALS

Nation	Gold	Silver	Bronze	Total
Soviet Union	8	5	3	16
East Germany	4	3	7	14
Switzerland	4	3	3	10
Netherlands	4	3	2	9
United States	3	2	3	8
West Germany	3	1	1	5
Norway	2	5	5	12
Italy	2	2	1	5
Austria	1	2	2	5
Sweden	1	1	2	4
Japan	1	1	1	3
Czechoslovakia	1	0	2	3
Spain	1	0	0	1
Poland	1	0	0	1
Finland	0	4	1	5
France	0	1	2	3
Canada	0	1	0	1[187]

1976   Innsbruck   Austria   February 4–15

Nations: Andorra, Argentina, Australia, Austria, Belgium, Bulgaria, Canada, Chile, Czechoslovakia, East Germany, Finland, France, Great Britain, Greece, Hungary, Iceland, Iran, Italy, Japan, Lebanon, Liechtenstein, Netherlands, New Zealand, Norway, Poland, Romania, San Marino, South Korea, Soviet Union, Spain, Sweden, Switzerland, Taiwan, Turkey, United States, West Germany, Yugoslavia

Sports: Alpine Skiing, Biathlon, Bobsled, Figure Skating, Ice Hockey, Luge, Nordic Skiing, Speed Skating

Sports for Women: Alpine Skiing, Figure Skating, Luge, Nordic Skiing, Speed Skating

MEDALS

Nation	Gold	Silver	Bronze	Total
Soviet Union	13	6	8	27
East Germany	7	5	7	19
United States	3	3	4	10
Norway	3	3	1	7
West Germany	2	5	3	10
Finland	2	4	1	7
Austria	2	2	2	6
Switzerland	1	3	1	5
Netherlands	1	2	3	6
Italy	1	2	1	4
Canada	1	1	1	3
Great Britain	1	0	0	1
Czechoslovakia	0	1	0	1
Sweden	0	0	2	2
Liechtenstein	0	0	2	2
France	0	0	1	1

1980   Lake Placid   USA   February 14–23

Nations: Andorra, Argentina, Australia, Austria, Belgium, Bolivia, Bulgaria, Canada, China, Costa Rica, Cyprus, Czechoslovakia, East Germany, Finland, France, Great Britain, Greece, Hungary, Iceland, Italy, Japan, Lebanon, Liechtenstein, Mongolia, Netherlands, New Zealand, North Korea, Norway, Poland, Romania, South Korea, Soviet Union, Spain, Sweden, Switzerland, Taiwan, United States, West Germany, Yugoslavia

Sports: Alpine Skiing, Biathlon, Bobsled, Figure Skating, Ice Hockey, Luge, Nordic Skiing, Speed Skating

Sports for Women: Alpine Skiing, Figure Skating, Luge, Nordic Skiing, Speed Skating

MEDALS

Nation	Gold	Silver	Bronze	Total
Soviet Union	10	6	6	22
East Germany	9	7	7	23
United States	6	4	2	12

Nation	Gold	Silver	Bronze	Total
Austria	3	2	2	7
Sweden	3	0	1	4
Liechtenstein	2	2	0	4
Finland	1	5	3	9
Norway	1	3	6	10
Netherlands	1	2	1	4
Switzerland	1	1	3	5
Great Britain	1	0	0	1
West Germany	0	2	3	5
Italy	0	2	0	2
Canada	0	1	1	2
Japan	0	1	0	1
Hungary	0	1	0	1
Bulgaria	0	0	1	1
Czechoslovakia	0	0	1	1
France	0	0	1	1

1984   Sarajevo   Yugoslavia   February 7–19

Nations: Andorra, Argentina, Australia, Austria, Belgium, Bolivia, Bulgaria, Canada, Chile, China, Chinese Taipei, Costa Rica, Cyprus, Czechoslovakia, East Germany, Egypt, Finland, France, Great Britain, Greece, Hungary, Iceland, Italy, Japan, Lebanon, Liechtenstein, Mexico, Monaco, Mongolia, Morocco, Netherlands, New Zealand, North Korea, Norway, Poland, Puerto Rico, Romania, San Marino, Senegal, South Korea, Soviet Union, Spain, Sweden, Switzerland, Turkey, United States, U.S. Virgin Islands, West Germany, Yugoslavia

Sports: Alpine Skiing, Biathlon, Bobsled, Figure Skating, Ice Hockey, Luge, Nordic Skiing, Speed Skating

Sports for Women: Alpine Skiing, Figure Skating, Luge, Nordic Skiing, Speed Skating

MEDALS

Nation	Gold	Silver	Bronze	Total
East Germany	9	9	6	24
Soviet Union	6	10	9	25
United States	4	4	0	8
Finland	4	3	6	13
Sweden	4	2	2	8
Norway	3	2	4	9
Switzerland	2	2	1	5
West Germany	2	1	1	4
Canada	2	1	1	4
Italy	2	0	0	2
Great Britain	1	0	0	1
Czechoslovakia	0	2	4	6
France	0	1	2	3
Japan	0	1	0	1
Yugoslavia	0	1	0	1

Nation	Gold	Silver	Bronze	Total
Liechtenstein	0	0	2	2
Austria	0	0	1	1

1988   Calgary   Canada   February 13–28

Nations: Andorra, Argentina, Australia, Austria, Belgium, Bolivia, Bulgaria, Canada, Chile, China, Chinese Taipei, Costa Rica, Cyprus, Czechoslovakia, Denmark, East Germany, Fiji, Finland, France, Great Britain, Greece, Guam, Guatemala, Hungary, Iceland, India, Italy, Jamaica, Japan, Lebanon, Liechtenstein, Luxembourg, Mexico, Monaco, Mongolia, Morocco, Netherlands Antilles, Netherlands, New Zealand, North Korea, Norway, Philippines, Poland, Portugal, Puerto Rico, Romania, San Marino, South Korea, Soviet Union, Spain, Sweden, Switzerland, Turkey, United States, U.S. Virgin Islands, West Germany, Yugoslavia

Sports: Alpine Skiing, Biathlon, Bobsled, Figure Skating, Ice Hockey, Luge, Nordic Skiing, Speed Skating

Sports for Women: Alpine Skiing, Figure Skating, Luge, Nordic Skiing, Speed Skating

MEDALS

Nation	Gold	Silver	Bronze	Total
Soviet Union	11	9	9	29
East Germany	9	10	6	25
Switzerland	5	5	5	15
Finland	4	1	2	7
Sweden	4	0	2	6
Austria	3	5	2	10
Netherlands	3	2	2	7
West Germany	2	4	2	8
United States	2	1	3	6
Italy	2	1	2	5
France	1	0	1	2
Norway	0	3	2	5
Canada	0	2	3	5
Yugoslavia	0	2	1	3
Czechoslovakia	0	1	2	3
Liechtenstein	0	0	1	1
Japan	0	0	1	1

1992   Albertville   France   February 8–23

Nations: Algeria, Andorra, Argentina, Australia, Austria, Belgium, Bermuda, Bolivia, Brazil, Bulgaria, Canada, Chile, China, Chinese Taipei, Costa Rica, Croatia, Cyprus, Czechoslovakia, Denmark, Estonia, Finland, France, Germany, Great Britain, Greece, Honduras, Hungary, Iceland, India, Ireland, Italy, Jamaica, Japan, Latvia, Lebanon, Liechtenstein, Lithuania, Luxembourg, Mexico, Monaco, Mongolia, Morocco, Netherlands Antilles, Netherlands, New Zealand, North Korea, Norway, Philippines, Poland, Puerto Rico, Romania, San Marino, Senegal, Slovenia, South

Korea, Spain, Swaziland, Sweden, Switzerland, Turkey, Unified Team, United States, U.S. Virgin Islands, Yugoslavia[188]

Sports: Alpine Skiing, Biathlon, Bobsled, Figure Skating, Freestyle Skiing, Ice Hockey, Luge, Nordic Skiing, Speed Skating

Sports for Women: Alpine Skiing, Biathlon, Figure Skating, Freestyle Skiing, Luge, Nordic Skiing, Speed Skating

MEDALS

Nation	Gold	Silver	Bronze	Total
Germany	10	10	6	26
Soviet Union (unified team	9	6	8	23
Norway	9	6	5	20
Austria	6	7	8	21
United States	5	4	2	11
Italy	4	6	4	14
France	3	5	1	9
Finland	3	1	3	7
Canada	2	3	2	7
South Korea	2	1	1	4
Japan	1	2	4	7
Netherlands	1	1	2	4
Sweden	1	0	3	4
Switzerland	1	0	2	3
China	0	3	0	3
Luxembourg	0	2	0	2
New Zealand	0	1	0	1
Czechoslovakia	0	0	3	3
Spain	0	0	1	1
North Korea	0	0	1	1

1994   Lillehammer   Norway   February 12–25

Nations: American Samoa, Andorra, Argentina, Armenia, Australia, Austria, Belarus, Belgium, Bermuda, Bosnia and Herzegovina, Brazil, Bulgaria, Canada, Chile, China, Chinese Taipei, Croatia, Cyprus, Czech Republic, Denmark, Estonia, Fiji, Finland, France, Georgia, Germany, Great Britain, Greece, Hungary, Iceland, Israel, Italy, Jamaica, Japan, Kazakhstan, Kyrgyzstan, Latvia, Liechtenstein, Lithuania, Luxembourg, Mexico, Moldova, Monaco, Mongolia, Netherlands, New Zealand, Norway, Poland, Portugal, Puerto Rico, Romania, San Marino, Senegal, Slovakia, Slovenia, South Africa, South Korea, Spain, Sweden, Switzerland, Trinidad and Tobago, Turkey, Unified Team, United States, U.S. Virgin Islands, Ukraine, Uzbekistan.

Sports: Alpine Skiing, Biathlon, Bobsled, Figure Skating, Freestyle Skiing, Ice Hockey, Luge, Nordic Skiing, Short-track Speed Skating, Speed Skating

Sports for Women: Alpine Skiing, Biathlon, Figure Skating, Freestyle Skiing, Luge, Nordic Skiing, Short-track Speed Skating, Speed Skating

MEDALS

Nation	Gold	Silver	Bronze	Total
Russia (unified team)	11	8	4	23
Norway	10	11	5	26

Nation	Gold	Silver	Bronze	Total
Germany	9	7	8	24
Italy	7	5	8	20
United States	6	5	2	13
South Korea	4	1	1	6
Canada	3	6	4	13
Switzerland	3	4	2	9
Austria	2	3	4	9
Sweden	2	1	0	3
Japan	1	2	2	5
Kazakhstan	1	2	0	3
Ukraine	1	0	1	2
Uzbekistan	1	0	0	1
Belarus	0	2	0	2
Finland	0	1	5	6
France	0	1	4	5
Netherlands	0	1	3	4
China	0	1	2	3
Slovenia	0	0	3	3
Great Britain	0	0	2	2
Australia	0	0	1	1

1998   Nagano   Japan   February 7–22

Nations: Andorra, Argentina, Armenia, Australia, Austria, Azerbaijan, Belarus, Belgium, Bermuda, Bosnia and Herzegovina, Brazil, Bulgaria, Canada, Chile, China, Chinese Taipei, Croatia, Cyprus, Czech Republic, Denmark, Estonia, Finland, France, Georgia, Germany, Great Britain, Greece, Hungary, India, Iceland, Iran, Ireland, Israel, Virgin Islands, Italy, Jamaica, Japan, Kazakhstan, Kenya, Kyrgyzstan, South Korea, Latvia, Liechtenstein, Lithuania, Luxembourg, Moldova, Mongolia, Macedonia, Monaco, Netherlands, North Korea, Norway, New Zealand, Poland, Portugal, Puerto Rico, Romania, Russia, Slovenia, South Africa, Slovakia, Spain, Sweden, Switzerland, Trinidad and Tobago, Turkey, Ukraine, United States, Uruguay, Uzbekistan, Venezuela, Yugoslavia

Sports: Alpine Skiing, Biathlon, Bobsled, Curling, Figure Skating, Freestyle Skiing, Ice Hockey, Luge, Nordic Skiing, Short-track Speed Skating, Snowboarding, Speed Skating

Sports for Women: Alpine Skiing, Biathlon, Curling, Figure Skating, Freestyle Skiing, Ice Hockey, Luge, Nordic Skiing, Short-track Speed Skating, Snowboarding, Speed Skating

MEDALS

Nation	Gold	Silver	Bronze	Total
Germany	12	9	8	29
Norway	10	10	5	25
Russia	9	6	3	18
Canada	6	5	4	15
United States	6	3	4	13
Netherlands	5	4	2	11
Japan	5	1	4	10

Nation	Gold	Silver	Bronze	Total
Austria	3	5	9	17
South Korea	3	1	2	6
Italy	2	6	2	10
Finland	2	4	6	12
Switzerland	2	2	3	7
France	2	1	5	8
Czech Republic	1	1	1	3
Bulgaria	1	0	0	1
China	0	6	2	8
Sweden	0	2	1	3
Denmark	0	1	0	1
Ukraine	0	1	0	1
Belarus	0	0	2	2
Kazakhstan	0	0	2	2
Belgium	0	0	1	1
Great Britain	0	0	1	1
Australia	0	0	1	1

Pacific Ocean Games

The inaugural Pacific Ocean Games in 1995 were centered in Cali, Colombia, with the cities of Buenaventura, Armenia, Pereira, Manizales and Popayan hosting other events.

Colombia's Olympic Committee president, Jorge Herrera Barona, was appointed general director of the games. Herrera had previously directed other major events in Colombia such as the Pan-American Games in Cali in 1971, the World Swimming Championships in 1975, and the World Basketball Championships in 1982.

Thirty-eight nations from around the Pacific Rim were invited. The games' emblem integrated a Colombian and Chinese dragon to symbolize the mixing of cultures from both sides of the Pacific Ocean.

The 1999 Pacific Ocean Games were scheduled to be held in Santiago, Chile, with the next games scheduled two years later in Vancouver, Canada. Both were canceled, with no plans yet for future games.

Year	Host City	Host Nation	Dates	Nations	Athletes	Sports
1995	Cali	Colombia	June 23–July 3	38	3000[189]	13

1995   Cali   Colombia   June 23–July 3

Nations: American Samoa, Australia, Brunei, Canada, Chile, China, China-Taipei, Colombia, Cook Islands, Costa Rica, Ecuador, El Salvador, Guam, Guatemala, Fiji Islands, Honduras, Hong Kong, Indonesia, Japan, Malaysia, Mexico, New Zealand, Nicaragua, North Korea, Panama, Papua New Guinea, Peru, Philippines, Russia, Singapore, Solomon Islands, South Korea, Thailand, Tonga, United States, Vanuatu, Vietnam, Western Samoa

Sports: Athletics, Baseball, Boxing, Cycling, Gymnastics, Judo, Roller-skating, Rhythmic Gymnastics, Swimming, Synchronized Swimming, Volleyball, Water Polo, Wrestling

Venues: Pascual Guerrero Stadium (Athletics), Jose J. Clark Stadium (Baseball), Alcides Nieto Patillo Velodrome (Cycling), El Pueblo Coliseum (Gymnastics), Pan American Pools (Swimming, Synchronized Swimming), Jose J. Clark Skate-o-drome (Roller Skating), Evangelista Mora Coliseum (Volleyball—Men), Municipal Coliseum, Buenaventura (Boxing), El Café Coliseum, Armenia (Rhythmic Gymnastics), Olympic Village Pools, Pereira (Water Polo), Rafael Cuartas Stadium, Pereira (Volleyball—Women), Jorge Arango Uribe Gymnasium, Manizales (Wrestling), La Estancia Coliseum, Popayan (Judo)

Pacific School Games

The first Pacific School Games, for children between the ages of eleven and nineteen, were held in Brisbane in 1982 in conjunction with the celebration of the Commonwealth Games.

The games are sanctioned by the Australian Sports Council and have so far been held in Australia on each occasion: Melbourne (1984), Sydney (1988), Darwin (1992) Perth (1996) and Sydney (2000). Teams from various Pacific nations are invited, with the school children from Australia competing in teams from their state or territory.

The accommodations for athletes in Perth in 1996 were split: some athletes stayed at a games village in the Perth University colleges; others stayed with families in homes in Perth. Walt and Tilda, two friendly wallaby mascots, kept the students' spirits high throughout the games.

The games are kept small in terms of the number of sports—athletics, gymnastics, swimming and diving were the disciplines offered in Perth. However, age groups brought the number of participants to 3200.

The 2000 games were held in Sydney in April and May. They used the facilities in place for the 2000 Olympic Games and gave the Sydney Olympic Organizing Committee another small test of its operations.

Year	Host City	Host Nation	Dates	Nations	Athletes	Sports
1982	Brisbane	Australia		NA	2000	NA
1984	Melbourne	Australia		NA	NA	NA
1988	Sydney	Australia		NA	NA	NA
1992	Darwin	Australia	April 3–13	22	2300	3
1996	Perth	Australia	December 7–13	30	3200	4
2000	Sydney	Australia	April 27–May 8	NA	NA	4

1992   Darwin   Australia   April 3–13

Sports: Athletics, Gymnastics, Swimming

1996   Perth   Australia   December 7–13

Sports: Athletics, Diving, Gymnastics, Swimming
Venues: Perth Superdrome, Perry Lakes Stadium

2000   Sydney   Australia   April 27–May 8

Sports: Athletics, Diving, Gymnastics, Swimming

Pan-American Games

The first Pan-American Games held in 1951 in Buenos Aires, Argentina, were the culmination of an idea for an Olympic festival for the western hemisphere that had been developing for well over a decade.

The first precursor to the Pan-American Games was the sporting events held in Dallas in the summer of 1937 as part of the Pan-American Exposition which took place from June 13 to November 1 of that year. Two hundred elite athletes from ten nations were specially invited to compete in athletics and football in the Cotton Bowl from July 15 to 18. There was also a boxing tournament held from August 12 to 14.

Most of the star athletes of the day were invited to the games. Glenn Cunningham won the 1500 meter run. The 800-meter Olympic champion, John Woodruff, and Elroy Robinson, who had broken the 880-yard world record the week before, faced off in the 800 meter event. Woodruff scored a convincing win and a world record of his own at the distance.

The round-robin football (soccer) tournament in the Cotton Bowl included Argentina, Canada (represented by the Winnipeg Irish club), and the U.S. champion, the Highlanders from Trenton, New Jersey. On three successive nights, Argentina beat the U.S. 9–1, Canada beat the U.S. 3–2, and Argentina beat Canada in the final game 8–1, to take the championship.

Dignitaries at the games included Lewis Johnson, the U.S. Assistant Secretary of War, while Brazil was represented by Oswaldo Aranja, the ambassador to the United States, and Sousa Coats, the Brazilian Minister of Finance. Brazil wanted to hold a similar sports festival in Rio de Janeiro in 1938, but the games were not arranged.

The next proposal for a Pan-American Games was in 1940, and this was largely inspired by the onset of World War II and the cancelation of the 1940 Olympic Games. On January 23, 1940, a *New York Times* headline read, "Pan-America Meet Sure To Go On." The games were proposed to be held in the United States in the summer of 1940, either in Philadelphia, New York, Los Angeles or San Francisco; despite the *Times* headline, though they did not go on. At the same time, Lake Placid offered to stage a winter Pan-American games in 1941, as the 1940 Olympic Winter Games had already been canceled. Games were again proposed for Buenos Aires in 1942, and the Argentineans were preparing facilities for them when the bombing of Pearl Harbor brought the U.S. into the war. The games were put off again until 1946. However, there was not enough time to prepare this event after the war, and the idea was set aside once more.

The Pan-American countries gathered together in London at the 1948 Olympic Games and decided to have Buenos Aires arrange a games for the nations of the Western hemisphere one more time. The first games were finally held in 1951. There was plenty of propaganda from Argentine dictator Juan Domingo Perón, who opened the very first games with a long speech rather than the standard brief declaration. The host crowds were strongly partisan, establishing a precedent of behavior that would plague the games throughout their history and prompting the Olympic Committee members present to state, "People must be taught to wish the 'best man' not 'our man' to win." The Argentines won the most medals and swept the titles in boxing, said to be due in a large part to biased officiating. Racing on the track was rough, and during the basketball final the fans threw rotten fruit onto the floor at the U.S. players. Mal Whitfield, the U.S. star, won two individual events—the 400 meters and 800 meters—

and was a member of the winning 1600 meter relay team. Despite the propaganda, questionable officiating and rowdy fan behavior, Avery Brundage, the president of the Pan-American Congress, called the games "a tremendous success."

At the 1955 games in Mexico City, Admehar Ferreira da Silva of Brazil, the 1952 Olympic champion, set a world record in the triple jump of 54 feet 4 inches. In the 400 meters, Lou Jones from the U.S. ran 45.4 seconds to establish a new world mark in that event. Argentinean Oswaldo Suarez won both the 5,000 and 10,000 meter runs, while Rodney Richard from the U.S. was a double gold medalist in the 100 and 200 meter dashes.

Bob Richards (pole vault), Franklin Held (javelin), Parry O'Brien (shot put) and Fortune Gordien (discus) swept the field events for the U.S. team.

The 1959 games were first awarded to Cleveland, but when it attempted to get federal funding and was denied, the city gave up the event. Washington, D.C., Philadelphia, Montevideo, Uruguay, and Guatemala City, Guatemala, were proposed as hosts, but eventually the games were given to Chicago just two years before they were to be held.

In preparation for the games, the asphalt auto racing track in Soldier Field was torn out and 485 tons of the state of the art "Tout-en-cas" brick and clay mixture was used to construct a new athletics racing surface. Organizers spent $750,000 on a new swimming pool.

When the games opened, foreign teams complained about the facilities in Chicago. The president of the Argentine delegation, Dr. Jose Oriani, said that "There is an air of improvisation about the games," and that the games "lacked sports specialists to take care of the sporting aspect." Transportation was a problem at the start, but was quickly improved.

Dr. Milton Eisenhower, the brother of U.S. President Eisenhower, addressed the opening ceremonies, while the President attended to business in Europe. The games torch was brought into the stadium after being relayed from the U.S.-Mexico border by 3000 Boy Scouts, a 1,464-mile route beginning at Laredo, Texas.

Francisco Sanchez Leonard, a boxer, and one other unnamed athlete from the Dominican Republic sought political asylum in the U.S. during the games. Leonard claimed that he feared execution by the ruling dictatorship if he returned home.

Once the games began, the U.S. dominated as expected. Ray Norton won three gold medals in the 100 meters, 200 meters and 4 by 100 meters relay. Brazil's Adhemar da Silva won the triple jump for the third consecutive time. The U.S. swept the 1500 meters with Dyrol Burleson, Jim Grelle and Ed Moran taking the medals. Althea Gibson came out of retirement to win the tennis competition, and hinted that she might turn professional if given the right offer. Such was the feeling towards professionalism at the time that the Pan-American Sports Organization (PASO) issued a strong statement which recommended that "the Executive Committee analyze the case and if the comments attributed to the winning athlete in individual tennis are found to be true, to make a public and energetic condemnation of such sports misconduct."

Chris von Saltza, a fifteen-year-old Californian, won five gold medals in swimming, while shooter Daniel Puckel had the largest individual tally of the games, winning nine gold medals.

The United States totally dominated the 1959 games winning 121 gold medals. Argentina was a distant second with nine golds.

São Paulo, Brazil, was selected over Winnipeg as host of the fourth Pan-American

Games to be held in 1963. The Cubans had not responded to invitations to the games sent as early as 1962, and a week before the event, Jose Flores of Mexico, the IOC's representative for the São Paulo games, sent another cable to Havana asking for Cuba's official entry. Avery Brundage had asked Flores to disallow a Cuban entry unless an official communication was received from the Cubans. The Cuban press turned this into a U.S. attack, quoting Fidel Castro as saying that the Americans were afraid of the Cuban athletes, and that "enemies of the revolution" were conspiring to keep the Cubans out of the games. A day later the impasse was solved when the games organizers accepted Cuba's official entry of 105 members in seven sports. The Cubans marched into Paçaembu stadium on April 20, each waving a small Brazilian flag.

The torch relay for the games was carried from Brazil's capital, Brasilia, to São Paulo. Jose Teles de Conceicao, one of Brazil's former Olympic high jumpers, carried the torch into the stadium and was joined for one lap of the track by Oswaldo Suarez, the distance running champion from Argentina, U.S. miler Jim Beatty, and Mexico's Eligio Batica.

On the first day of the games baseball tournament, Cuba crushed the U.S. team 13–1. Although Cuba went on to win the baseball competition, overall, the U.S. once again overwhelmed the competition, winning 109 gold medals.

Winnipeg was chosen to host the next games in four years' time over bids from Caracas, Venezuela, and Santiago, Chile.

At Canada's centennial in 1967, a record 2,438 athletes and 28 countries participated. England's Prince Philip opened the games under an unfortunate downpour of rain, but the skies cleared and warmer temperatures returned for most of the games.

Four members of the Canadian baseball team were declared ineligible for the games because of professionalism, and the U.S. finally beat the Cubans in baseball and went on to lock up the gold medal race again.

Van Nelson, a twenty-one-year-old U.S. team member, scored a double victory in the 5000 and 10,000 meter runs. U.S. swimmer Debbie Meyer broke world records in the 400 and 800 meter freestyle races. Canadian Elaine Tanner became an overnight Canadian heroine by setting world records in the 100 and 200 meter backstroke events.

The event went south of the equator in 1971 to Cali, Colombia. In one of the strangest incidents of an international games, a Cuban trainer jumped to his death from his hotel while denouncing Cuban Premier Castro. The Cubans claimed the death was accidental. When three Cubans were found missing during the games, Cuban officials claimed that one had defected and two had been kidnapped. One Puerto Rican athlete, A. Morales, resisted an order to return home after giving a black power salute on the awards stand during the U.S. national anthem, in protest over U.S. oppression of Puerto Rico.

The games village had fewer amenities than most. There was little or no hot water for showers, there were six athletes to a room, and the beds were made of nothing more than a foam pad on a wood board. Rats were frequently sighted. The food in the cafeteria fortunately drew high praise.

The U.S. basketball team struggled in Cali and lost the chance to determine its own destiny by losing to Cuba by four points. After beating Brazil by only two points, the U.S. team needed Cuba to beat Brazil in their match. If Brazil beat Cuba, the final teams would be decided by points scored for and against. If Cuba lost to Brazil by five or fewer points, both Brazil and Cuba would move to the finals. With less than three minutes left to play in the Brazil-Cuba match, Brazil was up by 13 points, but curiously began to miss easy shots and lose the ball on steals. Cuba made two free throws with 10 seconds left, and lost the game—by five points. A celebration ensued on the court, the Cubans and Brazilians dancing together, congratulating each other for having made the final round. The U.S. would not win a medal.

The by-now familiar pattern to root against the U.S. team was evident again, with Frank Shorter winning the 10,000 meter run while being booed and dodging garbage thrown at him from the stands. Shorter also won the marathon.

At a rally in Havana to welcome the Cuban athletes home, a large board boasted Cuba's medal count for the games, listing each team gold medal as several individual medals which dramatically increased the apparent total. Castro spoke for 55 minutes to the crowd, lauding the Cubans' victories, especially the upset of the U.S. in basketball and Pedro Perez' world record in the triple jump.

Two Pan-American Games traditions continued at the seventh games in Mexico City in 1975. Spectators jeered the U.S. team at every chance and the world record in the triple jump was broken again, the third time it had been bettered at the games. This time João Oliveira of Brazil used the altitude of Mexico City to his advantage to leap 58 feet 8½ inches to break the world record by 1 foot 5¾ inches.

The 1975 games had originally been awarded to Santiago, Chile, but Chilean dictators forced them to be moved. São Paulo was the first alternate chosen, but finances and a meningitis epidemic caused that plan to be canceled. Mexico City eventually rescued the games just 10 months before they were scheduled to begin.

The U.S. team was booed from the beginning, during the march past in the opening ceremonies and all through the games at every venue. On the race walk course, U.S. athletes were interfered with. Larry Scully filed an official protest after students on the course at the University of Mexico campus blocked his way and tugged his shirt and held him back.

Bruce Jenner won the decathlon, with 8045 points, a games record by one point. Cuba's Silvio Leonard won the 100 meters but ended up tumbling fifteen feet into the moat that surrounds the Aztec Stadium track. His injuries kept him from running the 200 meters.

Mexican President Luis Echeverria, the only person booed more loudly than the U.S. team at the opening ceremony, decided to skip the closing festivities.

Security was an issue at the 1979 games in San Juan, Puerto Rico, with factions favoring statehood for Puerto Rico closely watched by the authorities.

Bobby Knight, U.S. basketball coach, made the San Juan basketball competition memorable. Knight was accused of assaulting a Puerto Rican police officer. After trying and convicting him of this offense, the courts tried to impose a penalty of six months in jail and a $500 fine on Knight. Knight had already left the country, however, and efforts to have him extradited were not successful.

On the track, Alberto Juantorena was heckled just prior to his 400 meter race by expatriate Cubans yelling, "There is no food in Cuba." Juantorena had to be restrained from going into the stands to confront the hecklers. Cuba's Silvio Leonard defended his 100 meter title and was able to come back and win the 200 meter race as well.

The biggest news of the ninth Pan-American Games at Caracas, Venezuela in 1983, was the new drug testing equipment that had been installed at a Caracas laboratory. U.S. athletes left the games village and returned home without competing after other athletes had been found using steroids and other banned substances.

The next games were originally to be awarded to Ecuador, but the Ecuadorian government was not able to commit to them at meetings in Caracas. The deadline was extended and the decision was to be made at a meeting in Havana in June 1984, with the understanding that if Ecuador was not able to take the games that Cuba would be chosen as host. However, in the interim, Cuba decided to join the boycott of the 1984 Olympic Games, and the meeting in Havana was canceled. PASO changed its mind and the games were to be awarded to Indianapolis on December 15, 1984, if Ecuador was not able to accept them. Fidel Castro, in a letter written to IOC president Juan Antonio Samaranch in November 1984, expressed his frustration that the games were being awarded to nations with "large financial resources" who could exert political pressure and dictate where the event could go. Indianapolis was eventually chosen, but PASO awarded the following games to Havana for 1991.

In 1987, Olympic champion sprinter Wilma Rudolph lit the games torch at the Indianapolis Motor Speedway, while U.S. Vice President George Bush officially opened the tenth Pan-American Games.

The games were marred by brawls and protests between the U.S. team and the Cuban team. Security increased after a series of fights between Cubans and anti–Castro demonstrators at the baseball and boxing venues.

Cuba had considered boycotting these games. This could have put them in a precarious position, though, as the 1991 games had been awarded to Havana, so the Cubans ultimately participated. It was the largest delegation of Cuban athletes to compete in the U.S. since Castro came to power—some 450 athletes—which concerned the Cubans in terms of possible defections, but none was reported.

Other controversies abounded. Overcrowding was a problem in the village when hundreds of extra athletes showed up. The Puerto Ricans resurrected their attempt to have Bobby Knight extradited to serve his sentence for the 1979 assault incident. The U.S. State Department denied entry into the U.S. for one Chilean athlete, Francisco Zuniga, claiming it had evidence that Zuniga was part of the governmental reign of torture, murder and terror in Chile. Another Chilean athlete, Sergio Arrendondo Gonzalez, was allowed entry into the U.S. but was accused by two former Chilean citizens of being part of the same terror. The State Department said there was not evidence to bar Gonzalez from the games, but after a lawsuit was filed against Gonzalez, he quickly returned home to Chile. Puerto Rican gymnastics judge Heriberto Crerspo was dismissed from his position after he was found to be trying to influence other judges to lower the scores of American athletes and give higher scores to Cubans. The American Legion in Indianapolis refused to allow the closing ceremonies to be held in the Legion's War Memorial Plaza because the American flag would be lowered and the Cuban flag put in its place during the ceremony. The closing festivities were moved to the Hoosier Dome. Eight Dominican athletes, all members of the armed forces, disappeared from the games village, presumably as defectors. Drugs were not as big an issue in Indianapolis as they had been in Caracas, but six athletes were caught using banned substances.

In 1991, Havana, Cuba, finally got its chance to host the Pan-American Games, but not without difficulty. In July 1990, a U.S. federal judge ruled that the U.S. government could prevent ABC television from broadcasting the 1991 Pan-American Games from Cuba because paying the fees to a communist nation would violate the "Trading with the Enemy" Act. In December 1990, ABC, along with Turner Broadcasting, reached an agreement with the federal government to allow the broadcasts, but with a very limited fee paid to the Cubans.

Cuba surpassed the U.S. for the first time in the gold medal race, winning 140 to the U.S.'s 130 by dominating the boxing and weightlifting competitions and outperforming its rival in track and field. Cuban President Fidel Castro was so busy visiting all of the games venues to congratulate the Cuban victors that one news reporter likened him to a department store Santa, with one on every corner. The United States bright spot was the women's softball team which won all seven of its games by a combined score of 42–0.

This time around it was the Canadians' and Mexicans' turn to brawl at the games. They had a fight during the baseball competition that caused the game to be halted.

Mar del Plata, Argentina, was the site for the 1995 Pan-Am Games. The U.S. regained its top spot after sending its largest delegation ever to an international event— 746 athletes. The Cubans finished second with their largest delegation ever—490 athletes. The growth in delegations reflected the addition of several sports to the program, making thirty-four in total. The medals table also reflected this, with 432 gold medals handed out at the games.

A U.S. team shock was the baseball team that went 0–6. The U.S. representatives were the baseball squad from St. John's University which was chosen in lieu of creating a U.S. collegiate all-star team because of the March dates of the games, during the university sessions in the U.S. The Cubans won the baseball competition for the seventh games in a row.

The U.S. basketball team composed of Continental Basketball Association players won the silver medal, losing to Argentina 90–86. The U.S. soccer team, though allowed to use professional players, had just one on the team, and did not win a medal.

Even in track and field, the U.S. team won just one event—Roger Kingdom took the 110 meter hurdles. The March dates did not fit well into many of the northern hemisphere athletes' early season training. Where the Americans did win medals was in sports not on the Olympic program but included in the Pan-Ams, such as bowling, roller-skating and water-skiing. The women's basketball competition was canceled because too few teams were entered after Puerto Rico withdrew.

The *New York Times* wrote: "In too many events the Americans either received or provided inferior competition. It has come time for the United States to rethink the extent of its involvement in this quadrennial affair." It concluded by saying that "as preparation for the 1996 Atlanta Olympics, these events served little purpose."

The 1999 games returned to Winnipeg, Canada, site of the 1967 edition. The Pan-American torch was lit in the last week of June 1999 at the site of the ancient Aztec temple of Teotihuacan, and relayed to Winnipeg for the opening ceremonies on July 23. Canadians Alwyn Morris, double gold medalist in canoeing at the 1984 Olympic Games, and Silken Laumann, bronze medalist in rowing, were given the honor of being the final torchbearers to light the flame for the games. Tanya Dubnicoff, a cyclist born and raised in Winnipeg, carried the Canadian flag and led the Canadian contingent into the opening ceremony. As part of the ceremony, hand-made native blankets were given to representatives of each nation as gifts. Each blanket was made with the colors of the nation's flag. Princess Anne gave a welcoming message to the athletes.

As the games developed, the biggest questions were, how many Cubans would defect? (it turned out to be eleven) and did Javier Sotomayor really use cocaine?

The local newspaper, the *Winnipeg Sun*, offered a prize, a vacation to Cuba, to the reader who guessed the correct number of defections. Fidel Castro was not pleased with the treatment of the Cubans at the games, saying "We have never seen so many tricks, so much filth at the Pan-Am Games. We are competing on enemy territory." Sports agents were seen lurking around the games village and even shining flashlights from their cars into the windows of the top Cuban baseball talent. The Cubans called the games the "worst in history," and mentioned hosting the 2008 summer Olympic Games as a way to restore their pride.

Javier Sotomayor, the world record-holder in the high jump, had the gold medal taken away at the Pan-American Games for a reported positive drug test for cocaine, a ruling the Cubans continued to protest for months afterward. Three Cuban weightlifters tested positive for nandrolone, tests the Cuban government and sports federations hotly denied. The Cubans attacked the testing on every front possible, claiming that there was a drug-testing room for Cubans only, that they were forced to drink what was given to them and were not given a free choice from unopened bottles, that the lab in Montreal was corrupt, and that papers announcing a positive result for one of their athletes were dated August 2 when the test was completed on August 3.

Alberto Juantorena, president of the Cuban Athletics Federation, claimed that the Cubans filed a complaint with the International Amateur Athletic Federation. "We are awaiting a reply, because we're not going to sanction Sotomayor. We're going to defend him to the death and we will appeal through the courts if that's what we have to do to restore our athlete's honor, because we know he is incapable of having committed what he has been accused of."

The good news for Cuba was a world record lift of 205.5 kilos in the clean and jerk for Hidalberto Aranda in the 77 kilo division.

A brawl marred the Canada-Guatemala football game, and police protection was required to escort the U.S. referee from the field after the match. Four Guatemalans were suspended for the rest of the games.

Overall, the spirit of the games and the support of the fans and volunteers in Winnipeg made the event a tremendous success. The games set records for most participants and sports.

In December 1998, PASO selected Santo Domingo, Dominican Republic, as the host for the 2003 games over Medellín, Colombia, and Guadalajara, Mexico.

Year	Host City	Host Nation	Dates	Nations	Athletes	Sports
1951	Buenos Aires	Argentina	February 26–March 9	22	2513	19
1955	Mexico City	Mexico	March 12–26	19	2583	18
1959	Chicago	USA	August 27–September 7	25	2263	19
1963	São Paulo	Brazil	April 20–May 5	24	1665	20
1967	Winnipeg	Canada	July 23–August 6	28	2348	21
1971	Cali	Columbia	July 30–August 12	31	2996	18
1975	Mexico City	Mexico	October 12–26	33	3146	22
1979	San Juan	Puerto Rico	July 1–15	34	4000	22
1983	Caracas	Venezuela	August 15–29	36	3800	25
1987	Indianapolis	USA	August 7–23	38	6000	31
1991	Havana	Cuba	August 2–18	39	4519	31
1995	Mar del Plata	Argentina	March 14–25	42	5144	34
1999	Winnipeg	Canada	July 24–August 8	42	8949	41

1951   Buenos Aires   Argentina   February 26–March 9

Sports: Athletics, Baseball, Basketball, Boxing, Cycling, Equestrian, Fencing, Gymnastics, Modern Pentathlon, Polo (Horse), Rowing, Sailing, Shooting, Football, Swimming, Diving, Water Polo, Tennis, Weightlifting, Wrestling (Freestyle)

Sports for Women: Athletics, Equestrian, Fencing, Sailing, Shooting, Swimming (Swimming, Diving), Tennis

MEDALS

Nation	Gold	Silver	Bronze	Total
Argentina	57	41	33	131
United States	46	33	19	98
Chile	7	17	10	34
Cuba	6	7	10	23
Brazil	5	15	11	31
Mexico	5	6	22	33
Peru	2	3	4	9
Trinidad	1	3	0	4
Ecuador	1	0	1	2
Colombia	1	0	0	1
Venezuela	0	1	1	2
Costa Rica	0	1	0	1
Guatemala	0	0	3	3
Jamaica	0	0	3	3
Panama	0	0	2	2
Haiti	0	0	1	1

1955   Mexico City   Mexico   March 12–26

Sports: Athletics, Baseball, Basketball, Boxing, Cycling, Equestrian, Fencing, Football, Gymnastics, Modern Pentathlon, Rowing, Shooting, Swimming, Diving, Volleyball, Water Polo, Tennis, Weightlifting, Wrestling (Freestyle)

Sports for Women: Athletics, Basketball, Equestrian, Fencing, Shooting, Swimming (Swimming, Diving, Synchronized Swimming), Tennis, Volleyball

MEDALS

Nation	Gold	Silver	Bronze	Total
United States	83	57	35	175
Argentina	26	31	17	74
Mexico	16	11	34	61
Canada	4	5	3	12
Chile	3	4	13	20
Venezuela	2	4	11	17
Brazil	2	3	12	17
Colombia	1	3	1	5
Panama	1	1	0	2
Guatemala	1	0	1	2
Dominican Republic	1	0	0	1
Cuba	0	6	6	12
Uruguay	0	5	3	8
Puerto Rico	0	3	3	6
Jamaica	0	2	1	3
Netherlands Antilles	0	1	3	4
Trinidad and Tobago	0	1	0	1

1959   Chicago   USA   August 27–September 7

Nations: Argentina, Bahamas, Barbados, Bermuda, Brazil, British Guiana, Canada, Chile, Costa Rica, Cuba, Ecuador, El Salvador, Guatemala, Jamaica, Mexico, Netherlands Antilles, Panama, Paraguay, Peru, Puerto Rico, Trinidad and Tobago, United States, Uruguay, Venezuela (1 more)

Sports: Athletics, Baseball, Basketball, Boxing, Cycling, Equestrian, Fencing, Gymnastics, Modern Pentathlon, Rowing, Sailing, Shooting, Soccer, Swimming, Diving, Water Polo, Tennis, Volleyball, Weightlifting, Wrestling (Freestyle)

Sports for Women: Athletics, Basketball, Equestrian, Fencing, Gymnastics, Sailing, Shooting, Swimming (Swimming, Diving, Synchronized Swimming [Demonstration]), Tennis, Volleyball

Venues: Soldier Field

MEDALS

Nation	Gold	Silver	Bronze	Total
United States	121	72	52	245
Argentina	9	22	12	43
Brazil	8	8	6	22
Canada	7	21	27	55
Mexico	6	11	13	30
Chile	5	2	5	12
Cuba	2	5	4	11
West Indies	2	4	8	14
Bahamas	2	0	0	2
Venezuela	1	7	6	14
Uruguay	1	3	4	8
Panama	0	4	3	7
Peru	0	2	7	9
Puerto Rico	0	2	4	6
Haiti	0	1	0	1
British Guiana	0	0	3	3
Guatemala	0	0	1	1
Netherlands Antilles	0	0	1	1

1963   São Paulo   Brazil   April 20–May 5

Nations: Argentina, Bahamas, Barbados, Bermuda, Brazil, British Guiana, Canada, Chile, Costa Rica, Cuba, Ecuador, El Salvador, Guatemala, Jamaica, Mexico, Netherlands Antilles, Panama, Paraguay, Peru, Puerto Rico, Trinidad and Tobago, United States, Uruguay, Venezuela

Sports: Athletics, Baseball, Basketball, Boxing, Cycling, Equestrian, Fencing, Gymnastics, Judo, Modern Pentathlon, Rowing, Sailing, Shooting, Soccer, Swimming, Diving, Water Polo, Tennis, Volleyball, Weightlifting, Wrestling (Freestyle)

Sports for Women: Athletics, Basketball, Equestrian, Fencing, Gymnastics, Sailing, Shooting, Swimming (Swimming, Diving, Synchronized Swimming), Tennis, Volleyball

Venues: Pacaembu Stadium (opening ceremonies, Athletics), Bom Retiro Stadium (Baseball)

MEDALS

Nation	Gold	Silver	Bronze	Total
United States	109	49	35	193
Brazil	14	21	18	53
Canada	10	28	24	62
Argentina	8	16	18	42
Uruguay	5	1	7	13
Cuba	4	5	3	12
Mexico	2	7	18	27
Venezuela	2	6	5	13
Chile	2	1	6	9
Trinidad and Tobago	1	2	2	5
British Guiana	1	0	0	1
Netherlands Antilles	0	4	2	6
Panama	0	2	3	5
Guatemala	0	2	2	4
Jamaica	0	2	2	4
Puerto Rico	0	2	2	4
Peru	0	1	1	2
Barbados	0	0	3	3

1967   Winnipeg   Canada   July 23–August 6

Nations: Argentina, Bahamas, Barbados, Bermuda, Bolivia, Brazil, British Honduras, Canada, Chile, Costa Rica, Colombia, Cuba, Ecuador, El Salvador, Guyana, Guatemala, Jamaica, Mexico, Netherlands Antilles, Panama, Paraguay, Peru, Puerto Rico, Trinidad and Tobago, United States, Uruguay, Venezuela, Virgin Islands[190]

Sports: Athletics, Baseball, Basketball, Boxing, Cycling, Equestrian, Fencing, Field Hockey, Gymnastics, Judo, Rowing, Sailing, Shooting, Soccer, Swimming, Diving, Water Polo, Tennis, Volleyball, Weightlifting, Wrestling (Freestyle)

Sports for Women: Athletics, Basketball, Equestrian, Fencing, Gymnastics, Sailing, Shooting, Swimming (Swimming, Diving, Synchronized Swimming (Demonstration)), Tennis, Volleyball

Venues: University of Manitoba Stadium (Athletics), Miller Road (Shooting), Gimli, Lake Winnipeg (Yachting), Whiteshell (Cycling), Birds Hill Park (Equestrian), Winnipeg Civic Auditorium (Wrestling, Boxing, Weightlifting), Winnipeg Stadium (Baseball, Soccer, Equestrian), Alexander Park (Soccer), Winnipeg Velodrome (Cycling), Winnipeg Arena (Basketball, Volleyball), Highlander Club (Fencing), St. James Centenary Arena (Gymnastics and Judo), Assiniboia Downs (Equestrian Dressage), Assiniboine Park (Field Hockey), Pan-Am Pool (Swimming, Diving), Winnipeg Canoe Club (Tennis), Winnipeg Floodway (Canoeing and Rowing), Winnipeg Track and Skeet Club (Shooting), Carman, Portage la Prairie (Baseball)

MEDALS

Nation	Gold	Silver	Bronze	Total
United States	109	64	42	215
Canada	12	38	43	93
Brazil	11	10	4	25
Cuba	8	13	23	44

Nation	Gold	Silver	Bronze	Total
Argentina	8	13	12	33
Mexico	5	14	23	42
Trinidad and Tobago	2	2	3	7
Venezuela	1	4	5	10
Colombia	1	2	5	8
Puerto Rico	1	1	3	5
Chile	1	1	3	5
Peru	0	2	1	3
Uruguay	0	1	4	5
Panama	0	1	3	4
Bermuda	0	1	0	1
Ecuador	0	1	0	1
Barbados	0	1	0	1
Jamaica	0	0	3	3
Guyana	0	0	1	1

1971   Cali   Columbia   July 30–August 12

Nations: Argentina, Barbados, Brazil, Canada, Chile, Colombia, Cuba, Ecuador, Guatemala, Guyana, Jamaica, Mexico, Netherlands Antilles, Panama, Peru, Puerto Rico, Trinidad, United States, Uruguay, Venezuela (11 more)

Sports: Athletics, Baseball, Basketball, Boxing, Cycling, Equestrian, Fencing, Field Hockey, Gymnastics, Rowing, Sailing, Shooting, Soccer, Swimming, Diving, Water Polo, Volleyball, Weightlifting, Wrestling (Freestyle)

Sports for Women: Athletics, Basketball, Equestrian, Fencing, Gymnastics, Sailing, Shooting, Swimming (Swimming, Diving, Synchronized Swimming), Volleyball

Venues: Estadio Pascual Guerrero (Athletics, Soccer), Gimnasio Universidad Deportivo Alberto Galindo H (Basketball, Weightlifting), Diamante Universidad Deportivo Panamericana (Baseball) Plaza de Toros Universidad Deportivo A Galindo H (Boxing), Velódromo Universidad Deportivo A Galindo H (Cycling), Club Campestre (Equestrian. Tennis), Club San Fernando (Fencing), Canchas A.B.C. (Soccer), Gimnasio Universidad Deportivo San Fernando (Gymnastics, Judo, Wrestling), Piscina Universidad Deportivo Panamericana (Swimming, Diving, Water Polo), Club Cazadores (Shooting), Lago Calima (Sailing), Gimnasio Universidad Deportivo Panamericana (Volleyball)

MEDALS

Nation	Gold	Silver	Bronze	Total
United States	105	73	40	218
Cuba	30	50	25	105
Canada	19	20	41	80
Brazil	9	7	14	30
Mexico	7	11	23	41
Argentina	6	4	12	22
Colombia	5	9	14	28
Jamaica	4	3	6	13
Puerto Rico	2	4	5	11
Venezuela	2	4	3	9
Trinidad	1	2	4	7

Nation	Gold	Silver	Bronze	Total
Panama	1	2	3	6
Netherlands Antilles	1	1	1	3
Ecuador	1	0	2	3
Guatemala	1	0	0	1
Chile	0	3	3	6
Peru	0	1	4	5
Barbados	0	1	0	1
Uruguay	0	0	3	3
Guyana	0	0	1	1

1975   Mexico City   Mexico   October 12–26

Nations: Argentina, Bahamas, Brazil, Canada, Chile, Colombia, Cuba, Dominican Republic, Ecuador, Guyana, Jamaica, Mexico, Netherlands Antilles, Panama, Peru, Puerto Rico, Trinidad, United States, Uruguay, Venezuela (13 more)

Sports: Athletics, Baseball, Basketball, Boxing, Cycling, Equestrian, Fencing, Field Hockey, Gymnastics, Judo, Rowing, Sailing, Shooting, Soccer, Swimming, Diving, Water Polo, Tennis, Volleyball, Weightlifting, Wrestling (Freestyle, Greco-Roman)

Sports for Women: Athletics, Basketball, Equestrian, Fencing, Gymnastics, Sailing, Shooting, Swimming (Swimming, Diving, Synchronized Swimming), Tennis, Volleyball

MEDALS

Nation	Gold	Silver	Bronze	Total
United States	116	82	46	244
Cuba	55	45	30	130
Canada	18	34	39	91
Mexico	9	34	39	82
Brazil	8	13	23	44
Argentina	3	5	8	16
Colombia	2	3	4	9
Ecuador	1	1	1	3
Peru	1	1	0	2
Guyana	1	1	0	2
Puerto Rico	0	2	7	9
Panama	0	2	4	6
Venezuela	0	1	11	12
Dominican Republic	0	1	8	9
Jamaica	0	1	4	5
Bahamas	0	1	1	2
Netherlands Antilles	0	1	0	1
Trinidad	0	1	0	1
Chile	0	0	2	2
Uruguay	0	0	2	2

1979   San Juan   Puerto Rico   July 1–15

Nations: Argentina, Bahamas, Belize, Brazil, Canada, Chile, Colombia, Cuba, Dominican Republic, Ecuador, El Salvador, Guyana, Jamaica, Mexico, Netherlands

Antilles, Panama, Peru, Puerto Rico, United States, U.S. Virgin Islands, Venezuela (13 more)

Sports: Archery, Athletics, Baseball, Basketball, Boxing, Cycling, Equestrian, Fencing, Field Hockey, Gymnastics, Judo, Roller Skating, Rowing, Sailing, Shooting, Soccer, Softball, Swimming, Diving, Water Polo, Tennis, Volleyball, Weightlifting, Wrestling (Freestyle, Greco-Roman)

Sports for Women: Archery, Athletics, Basketball, Equestrian, Fencing, Gymnastics, Roller-skating, Sailing, Shooting, Softball, Swimming (Swimming, Diving, Synchronized Swimming), Tennis, Volleyball

Venues: Hiram Bithorm Municipal Stadium (Opening, Closing Ceremonies), Sixto Escobar Stadium (Athletics Football), Rio Hondo Canal (Rowing), Roberto Clemente Coliseum (Basketball, Boxing, Gymnastics), Pepin Cetero Hall, Bayamon (Basketball), Canovanas Hall (Basketball), Trujillo Alto Gymnasium (Boxing), Coamo Velodrome (Cycling), Equestrian Park in Stop (Equestrian), Manuel Carrasquillo Herpen Hall (Fencing, Roller-skating), Country Club Grounds (Football), San Juan Regional Park, Barrio Los Corozos (Hockey and Tennis), Baldrich Field (Hockey), Guaynabo Municipal Coliseum (Judo, Wrestling), Escambron Swimming Pool (Swimming, Water Polo), University Swimming Pool, Rios Pedras (Water Polo), Bairoa 25 Shooting Range, Caguas (Shooting), Metropolitan Shooting Club (Shooting), Roberto Clemente Center (Archery), Caguas Municipal Coliseum (Volleyball), Rio Pedras Gymnasium (Weightlifting), Ponce Yacht Club (Yachting), Juan Ramon Loubriel Stadium, Bayamon (Baseball), Ildefonso Sola Morales Stadium, Caguas (Baseball), Guaynabo Municipal Stadium (Softball), Villa Nevarez Field (Softball), "Summit Hills" Park (Softball)

MEDALS

Nation	Gold	Silver	Bronze	Total
United States	127	92	45	264
Cuba	65	49	32	146
Canada	24	44	68	136
Argentina	12	7	17	36
Brazil	9	13	18	40
Mexico	3	6	28	37
Puerto Rico	2	9	11	22
Venezuela	1	4	7	12
Chile	1	4	6	11
Dominican Republic	0	5	7	12
Panama	0	3	1	4
Jamaica	0	3	0	3
Guyana	0	2	1	3
Colombia	0	1	8	9
Peru	0	1	2	3
Bahamas	0	1	0	1
Ecuador	0	0	2	2
Belize	0	0	1	1
Netherlands Antilles	0	0	1	1
El Salvador	0	0	1	1
U.S. Virgin Islands	0	0	1	1

1983   Caracas   Venezuela   August 15–29

Nations: Argentina, Brazil, Canada, Chile, Colombia, Cuba, Dominican Republic, Ecuador, Jamaica, Mexico, Panama, Peru, Puerto Rico, Trinidad, United States, Uruguay, Venezuela (19 more)

Sports: Archery, Athletics, Baseball, Basketball, Boxing, Cycling, Equestrian, Fencing, Field Hockey, Gymnastics, Judo, Roller-skating, Rowing, Sailing, Shooting, Soccer, Softball, Swimming, Diving, Water Polo, Table Tennis, Tennis, Volleyball, Weightlifting, Wrestling (Freestyle, Greco-Roman, Sambo)

Sports for Women: Archery, Athletics, Basketball, Equestrian, Fencing, Gymnastics, Judo, Rowing, Sailing, Shooting, Softball, Swimming (Swimming, Diving, Synchronized Swimming), Table Tennis, Tennis, Volleyball, Wrestling (Sambo)

MEDALS

Nation	Gold	Silver	Bronze	Total
United States	136	92	56	284
Cuba	79	53	43	175
Canada	18	44	47	109
Brazil	14	20	22	56
Venezuela	12	26	35	73
Mexico	7	11	24	42
Argentina	2	11	22	35
Puerto Rico	2	7	6	15
Colombia	1	7	13	21
Chile	1	3	9	13
Peru	1	1	4	6
Uruguay	1	0	2	3
Ecuador	1	0	0	1
Dominican Republic	0	5	9	14
Trinidad	0	1	2	3
Jamaica	0	0	6	6
Panama	0	0	3	3
(Others)	0	2	3	5

[the official medals table for this games simply lists "others" at the end]

1987   Indianapolis   USA   August 7–23

Nations: Antigua, Aruba, Argentina, Bahamas, Barbados, Belize, Bermuda, Bolivia, Brazil, British Virgin Islands, Canada, Cayman Islands, Chile, Colombia, Costa Rica, Cuba, Dominican Republic, Ecuador, El Salvador, Granada, Guatemala, Guyana, Haiti, Honduras, Jamaica, Mexico, Netherlands Antilles, Nicaragua, Panama, Paraguay, Peru, Puerto Rico, Suriname, Trinidad and Tobago, United States, Uruguay, Venezuela, Virgin Islands

Sports: Archery, Athletics, Baseball, Basketball, Boxing, Canoe/Kayak, Cycling, Equestrian, Fencing, Field Hockey, Gymnastics, Judo, Modern Pentathlon, Roller-skating, Rowing, Sailing, Shooting, Soccer, Softball, Swimming, Diving, Water Polo, Table Tennis, Tae Kwon Do, Team Handball, Tennis, Volleyball, Weightlifting, Wrestling (Freestyle, Greco-Roman)

Sports for Women: Archery, Athletics, Basketball, Canoe/Kayak, Cycling, Equestrian, Fencing, Field Hockey, Gymnastics (Artistic and Rhythmic), Judo, Roller-skating,

Rowing, Sailing, Shooting, Softball, Swimming (Swimming, Diving, Synchronized Swimming), Table Tennis, Team Handball, Tennis, Volleyball

MEDALS

Nation	Gold	Silver	Bronze	Total
United States	168	118	83	369
Cuba	75	52	48	175
Canada	30	57	75	162
Brazil	14	14	33	61
Argentina	12	14	22	48
Mexico	9	11	18	38
Venezuela	3	11	12	26
Colombia	3	8	13	24
Costa Rica	3	4	4	11
Puerto Rico	2	5	20	27
Jamaica	2	3	8	13
Uruguay	2	2	3	7
Chile	1	2	4	7
Suriname	1	0	1	2
Peru	0	4	2	6
Dominican Republic	0	3	9	12
Panama	0	3	1	4
Bahamas	0	2	3	5
Ecuador	0	1	5	6
Trinidad and Tobago	0	1	1	2
Virgin Islands	0	1	1	2
Guatemala	0	0	2	2
Bermuda	0	0	1	1
El Salvador	0	0	1	1
Guyana	0	0	1	1
Netherlands Antilles	0	0	1	1
Paraguay	0	0	1	1

1991   Havana   Cuba   August 2–18

Nations: Argentina, Bahamas, Bolivia, Brazil, Canada, Chile, Colombia, Costa Rica, Cuba, Dominican Republic, Ecuador, Guatemala, Guyana, Haiti, Jamaica, Mexico, Nicaragua, Panama, Peru, Puerto Rico, Suriname, Trinidad, United States, Uruguay, U.S. Virgin Islands, Venezuela (13 more)

Sports: Archery, Athletics, Baseball, Basketball, Bowling, Boxing, Canoe/Kayak, Cycling, Equestrian, Fencing, Field Hockey, Gymnastics, Judo, Roller-skating, Rowing, Sailing, Shooting, Soccer, Softball, Swimming, Diving, Water Polo, Table Tennis, Tae Kwon Do, Team Handball, Tennis, Volleyball, Weightlifting, Wrestling (Freestyle, Greco-Roman)

Sports for Women: Archery, Athletics, Basketball, Bowling, Canoe/Kayak, Cycling, Equestrian, Fencing, Field Hockey, Gymnastics (Artistic and Rhythmic), Judo, Roller-skating, Rowing, Sailing, Shooting, Softball, Swimming (Swimming, Diving, Synchronized Swimming), Table Tennis, Tennis, Volleyball

Nation	MEDALS			
	Gold	Silver	Bronze	Total
Cuba	140	62	97	299
United States	130	125	63	318
Canada	22	46	59	127
Brazil	21	21	37	79
Mexico	14	23	38	75
Argentina	11	15	29	55
Colombia	5	15	21	41
Venezuela	4	14	20	38
Puerto Rico	3	13	11	27
Chile	2	1	7	10
Jamaica	2	1	5	8
Suriname	1	2	1	4
Trinidad	1	1	0	2
Costa Rica	1	0	1	2
Dominican Republic	0	5	4	9
Guatemala	0	1	5	6
Nicaragua	0	1	2	3
Bahamas	0	1	1	2
Ecuador	0	1	1	2
Bolivia	0	1	0	1
Panama	0	1	0	1
Uruguay	0	1	0	1
Peru	0	0	3	3
Guyana	0	0	2	2
U.S. Virgin Islands	0	0	2	2
Haiti	0	0	1	1

1995   Mar del Plata   Argentina   March 14–25

Nations: Antigua, Argentina, Bahamas, Bermuda, Brazil, Canada, Chile, Colombia, Costa Rica, Cuba, Dominica, Dominican Republic, Ecuador, El Salvador, Guatemala, Honduras, Jamaica, Mexico, Netherlands Antilles, Nicaragua, Panama, Paraguay, Peru, Puerto Rico, St. Vincent, Suriname, Trinidad and Tobago, United States, U.S. Virgin Islands, Uruguay, Venezuela (11 more)

Sports: Archery, Athletics, Baseball, Basketball, Bowling, Boxing, Canoe/Kayak, Cycling, Equestrian, Fencing, Field Hockey, Gymnastics, Judo, Karate, Pelota, Racquetball, Roller-skating, Rowing, Sailing, Shooting, Soccer, Softball, Squash, Swimming, Diving, Water Polo, Table Tennis, Tae Kwon Do, Team Handball, Tennis, Triathlon, Volleyball, Water Skiing, Weightlifting, Wrestling (Freestyle, Greco-Roman)

Sports for Women: Archery, Athletics, Badminton, Basketball, Bowling, Canoe/Kayak, Cycling, Equestrian, Fencing, Field Hockey, Gymnastics (Artistic and Rhythmic), Judo, Karate, Pelota, Racquetball, Roller-skating, Rowing, Sailing, Shooting, Softball, Squash, Swimming (Swimming, Diving, Synchronized Swimming), Table Tennis, Tae Kwon Do, Team Handball, Tennis, Triathlon, Volleyball, Water Skiing

Nation	MEDALS			
	Gold	Silver	Bronze	Total
United States	169	146	109	424
Cuba	112	66	60	238

Nation	Gold	Silver	Bronze	Total
Canada	48	60	69	177
Argentina	40	45	74	159
Mexico	23	20	37	80
Brazil	18	27	37	82
Venezuela	9	14	25	48
Colombia	5	15	28	48
Chile	2	6	10	18
Puerto Rico	1	9	12	22
Uruguay	1	4	3	8
Guatemala	1	1	6	8
Dominican Republic	1	1	5	7
Netherlands Antilles	1	1	4	6
Ecuador	1	1	3	5
Peru	0	3	4	7
U.S. Virgin Islands	0	3	0	3
Jamaica	0	2	2	4
Nicaragua	0	2	2	4
Bahamas	0	2	1	3
Paraguay	0	1	2	3
Costa Rica	0	1	1	2
Panama	0	1	0	1
El Salvador	0	1	0	1
Dominica	0	1	0	1
Trinidad and Tobago	0	0	6	6
Honduras	0	0	2	2
Suriname	0	0	2	2
St. Vincent	0	0	1	1
Antigua	0	0	1	1
Bermuda	0	0	1	1

1999   Winnipeg   Canada   July 24–August 8

Nations: Antigua, Argentina, Aruba, Bahamas, Barbados, Belize, Bermuda, Bolivia, Brazil, British Virgin Islands, Canada, Cayman Islands, Chile, Colombia, Costa Rica, Cuba, Dominica, Dominican Republic, Ecuador, El Salvador, Grenada, Guatemala, Guyana, Haiti, Honduras, Jamaica, Mexico, Netherlands Antilles, Nicaragua, Panama, Paraguay, Peru, Puerto Rico, St. Kitts and Nevis, St. Lucia, St. Vincent and the Grenadines, Suriname, Trinidad and Tobago, United States, Uruguay, Venezuela, Virgin Islands

Sports: Aquatics (Swimming, Diving, Water Polo, Synchronized Swimming), Archery, Athletics, Badminton, Baseball, Basketball, Bowling (Ten-pin), Boxing, Canoeing, Cycling, Equestrian, Fencing, Football, Field Hockey, Gymnastics (Artistic and Rhythmic), Judo, Karate, Modern Pentathlon, Racquetball, Roller-skating, Rowing, Sailing, Shooting (Trap, Skeet, Handgun, Rifle), Softball, Squash, Table Tennis, Tae Kwon Do, Team Handball, Tennis, Triathlon, Volleyball, Water Skiing, Weightlifting, Wrestling

MEDALS

Nation	Gold	Silver	Bronze	Total
United States	106	110	80	296
Cuba	69	40	47	156

Nation	Gold	Silver	Bronze	Total
Canada	64	52	80	196
Brazil	25	32	44	101
Argentina	25	19	28	72
Mexico	11	16	30	57
Colombia	7	17	18	42
Venezuela	7	16	17	40
Jamaica	3	4	6	13
Guatemala	2	1	1	4
Bahamas	2	0	1	3
Puerto Rico	1	3	9	13
Chile	1	3	7	11
Dominican Republic	1	3	5	9
Ecuador	1	2	5	8
Bermuda	1	2	0	3
Suriname	1	0	1	2
Netherlands Antilles	1	0	0	1
Peru	0	2	6	8
Uruguay	0	1	3	4
Barbados	0	1	1	2
Panama	0	1	1	2
Cayman Islands	0	1	0	1
Honduras	0	1	0	1
Trinidad and Tobago	0	0	1	1
Costa Rica	0	0	1	1
El Salvador	0	0	1	1

Pan-American Games for Patients with Asthma

The first Pan-American Games for Patients with Asthma, Juegos Deportivos Panamericanos para Pacientes con ASMA, were held September 22–23, 2000, in River Plate, Argentina. The games were for boys aged 12 to 14 and comprised two sports, athletics and swimming. The goal of the games is to show that with proper treatment, exercise can be a part of life for those with asthma.

The games are sponsored by the Union Panamericana de fundaciones de Asma y Alergia (UNASMA). UNASMA plans to hold the next games in Monterrey, Mexico, in July 2002.

Year	Host City	Host Nation	Dates	Nations	Athletes	Sports
2000	River Plate	Argentina	September 22–23	4	54	2

Nations: Argentina, Mexico, Panama, Uruguay
Sports: Athletics, Swimming

Pan-American Games for the Blind

The Pan-American Games for the Blind were begun in 1997 and first held in Buenos Aires, Argentina. The games are for visually impaired athletes from both North and South America who compete in track and field, swimming, and goalball. Mexico City held the second games in 1999.

The third Pan-American Games for the Blind were scheduled to be held in Spartanburg, South Carolina, in the summer of 2001.

Year	Host City	Host Nation	Dates	Nations	Athletes	Sports
1997	Buenos Aires	Argentina	NA	NA	NA	NA
1999	Mexico City	Mexico	NA	NA	NA	NA

Pan-American Games for the Deaf

The Pan-American Games for the Deaf have been held on two occasions: in Maracaibo, Venezuela, in 1975, and in 1999 in Havana, Cuba.

Year	Host City	Host Nation	Dates	Nations	Athletes	Sports
1975	Maracaibo	Venezuela	November 15–22	11	300	5
1999	Havana	Cuba	August 16–26	NA	NA	NA

1975   Maracaibo   Venezuela   November 15–22

Sports: Athletics, Football, Table Tennis, Swimming, Volleyball

Pan-American Maccabi Games

With the establishment of the Maccabiah Games in 1932 and the European Maccabi Games in 1959, the Maccabi movement branched into another region and established the Pan-American Maccabi Games in 1964.

The games are for Jewish competitors, and are meant to help establish Jewish identity, with cultural activities an integral part of the experience.

The games have been hosted only by nations in Central and South America, although Canada and the United States have been regular participants.

The 1999 games were held in Mexico City, Mexico, with sports in several age categories including junior, open and masters.

Year	Host City	Host Nation	Dates	Nations	Athletes	Sports
1964	Buenos Aires	Argentina	Sept. 27–Oct. 1	9	500	10
1967	São Paulo	Brazil	August 23–28	11	700	11
1976	Lima	Peru	July 23–29	11	700	8
1979	Mexico City	Mexico	August 21–29	17	1100	13
1983	São Paulo	Brazil	December 20–30	10	1000	11
1987	Caracas	Venezuela	July 19–26	21	1700	19
1991	Montevideo	Uruguay	July	13	NA	19
1995	Buenos Aires	Argentina	Dec. 24–Jan. 4	14	1800	21
1999	Mexico City	Mexico	July 8–20	14	NA	13

1964   Buenos Aires   Argentina   September 27–October 1

Nations: Argentina, Brazil, Canada, Chile, Mexico, Paraguay, Peru, United States, Uruguay

Sports: Basketball, Chess, Football, Judo, Mini-football, Swimming, Table Tennis, Tennis, Wrestling, Volleyball

1967   São Paulo   Brazil   August 23–28

Nations: Argentina, Brazil, Canada, Chile, Colombia, Mexico, Paraguay, Peru, United States, Uruguay, Venezuela
Sports: Basketball, Chess, Diving, Football, Gymnastics, Judo, Mini-football, Swimming, Table Tennis, Tennis, Volleyball

1976   Lima   Peru   July 23–29

Nations: Argentina, Brazil, Chile, Costa Rica, Ecuador, Guatemala, Mexico, Peru, United States, Uruguay, Venezuela
Sports: Basketball, Bridge, Chess, Football, Swimming, Table Tennis, Tennis, Volleyball

1979   Mexico City   Mexico   August 21–29

Nations: Argentina, Brazil, Canada, Chile, Colombia, Ecuador, Guatemala, Mexico, Panama, Peru, United States, Uruguay, Venezuela
Sports: Athletics, Basketball, Bowling, Bridge, Chess, Fencing, Football, Judo, Karate, Mini-football, Gymnastics, Golf, Swimming, Softball, Table Tennis, Tennis, Volleyball

1983   São Paulo   Brazil   December 20–30

Nations: Argentina, Bolivia, Brazil, Canada, Chile, Colombia, Mexico, Peru, United States, Venezuela
Sports: Athletics, Basketball, Bridge, Chess, Football, Mini-football, Golf, Handball, Squash, Volleyball, Water Polo

1987   Caracas   Venezuela   July 19–26

Nations: Argentina, Bahamas, Barbados, Brazil, Bolivia, Canada, Chile, Colombia, Costa Rica, Dominican Republic, Ecuador, Guatemala, Israel, Mexico, Panama, Paraguay, Peru, Puerto Rico, United States, Uruguay, Venezuela
Sports: Athletics, Badminton, Basketball, Bowling, Bridge, Chess, Football, Golf, Mini-football, Gymnastics, Karate, Shooting, Swimming, Softball, Squash, Table Tennis, Tennis, Volleyball, Water Polo

1991   Montevideo   Uruguay   July

Nations: Argentina, Aruba, Australia, Brazil, Chile, Ecuador, Israel, Mexico, Panama, Peru, United States, Uruguay, Venezuela
Sports: Athletics, Basketball, Bowling, Bridge, Chess, Football, Golf, Half-marathon, Handball, Mini-football, Gymnastics, Karate, Rugby, Swimming, Softball, Squash, Tennis, Volleyball, Water Polo

1995   Buenos Aires   Argentina   December 24–January 4

Nations: Argentina, Australia, Brazil, Canada, Chile, Colombia, Costa Rica, Guatemala, Israel, Mexico, Panama, South Africa, United States, Venezuela

Sports: Athletics, Basketball, Chess, Football, Golf, Half-marathon, Handball, Hockey, Indoor Football, Mini-football, Judo, Karate, Rugby, Swimming, Softball, Squash, Table Tennis, Tennis, Triathlon, Volleyball, Water Polo

1999   Mexico City   Mexico   July 8–20

Sports: *Open:* Basketball (m), Golf, Gymnastics (w), Judo, Softball (m), Swimming (m, w), Tennis, Ten-pin Bowling, Track/Half-marathon, Volleyball (w). *Juniors:* Baseball (m), Basketball (m), Football (m), Swimming (m, w), Tennis. *Masters:* Basketball (m), Squash, Tennis (m), Tennis (w), Track/Half-marathon.

Pan-American Medical Games

The Pan-American Medical Games, Juegos Panamericanos de la Medecina, are an independent competition for medical professionals held in the Pan-American region. Not affiliated with the World Medical Games, the games were begun by the Medical Federation of the Federal Capital, FEMECA, in Buenos Aires, Argentina. FEMECA held annual Medical Olympic Games and Medical Football Tournaments in Buenos Aires for several years, and in 1998 decided to expand and host other countries for the first Pan-American Medical Games.

The rules are similar to those of the World Medical Games—athletes represent an association, federation, city or hospital, or compete as individuals. Doctors, pharmacists, dentists, veterinarians, psychologists, biochemists, and senior university students are eligible to compete.

Age groups start at 35 and are divided into ten-year increments up to 65 and over.

Included at each games is the Cultural Meeting of America, an exhibition of paintings, sculptures and theater, and a sports medicine symposium.

Argentina, Chile, Brazil and Uruguay participated in the first games held in Mar del Plata, Argentina. Despite their name, the games are not restricted to athletes from the Pan-American region. Participants from Croatia, Italy, and Portugal joined in the second edition of the games.

Year	Host City	Host Nation	Dates	Nations	Athletes	Sports
1998	Mar del Plata	Argentina	March 22–29	4	300	10
1999	Punte del Este	Uruguay	December 4–11	8	500	NA
2000	Foz de Iguazi	Brazil	November 18–25	NA	NA	10

1998   Mar del Plata   Argentina   March 22–29

Nations: Argentina, Brazil, Chile, Uruguay
Sports: Athletics, Aerobics, Basketball, Football, Golf, Swimming, Tennis, Table Tennis, Shooting, Volleyball

1999   Punte del Este   Uruguay   December 4–11

Nations: Argentina, Bolivia, Brazil, Croatia, Italy, Portugal, Uruguay, Venezuela

2000   Foz de Iguazi   Brazil   November 18–25

Sports: Athletics, Basketball, Chess, Cycling, Football, Golf, Swimming, Table Tennis, Tennis, Volleyball

Pan-American Wheelchair Games

One year before the 1967 Winnipeg Pan-American Games, a group of representatives from the Pan-American region gathered to discuss the establishment of a games for wheelchair athletes. The Pan-American Wheelchair Games were established and held in Winnipeg, a few weeks after the 1967 Pan-American Games were completed. The only other Pan-American Wheelchair Games held in the same year and location as the Pan-American Games were the 1975 games in Mexico City.

Mexico City also held the most recent edition, in November 1999.

Year	Host City	Host Nation	Dates[191]	Nations	Athletes	Sports
1967	Winnipeg	Canada	August 24–	5	NA	NA
1969	Buenos Aires	Argentina	May 25–	NA	250	NA
1971	Kingston	Jamaica	September 12–	NA	NA	NA
1973	Lima	Peru	November 17–	NA	NA	NA
1975	Mexico City	Mexico	August 9–	NA	NA	NA
1978	Rio de Janeiro	Brazil	November 28–	NA	NA	NA
1982	Halifax	Canada	July 21–	NA	NA	NA
1986	San Juan	Puerto Rico	October 1–Oct. 11	NA	NA	NA
1990	Caracas	Venezuela	September 1–9	NA	NA	NA
1995	Buenos Aires	Argentina	September 17–30	NA	NA	NA
1999	Mexico City	Mexico	November 1–8	NA	NA	NA

Pan-Armenian Games

Ashot Melik-Shahnazarian, a vice-president of the Armenian Olympic Committee, is credited with the inspiration for the Pan-Armenian Games, a gathering for people of Armenian descent living throughout the world.

After originally being scheduled for 1997, the first games were first held in 1999 in Yerevan, the Armenian capitol. Delegations competed as representatives of their cities, not nations, but 27 nations were represented at the games.

With the success of the 1999 games, a second edition was scheduled for 2001.

Year	Host City	Host Nation	Dates	Nations	Athletes	Sports
1999	Yerevan	Armenia	Aug. 28–Sept. 5	27	1,600	7

Sports: Athletics, Basketball, Chess, Football, Table Tennis, Tennis, Volleyball

Paralympic Games

The goal of the Paralympic Games, according to the International Paralympic Committee handbook, is "to provide the opportunity for persons with a disability to engage in a high level of competitive sport."

The Paralympics have an involved history that intertwines numerous sports organizations and governing bodies. These organizations, since 1992, have been under the umbrella of the International Paralympic Committee (IPC). The games were originally for wheelchair athletes but have been expanded so that in the 2000 games in Sydney there were classifications for athletes with amputations, cerebral palsy, dwarfism, blindness, deafness and mental impairment. Due to the nature of the divisions, there were 700 medal events in the Paralympics of 1996—double the number of events in the Olympic Games.

Specifically at the 2000 Sydney Paralympic Games, the divisions were:

Classes 11, 12, 13—Blind Athletes (International Blind Sports Association, IBSA).

Class 20—Intellectually Disabled Athletes (International Sports Organization for the Disabled, INAS-FID).

Classes 33–38—different levels of Cerebral Palsy (Cerebral Palsy-International Sports and Recreation Association, CP-ISRA).

Classes 42–46—different levels of amputees and "other disabilities," known as Les Autres (International Sports Organization for Disabled, ISOD).

Classes 51–58—those with spinal cord injuries and amputee athletes competing in wheelchairs (International Stoke Mandeville Wheelchair Sports Federation [ISMWSF]).

In 1960, the International Working Group on Sport for the Disabled was set up to help establish sporting events and rules for the blind, for amputees, and for athletes with cerebral palsy, who up to that time had no sports organizations. In 1964 this group became known as ISOD, the International Sport Organization for the Disabled.[192]

In 1982, an International Coordinating Committee (ICC) for World Sports Organizations for the Disabled was begun. This group had four international federations as members: International Sports Organization for the Disabled (ISOD), the International Stoke Mandeville Wheelchair Sports Federation (ISMWSF), the International Blind Sports Association (IBSA), and the Cerebral Palsy International Sports and Recreation Association (CP-ISRA). In 1992, the name of this umbrella organization was changed to the International Paralympic Committee (IPC).

The first games to become known as the Paralympic Games were held in Rome in 1960, though at the time they were not called the Paralympic Games. From 1964 to 1972, they were called the International Stoke Mandeville Games—Olympics of the Paralyzed, and the games were only open to athletes with spinal cord injuries.

The 1960 games were organized by the International Stoke Mandeville Games Federation that had been holding the Stoke Mandeville Wheelchair Games in England since 1948 under the guidance of Sir Ludwig Guttman. The first year that Guttman was successful in holding the games in the same city as the Olympic Games was 1960. Pope John XXIII made a special appearance and addressed the athletes.

The games of 1964 took place in Tokyo using the Olympic village and facilities in the same way the 1960 games used the Olympic facilities of Rome. Prince Akihito and Princess Michiko were present at the opening ceremony. Media coverage was good, with newspapers, radio and television all covering the events. The 1964 games were the first in which athletes actually raced in their wheelchairs.

Mexico City was not able to hold the 1968 games—altitude and problems of organization the two main considerations—so Israel volunteered to hold them. One athlete, Roberto Marson of Italy, won nine gold medals in three sports—swimming, fencing and athletics.

The 1972 and 1976 games were held in Heidelberg, West Germany, and Toronto, Canada, the nations if not the cities of the Olympic hosts of those years. The West German hosts wanted to stage the games in Munich after the Olympics but were not able to get permission to use the village and facilities in Munich. The games did branch out with the first events for quadriplegics and demonstration goalball for blind athletes.

The first instance of political disturbances in the games was in 1976, over the inclusion of a team from South Africa. Kenya and Yugoslavia decided ahead of time not to send teams to the games if South Africa was included. Cuba, Hungary, India and Jamaica arrived at the games and then withdrew. Poland pulled out in the middle of the games after winning a number of medals.

The inclusion of South Africa had financial implications for the games as well. When the Canadian federal government withdrew its support of $500,000 over the South African issue, the provincial government of Ontario was compelled to make up the difference.

Ironically, South Africa was one of the nations bidding for the games of 1980. Dr. Guttman defended South Africa in a press conference, saying that the South African Disabled Sport Association had rewritten its constitution to eliminate any references to segregation, and during his visit to South Africa he had personally witnessed mixed teams competing together.

One Hungarian athlete took the opportunity to defect during the 1976 games. He had the good fortune of hailing a taxi outside the village in the middle of the night, a taxi that happened to be driven by a former Hungarian citizen who was able to understand his every word.

A final controversy of the 1976 games was the revelation that some athletes were inclined to cheat during the physical evaluations which were used to place them in classifications to ensure fair competition. Canadian swimmer Barney Fegyverneki was quoted as saying, "classification is really not that hard to beat. All you have to do to bugger them up is to pretend you are having difficulty doing whatever they ask you to do and they will put you in a lower class." Much was made of the comments, with many doctors admitting that the classification system had weaknesses and that it was not an easy task to classify disabled athletes. Bob Steadward, a Canadian official who was later to become president of the International Paralympic Committee, defended the classification system and the doctors' abilities to correctly classify the athletes.

After Moscow refused to agree to hold the Paralympic Games of 1980, Arnhem, Netherlands, was chosen as host. The Dutch decided not to accept the entry of the South African delegation, hoping to avoid the protest and rancor of the 1976 games over this issue. Dr. Guttman died in March 1980, before the South Africa question could be resolved. The 1980 games were the first to include the participation of athletes with cerebral palsy.

The 1984 games were broken into two parts when Los Angeles refused to hold them. The blind, and those with cerebral palsy and with disabilities other than wheelchair athletes, competed in New York in June 1984 under the eye of IBSA, CP-ISRA and ISOD. U.S. President Ronald Reagan officially opened these games.

The wheelchair athletes from the International Stoke Mandeville Games Federation (ISMGF) who were originally scheduled to compete in Illinois, competed in the "VIIth World Wheelchair Games Paralympics" in Aylesbury, England, from July 22 to August 1.

The term "Paralympics," though used occasionally, had still not come into consistent use by this time, Guttman himself preferring to use the term "Olympics of the Paralyzed," and the press terming the games the "Wheelchair Olympics" or "Olympics of the Disabled." The IOC had never fully approved the use of the term "Olympic" but had not strongly disapproved it either. When the word "Paralympic" was proposed in 1984, the IOC had no difficulties accepting this term. In February 1985, the ICC and IOC came to more formal terms over the issue. The IOC would provide support and financial aid for the disabled athletes, while the disabled sport movement would forgo the use of the word "Olympic" and use "Paralympic" in its place.

The games in Seoul in 1988 were organized by SPOC, the Seoul Paralympic Organizing Committee, which worked in conjunction with the Seoul Olympic Organizing Committee. With 61 nations and 3,053 athletes, the games were a huge leap in size over previous games.

In 1992, the Barcelona Olympic Organizing Committee set up a division of its organization specifically to organize the Paralympics. After the Barcelona Games the name International Coordinating Committee (ICC) was changed to IPC, the International Paralympic Committee.

Drug testing became an accepted reality of the games. Five athletes were caught and suspended, three for steroid violations. In the first real scandal involving doping at the games, the United States lost the wheelchair basketball gold medal when one player tested positive for banned pain-killing drugs. The result was protested, and for a short time the ruling was reversed, but eventually the case was heard before the Court of Arbitration for Sport and the U.S. team was disqualified. The rules in team sports were then changed and now read that only a guilty player is disqualified, not the entire team and results stand.

At the Atlanta Games in 1996, actor Christopher Reeve, paralyzed after an earlier show-jumping accident, was the master of ceremonies at the opening ceremony. U.S. Vice-President Al Gore opened the games and Aretha Franklin, Liza Minelli and Carly Simon provided the musical entertainment. The 1996 Paralympics were the first to include athletes with mental disabilities.

The 1500 meter wheelchair event saw a world record by Australia's Louise Sauvage when she beat out Chantal Petitclerc of Canada and Jean Driscoll of the United States. Sauvage's world record time was 3:30.45. The first six places were under the old world record of 3:36.66. Sauvage also set a world record in the 5,000 meter race in a time of 12:40.71 and also won the 400 and 800 meter races in her division. Petitclerc won the gold in the 100 meters, and silver medals in the 200, 400, 800 and 1500 meters. Finally, Jean Driscoll, third in the 1500, was second in the 5000 and won both the 10,000 (in a world record of 24:21.64) and marathon events. In total, 268 world records were broken in all sports at the Atlanta Paralympics.

The Sydney 2000 Paralympic Games were highly acclaimed and highly successful with 3900 competitors from 122 countries, plus two independent athletes from East Timor. When the East Timorese athletes arrived in Australia, customs agents noticed that they had very little equipment or even clothing with them. They roused the Australian citizens who donated clothing and uniforms.

1.2 million tickets were sold for the games—more than double the number for Atlanta. The athletes competed for 550 gold medals in 18 sports. The Australian people supported the games strongly, purchasing the vast majority of the tickets.

The Paralympic torch was brought into the stadium by Australian Paralympian Katrina Webb, and relayed around the track to Louise Sauvage who lit a special cauldron on the stadium floor which then lit the Paralympic flame above the stadium.

The games were not without several controversies. After physical examinations, athletes of several nationalities were reclassified, causing the British to complain that they would lose several gold medals as a result. Britain's director of swimming performance said, "You've worked to get a world record, but you still get beaten by someone you didn't even know was going to be there."

Classifications are reviewed every two years and changed in many cases, especially for athletes with degenerative conditions. Athletes may even at times be reclassified after participating in qualifying heats if they show more functionality during the race than they showed during testing.

Bob Matthews of Britain made up for some of the disappointment when he won the 10,000 meter blind race. Matthews had won the 5,000 meter gold in Barcelona and finished second in the Atlanta 5,000 meters, but had been disqualified in that race after his guide runner crossed the line ahead of him.

Another eligibility issue arose when the discus event in the Cerebral Palsy category (F34) was canceled. Shot putter Hamish MacDonald, the Atlanta gold medalist, hoped to switch divisions and compete in the F56 wheelchair division. The Court of Arbitration for Sport ordered a medical evaluation but the medical panel ruled that he did not qualify for the new division.

Some 700 drug tests were carried out at the games, with the result being the highest-profile drug case at a Paralympic games. Brian Frasure of the United States, at the time the 100 meter world record-holder in his division, tested positive for nandrolone after winning two silver medals. He was allowed to keep his medal for the 100 meters but was stripped of the 200 meters medal and given a four-year suspension which was appealed. Ten athletes in total failed drug tests at the games. The other nine were from the sport of powerlifting.

After the games, another troubling development came to light when it was revealed by one of the team members that Spain's intellectually disabled Paralympic basketball team comprised some players who were not intellectually disabled. Some 10 of its 12 members, allegedly, were not handicapped. The incident had immediate and perhaps far-reaching ramifications. The Spanish team returned the gold medals, and the vice president of Spain's Paralympic Committee and president of the Sports Federation for the Intellectually Handicapped, Fernando Martin Vicente, resigned.

Just after the Paralympics, basketball player Carlos Ribagorda wrote in Spain's *Capital* magazine that he and other medal winners were not mentally disabled. Ribagorda claimed that up to 15 members of Spain's Paralympic team in track and field, table tennis and swimming were not handicapped.

Several weeks later the International Paralympic Committee moved to suspend all intellectually disabled athletes from the Paralympic Games. The International Paralympic Committee concluded that there are "serious problems regarding the determination of eligibility of athletes" in the intellectually disabled class. The IPC also suspended the International Sports Federation for Athletes with an Intellectual Disability.

The beneficiaries of Spain's disqualification were the Russian basketball team. The Russians had been awarded the silver medal and $2000 each from their federation. When the silver medals were upgraded to gold, the Russian federation gave each $3000 more to equal the promised $5000 to each gold-medal winner.

International Paralympic Committee president Dr. Robert Steadward was very pleased with the outcome of the games. He called them "near perfect," and was pleased that Sydney Olympic and Paralympic organizers had worked side by side.

Before the Sydney Games, Athens had not formally signed a contract with the IPC to host the 2004 Paralympic Games. This was taken care of at Sydney, however.

During the games, the IOC and IPC signed another agreement which stated that "the IOC will formalize its relationship with the International Paralympic Committee (IPC) through a contract or memorandum of understanding. Clear rules concerning the link between the Olympic Games and the Paralympic Games must be set."

The agreement went on to say that "the Paralympics must be organized in the same city as the Olympic Games." The obligation for the host city to organize the Paralympic Games, it added, must be included in the host city contract and the Paralympics must always follow the Olympic Games. The IPC would also be represented on IOC commissions covering such issues as the evaluation of candidate cities for the Olympic Games, coordination for the Olympic Games, culture and Olympic education and athletes, and on the working group addressing women and sport. The IOC would also continue to give financial support to the Paralympic movement, the agreement concluded.

Year	Host City	Host Nation	Dates	Nations	Athletes[193]	Sports
1960	Rome	Italy	September 17–22	23	400	8
1964	Tokyo	Japan	November 6–14	22	390	9
1968	Tel Aviv	Israel	November 5–13	28	750	10
1972	Heidelberg	West Germany	August 2–10	44	1000	10
1976	Toronto	Canada	August 3–11	42	1600	13
1980	Arnhem	Netherlands	June 21–July 5	42	2500	12
1984	New York	USA	June 16–30	45	1750	15
1984	Aylesbury	England	July 22–Aug.1	41	1100	10
1988	Seoul	South Korea	October 15–25	61	3053	17
1992	Barcelona	Spain	September 3–14	82	3020	15
1996	Atlanta	USA	August 15–25	120	3195	17
2000	Sydney	Australia	October 14–24	122	3900	18

1960   Rome   Italy   September 17–22

Sports: Archery, Athletics, Basketball, Dartchery, Fencing, Snooker, Swimming, Table Tennis

Sports for Women: Archery, Athletics, Dartchery, Fencing, Swimming, Table Tennis

MEDALS

Nation	Gold	Silver	Bronze	Total
Italy	29	26	18.5	73.5
Great Britain	21	15	18	54
West Germany	14	7	8	29
Austria	11	8	9	28
United States	10	7	7	24
Norway	7	5	4	16
France	4	1	3	8
Australia	3	6	2	11
Netherlands	2	6	0	8
Malta	2	4	1.5	7.5
Argentina	2	3	2	7
Rhodesia	2	1	2	5
Ireland	2	0	0	2
Switzerland	1	3	0	4
Belgium	1	1	0	2
Finland	1	0	0	1
Israel	0	2	2	4

1964   Tokyo   Japan   November 6–14

Sports: Archery, Athletics, Basketball, Dartchery, Fencing, Powerlifting, Snooker, Swimming, Table Tennis

Sports for Women: Archery, Athletics, Dartchery, Fencing, Swimming, Table Tennis

MEDALS

Nation	Gold	Silver	Bronze	Total
United States	50	41	31	122
Great Britain	18	23	19	60
Italy	14	15	24	53
Australia	11	11	8	30
Rhodesia	10	5	2	17
South Africa	8	8	3	19
Israel	7	3	10	20
Argentina	6	15	16	37
West Germany	5	2	3	10
Netherlands	4	6	3	13
France	4	2	4	10
Austria	4	1	4	9
Japan	1	5	3	9
Belgium	1	0	2	3
Switzerland	0	1	0	1
Malta	0	0	2	2
Sweden	0	0	1	1

1968   Tel Aviv   Israel   November 5–13

Nations: Argentina, Australia, Austria, Belgium, France, Germany, Great Britain, Ireland, Israel, Italy, Jamaica, Japan, Netherlands, New Zealand, Norway, Rhodesia, South Africa, Spain, Sweden, Switzerland, United States (21 of 28 participating nations)

Sports: Archery, Athletics, Basketball, Dartchery, Fencing, Lawn Bowls, Powerlifting, Snooker, Swimming, Table Tennis

Sports for Women: Archery, Athletics, Basketball, Dartchery, Fencing, Lawn Bowls, Swimming, Table Tennis

MEDALS

Nation	Gold	Silver	Bronze	Total
United States	30	24	33	87
Great Britain	27	16	17	60
Israel	15	20	17	52
Australia	15	14	7	36
Germany	13	11	13	37
France	12	7	7	26
Netherlands	12	4	6	22
Italy	11	11	13	35
South Africa	8	8	9	25
Argentina	6	6	6	18
Rhodesia	4	9	6	19
Norway	4	3	1	8

Nation	Gold	Silver	Bronze	Total
Jamaica	3	1	1	5
Austria	2	7	9	18
Japan	2	2	8	12
Sweden	1	5	4	10
New Zealand	1	2	1	4
Ireland	0	3	6	9
Belgium	0	3	2	5
Spain	0	3	1	4
Switzerland	0	2	5	7

1972 Heidelberg West Germany August 2–10

Sports: Archery, Athletics, Basketball, Dartchery, Fencing, Lawn Bowls, Powerlifting, Snooker, Swimming, Table Tennis

Sports for Women: Archery, Athletics, Basketball, Dartchery, Fencing, Lawn Bowls, Powerlifting, Swimming, Table Tennis

MEDALS

Nation	Gold	Silver	Bronze	Total
West Germany	28	15	24	67
United States	17	28	28	73
South Africa	16	12	13	41
Great Britain	15	15	20	50
Netherlands	14	13	11	38
Poland	14	12	7	33
France	10	8	12	30
Israel	9	10	9	28
Italy	8	3	5	16
Jamaica	8	3	4	15
Australia	6	9	10	25
Canada	6	6	8	20
Austria	6	6	5	17
Sweden	5	5	5	15
Japan	4	5	3	12
Rhodesia	3	5	4	12
New Zealand	3	3	3	9
Switzerland	3	2	3	8
Korea	3	2	1	6
Argentina	2	5	3	10
Ireland	2	4	2	8
Kenya	2	0	0	2
Norway	1	5	5	11
Belgium	1	2	2	5
Yugoslavia	1	1	2	4
India	1	0	0	1
Spain	0	4	1	5
Finland	0	2	2	4
Hong Kong	0	1	1	2
Soviet Union	0	0	1	1
Hungary	0	0	1	1

1976   Toronto   Canada   August 3–11

Nations: Argentina, Australia, Austria, Belgium, Brazil, Burma, Canada, Denmark, Egypt, Fiji, Finland, France, Great Britain, Guatemala, Hong Kong, Indonesia, Ireland, Israel, Italy, Japan, Mexico, Netherlands, New Zealand, Norway, Peru, Poland, South Africa, South Korea, Spain, Sweden, Switzerland, United States, West Germany (nine more)

Sports: Archery, Athletics, Basketball, Dartchery, Fencing, Goalball, Lawn Bowls, Powerlifting, Shooting, Snooker, Swimming, Table Tennis, Volleyball

Sports for Women: Archery, Athletics, Basketball, Dartchery, Fencing, Lawn Bowls, Swimming, Table Tennis

MEDALS

Nation	Gold	Silver	Bronze	Total
United States	66	44	45	155
Netherlands	45	25	14	84
Israel	39	13	16	68
West Germany	37	33	26	96
Great Britain	29	29	36	94
Canada	25	26	26	77
Poland	24	17	12	53
France	23	22	14	59
Sweden	22	27	25	74
Austria	18	16	17	51
Australia	16	18	10	44
Mexico	16	14	9	39
Finland	12	20	18	50
Japan	10	6	3	19
Switzerland	9	12	10	31
Norway	9	6	4	19
South Africa	7	9	12	28
Belgium	7	7	8	22
New Zealand	7	1	5	13
Egypt	5	2	1	8
Ireland	4	10	6	20
Spain	4	6	2	12
Argentina	3	4	6	13
Denmark	3	0	3	6
Italy	2	5	11	18
Indonesia	2	1	4	7
South Korea	1	2	1	4
Burma	1	1	1	3
Peru	1	0	2	3
Hong Kong	0	1	2	3
Brazil	0	1	0	1
Guatemala	0	0	1	1

1980   Arnhem   Netherlands   June 21–July 5

Nations: Argentina, Australia, Austria, Bahamas, Belgium, Canada, Colombia, Czechoslovakia, Denmark, Egypt, Finland, France, Great Britain, Hong Kong, Iceland, Indonesia, Ireland, Israel, Italy, Jamaica, Japan, Kenya, Korea, Kuwait, Luxembourg, Malta, Mexico, Netherlands, New Zealand, Norway, Poland, Spain, Sudan, Sweden, Switzerland, United States, West Germany, Yugoslavia, Zimbabwe (3 more)

Sports: Archery, Athletics, Basketball, Fencing, Goalball, Lawn Bowls, Powerlifting, Shooting, Swimming, Table Tennis, Volleyball, Wrestling

Sports for Women: Archery, Athletics, Basketball, Fencing, Lawn Bowls, Shooting, Swimming, Table Tennis

MEDALS

Nation	Gold	Silver	Bronze	Total
United States	62	58	54	174
West Germany	61	47	41	149
Canada	53	27	31	111
Poland	51	51	47	149
Great Britain	43	29	20	92
Netherlands	32	27	33	92
Sweden	25	35	24	84
France	25	23	24	72
Mexico	20	16	4	40
Israel	12	18	11	41
Norway	11	11	7	29
Belgium	11	9	13	33
Austria	9	12	4	25
Switzerland	9	10	9	28
Australia	8	19	18	45
Japan	8	10	6	24
Finland	6	15	12	33
Italy	6	4	9	19
New Zealand	5	6	5	16
Jamaica	5	6	4	15
Egypt	4	7	3	14
Argentina	4	4	6	14
Yugoslavia	3	5	9	17
Denmark	3	4	6	13
Ireland	2	2	10	14
Kuwait	2	2	1	5
Iceland	2	0	1	3
Spain	1	14	9	24
Korea	1	2	1	4
Kenya	1	2	0	3
Indonesia	1	0	4	5
Colombia	1	0	1	2
Sudan	1	0	0	1
Zimbabwe	0	7	4	11
Bahamas	0	1	2	3
Hong Kong	0	0	2	2
Czechoslovakia	0	0	1	1
Malta	0	0	1	1
Luxembourg	0	0	1	1

1984   New York   USA   June 16–30

Sports: Archery, Athletics, Basketball, Boccia, Cycling, Dressage, Football, Goalball, Lawn Bowls, Powerlifting, Shooting, Swimming, Table Tennis, Volleyball, Wrestling

MEDALS

Nation	Gold	Silver	Bronze	Total
United States	101	91	84	276
Great Britain	75	80	85	240
Sweden	51	30	22	103
Canada	48	52	49	149
West Germany	44	42	29	115
Netherlands	44	40	17	101
France	37	39	23	99
Australia	29	38	26	93
Norway	22	24	20	66
Denmark	22	6	11	39
Spain	21	8	12	41
Poland	20	15	13	48
Finland	15	10	17	42
Ireland	13	11	20	44
Hungary	12	12	3	27
Belgium	9	11	6	26
Yugoslavia	7	9	8	24
Austria	5	13	7	25
Switzerland	5	2	2	9
Portugal	4	2	7	13
Italy	3	7	6	16
Japan	3	2	5	10
China	2	12	8	22
Israel	2	6	7	15
New Zealand	2	3	1	6
Egypt	2	0	3	5
Trinidad and Tobago	2	0	1	3
Luxembourg	1	4	1	6
Brazil	1	3	2	6
Burkina Faso	1	1	2	4
Mexico	0	3	3	6
Iceland	0	2	6	8
East Germany	0	2	1	3
India	0	2	1	3
Indonesia	0	1	1	2
Zimbabwe	0	1	0	1
Korea	0	0	1	1
Hong Kong	0	0	1	1

1984   Aylesbury   England   July 22–Aug. 1

Sports: Archery, Athletics, Basketball, Fencing, Lawn Bowls, Shooting, Snooker, Swimming, Table Tennis, Powerlifting

MEDALS

Nation	Gold	Silver	Bronze	Total
West Germany	37	32	41	110
Canada	35	22	16	73
France	34	30	23	87

Nation	Gold	Silver	Bronze	Total
United States	30	34	48	112
Sweden	30	13	8	51
Great Britain	27	28	27	82
Poland	24	18	8	50
Australia	18	16	22	56
Switzerland	13	12	10	35
Belgium	13	10	8	31
Israel	9	15	5	29
Netherlands	8	10	9	27
Austria	7	7	3	17
Brazil	6	14	2	22
Mexico	6	12	13	31
Denmark	6	6	15	27
New Zealand	6	6	5	17
Japan	6	5	14	25
Ireland	6	4	18	28
Italy	5	12	26	43
Norway	5	6	16	27
Hong Kong	3	5	16	24
Yugoslavia	2	1	5	8
Finland	1	3	12	16
Kuwait	1	2	7	10
Kenya	1	1	3	5
Korea	0	2	3	5
Bahamas	0	2	2	4
Jordan	0	1	3	4
Bahrain	0	0	2	2
Egypt	0	0	2	2
Iceland	0	0	2	2
Zimbabwe	0	0	2	2

1988   Seoul   South Korea   October 15–25

Sports: Archery, Athletics, Basketball, Boccia, Cycling, Fencing, Football, Goal Ball, Judo, Lawn Bowls, Powerlifting, Shooting, Snooker, Swimming, Table Tennis, Tennis, Weightlifting

Sports for Women: Archery, Athletics, Basketball, Boccia, Fencing, Goal Ball, Lawn Bowls, Powerlifting, Shooting, Swimming, Table Tennis, Tennis

MEDALS

Nation	Gold	Silver	Bronze	Total
United States	92	61	85	238
Germany	77	64	48	189
Great Britain	62	66	51	179
Canada	54	42	57	153
France	45	48	49	142
Sweden	42	38	22	102
Korea	40	35	19	94
Netherlands	30	23	29	82
Denmark	25	18	22	65

Nation	Gold	Silver	Bronze	Total
Australia	23	34	37	94
Poland	22	25	34	81
Russia	21	19	15	55
Spain	18	13	12	43
China	17	17	9	43
Italy	16	15	27	58
Japan	16	12	17	45
Belgium	15	17	9	41
Israel	15	13	15	43
Ireland	13	13	18	44
Austria	13	7	15	35
Switzerland	12	12	10	34
Finland	11	23	15	49
Norway	11	11	13	35
Mexico	8	9	6	23
Brazil	4	9	14	27
Kuwait	4	6	8	18
Yugoslavia	4	4	11	19
Iran	4	1	3	8
Portugal	3	4	5	12
New Zealand	2	4	11	17
Iceland	2	2	8	12
Bulgaria	2	1	0	3
Jamaica	1	4	3	8
Faroe Islands	1	3	3	7
Egypt	1	2	3	6
Puerto Rico	1	2	0	3
Bahrain	1	1	1	3
Guatemala	1	0	0	1
Argentina	0	7	2	9
Hungary	0	4	7	11
Kenya	0	4	1	5
Hong Kong	0	2	7	9
Greece	0	1	3	4
Thailand	0	1	0	1
Czechoslovakia	0	1	0	1
Indonesia	0	1	0	1
Tunisia	0	0	2	2

1992   Barcelona   Spain   September 3–14

Sports: Archery, Athletics, Basketball, Boccia, Cycling, Fencing, Football, Goal Ball, Judo, Powerlifting, Shooting, Swimming, Table Tennis, Tennis, Volleyball

Sports for Women: Archery, Athletics, Basketball, Boccia, Cycling, Fencing, Goal Ball, Shooting, Swimming, Table Tennis, Tennis

MEDALS

Nation	Gold	Silver	Bronze	Total
United States	76	51	48	175
Germany	60	50	60	170

Nation	Gold	Silver	Bronze	Total
Great Britain	40	46	41	127
France	36	35	33	104
Spain	34	31	42	107
Canada	28	21	26	75
Australia	24	27	25	76
Unified Team	17	14	15	46
Netherlands	13	15	11	39
Norway	13	12	7	32
Denmark	12	22	12	46
China	11	7	7	25
Korea	10	14	18	42
Italy	10	7	18	35
Finland	8	6	11	25
Sweden	7	22	9	38
Poland	7	10	7	24
Japan	7	8	15	30
Switzerland	6	16	12	34
Austria	5	4	13	22
Belgium	5	4	6	15
Egypt	5	4	4	13
New Zealand	5	1	0	6
Czechoslovakia	4	3	6	13
Hungary	4	3	4	11
Yugoslavia	4	3	1	8
South Africa	4	1	3	8
Hong Kong	3	4	4	11
Cuba	3	3	3	9
Portugal	3	3	1	7
Iceland	3	2	12	17
Brazil	3	0	4	7
Israel	2	4	5	11
Slovenia	2	0	1	3
Nigeria	2	0	0	2
Kuwait	1	3	1	5
Iran	1	2	1	4
Panama	1	2	0	3
Bulgaria	1	2	0	3
Argentina	1	1	0	2
Kenya	1	0	1	2
Lithuania	0	4	3	7
Ireland	0	3	3	6
Estonia	0	2	1	3
Greece	0	2	1	3
Mexico	0	1	10	11
Malaysia	0	1	2	3
Jamaica	0	1	2	3
Faroe Islands	0	1	0	1
Venezuela	0	0	1	1
Croatia	0	0	1	1
Chinese Taipei	0	0	1	1
Iraq	0	0	1	1

Nation	Gold	Silver	Bronze	Total
Bahrain	0	0	1	1
Thailand	0	0	1	1

1996   Atlanta   USA   August 15–25

Sports: Archery, Athletics, Basketball, Boccia, Cycling, Fencing, Football, Goal Ball, Judo, Powerlifting, Shooting, Swimming, Table Tennis, Tennis, Volleyball, Wheelchair Rugby, Yachting

Sports for Women: Archery, Athletics, Basketball, Boccia, Cycling, Fencing, Goal Ball, Shooting, Swimming, Table Tennis, Tennis

Nations: Algeria, Argentina, Australia, Austria, Belarus, Belgium, Brazil, Bulgaria, Canada, China, Chinese Taipei, Cuba, Czech Republic, Denmark, Dominican Republic, Egypt, Estonia, Finland, France, Germany, Great Britain, Greece, Hong Kong, Hungary, Iceland, Iran, Ireland, Israel, Italy, Ivory Coast, Jamaica, Japan, Jordan, Kenya, Kuwait, Lithuania, Mexico, Moldova, Netherlands, New Zealand, Nigeria, Norway, Panama, Peru, Poland, Portugal, Russia, Slovakia, Slovenia, South Africa, South Korea, Spain, Sweden, Switzerland, Thailand, Tunisia, Ukraine, United States, Uruguay, Yugoslavia (60 more)

MEDALS

Nation	Gold	Silver	Bronze	Total
United States	46	46	65	157
Australia	42	37	27	106
Germany	40	58	51	149
Great Britain	39	42	41	122
Spain	39	31	36	106
France	35	29	31	95
Canada	24	21	24	69
Netherlands	17	11	17	45
China	16	13	10	39
Japan	14	10	12	36
Poland	13	14	8	35
South Korea	13	2	15	30
Sweden	12	14	10	36
Italy	11	20	15	46
South Africa	10	8	10	28
Russia	9	7	11	27
Norway	9	7	4	20
Switzerland	9	6	6	21
New Zealand	9	6	3	18
Iran	9	5	3	17
Egypt	8	11	11	30
Belgium	8	10	7	25
Cuba	8	3	0	11
Denmark	7	17	17	41
Austria	6	6	10	22
Portugal	6	4	4	14
Hong Kong	5	5	5	15
Iceland	5	4	5	14

Nation	Gold	Silver	Bronze	Total
Hungary	5	2	3	10
Finland	4	5	4	13
Mexico	3	5	4	12
Estonia	3	4	2	9
Belarus	3	3	7	13
Lithuania	3	2	6	11
Nigeria	3	2	3	8
Czech Republic	2	7	1	10
Brazil	2	6	13	21
Argentina	2	5	2	9
Slovakia	2	4	5	11
Algeria	2	2	3	7
Yugoslavia	2	2	0	4
Ivory Coast	2	0	0	2
Panama	2	0	0	2
Ukraine	1	4	2	7
Ireland	1	3	6	10
Greece	1	1	3	5
Kuwait	1	1	1	3
Kenya	1	1	0	2
Chinese Taipei	1	0	2	3
Dominican Republic	1	0	0	1
Peru	1	0	0	1
Israel	0	4	5	9
Slovenia	0	2	3	5
Tunisia	0	2	0	2
Bulgaria	0	1	1	2
Jordan	0	1	0	1
Moldova	0	0	2	2
Thailand	0	0	2	2
Jamaica	0	0	1	1
Uruguay	0	0	1	1

2000   Sydney   Australia   October 14–24

Nations: Algeria, Angola, Argentina, Armenia, Australia, Austria, Azerbaijan, Bahrain, Barbados, Belarus, Belgium, Benin, Bermuda, Bosnia and Herzegovina, Brazil, Bulgaria, Burkina Faso, Cambodia, Cameroon, Canada, Chile, China, Chinese Taipei, Columbia, Costa Rica, Côte d'Ivoire, Croatia, Cuba, Cyprus, Czech Republic, Denmark, East Timor, Ecuador, Egypt, El Salvador, Estonia, Faroe Islands, Fiji, Finland, FYR of Macedonia, France, Germany, Great Britain, Greece, Guatemala, Guinea Republic, Honduras, Hong Kong, Hungary, Iceland, India, Indonesia, Iraq, Ireland, Islamic Republic of Iran, Israel, Italy, Japan, Jamaica, Jordan, Kazakhstan, Kenya, Korea, Kuwait, Kyrgyzstan, Laos, Latvia, Lebanon, Lesotho, Libya, Lithuania, Macau, Madagascar, Malaysia, Mali, Mauritania, Mexico, Mongolia, Morocco, Netherlands, New Zealand, Niger, Nigeria, Norway, Oman, Pakistan, Palestine, Panama, Papua New Guinea, Peru, Philippines, Poland, Portugal, Puerto Rico, Qatar, Republic of Moldova, Romania, Russian Federation, Rwanda, Samoa, Saudi Arabia, Sierra Leone, Singapore, Slovakia, Slovenia, South Africa, Spain, Sri Lanka, Sudan, Sweden, Switzerland, Syrian Arab Republic, Thailand, Tonga, Tunisia, Turkey, Turkmenistan, Uganda, Ukraine,

United Arab Emirates, United States, Uruguay, Vanuatu, Venezuela, Vietnam, Yugoslavia, Zambia, Zimbabwe[194]

Sports: Archery, Athletics, Basketball, Boccia, Cycling, Equestrian, Fencing, Football, Goalball, Judo, Powerlifting, Sailing, Shooting, Swimming, Table Tennis, Tennis, Volleyball (sitting and standing), Wheelchair Rugby

Sports for Women: Archery, Athletics, Basketball, Boccia, Cycling, Equestrian, Fencing, Goalball, Powerlifting, Shooting, Swimming, Table Tennis, Tennis, Wheelchair Rugby

MEDALS

Nation	Gold	Silver	Bronze	Total
Australia	63	39	47	149
Great Britain	41	43	47	131
Spain	39	30	38	107
Canada	38	33	25	96
United States	36	39	34	109
China	34	22	16	72
France	30	28	28	86
Poland	19	22	12	53
Korea	18	7	7	32
Germany	15	42	38	95
Czech Republic	15	15	13	43
Japan	13	17	11	41
South Africa	13	12	13	38
Russia	12	11	12	35
Netherlands	12	9	9	30
Iran	12	4	7	23
Mexico	10	12	12	34
Italy	9	8	10	27
Denmark	8	8	14	30
Switzerland	8	4	8	20
Hong Kong	8	3	7	18
Nigeria	7	1	5	13
Egypt	6	11	11	28
Brazil	6	10	6	22
New Zealand	6	8	3	17
Portugal	6	5	4	15
Tunisia	6	4	1	11
Belarus	5	8	10	23
Sweden	5	6	10	21
Thailand	5	4	2	11
Ireland	5	3	1	9
Hungary	4	5	14	23
Greece	4	4	3	11
Cuba	4	2	2	8
Ukraine	3	20	14	37
Slovakia	3	5	5	13
Israel	3	2	1	6
Algeria	3	0	0	3
Austria	2	7	6	15
Norway	2	6	7	15

Nation	Gold	Silver	Bronze	Total
Iceland	2	0	2	4
Belgium	1	4	4	9
Finland	1	3	6	10
Chinese Taipei	1	2	4	7
Estonia	1	1	3	5
Kenya	1	1	2	4
Azerbaijan	1	1	0	2
Peru	1	1	0	2
Ivory Coast	1	0	1	2
Zimbabwe	1	0	0	1
Jordan	1	0	0	1
Bulgaria	1	0	0	1
United Arab Emi.	0	3	1	4
Faroe Islands	0	3	1	4
Argentina	0	2	3	5
Slovenia	0	2	2	4
Lithuania	0	2	1	3
Kuwait	0	1	4	5
Bahrain	0	1	1	2
Panama	0	1	1	2
Yugoslavia	0	1	0	1
Bosnia/Herz.	0	1	0	1
Latvia	0	0	3	3
Venezuela	0	0	1	1
Libya	0	0	1	1
Philippines	0	0	1	1
Palestine	0	0	1	1
Puerto Rico	0	0	1	1

Peace Arch Games

The Peace Arch Games were a short-lived event begun in 1987 and ending in 1992. They took their name from the Peace Arch monument which straddles the border between British Columbia, Canada, and the state of Washington in the Northwest United States, on the Pacific Ocean.

The games, designed for the athletes from Washington and British Columbia, were inspired by the mayor of the city of Bellingham, Tim Douglas, and organized by the Bellingham Parks and Recreation Department with the hope of creating a summer tourist draw to their city. The plan was to let local sports clubs arrange the events, independently of one another. All the events together would then be called the Peace Arch Games. Throughout their existence, the games were designed to last over two or three weeks, with events held only on the weekends.

Organizers had very high expectations for the first edition of the games in 1987, with plans for thirty-two events, 7,000 athletes, and plenty of spectators. The organization of such a large undertaking proved to be problematic, however. In the end, there were twenty-one sports with 1,923 participants and low spectator interest. Both the governor of Washington State and the premier of British Columbia were invited to the games opening ceremonies but both declined.

After a few years, organizers from Bellingham attempted to share the organizing duties with the Canadians and to get them involved on the board of directors and in hosting some of the events. In 1989, the horseshoe competition was held across the border in Cloverdale, British Columbia, the only event in the six years of the games to be held in Canada.

Opening ceremonies for the second games in 1988 were held at the U.S.-Canada border at Peace Arch Park in an effort to involve more Canadian participants.

The games were intended for citizen participation, but the occasional star did show up. In 1988, Brian Oldfield, the former world record shot putter, was in the area visiting friends and decided to compete. He won the shot put.

Organizers were perennially frustrated by the lack of spectators and the difficulty in establishing the games' identity. Many people were confused by the name of the games, which implied the event was held in Blaine, Washington, the border town where the Peace Arch is located. With events spread out over a wide geographic area, spectators were not always aware of all the activities in the games.[195]

The Bellingham Parks and Recreation Department had voiced plans for a winter Peace Arch Games to be held in 1991, but these were never organized.[196]

The games continued to dwindle in 1991 and 1992. The 1992 event, which ended up being the last, comprised of just five sports: athletics, gymnastics, handball, tennis and triathlon.

Year	Host City	Host Nation	Dates*	Nations	Athletes	Sports
1987	Bellingham	USA	June 28–July 5	2	1923	21
1988	Bellingham	USA	June 26–July 5	2	2205	26
1989	Bellingham	USA	June 24–July 9	2	2000	14
1990	Bellingham	USA	June 20–July 8	2	2000	14
1991	Bellingham	USA	June 29–July 7	2	NA	NA
1992	Bellingham	USA	June–July	2	NA	5

*events were held only on the weekends at each edition of these games

1987   Bellingham   USA   June 28–July 5

Sports: Athletics, Autocross, Baseball, Bicycling, Board Sailing, Bocci, Bowling, Gymnastics, Handball (doubles), Polo, Racewalking, Racquetball, Rifle, Softball, Tennis, Trap Shooting, Triathlon, Road Racing, Rugby, Running Relay, Waterskiing

Venues: Civic Stadium (Athletics), Port of Bellingham (Autocross), Joe Martin Field (Baseball), Point Roberts (Bicycling), Boulevard Park (Board Sailing), Peace Arch Park (Bocci), Bowling, Whatcom County (Gymnastics—Men), Academy of Northwest Gymnastics (Gymnastics—Women), Muenscher Courts (Handball—Doubles), Bellingham Polo Club (Polo), Beach School (Racewalking), Park Athletic and Recreation Club (Racquetball), Plantation Rifle Range (Rifle), Frank Geri Fields (Softball), Sportsman's Club (Trap Shooting), Lake Padden (Triathlon), Mt. Baker to Bellingham (Running Relay), Borderline Sports (Waterskiing)

1988   Bellingham   USA   June 26–July 5

Sports: Amputee Soccer, Athletics, Autocross, Baseball, Bicycle Motocross, Board Sailing, Bocci, Bowling, Catch n' Fetch, Football, Gymnastics, Handball (doubles), Horseshoes, Polo, Racewalking, Rifle, Sailing, Softball, Squash, Tennis, Triathlon, Road Racing, Rugby, Running Relay, Volleyball, Waterskiing

Venues: Shuksan Middle School (Amputee Football, Football), Civic Stadium (Athletics, Bicycle Motocross, Catch N' Fetch, Racewalking), Downtown Bellingham City Hall (Autocross), Joe Martin Field (Baseball), Lakewood, Lake Whatcom (Board Sailing, Sailing), Peace Arch Park (Bocci, Opening Ceremonies, Road Race), Park Bowl and Mount Baker Lanes (Bowling), Whatcom County Gymnastics (Gymnastics—Men), Academy of Northwest Gymnastics (Gymnastics—Women), Muenscher Athletic Courts (Handball—Doubles), Cornwall Park (Horseshoes), Ferndale Polo Grounds (Polo), Frank Geri Fields (Softball), Sudden Valley Tennis Courts (Tennis), Lake Padden (Triathlon), Ferndale Polo Grounds (Rugby), Mt. Baker Ski Area to Downtown Bellingham (Running Relay), Borderline Lake (Waterskiing), Plantation Rifle Range (Rifle), Bellingham YMCA (Squash, Volleyball),

1989   Bellingham   USA   June 24–July 9

Sports: Athletics, Board Sailing, Bowling, Catch 'n Fetch, Gymnastics, Football, Horseshoes, Polo, Race Walking, Road Race, Road Relay, Softball, Tennis, Triathlon

1990   Bellingham   USA   June 20–July 8

Sports: Athletics, Catch 'n Fetch, Fencing, Football, Handball, Horseshoes, Polo, Road Race, Road Relay, Softball (coed), Slowpitch Softball (women), Tennis, Triathlon, Water Skiing

1992   Bellingham   USA   June–July

Sports: Athletics, Gymnastics, Handball, Tennis, Triathlon

Renaissance Games

The uniquely formatted Renaissance Games, a competition organized by the Institute for International Sport, were created to test the skills of both the scholar and the athlete. Each competitor is required to participate in two athletic events and two academic/cultural events.

The initial Renaissance Games were held at Bates College in Lewiston, Maine, in 1998. They were very small; about 40 scholar athletes were invited from areas of the world that have traditionally been in conflict. Four students, two Catholic and two Protestant, were invited from the University of Belfast. Four other students, two Jewish, one Arab and one Muslim, were invited from the University of Tel Aviv. Six students from McGill University in Canada, four students from South Africa, and students from six U.S. colleges were also invited. Twenty other nations, chosen from among the group of participants at the 1997 World Scholar Athlete Games in Newport, Rhode Island, had one student representative each.

The participants in the games were divided into two teams, named Sparta and Athens. Each student chose two academic events from a list of creative writing, performance (music, instrument, voice, theater), debate/public speaking, photography/art, spelling bee, mathletics, library research and scientific discovery. Each student also chose two athletic events from among basketball, football (soccer), softball, swimming, tennis, track and field and volleyball. Points were awarded for each event and totaled at the end of the competition.

More Renaissance Games are scheduled for the future. The Institute for International Sport is planning to begin a series of competitions between American students and students from other colleges and universities around the world.[197,198]

Year	Host City	Host Nation	Dates	Nations	Athletes	Sports
1998	Lewiston ME	USA	April 17–19	9	40	7

Nations: U.S., Bahamas, Canada, Irish Republic, Israel, Northern Ireland, Norway, South Africa, Turkey (and one student each from about twenty other countries from among those which sent scholar-athletes to the 1997 World Scholar Athlete Games.

Sports: Athletics, Basketball, Football, Softball, Swimming, Tennis, Volleyball

Academic/Cultural events: Creative Writing, Performance (Voice Choir, Instrumental Music, Theater), Debate/Public Speaking, Photography/Art, Spelling Bee, College Bowl, Library Research, Mathletics, Scientific Discovery

Robin Hood Games

The Robin Hood Games, also known as the CP-ISRA [Cerebral Palsy-International Sports and Recreation Association] World Games, are specifically for athletes with cerebral palsy.

Nottingham, England, has hosted all three games. The first two editions in 1989 and 1993 were essentially developmental events. The focus for the 1997 games was to provide a high level of competition in certain events, and provide other events designed for wide participation.

Athletes from 38 nations marched into Harvey Hadden Stadium in 1997 to participate in athletics, boccia, swimming, powerlifting, cycling, table tennis, football, lawn bowling, polybat and kayaking. The athletics, swimming, cycling and table tennis events were also the CP-ISRA World Championships for their disciplines. Thirty-seven CP-ISRA world records were set in athletics and forty-seven world records in swimming.

Nottingham was planning to hold the fourth edition of the Robin Hood Games in 2001.

Year	Host City	Host Nation	Dates	Nations	Athletes	Sports
1989	Nottingham	England		NA	400	NA
1993	Nottingham	England		NA	600	NA
1997	Nottingham	England	July 18–28	38	850	10

1997   Nottingham   England   July 18–28

Sports: Athletics, Boccia, Bowls, Cycling, Football, Kayaking, Polybat, Powerlifting, Swimming, Table Tennis

Venues: Harvey Hadden Stadium (Opening ceremonies, Athletics, Cycling), Darley Moor, Derbyshire (Cycling Road Race), University of Nottingham Pool (Swimming), Nottingham Trent University Gymnasium (Powerlifting), Holme Pierrepont National Watersports Centre Sports Hall (Table Tennis), University of Nottingham Sports Centre (Boccia)

SCFA Summer Spartakiade

The Sports Committee of Friendly Armies (SCFA) was established in 1958 by twelve nations—Albania, Bulgaria, China, Czechoslovakia, German Democratic Republic, Hungary, Mongolia, North Korea, North Vietnam, Romania, and the USSR—to provide sporting opportunities for soldiers from its member nations. The first Summer Spartakiade competition was in Leipzig, East Germany, the same year, with 1,500 participants in 12 sports. The final SCFA Spartakiade in Sofia, Bulgaria had 2,080 participants from 33 nations in 19 sports.

In 1991, the SCFA, with 23 member states and 11 observer states, was integrated with the Conseil International du Sport Militaire (CISM), an organization established in 1948 by the military sports personnel of western nations.

Year	Host City	Host Nation	Dates	Nations	Athletes	Sports
1958	Leipzig	East Germany		12	1500	12
1969	Kiev	Soviet Union		11	1650	10
1973	Prague	Czechoslovakia		12	1600	13
1977	Havana	Cuba	September	23	1500	15
1981	Budapest	Hungary		25	1700	11
1985	Warsaw	Poland		14	1427	10
1989	Sofia	Bulgaria		33	2080	17

1958   Leipzig   East Germany

Sports: Athletics, Basketball, Boxing, Football, Gymnastics, Handball, Pentathlon, Triathlon, Shooting, Swimming, Weightlifting, Wrestling (Greco-Roman)

1969   Kiev   Soviet Union

Sports: Athletics, Basketball, Boxing, Handball, Shooting, Swimming, Triathlon, Volleyball, Weightlifting, Wrestling,

1973   Prague   Czechoslovakia

Sports: Athletics, Basketball, Boxing, Cycling (track), Gymnastics, Handball, Motorcycling, Parachuting, Shooting, Swimming, Weightlifting, Wrestling, Volleyball.

1977   Havana   Cuba   September

Sports: Athletics, Basketball, Boxing, Cycling (Road), Gymnastics, Handball, Judo, Motorcycling, Parachuting, Pentathlon, Shooting, Swimming, Triathlon, Volleyball, Water Polo

1981   Budapest   Hungary

Sports: Athletics, Basketball, Boxing, Gymnastics, Handball, Judo, Parachuting, Pentathlon, Shooting, Swimming, Wrestling (Greco-Roman)

1985   Warsaw   Poland

Sports: Athletics, Boxing, Cycling (Road), Gymnastics, Handball, Horsemanship, Shooting, Swimming, Volleyball, Weightlifting, Wrestling (Greco-Roman)

1989 Sofia Bulgaria

Sports: Acrobatics, Athletics, Boxing, Canoeing, Cross Country, Gymnastics, Horsemanship, Judo, Parachuting, Pentathlon, Sailing, Shooting, Swimming, Volleyball, Water Polo, Weightlifting, Wrestling, (Greco-Roman and Freestyle).

SCFA Winter Spartakiade

The first Spartakiade in winter was held in 1961 in Poland. The SCFA (Sports Committee of Friendly Armies) held some winter events for soldiers in 1963, 1965 and 1967 in Romania, the Soviet Union and East Germany but it was not until 1969 that full winter Spartakiades were held regularly. The winter version of the SCFA Spartakiades were organized every two years while those in the summer were held every four years.

Eleven Winter Spartakiades were held from 1969 to 1989. The core participating nations were the Soviet Union, East Germany, Czechoslovakia, Bulgaria, Poland, Romania and Hungary. Between 240 and 400 athletes competed in each games, with the events covering the traditional winter sports of alpine and Nordic skiing, biathlon, ski jumping, Nordic combined, hockey, toboggan, bobsled, and military ski patrol.[199]

Year	Host City	Host Nation	Dates	Nations	Athletes	Sports
1961		Poland		NA	NA	6
1969	Spindleruv Mlyn	Czechoslovakia		9	280	4
1971	Zakopane	Poland		NA	NA	4
1973	Pamporovo	Bulgaria		NA	NA	3
1975	Leningrad	Soviet Union	Feb. 21–March 3	NA	NA	5
1977	Spindleruv Mlyn (Liberec)	Czechoslovakia	February	9	280	5
1979	Novi-Targ	Poland	Feb. 27–March 2	NA	NA	5
1981	Borovec	Bulgaria		NA	NA	5
1983	Strbske Pleso	Czechoslovakia		8	250	6
1985	Minsk	Soviet Union	Feb. 23–March 2	NA	NA	6
1987	Bucharest	Romania	Feb. 27–March 4	NA	NA	8
1989	Jasna, Osrblie, Strbske Pleso	Czechoslovakia		10	290	6

1961 Poland

Sports: Biathlon, Nordic Combined, Hockey, Skiing, Ski Jumping, Ski Patrol

1969 Spindleruv Mlyn Czechoslovakia

Sports: Biathlon, Skiing, Ski Jumping, Nordic Combined

1971 Zakopane Poland

Sports: Biathlon, Nordic Combined, Skiing, Ski Jumping

1973 Pamporovo Bulgaria

Sports: Biathlon, Skiing, Ski Jumping

1975   Leningrad   Soviet Union
February 21–March 3

Sports: Biathlon, Hockey, Nordic Combined, Skiing, Ski Jumping

1977   Spindleruv Mlyn (Liberec)   Czechoslovakia

Sports: Biathlon, Hockey, Nordic Combined, Skiing, Ski Jumping

1979   Novi-Targ   Poland   February 27–March 2

Sports: Biathlon, Hockey, Nordic Combined, Skiing, Ski Jumping

1981   Borovec   Bulgaria

Sports: Biathlon, Hockey, Nordic Combined, Skiing, Ski Jumping

1983   Strbske Pleso   Czechoslovakia

Sports: Bobsleigh, Biathlon, Nordic Combined, Skiing, Ski Jumping, Toboggan,

1985   Minsk   Soviet Union   February 23–March 2

Sports: Biathlon, Nordic Combined, Hockey, Skiing, Ski Jumping, Ski-Patrol

1987   Bucharest   Romania   February 27–March 4

Sports: Bobsleigh, Biathlon, Hockey, Nordic Combined, Skiing, Ski Jumping, Ski-Patrol, Toboggan

1989   Jasna, Osrblie, Strbske Pleso   Czechoslovakia

Sports: Biathlon, Bobsleigh, Nordic Combined, Skiing, Ski Jumping, Toboggan

SELL Games (Summer)

In 1923, the student unions of Finland, Estonia, Latvia and Lithuania began to organize sporting competitions between the universities in those countries. They were originally called the "Baltic Students Olympics," but the name was changed to the SELL Games, SELL being an acronym for the participating countries (Suomi [Finland], Estonia, Latvia, Lithuania).

The summer games were held until 1938. The games to be held in 1939 in Riga, Latvia, were canceled due to the impending war.

Five editions of SELL Winter Games were held from 1929 to 1940. One edition, planned for 1933, was cancelled. Separate chess tournaments were held in 1937, 1938 and 1939.

The summer games did not take place for sixty years before they were revived in 1998. Then, they were opened to athletes from universities all over the world. Some 790 athletes from 52 universities in thirteen countries participated.

The games are now scheduled once again on an annual basis.

Year	Host City	Host Nation	Dates	Nations	Athletes	Sports
1923	Tartu	Estonia		NA	NA	3
1924	Riga	Latvia		NA	NA	NA
1926	Helsinki	Finland		NA	NA	NA
1929	Kaunas	Lithuania		NA	NA	NA
1930	Tallin	Estonia		NA	NA	NA
1931	Riga	Latvia		NA	NA	NA
1932	Helsinki	Finland		NA	NA	NA
1933	Kaunas	Lithuania		NA	NA	NA
1934	Tartu	Estonia		NA	NA	NA
1935	Riga	Latvia		NA	NA	NA
1936	Helsinki	Finland		NA	NA	NA
1937	Kaunas	Lithuania		NA	NA	NA
1938	Tartu	Estonia		NA	NA	NA
1998	Tartu	Estonia	May 1–10	13	790	8
1999	Kaunas	Lithuania	May 11–17	NA	NA	NA
2000	Jelgava	Latvia	May 18–27	NA	NA	NA

1998   Tartu   Estonia   May 1–10

Nations: Austria, Azerbaijan, Belarus, England, Estonia, Finland, Germany, Latvia, Lithuania, Netherlands, Norway, Russia, Switzerland

Sports: Athletics, Badminton, Basketball, Gymnastics, Judo, Karate, Orienteering, Volleyball

MEDALS

Nation	Gold	Silver	Bronze	Total
Estonia	47	42	40	129
Latvia	10	11	8	29
Lithuania	9	9	8	26
Russia	3	3	4	10
Netherlands	3	2	2	7
Belarus	2	5	4	11
Switzerland	2	1	1	4
England	1	1	0	2
Germany	1	0	2	3
Azerbaijan	0	1	0	1
Austria	0	1	0	1
Finland	0	0	2	2

SELL Games (Winter)

Year	Host City	Host Nation	Dates	Nations	Athletes	Sports
1929	Riga	Latvia		NA	NA	NA
1931	Helsinki	Finland		NA	NA	NA
1935	Riga, Sigulda	Latvia		NA	NA	NA
1938	Zarasai	Lithuania		NA	NA	NA
1940	Otepaa	Estonia	March 2–3	NA	NA	NA

Games planned for 1933 in Kaunas, Lithuania, were not held.

Socialist Olympics

The "worker sports" movement, which had its peak between the world wars of the 20th century, grew out of the belief that everyone should have access to physical activity and sport, not just the upper classes.

While Pierre de Coubertin was establishing the International Olympic Committee and reviving the Olympic Games, clubs and organizations specifically for the working class were being established in Germany and other parts of Europe. The worker sports movement, when it began, stood in opposition to the methods of the Olympic movement, catering instead to mass participation, noncompetitive displays, internationalism over nationalism, and any form of racism, sexism or social barriers. In the end, however, the Red Sport International, the Communist wing of the worker sport movement, was leaning towards trying to outperform the bourgeois athletes at their own game.

The climate of the international labor movement during the period between the wars led to the establishment of two separate organizations with differing ideologies: the Socialist Worker Sports International (SWSI), formed in September 1920, and the Red Sport International, established in July 1921. The Socialist Worker Sports International attempted to distance itself both from all political parties and from "bourgeois" sport, or the Olympic movement. The Red Sport International (RSI) decided that sport should be used to help promote the revolution, and tended to focus on achieving athletic performances that would outshine those of the west.[200]

A convoluted history developed, with games being called Spartakiades, Worker Olympiads, Workers Games and combinations of all of these names.[201] The SWSI at times cooperated with the RSI, and at other times relationships were antagonistic. The SWSI banned the participation of RSI athletes from its 1925 and 1931 Socialist Olympics, and banned SWSI members from participating in the RSI Spartakiade in Moscow in 1928.[202]

Mass participation was a hallmark of these games. In 1931, some 80,000 people from 26 nations participated. At the 1934 Prague games, 100,000 people were said to have participated, but not necessarily competed. The figures account for all of the participants in mass drills and gymnastics displays that were a staple of the worker sports movements.

Certain games were organized in protest at the ideals of the Olympic Games. In 1932 in Chicago, the Communist Party of the United States of America organized a small "Counter Olympics" with about 400 worker athletes.[203]

In 1936, games in opposition to the Berlin Olympics were to be held in Barcelona, Spain, but the Spanish civil war broke out two days before they were to start on July 19.

The final worker games were held in Antwerp, Belgium, in 1937. Games had been planned for Prague in 1940 but were not held due to the war.[204]

Year	Host City	Host Nation	Dates	Nations	Athletes	Sports
Socialist Olympics						
1921	Prague	Czechoslovakia		NA	NA	NA
1925	Frankfurt	Germany	July 22–25	NA	NA	NA
1927	Prague	Czechoslovakia		NA	NA	NA
1931	Vienna	Austria	July 16–26	NA	NA	NA
1934	Prague	Czechoslovakia	July 4–9	NA	NA	NA
1937	Antwerp	Belgium	July 25–Aug. 11	5	14000	NA

Year	Host City	Host Nation	Dates	Nations	Athletes	Sports
Red Sport International Spartakiade						
1921	Prague	Czechoslovakia	June 19–26	NA	NA	NA
1924	Paris	France	July 13–14	NA	NA	NA
1928	Moscow	Soviet Union	August 12–28	14	4000	NA
1931	Moscow	Soviet Union	July 5–19	NA	NA	NA
Socialist Worker Sports International Winter Worker Olympiad						
1925	Schrieberhau (Riesenberge)	Germany	Jan. 31–Feb. 2	NA	NA	NA
1931	Murzzuschlag	Austria	February 5–8	NA	NA	NA
1937	Johannesbad	Czechoslovakia	February 18–21	NA	NA	NA
Red Sport International Winter Spartakiade						
1928	Oslo	Norway	February 17–28	NA	NA	NA
1928	Moscow	Soviet Union	December	NA	638	3
Counter Olympics						
1932	Chicago	USA	July 28–Aug. 1	NA	400	7

South American Games

The current series of South American Games began in 1978 and have been held regularly every four years.

One of the first games in the region, now known as the Latin American Games or South American Olympics, was much earlier in the century when, in 1922, Argentina, Uruguay and Chile were invited to join Brazil for events commemorating the 100-year anniversary of its independence. Just two sports, soccer and athletics, were contested. The games were very small, and though a second games was proposed, it was never organized.

The modern games are governed by ODESUR (Organizacíon Deportiva Sud-americana). The first edition in November 1978 in La Paz in 1977, Bolivia (with some events in Cochabamba and Santa Cruz), were held just thirteen months after the eighth Bolivarian Games which had also been held in La Paz in 1977. These two events marked the first occasions that Bolivia had hosted international competitions on this scale.

Both the first and second editions of the modern games, in 1978 and 1982, were known as Los Juegos Deportivos Cruz del Sur, which roughly translated means the Southern Cross Games. However, the games are now called Los Juegos Deportivos Sudamericanos, or South American Games, but are sometimes cited as Los Juegos ODESUR (ODESUR Games).

Argentina, Bolivia, Chile, Ecuador, Paraguay, Peru and Uruguay participated in the first games in 1978. Brazil was invited but did not come.

The Argentineans have won the most gold medals on each occasion.

Year	Host City	Host Nation	Dates	Nations	Athletes	Sports
1978	La Paz	Bolivia	November 3–13	7	480	15
1982	Rosario/Santa Fe	Argentina	Nov. 26–Dec 5	10	961	20
1986	Santiago	Chile	Nov. 29–Dec. 7	10	969	15
1990	Lima	Peru	December 1–10	10	1070	16

Year	Host City	Host Nation	Dates	Nations	Athletes	Sports
1994	Valencia	Venezuela	November 19–28	14	1599	19
1998	Cuenca	Ecuador	October 21–31	15	NA	27

1978   La Paz   Bolivia   November 3–13

Nations: Argentina, Bolivia, Chile, Ecuador, Paraguay, Peru, Uruguay
Sports: Athletics, Basketball, Boxing, Cycling, Equestrian, Fencing, Football, Gymnastics, Judo, Shooting, Swimming, Tennis, Volleyball, Weightlifting, Wrestling

MEDALS

Nation	Gold	Silver	Bronze	Total
Argentina	91	53	45	189
Bolivia	20	42	44	106
Chile	32	25	20	77
Peru	9	16	10	35
Uruguay	4	16	12	32
Ecuador	18	8	6	32
Paraguay	2	3	4	9

(*Olympic Review*, March-April 1979, p. 111, says that Brazil was invited but did not compete at these games. However, the Cuenca 1998 website lists Brazil as having won one gold medal at the 1978 games.)

1982   Rosario/Santa Fe   Argentina
November 26–December 5

Nations: Argentina, Bolivia, Brazil, Chile, Colombia, Ecuador, Paraguay, Peru, Uruguay, Venezuela

MEDALS

Nation	Gold	Silver	Bronze	Total
Argentina	114	75	47	236
Chile	37	51	47	135
Brazil	29	34	12	75
Uruguay	13	17	22	52
Peru	30	18	2	50
Ecuador	11	14	12	37
Venezuela	8	3	13	24
Colombia	6	2	6	14
Bolivia	1	1	8	10
Paraguay	0	3	3	6

1986   Santiago   Chile   November 29–December 7

Nations: Argentina, Bolivia, Brazil, Chile, Colombia, Ecuador, Paraguay, Peru, Uruguay, Venezuela

MEDALS

Nation	Gold	Silver	Bronze	Total
Argentina	80	44	45	169
Chile	50	66	60	176

Nation	Gold	Silver	Bronze	Total
Peru	13	26	35	74
Ecuador	16	17	25	58
Uruguay	17	15	12	44
Brazil	14	10	12	36
Paraguay	1	6	8	15
Bolivia	2	2	6	10
Venezuela	0	1	1	2
Colombia	0	1	0	1

1990   Lima   Peru   December 1–10

Nations: Argentina, Bolivia, Brazil, Chile, Ecuador, Paraguay, Peru, Suriname, Uruguay, Venezuela

MEDALS

Nation	Gold	Silver	Bronze	Total
Argentina	68	73	46	187
Peru	50	59	76	185
Chile	40	38	60	138
Brazil	37	21	19	77
Venezuela	27	22	15	64
Ecuador	21	23	18	62
Uruguay	13	13	15	41
Bolivia	2	9	24	35
Paraguay	0	4	2	6
Suriname	2	0	1	3

1994   Valencia   Venezuela   November 19–28

Nation: Argentina, Aruba, Bolivia, Brazil, Chile, Colombia, Dutch Antilles, Ecuador, Panama, Paraguay, Peru, Suriname, Uruguay, Venezuela

MEDALS

Nation	Gold	Silver	Bronze	Total
Argentina	108	61	64	233
Venezuela	78	73	82	233
Colombia	41	54	33	128
Brazil	30	32	39	101
Peru	15	28	39	82
Chile	18	17	42	77
Ecuador	2	17	20	39
Uruguay	4	10	10	24
Bolivia	2	5	15	22
Dutch Antilles	3	5	6	14
Panama	4	2	5	11
Paraguay	3	0	7	10
Aruba	0	5	0	5
Suriname	0	3	0	3

South Asian Federation Games

The South Asian Sports Federation was created in 1981 after meetings between seven South Asian nations at the International Olympic Committee Congress in Baden-Baden.

The intent was to establish a regional games that would be held on an annual basis for the first five years. After that time, the games would be held on a biennial schedule. The games were to be hosted by each nation—Bangladesh, Bhutan, India, the Maldives, Nepal, Pakistan and Sri Lanka—in alphabetical order, but this rule has not been adhered to. The first two games were held in 1984 and 1985 and the event was put on a biennial schedule thereafter until 1997. At that point, the games scheduled for Kathmandu had to be postponed until 1999.

The initial games in Kathmandu in 1984 had just five sports: athletics, boxing, football, swimming and weightlifting. Kabbadi and wrestling were added the following year at the games in Bangladesh—two sports exclusively for male participants to a schedule that was already heavy with men-only events. India finished well ahead of the other nations in the medal tables on both occasions.

The third games were opened in Calcutta, India, in 1987 by President Ramaswamy Venkataraman. A games torch was relayed from Bangladesh, the previous host city, to Calcutta and P.T. Usha, India's sprint queen, took the athlete's oath. Usha went on to win five gold medals in sprints and relays. [205]

Muhammad Ali was an honored guest at the opening ceremony of the 1989 games in Islamabad, Pakistan, which were opened by President Ghulam Ishaq Khan under the theme "Together in Sports, together in Friendship." The Chinese gave assistance to Pakistan in refurbishing Islamabad's Jinnah Stadium. Mohammed Rashid, Pakistan's javelin champion from the 1987 games, read the athlete's oath. India's Khajan Singh walked away from the games with seven swimming gold medals.

India continued its streak of domination on the sports fields at the 1991 games in Colombo, Sri Lanka, and at the 1993 games held for the second time in Dhaka, Bangladesh. Dhaka tried to put on its best face for the games, spending millions on new stadiums, and sweeping beggars, prostitutes and thieves off of the streets in the weeks before the event. Some 12,000 policemen and volunteer security personnel were on hand for the games. Women's events were included,[206] with Pakistani long jumper Shabana Akhter winning the first ever women's gold medal in athletics for Pakistan.

Protests were the story at the games in Madras, India, in December 1995. Two days prior to the opening, Abdul Rahoof, a 24-year-old office worker, committed self-immolation by pouring kerosene over his body and setting himself ablaze. His protest was in support of an independent homeland for the Eelam Tamils. Before his act, Rahoof wrote a message calling for a boycott of the South Asian Federation Games on a bulletin board at his work. He died later the same day in the hospital.[207] In addition, the Indian government was accused by the opposition parties of finance irregularities during the course of staging the games.[208]

P.T. Usha once again took the athlete's oath, as she had for the games eight years previously in Calcutta. On the track, she was surpassed by Sri Lankan Susanthika Jayasinghe who won the gold medals in the 100 and 200 meters.

The games were to return to their birthplace, Kathmandu, Nepal, in 1997, but facilities could not be made ready in time and the event was postponed two years until

1999. With the help of the Chinese, Nepal was finally able to ready its athletic stadium, swimming pool and other facilities in time.

King Birendra Bir Bikram Shah Deva opened the eighth South Asian Federation (SAF) Games in Dashrath Stadium in Nepal. Special security arrangements had to be made for athletes from rivals India and Pakistan to protect them from possible terrorist threats.

Host Nepal swept all six gold medals in tae kwon do, and overall finished a surprising second place to India in the gold medals race. Indian had never been threatened for the games medals lead. The team was led by 41-year-old Raj Kumar Rai who won gold in the middleweight category. Rai had won tae kwon do at the Asian Games in 1986 in Seoul. Bangladesh defeated host Nepal by 1–0 for the coveted football gold.

On the track two women had great success. Damayanthi Darsha of Sri Lanka won three women's sprint golds, and India's Sunita Rani won the women's 1,500, 5,000 and 10,000 meter runs.

Three of the athletes who participated at the eighth South Asian Federation Games tested positive to banned substances.

The ninth SAF Games were to be held in Pakistan in 2001.

Year	Host City	Host Nation	Dates	Nations	Athletes	Sports
1984	Kathmandu	Nepal		7	NA	5
1985	Dhaka	Bangladesh	December 20–26	7	NA	7
1987	Calcutta	India	November 20–27	7	NA	10
1989	Islamabad	Pakistan	October 20–27	7	800	10
1991	Colombo	Sri Lanka	Nov. or Dec.	7	NA	10
1993	Dhaka	Bangladesh	December 20–27	7	1183	11
1995	Madras	India	December 18–26	7	NA	NA
1999	Kathmandu	Nepal	Sept. 25–Oct. 4	7	1069	12

1984   Kathmandu   Nepal

Nations: Bangladesh, Bhutan, India, Maldives, Nepal, Pakistan, Sri Lanka
Sports: Athletics, Boxing, Football, Swimming, Weightlifting

MEDALS

Nation	Gold	Silver	Bronze	Total
India	44	28	16	88
Sri Lanka	7	11	19	37
Pakistan	5	3	2	10
Nepal	4	12	8	24
Bangladesh	2	8	13	23
Bhutan	0	0	2	2
Maldives	0	0	1	1

1985   Dhaka   Bangladesh   December 20–26

Nations: Bangladesh, Bhutan, India, Maldives, Nepal, Pakistan, Sri Lanka
Sports: Athletics, Boxing, Football, Kabbadi, Swimming, Weightlifting, Wrestling

MEDALS

Nation	Gold	Silver	Bronze	Total
India	61	32	10	103
Pakistan	20	26	12	58

Nation	Gold	Silver	Bronze	Total
Bangladesh	9	17	38	64
Sri Lanka	2	7	9	18
Nepal	1	9	22	32
Bhutan	0	0	4	4
Maldives	0	0	0	0

1987   Calcutta   India   November 20–27

Nations: Bangladesh, Bhutan, India, Maldives, Nepal, Pakistan, Sri Lanka
Sports: Athletics, Basketball, Boxing, Football, Kabbadi, Swimming, Table Tennis, Volleyball, Weightlifting, Wrestling

MEDALS

Nation	Gold	Silver	Bronze	Total
India	91	45	19	155
Pakistan	16	35	14	65
Sri Lanka	4	7	23	34
Bangladesh	3	21	31	55
Nepal	2	7	33	42
Bhutan	0	0	5	5
Maldives	0	0	0	0

1989   Islamabad   Pakistan   October 20–27

Nations: Bangladesh, Bhutan, India, Maldives, Nepal, Pakistan, Sri Lanka
Sports: Athletics, Boxing, Football, Kabbadi, Squash, Swimming, Table Tennis, Volleyball, Weightlifting, Wrestling

MEDALS

Nation	Gold	Silver	Bronze	Total
India	61	43	20	124
Pakistan	42	33	22	97
Sri Lanka	6	10	21	37
Nepal	1	13	32	46
Bangladesh	1	12	24	37
Bhutan	0	0	3	3
Maldives	0	0	0	0

1991   Colombo   Sri Lanka   November or December

Nations: Bangladesh, Bhutan, India, Maldives, Nepal, Pakistan, Sri Lanka

MEDALS

Nation	Gold	Silver	Bronze	Total
India	64	59	41	164
Sri Lanka	44	33	41	118
Pakistan	28	33	24	85
Bangladesh	4	8	29	41

Nation	Gold	Silver	Bronze	Total
Nepal	2	8	30	40
Maldives	0	1	0	1
Bhutan	0	0	0	0

1993   Dhaka   Bangladesh   December 20–27

Nations: Bangladesh, Bhutan, India, Maldives, Nepal, Pakistan, Sri Lanka
Sports: Athletics, Boxing, Football, Swimming, Kabbadi, Lawn Tennis, Volleyball, Table Tennis, Wrestling, Shooting, Judo (possibly two more)

MEDALS

Nation	Gold	Silver	Bronze	Total
India	61	47	31	139
Pakistan	23	22	21	66
Sri Lanka	21	23	39	83
Bangladesh	11	19	34	64
Nepal	1	6	15	22
Maldives	0	0	0	0
Bhutan	0	0	0	0

1995   Madras   India   December 18–26

Nations: Bangladesh, Bhutan, India, Maldives, Nepal, Pakistan, Sri Lanka
Sports: Athletics, Football, Field Hockey, Judo, Kabbadi, Shooting, Swimming, Table Tennis, Tennis, Volleyball, Weightlifting (three more)

MEDALS

Nation	Gold	Silver	Bronze	Total
India	106	60	19	185
Sri Lanka	16	25	50	91
Pakistan	10	33	36	79
Bangladesh	7	17	35	59
Nepal	4	8	16	28
Maldives	0	0	1	1
Bhutan	0	0	2	2

1999   Kathmandu   Nepal   September 25–October 4

Nations: Bangladesh, Bhutan, India, Maldives, Nepal, Pakistan, Sri Lanka
Sports: Athletics, Boxing, Football, Karate, Kabbadi, Shooting, Swimming, Table Tennis, Tae Kwon Do, Volleyball, Weightlifting, Wrestling
Sports for Women: Athletics, Karate, Shooting, Swimming, Table Tennis, Tae Kwon Do, Volleyball
Venues: Dasharatha Stadium (Opening Ceremony, Closing Ceremony, Athletics, Football), Shahanshah Hall (Boxing), Tripuweshwor Covered Hall (Karate, Volleyball), Sanogauchpr Gyaneshwor (Kabbadi), BIS Complex Satdobato (Shooting, Swimming), Lainchour Covered Hall (Table Tennis), Sansha Hall (Table Tennis), Royal Nepal Academy (Weightlifting), Smitri Bwan TU (Wrestling)

| | MEDALS | | | |
Nation	Gold	Silver	Bronze	Total
India	102	58	37	197
Nepal	31	10	24	65
Sri Lanka	16	42	62	120
Pakistan	10	36	30	76
Bangladesh	2	10	35	47
Bhutan	1	6	7	14
Maldives	0	0	4	4

South East Asian Games

The South East Asian Games (SEA Games) began as the South East Asian Peninsular Games, first held in Thailand in 1959. The original participants were Burma, Laos, Malaysia, Singapore, Thailand and Vietnam.

The name South East Asian Peninsular Games was used up until 1975 when the SEAP Games Federation accepted Indonesia and the Philippines as members. The name was then changed to South East Asian Games. Lord Killanin, then President of the IOC, showed his support for the South East Asian Games movement by attending the 1977 games in Kuala Lumpur, Malaysia.

The huge 100,000-seat Gelora Senayan Stadium, originally built for the 1962 Asian Games, was host to the 1979 South East Asian Games in Jakarta, Indonesia.

The 1989 games in Kuala Lumpur saw the return of teams from Vietnam and Laos, who had last attended in 1973.

Chiang Mai, Thailand, in 1995 was the first noncapital city to host the games. The event was part of the 700th anniversary celebration of the city.

The South East Asian Games Federation intends to rotate the hosts alphabetically by nation name which removes some of the politics, planning time, and uncertainty as to who will host the next edition. Nonetheless, even with this arrangement some nations have not been ready for their turn.

Many athletes have had the opportunity to star at the games. Malaysia's Nurul Hada Abdullah won eight gold and two silver medals in women's swimming in 1989. The same year, Eric Buhain, a Philippine swimmer, won three gold, two silver and two bronze medals. Singapore's Joscelin Yao won nine swimming events in 1993. In 1999, Elma Muros of the Philippines won her eighth gold medal in the long jump, extending a string going back to the Singapore games in 1983, broken only in 1987 when she did not participate. Asked when she would retire she said, "I will go when the desire to win is no longer there. Right now the body is still willing." Muros won her first medal at the age of 16 and was 32 when she won her eighth gold.

The *Bangkok Nation Newspaper* wrote of the 1997 games in Jakarta: "As always, the theme is regional brotherhood. But as expected, the games nearly ended in a riot." Endless squabbles over rulings in gymnastics, boxing and tae kwon do and hostility to visiting athletes by spectators disrupted the friendly spirit of the games. The soccer tournament was especially raucous, with fans smashing and burning the wooden seats inside the stadium and overturning cars outside. The Asian Football Confederation threatened to cancel the football final if organizers could not guarantee that the crowds could be controlled. Though security was massive, the crowd was still unruly, throwing stones onto the field and starting fires in the stands. The game was delayed 45 minutes between halves so that order could be restored. Many were injured and dozens arrested. The crowd again began destroying property and overturning cars after the host Indonesia lost the final to Thailand.

Indonesia's Eduardus Nabunome made a comeback to win the marathon in 2:20.27. Nabunome had not competed in the SEA Games since 1991. He had gained five gold and two silver medals in the 10,000 meters and 5,000 meters events in the SEA Games from 1985 to 1991.

The 1999 games were held in the tiny oil-rich kingdom of Brunei, in Bander Seri Bagawan. Organizers expected little trouble with crowd control due to the strict Islamic laws enforced in Brunei.

The Sultan of Brunei also declared that his subjects could watch the games for free.

Brunei's only three gold medal–winning athletes from the games—Umi Kalthum Abdul Karim (a female star in the martial arts discipline of pencak silat), Dato Kol Mohamed Samid Abdul Aziz and Zabidi Ali—were given the honor of lighting the 20th SEA Games' flame at the opening ceremony in Sultan Hassanal Bolkiah stadium.

Once again, the regional pollution problems affected the games, with fires from Malaysia causing a haze.

The 2001 games were to be held in Kuala Lumpur, Penang and Johor in Malaysia.

Year	Host City	Host Nation	Dates	Nations	Athletes	Sports
1959	Bangkok	Thailand	December 12–17	6	NA	NA
1962	Rangoon	Burma	December 11–16	7	NA	NA
1965	Kuala Lumpur	Malaysia	December 14–21	7	NA	NA
1967	Bangkok	Thailand	December 9–16	6	NA	NA
1969	Rangoon	Burma	December 6–13	NA	NA	NA
1971	Kuala Lumpur	Malaysia	December 11–18	7	NA	NA
1973	Singapore	Singapore	September 1–8	7	NA	NA
1975	Bangkok	Thailand	December 9–16	NA	NA	NA
1977	Kuala Lumpur	Malaysia	November 19–26	7	2000	18
1979	Jakarta	Indonesia	September 21–30	7	NA	NA
1981	Manila	Philippines	December 6–15	7	2000	NA
1983	Singapore	Singapore	May 28–June 6	8	NA	NA
1985	Bangkok	Thailand	December 8–17	8	NA	NA
1987	Jakarta	Indonesia	September 9–20	8	NA	NA
1989	Kuala Lumpur	Malaysia	August 20–31	9	2355	NA
1991	Manila	Philippines	November 24–Dec.5	9	NA	NA
1993	Singapore	Singapore	June 12–20	9	3000	29
1995	Chiang Mai	Thailand	December 9–17	10	3226	NA
1997	Jakarta	Indonesia	October 11–19	10	4300	34
1999	Bandar Seri Bagawan	Brunei	August 8–14	10	4000	21

1959   Bangkok   Thailand   December 12–17

Nations: Burma, Laos, Malaysia, Singapore, Thailand, Vietnam

MEDALS

Nation	Gold	Silver	Bronze	Total
Thailand	35	26	16	77
Burma	11	15	14	40

Nation	Gold	Silver	Bronze	Total
Malaysia	8	15	11	34
Singapore	8	7	18	33
Vietnam	5	5	5	15
Laos	0	0	0	0

1962   Rangoon   Burma   December 11–16

Nations: Burma, Cambodia, Laos, Malaysia, Singapore, Thailand, Vietnam

MEDALS

Nation	Gold	Silver	Bronze	Total
Burma	35	25	22	82
Thailand	21	18	22	61
Malaysia	12	16	16	44
Vietnam	6	1	3	10
Singapore	4	13	11	28
Cambodia	1	6	4	11
Laos	0	0	0	0

1965   Kuala Lumpur   Malaysia   December 14–21

Nations: Burma, Cambodia, Laos, Malaysia, Singapore, Thailand, Vietnam

MEDALS

Nation	Gold	Silver	Bronze	Total
Thailand	38	33	35	106
Malaysia	33	36	29	98
Singapore	26	23	27	76
Burma	18	14	16	48
Cambodia	15	19	17	51
Vietnam	5	7	7	19
Laos	0	0	0	0

1967   Bangkok   Thailand   December 9–16

Nations: Burma, Laos, Malaysia, Singapore, Thailand, Vietnam

MEDALS

Nation	Gold	Silver	Bronze	Total
Thailand	77	48	47	172
Singapore	28	31	28	87
Malaysia	23	29	43	95
Burma	11	26	32	69
Vietnam	6	10	17	33
Laos	0	0	3	3

1971   Kuala Lumpur   Malaysia   December 11–18

Nations: Burma, Cambodia, Laos, Malaysia, Singapore, Thailand, Vietnam

MEDALS			
Nation	Gold	Silver	Bronze	Total
Thailand	44	27	38	109
Malaysia	41	43	55	139
Singapore	32	33	31	96
Burma	20	28	13	61
Cambodia	17	18	18	53
Vietnam	3	6	9	18
Laos	0	1	4	5

1973   Singapore   Singapore   September 1–8

Nations: Burma, Cambodia, Laos, Malaysia, Singapore, Thailand, Vietnam

MEDALS			
Nation	Gold	Silver	Bronze	Total
Thailand	47	24	28	99
Singapore	45	50	47	142
Malaysia	30	35	49	114
Burma	28	25	15	68
Cambodia	9	12	20	41
Vietnam	2	13	9	24
Laos	0	5	4	9

1975   Bangkok   Thailand   December 9–16

Nations: Burma, Malaysia, Singapore, Thailand (incomplete)

MEDALS*			
Nation	Gold	Silver	Bronze	Total
Thailand	80	45	39	164
Singapore	38	42	49	129
Burma	28	35	33	96
Malaysia	27	39	51	117

*Incomplete

1977   Kuala Lumpur   Malaysia   November 19–26

Nations: Brunei, Burma, Indonesia, Malaysia, Philippines, Singapore, Thailand
Sports: Archery, Athletics, Badminton, Basketball, Bowling, Boxing, Cycling, Football, Hockey, Judo, Rugby, Sepak Takraw, Shooting, Swimming, Table Tennis, Tennis, Volleyball, Weightlifting
Venues: Merdeka Stadium (Opening and Closing Ceremonies, Athletics, Football), Kota Raja Kelang Stadium (Cycling), Negara Stadium (Basketball, Boxing, Badminton), Kolam Bandaraya Swimming Pool (Swimming)

MEDALS			
Nation	Gold	Silver	Bronze	Total
Indonesia	62	41	34	137
Thailand	37	35	33	105

Nation	Gold	Silver	Bronze	Total
Malaysia	31	30	30	91
Burma	25	42	43	110
Singapore	21	17	21	59
Philippines	14	21	28	63
Brunei	0	0	3	3

1979   Jakarta   Indonesia   September 21–30

Nations: Brunei, Burma, Indonesia, Malaysia, Philippines, Singapore, Thailand
Sports: Archery, Athletics, Badminton, Basketball, Boxing, Cycling, Football, Gymnastics, Field Hockey, Judo, Sepak Takraw, Shooting, Softball, Swimming, Table Tennis, Tennis, Volleyball, Weightlifting, (demonstration Sport, Pencak Silak, an Indonesian martial arts discipline)

MEDALS

Nation	Gold	Silver	Bronze	Total
Indonesia	92	78	52	222
Thailand	50	46	29	125
Burma	26	26	24	76
Philippines	24	31	38	93
Malaysia	19	23	39	81
Singapore	16	20	36	72
Brunei	0	1	0	1

1981   Manila   Philippines   December 6–15

Nations: Brunei, Burma, Indonesia, Malaysia, Philippines, Singapore, Thailand

MEDALS

Nation	Gold	Silver	Bronze	Total
Indonesia	85	73	56	214
Thailand	62	45	41	148
Philippines	55	55	71	181
Malaysia	16	27	31	74
Burma	15	19	27	61
Singapore	12	26	33	71
Brunei	0	0	0	0

1983   Singapore   Singapore   May 28–June 6

Nations: Brunei, Burma, Cambodia, Indonesia, Malaysia, Philippines, Singapore, Thailand
Sports: Archery, Athletics, Badminton, Basketball, Board Sailing, Boxing, Equestrian, Field Hockey, Football, Judo, Sailing, Sepak Takraw, Shooting, Swimming, Table Tennis, Tennis, Volleyball, Water Skiing, Weightlifting

MEDALS

Nation	Gold	Silver	Bronze	Total
Indonesia	64	67	54	185
Philippines	49	48	53	150

Nation	Gold	Silver	Bronze	Total
Thailand	49	40	38	127
Singapore	38	38	58	134
Burma	18	15	17	50
Malaysia	16	25	40	81
Brunei	0	0	5	5
Cambodia	0	0	0	0

1985   Bangkok   Thailand   December 8–17

Nations: Brunei, Burma, Cambodia, Indonesia, Malaysia, Philippines, Singapore, Thailand

MEDALS

Nation	Gold	Silver	Bronze	Total
Thailand	93	65	52	210
Indonesia	62	73	74	209
Philippines	43	54	32	129
Malaysia	26	28	32	86
Singapore	16	11	23	50
Burma	13	19	34	66
Brunei	0	0	3	3
Cambodia	0	0	0	0

1987   Jakarta   Indonesia   September 9–20

Nations: Brunei, Burma, Cambodia, Indonesia, Malaysia, Philippines, Singapore, Thailand

MEDALS

Nation	Gold	Silver	Bronze	Total
Indonesia	185	136	84	405
Thailand	63	59	67	189
Philippines	59	77	69	205
Malaysia	36	40	63	139
Singapore	19	38	64	121
Burma	13	16	22	51
Brunei	1	6	17	24
Cambodia	0	1	9	10

1989   Kuala Lumpur   Malaysia   August 20–31

Nations: Brunei, Indonesia, Laos, Malaysia, Myanmar, Philippines, Singapore, Thailand, Vietnam

MEDALS

Nation	Gold	Silver	Bronze	Total
Indonesia	102	78	70	250
Malaysia	67	58	75	200
Thailand	62	63	66	191
Singapore	32	38	47	117

Nation	Gold	Silver	Bronze	Total
Philippines	26	37	64	127
Myanmar	10	14	20	44
Vietnam	3	11	5	19
Brunei	1	2	24	27
Laos	0	1	0	1

1991 Manila Philippines November 24–December 5

Nations: Brunei, Indonesia, Laos, Malaysia, Myanmar, Philippines, Singapore, Thailand, Vietnam

MEDALS

Nation	Gold	Silver	Bronze	Total
Indonesia	92	86	69	247
Philippines	91	62	84	237
Thailand	72	80	91	243
Malaysia	36	38	65	139
Singapore	18	32	45	95
Myanmar	12	16	28	56
Vietnam	7	12	10	29
Brunei	0	0	8	8
Laos	0	0	0	0

1993 Singapore Singapore June 12–20

Nations: Brunei, Indonesia, Laos, Malaysia, Myanmar, Philippines, Singapore, Thailand, Vietnam

MEDALS

Nation	Gold	Silver	Bronze	Total
Indonesia	88	81	84	253
Thailand	63	70	63	196
Philippines	57	59	72	188
Singapore	50	40	74	164
Malaysia	43	45	65	153
Vietnam	9	6	19	34
Myanmar	8	13	16	37
Brunei	1	3	18	22
Laos	0	1	0	1

1995 Chiang Mai Thailand December 9–17

Nations: Brunei, Cambodia, Indonesia, Laos, Malaysia, Myanmar, Philippines, Singapore, Thailand, Vietnam

MEDALS

Nation	Gold	Silver	Bronze	Total
Thailand	157	98	91	346
Indonesia	77	67	77	221
Philippines	33	48	62	143

Nation	Gold	Silver	Bronze	Total
Malaysia	31	49	69	149
Singapore	26	27	42	95
Vietnam	10	18	24	52
Myanmar	4	21	37	62
Brunei	0	2	6	8
Laos	0	1	6	7
Cambodia	0	0	2	2

1997   Jakarta   Indonesia   October 11–19

Nations: Brunei, Cambodia, Indonesia, Laos, Malaysia, Myanmar, Philippines, Singapore, Thailand, Vietnam
Sports: Archery, Athletics, Badminton, Basketball, Billiards, Bodybuilding, Bowling, Boxing, Canoeing, Cycling, Fencing, Field Hockey, Football, Golf, Gymnastics, Judo, Karatedo, Pencak Silat, Rowing, Sepak Takraw, Shooting, Softball, Squash, Swimming, Table Tennis, Tae Kwon Do, Tennis, Traditional Boat Racing, Volleyball, Water Skiing, Weightlifting, Wrestling, Wushu, Yachting

MEDALS

Nation	Gold	Silver	Bronze	Total
Indonesia	194	101	115	410
Thailand	83	97	78	258
Malaysia	55	68	75	198
Philippines	43	56	108	207
Vietnam	35	48	50	133
Singapore	30	26	50	106
Myanmar	8	34	44	86
Brunei	0	2	4	6
Laos	0	0	7	7
Cambodia	0	0	6	6

1999   Bandar Seri Bagawan   Brunei   August 8–14

Nations: Brunei, Cambodia, Indonesia, Laos, Malaysia, Myanmar, Philippines, Singapore, Thailand, Vietnam
Sports: Athletics, Badminton, Basketball, Billiards, Boxing, Cycling, Field Hockey, Football, Karate, Lawn Bowls, Pencak Silat, Shooting, Swimming, Sepak Takraw, Squash, Table Tennis, Tae Kwon Do, Ten-pin Bowling, Tennis, Traditional Boat Racing, Weightlifting

South Pacific Games

In March 1961, nine South Pacific nations gathered to discuss the creation of sports competitions that would serve to bring the region closer together. Dr. A.H. Sahu Khan, a Fijian originally from India, was responsible for the initial proposal.

One of the first items to be instituted in the South Pacific Games' charter was a rule requiring all participants to be residents of the South Pacific Islands and not just

New Zealanders, Australians or French that happened to be stationed there. The over-seas residents could compete but only after establishing residency of more than two years.

An ongoing discussion in the South Pacific Games has been the issue of sched-uling events on Sundays. Many nations prohibited their teams from competing on Sun-days, and on the island of Tonga it was actually against the law to participate in sporting events on the Sabbath.

Thirteen nations participated in the first games held in Suva, Fiji, in 1963. Many of the competing nations used the British or French flag and anthems based on their historic colonial ties which made it quite difficult to distinguish the various teams one from another.

One humorous anecdote from the first South Pacific Games has the Solomon Islands football team refusing to wear the heavy cleated boots that their team man-agers had purchased for them, preferring to play barefoot as they did at home. Facing off with the team from New Hebrides, the Solomon Islanders were at first fearful of the boots worn by the other team and were quickly down by two goals. Finally a Solomon Islander was trounced by the boots and bounced up unhurt, yelling in per-fect pidgin, "No matter long boots. Me feller no fright now!" He and his inspired teammates came back to win the game 6 to 3.[209]

Good sportsmanship was upheld. The team from Tonga was awarded the bronze medal in football because the team from the Gilbert and Ellice Islands showed up late for the game. The Tongans offered to play for the medal and the tardy team from Gilbert and Ellice Islands won.

Fiji outdistanced all other teams in the medal race with 34 gold, 23 silver and 27 bronze. Papua New Guinea had nine gold; New Caledonia seven.

The honor of hosting the second games was given to Nouméa, New Caledonia, which spent a great deal of money to construct an Olympic stadium, Olympic pool, velodrome and other facilities for the event held in December 1966.

When the official schedule came out one year in advance of the games, the Fijians protested that some events were scheduled for Sundays, but these concerns were not addressed by the organizers.

The New Caledonians spent most of their money on facilities but not on accom-modations. In one case, twenty-eight athletes were expected to be housed in one small twenty-five by twenty-seven foot classroom. The 400 athletes at La Perouse High School were expected to make do with four showers and eleven toilets for the dura-tion of the games. Food poisoning knocked some of the Fijian weightlifters out of their events.

The issue of the Sunday schedule was never resolved and some Tongan athletes chose not to compete in the finals of their events, rather than break Tongan law which forbade competition on Sundays.

The cycling competition was diminished midway through the games when one of the bicycles was stolen from the New Hebrides team and it had to forfeit the rest of the competition.

In order to try to distinguish the teams one from another, most of the countries and territories had special tunes to replace the anthems of France and Britain which had been played repeatedly at the games in Suva. French Polynesia and New Caledo-nia kept "The Marsellaise."

In meetings during the games, the residential qualification rule was extended to three years. Papua New Guinea wanted the rule kept at two years, Tonga would have preferred four years, while Western Samoa wanted a full five years.

The host New Caledonians vaulted over the Fijians to win the most medals. New Caledonia gathered 39 gold, 30 silver and 30 bronze. Fiji was second with 19 gold, and French Polynesia third with 13 gold.

The next games were awarded to Papua New Guinea and were to be held in 1969, though the New Guinea House of Assembly had initially passed a resolution against accepting them. Strong lobbying by the leader of the games committee, Don Barnett, changed their minds.

By the time the games were to be held, the government had given its full support, advertising the event in Japan, the U.S. and the Philippines to attract tourists. The government even went so far as to drop leaflets by airplane into remote villages in New Guinea to inform citizens there of the games. No competitions were scheduled on Sundays, and during the South Pacific Games committee meetings, a rule was passed to say that in the future no sports could ever be scheduled on a Sunday. During the games the French- and English-speaking athletes were segregated in separate villages.

At the opening ceremonies in Port Moresby, it was decided to let over 5,000 people enter the stadium at the last minute for free when it became apparent that they could not all purchase tickets and be seated without delaying the function. This cost the Organizing Committee much needed funds, but in the end ticket revenues for the games exceeded the original estimates anyway.

The facilities were a combination of old and new. A brand-new athletics stadium was created using an old technology, a grass track. The timing equipment was new technology, the same electronic Omega system from Switzerland that was used for the 1968 Mexico City Olympic Games.

Accommodations were again crowded. The students of the Administrative College were moved out of their dormitories and housed in tents on the outskirts of Port Moresby to make room for the athletes during the games.

The food preparations were taken care of by two of Australia's largest catering services, one of which had provided the food services for the Melbourne Olympics in 1956 and the other the food services for the Perth Commonwealth Games in 1962.

The Duke of Kent was on hand to officially open the games. The opening ceremonies were disrupted when some of the visiting athletes ran across the field for a closer look and to take pictures of the native Papua New Guinean dancers—some of them were women and topless in their native garb.

Kate Tongi was the only athlete from Tonga to compete at the games, but she won four events: the 100 meters, 200 meters, 80 meter hurdles and the pentathlon. At the end of the games, the French sports magazine *L'Equipe* gave her an award for the best performer. Peter Snell, the New Zealand Olympic Champion middle-distance runner, assisted with the coaching of the runners from Western Samoa.

New Caledonia held on to its spot on top of the medals table with 36 gold medals. Papua New Guinea improved to second with 23 gold, and Fiji was third with 13 first-place medals.

The fourth games were held in 1971 in Papeete, Tahiti. The South Pacific Games regulations stated that the games should be held every three years unless it was an Olympic year. In that case, the host nation had the choice of holding the games in the year before or the year after the Olympic Games.

This was the only time the rule was applied, however, as the games council made the decision to go with the more traditional quadrennial schedule thereafter. CBS television covered these games in the United States.

The 1971 Papeete games also had two villages, but rather than dividing the French and English competitors, this time the men and women had separate accommodations. The rooms were still not spacious, though. Fautaue Stadium was remodeled for the games with a new concrete cycling track installed. Once again, the athletics track was grass.

A contest to design the emblem for the games was won by André Henry of New Caledonia who had also won the competition to design the emblem for the 1966 games.

The stars of the games were the swimmer Marie-Jose Kersaudy, a New Caledonian who won seven gold medals for the third games in a row for a career total of twenty-one golds, and Usaia Sotutu of Fiji, who won the 5,000 meter run in addition to defending his 10,000 meter and 3,000 meter steeplechase titles claimed in Port Moresby.

A small protest occurred when judo competitors from Guam demonstrated on the medal stand: one, Rainardo Santos, raising a clenched fist in a "brown power salute," and in a separate incident, Ricardo Blas standing with his back to the French flag. This deeply offended the French, who responded later by removing the American flag from the judo hall. The Guamanians answered that the demonstration was not political but that they were protesting the poor judging and organization of the events, and that things had improved after the protests. Guam was selected as the next host of the Games but only after an apology was made to the French.

The group responsible for the organization of the fifth South Pacific Games in Guam was the AAU (Amateur Athletic Union) of the U.S., based in Indianapolis. Guam's Governor Camacho announced in February 1973 that Guam would not be able to host the games due to U.S. President Richard Nixon's announced budget cutbacks. In June, Camacho was convinced to change his mind and the games went on as scheduled in 1975.

Rainy weather disrupted the schedules for many of the events, and the marathon was started at 4 A.M. to escape the heat of the day.

The 1979 games were held once again in Suva, Fiji. They had originally been awarded to the New Hebrides during meetings in Guam at the 1975 games. However, the New Hebrides, the Solomon Islands and Guam all bid for them, but technically all three bids were illegal according to the South Pacific Games charter. New Hebrides and Solomon Islands submitted their bids the week of the meetings, instead of three months ahead as required. Fiji volunteered to host the games in 1979 rather than 1978, and was the eventual selection.

A record 2700 athletes from twenty nations competed in the 1983 games in Apia, Western Samoa, which were opened by the head of state, Susuga Malietoa Tanumafili II. The event gave Western Samoa an opportunity to upgrade its outdated sports facilities, with China supplying labor and expertise to help build a gymnasium, football fields, and an all-weather track at the Apia Park Complex. The boxing venue was a large converted storage shed on the city's wharf which was made to seat 5,000 spectators. Australia, New Zealand, Canada and the United States (through the Peace Corps and U.S. Army) supported the games by providing funds, personnel, food and equipment.

The male athletes were housed at the Malifa Education Compound, while the women had their own village at Samoa College.

In 1991, the games were held in Port Moresby which was under curfew at the time due to the general unrest and violence in the Papua New Guinea capital.

The 1995 games in Papeete, Tahiti, were boycotted by a number of nations due to France's continued testing of nuclear weapons in Tahiti.

The 1999 games were held in Guam for the second time, with stunning South Pacific sunsets gracing the opening and closing ceremonies.

The New Caledonians, as they had been several times before, were winners of the overall medals race in 1999. The individual stars of the games were Oliver Saminadin, who won 12 gold medals and one silver in swimming, and Fiji's Caroline Pickering, who won six gold medals in athletics. Nauru continued its tradition of weightlifting prowess. Ten-year-old Cyrine Sam was the games' youngest competitor, participating in table tennis.

Avoiding the controversies of the past, the organizers made Sunday June 6 a day off from competition in 1999.

Suva, Fiji, is scheduled to be the host of the 2003 games.

Year	Host City	Host Nation	Dates	Nations	Athletes	Sports
1963	Suva	Fiji	Aug. 29–Sept. 7	13	646	9
1966	Nouméa	New Caledonia	December 8–18	14	1182	12
1969	Port Moresby	Papua New Guinea	August 13–23	12	1154	15
1971	Papeete	Tahiti	September 8–19	14	1350	17
1975	Tumon	Guam	August 1–10	13	NA	17
1979	Suva	Fiji	Aug. 27–Sept. 8	19	NA	NA
1983	Apia	Western Samoa	September 5–16	20	2700	13
1987	Nouméa	New Caledonia		NA	NA	NA
1991	Port Moresby/Lae	Papua New Guinea	Sept. 2–23	16	NA	17
1995	Papeete	Tahiti	August 12–26	NA	NA	NA
1999	Agana	Guam	May 29–June 12	21	2591	24

1963   Suva   Fiji   August 29–September 7

Nations: American Samoa, Cook Islands, Fiji, French Polynesia, Gilbert and Ellice Islands, Nauru, New Caledonia, New Hebrides, Niue, Papua New Guinea, Solomon Islands, Tonga, Western Samoa

Sports: Athletics, Basketball, Boxing, Football, Rugby, Swimming, Table Tennis, Tennis, Volleyball

Sports for Women: Athletics, Basketball, Swimming, Volleyball

Venues: Buckhurst Park (Opening Ceremony, Closing Ceremony, Athletics, Football, Rugby, Men's Basketball), Albert Park (Women's Volleyball, Women's Basketball), Suva Town Hall (Boxing), Suva Sea Baths (Swimming) Recreation Hall, LDS Church (Table Tennis)

MEDALS

Nation	Gold	Silver	Bronze	Total
Fiji	34	23	27	84
Papua New Guinea	9	12	11	32
New Caledonia	7	9	11	27
French Polynesia	4	2	4	10
Tonga	2	4	2	8
Cook Islands	2	3	0	5
American Samoa	1	2	4	7
Western Samoa	0	1	2	3
Gilbert and Ellice Islands	0	1	1	2
New Hebrides	0	1	0	1

1966 Nouméa New Caledonia December 8–18

Nations: American Samoa, Cook Islands, Fiji, French Polynesia, Gilbert and Ellice Islands, Guam, Nauru, New Caledonia, New Hebrides, Papua New Guinea, Solomon Islands, Tonga, Wallis and Futuna, Western Samoa

Sports: Athletics, Basketball, Boxing, Cycling, Football, Netball, Rugby, Swimming, Table Tennis, Tennis, Volleyball, Weightlifting

Sports for Women: Athletics, Basketball, Netball, Swimming, Table Tennis, Tennis, Volleyball

MEDALS

Nation	Gold	Silver	Bronze	Total
New Caledonia	39	30	30	99
Fiji	19	23	17	59
French Polynesia	13	8	9	30
Papua New Guinea	5	11	13	29
Western Samoa	4	4	0	8
Nauru	4	2	0	6
American Samoa	1	4	1	6
Tonga	1	0	1	2
Wallis and Futuna	0	2	12	14
New Hebrides	0	0	2	2
Cook Islands	0	1	0	1
Guam	0	0	1	1
Solomon Islands	0	0	1	1

1969 Port Moresby Papua New Guinea August 13–23

Nations: American Samoa, Fiji, French Polynesia, Guam, Nauru, New Caledonia, New Hebrides, Papua New Guinea, Solomon Islands, Tonga, Wallis and Futuna, Western Samoa

Sports: Athletics, Basketball, Boxing, Cycling, Football, Golf, Judo, Netball, Rugby, Swimming, Table Tennis, Tennis, Volleyball, Weightlifting, Yachting

Sports for Women: Athletics, Basketball, Golf, Netball, Swimming, Table Tennis, Tennis, Volleyball

Venues: Sir Hubert Murray Stadium (Athletics, Football), Borko Recreation Reserve (Boxing, Rugby, Netball, Volleyball), Borko Tennis Club (Tennis), Lae Golf Course (Golf), Olympic Pool at Taurama Road (Swimming), Murray Barracks Main Hall (Table Tennis), Murray Barracks Gymnasium (Weightlifting), Taurama Barracks Main Hall (Judo), Paga Point, Fairfax Harbour (Yachting)

MEDALS

Nation	Gold	Silver	Bronze	Total
New Caledonia	36	20	21	77
Papua New Guinea	23	23	18	64
Fiji	13	18	25	56
French Polynesia	8	11	13	32
Tonga	6	4	2	12
Western Samoa	4	4	1	9
Wallis and Futuna	1	5	1	7

Nation	Gold	Silver	Bronze	Total
New Hebrides	1	4	2	7
Nauru	1	2	4	7
Guam	1	3	2	6
American Samoa	1	0	5	6
Solomon Islands	0	2	1	3

1971   Papeete   Tahiti   September 8–19

Nations: American Samoa, Cook Islands, Fiji, French Polynesia, Gilbert and Ellice Islands, Guam, Nauru, New Caledonia, New Hebrides, Papua New Guinea, Solomon Islands, Tonga, Wallis and Futuna, Western Samoa

Sports: Archery, Athletics, Basketball, Boxing, Cycling, Football, Golf, Judo, Rugby, Spearfishing, Swimming, Table Tennis, Tennis, Volleyball, Weightlifting, Yachting (one more)

Sports for Women: Athletics, Basketball, Golf, Swimming, Table Tennis, Tennis, Volleyball

Venues: Pater Olympic Stadium (Athletics), Fautae Stadium (Cycling, Basketball, Volleyball, Rugby, Football, Tennis), Tipaerui Hall (Volleyball), Olympic Pool, Tipaerui (Swimming), Maison des Jeunes (Weightlifting), Mormon Mission (Judo), Mormon School (Table Tennis), St. Paul's Roman Catholic Hall (Basketball), Atimaono Golf Course (Golf)

MEDALS

Nation	Gold	Silver	Bronze	Total
New Caledonia	33	32	27	92
Papua New Guinea	28	28	21	77
French Polynesia	22	24	24	70
Fiji	16	17	13	46
Western Samoa	9	3	5	17
Tonga	4	3	4	11
Guam	3	3	8	14
Wallis and Futuna	2	1	6	9
American Samoa	0	2	12	14
Solomon Islands	0	2	2	4
New Hebrides	0	1	4	5
Cook Islands	0	1	3	4

1975   Tumon   Guam   August 1–10

Nations: American Samoa, Fiji, French Polynesia, Guam, Micronesia, Nauru, New Caledonia, New Hebrides, Papua New Guinea, Solomon Islands, Tonga, Wallis & Futuna, Western Samoa

Sports: Archery, Athletics, Basketball, Boxing, Football, Golf, Judo, Rugby, Softball, Spearfishing, Swimming, Table Tennis, Tennis, Volleyball, Weightlifting, Yachting (one more)

Sports for Women: Athletics, Basketball, Golf, Softball, Swimming, Table Tennis, Tennis, Volleyball

Venues: John F. Kennedy High School (Athletics, Table Tennis), Northwest Field (Cycling), Desedo Junior High (Judo, Weightlifting), George Washington Senior High

School (Basketball, Football), Agueda Johnson Junior High School (Archery), Windward Hills Club (Tennis), Notre Dame High (Volleyball), Country Club of the Pacific (Golf), Apra Harbor (Yachting), Guam Recreation Center (Boxing), Paseo de Susana Park (Softball), Agana Swimming Pool (Swimming)

MEDALS

Nation	Gold	Silver	Bronze	Total
New Caledonia	37	31	34	102
French Polynesia	27	28	39	94
Papua New Guinea	22	25	18	65
Fiji	13	13	11	37
Western Samoa	9	4	5	18
Guam	3	5	5	13
American Samoa	3	4	5	12
Tonga	2	1	1	4
New Hebrides	1	3	4	8
Wallis and Futuna	1	2	8	11
Solomon Islands	1	2	3	6
Micronesia	0	2	0	2
Nauru	0	0	1	1

1979   Suva   Fiji   August 27–September 8

Nations: American Samoa, Cook Islands, Fiji, Gilbert Islands, Guam, Nauru, New Caledonia, New Hebrides, Northern Marianas, Niue, Papua New Guinea, Solomon Islands, Tahiti, Tokelau, Tonga, Tuvalu, Vanuatu, Western Samoa, Wallis and Futuna
Sports: Athletics, Basketball, Boxing, Cricket, Football, Field Hockey, Golf, Judo, Lawn Bowls, Netball, Rugby, Squash, Swimming, Table Tennis, Tennis, Weightlifting, Volleyball, Yachting

1983   Apia   Western Samoa   September 5–16

Nations: American Samoa, Cook Islands, Fiji, French Polynesia, Guam, Nauru, Niue, New Caledonia, Norfolk Island, Northern Marianas, Papua New Guinea, Solomon Islands, Tahiti, Tokelau, Tonga, Vanuatu, Wallis and Futuna, Western Samoa (2 more)
Sports: Athletics, Basketball, Bowling, Boxing, Golf, Netball, Rugby, Soccer, Squash, Table Tennis, Tennis, Volleyball, Weightlifting
Venues: Apia Sports Complex (Basketball, Bowling, Netball, Rugby, Soccer, Tennis, Volleyball), Apia Park Stadium (Athletics), Feiloaimauso Hall (Weightlifting), Apia Wharf Customs Shed (Boxing), Royal Samoan Country Golf Club (Golf), C.C.W.S. (Volleyball), LDS Hall, Lotopa (Table Tennis), Squash Center (Squash), (Villages—Malifa Compound, Men; Samoa College, Women; USP Alafua, Officials)

1991   Port Moresby-Lae
Papua New Guinea   September 2–23

Nations: American Samoa, Cook Islands, Fiji, French Polynesia, Guam, Nauru,

New Caledonia, Norfolk Island, Northern Marianas, Niue, Papua New Guinea, Solomon Islands, Tonga, Western Samoa, Vanuatu, Wallis and Futuna

Sports: Athletics, Basketball, Boxing, Cricket, Golf, Lawn Bowls, Lawn Tennis, Netball, Rugby, Soccer, Softball, Squash, Swimming, Table Tennis, Volleyball, Weightlifting, Yachting (Boardsailing and Hobie Cat)

1999   Agana   Guam   May 29–June 12

Nations: American Samoa, Cook Islands, Federated States of Micronesia, Fiji, Guam, Kiribati, Marshall Islands, Nauru, New Caledonia, Niue, Norfolk Island, Northern Marianas, Palau, Papua New Guinea, Solomon Islands, Tahiti, Tonga, Tuvalu, Vanuatu, Wallis and Futuna, Western Samoa

Sports: Athletics, Archery, Body Building, Basketball, Boxing, Canoeing/Outrigger, Cycling, Golf, Judo, Karate, Lawn Tennis, Netball, Sailing, Softball, Football (Soccer), Surfing, Swimming, Tae Kwon Do, Triathlon, Table Tennis, Underwater Fishing, Volleyball, Weightlifting, Wrestling

MEDALS

Nation	Gold	Silver	Bronze	Total
New Caledonia	72	54	44	170
Nauru	27	8	7	42
Tahiti	26	18	34	78
Fiji	22	32	37	91
Papua New Guinea	19	31	34	84
Western Samoa	19	9	4	32
Guam	14	32	26	72
American Samoa	7	3	5	15
Fed. St. of Micronesia	4	2	6	12
Solomon Islands	3	6	12	21
Wallis and Futuna	3	6	11	20
Vanuatu	2	8	12	22
N. Marianas	2	6	8	16
Tonga	2	3	10	15
Norfolk Island	1	0	1	2
Palau	0	7	3	10
Kiribati	0	3	3	6
Marshall Islands	0	2	5	7
Cook Islands	0	1	0	1
Tuvalu	0	0	0	0
Niue	0	0	0	0

South Pacific Mini Games

The first two editions of the South Pacific Mini Games were held in Honiara, Solomon Islands, in 1981 and Rarotonga, Cook Islands, in 1985. At the third edition in 1989 in Nukualofa, Tonga, the International Olympic Committee sanctioned the games as an official regional games. Port Vila, Vanuatu, hosted the 1993 games. On each occasion, the South Pacific Mini Games has provided the first opportunity for each of the small nations to host an international games.

The games invite the smallest of the South Pacific nations, giving them a chance for equitable competition, and a chance to host an international event of a manageable scale.

Despite the games' size, they are attended by each nations' dignitaries. King Taufa'ahua Tupov IV opened the games in Tonga in 1989, while Tonga's Princess Pilolevu as president of Tonga's National Olympic Committee also served as head of the games organizing committee. France and Taiwan assisted the Tongans in preparing facilities for the games.

Organizing a games for the first time has its difficulties. The 1997 games in Pago Pago, American Samoa, were reported to have been disorganized because the hosts, although they had been awarded the games in 1991, left most of the preparations until the year of the event. Poor advertising of the games meant that few people showed up for the opening ceremonies, even though Miss South Pacific, Ah Ching of Western Samoa, led the athletes in the march into the stadium. Some 3000 people, reportedly a much larger crowd than at the opening, showed up for the closing ceremonies.

The other nations did not make it easy on the organizers by canceling their participation in some of the team events, throwing the scheduling into chaos. Tahiti, Papua New Guinea, Wallis and Futuna and Tonga all dropped out of the rugby sevens competition. Guam, Tonga, Palau and Papua New Guinea dropped out of women's volleyball. The team from Guam pulled out as a direct result of the crash of a Korean airliner in Guam. The plane was supposed to be their transportation to the games.

In men's volleyball, Kiribati, Niue, Papua New Guinea, Palau and Tonga withdrew. Kiribati and Wallis and Futuna ended up sending no athletes to the games.

All of this led to the event being called the most disorganized South Pacific Mini Games ever. South Pacific Mini Games secretary Vidyha Lakhan disputed the press reports and said the difficulties were normal for any event of this type, but others concurred with the press reports including the President of Guam's Olympic Committee who said that he was disappointed that at the opening ceremonies the flagpoles for the participating nations' banners had not been made ready in time.

In the end most of the athletes made do and enjoyed the games. Fiji won 91 total medals to lead all nations.

The 2001 games were scheduled for Norfolk Island.

Year	Host City	Host Nation	Dates	Nations	Athletes	Sports
1981	Honiara	Solomon Islands		NA	NA	NA
1985	Rarotonga	Cook Islands		NA	NA	NA
1989	Nukualofa	Tonga	Aug. 22–Sept. 1	16	832	6
1993	Port Vila	Vanuatu		NA	NA	NA
1997	Pago Pago	American Samoa	August 12–26	17	NA	11

1989   Nukualofa   Tonga   August 22–September 1

Sports: Athletics, Boxing, Golf, Netball, Tennis, Weightlifting
Venues: Atele Multipurpose Gymnasium and Tennis Courts

1997   Pago Pago   American Samoa   August 12–26

Nations: American Samoa, Cook Islands, Federated States of Micronesia, Fiji, Guam, Nauru, New Caledonia, Niue, Norfolk Island, Northern Marianas, Palau, Papua New Guinea, Solomon Islands, French Polynesia, Tonga, Vanuatu, Western Samoa

Sports: Athletics, Basketball, Boxing, Golf, Netball, Powerlifting, Rugby 7s, Tennis, Volleyball, Weightlifting, Yachting

Sports for Women: Athletics, Basketball, Golf, Netball, Powerlifting, Tennis, Volleyball, Weightlifting, Yachting

Venues: Veterans Stadium, Tafuna (Opening Ceremonies, Closing Ceremonies, Athletics, Rugby 7s), ASCC Gymnasium, Malaeimi (Basketball), Tafuna High School (Boxing), Ililli Golf Course (Golf), Tafuna Park, Tafuna (Netball), Lee Auditorium, Utulei (Powerlifting, Weightlifting), Lions Park, Tafuna (Tennis), Kanana Fou, Tafuna (Volleyball), Utulei Beach Park, Utulei (Yachting)

Special Olympics

The Special Olympics have developed from one person's dreams and efforts into a movement that has, in 25 years, inspired over 500,000 volunteers to help with sports competitions for those with mental disabilities around the world.

Eunice Kennedy Shriver (sister to U.S. President John F. Kennedy) in the summer of 1963 started a summer day camp at her home in Maryland, with the goal to help develop the physical capabilities of those with mental handicaps. In five years' time, this idea had spawned a movement, and activities for athletes with mental disabilities were being held across the United States.

In 1968, the Kennedy Foundation financed the very first Special Olympics (also known as the Special Olympics Summer World Games) held in 1970 at Soldier Field in Chicago in July. It was international in that athletes from 26 U.S. states and Canada took part in three sports: track and field, floor hockey, and aquatics.

"Let me win, but if I cannot win, let me be brave in the attempt," has become the motto for the Special Olympics movement. Medals are awarded to all athletes and no anthems or flags are used at the medal ceremonies. Medal tables are not kept at the Special Olympics.

The second Special Olympics Summer World Games were again held in 1970 at Soldier Field in Chicago with 2000 athletes, representing all 50 states, France and Puerto Rico. A year later, the U.S. Olympic Committee gave the Special Olympics the uncommon privilege of being able to use the word "Olympic" in its name.

The games grew, with ten nations in 1975 and twenty in 1979. Along with the increased international participation came some of the political issues that have affected other games. In 1983 at the games in Baton Rouge, Louisiana, the team from Taiwan did not take part after a dispute over whether their delegation should be called Chinese Taipei, the name they preferred, or Taiwan, Republic of China, the name declared by the Kennedy Foundation.

The movement continued to gain prestige over the years with 1986-87 declared the International Year of the Special Olympics by the United Nations. In 1988, the Special Olympics were endorsed by the International Olympic Committee when it allowed them to officially use the Olympic name, reinforcing the agreement that Special Olympics International had negotiated with the United States Olympic Committee in 1971.

Over the years, the Kennedy Foundation has been able to garner support from numerous sports and entertainment celebrities. At the 1991 games in Minneapolis-St. Paul, sports stars such as Wayne Gretzky, Pelé, Dick Fosbury, Nadia Comaneci, Bart Conner, John Naber and Florence Griffith-Joyner gave clinics for the Special Olympians.

The Special Olympics have grown into one of the world's largest international multisport gatherings, with over 7000 athletes and 140 nations competing at the 1995 games in New Haven, Connecticut. Special Olympics International now has programs in over 150 nations and has begun to branch out into regional Special Olympic competitions. European Special Olympics have been held since 1981. Since 1996, regional games have been held in West Africa, the Mediterranean, the Arab Gulf, and the Asia Pacific region. A Special Olympics Small Nations Games has also been staged. Special Olympics International is still in the process of deciding whether these games will be organized on an ongoing basis.

One of the goals of Special Olympics International has always been to try as much as possible to integrate those with mental handicaps into everyday life. The Unified Sports program was begun in 1987 to combine those with and without mental handicaps into one team. The program is designed to give confidence to those athletes with disabilities and help the athletes without disabilities to learn about those with mental handicaps. In some instances, however, the program has allowed nonhandicapped athletes to participate while handicapped athletes stayed home, prompting the coaches and administrators to consider making adjustments to the program so that every handicapped athlete would be able to compete.[210]

Raleigh-Durham, North Carolina, served as the host for the 1999 Special Olympics Summer World Games.

The Special Olympics torch was lit in Athens, Greece, on May 5 and relayed around the Greek capital. The torch arrived in North Carolina on June 20 and was relayed to over 100 cities and towns throughout the state, finally arriving in Raleigh on June 26 for the opening ceremony.

The games took place under a broiling Raleigh-Durham sun, but the North Carolina hosts did their best to ensure that it was the best Special Olympics ever.

Over one third of the athletes came from the United States, a percentage expected to drop when the games are held in Dublin, Ireland, in the year 2003. While U.S. participation may drop, European participation may rise accordingly, as this will be the very first time that the Special Olympics World Summer Games will be held outside the United States.

At the closing ceremony of the North Carolina games, a moment of silence was observed to acknowledge three individuals, a volunteer, an athlete and an organizer, who died during the games. Neale Orrok, a 62-year-old volunteer, died after assisting at the opening ceremonies. Mohamed Abdul Baset Barin, a 14-year-old athlete from Egypt, died of an epileptic seizure. Michael Hooker, chancellor of the University of North Carolina and on the board of directors for the Special Olympics, died after a long bout with cancer.

With 7,000 athletes and some 400,000 spectators over the course of the event, the games were the largest to date. They worked, but pushed the limits of what could realistically be done, according to the organizers. In response to this, Special Olympics International discussed plans to continue the regionalization of the Special Olympics to make the size of each games more manageable.

Nearly all of the over 150 nations that sponsor Special Olympics programs hold national games. Many times, athletes from several other nations will be invited to participate, making these events international in scope though national in name.

Year	Host City	Host Nation	Dates	Nations	Athletes	Sports
1968	Chicago	USA	July 19–20	2	1000	3
1970	Chicago	USA	August 13–15	3	2000	3
1972	Los Angeles	USA	August 13–18	NA	2500	NA
1975	Mt. Pleasant	USA	August 7–11	10	3200	NA
1979	Brockport	USA	August 8–13	20	3500	NA
1983	Baton Rouge	USA	July 12–18	NA	4000	NA
1987	South Bend	USA	July 31–Aug. 8	70	4700	NA
1991	Minneapolis	USA	July 19–27	100	6000	16
1995	New Haven	USA	July 1–9	140	7000	21
1999	Raleigh-Durham	USA	June 26–July 4	147	7000	18

1968   Chicago   USA   July 19–20

Nations: Canada, United States
Sports: Athletics, Floor Hockey, Aquatics
Venues: Soldier Field

1970   Chicago   USA   August 13–15

Nations: France, United States
Venues: Soldier Field

1987   South Bend   USA   July 31–August 8

Sports: Athletics, Aquatics, Basketball, Bowling, Gymnastics, Soccer, Softball, Volleyball (demonstration sports—Cycling, Equestrian, Roller-skating, Table tennis, Tennis, Weightlifting)

1995   New Haven   USA   July 1–9

Sports: Athletics, Aquatics, Badminton, Basketball, Bocce, Bowling, Croquet, Cycling, Equestrian, Football, Golf, Gymnastics, Powerlifting, Roller-skating, Rowing, Sailing, Softball, Table Tennis, Team Handball, Tennis, Volleyball

1999   Raleigh-Durham
USA   June 26–July 4

Sports: Aquatics, Athletics, Badminton, Bocci, Bowling, Cycling, Equestrian, Football, Golf, Gymnastics, Handball, Powerlifting, Sailing, Skating, Softball, Table Tennis, Tennis, Volleyball

Special Olympics Asia-Pacific Games

Year	Host City	Host Nation	Dates	Nations	Athletes	Sports
1996	Shanghai	China	Nov. 8–11	15	750	5

Nations: Bangladesh, China, Chinese Taipei, Hong Kong, India, Indonesia, Japan, Korea, Macao, Malaysia, Nepal, Pakistan, Philippines, Singapore, Thailand
Sports: Athletics, Basketball, Football, Swimming, Table Tennis
Venues: Shanghai Stadium (Opening Ceremonies)

Special Olympics Gulf Games

Year	Host City	Host Nation	Dates	Nations	Athletes	Sports
1996	Abu Dhabi	United Arab Emirates	Nov. 1–10	NA	NA	NA
1998	Doha	Qatar	Nov. 21–26	6	NA	NA

Special Olympics Mediterranean Games

Year	Host City	Host Nation	Dates	Nations	Athletes	Sports
1998	Athens	Greece	April 6–10	24	5	NA

1998   Athens   Greece   April 6–10

Nations: Albania, Algeria, Austria, Azerbaijan, Belgium, Bulgaria, Cyprus, Denmark, Egypt, France, Germany, Greece, Italy, Jordan, Lebanon, Morocco, Palestine, Romania, San Marino, Saudi Arabia, Slovenia, Spain, Syria, United Kingdom
Sports: Athletics, Basketball, Football, Swimming, Table Tennis
Venues: Olympic Indoor Basketball Hall (Opening Ceremonies)

Special Olympics Small Nations Games

Year	Host City	Host Nation	Dates	Nations	Athletes	Sports
1996	Monte Carlo	Monaco	May 10–12	NA	NA	NA

Special Olympics West African Games

Year	Host City	Host Nation	Dates	Nations	Athletes	Sports
1996	Abidjan	Ivory Coast		NA	NA	NA

Special Olympics Winter World Games

In 1977, nine years after the establishment of the Special Olympics Summer Games, the first winter games for athletes with mental retardation and mental disabilities were held in Steamboat Springs, Colorado, with 500 athletes competing in two sports, skiing and skating.

Four years later, in 1981, Olympic speed-skating star Eric Heiden was honorary head coach of the second Special Olympic Winter World Games in Smugglers Cove and Stowe, Vermont.

The third games in Park City, Utah, in 1985 saw a total of fourteen nations competing, and the fourth games in Reno in 1991 saw 18 nations take part.

The first winter games held outside the U.S. were in Salzburg/Schladming, Austria, in 1993. The games returned to North America in 1997 when a record 2000 athletes from eighty nations competed in seven sports in Toronto and the Collingwood area of Canada. Nadia Comaneci and Kerri Strug were on hand to give a special gymnastics demonstration to the athletes in Toronto.

An international team of police officers from twenty-five countries carried the Special Olympics flame, which was lit in Athens, Greece, and after reaching Toronto, was carried around Canada in a 100 mile relay for five days before the games.

As the games have grown, they have taken on the elements of all major international sports gatherings. Pin trading has become one of the most popular sports at the games, and "Olympic Town" provides games and entertainment for the athletes when they are not competing.

Special Olympics International also arranged for dental and eye exams for some of the international athletes while they were in Toronto. Many of them had had little access to medical and dental care in their own countries.

Special Olympics International goes out of its way to make sure everyone can participate. When the Kuwaiti floor hockey team showed up with one short of the number required for a full team, organizers agreed to bend the rules and arranged a special rotation for the Kuwaiti team, in their first winter Special Olympics appearance.

Consistent with the summer games, medals are awarded but no anthems or flags are used at the medal ceremonies and medal tables are not kept.

Anchorage, Alaska, outbid Salt Lake City, Vail, and Lake Placid for the privilege of hosting the 2001 Special Olympics Winter World Games.

Year	Host City	Host Nation	Dates	Nations	Athletes	Sports
1977	Steamboat Springs	USA	February 5–11	NA	500	2
1981	Smugglers Cove	USA	March 8–13	NA	600	3
1985	Park City	USA	March 24–29	14	NA	2
1989	Reno	USA	April 1–8	18	1000	NA
1993	Salzburg/Schladming	Austria		50	1600	5
1997	Toronto/Collingwood	Canada	February 7–11	80	2000	7

1977   Steamboat Springs   USA   February 5–11

Sports: Skiing, Skating

1981   Smugglers Cove   USA   March 8–13

Sports: Alpine Skiing, Cross-country Skiing, Ice Skating

1985   Park City   USA   March 24–29

Sports: Skiing, Skating

1997   Toronto/Collingwood   Canada   February 7–11

Sports: Alpine Skiing, Cross Country Skiing, Eistocksport, Figure Skating, Floor Hockey, Snowshoeing, Speed Skating
Venues: Toronto Skydome (Opening Ceremonies)

Stockholm Summer Games

The city of Stockholm, in the midst of its bid for the 2004 Olympic Games, instituted a competition for young athletes called the Stockholm Summer Games. The games are open to any youth aged 10 to 18. The first edition of the games was held in 1996 with approximately 6000 participants, and the event has been an annual one since that time. The games of 1998 provided competition in 20 sports, and offered the participants rare opportunities to compete in motocross and minigolf at an international level. The athletic events give young athletes the chance to compete in the 1912 Olympic Stadium.

The participants pay their own way to the games and Stockholm's elementary schools are used as housing for the event. Registration fees provide for lodging, food, and transportation during the games. Fun activities are important and include a disco where kids from all over the world teach each other the latest moves and vote on who has the coolest hairdo of the games.

Despite losing out on the bid for the 2004 Olympic Games, Stockholm plans to keep its summer youth games on the schedule.

Year	Host City	Host Nation	Dates	Nations	Athletes	Sports
1996	Stockholm	Sweden	July*	NA	6000	NA
1997	Stockholm	Sweden	June 29–July 5	NA	9000*	19
1998	Stockholm	Sweden	June 28–July 4	16	10000*	20
1999	Stockholm	Sweden	July 4–10	NA	NA	NA
2000	Stockholm	Sweden	July 2–8	NA	NA	16

*Pregames estimates of participation.

1997   Stockholm   Sweden   June 29–July 5

Sports: Athletics, Badminton, Basketball, Beach Volleyball, Bowling, Canoeing, Equestrian sports, Floorball, Golf, Gymnastics, Handball, Motocross, Mountain Biking, Orienteering, Soccer, Swimming, Table Tennis, Tae Kwon Do, Wrestling
Venues: Stockholm Olympiastadion (Opening Ceremonies, Athletics), Stockholm Badmintonhall in Stockholm (Badminton), Gärdets Sportsfield (Beach Volleyball), Enskede Bowlingcenter, Stockholm (Bowling), Lake Norrviken, Sollentuna (Canoeing), Ryttarstadion (Equestrian Sports), various golf courses in the Stockholm

region, (Golf), Åkeshovshallen in Stockholm (Gymnastics), Gärdets Sportsfield in Stockholm (Handball), Barkarby Motorstadium (Motocross), Grimsta Sportsfield, Spånga in Stockholm (Mountain Biking), Northern Stockholm (Orienteering), a total of 20 grass pitches (Soccer). No venues listed (Basketball, Floorball, Swimming, Tables Tennis, Tae Kwon Do, Wrestling)

1998   Stockholm   Sweden   June 28–July 4

Nations: Brazil, Belarus, Colombia, Denmark, Finland, Guatemala, Estonia, Latvia, Norway, Pakistan, Poland, Russia, Sweden, USA, Taiwan, Turkey
Sports: Athletics, Badminton, Basketball, Beach Volleyball, Bowling, Canoeing, Equestrian Sport, Frisbee, Golf, Gymnastics, Handball, Inline Skating, Minigolf, Motocross, Orienteering, Soccer, Swimming, Tae Kwon Do, Volleyball, Wrestling
Venues: Sergels Torg (Opening Ceremonies), Stockholm Olympiastadion (Athletics), Stockholm Badminton Hall (Badminton), Brannkyrkahallen (Basketball), Gärdet Sportsfield (Beach Volleyball, Frisbee, Handball), Enskede Bowling Center (Bowling), Magelungen (Canoeing), Ryttarstadion (Equestrian Sport), various golf courses (Golf), Akeshovshallen (Gymnastics), Centrala Stockholm (Inline Skating), Ersta MGK (Minigolf), Barkarby Motorstadion (Motocross), North Stockholm (Orienteering), Spånga Sportsfield, Grimsta Sportsfield, Hasselby IP, Angby IP, Glantans IP, Akeshovs IP, Hjorthagen IP, Bromstens IP, Kristinebergs IP, Soderstadion (Football), Erikdalsbadet (Swimming), Forsgrenska Hallen (Tae Kwon Do), Solnhallen (Volleyball), Enskedehallen (Wrestling)

2000   Stockholm   Sweden   July 2–8

Sports: Archery, Athletics, Beach Volleyball, Bowling, Football, Frisbee, Golf, Gymnastics, Inline Skating, Judo, Minigolf, Motocross, Orienteering, Swimming, Triathlon, Wrestling

Stoke Mandeville Wheelchair Games

A defining moment in international sports occurred when Dr. Ludwig Guttman was asked by the British government to begin a special center at the Stoke Mandeville Hospital in Buckinghamshire, England, for service personnel from World War II who had suffered spinal cord injuries.

From 1944 to 1948, Dr. Guttman integrated general rehabilitative sports activities into the treatment of the injured servicemen. After the war, when the Olympics were to resume and were to be held in London, Dr. Guttman was inspired to hold a competition for the patients in his program and the Stoke Mandeville Games, the first a very modest affair, were born. On July 28, one day before the 1948 London Olympic opening ceremonies, sixteen athletes from Stoke Mandeville and the Star and Garter Home for disabled servicemen competed in an archery tournament. Groups from five hospitals competed the following year, and the annual games had truly begun.

In 1952, the games became international for the first time with participation from the Netherlands. One hundred and thirty competitors took part. By the tenth edition, in 1957, 360 athletes from 24 nations were competing at Stoke Mandeville. Rules and regulations were drawn up by the International Stoke Mandeville Games Federation (ISMGF) and modified on an annual basis.

The games took a leap forward in 1960 when the organizers, on the proposal of Professor Antonio Maglio, director of the INAIL Spinal Injuries Centre in Rome, Italy, shifted the venue from Stoke Mandeville to Rome, the site of the 1960 Olympic Games. These would eventually be called the first Paralympics. For several editions, the terms Stoke Mandeville Wheelchair Games and Paralympics were both used to describe the editions of the games which were held during Olympic years. In Rome, the athletes were housed in the Olympic Village and used the same sports facilities as the Olympic games participants. A private audience with the Pope was part of the experience for the athletes in Rome.

The games returned on an annual basis to Stoke Mandeville the following three years and in 1964 were held in Tokyo, Japan. Though the intent was to have the Paralympics use the very same facilities in the same city as the Olympic Games, either just before or after, this has proven to be difficult on a number of occasions. In 1968, the Paralympics were held in Tel Aviv, Israel, when it was determined that the high altitude of Mexico City would cause concerns for the athletes.

The British Paraplegic Sports Society in 1968 decided to build a permanent stadium at Stoke Mandeville to use for the games, the first stadium of its kind dedicated and designed specifically for wheelchair and other disabled athletes. Queen Elizabeth II dedicated the facility, the Stoke Mandeville Sports Stadium, on August 2, 1969, and except for Olympic years, the Stoke Mandeville Wheelchair Games have been held in this stadium every year since it was built.

In 1972, Heidelberg, West Germany, hosted the games, with the 1976 edition in Toronto, Canada. The games had to that point been primarily for athletes with spinal cord injuries, competing in wheelchairs. In 1976, the ISMGF invited athletes from ISOD, the International Sports Organization for the Disabled, to join the games. This opened the event to blind athletes and those with cerebral palsy. When Moscow was unable to host the 1980 edition, Arnhem, Netherlands, accepted the assignment. The ISOD, undergoing further development, spawned two more branches: the Cerebral Palsy-International Sports and Recreation Association (CP-ISRA), and IBSA, the International Blind Sports Association. In 1982, the four federations formed a coalition, the International Coordinating Committee (ICC) to coordinate games and championships that would have more than one organization present. In 1986, the ICC admitted two more disabled sports organizations: CISS (the Comité International des Sports des Sourds), the organization overseeing sports for the deaf, and INAS-FMH, the International Sports Federation for Persons with Mental Handicap. The 1988 games in Seoul, Korea, were the first to be organized under the guidance of the ICC.

In 1984, financial difficulties split the event into two parts. The games for the athletes of the ISOD, IBSA and CP-ISRA were held in New York, with U.S. President Ronald Reagan presiding over the opening ceremonies. The wheelchair sports were scheduled to be held in Illinois but had to be switched at the last minute back to Stoke Mandeville's Ludwig Guttman Sports Centre. Prince Charles, the Prince of Wales opened these games. With 1750 athletes in the U.S., and 1100 in Great Britain, they were the largest to date.

Since 1988, the Paralympics have been held in the Olympic cities of Barcelona in

1992 and Atlanta in 1996, and the Stoke Mandeville Wheelchair Games have been held all non-summer Olympic years in England. In 1996, along with the Paralympic Games in Atlanta, the ISMWGF hosted a World Wheelchair Games in Stoke Mandeville, which was designed to be developmental and open to young, less-experienced athletes.

In 1999, the Stoke Mandeville Wheelchair Games broke with tradition and were held in Christchurch, New Zealand, instead of Stoke Mandeville and continued to be known as the World Wheelchair Games. The archery event in Christchurch was also the archery world championships for disabled shooters. New Zealand's 1982 Commonwealth Games archery champion, Neroli Fairhall, was a participant.

The 2000 Paralympic Games were held in Sydney, Australia.

Year	Host City	Host Nation	Dates	Nations	Athletes	Sports
1948	Buckinghamshire	England	July 28	1	16	1
1949	Buckinghamshire	England	[211]	1	NA	NA
1950	Buckinghamshire	England		1	NA	NA
1951	Buckinghamshire	England		1	NA	NA
1952	Buckinghamshire	England		2	130	NA
1953	Buckinghamshire	England		NA	NA	NA
1954	Buckinghamshire	England		NA	NA	NA
1955	Buckinghamshire	England		NA	NA	NA
1956	Buckinghamshire	England		NA	NA	NA
1957	Buckinghamshire	England		24	360	NA
1958	Buckinghamshire	England		NA	NA	NA
1959	Buckinghamshire	England		NA	NA	NA
1961	Buckinghamshire	England		NA	NA	NA
1962	Buckinghamshire	England		NA	NA	NA
1963	Buckinghamshire	England		20	371	NA
1965	Buckinghamshire	England	July 27–30	NA	NA	NA
1966	Buckinghamshire	England		NA	NA	NA
1967	Buckinghamshire	England		NA	NA	NA
1969	Buckinghamshire	England		NA	NA	NA
1970	Buckinghamshire	England		NA	NA	NA
1971	Buckinghamshire	England		NA	NA	NA
1973	Buckinghamshire	England		NA	NA	NA
1974	Buckinghamshire	England		NA	NA	NA
1975	Buckinghamshire	England		NA	NA	NA
1977	Buckinghamshire	England	July 23–31	NA	NA	4
1978	Buckinghamshire	England	July 22–30	NA	NA	NA
1979	Buckinghamshire	England	July 21–29	NA	NA	NA
1981	Buckinghamshire	England	July 25–Aug. 2	NA	NA	NA
1982	Buckinghamshire	England	July 24–Aug. 1	NA	NA	NA
1983	Buckinghamshire	England	July 23–31	NA	NA	NA
1985	Buckinghamshire	England	July 20–28	NA	NA	NA
1986	Buckinghamshire	England	July 19–27	NA	NA	NA
1987	Buckinghamshire	England	July 18–26	NA	NA	NA
1989	Buckinghamshire	England	July 22–30	NA	NA	NA
1990	Buckinghamshire	England	July 21–29	NA	NA	NA
1991	Buckinghamshire	England	July 20–28	NA	NA	NA
1993	Buckinghamshire	England	July 24–Aug. 1	NA	NA	NA
1994	Buckinghamshire	England	July 23–31	NA	NA	NA
1995	Buckinghamshire	England	July 22–30	NA	NA	NA

Year	Host City	Host Nation	Dates	Nations	Athletes	Sports
1996	Buckinghamshire	England		NA	NA	NA
1997	Buckinghamshire	England	July 27–Aug. 2	NA	NA	NA
1998	Buckinghamshire	England	Aug. 20–31	NA	NA	NA
1999	Christchurch	New Zealand	October 8–18	NA	NA	NA

Tailteann Games

The Tailteann Games, like the Olympic Games, have been both ancient and modern. While the modern revival of the Olympic games continues, the Tailteann revival was short-lived. As an "Irish Olympics," the modern Tailteann Games were open to citizens of Ireland or individuals of Irish extraction (at least one grandparent born in Ireland) throughout the world. The modern games not only had sporting events but also cultural exhibitions and competitions in music, singing, and a wide variety of dancing styles. Age groups made this a competition open to all.

Irish history records the ancient Tailteann Games (or Aonach Tailteann, meaning Public National Assembly) as having begun in 632 B.C.[212] The games were founded as funeral festivities upon the death of Queen Tailte, a royal princess who was married to Irish King Eochaidh Mac Erc and had come to Ireland from Spain. Tailte was said to be beautiful and educated, and to have learned every science and art in both Europe and the eastern world.

The Aonach, of which the Aonach Tailteann was one of many,[213] were first of all festivals used to honor the dead. A second function was as a forum to discuss law. After this business was complete, there followed a time of games and entertainment. The first days of the Aonach, one to three depending on the stature of the dead, were taken up with funeral rites. The days following, the king and the noblemen would teach and review the laws of the land so that each person understood his legal rights as well as his duties under the law.

The funeral games were the final part of the Aonach and included contests of athletic and gymnastic skill, equestrian events, hurling, quoit throwing, spear throwing, swordsmanship with shields, contests with slings and bows and arrows, wrestling, swimming, boxing, horse racing, chariot racing and pole jumping. Once established, the funeral games of the major Aonach were observed on an annual basis. Chiefs and military officers would attend the Aonach each year to recruit the best men into their armies. A strict truce was declared for the duration of the Aonach, and women, rather than being excluded as was the custom of the ancient Olympic games, were given places of honor at the event. As the Aonach Tailteann developed, it took on the aspects of a great fair, with all manner of goods sold. The games also included singing, dancing, music, oratory and literary contests, as well as competitions for artisans, goldsmiths, jewelers, makers of weapons, spinners, weavers and dyers.

One of the more curious aspects that developed from the Aonach Tailteann was that of matchmaking. Parents would assemble and find marriage matches for their children. If the marriage was not a satisfactory one, the couple could return the following year and through an elaborate and lengthy public ceremony, dissolve the union. One year and one day was the time allotted for this decision to be made, after this time the marriage was final.

Queen Tailte had chosen her burial place before her death on a hill some 12 miles from Teltown, and at this location the Aonach Tailteann lasted annually from 632 B.C. until 1169 A.D. It was always held in the first week of August. At its peak, the assembly grew so large that the crowds would extend in camps for seven miles across the Irish plains. After the Aonach Tailteann ended, the Teltown fair continued well into the 19th century.[214]

After the founding of the Irish Free State in 1921, the modern games were revived in 1924, by the suggestion and under the direction of Mr. J. J. Walsh, with Dublin as host. Many stars from the 1924 Paris Olympic Games, including sprinter Jackson Scholz (gold in the 200 meters, and silver in the 100 meters in Paris) and multievent star Harold Osborn (gold medals in the decathlon and high jump in Paris), traveled from Paris to Dublin to take part in the Tailteann Games which opened August 2, a week after the closing of the Olympic Games. In total, 3,000 people participated in the sports competitions, which ranged from motorcycling, golf and yachting, to the Irish sports of hurling and camogie. Most of the athletes were from Ireland, but Australia, Canada, England, Newfoundland, New Zealand, Scotland, South Africa, the United States and Wales were also represented. Another 3,500 people competed in the music, dancing and art competitions. The music competitions included contests for pipes, flutes, harps and fiddles, massed bands and solo and group singing. The dancing contests were numerous, including jigs, reels and caps, while the arts and crafts competitions included everything from painting to lingerie design. Some 100,000 spectators passed through the gates in sixteen days of competition, which meant that the games were able to pay for themselves.[215]

Internal political bickering threatened the games throughout their existence.[216] Eamon De Valera's party called for a boycott of the 1924 event, then complained bitterly when President Cosgrave ignored the games of 1928. Cosgrave declined to attend the opening ceremonies, choosing instead to attend horse races at Phoenix Park and a garden party given by the German consul to celebrate the anniversary of the signing of the Weimar Constitution. In 1932, after De Valera became prime minister, he was the guest of honor at the opening ceremony and threw out the first ball for the hurling match.

The 1928 Tailteann Games star was Ireland's hammer thrower Patrick O'Callaghan. Fresh from winning at the 1928 Amsterdam Olympics with a throw of 168 ft. 7½ in., he would better his Olympic mark and set a new Irish record by throwing 170 ft. 1 in. Canada's Percy Williams, gold medalist in the 100 meters and 200 meters in Amsterdam, declined to run his individual specialties but helped with Canada's relay teams. A number of other athletes, mostly from the U.S., traveled from Amsterdam, and although they did not meet the criteria of being Irish or of Irish extraction, were allowed to compete anyway. The organizers did not want to cause a scene by turning them away, while appreciating the added draw to the gate.

World champion boxer Gene Tunney was invited to be a guest at the games and was a frequent presence at the boxing events. He even addressed the city of Dublin over the radio regarding the activities at the boxing matches.

The organizers wanted to revive an event from the ancient games, chariot racing, and add it as a spectacle to the modern games. The owners of the Phoenix Park racetrack were convinced the chariot wheels would destroy the turf track and turned the idea down.

The decision was made to move the next games up to 1931 so as to not conflict with the Los Angeles 1932 Olympic Games. This decision was later reversed, and the dates of the games were merely moved up a month or so to June and July 1932 to give the Irish athletes a competitive test right before making the long trip to California. The star power of the games was greatly diminished by not having the recently crowned Olympic champions, and many of the events were more domestic than they had been in the past.

On the eve of the 1932 games, the organizers proclaimed in the program "Yes! Aonach Tailteann is here to stay—a permanent and significant revival of an age old August Festival, an evidence of our distinct Nationality; a gesture to the scattered units of the Gaelic race, telling them of our rejuvenescence and virility, of our optimism for the future and our pride in the past."[217]

Despite this proclamation, the worldwide depression during the 1930s and the world war of the 1940s ended the gatherings and they have not been revived since.

Year	Host City	Host Nation	Dates	Nations	Athletes	Sports
1924	Dublin	Ireland	August 2–18	10	6500	NA
1928	Dublin	Ireland	August 11–22	13	NA	NA
1932	Dublin	Ireland	June 29–July 10	6	NA	16

1924   Dublin   Ireland   August 2–18

Nations: Australia, Canada, England, Ireland, Newfoundland, New Zealand, Scotland, South Africa, United States, Wales

Venues: Croke Park

Sports: Athletics, Boxing, Camogie, Clay Trap Shooting, Gaelic Football, Golf, Handball, Hurling, Motor Cycling, Shinty, Swimming, Tennis, Yachting

1928   Dublin   Ireland   August 11–22

Nations: Australia, Austria, Brazil, Canada, England, France, Ireland, New Zealand, Rhodesia, Scotland, South Africa, United States, Wales

Sports: Athletics, Billiards, Boxing, Chess, Football, Golf, Gymnastics, Handball, Hurling, Motor Cycling, Rowing, Shinty, Swimming, Yachting

Venues: Croke Park

1932   Dublin   Ireland   June 29–July 10

Nations: Australia, Canada, Ireland, Scotland, United States, Wales

Sports: Athletics, Boxing, Cycling, Football, Hurling, Shinty, Camogie, Rowing, Handball (Hardball and Softball), Yachting, Golf, Gymnastics, Motor Boat Racing, Swimming, Lawn Bowling, Chess

Venues: Boyne River (Rowing), Phoenix Park (Handball), Croke Park (Opening Ceremonies, Athletics, Boxing, Cycling, Football, Hurling, Shinty, Camogie), Dublin Bay National Yacht Club (Yachting), Woodbrook Golf Club (Ladies Golf), Milltown Golf Club (Men's Golf), Mansion House (Women's Gymnastics), Portobello Barracks (Men's Gymnastics), Blackrock Baths (Swimming), Shannon River (Motor Boat Racing), Blackrock, Clontarf, Kenilworth, Leinster, St. James Gate, Railway Union (Lawn Bowling), Regent House, Trinity College (Chess)

UK & Ireland Corporate Games

The UK & Ireland Corporate Games are hosted throughout the United Kingdom and Ireland. They are open to participants from anywhere in the world as a regional version of the World Corporate Games sponsored by Sport For Life.

Year	Host City	Host Nation	Dates	Nations	Athletes	Sports
1993	Milton Keynes	England		NA	NA	NA
1994	Milton Keynes	England		NA	NA	NA
1995	Peterborough	England		NA	NA	NA
1996	Aberdeen	Scotland	June 14–16	NA	NA	NA
1997	Belfast	Northern Ireland	June 13–15	NA	NA	NA
1998	Bracknell	England	June 12–14	NA	NA	20
1999	Limerick	Ireland		NA	NA	NA

Victorian Corporate Games

The state of Victoria in Australia hosts the Victorian Corporate Games, a regional corporate games. Participation is open to any nation, but most participants are from Australia.

Year	Host City	Host Nation	Dates	Nations	Athletes	Sports
1997	Melbourne	Australia		NA	NA	NA
1998	Melbourne	Australia	Nov. 20–22	NA	NA	9
1999	Melbourne	Australia		NA	NA	NA
2000	Melbourne	Australia	Nov. 24–26	NA	NA	NA

West African University Games

The West African University Games were held on a biennial basis from 1965 to 1977. After a long pause, they were held again in 1989 but then not held until 1995.[218]

Year	Host City	Host Nation
1965	Ibadan	Nigeria
1967	Legon	Ghana
1969	Freetown	Sierra Leone
1971	Lagos	Nigeria
1973	Kumasi	Ghana
1975	Ife	Nigeria
1977	Yamoussoukro	Ivory Coast
1989	Ouagadougou	Burkina Faso
1995	Benin City	Nigeria
1999	Cotonou	Benin

West Asian Games

The first West Asian Games, created with the goal of helping to foster peace and harmony among the nations of western Asia, were held in November 1997 in Tehran, Iran, with eleven nations in attendance.

Iranian President Seyed Mohammad Khatami, speaking to the Iranian High Council of Sport at the beginning of the games, said "sports … [are] inseparable from economic, cultural and political issues and … due attention should be paid to sports in Iranian society."

The games were open to male athletes only, and Tehran hosted the 1997 Muslim Women's Games a few weeks later. President Khatami addressed the need for more sports facilities for women, noting that women had always suffered deprivation and discrimination in the area of access to opportunities in sports.[219]

Beirut, Lebanon, was tasked with organizing the second edition of the games in the year 2001.

Year	Host City	Host Nation	Dates	Nations	Athletes	Sports
1997	Tehran	Iran	November 19–28	11	1200	22

1997   Tehran   Iran   November 19–28

Nations: Iran, Jordan, Kuwait, Kyrgyzstan, Lebanon, Oman, Syria, Qatar, Tajikistan, Turkmenistan, Yemen

Sports[220]**:** Athletics, Badminton, Basketball, Boxing, Canoeing, Cycling, Diving, Equestrian, Fencing, Football, Gymnastics, Handball, Judo, Karate, Shooting, Swimming, Table Tennis, Tennis, Volleyball, Water Polo, Weightlifting, Wrestling

Venues: Shahid Mofatteh Sport Complex (Athletics), Tehran Azadi Sports Complex (Basketball, Cycling, Judo, Shooting, Water Polo), Afrasiabi Hall, Shahid Shiroodi Complex (Boxing), Shohad Equestrian Complex (Equestrian), Azadi Fencing Hall (Fencing), Haft-e-Tir Stadium (Football, Wrestling), Haftom-e-Tir Hall (Karate, Tae Kwon Do), Azadi Swimming Complex (Swimming), Five Halls Azadi (Table Tennis), Englehab Sports (Tennis), Azadi Hall Number Two (Volleyball), Azadi Weightlifting Hall (Weightlifting)

Western Asiatic Games

When political difficulties between China and Japan ended the Far East Championships, and the Far Eastern Athletic Association unraveled, G.D. Sondhi of India laid plans for the first Western Asiatic Games in Delhi and Patalia in March 1934. The invitees included Afghanistan, Burma, Ceylon, Federated Malay States, Hedjaz, Iraq, Nepal, Palestine, Persia, Siam, the Straits Settlements, Syria and Turkey. However, only Afghanistan, Ceylon and Palestine joined India for the event.

The games' "Olympic Village" was unique. Several tents were set up and in the evenings the eighty-two participants, all male, would gather around a bonfire in the middle of the village to sing and share stories.

Athletics, swimming and field hockey were on the schedule. Tennis was dropped at the last moment.

The Western Asiatic Games Federation was established at the games and the members set up rules for the continuation of the event. Along with the four participating countries, Persia had a representative at the meeting. The five countries decided that the games should rotate through the remaining host countries alphabetically. Afghanistan would hold the next edition followed by Ceylon, Palestine and Persia.

Any countries west of Singapore and east of Suez were eligible to join the federation. If a country could not guarantee that it could hold the games, the duties would pass on to the next available member state.[221]

However, this was not what happened in the case of the second western Asiatic Games. They were to be organized in Tel Aviv in Palestine in 1938 but were not held there or anywhere due to the impending war. They were never held again.

Year	Host City	Host Nation	Dates	Nations	Athletes	Sports
1934	Delhi-Patalia	India		4	82	3

Nations: Afghanistan, Ceylon, India, Palestine
Sports: Athletics, Field Hockey, Swimming

Windsor Classic Indoor Games

The Windsor Classic Indoor Games are organized by the city of Windsor, Ontario, Canada, on an annual basis for athletes who are blind, in a wheelchair, are amputees, or those who have cerebral palsy. The games are organized to give athletes the opportunity to retain their fitness by having a competition indoors in the winter.

The United States and Canada have participated on each occasion, and teams from Mexico, Australia, Colombia and England have joined in from time to time. Organizers are working to make the games more international.

The games draw an average over 750 athletes, 500 volunteers and 200 coaches. Currently, athletics, boccia, powerlifting, sledge hockey, swimming, wheelchair rugby and wheelchair tennis are included in the games.

Year	Host City	Host Nation	Dates	Nations	Athletes	Sports
1982	Windsor	Canada	March	NA	NA	NA
1983	Windsor	Canada		NA	NA	NA
1984	Windsor	Canada		NA	NA	NA
1985	Windsor	Canada		NA	NA	NA
1986	Windsor	Canada		NA	NA	NA
1987	Windsor	Canada		NA	NA	NA
1988	Windsor	Canada		NA	NA	NA
1989	Windsor	Canada		NA	NA	NA
1990	Windsor	Canada		NA	NA	NA
1991	Windsor	Canada		NA	NA	NA
1992	Windsor	Canada		NA	NA	NA
1993	Windsor	Canada		NA	NA	NA
1994	Windsor	Canada		NA	NA	NA
1995	Windsor	Canada		NA	NA	NA
1996	Windsor	Canada		NA	NA	NA
1997	Windsor	Canada		NA	NA	NA
1998	Windsor	Canada		NA	NA	NA
1999	Windsor	Canada		NA	NA	NA
2000	Windsor	Canada	March 24–26		800	7

2000   Windsor   Canada   March 24–26

Sports: Athletics, Boccia, Powerlifting, Sledge Hockey, Swimming, Wheelchair Rugby, Wheelchair Tennis

Winter Australian Corporate Games

The Winter Australian Corporate Games, one of the regional corporate games, are open to anyone but up to now have been attended primarily by Australians.

Year	Host City	Host Nation	Dates	Nations	Athletes	Sports
1996	Thredbo	Australia		NA	NA	NA
1997	Thredbo	Australia		NA	NA	NA
1998	Thredbo	Australia	August 7–9	NA	NA	5
1999	Thredbo	Australia		NA	NA	NA
2000	Thredbo	Australia		NA	NA	NA

1998   Thredbo   Australia   August 7–9

Sports: Alpine Skiing, Cross-country Skiing, Snow Boarding, Snow Tubing, Snow Volleyball 4-a-side

Winter Games for the Disabled

The Vasternorrland Association for Disabled Sports has held a biannual winter games in Sollefteå, Sweden, since 1995. Sollefteå is the largest town in the county of Vasternorrland.

Currently biathlon, Nordic skiing, alpine skiing and sledge hockey are on the schedule. Short track speed skating and mushing are possible new sports for 2001.

Year	Host City	Host Nation	Dates	Nations	Athletes	Sports
1995	Sollefteå	Sweden	February 23–26	NA	NA	NA
1997	Sollefteå	Sweden	March 11–16	NA	NA	NA
1999	Sollefteå	Sweden	March 5–13	18	NA	4

1999   Sollefteå   Sweden   March 5–13

Sports: Alpine Skiing, Biathlon, Nordic Skiing, Sledge Hockey

Winter International School Children's Games

Year	Host City	Host Nation	Dates	Nations	Athletes	Sports
1994	Ravne na Koroskem	Slovakia	February 10–13	8	NA	3
1995	Prakovce-Helcmanovc	Slovenia	February 2–3	4	NA	3
1999	Maribor	Slovenia		6	NA	2

1994   Ravne na Koroskem   Slovakia   February 10–13

Nations: Austria, Canada, Germany, Italy, Slovakia, Slovenia, Switzerland, Ukraine

Sports: Giant Slalom, Cross Country (classic), Ski Jump

1995   Prakovce-Helcmanovc   Slovenia   February 2–3

Nations: Czech Republic, Slovakia, Slovenia, Ukraine
Sports: Giant Slalom, Cross Country (classic), Sleighing

1999   Maribor   Slovenia   February 2–3

Nations: Austria, Germany, Hungary, Slovakia, Slovenia, Ukraine
Sports: Alpine Skiing, Nordic Skiing

Winter Pan-American Games

The Pan-American Winter Games were to be established as the quadrennial sister of the Pan-American summer games, but have not met with the greatest success so far.

The first suggestion of a Pan-American winter games came at the same time as the first mentions of the summer games. An event was originally scheduled to be held in Argentina in 1942, but World War II intervened.

The International Olympic Committee mentioned another attempt by U.S. winter sports federations at establishing a winter Pan-American games in its February 15, 1958, *Bulletin*. Lake Placid had been proposed as the site for a 1959 games as long as five member nations from the Pan-American Sports Organization (PASO) agreed to compete. Political unrest and unfavorable exchange rates were cited by the South American countries as reasons for not being able to send teams, and the idea was set aside once again.

When the idea was reborn almost thirty years later, the inaugural games were scheduled for September of 1989 in Las Lenas, Argentina. Lack of snow forced them to be postponed until August 1990, but at that point the snow conditions still refused to cooperate. The games were finally held, on a very abbreviated schedule, from September 18 to 22, 1990. Sixteen countries had originally intended to compete in alpine skiing, biathlon, and cross-country and freestyle skiing. In the end, the only events to be held were the alpine events. The United States and Canada won the majority of the medals—eligibility rules permitted more than the usual three individuals per event for each nation. The United States men skiers took the first six places in the super giant slalom, and nine of the top ten places in the giant slalom.

The intention was for the games to alternate between North and South America. However, the second games planned for Santiago, Chile, in 1993 were also canceled due to the lack of snow.

Salt Lake City had contemplated bidding for the 1997 edition, but so far the games have not been organized beyond the first edition.

Year	Host City	Host Nation	Dates	Nations	Athletes	Sports
1990	Las Lenas	Argentina	Sept. 18–22	8	NA	1

Nations: Argentina, Canada, United States (5 more)
Sports: Alpine Skiing (Downhill, Giant Slalom, Super Giant Slalom). Cancelled—Cross Country, Freestyle Skiing, Biathlon
Venues: Valle de Las Lenas Resort

Winter Paralympic Games

The original multisport competitions for winter athletes were called the Winter Games for the Disabled and were small and all but invisible to the press. Ornsköldsvik, Sweden (1976), Geilo, Norway (1980), and Innsbruck, Austria (1984), were the venues for first Winter Games for the Disabled.

In 1984, the inclusion of a few demonstration events for the disabled in the 1984 Sarajevo Olympic Winter Games helped to bring some visibility to winter sports for the disabled.

In 1988, the name of the games was changed to the Winter Paralympic Games and the event was held once again in Innsbruck. The games have been more closely linked with the Olympic Games since 1992 when they were held in the Olympic city Albertville for the first time.

Two years later, following the schedule set by the International Olympic Committee and by staggering the summer and winter games two years apart, the Paralympic Games were held in Lillehammer, Norway, in 1994, with thirty-one nations participating. The games were noted for their increased level of competition over previous editions. Speed skating and ice hockey were added as new events.

Norwegian Nordic skier Ragnhild Halvore Myklebust won nine medals—five gold, two silver and two bronze—to add to her collection of six gold and one silver from the previous two Paralympic Games.

The 1998 Nagano Paralympic Games stood out for the enthusiasm of the host Japanese fans who packed the stadiums throughout the games. The torch relay began in Tokyo on February 25, days after the closing ceremony of the Olympic Games. The torch arrived in Nagano on March 4, a day before the opening ceremony of the Paralympic Games. The Japanese Broadcasting Corporation had intended to televise only the opening ceremonies of the games, but after the enthusiastic response to them and the many requests, the closing ceremonies were also shown on live television in Japan.

The 2002 Winter Paralympic Games are being planned for Salt Lake City, Utah, and are scheduled to be held in the weeks after the conclusion of the Winter Olympic Games.

Year	Host City	Host Nation	Dates	Nations	Athletes	Sports
1976	Ornsköldsvik	Sweden	February 23–28	14	250	NA
1980	Geilo	Norway		18	350	NA
1984	Innsbruck	Austria	January 11–20	22	500	NA
1988	Innsbruck	Austria	January 17–24	22	700	NA
1992	Albertville	France	March 25–April 1	24	498	NA
1994	Lillehammer	Norway	March 10–19	31	1054	NA
1998	Nagano	Japan	March 5–14	32	571	5

1976   Ornsköldsvik   Sweden   February 23–28

Nation	MEDALS			
	Gold	Silver	Bronze	Total
West Germany	9	12	6	27
Switzerland	9	1	1	11

Nation	Gold	Silver	Bronze	Total
Finland	8	7	7	22
Sweden	6	7	7	20
Austria	5	16	14	35
Norway	5	3	2	10
Czechoslovakia	3	0	0	3
France	2	0	3	5
Canada	1	0	2	3

1984   Innsbruck   Austria   January 11–20

MEDALS

Nation	Gold	Silver	Bronze	Total
Austria	41	21	20	82
Finland	19	9	6	34
Norway	15	14	12	41
West Germany	12	13	13	38
United States	10	17	15	42
Switzerland	6	20	20	46
Sweden	6	4	5	15
Canada	4	8	7	19
France	4	4	0	8
Poland	3	2	8	13
New Zealand	2	4	3	9
Great Britain	0	4	6	10
Italy	0	1	1	2
Yugoslavia	0	0	1	1

1988   Innsbruck   Austria   January 17–24

MEDALS*

Nation	Gold	Silver	Bronze	Total
Norway	25	0	0	25
Austria	20	0	0	20
Finland	9	0	0	9
Germany	9	0	0	9
Switzerland	8	0	0	8
United States	7	0	0	7
Canada	5	0	0	5
France	5	0	0	5
Italy	3	0	0	3
Sweden	3	0	0	3
Poland	1	0	0	1
Spain	1	0	0	1
Russia	0	0	0	0
Japan	0	0	0	0
New Zealand	0	0	0	0

*silver and bronze medal data incomplete

1992   Albertville   France   March 25–April 1

| Nation | MEDALS | | | |
	Gold	Silver	Bronze	Total
United States	21	15	9	45
Germany	12	17	9	38
Unified Team	10	8	3	21
Austria	8	3	9	20
Finland	8	2	4	14
France	6	4	9	19
Norway	5	5	4	14
Switzerland	3	8	4	15
Canada	2	4	6	12
Poland	2	0	3	5
New Zealand	2	0	0	2
Australia	1	1	2	4
Sweden	1	1	2	4
Czech Republic	0	4	2	6
Great Britain	0	1	4	5
Italy	0	1	3	4
Spain	0	1	3	4
Denmark	0	1	0	1
Japan	0	0	2	2

1994   Lillehammer   Norway   March 10-19

| Nation | MEDALS | | | |
	Gold	Silver	Bronze	Total
Norway	29	22	13	64
Germany	25	21	18	64
United States	24	12	7	43
France	14	6	11	31
Russia	10	12	8	30
Austria	7	16	12	35
Finland	7	6	11	24
Sweden	3	3	2	8
Australia	3	2	4	9
New Zealand	3	0	3	6
Switzerland	2	9	5	16
Poland	2	3	5	10
Spain	1	6	3	10
Canada	1	2	5	8
Netherlands	1	0	3	4
Denmark	1	0	2	3
Italy	0	7	6	13
Japan	0	3	3	6
Slovakia	0	3	2	5
Great Britain	0	0	5	5
Liechtenstein	0	0	1	1
Belgium	0	0	1	1
Czech Republic	0	0	1	1
Estonia	0	0	1	1

1998   Nagano   Japan   March 5–14

Sports: Alpine Skiing, Biathlon, Cross Country, Ice Sledge Racing, Ice Sledge Hockey

Sports for Women: Alpine Skiing, Biathlon, Cross Country, Ice Sledge Racing, Ice Sledge Hockey

| | MEDALS | | | |
Nation	Gold	Silver	Bronze	Total
Norway	18	9	13	40
Germany	14	17	13	44
United States	13	8	13	34
Japan	12	16	13	41
Russia	12	10	9	31
Switzerland	10	5	8	23
Spain	8	0	0	8
Austria	7	16	11	34
Finland	7	5	7	19
France	5	9	8	22
New Zealand	4	1	1	6
Italy	3	4	3	10
Czech Republic	3	3	1	7
Ukraine	3	2	4	9
Canada	1	9	5	15
Denmark	1	0	1	2
Australia	1	0	1	2
Slovakia	0	6	4	10
Sweden	0	1	5	6
Netherlands	0	1	1	2
Poland	0	0	2	2

Winter World Corporate Games

The Winter World Corporate Games are sponsored by Sport for Life, which organizes the summer games of the same name. The games are open to all, with no restrictions on age and sex, and there are no qualification standards.

The first Winter World Corporate Games were held in Steamboat Springs, Colorado, in 1991. The next games were scheduled for Sarajevo, Yugoslavia, in 1993, but war in the region meant that they had to be canceled. Seefeld, Austria, eventually hosted the second games in 1996, and it and nearby Gastein have served as host annually since then.

Among the unique events held at the games are snow volleyball, alpine curling, Nordic triathlon and snow tubing, as well as the more standard winter sports of alpine and cross-country skiing and ice hockey.

Year	Host City	Host Nation	Dates	Nations	Athletes	Sports
1991	Steamboat Springs	United States		NA	NA	NA
1996	Seefeld	Austria		NA	NA	NA
1997	Seefeld	Austria	March 9–14	NA	NA	NA

Year	Host City	Host Nation	Dates	Nations	Athletes	Sports
1998	Seefeld	Austria	March 15–20	NA	NA	9
1999	Gastein	Austria	March 26–28	NA	NA	NA
2000	Gastein	Austria	January 28–30	NA	NA	7

1998   Seefeld   Austria   March 15–20

Sports: Alpine Curling, Alpine Skiing, Alpine Nordic Triathlon, Cross-country Skiing, Curling, Ice Hockey, Snow Boarding, Snow Tubing, Snow Volleyball

2000   Gastein   Austria   January 28–30

Sports: Alpine Curling, Alpine Skiing, Cross-country Skiing, Ice Hockey, Snowboarding, Snow Volleyball, Tobogganing

Winter World Games for the Deaf

Twenty-five years after the establishment of the summer World Games for the Deaf, and after the conclusion of World War II, CISS (Comité International des Sports des Sourds) began its first winter games for deaf athletes. The games have always been relatively small affairs, both in terms of competitors and nations. Sixteen nations and 268 competitors were the records until 1991.[222]

The 1999 games were to be held in Davos, Switzerland, as part of the 75th Anniversary celebrations of CISS. Alpine skiing, cross-country skiing and ice hockey were on the schedule, with snowboarding a demonstration event.

Sundsvall, Sweden, was chosen as the venue for the 2003 winter games.

Year	Host City	Host Nation	Dates	Nations	Athletes	Sports
1949	Seefeld	Austria	Feb. 26–March 2	5	33	2
1953	Oslo	Norway	February 20–24	6	43	3
1955	Oberammergau	West Germany	February 10–13	8	57	3
1959	Montana-Vermala	Switzerland	January 27–30	8	56	3
1963	Are	Sweden	March 11–16	8	53	2
1967	Berchtesgaden	West Germany	February 20–25	12	86	2
1971	Adelboden	Switzerland	January 25–29	13	92	2
1975	Lake Placid	USA	February 11–16	15	268	2
1979	Meribel	France	January 21–27	14	94	2
1983	Madonna di Campoglio	Italy	January 16–22	16	143	3
1987	Oslo	Norway	February 7–14	15	136	NA
1991	Banff	Canada	March 2–9	16	287	NA
1995	Yllas	Finland	March 14–19	NA	312	NA
1999	Davos	Switzerland	March 8–14	18	273	4

1949   Seefeld   Austria   February 26–March 2

Nations: Austria, Finland, Sweden, Switzerland (1 more)
Sports: Alpine Skiing, Nordic Skiing

MEDALS

Nation	Gold	Silver	Bronze	Total
Switzerland	3	0	1	4
Finland	1	2	0	3
Sweden	1	0	1	2
Austria	0	3	3	6

1953   Oslo   Norway   February 20–24

Nations: Austria, Finland, Norway, Switzerland, Yugoslavia (one more)
Sports: Alpine Skiing, Nordic Skiing, Ski Jumping

MEDALS

Nation	Gold	Silver	Bronze	Total
Norway	4	3	4	11
Finland	3	2	2	7
Austria	1	1	0	2
Sweden	0	2	1	3
Yugoslavia	0	1	1	2
Switzerland	0	0	1	1

1955   Oberammergau   West Germany   February 10–13

Nations: Austria, Finland, West Germany, Norway, Sweden (three more)
Sports: Alpine Skiing, Nordic Skiing, Ski Jumping

MEDALS

Nation	Gold	Silver	Bronze	Total
Norway	9	6	5	20
Austria	1	1	0	2
Finland	0	2	2	4
West Germany	0	1	3	4

1959   Montana-Vermala   Switzerland   January 27–30

Nations: Austria, Finland, West Germany, Norway, Sweden, Switzerland (two more)
Sports: Alpine Skiing, Nordic Skiing, Ski Jumping

MEDALS

Nation	Gold	Silver	Bronze	Total
Norway	6	4	5	15
West Germany	3	3	2	8
Finland	3	1	2	6
Austria	0	2	1	3
Sweden	0	1	0	1
Switzerland	0	1	0	1

1963   Are   Sweden   March 11–16

Nations: Austria, Finland, West Germany, Italy, Norway, Sweden, Switzerland (one more)
Sports: Alpine Skiing, Nordic Skiing

MEDALS

Nation	Gold	Silver	Bronze	Total
Austria	4	0	0	4
Norway	3	3	2	8
Finland	2	1	0	3
Switzerland	1	3	5	9
Italy	1	0	1	2
West Germany	0	4	2	6
Sweden	0	0	1	1

1967   Berchtesgaden   West Germany   February 20–25

Nations: Austria, Finland, Italy, Norway, Sweden, Switzerland, United States, West Germany (five more)
Sports: Alpine Skiing, Nordic Skiing

MEDALS

Nation	Gold	Silver	Bronze	Total
Norway	3	2	3	8
Italy	2	0	0	2
United States	2	0	0	2
Switzerland	1	3	2	6
Finland	1	2	2	5
Austria	1	0	1	2
West Germany	0	3	2	5
Sweden	0	1	0	1

1971   Adelboden   Switzerland   January 25–29

Nations: Finland, Italy, Norway, Switzerland, United States, USSR, West Germany (six more)
Sports: Alpine Skiing, Nordic Skiing

MEDALS

Nation	Gold	Silver	Bronze	Total
Switzerland	2	6	2	10
USSR	2	3	2	7
United States	2	1	0	3
Norway	2	0	2	4
Italy	2	0	0	2
Finland	1	1	0	2
West Germany	0	0	3	3

1975   Lake Placid   USA   February 11–16

Nations: Austria, Finland, France, Italy, Sweden, Switzerland, United States, USSR (seven more)
Sports: Alpine Skiing, Nordic Skiing

MEDALS

Nation	Gold	Silver	Bronze	Total
USSR	4	5	3	12
Switzerland	4	1	1	6
France	1	3	1	5
Finland	1	0	1	2
Italy	1	0	1	2
United States	0	1	2	3
Austria	0	1	1	2
Sweden	0	0	1	1

1979   Meribel   France   January 21–27

Nations: Austria, Finland, France, Italy, Norway, Sweden, Switzerland, USSR, West Germany (five more)
Sports: Alpine Skiing, Nordic Skiing

MEDALS

Nation	Gold	Silver	Bronze	Total
USSR	5	5	3	13
France	2	4	1	7
Austria	2	1	0	3
Switzerland	2	0	2	4
Finland	1	0	2	3
Norway	0	2	0	2
Italy	0	0	2	2
Sweden	0	0	1	1
West Germany	0	0	1	1

1983   Madonna di Campoglio
Italy   January 16–22

Nations: Austria, France, Italy, Norway, Sweden, Switzerland, USSR, West Germany (eight more)
Sports: Alpine Skiing, Nordic Skiing, Speed Skating

MEDALS

Nation	Gold	Silver	Bronze	Total
USSR	6	4	4	14
France	3	3	1	7
Norway	2	1	3	6
Austria	2	1	0	3
West Germany	1	0	3	4
Italy	0	2	2	4
Sweden	0	2	0	2
Switzerland	0	1	1	2

1999   Davos   Switzerland   March 8–14

Nations: Austria, Canada, Czech Republic, Finland, France, Germany, Italy, Japan, Lithuania, Norway, Russia, Slovakia, Slovenia, Sweden, Switzerland, United States

Sports: Alpine Skiing, Cross-country Skiing, Ice Hockey, Speed Skating

MEDALS

Nation	Gold	Silver	Bronze	Total
Russia	4	4	2	10
Czech Republic	4	0	0	4
Norway	3	0	1	4
Sweden	2	1	0	3
Italy	1	3	0	4
Slovenia	1	1	1	3
France	1	0	1	2
Slovakia	1	0	0	1
Canada	1	0	0	1
Austria	0	2	3	5
United States	0	2	1	3
Japan	0	1	1	2
Lithuania	0	1	0	1
Finland	0	0	4	4
Germany	0	0	2	2
Switzerland	0	0	1	1

Winter World Transplant Games

After sixteen successful years of summer World Transplant Games, the World Transplant Games Federation instituted its first Winter World Transplant Games in 1994 for athletes who had had heart, liver, lung, kidney, pancreas or bone marrow transplants.

The first two games held in France brought to light the differing definitions of the concept of a transplant among nations. The French provided facilities for dialysis patients to participate alongside those athletes with organ transplants. While the French consider the dialysis process to qualify as a form of transplant, the rest of the world has not accepted this definition.

Though very small, with 89 competitors, the second games in Pra-Loup in 1996 were well-organized and professionally run. A highlight was an evening parade down the ski slope with each athlete carrying a torch to light his or her way.

The 1999 games were held in Salt Lake City at the Snowbird Ski Resort, with the opening ceremony a tribute to those who had donated organs and a celebration of the lives that had been extended by those donations. Athletes from thirteen nations competed in five age categories: children/juniors 8–15, adults 16–34, senior 35–44, veteran 45–59 and super veteran over 60. Events included slalom, giant slalom, dual gate racing, biathlon and nordic races.

Year	Host City	Host Nation	Dates	Nations	Athletes	Sports
1994	Tignes	France		NA	NA	NA
1996	Pra-Loup	France	January 7–13	NA	89	NA
1999	Salt Lake City	United States	January 10–15	13	NA	2

1999   Salt Lake City   United States   Jan. 10–15

Nations: Austria, Canada, Czech Republic, Denmark, Finland, France, Germany, Great Britain, Hungary, Norway, Slovenia, Switzerland, United States
Sports: Alpine Skiing, Nordic Skiing

Winter World University Games

The Winter World University Games or Winter Universiade has the same historical roots as the summer university games, having first been organized by the Confédèration Internationale d'Étudiants (CIE) in 1928 in Cortina d'Ampezzo, Italy. A precursor to these games was the International Collegiate Skiing Meeting held in St. Moritz, January 18–19, 1926, with competitions in downhill skiing, slalom and ski jumping.

The 1928 Cortina Games were very small in terms of the number of events. Only nine medals were awarded in three disciplines: cross-country skiing, figure skating and speed skating. No women's events were on the schedule.

Davos, Switzerland, expanded the schedule in 1930 with seven events: alpine skiing, bobsled, cross-country skiing, figure skating, hockey, ski jumping and speed skating. Women competed in figure skating.

Bardonecchia, Italy, hosted the games of 1933. Figure skating was dropped and with it the chance for women to participate.

Women were welcomed back at the next games in St. Moritz in 1935, with both figure skating and skiing on the program. Zeel am See, Austria, and Lillehammer, Norway, held the 1937 and 1939 editions of the games before World War II ended organized sporting activities across the globe.

The Union Internationale d'Étudiants (UIE) replaced CIE after the war and organized the winter games in Davos, Switzerland, in 1947. Helsinki, Finland, was originally chosen as host of the 1949 UIE games, but could not fulfill its duties. A little later, the East-West rift split UIE. FISU (Federation Internationale du Sport Universtaire) was established in 1949 and the two organizations staged separate games for the next decade. After much discussion between them, the rival factions, the UIE and FISU, rejoined for good at the 1959 summer Universiade in Turin, Italy.

The games get little coverage in the world press, and have been relatively small. After the reunification, it took some time to get the event going again. The 1960 games in Chamonix, France, had just 143 participants. They opened on February 28, the same day as the closing ceremony of the Squaw Valley Olympic Winter Games.

Of the 19 editions of the games since 1960, 16 have been held in Europe. The U.S. held the games in Lake Placid in 1972, Japan hosted them in 1991, and South Korea staged the 1997 event.

The Sapporo games of 1991 had a record thirty-three nations participate. The games continued to grow, with forty-one nations at the next two games in 1993 and 1995, and forty-eight nations and 877 athletes at the 1997 games in Chonju-Moju, Korea.

Strong environmental protests were lodged against the Chonju-Moju games, when it was feared that damage would be caused to the national forest where the downhill ski run was located. Japan and Russia tied with nine gold medals each.

The 1999 games were held in Poprad, Slovakia, with the Russians turning in the best performances. Ukraine's Valentina Shevchenko won three gold medals in Nordic skiing.

Zakopane, Poland, one of the cities which had bid for the 2006 Winter Olympic Games, was selected in July 1999 to host the 2001 Winter World University Games. Zakopane has hosted the student games on two previous occasions, in 1956 and 1993. Vancouver, Calgary, and Reno, Nevada, had also expressed interest in hosting the 2001 games.

Year	Host City	Host Nation	Dates	Nations	Athletes	Sports
1928	Cortina D'Ampezzo	Italy	Jan. 22–29	15	NA	3
1930	Davos	Switzerland	Jan. 4–12	12	NA	7
1933	Bardonecchia	Italy	Jan. 29–Feb. 5	15	NA	7
1935	St. Moritz	Switzerland	Feb. 4–10	13	NA	8
1937	Zeel am See	Austria	Feb. 2–10	15	317	8
1939	Lillehammer	Norway	Feb. 19–23	11	NA	3
1947	Davos	Switzerland	Jan. 19–26	13	301	NA
1960	Chamonix	France	Feb. 28–Mar. 6	15	143	NA
1962	Villars	Switzerland	March 6–12	22	283	NA
1964	Spindleruv-Mlyn	Czechoslovakia	Feb. 11–17	NA	410	NA
1966	Sestriere	Italy	Feb. 5–13	NA	420	NA
1968	Innsbruck	Austria	Jan. 18–28	NA	580	NA
1970	Rovaniemi	Finland	April 3–9	NA	460	NA
1972	Lake Placid	USA	Feb. 26–March 5	NA	220	NA
1975	Livigno	Italy	April 6–13	NA	200	NA
1978	Spindleruv-Mlyn	Czechoslovakia	Feb. 5–12	21	450	NA
1981	Jaca	Spain	Feb. 23–March 4	28	583	NA
1983	Sofia	Bulgaria	Feb. 17–27	31	812	NA
1985	Belluno	Italy	Feb. 16–24	29	844	NA
1987	Strbske Pleso	Czechoslovakia	Feb. 21–28	28	941	NA
1989	Sofia	Bulgaria	March 2–12	32	1079	NA
1991	Sapporo	Japan	March 2–10	33	1040	6
1993	Zakopane	Poland	Feb. 6–14	41	668	8
1995	Jaca	Spain	Feb. 18–26	41	765	8
1997	Chonju-Moju	South Korea	Jan. 24–Feb. 2	48	877	7
1999	Poprad	Slovakia	Jan. 22–30	NA	929	7

University Sports Week Winter (FISU)

Year	Host City	Host Nation	Dates	Nations	Athletes	Sports
1951	Gastein	Austria	Jan. 22–28	9	NA	1
1953	St. Moritz	Switzerland	March 2–8	17	220	1
1955	Mt. Jahorina	Yugoslavia	April 1–7	6	92	1
1957	Oberammergau	West Germany	Feb. 19–24	10	83	NA
1958	Zeel am See	Austria	Feb. 16–21	7	NA	NA

World Student Championships Winter (UIE)

Year	Host City	Host Nation	Dates	Nations	Athletes	Sports
1949	Spindleruv-Mlyn	Czechoslovakia	Jan. 29–Feb. 6	7	311	3
1951	Poiana	Romania	Jan. 28–Feb. 7	15	326	5

Year	Host City	Host Nation	Dates	Nations	Athletes	Sports
1953	Semeringen-Vienna	Austria	Feb. 23–March 1	15	508	4
1956	Zakopane	Poland	March 7–13	NA	NA	3

1928   *Cortina D'Ampezzo*   *Italy*   *January 22–29*

Nations: Austria, Belgium, Czechoslovakia, Denmark, France, Hungary, Italy, Japan, Latvia, Luxembourg, Norway, Poland, Sweden, Switzerland, Yugoslavia
Sports: Cross-country skiing, Figure Skating, Speed Skating

	MEDALS			
Nation	Gold	Silver	Bronze	Total
Hungary	1	2	0	3
Czechoslovakia	1	1	0	2
Norway	1	0	0	1
Italy	0	0	2	2
Belgium	0	0	1	1

1930   *Davos*   *Switzerland*   *January 4–12*

Nations: Australia, Austria, Czechoslovakia, England, France, Germany, Holland, Hungary, Italy, Poland, Romania, Switzerland

	MEDALS			
Nation	Gold	Silver	Bronze	Total
Holland	5	0	0	5
Austria	3	7	7	17
Germany	3	1	0	4
Switzerland	2	1	1	4
Czechoslovakia	1	2	1	4
Italy	1	1	1	3
Hungary	0	2	1	3
Romania	0	1	0	1
Poland	0	0	1	1
France	0	0	1	1
England	0	0	1	1
Australia	0	0	0	0

1933   *Bardonecchia*   *Italy*   *January 29–February 5*

Nations: Argentina, Columbia, Czechoslovakia, Denmark, England, France, Hungary, Italy, Latvia, Netherlands, Norway, Poland, Romania, Switzerland, United States

	MEDALS			
Nation	Gold	Silver	Bronze	Total
Latvia	6	2	0	8
Italy	3	3	4	10
Norway	1	1	0	2

Nation	Gold	Silver	Bronze	Total
France	0	1	2	3
Switzerland	0	1	1	2
Netherlands	0	1	0	1
England	0	1	0	1
Romania	0	0	2	2
Czechoslovakia	0	0	1	1
Hungary	0	0	0	0

1935   St. Moritz   Switzerland   February 4–10

Nations: Austria, Czechoslovakia, England, France, Germany, Hungary, Italy, Latvia, Netherlands, Norway, Poland, Switzerland (one more)

MEDALS

Nation	Gold	Silver	Bronze	Total
Germany	4	3	2	9
Austria	4	2	2	8
Latvia	4	1	0	5
Italy	2	1	3	6
Netherlands	1	4	1	6
Hungary	1	3	5	9
Switzerland	1	1	0	2
Norway	1	1	0	2
France	0	1	0	1
England	0	1	0	1
Poland	0	0	3	3
Czechoslovakia	0	0	2	2

1937   Zeel am See   Austria   February 2–10

Nations: Austria, Czechoslovakia, France, Germany, Hungary, Italy, Norway, Poland, Switzerland (six more)

MEDALS

Nation	Gold	Silver	Bronze	Total
Austria	5	3	7	15
Germany	5	2	2	9
Norway	4	4	5	13
Hungary	2	2	2	6
Poland	1	1	0	2
France	1	1	0	2
Switzerland	0	4	0	4
Czechoslovakia	0	1	0	1
Italy	0	0	1	1

1939   Lillehammer   Norway   February 19–23

Nations: Austria, Czechoslovakia, Finland, France, Germany, Hungary, Latvia, Norway, Poland, Sweden, Switzerland

Nation	MEDALS			
Nation	*Gold*	*Silver*	*Bronze*	*Total*
Germany	6	4	3	13
Norway	3	8	3	14
Hungary	1	1	0	2
Finland	1	1	0	2
Sweden	1	0	2	3
Switzerland	1	0	1	2
Czechoslovakia	1	0	0	1
Latvia	0	0	2	2
Poland	0	0	1	1
France	0	0	1	1
Austria	0	0	1	1

1947   Davos   Switzerland   January 19–16

Nations: Austria, Czechoslovakia, Finland, Hungary, Italy, Poland, Switzerland (six more)

Nation	MEDALS			
Nation	*Gold*	*Silver*	*Bronze*	*Total*
Austria	9	2	2	13
Finland	6	1	0	7
Hungary	2	7	6	15
Switzerland	2	2	6	10
Czechoslovakia	1	4	3	8
Poland	1	2	2	5
Italy	0	1	0	1

1949   Spindleruv-Mlyn   Czechoslovakia January 29–February 6   (UIE)

Nations: Bulgaria, Czechoslovakia, Finland, France, Hungary, Poland, Romania

Nation	MEDALS			
Nation	*Gold*	*Silver*	*Bronze*	*Total*
Czechoslovakia	8	4	11	23
Hungary	7	8	2	17
Poland	5	6	5	16
Finland	1	0	0	1
France	0	3	4	7

1951   Gastein   Austria   January 22–28   (FISU)

Nations: Austria, Italy, Switzerland, West Germany, Yugoslavia (four more)

Nation	MEDALS			
Nation	*Gold*	*Silver*	*Bronze*	*Total*
Austria	5	4	4	13
West Germany	2	3	2	7
Switzerland	2	1	0	3

Nation	Gold	Silver	Bronze	Total
Yugoslavia	1	1	2	4
Italy	0	1	2	3

1951   Poiana   Romania   January 28–February 7   (UIE)

Nations: Austria, Bulgaria, Czechoslovakia, East Germany, England, Finland, Hungary, Poland, Romania, Soviet Union (five more)

MEDALS

Nation	Gold	Silver	Bronze	Total
Soviet Union	16	14	14	44
Czechoslovakia	6	4	3	13
Poland	4	3	6	13
Finland	2	1	2	5
Romania	1	3	1	5
Hungary	1	2	2	5
England	1	0	0	1
East Germany	0	2	1	3
Bulgaria	0	1	2	3
Austria	0	1	0	1

1953   St. Moritz   Switzerland   March 2–8   (FISU)

Nations: Austria, Finland, Italy, Norway, Switzerland, West Germany, Yugoslavia (ten more)

MEDALS

Nation	Gold	Silver	Bronze	Total
Switzerland	3	6	1	10
West Germany	3	1	3	7
Finland	2	1	3	6
Austria	1	1	3	5
Norway	1	0	0	1
Yugoslavia	1	0	0	1
Italy	0	2	1	3

1953   Semeringen-Vienna   Austria   February 23–March 1   (UIE)

Nations: Austria, Czechoslovakia, East Germany, Hungary, Norway, Poland, Soviet Union (eight more)

MEDALS

Nation	Gold	Silver	Bronze	Total
Soviet Union	13	10	10	33
Czechoslovakia	7	10	4	21
Poland	4	5	8	17
East Germany	1	0	1	2
Hungary	1	0	1	2
Norway	0	1	0	1
Austria	0	0	1	1

1955   Mt. Jahorina   Yugoslavia   April 1–7   (FISU)

Nations: Austria, East Germany, Finland, Italy, Switzerland, Yugoslavia

MEDALS

Nation	Gold	Silver	Bronze	Total
East Germany	3	4	4	11
Yugoslavia	2	2	4	8
Austria	2	1	1	4
Switzerland	1	1	0	2
Finland	1	0	0	1
Italy	0	1	0	1

1956   Zakopane   Poland   March 7–13   (UIE)

Nations: Austria, Bulgaria, Czechoslovakia, Finland, Hungary, Poland, Romania, Soviet Union

MEDALS

Nation	Gold	Silver	Bronze	Total
Soviet Union	10	4	4	18
Czechoslovakia	6	4	4	14
Hungary	2	0	0	2
Poland	1	7	8	16
Austria	0	2	1	3
Romania	0	2	0	2
Finland	0	0	1	1
Bulgaria	0	0	1	1

1957   Oberammergau   West Germany   February 19–24   (FISU)

Nations: Austria, Czechoslovakia, East Germany, France, Iceland, Italy, Norway, Poland, Spain, Yugoslavia

1993   Zakopane   Poland   February 6—14

Nations: Andorra, Australia, Austria, Belarus, Belgium, Bulgaria, Canada, China, Czech Republic, Denmark, Finland, France, Germany, Great Britain, Greece, Hungary, Independent Participants, Israel, Italy, Japan, Kazakhstan, Latvia, Liechtenstein, Lithuania, Mongolia, Netherlands, New Zealand, North Korea, Norway, Poland, Romania, Russia, Slovakia, South Korea, Spain, Sweden, Switzerland, Taipei, Turkey, Ukraine, United States

Sports: Alpine Skiing, Biathlon, Figure Skating, Ice Hockey, Nordic Combined, Nordic Skiing, Ski Jump, Speed Skating

Sports for Women: Alpine Skiing, Biathlon, Figure Skating, Nordic Skiing, Speed Skating

MEDALS

Nation	Gold	Silver	Bronze	Total
Russia	6	3	5	14
China	6	2	4	12

Nation	Gold	Silver	Bronze	Total
Japan	5	7	4	16
Korea	5	2	3	10
United States	4	4	5	13
France	2	2	0	4
Slovakia	2	0	1	3
Switzerland	2	0	0	2
Italy	1	6	2	9
Austria	1	2	6	9
Poland	1	2	2	5
Germany	1	1	1	3
Belarus	1	1	1	3
Ukraine	1	0	0	1
Czech Republic	1	0	0	1
North Korea	0	5	3	8
Lithuania	0	1	0	1
Kazakhstan	0	1	0	1
Finland	0	0	2	2

1995   Jaca   Spain   February 18–26

Sports: Alpine Skiing, Figure Skating, Ice Hockey, Nordic Skiing, Nordic Combined, Short Track Speed Skating, Ski Jumping, Snowboarding

1997   Chonju-Moju   South Korea   January 24–February 2

Sports: Alpine Skiing, Biathlon, Figure Skating, Ice Hockey, Short-track Speed Skating, Speed Skating, Nordic Skiing (Ski Jumping, Cross-country Skiing, Nordic Combined)

	MEDALS			
Nation	Gold	Silver	Bronze	Total
Japan	9	8	7	24
Russia	9	6	9	24

1999   Poprad   Slovakia   January 22–30

Sports: Alpine Skiing, Biathlon, Figure Skating, Ice Hockey, Short-track Speed Skating, Snowboarding, Nordic Skiing (Ski Jumping, Cross-country Skiing, Nordic Combined)

	MEDALS			
Nation	Gold	Silver	Bronze	Total
Russia	8	11	10	29
Austria	7	2	0	9
Japan	5	6	7	18
Poland	5	2	3	10
Slovakia	4	7	8	19
Ukraine	4	1	2	7
Italy	4	0	2	6
France	4	0	1	5

Nation	Gold	Silver	Bronze	Total
China	3	5	5	13
Bulgaria	3	0	1	4
Belarus	2	2	3	7
Sweden	2	2	2	6
Canada	1	2	1	4
Germany	1	0	3	4
Switzerland	0	4	0	4
Czech Republic	0	2	1	3
United States	0	2	0	2
Slovenia	0	1	2	3
Spain	0	1	0	1
Belgium	0	1	0	1

Winter X Games

ESPN's phenomenal success showcasing extreme sports with the X Games in the summers of 1995 and 1996, persuaded the channel to create an event for extreme sports of the winter variety. ESPN sold out its advertising months in advance. The games were broadcast over ESPN and its affiliates to over 150 countries with $200,000 in prize money offered in the inaugural competition.

Snow Summit Mountain Resort in Big Bear Lake, California, was chosen as the host for the first Winter X Games. A variety of new events were introduced to the international sports world, such as supermodified shovel racing and snow mountain biking. The games also included a variety of events for snowboarders (big air, half-pipe, slope style and mass board race); ice climbing for speed and difficulty was also included in the first games.

The 1998 games introduced sno-cross, snowmobile racing on a motocross-style course. Both the 1998 and 1999 games at Crested Butte, Colorado, were hampered by heavy snow which wreaked havoc with the schedules of many events.

Mount Snow, Vermont, held the 2000 edition of the games and broke records for spectator attendance.

Year	Host City	Host Nation	Dates	Nations	Athletes	Sports
1997	Big Bear Lake	USA	January 30–Feb. 2	NA	200	5
1998	Crested Butte	USA	January 15–18	16	200	6
1999	Crested Butte	USA	January 14–17	NA	NA	NA
2000	Mount Snow	USA	February 3–6	NA	NA	NA

1997   Big Bear Lake   USA   January 30–February 2

Events: Snowboarding (Slope-style, Big Air, Half-pipe, Mass Board Race), Ice Climbing (Difficulty, Speed), Snow Bicycling (Dual-speed Downhill, Dual Downhill Racing), Supermodified Shovel Racing, Cross Over (a combination of summer and winter sports, snowboarding and in-line skating, skateboarding, and bicycle stunt vert)

1998   Crested Butte   USA   January 15–18

Sports: Snowboarding, Snow Mountain Bike Racing, Ice Climbing, Skiboarding, Sno-cross, Free Skiing

	Medals			
Nation	*Gold*	*Silver*	*Bronze*	*Total*
United States	15	13	17	45
Canada	1	2	0	3
France	1	1	1	3
Sweden	1	0	1	2
Finland	1	0	0	1
South Korea	0	2	0	2
Germany	0	0	1	1

1999　Crested Butte　USA　January 15–18

Sports: Free Skiing, Ice Climbing, Sno-Boarding, Snocross, Snow Mountain Bike Racing

World Air Games

The Fédération Aéronautique Internationale (FAI), the world governing body of air sports founded in 1905, held their first World Air Games in 1997 after a decade of proposals which had not produced an event.

The federations governing the sports of aerobatics, aeromodeling, ballooning, hang gliding, helicoptering, flying microlights, parachuting and paragliding join together under the umbrella of the FAI to make this a multisport event.

The first proposal for the games was by the Aero Club de France (AeCF) in the FAI council meetings of 1986. The proposed venue was to be the Midi-Pyrenees region centered around Toulouse, France. The FAI preliminarily approved the event and asked the Union des Fédérations Française Aéronautiques et Sportives (UFFAS) and the AeCF to reach a cooperative agreement on how the games were to be run. By October 1990, an agreement between UFFAS and the AeCF had not been reached and the FAI withdrew its preliminary sanction for the games.

In the meantime at the FAI council meetings of 1988, the National Aero Club (NAC) of Greece had offered to host the second World Air Games in 1995. When the Toulouse proposal fell through, the Greeks maintained their intention to hold the games, calling them the IKARIADA, in reference to Icarus. In March 1993, the FAI and the Greek organizing body signed an agreement to go ahead with the games. In October 1993, Greek elections brought in a new government which withdrew financial support and the games were canceled again.

One year later, the FAI asked once again for bids and had proposals from South Africa, Australia and Turkey. By June 1995, the South African and Australian proposals had been withdrawn and the Turk Hava Kurumu (Turkish Air Association) was awarded the event. The Turks quickly moved to organize the games, with a series of test competitions, an international event in itself, organized in September 1996.

The 1997 games were televised live on the Eurosport cable network, with the events—aeromodeling, ballooning, gliding, hang gliding, parachuting, and microlight flying—spread out among many cities and venues in Turkey. The long-distance air race began in Iceland, with the route going through France, Spain, Italy, Egypt, Jordan, and Israel before finishing in Turkey.

Entry fees for participants ranged from U.S. $250 to $600, depending on the event.

The bidders for the 2001 games were Austria, Poland, Spain and Turkey. In May 1998, the region of Andalusia, Spain, was chosen. Seville was to serve as the main venue, with events spread out across the region.

Year	Host City	Host Nation	Dates	Nations	Athletes	Sports
1996	Ankara	Turkey	August 28–Sept. 22	NA	NA	8
1997	Ankara	Turkey	September 3–21	60	3000	9

1996   Ankara   Turkey   August 28–September 22

Sports: Aeromodeling, Ballooning, Gliding, Hang Gliding, Parachuting, General Aviation (Air Rally Flying, Paragliding, Microlight Flying)
Venues: Aeromodeling (Ankara), Ballooning (Urgup), Gliding (Inonu), Hang Gliding (Denizli), Parachuting (Efes), Air Rally Flying (Antalya), Microlight Flying (Efes)

1997   Ankara   Turkey   September 3–21

Sports: Aerobatics, Gliding, Hang Gliding, Parachuting, General Aviation, Aeromodeling, Microlight Flying, Rotorcrafts, Ballooning
Venues: Aerobatics (Antalya), Gliding (Inonu), Hang Gliding (Denizli), Parachuting (Efes), General Aviation (Antalya), Aeromodeling (Ankara), Microlight Flying (Aydin), Rotorcrafts (Istanbul), Ballooning (Urgup)

World Corporate Games

The World Corporate Games, sponsored by Sport for Life, in theory can claim to be the most inclusive international games, with competition open to everyone. There are no qualifying standards, competition is divided into age divisions, and disabled competitors are welcomed. Participants must compete as a team, not as individuals. However, teams may include nearly anyone; family, friends, colleagues or clients may all join together.

Teams are divided into eight divisions based on team size. In the smallest division, teams may have as few as five entrants; in the largest division, as many as 200. The emphasis is on participation rather than competition, with the Sport for Life Grand Award given to the corporation with the most entries.

The World Corporate Games have raised hundreds of thousands of dollars which are donated to charities involved in medical research, to programs for the disabled, including disabled sports, to the International Red Cross, and to UNICEF.

In the past few years, the World Corporate Games movement has attempted to expand into regional competitions with varying success. Events such as the Russian Corporate Games and the Mediterranean Corporate Games have been proposed but not held.

Year	Host City	Host Nation	Dates	Nations	Athletes	Sports
1988	San Francisco	USA		NA	NA	NA
1989	Concord	USA		NA	NA	NA

Year	Host City	Host Nation	Dates	Nations	Athletes	Sports
1990	Oahu	USA	October 6–13	NA	NA	20
1991	Lille	France		NA	NA	NA
1992	London	England		NA	NA	NA
1993	Kuala Lumpur	Malaysia		NA	NA	NA
1994	Johannesburg	South Africa	October	NA	NA	NA
1995	Geneva	Switzerland	September 2–9	NA	NA	NA
1996	Stuttgart	Germany	September 7–14	NA	NA	NA
1997	Oranjestad	Aruba	September 13–20	NA	NA	NA
1998	The Hague	Netherlands	August 29–Sept. 5	NA	NA	21
1999	Montevideo	Uruguay	Dec. 13–16	NA	NA	NA
2000	Aberdeen	Scotland	July 13–16	NA	NA	24

1990   Oahu   USA   October 6–13

Sports: Basketball, Beach Volleyball, Board Sailing, Bowling, Cycling, Diving, Golf, Outrigger Canoe, Road Running, Sailing, Soccer, Softball, Surfing, Surf-ski Paddling, Swimming, Table Tennis, Tennis, Track (and Beach Sprints), Triathlon, Volleyball

Venues: Sub Base Pearl Harbor (Basketball), Kapiolani Beach Park (Beach Volleyball), Kailua Bay Beach Park (Board Sailing), Hickam Air Force Base (Bowling), Barbers Point Naval Air Station (Cycling), University of Hawaii (Diving), Klahuna, Westin Lagoons, Westin Kiele Kauai (Golf), Waikiki Beach (Outrigger Canoe), Schofield Barracks (Road Running), Waikiki Yacht Club (Sailing), Ala Wai Field Schofield Leader Park (Soccer), Hickam Air Force Base (Softball), Haleiwa (Surfing), Waikiki Beach (Surf-ski Paddling), University of Hawaii (Swimming), Bloch Arena, Pearl Harbor (Table Tennis), Klahuna Club Westin Lagoons, Kauai (Tennis), Kaiser High School (Track), Ala Moana Beach (Beach Sprints), Kapiolani Park (Triathlon), BYU-Hawaii (Volleyball)

1998   The Hague   Netherlands   August 29–September 5

Sports: Badminton, Basketball, Basketball 3-on-3, Beach Volleyball, Cycling, Dragon-boat Racing, Field Hockey, Golf, Indoor Carting, Mountain Biking, Petanque, Road Running, Sailing Hobie Cat, Soccer, Soccer 6-a-side, Squash, Table Tennis, Tennis, Ten-pin Bowling, Triathlon, Volleyball

2000   Aberdeen   Scotland   July 13–16

Sports: Badminton, Basketball, Basketball 3–on–3, Cycling, Cricket 8s, Dragonboat Racing, Field Hockey, Football, Football 6s, Golf, Karting, Lawn Bowling, Mountain Biking, Netball, Petanque, Rugby 7s, Running, Squash, Table Tennis, Tennis, Ten-pin Bowling, Touch Rugby, Triad and Triathlon, Volleyball

World Dwarf Games

The Dwarf Athletic Association of America (DAAA) was formed in 1985 to develop, promote and provide quality amateur-level athletic opportunities for dwarf athletes in the United States. The DAAA represents athletes who are dwarves (those 4 ft. 10 in. or less, adult height) as a result of chondrodysplasia or related causes.

The DAAA began sponsoring national Dwarf Games on an annual basis in 1986 and these led to the first World Dwarf Games in Chicago, Illinois, in July 1993. 165 athletes from ten nations participated in eight sports: athletics, basketball, boccia, powerlifting, soccer, swimming, table tennis and volleyball. During the meeting in Chicago, the International Dwarf Athletic Federation (IDAF) was created, to join together the national federations that had been established around the world.

The second World Dwarf Games were held in Peterborough, England, July 18–25, 1997. British Olympian and world champion javelin thrower Fatima Whitbread was the games' patron. Two hundred athletes participated from Canada, Denmark, Finland, France, Germany, Great Britain, New Zealand, the Philippines and the United States.

Year	Host City	Host Nation	Dates	Nations	Athletes	Sports
1993	Chicago	USA	July 1–6	10	165	8
1997	Peterborough	England	July 18–25	9	200	10

1993   Chicago   USA   July 1–6

Sports: Athletics, Basketball, Boccia, Powerlifting, Swimming, Soccer, Table Tennis, Volleyball

1997   Peterborough   England   July 18–25

Sports: Athletics, Basketball, Badminton, Boccia, Field Hockey, Powerlifting, Soccer, Swimming, Table Tennis, Volleyball (Sailing as demonstration sport)
Nations: Canada, Denmark, Finland, France, Germany, Great Britain, New Zealand, Philippines, United States

World Equestrian Games

The World Equestrian Games, organized under the auspices of the Fédération Équestre Internationale (FEI), are the international multisport competition dedicated to the disciplines of dressage, jumping, three-day event, driving, vaulting and endurance riding. In addition to the preparations for the human participants, organizers also need to make arrangements for at least as many horses.

Stockholm, Sweden, hosted the first games in July 1990 in Stockholm Stadium, the venue for the 1912 Olympic Games and for the equestrian events of the 1956 Olympic Games, when Australia's strict horse quarantine laws prevented the equestrian events from being held in Melbourne. The 1990 games were regarded as highly organized and efficient with each of the events serving as the world championships for their respective disciplines. The games were well attended; 100,000 spectators passed through the gates for the driving championships alone.

West Germany won four medals of each color, in the team and individual dressage and the male and female individual vaulting titles.

The second games in 1994 at The Hague, Netherlands, were beset with budgeting and organizational difficulties. The participants complained about the lack of accommodations for grooms and riders and some horses were boarded at a great distance from the venues.

Such was the view of the games at The Hague that when the 1996 Olympic Games equestrian events came under similar criticism for their lack of organization, Hugh Thomas, the technical director of the FEI who filed a formal complaint against the Atlanta organizers, said, "We shouldn't compare this to The Hague. It's fractionally better than that, but there were ships that were fractionally better than the Titanic. They just sank more slowly."[223]

The main games stadium at Zuiderpark was a temporary structure with space for 26,000 spectators, said to be the largest temporary stadium ever constructed in Europe.[224] Though the facilities and organization left something to be desired (the official reports from the FEI for all five disciplines all mention the poor organization), the competition itself was considered to be of a very high standard.

A unified Germany won a total of seven gold medals, with winning performances in both team and individual driving, jumping, dressage and the team Grand Prix special. So dominating were the Germans that no other team won more than one gold medal. Seven other nations split the rest of the events with one win apiece.

The World Equestrian Games ran into more trouble in the preparations for the third edition which was awarded to Dublin, Ireland, and scheduled to be held in 1998. The Irish government pulled its financial support for the games late in 1996, forcing the organizers to find a title sponsor. Nissan was signed on preliminarily to fund the games. Plans seemed to be progressing well in early 1997 when the Royal Dublin Society (RDS) and the games organizers could not reach an agreement on the use of the RDS facilities. All of the events were then moved to Punchestown, 25 miles from Dublin, where some events had already been scheduled. In May 1997, when a television guarantee could not be reached (a guarantee was one of the stipulations of Nissan's sponsorship agreement), Nissan pulled its title sponsorship. The games were called off in July.

The FEI reopened its bidding process, with Great Britain, Portugal, Germany and Italy among the candidates. Italy was selected at the end of August 1997. The games were scheduled for the first two weeks of October 1998, and would use the Pratoni del Vivaro, the facility used in the 1960 Rome Olympic Games, the Stadio Flaminio, and the Tenuta Santa Barbara.

A tremendous amount of work and cooperation between the FEI and the Italian organizers took place in the next year in order to prepare for the games. The Italians hired internationally renowned equestrian course designers Albino Garbari and Marcello Mastronardi to create courses for eventing and show jumping. Equally respected Herman Duckek was chosen to prepare the arena surface for the dressage and jumping competitions.

To open the games, the World Equestrian Games flag was carried from Lausanne, the headquarters of the FEI, to Rome on horseback. The ceremony was opened by IOC member (and president of the FEI) the Infanta Doña Pilar de Borbón, IOC President Juan Antonio Samaranch, and Italy's IOC representatives, Franco Carraro, Mario Pescante and Primo Nebiolo.

While horse racing was not part of the World Equestrian Games, both of Rome's racecourses, Capannelle and Tor di Valle, offered free entry to any person participating in or attending any World Equestrian Games event.

Germany once again showed its equestrian strength by winning gold medals in individual and team dressage, women's vaulting, team vaulting and show jumping. New

Zealand won the team and individual gold medals in the three-day event. Blyth Tait, the 1990 Games champion, was the individual medalist. Netherlands won the team driving event; Werner Ulrich of Switzerland won the individual driving gold. Rodrigo Pessoa of Brazil won the last event of the games, the individual show jumping. Also competing in the event was his father, Nelson Pessoa. Rodrigo dedicated his gold medal to his father, acknowledging his influence on his career.

The closing ceremonies of the games featured the Carosello, the mounted performance of the Italian police service, the Carabinieri. The flag of the games was turned over to Jerez de la Frontera, Spain, which was scheduled to host the next edition of the games in 2002.

Year	Host City	Host Nation	Dates	Nations	Athletes	Sports
1990	Stockholm	Sweden	July 24–Aug. 2	27[225]	546	5
1994	The Hague	Netherlands	July 27–Aug. 7th	27[226]	596	6
1998	Rome	Italy	October 1–11	43	800	5

1990   Stockholm   Sweden   July 24–Aug. 2

Nations: France, Great Britain, United States, Australia, Austria, Belgium, Canada, Denmark, West Germany, Holland, Italy, Sweden, Switzerland, USSR, Yugoslavia, South Korea, Mexico, Netherlands Antilles, Norway, Poland, Ireland, Finland, Czechoslovakia, East Germany, Hungary, Poland, Portugal (at least 27 nations in all; partial list)

Sports: Dressage, Driving, Endurance Riding, Show Jumping, Three-day Event

Venues: Stockholm Olympic Stadium (Jumping, Dressage), Royal Park (Three-day Event—Dressage and Endurance, Driving—Dressage, Driving—Endurance)

MEDALS

Nation	Gold	Silver	Bronze	Total
West Germany	4	4	4	12
Holland	2	0	0	2
New Zealand	2	0	0	2
France	2	0	1	3
Great Britain	1	4	1	6
United States	1	0	2	3
Switzerland	1	0	1	2
Sweden	0	2	0	2
Hungary	0	0	2	2
Belgium	0	1	0	1
Finland	0	1	0	1
Soviet Union	0	1	0	1
Australia	0	0	1	1
Spain	0	0	1	1

1994   The Hague   Netherlands   July 27–August 7

Nations: Australia, Belgium, Brazil, France, Germany, Great Britain, Netherlands, New Zealand, Sweden, Switzerland, United States (at least 27 nations in all; partial list)

Sports: Dressage, Driving, Endurance Riding, Show Jumping, Three-day Event, Vaulting

Venues: Zuiderpark (Jumping, Dressage, Three-day Event), Duindigt (Endurance Riding), De Vlassakers (Driving—Endurance)

MEDALS

Nation	Gold	Silver	Bronze	Total
Germany	7	4	5	16
France	1	4	1	6
United States	1	2	1	4
Holland	1	1	3	5
Great Britain	1	1	1	3
Switzerland	1	0	1	2
New Zealand	1	0	0	1
Denmark	1	0	0	1
Sweden	0	1	1	2
Belgium	0	1	0	1
Australia	0	0	1	1

1998   Rome   Italy   October 1–11

Sports: Dressage, Driving, Show Jumping, Three-day Event, Vaulting
Venues: Stadio Flaminio (Show Jumping and Dressage), Pratoni del Vivaro (Three-day Event, Driving), Tor di Quinto (Vaulting)
Nations: Argentina, Australia, Austria, Belarus, Belgium, Bermuda, Brazil, Bulgaria, Canada, Chile, Denmark, Egypt, Finland, France, Germany, Great Britain, Greece, Hungary, Israel, Italy, Jamaica, Japan, Lithuania, Luxembourg, Mexico, Netherlands, New Zealand, Norway, Poland, Portugal, Russia, Saudi Arabia, South Africa, Spain, Sweden, Switzerland, Ukraine, United States, Venezuela (possibly 2 more)

MEDALS

Nation	Gold	Silver	Bronze	Total
Germany	5	2	4	11
New Zealand	2	1	0	3
Netherlands	1	2	1	4
United States	1	1	1	3
Switzerland	1	1	0	2
Brazil	1	0	0	1
France	0	4	0	4
Sweden	0	0	3	3
Great Britain	0	0	2	2

World Ex-Service Wheelchair and Amputee Games

The Royal British Legion, the premier charity organization for ex-servicemen in the United Kingdom, organized the first World Ex-Service Wheelchair and Amputee Games to bring together former soldiers, sailors and airmen "in an atmosphere of reconciliation, shared common experiences and to form strong bonds of friendship."

Twenty countries participated in the inaugural games in 1993, including athletes from the 1992 Barcelona Paralympics. They used the established facilities at the Stoke Mandeville Sports Stadium. King Hussein of Jordan helped open the games.

The 1993 games were also known as "Challenge 93," the 1997 games as "Challenge 97."

Year	Host City	Host Nation	Dates	Nations	Athletes	Sports
1993	Aylesbury	England	July 10–16	20	200	10
1997	Pretoria	South Africa	Sept. 20–28	NA	NA	11

1993   Aylesbury   England   July 10–16

Sports: Archery, Athletics, Basketball, Lawn Bowling, Shooting, Snooker, Swimming, Table Tennis, Weightlifting (Fencing—exhibition)

1997   Pretoria   South Africa   September 20–28

Sports: Archery, Athletics, Basketball, Lawn Bowls, Quad Rugby, Shooting, Snooker, Swimming, Table Tennis, Tennis, Weightlifting

World Games

The World Games are the "Olympic Games" for sports that have not yet been included in the Olympic Games. Most of the sports are working hard through their International Federations to gain the recognition of the International Olympic Committee with the hopes of being included in future Olympic competitions. This will be an increasingly difficult task, however, given that the Olympic movement is taking measure to keep the size of the Olympic Games from growing.

The games differ drastically from the Olympics in that there are no flags, anthems, or national teams. The athletes are housed by sport and march into the opening ceremony by sport and not by nation.

The organizers have established a limit of entries to about 2,500 for each games, to lessen their impact on the host city and to control the cost. The rules also specify that each host city must be able to stage the games with existing infrastructure. No new facilities are to be added solely for the games.

Some of the sports included in past World Games are: acrobatics, aerobics, bodybuilding, bowling, casting, ballroom dancing, field archery, fin swimming, fistball (faustball), ju-jitsu, karate, korfball, lifesaving, parachuting, petanque, powerlifting, roller-skating, squash, trampoline, triathlon, tug of war, tumbling, water skiing, and weightlifting (for women). While the games are meant to showcase the non–Olympic sports, during the very first games sports already on the Olympic program were not excluded. This decision was made so that the Olympic Games could not claim that they were excluded from the World Games, and therefore argue that sports in the World Games should be excluded from the Olympic Games. In practice, the emphasis is on sports not in the Olympic Games.

The idea for the games came out of the 1974 meetings of GAISF, the General Association of International Sports Federations. At the time, 27 of the 51 federations of GAISF were not included in the Olympic Games and decided to create a competition that would give the athletes from their respective federations an Olympic type of experience. The original intention was to hold the games every two years, but they have been held on a four-year cycle since their inception.

The first games were held at the University of Santa Clara in 1981 and nearby San Jose, California. The games used existing facilities which kept the costs for the first games low.

The next edition in London in 1985 showed how far the sports in the World Games have to go to earn the respect of the public and the media. London *Times* headlines belittled the games, calling the sports silly and a "joke." "Nobody died except perhaps of laughter" read the headline on the games' final day. Ticket sales lagged with only 30,000 spectators showing up during the eleven days of competition. Japanese shipbuilder Ryoichi Sasakawa promised to underwrite that games with a bill expected to be around 300,000 pounds.

The 1989 Games in Karlsruhe, West Germany, gained respect, were considered to be well-organized, and had the support of the IOC. Juan Antonio Samaranch helped open them, along with Dr. Un Yong Kim of Korea, one of the founders of the International World Games Association. Some 250,000 spectators passed through the games' turnstiles, and television coverage was extensive.

Underwater swimmer Serghei Akhapov from the Soviet Union set a world record in the 200 meter underwater finswimming event with a time of 1:25.70.

The Hague, Netherlands, hosted the 1993 games, with 74 nations providing fine athletic performances. The event was notably disorganized, however, and considered to be a disappointment after the rousing success of 1989. ESPN gave daily coverage to the games, helping to promote their popularity in the United States.

French water skier Patrice Martin won his fourth consecutive World Games title. Great Britain's Andrea Holmes won her third straight duo trampoline title. She also won the singles trampoline event in the 1985 and 1989 games.

The 1997 games in Lahti, Finland, were originally scheduled for Port Elizabeth, South Africa. Lahti had been selected as the host for the 2001 World Games, but Port Elizabeth canceled in 1995 and Lahti was asked to step in on two years' notice and organize them.

Finnish television covered the games extensively with IMG and Transworld International broadcasting them internationally. The IOC continued to help advertise the World Games, with Samaranch again present at the opening ceremony. Since 1993, the IOC has also helped with the costs related to drug testing for the games.

After the 2000 Sydney Olympic Games, the International Olympic Committee and International World Games Association (IWGA) signed an historic agreement for further cooperation. The agreement, signed by IOC president Juan Antonio Samaranch and IWGA president Ron Froehlich, stated that the IOC would grant patronage to the World Games, provide technical assistance through the IOC's transfer-of-knowledge program, and encourage the National Olympic Committees to support and assist their national multisport delegations to take part in the World Games.

The IWGA also committed itself to continue to work with the World Anti-Doping Agency (WADA), and the IOC agreed to grant funding for antidoping control to the organizing committee of a World Games event.

Akita, Japan, held the sixth edition of the games in 2001.

Year	Host City	Host Nation	Dates	Nations	Athletes	Sports
1981	Santa Clara	USA	July 24–August 2	18	1265	18
1985	London	England	July 25–August 4	48	1550	23
1989	Karlsruhe	West Germany	July 20–30	54	1965	19
1993	The Hague	Netherlands	July 22–August 1	74	2275	25
1997	Lahti	Finland	August 7–17	71	2500	25

1981   Santa Clara   USA   July 24–August 2

Sports: Badminton, Baseball, Bodybuilding, Bowling, Casting, Fin Swimming, Karate, Powerlifting, Racquetball, Roller-skating Artistic, Roller-skating Hockey, Roller-skating Speed, Softball, Tae Kwon Do, Trampoline, Tug of War (men), Tumbling, Water Skiing

1985   London   England   July 25–August 4

Sports: Bodybuilding, Bowling, Casting, Field Archery, Fin Swimming, Fistball (Faustball), Karate, Korfball, Lifesaving, Netball, Petanque, Powerlifting, Racquetball, Roller-skating Artistic, Roller-skating Hockey, Roller-skating Speed, Softball, Sombo, Tae Kwon Do, Trampoline, Tug of War (men), Tumbling, Water Skiing

Venues: Wembley Conference Center (Opening Ceremonies, Power Lifting, Body Building, Princes Club, Bedfont [Water Skiing]), Tolmers Scout Camp (Field Archery), David Lloyd Club (Racquetball), Crystal Palace (Roller Hockey), Speed Roller-skating, Artistic Roller-skating, Karate, Life Saving, Fin Swimming, Trampoline, Korfball, Sombo, Netball, Tae Kwon Do, Wimbledon Stadium (Speedway), Copthall Stadium (Softball, Faustball, Casting, Petanque, Tug of War), Stevenage Bowling Center (Bowling)

1989   Karlsruhe   West Germany   July 20–30

Sports: Bodybuilding, Bowling, Field Archery, Fin Swimming, Fistball (Faustball), Karate, Korfball, Lifesaving, Netball, Petanque, Powerlifting, Roller-skating Artistic, Roller-skating Hockey, Roller-skating Speed, Tae Kwon Do, Trampoline, Tug of War (men), Tumbling, Water Skiing

1993   The Hague   Netherlands   July 22–August 1

Nations: Australia, Belgium, Brazil, Bulgaria, China, Chinese Taipei, Czech Republic, Denmark, Egypt, Equatorial Guinea, Finland, France, Germany, Great Britain, Hungary, Japan, Mexico, Netherlands, New Zealand, Poland, Portugal, Russia, Singapore, South Korea, Spain, Sweden, Switzerland, Ukraine, United States (forty-five more)

Sports: Beach Volleyball, Bodybuilding, Bowling, Casting, Field Archery, Fin Swimming, Fistball (Faustball), Karate, Korfball, Lifesaving, Netball, Petanque, Powerlifting, Racquetball, Roller-skating Artistic, Roller-skating Hockey, Roller-skating Speed, Sombo, Tae Kwon Do, Trampoline, Triathlon, Tug of War (men), Tumbling, Water Skiing

1997   Lahti   Finland   July 7–17

Nations: Argentina, Australia, Austria, Belarus, Belgium, Brazil, Bulgaria, Canada, China, Chinese Taipei, Colombia, Czech Republic, Denmark, Egypt, Finland, France,

Germany, Great Britain, Greece, Hungary, Indonesia, Italy, Japan, Kazakhstan, Malaysia, Netherlands, Norway, Poland, Russia, Saudi Arabia, Slovakia, Slovenia, South Africa, South Korea, Spain, Sweden, Switzerland, Ukraine, United States, Uzbekistan (31 more)

Sports: Aerobics, Bodybuilding, Bowling, Casting, Ballroom Dancing, Field Archery, Fin Swimming, Fistball (Faustball), Jujitsu, Karate, Korfball, Lifesaving, Parachuting, Petanque, Powerlifting, Roller-skating Artistic, Roller-skating Hockey, Roller-skating Speed, Sport Acrobatics, Squash, Trampoline, Triathlon, Tug of War (men), Tumbling, Water Skiing, Weightlifting (Women) (Exhibition sports: Aikido, Boule Lyonnaise, Floorball, Pesapallo, Indoor Tug of War, Military Pentathlon)

Venues: Sport Center (Opening Ceremonies), Suurhalli Sportshall (Karate, Sport Acrobatics, Weightlifting, Powerlifting, Trampolining, Tumbling, Floorball, Tug of War), Suurhalli Exhibition Hall (Squash), Urheilutalo A, (Sport Dancing, Korfball), Urheilutalo B (Aikido, Jujitsu), Kispuisto Sportspark (Petanque, Boule Lyonnaise, Casting, Pesapallo, Tug of War), Jaahalli Icehall (Artistic Roller-skating, Roller Hockey), Lahti City Theater (Bodybuilding), Jokimaa, Horse Racing Centre (Parachuting), Bowling Centre (Bowling), Salpausselka Ridges (Field Archery), Hennala/ Halvala (Military Pentathlon), Squash Centres (Squash)

MEDALS

Nation	Gold	Silver	Bronze	Total
United States	17	18	10	45
Germany	16	16	10	42
China	16	13	7	36
Russia	16	11	14	41
Italy	12	12	15	39
Sweden	8	6	9	23
Great Britain	6	8	7	21
Japan	6	3	5	14
Belgium	6	3	4	13
France	5	12	7	24
Czech Republic	5	5	4	14
Australia	5	4	5	14
Spain	5	2	7	14
Ukraine	4	8	0	12
Netherlands	4	6	7	17
Chinese Taipei	4	2	3	9
Belarus	3	1	3	7
Canada	3	0	3	6
Hungary	2	2	4	8
Colombia	2	2	2	6
Egypt	2	1	1	4
South Africa	2	0	4	6
Austria	1	3	1	5
Slovakia	1	2	2	5
Denmark	1	2	1	4
Norway	1	1	4	6
Slovenia	1	1	2	4
South Korea	1	1	2	4
Greece	1	1	1	3

Nation	Gold	Silver	Bronze	Total
Switzerland	1	1	1	3
Bulgaria	1	1	0	2
Indonesia	1	1	0	2
Uzbekistan	1	1	0	2
Brazil	1	0	2	3
Argentina	1	0	1	2
Kazakhstan	1	0	1	2
Malaysia	1	0	0	1
Saudi Arabia	1	0	0	1
Finland	0	9	10	19
Poland	0	2	5	7

World Games for the Deaf

The World Games for the Deaf were established in 1924 in Paris, France, with one hundred and thirty-three athletes from nine countries participating.[227] During these first games, leaders from the participating nations met to establish the International Committee of Silent Sports which would later become the CISS, the Comité International des Sports des Sourds.[228] The CISS sets the rules for deaf sport, the first of which is that to participate in the deaf games, individuals must have a hearing loss of greater than 55 decibels in the better ear.

Periodic congresses are held by the CISS to discuss matters related to deaf sport. The first Congress in 1926 in Brussels established the statutes for the CISS. The Congress of 1933 in Copenhagen established a world records commission to keep track of all-time world bests for deaf athletes in swimming and athletics. The United States became the first non–European member of the CISS during the fourth games in 1935 in London. In 1955 the International Olympic Committee recognized the CISS for the first time as an "International Federation with Olympic Standing," and in 1957 the CISS agreed to amend its statutes to comply with IOC rules and forgo the use of the word Olympic and the use of Olympic symbols. In 1966, the IOC awarded the Coubertin Cup to the CISS for its efforts in the promotion of international sports.

The 1965 games in Washington, D.C., were a fascinating example of the Cold War reaching to all areas of society, even deaf sport. Competition was strong between the Russians and United States. Both teams finished with fifty-three total medals, though the *Washington Post* published the medals table and placed the United States, with its nine gold medals, above Russia with twenty-nine gold medals.

In 1974, the 50-year anniversary of the CISS, the Italian Deaf Sport Federation established a CISS Museum in Rome which still exists today. Tehran, Iran, was to host the 1981 games but internal political strife forced them to be moved to Cologne.

South Africa was given membership in the CISS in 1979, but not allowed to participate in international competitions until 1983, and only if every other participating nation agreed. At the same Congress in 1983, hearing aids were made illegal in competition.

In 1985, the trend in competitions for athletes with physical handicaps was to integrate as much as possible. The Paralympic Games, which had begun with wheelchair athletes, had expanded to include amputees and athletes with visual impairments and cerebral palsy. The CISS was asked by the International Olympic Committee to join the International Coordinating Committee (ICC, which later became the IPC, International Paralympic Committee) to help coordinate all sports for disabled athletes under one organization. The CISS agreed to join, but only after it had been assured by the IOC that it could continue with its own World Games for the Deaf. After much disagreement over the sharing of revenues, after the decision to include deaf athletes in the Paralympic Games (the International Paralympic Committee had never made the arrangements for deaf athletes to be included in the Paralympics), and after confusion over whether National Olympic Committees or the national disabled sport federations had jurisdiction over deaf sports, the CISS decided in 1993 to leave the IPC and once again organize its events independently of any other organization.[229]

The hosting of the World Games for the Deaf has primarily been the domain of the European nations—the event has been held on the European continent 15 times through the 1997 Games. The United States has hosted the competition twice and New Zealand once.

The 1997 Games in Copenhagen, Denmark were the largest to date with 2,078 athletes from 70 nations.

Rome was chosen to host the 2001 games.

Year	Host City	Host Nation	Dates	Nations	Athletes	Sports
1924	Paris	France	August 10–17	9	133	5
1928	Amsterdam	Netherlands	August 18–26	10	210	5
1931	Nürnberg	Germany	August 19–25	14	316	6
1935	London	England	August 18–24	12	283	6
1939	Stockholm	Sweden	August 24–27	13	264	6
1949	Copenhagen	Denmark	August 12–16	14	393	7
1953	Brussels	Belgium	August 15–19	16	524	7
1957	Milan	Italy	August 25–30	25	626	10
1961	Helsinki	Finland	August 6–10	24	595	11
1965	Washington DC	USA	June 27–July 3	27	697	9
1969	Belgrade	Yugoslavia	August 9–16	33	1183	12
1973	Malmö	Sweden	July 21–28	32	1061	11
1977	Bucharest	Romania	July 17–27	32	1118	12
1981	Cologne	West Germany	July 24–August 2	32	1213	12
1985	Los Angeles	USA	July 10–20	29	1053	12
1989	Christchurch	New Zealand	January 17–30	30	959	NA
1993	Sofia	Bulgaria	July 24–August 2	51	1706	NA
1997	Copenhagen	Denmark	July 13–23	70	2078	15

1924　Paris　France　August 10–17

Nations: Belgium, Czechoslovakia, France, Great Britain, Holland, Poland, Hungary,* Italy,* Romania*

*Athletes from these nations participated but these countries did not have organized national federations

Sports: Athletics, Cycling, Football, Shooting, Swimming

MEDALS

Nation	Gold	Silver	Bronze	Total
France	21	27	8	56
Holland	3	5	2	10

Nation	Gold	Silver	Bronze	Total
Great Britain	3	2	5	10
Italy	2	0	0	2
Belgium	1	4	12	17
Poland	0	1	0	1

1928   Amsterdam   Netherlands   August 18–26

Nations: Belgium, Czechoslovakia, France, Germany, Great Britain, Holland, Hungary, Poland, Switzerland (1 more)
Sports: Athletics, Cycling, Football, Swimming, Tennis

MEDALS

Nation	Gold	Silver	Bronze	Total
Germany	14	11	5	30
France	11	14	6	31
Great Britain	4	2	9	15
Belgium	2	4	4	10
Poland	2	2	0	4
Hungary	2	0	0	2
Holland	0	1	6	7
Czechoslovakia	0	1	0	1
Switzerland	0	0	1	1

1931   Nürnberg   Germany   August 19–25

Nations: Austria, Belgium, Czechoslovakia, Denmark, Finland, France, Germany, Great Britain, Holland, Hungary, Italy, Norway, Sweden (1 more)
Sports: Athletics, Cycling, Football, Shooting, Swimming, Tennis

MEDALS

Nation	Gold	Silver	Bronze	Total
Germany	13	14	10	37
Denmark	10	2	5	17
France	8	8	9	25
Sweden	4	4	0	8
Belgium	3	1	3	7
Finland	2	5	2	9
Hungary	2	2	1	5
Norway	1	1	2	4
Holland	1	1	0	2
Italy	1	1	0	2
Austria	0	3	4	7
Great Britain	0	2	8	10
Czechoslovakia	0	0	1	1

1935   London   England   August 18–24

Nations: Austria, Belgium, Denmark, Finland, France, Germany, Great Britain, Holland, Hungary, Norway, Sweden, United States
Sports: Athletics, Cycling, Football, Shooting, Swimming, Tennis

MEDALS

Nation	Gold	Silver	Bronze	Total
Great Britain	9	8	8	25
France	8	4	5	17
Germany	8	3	9	20
Finland	5	3	6	14
Sweden	3	10	3	16
Belgium	2	3	0	5
Holland	2	2	1	5
Norway	1	4	2	7
Denmark	1	2	4	7
Hungary	1	2	2	5
United States	1	1	1	3
Austria	0	1	1	2

1939   Stockholm   Sweden   August 24–27

Nations: Belgium, Denmark, Finland, France, Germany, Great Britain, Holland, Norway, Poland, Sweden, United States (2 more)
Sports: Athletics, Cycling, Football, Shooting, Swimming, Tennis

MEDALS

Nation	Gold	Silver	Bronze	Total
Germany	14	11	7	32
Sweden	13	8	6	27
Finland	6	6	5	17
France	4	9	8	21
Great Britain	4	4	7	15
Belgium	2	1	3	6
Norway	1	3	4	8
Holland	1	0	0	1
Denmark	0	2	2	4
United States	0	1	0	1
Poland	0	0	4	4

1949   Copenhagen   Denmark   August 12–16

Nations: Belgium, Czechoslovakia, Denmark, Finland, France, Great Britain, Holland, Italy, Norway, Sweden, Switzerland, United States, Yugoslavia, (one more)
Sports: Athletics, Cycling, Football, Shooting, Swimming, Tennis, Water Polo

MEDALS

Nation	Gold	Silver	Bronze	Total
Denmark	11	9	10	30
Finland	11	4	8	23
Holland	7	5	1	13
Sweden	6	15	8	29
Great Britain	5	1	0	6
France	4	6	6	16
Norway	4	3	6	13

Nation	Gold	Silver	Bronze	Total
Italy	1	1	3	5
Belgium	0	3	1	4
United States	0	1	0	1
Czechoslovakia	0	0	2	2
Switzerland	0	0	2	2
Yugoslavia	0	0	1	1

1953   Brussels   Belgium   August 15–19

Nations: Belgium, Denmark, East Germany, Finland, France, Great Britain, Holland, Italy, Norway, Sweden, Switzerland, United States, West Germany, Yugoslavia, (three more)

Sports: Athletics, Basketball, Cycling, Football, Shooting, Swimming, Tennis

MEDALS

Nation	Gold	Silver	Bronze	Total
West Germany	16	9	12	37
Great Britain	7	5	3	15
Finland	7	4	3	14
Sweden	6	8	7	21
Denmark	5	4	6	15
Norway	4	9	6	19
Holland	3	4	4	11
Belgium	2	2	2	6
Switzerland	2	0	2	4
United States	2	0	1	3
Italy	1	4	2	7
Yugoslavia	1	0	0	1
France	0	5	7	12
East Germany	0	0	1	1

1957   Milan   Italy   August 25–30

Nations: Belgium, Bulgaria, Czechoslovakia, Denmark, East Germany, Finland, France, Great Britain, Holland, Hungary, Italy, Poland, Romania, Soviet Union, Switzerland, United States, West Germany, Yugoslavia, (seven more)

Sports: Athletics, Basketball, Cycling, Football, Gymnastics, Shooting, Swimming, Table Tennis, Tennis, Water Polo

MEDALS

Nation	Gold	Silver	Bronze	Total
West Germany	14	10	11	35
Italy	13	9	20	42
Soviet Union	13	8	4	25
Hungary	10	4	2	16
United States	7	6	10	23
Bulgaria	5	4	3	12
Czechoslovakia	5	2	4	11
Switzerland	5	0	0	5

Nation	Gold	Silver	Bronze	Total
Poland	4	5	5	14
Denmark	4	1	2	7
Yugoslavia	3	5	4	12
Great Britain	1	9	1	11
France	1	6	5	12
Holland	1	5	1	7
Finland	1	3	3	7
Romania	0	6	3	9
Belgium	0	1	2	3
East Germany	0	0	1	1

1961   Helsinki   Finland   August 6–10

Nations: Belgium, Bulgaria, Canada, Czechoslovakia, Denmark, Finland, France, Great Britain, Holland, Hungary, Iran, Italy, New Zealand, Norway, Poland, Romania, Soviet Union, Sweden, Switzerland, United States, West Germany, Yugoslavia, (two more)

Sports: Athletics, Basketball, Cycling, Football, Gymnastics, Shooting, Swimming, Table Tennis, Tennis, Water Polo, Wrestling

MEDALS

Nation	Gold	Silver	Bronze	Total
Soviet Union	33	20	17	70
United States	14	13	13	40
West Germany	12	9	10	31
Italy	11	11	8	30
Hungary	9	6	3	18
Poland	5	7	12	24
Czechoslovakia	4	4	3	11
Iran	3	1	2	6
Finland	2	7	2	11
Denmark	2	6	3	11
Bulgaria	2	5	4	11
Great Britain	1	2	3	6
Holland	1	1	1	3
Norway	1	1	0	2
Yugoslavia	1	0	1	2
Romania	1	0	0	1
Canada	0	2	1	3
Switzerland	0	1	2	3
New Zealand	0	1	1	2
Belgium	0	1	0	1
Sweden	0	1	0	1
France	0	0	2	2

1965   Washington DC   USA   June 27–July 3

Nations: Argentina, Australia, Belgium, Canada, Denmark, Finland, France, Germany, Great Britain, Holland, Hungary, Iran, Italy, Japan, New Zealand, Norway, Poland, Soviet Union, Sweden, Switzerland, United States, Yugoslavia, (five more)

Venues: University of Maryland (Tennis, Soccer), UM Byrd Stadium (Athletics), UM Cole Field House (Basketball, Diving), Hains Point (Swimming), American University (Soccer), Gallaudet (Table Tennis, Basketball), Mount Vernon Parkway (Cycling), Ft. Reno, Quantico

Sports: Athletics, Basketball, Diving, Soccer, Swimming, Table Tennis, Tennis (list may be incomplete; these are the sports listed in *Washington Post*)

MEDALS

Nation	Gold	Silver	Bronze	Total
Soviet Union	29	15	9	53
United States	9	21	23	53
Poland	9	9	6	24
Italy	9	6	11	26
Hungary	7	8	4	19
Germany	5	4	8	17
Iran	4	6	0	10
Denmark	4	1	3	8
Canada	4	1	3	8
Great Britain	3	6	4	13
Finland	1	3	4	8
Yugoslavia	1	2	2	5
Norway	1	2	1	4
Australia	1	1	0	2
Switzerland	1	0	1	2
France	0	1	1	2
Japan	0	1	1	2
Argentina	0	1	0	1
Holland	0	1	0	1
Sweden	0	0	3	3
Belgium	0	0	1	1
New Zealand	0	0	1	1

1969   Belgrade   Yugoslavia   August 9–16

Nations: Argentina, Australia, Bulgaria, Canada, Colombia, Czechoslovakia, Denmark, East Germany, Finland, France, Great Britain, Holland, Hungary, Iran, Italy, Japan, Norway, Poland, Romania, Soviet Union, Sweden, United States, West Germany, Yugoslavia, (eleven more)

Sports: Athletics, Basketball, Cycling, Football, Gymnastics, Handball, Shooting, Swimming, Table Tennis, Tennis, Volleyball, Wrestling

MEDALS

Nation	Gold	Silver	Bronze	Total
Soviet Union	42	32	20	94
United States	22	25	23	70
Italy	13	10	12	35
Hungary	9	6	8	23
West Germany	6	2	4	12
Iran	5	4	3	12
Poland	4	6	9	19

Nation	Gold	Silver	Bronze	Total
Yugoslavia	3	4	12	19
Great Britain	3	3	1	7
East Germany	3	2	3	8
Canada	2	4	1	7
Finland	2	3	3	8
Denmark	1	4	1	6
Sweden	1	2	4	7
Czechoslovakia	1	2	1	4
Argentina	1	1	0	2
Norway	1	0	0	1
Bulgaria	0	6	6	12
Japan	0	3	0	3
Australia	0	1	0	1
Holland	0	0	3	3
Romania	0	0	3	3
Colombia	0	0	1	1
France	0	0	1	1

1973   Malmö   Sweden   July 21–28

Nations: Australia, Belgium, Bulgaria, Canada, Czechoslovakia, Denmark, East Germany, Finland, France, Great Britain, Holland, Hungary, Iran, Italy, Japan, Norway, Poland, Romania, Soviet Union, Sweden, Switzerland, United States, West Germany, Yugoslavia, (eight more)

Sports: Athletics, Basketball, Cycling, Football, Handball, Shooting, Swimming, Table Tennis, Tennis, Volleyball, Wrestling

MEDALS

Nation	Gold	Silver	Bronze	Total
United States	28	20	31	79
Soviet Union	27	16	7	50
Italy	10	4	6	20
West Germany	4	10	5	19
Hungary	4	2	7	13
Japan	4	2	0	6
Bulgaria	3	5	8	16
East Germany	3	3	2	8
France	3	3	1	7
Great Britain	2	6	3	11
Sweden	2	6	2	10
Iran	2	4	1	7
Yugoslavia	2	3	4	9
Finland	2	2	3	7
Norway	2	1	0	3
Poland	1	6	6	13
Belgium	1	3	3	7
Denmark	1	2	4	7
Canada	0	1	3	4
Czechoslovakia	0	1	1	2
Holland	0	1	1	2

Nation	Gold	Silver	Bronze	Total
Australia	0	1	0	1
Romania	0	0	2	2
Switzerland	0	0	2	2

1977   Bucharest   Romania   July 17–27

Nations: Australia, Belgium, Bulgaria, Canada, Denmark, East Germany, Finland, France, Hungary, Iran, Ireland, Italy, Japan, Norway, Poland, Romania, Soviet Union, Sweden, United States, West Germany, Yugoslavia, (eleven more)

Sports: Athletics, Basketball, Cycling, Football, Handball, Swimming, Shooting, Volleyball, Table Tennis, Tennis, Water Polo, Wrestling

MEDALS

Nation	Gold	Silver	Bronze	Total
United States	38	34	30	102
Soviet Union	27	16	21	64
Iran	8	5	2	15
Italy	6	3	7	16
Japan	5	2	0	7
West Germany	4	9	5	18
Yugoslavia	4	4	1	9
Sweden	3	2	1	6
Romania	3	0	4	7
Canada	2	6	7	15
Bulgaria	1	7	5	13
Hungary	1	3	3	7
Belgium	1	3	1	5
Denmark	1	2	1	4
East Germany	1	1	3	5
Norway	1	1	0	2
Australia	1	0	5	6
Poland	0	4	7	11
France	0	4	1	5
Finland	0	1	3	4
Ireland	0	1	0	1

1981   Cologne   West Germany   July 24–August 2

Nations: Australia, Austria, Belgium, Bulgaria, Canada, Denmark, East Germany, Finland, France, Great Britain, Holland, Hungary, India, Iran, Italy, Japan, New Zealand, Norway, Poland, Soviet Union, Spain, Sweden, Switzerland, United States, West Germany, Yugoslavia, (six more)

Sports: Athletics, Basketball, Cycling, Football, Handball, Shooting, Swimming, Table Tennis, Tennis, Volleyball, Water Polo, Wrestling

MEDALS

Nation	Gold	Silver	Bronze	Total
United States	45	30	36	111
Soviet Union	22	18	13	53

Nation	Gold	Silver	Bronze	Total
Iran	7	5	2	14
Japan	7	4	2	13
Italy	6	9	4	19
Yugoslavia	5	0	2	7
West Germany	3	9	17	29
Bulgaria	3	6	6	15
Finland	3	0	0	3
Australia	2	3	3	8
Austria	2	2	0	4
France	1	5	6	12
Hungary	1	3	2	6
East Germany	1	3	0	4
Poland	1	2	4	7
New Zealand	1	2	0	3
Denmark	1	1	4	6
Sweden	1	1	1	3
Holland	1	0	0	1
Canada	0	4	6	10
India	0	2	1	3
Switzerland	0	2	0	2
Great Britain	0	1	5	6
Belgium	0	1	1	2
Norway	0	1	1	2
Spain	0	0	1	1

1985   Los Angeles   USA   July 10–20

Nations: Australia, Austria, Belgium, Canada, Colombia, Denmark, Spain, Finland, France, Great Britain, Hong Kong, Holland, Hungary, India, Ireland, Israel, Italy, Japan, Mexico, Norway, New Zealand, Poland, South Korea, Switzerland, Sweden, United States, West Germany, Venezuela, Yugoslavia

Sports: Athletics, Badminton, Basketball, Cycling, Football, Handball, Shooting, Swimming, Table Tennis, Tennis, Volleyball, Water Polo

Sports for Women: Athletics, Badminton, Basketball, Swimming, Table Tennis, Tennis, Volleyball

Venues: Drake Stadium (Opening Ceremonies, Athletics, Closing Ceremonies), Memorial Park Santa Monica (Badminton), Pepperdine University (Basketball, Swimming, Volleyball, Tennis, Water Polo), Griffith Park, Los Angeles, Emma Wood Park, Ventura, Santa Monica (roads) (Cycling), Palisades High School (Football, Volleyball), Prado Range, Corona (Shooting), Santa Monica City College (Table Tennis, Handball)

MEDALS				
Nation	Gold	Silver	Bronze	Total
United States	46	30	33	109
West Germany	8	21	14	43
Japan	8	5	2	15
France	6	9	8	23
Great Britain	5	11	10	26

Nation	Gold	Silver	Bronze	Total
Australia	5	1	3	9
Italy	4	2	8	14
Norway	4	2	3	9
Ireland	4	1	1	6
Denmark	2	1	3	6
New Zealand	2	1	0	3
Poland	1	4	4	9
Belgium	1	2	2	5
Finland	1	2	1	4
Canada	1	1	1	3
Holland	1	0	0	1
Yugoslavia	1	0	0	1
Sweden	0	4	1	5
Austria	0	2	0	2
Hungary	0	1	2	3
Switzerland	0	0	2	2
India	0	0	1	1
Colombia	0	0	0	0
Israel	0	0	0	0
South Korea	0	0	0	0
Spain	0	0	0	0
Venezuela	0	0	0	0

1997   Copenhagen   Denmark   July 13–23

Sports: Athletics, Badminton, Basketball, Bowling, Cycling, Football, Handball, Orienteering, Shooting, Swimming, Table Tennis, Tennis, Volleyball, Water Polo, Wrestling

Nations: Algeria, Argentina, Australia, Austria, Azerbaijan, Bangladesh, Belarus, Belgium, Canada, China, Croatia, Cuba, Cyprus, Czech Republic, Denmark, Estonia, Finland, France, Georgia, Germany, Greece, Hong Kong, Hungary, Iceland, India, Indonesia, Iran, Ireland, Israel, Italy, Japan, Kazakhstan, Kenya, Kuwait, Latvia, Lithuania, Macau, Macedonia, Malaysia, Mexico, Moldova, Mongolia, Netherlands, New Zealand, Norway, Pakistan, Poland, Portugal, Romania, Russia, Slovakia, Slovenia, South Africa, South Korea, Spain, Swaziland, Sweden, Switzerland, Taipei, Turkey, Turkmenistan, Uganda, Ukraine, United Kingdom, United States, Uzbekistan, Venezuela, Yugoslavia, Zambia, Zimbabwe

MEDALS

Nation	Gold	Silver	Bronze	Total
United States	24	21	23	68
Russia	10	12	12	34
Canada	9	4	4	17
Sweden	9	4	2	15
Germany	8	16	20	44
Iran	8	5	3	16
Italy	7	4	4	15
Japan	6	0	0	6
South Africa	5	2	2	9

Nation	Gold	Silver	Bronze	Total
Netherlands	4	5	6	15
Czech Republic	4	1	1	6
Australia	3	2	3	8
Ireland	3	2	1	6
Ukraine	2	9	3	14
Denmark	2	2	2	6
United Kingdom	2	1	2	5
Belarus	2	0	3	5
Yugoslavia	2	0	2	4
Belgium	1	4	3	8
Greece	1	3	2	6
Finland	1	3	1	5
Estonia	1	2	0	3
India	1	2	0	3
Hungary	1	1	0	2
Switzerland	1	1	0	2
Lithuania	1	0	1	2
Kazakhstan	1	0	1	2
China	1	0	0	1
Turkey	0	4	3	7
Romania	0	2	1	3
Poland	0	2	1	3
Algeria	0	2	0	2
France	0	1	3	4
Spain	0	1	2	3
Latvia	0	1	0	1
Moldova	0	1	0	1
Croatia	0	1	0	1
Taipei	0	0	2	2
Mongolia	0	0	1	1
Cuba	0	0	1	1
South Korea	0	0	1	1

World Masters Games

The World Masters Games can rightfully claim to be the largest international multisport competition in the world in terms of the number of athletes involved. In 1994, 24,000 masters athletes converged on Brisbane, Australia for the largest international multisport games ever held.

The International Masters Games Association in Copenhagen, Denmark, governs the games. Its goals are:

• To promote and encourage individuals of any age from all over the world to practice sports and to participate in the World Masters Games with the awareness that competitive sports can continue through life.

• To establish, every four years, an international multisport festival for mature people of any age, condition or standard, called the "World Masters Games."

• To promote, through the World Masters Games, friendship and understanding among mature sports people, regardless of age, gender, race, religion or sports status.

The games are open to all competitors, with no qualifying restrictions, other than age. The age divisions vary by sport, with the minimum ages ranging from 25 for diving, to 40 for fencing and golf. Athletes compete as individuals or teams but not on a national basis. The athletes are responsible for their own travel and housing expenses.

"Reunion competitions" are arranged at some games with athletes from other eras matched up to compete against each other again.

Toronto, Canada, welcomed athletes from sixty nations to the first games in 1985, though twelve of those nations were represented by just one competitor. At the last minute, the provincial government of Ontario and the Canadian federal government had to bail out the games with an extra $300,000 in funding, which strained the relations between the organizers and government officials.[230] Ticket sales below expectations also contributed to the financial disappointment.

Air guns were used in the shooting events to get around Canada's restrictive firearms laws. The International Cycling Union (UIC) refused to sanction the cycling races for anyone over the age of 65 as it did not issue racing licenses to athletes that old. The older age groups raced anyway, with the UIC conveniently looking the other way. Australian Olympic swimming star Dawn Fraser participated in four swimming events.

The games survived their rough initial outing and grew rapidly, with 15,000 participants in Denmark in 1989 and 24,000 in Brisbane in 1994.

In light of those numbers, the organizers for the 1998 games in Portland, Oregon, were disappointed when only 11,000 masters athletes showed up. Organizers had expected 25,000 athletes to participate and a financial windfall to result. A steep entry fee of $200 per person was the most mentioned factor for reducing the number of participants.

Past Olympic stars Dick Fosbury (high jump), Lee Evans (400 meters), and Joan Benoit-Samuelson (marathon), legendary track coach Payton Jordan, and long jumper and NFL star James Lofton, participated in the games. Benoit-Samuelson, running in the 40–44 age division, won the 5000 meters in a time of 17:03. Jordan, in the 80–84 age division, won gold medals in the 100 meters with 14.60 and the 200 meters with 31.62.

The two oldest competitors at the Portland games were 97-year-old diver Viola Krahn and 103-year-old shot putter Ben Levinson. When asked to say a few words at the opening ceremonies, Levinson responded, "I'm very happy to be here. Then again at my age, I'm very happy to be anywhere." When Krahn's turn came, she said, "I like older men."

The games were scheduled to return to Australia in the year 2002, when Melbourne was slated to serve as host.

Year	Host City	Host Nation	Dates	Nations	Athletes	Sports
1985	Toronto	Canada	August 7–25	60	7769	22
1989	Henning, Århus, Aalborg	Denmark		NA	15000	NA
1994	Brisbane	Australia	Sept. 26–Oct. 8	71	24000	30
1998	Portland	USA	August 9–22	102	11000	25

1998   Portland   USA   August 9–22

Sports: Athletics, Badminton, Baseball, Basketball, Bowling, Canoe/Kayak, Cycling, Diving, Fencing, Football, Golf, Orienteering, Rowing, Rugby, Sailing/Windsurfing, Shooting, Softball, Squash, Swimming, Table Tennis, Tennis, Triathlon, Volleyball, Water Polo, Weightlifting

Athletics(Track and Field, Cross Country, min. age 30); Badminton (min. age 30); Baseball (min. age 30); Basketball (Men, min. age 35; women, min. age 30); Bowling—Ten-pin, Singles, Doubles, Teams (min. age 30); Canoe/Kayak—Whitewater, Sprint, Marathon (min. age 30); Cycling—Road, Track, Mountain (min. age 30); Diving—Springboard, Platform (min. age 25); Fencing—Epee, Foil, Saber (min. age 40); Soccer (min. age 30); Golf (min. age 40); Orienteering (min. age 35); Rowing (min. age 27); Rugby (min. age 35); Sailing/Windsurfing (min. age 35); Shooting (min. age 35); Softball—Fastpitch (min. age 35); Slowpitch (men, min. age 40; women, min. age 35); Squash (min. age 30); Swimming (min. age 25); Table Tennis (min. age 30); Tennis (min. age 30); Triathlon—1.5 km swim, 40 km bike, 10 km run (men, min. age 40; women, min. age 35); Volleyball—Outdoor 6 Person Teams; Indoor 4 Person Teams (min. age 30); Water Polo (min. age 30); Weightlifting (min. age 35). All sports are for both men and women except baseball, which is for men only. Age is determined on the opening date of the games.

Venues: Multnomah Athletic Club, Tualatin Hills Park and Recreation Center (Badminton), Volcanoes Stadium, Chemetka Community College, South Salem High School, Willamette University, McKay High School, McNary High School, Western Baptist College, Sprague High School, Western Oregon University (Baseball), The Hoop, Vancouver, Wa., The Hoop, Beaverton (Basketball), Cascade Lanes (Bowling), Vancouver Lake and Lake River (Canoe/Kayak, Marathon), Big Eddy Rapid (Canoe/Kayak, Down River, Freestyle), First Street Rapid, Flume Park (Canoe/Kayak, Slalom), Mt. Hood Community College to Dodge Park (Cycling Road Race), Gresham (Cycling Criterium), West Leg Road (Cycling Hill Climb), Marine Drive (Cycling Time Trial), Alpenrose Velodrome (Cycling Sprints, Track), Flying M Ranch (Cycling, Mountain Bike), Tualatin Hills Aquatic Center (Diving, Water Polo), Double Tree Hotel Ballroom, Jantzen Beach (Fencing), Heron Lakes Golf Course, Eastmoreland Golf Course, Rose City Golf Course, Broadmoor Golf Course (Golf), Powell Butte Nature Park and Brooks Memorial State Park (Orienteering), Vancouver Lake and Park (Rowing), Tualatin Hills Fields (Rugby, Soccer), Port of Cascade Locks Marine Park (Sailing), Hillsboro Gun Club (Shooting), Powerlines Park, Delta Park Complex (Soccer), William V. Owens Complex and East Delta Park (Softball), River Place Athletic Club, Reed College Sports Center, Lloyd Athletic Center, Metro Family YMCA, MAC Club (Squash), Mt. Hood Community College (Swimming), Portland State University (Table Tennis), Tualatin Hills Tennis Center, Mountain Park Racquet Club, West Hills Racquet and Fitness Club (Tennis), University of Oregon—Hayward Field, Lane Community College (Athletics), Alton Baker Park (Cross Country), Henry Hagg Lake/Scroggins Valley Park (Triathlon), Tualatin Hills Softball Fields (Outdoor Volleyball), Tualatin Hills Athletic Center (Indoor Volleyball), Port of Hood River (Windsurfing), Oregon Convention Center (Weightlifting)

World Medical Games

Doctors, pharmacists, dental surgeons, veterinarians, internists, and final-year medical students (with written proof), are eligible to participate in the World Medical Games. Companions and spouses are eligible to participate but not included in the results. Participants compete as representatives of their hospitals, cities or universities. National flags, anthems and uniforms are expressly banned by the organizing body.

The games are broken into age divisions, starting with those under 35 and following in ten year increments up to age 65 and over.

Only twice have the games been outside Europe (through 2000): Casablanca in 1987 and Montreal in 1989. The games are generally accompanied by a medical symposium and have attracted over 2,000 participants (includes conference participants) on each occasion. American participation in the games has always been very limited. Fifty-three U.S. representatives went to the Montreal games, but generally only a handful of Americans participate each year. The organizers hope to expand the games, focusing on greater participation from those outside Europe.

One American who has enjoyed participating in the games is Dr. Lawrence Cohen. A swimmer, Dr. Cohen has competed in five World Medical Games and won 29 gold medals.

The 1999 games set records, with 2300 participants from 42 nations. Australia, Bosnia, Latvia, Liechtenstein and Turkey were represented for the first time. Thirty-two percent of the participants were from France. Specialists made up 41.8 percent of the participants, general practitioners 21.8 percent, physiotherapists 10.9 percent, dentists 10 percent, pharmacists 8.8 percent, students 5.2 percent and veterinarians 1.5 percent.

The 2000 games were held in Cannes, France, their birthplace, in July.

Year	Host City	Host Nation	Dates	Nations	Athletes	Sports
1978	Cannes	France	June 24–July 1*	24	1200	NA
1980	Cannes	France	June 28–July 5*	NA	NA	NA
1982	Cannes	France	June 26–July 3*	NA	NA	NA
1983	Paris	France	June 25–July 2*	NA	NA	NA
1984	Abano Terme	Italy	June 30–July 7*	NA	NA	NA
1985	Monte Carlo	Monaco	June 29–July 6*	NA	NA	NA
1986	Montecatin Terme	Italy	June 28–July 5*	NA	NA	NA
1987	Casablanca	Morocco	June 27–July 4*	NA	NA	NA
1988	Lyon	France	June 25–July 2*	NA	NA	NA
1989	Montreal	Canada	June 24–July 1*	NA	NA	NA
1990	Perpignan	France	June 30–July 7*	NA	NA	NA
1991	Heraklion	Greece	June 29–July 6*	NA	NA	NA
1992	Osturi	Italy	June 27–July 5*	NA	NA	NA
1993	Saint-Malo	France	June 26–July 4*	NA	NA	16
1994	Évian	France	June 25–July 3*	NA	NA	NA
1995	Limerick	Ireland	June 24–July 2*	NA	NA	NA
1996	Lisbon	Portugal	June 29–July 6	NA	NA	19
1997	Le Touquet	France	June 28–July 5	31	1700	20
1998	Klagenfurt	Austria	June 27–July 4	33	1500	21
1999	Saint-Tropez	France	June 26–July 3	40	2300	16
2000	Cannes	France	July 1–8	45	NA	21

*The dates of the games are generally scheduled for this time period, but exact dates are not available from the organizers.

1996   Lisbon   Portugal   June 29–July 6

Sports: Athletics, Basketball, Cycling, Fencing, Golf, Athletic Strength, Judo, Handball, Swimming, Rugby Sevens, Squash, Tennis, Table Tennis, Dinghy Sailing, Windsurfing, Volleyball, Shooting, Triathlon, Soccer

1997   Le Touquet   France   June 28–July 5

Nations: Algeria, Argentina, Austria, Belgium, Canada, Chile, Denmark, Estonia, France, Germany, Greece, Hungary, Ireland, Israel, Italy, Japan, Lithuania, Luxembourg, Morocco, Moldavia, Netherlands, Norway, Portugal, Slovakia, Slovenia, South Africa, South Korea, Sweden, Switzerland, United States, Yugoslavia

Sports: Athletics (inc. Half-marathon), Basketball, Cycling, Mountain Biking, Fencing, Golf, Athletic Strength, Judo, Handball, Swimming, Rugby Sevens, Squash, Tennis, Table Tennis, Dinghy Sailing, Windsurfing, Volleyball, Shooting (Clay Pigeon, Rifle, Pistol), Triathlon, Football

1998   Klagenfurt   Austria   June 27–July 4

Sports: Athletic Strength, Athletics, Basketball, Beach Volleyball, Cycling, Fencing, Football (11-a-side, 6-a-side), Golf, Judo, Mountain Biking, Swimming, Rugby Sevens, Half Marathon, Table Tennis, Tennis, Shooting (Rifle, Pistol, Clay Pigeon), Triathlon, Volleyball

1999   Saint-Tropez   France   June 26–July 3

Nations: Algeria, Argentina, Australia, Belgium, Brazil, Bosnia, Canada, Chile, Croatia, Czech Republic, Denmark, Estonia, Finland, France, Germany, Greece, Hungary, Ireland, Israel, Italy, Japan, Latvia, Liechtenstein, Lithuania, Luxembourg, Morocco, Netherlands, Poland, Portugal, Slovakia, Slovenia, South Africa, South Korea, Spain, Sweden, Switzerland, Tunisia, United Kingdom, Uruguay, United States

Sports: Athletics, Athletic Strength, Basketball, Cycling, Fencing, Football (11-a-side, 6-a-side), Golf, Judo, Mountain Biking, Rugby, Shooting (Rifle, Clay Pigeon, Pistol), Swimming, Table Tennis, Tennis, Triathlon, Volleyball

2000   Cannes   France   July 1–8

Sports: Athletics, Athletic Strength, Badminton, Basketball, Beach Volleyball, Cross Country, Cycling, Equestrian, Fencing, Football (11-a-side, 6-a-side), Golf, Judo, Mountain Biking, Rugby, Sailing, Shooting, Swimming, Table Tennis, Tennis, Triathlon, Volleyball

Venues: Sports Complex Maurice Chevalier (Athletics), Gymnasium Jules Ferry (Badminton), Gymnasium Ranguin (Basketball), Plage des Festival's Beach Majestic (Beach Volleyball), Gymnasium Les Muriers (Fencing), Sports Center Cannes (Athletic Strength, Judo, Volleyball), Golf Riviera, Golf Old Course (Golf), Cazagnaire Beach (Windsurfing, Sailing), Sports Complex Saint Cassein (Rugby), Tennis Club of the Red Country House (Tennis), Principiano Room, Le Cannet (Table Tennis), Stadium Pierre de Coubertin, Stadium Gioanni, Stadium Maurice Chevalier, Stadium of Saint Cassien, Stadium Estivals, Stadium Pegomas (Football)

World Nature Games

Brazilian President Fernando Henrique Cardoso and Brazilian Minister of Sport Edson Arantes do Nascimento, better remembered as football star Pelé, opened the first World Nature Games on September 27, 1997, at the spectacular Iguaçu Falls, where Brazil, Paraguay and Uruguay intersect, in front of 2000 spectators.

The World Nature Games focus on events that can be enjoyed in the great outdoors. The first edition took place in eleven cities and towns in the province of Parana, Brazil, with the Iguaçu Falls the center of attention. Athletes from fifty-five nations competed in the games.

Unique events and adaptations of events are the highlights of these games. Sky surfing (also contested in the World Air Games and the X-Games) was part of the parachuting competition. The ballooning competition was a test of accuracy in which the balloon pilots threw weighted banners as close to various targets as possible. In the fishing competition, fish were caught, weighed and then released back into the lake.

Archery orienteering was introduced at the World Nature Games as a new sport. The competition ran for three days, and comprised two races each day. Each course was between seven and eight kilometers long and athletes used compasses and maps to find the ten objectives, or control points, per course. Once found, the athletes shot three arrows at each control point from distances of 10 to 20 meters. The total time of the six races is also included in determining the winner.

The cycling, canoeing, equestrian and sailing competitions were all long-distance endurance races contested over a number of days. Cycling was contested on mountain bikes on rough rural roads, rather than the traditional road course. Golf, rafting, triathlon and a climbing exhibition filled out the schedule of events.

The organizers of the World Nature Games intend to hold the event on a quadrennial basis.

Year	Host City	Host Nation	Dates	Nations	Athletes	Sports
1997	Foz do Iguazi	Brazil	Sept. 27–Oct. 5	55	809	13

Nations: (partial list) Argentina, Austria, Belgium, Bulgaria, Chile, Colombia, Costa Rica, Cuba, Czech Republic, Denmark, Finland, France, Germany, Great Britain, Guatemala, Ireland, Israel, Italy, Japan, Luxembourg, Netherlands, Norway, Papua New Guinea, Poland, Portugal, Paraguay, Russia, South Africa, Sweden, Switzerland, Scotland, Slovakia, Ukraine, United States, Uruguay, Venezuela

Sports: Triathlon, Rafting, Canoeing, Endurance Horse Riding, Sailing (Hobie Cat and Laser), Archery Orienteering, Fishing, Cycling, Ballooning, Parachuting, Golf, Kayaking

Sports for Women: Triathlon, Equestrian, Archery Orienteering

Venues: Foz de Iguazi (Triathlon, Rafting, Canoeing—Slalom, Climbing), Guaíra, Porto Mendes, Entre Rios, Missal, Três Lagaos (Canoeing—Endurance, Sailing—Hobie Cat and Laser), Santa Helena, Entre Rios, Porto Mendes, Itaipulândia, Santa Helena (Endurance Horse Riding), Arroio Guaçu (Archery Orienteering), Guaíra (Fishing), Porto Mendes, Guaíra, Pato Bragado, Entre Rios, Itaipulândia, Três Lagaos (Cycling), various courses around Foz, São Miguel, Itaipulândia, Sta Terezhina, Missal, Guaíra, Mal Rondon, Porto Mendes, Santa Helena, Entre Rios, Pato Bragado (Ballooning), São Miguel (Parachuting)

World Peace Games/Jeux Mondiaux de le Paix

Frenchman Yves Angelloz founded the World Peace Games (Jeux Mondiaux de le Paix) in 1983. The International Committee for the World Peace Games (ICWPG) oversees the competitions and is sanctioned by cooperative agreements signed by UNESCO/FIDEPS, the United Towns Organization, and the University for Peace of the United Nations.

Participation is open to anyone, regardless of religion, citizenship, age or political convictions, with events in age categories ranging from under 19 years to over 80 years. Disabled athletes also have events on the schedule.

The games have lofty goals. Part of their charter reads, "Convinced that sports meetings carry an atmosphere of fair emulation and bring peoples together in a peaceful manner, that therefore they have an important part to play in the understanding and friendship between man and civilizations." The games have included cultural, humanitarian and economic components on each occasion.

The intent of the ICWPG is to hold the games every two years. The 1989 games in Morocco were deferred to 1990, and games scheduled to be held in 1994 in Malta had to be canceled altogether.

Year	Host City	Host Nation	Dates	Nations	Athletes	Sports
1983	Bellegarde	France		14	1500	NA
1985	Echiroles	France		28	10200	NA
1987	Neuchâtel/ Marignane	Switzerland/ France		30	18000	NA
1990	Fes/Ifrane/ Meknes	Morocco	July 17–22	42	22000	NA
1998	Dubai	United Arab Emirates	March 19–Apr. 18	75	28000	22

1998   Dubai   United Arab Emirates   March 19–April 18

Sports: Arm Wrestling, Athletics, Bowling, Beach Volleyball, Chess, Cycling, Desert Marathon, Football, Golf, Ice Hockey, Open Water Swimming, Road Race, Roller Bowl, Rowing, Snooker, Squash, Swimming, Table Tennis, Tennis, Trap Shooting, Triathlon, Tug of War (Parachuting demonstrations daily)

Venues: Hata, Dubai (Desert Marathon), Officers' Club (Athletics, Football, Chess, Squash, Roller Bowl), Emirates Hall (Snooker), Al Nasr Club (Tennis), Al Ahli Club (Table Tennis), Dubai City (Cycling Road Race, Running Road Race), Golf Club (Golf), Leisure Land (Bowling, Ice Hockey), Memzar Beach (Open Water Swim, Rowing), Al Khor Park (Beach Volleyball), Marine Club (Triathlon, Tug of War, Arm Wrestling), Jebel Ali (Trap Shooting)

World Police and Fire Games

The World Police and Fire Games are organized by the World Police and Fire Games Federation. Both the games and the organization grew from the development of the California Police Olympics which have been held in California on an annual basis since 1967. As the California games grew, the California Police Athletic Federation decided to take the idea to the international level.

The first international games held in San Jose, California, in 1985 were an immediate success, with 20 nations and 4713 athletes competing in 41 sports. In 1987 at the games in San Diego, Bob Hope performed at the opening ceremonies. On a sadder note, that same year, James Lynch, a firefighter from New York City, died suddenly after competing in the rowing event.

To be eligible to compete, a person must satisfy at least one of the following requirements:

• One must be publicly employed as a law enforcement officer or firefighter.

• One must have formal training as a law enforcement officer or firefighter.

• One's primary occupation must be as a law enforcement officer or firefighter.

• One must have been sworn in or appointed as a law enforcement officer or firefighter 180 days prior to the first day of the actual competition.

• One must be a member of an eligible agency.

• One must be a retired law enforcement officer or firefighter from an eligible agency.

The games focus on camaraderie and friendly competition, with the sports ranging from angling and archery to motorcycle riding, windsurfing and wrestling. Muster, S.W.A.T., scuba and police service dogs events use job skills as the basis for competition.

Both dogs and handlers are awarded medals in the police service dogs competitions. The teams compete in contests of obedience and agility, box search, protection, and narcotic detection.

The S.W.A.T. competition is a five-member team event that consists of negotiating an obstacle course, live fire house clearing, open-air range shooting, and rough-country orienteering. The competition is held over two days. Competitors are required to bring their own assault rifles and handguns, and carry a small first-aid kit, canteen, and a rappel seat with carabiner for the rough-country orienteering course.

The scuba competitors compete in a timed swim, over a buoyancy-obstacle course, in an equipment exchange, in a lift bag event, and over a navigation course.

The Calgary games in 1997 included a toughest competitor alive competition, which comprised a 5 km run, the shot put, a 100 meter dash, a 100 meter swim, a 6.1 meter (20 feet) rope climb, bench pressing, pull-ups, and an obstacle course.

Perhaps one of the most unique events ever held at an international games was the rodeo staged in Calgary. Competitors could participate in bareback bronco riding, bull riding, calf roping, steer wrestling, and a wild horse race (on a three-person team). The Calgary Fire Department, Royal Canadian Mounted Police and Calgary Police service teams swept the gold, silver and bronze medals in the wild cow milking contests!

The games include far more than sports events. There are also social activities, exhibitions of the latest police and firefighting equipment, and training seminars.

Ironically, during the 1995 Melbourne Games, with thousands of firefighters in attendance, one of the largest bush fires in the history of the State of Victoria broke out an hour north of Melbourne. Three days after the conclusion of competition, a fully loaded fuel truck rolled over directly in front of the Sports and Entertainment Center used for the games, exploding into a ball of flame and badly damaging the building. Organizers acknowledged how fortunate it was that no one was in the building, which had been packed with games participants the previous week.

The games also have provided their humorous moments. In the 1995 golf competition, John Kaninsky hit his tee shot far out of bounds. He took a two-stroke penalty and teed off again for a hole in one, to make par on the par three hole. During the bucket brigade event, it was noted that a number of competitors suffered minor injuries when teammates dropped buckets on their heads.

The Victoria Police Recruitment Center announced that any police officer wishing to stay in Australia would be welcome. There was at least one "defection" when a Canadian police officer took up the offer.

Criminals should take a look at the sports schedules and clear out before the World Police and Fire Games come to town. In 1997, at the games in Calgary, Alberta, detectives from neighboring Regina, Saskatchewan, caught a fugitive whom they recognized from their hometown.

The games were held in Europe for the first time in 1999. Stockholm, Sweden, hosted them after outbidding Barcelona, Indianapolis and Milwaukee in 1995. A total of 68 sports were included in the Stockholm edition.

The ninth games were scheduled for Indianapolis, Indiana, in 2001, and the tenth games for Barcelona in 2003.

Year	Host City	Host Nation	Dates	Nations	Athletes	Sports
1985	San Jose	USA	August 4–11	20	4713	41
1987	San Diego	USA	August 1–9	15	4972	43
1989	Vancouver	Canada	July 29–August 6	18	4373	43
1991	Memphis	USA	June 22–30	21	4097	41
1993	Colorado Springs	USA	July 31–August 7	26	5375	48
1995	Melbourne	Australia	February 26–March 4	43	6692	56
1997	Calgary	Canada	June 27–July 4	39	8900	64
1999	Stockholm	Sweden	July 16–24	NA	NA	68

1985   San Jose   USA   August 4–11

Sports: Archery, Athletics, Badminton, Basketball, Bowling, Boxing, Cross Country, Cycling, Equestrian, Golf, Handball, Horseshoes, Judo, Karate, Motocross, Muster, Pistol, Pocket Billiards, Police Service Dogs, Powerlifting, Rifle—Large-bore, Rifle—Small-bore, Road Race, Rowing, Scuba, Skeet, Soccer, Softball—Fast-pitch, Softball—Slow-pitch, Surfing, Swimming, Table Tennis, Toughest Competitor Alive, Tennis, Trap, Triathlon, Tug of War, Volleyball, Waterskiing, Wrestling, Wrist Wrestling

1987   San Diego   USA   August 1–9

Nations: Australia, Austria, Belgium, Bermuda, Canada, England, Ireland, Liechtenstein, New Zealand, Scotland, Sweden, Trinidad and Tobago, Netherlands, United States, West Germany

Sports: Archery, Arm Wrestling, Badminton, Basketball (5-on-5, 3-on-3), Bowling, Boxing, Cross Country, Cycling, Equestrian, Golf, Handball, Horseshoes, Judo, Karate, Motocross, Muster, Open-water Swim, Over the Line, Pistol, Pocket Billiards, Police Service Dogs, Powerlifting, Racquetball, Rifle (Large-bore, Small-bore), Road Race (Half-marathon, Marathon), Rowing, Sailing, Scuba, Skeet, Soccer, Softball (Fast-pitch, Slow-pitch), Surfing, Swimming, Table Tennis, The Complete Athlon, Tennis, Track and Field, Trap Shooting, Triathlon, Tug of War, Volleyball, Water Skiing, Wrestling

1989   Vancouver   Canada   July 29–August 6

Nations: Australia, Austria, Belgium, Bermuda, Canada, "Europe," Finland, Germany, Great Britain, Hong Kong, Ireland, Italy, Japan, Netherlands, New Zealand, Puerto Rico, Trinidad and Tobago, United States

Sports: Archery, Athletics, Badminton, Basketball (5-on-5, 3-on-3), Bowling, Boxing, Cross Country, Cycling, Equestrian, Golf, Handball, Horseshoes, Judo, Karate, Motocross, Muster, Open-water Swim, Pistol, Pocket Billiards, Police Service Dogs, Powerlifting, Racquetball, Rifle (Large-bore, Small-bore), Road Race (Half-marathon, Marathon), Rowing, Rugby, Sailing, Scuba, Skeet, Soccer, Softball (Fast-pitch, Slow-pitch), Swimming, Table Tennis, The Complete Athlon, Tennis, Trap Shooting, Triathlon, Tug of War, Volleyball, Water Skiing, Wrestling, Wrist Wrestling

1991   Memphis   USA   June 22–30

Nations: Australia, Austria, Belgium, Canada, "Europe," Finland, France, Germany, Great Britain, Hong Kong, Hungary, Ireland, Japan, Netherlands, New Zealand, Puerto Rico, Sweden, Trinidad and Tobago, USSR, United States, U.S. Virgin Islands

Sports: Archery, Athletics, Badminton, Basketball (5-on-5, 3-on-3), Bodybuilding, Bowling, Boxing, Cross Country, Cycling, Flag Football, Golf, Handball, Horseshoes, Judo, Karate, Motocross, Muster, Open-water Swim, Over the Line, Pistol, Pocket Billiards, Police Service Dogs, Powerlifting, Racquetball, Rifle (Large-bore, Small-bore), Road Race (Half-marathon, Marathon), Skeet, Soccer, Softball (Fast-pitch, Slow-pitch), Swimming, Table Tennis, The Complete Athlon, Tennis, Trap Shooting, Triathlon, Tug of War, Volleyball, Water Skiing, Wrestling, Wrist Wrestling

1993   Colorado Springs   USA   July 31–August 7

Nations: Australia, Austria, Belgium, Canada, Cayman Islands, England, Estonia, "Europe," Finland, France, Germany, Hong Kong, Hungary, India, Ireland, Latvia, Japan, Netherlands, New Zealand, Puerto Rico, Scotland, South Africa, Sweden, Trinidad and Tobago, United States, U.S. Virgin Islands

Sports: Archery, Athletics, Badminton, Basketball (5-on-5, 3-on-3), Bench Press, Biathlon, Bodybuilding, Bowling, Boxing, Cross Country, Cycling, Darts, Equestrian, Golf, Handball, Horseshoes, Ice Hockey, Karate, Motocross, Muster, Open-water Swim, Over the Line, Pistol, Pocket Billiards, Police Action Pistol, Police Service Dogs, Powerlifting, Racquetball, Rifle (Large-bore, Small-bore), Road Race (Half-marathon, Marathon), Rodeo, Rowing, Skeet, Soccer, Softball (Fast-pitch, Slow-pitch), Swimming, Table Tennis, The Complete Athlon, Tennis, Trap Shooting, Triathlon, Tug of War, Volleyball, Water Skiing, Wrestling, Wrist Wrestling

1995   Melbourne   Australia   February 26–March 4

Nations: Australia, Austria, Belgium, British West Indies, Bulgaria, Canada, Cayman Islands, Cook Islands, Croatia, Cyprus, Czech Republic, England/United Kingdom,

Estonia, European Union, Fiji, Finland, France, Germany, Hong Kong, Hungary, India, Ireland, Italy, Jamaica, Japan, Latvia, Malaysia, Netherlands, New Caledonia, New Zealand, North Marianas, Papua New Guinea, Puerto Rico, Russia, Scotland, Singapore, South Africa, Spain, Sweden, Switzerland, Ukraine, United States, Vanuatu

Sports: Angling—Salt Water, Angling—Fresh Water, Archery, Athletics, Badminton, Basketball (5-on-5, 3-on-3), Bench Press, Biathlon, Bodybuilding, Bowling, Boxing, Cross Country, Cycling, Darts, Equestrian, Golf, Handball, Horseshoes, Karate, Lawn Bowls, Motorcycling (Street), Motorcycling (Dirt), Mountain Biking, Muster, Netball, Open-water Swim, Pistol, Pocket Billiards, Police Action Pistol, Powerlifting, Racquetball, Rifle (Large-bore, Small-bore), Road Race (Half-marathon, Marathon), Rowing—Crew (Outdoor), Rowing (Indoor), Sailing, Scuba, Skeet, Soccer, Softball (Fast-pitch, Slow-pitch), Sporting Clays, Squash, Surfing, Swimming, Table Tennis, Toughest Competitor Alive, Tennis, Trap Shooting, Triathlon, Tug of War, Volleyball (Indoor), Volleyball (Outdoor), Water Skiing, Wrestling, Wrist Wrestling

1997   Calgary   Canada   June 27–July 4

Nations: Australia, Austria, Belgium, Brazil, Bulgaria, Canada, Cayman Islands, Croatia, Czech Republic, England, El Salvador, Estonia, Finland, France, Germany, Hong Kong, Hungary, India, Ireland, Italy, Japan, Latvia, Malaysia, Netherlands, New Zealand, Northern Ireland, Poland, Puerto Rico, Russia, Scotland, Singapore, South Africa, Spain, Sweden, Switzerland, Trinidad and Tobago, United Nations, United States, Uruguay[231]

Sports: Angling, Archery, Badminton, Basketball (5 × 5), Basketball (3 × 3), Bench Press, Biathlon, Body Building, Bowling, Boxing, Cross Country, Curling, Cycling, Mountain Cycling, Darts, Decathlon, Equestrian, Flag Football, Golf, Handball, Heptathlon, Horseshoes, Ice Hockey, Karate, Lawn Bowls, Motocross—Dirt Bikes, Motocross—Street Bikes, Muster, Open Water Swim, Pistol (P.A.P.), Pistol (P.P.C.), Pocket Billiards, Police Service Dogs, Power Lifting, Racquetball, Rifle (Large-bore, Small-bore), Road Race—Half-marathon, Rodeo, Rowing (Indoor), Rowing (Outdoor), Rugby (Touch), Sailing, Laser I, Scuba, Soccer, Softball (Fast-pitch, Slow-pitch), Sporting Clay, Squash, S.W.A.T., Swimming, Table Tennis, Tennis, Toughest Competitor Alive, Track and Field, Trap and Skeet, Triathlon, Tug of War, Volleyball (Indoor), Volleyball (Outdoor), Waterskiing, Wrist Wrestling, Wrestling

1999   Stockholm   Sweden   July 16–24

Sports: Athletics, Angling (Fresh-water, Salt-water), Archery, Badminton, Basketball (5 × 5, 3 × 3), Bench Press, Biathlon, Boule Petanque, Bowling (Ten-pin), Boxing, Canoe (Flat-water, Slalom), Cross Country, Cycling, Darts, Decathlon, Equestrian, Equestrian Western, Fencing, Floorball, Football, Golf, Heptathlon, Horseshoes, Ice Hockey, Judo, Karate, Motocross, Muster, Open-water Swim, Orienteering, Pistol, Pocket Billiards, Police Pentathlon, Powerlifting, Rifle, Road Race, Roller-skating, Rowing (Outdoor, Indoor), Rugby, Sailing, Skeet, Snooker, Softball, Sporting Clays, Squash, S.W.A.T., Swimming, Table Tennis, Team Handball, Tennis, Toughest Competitor Alive, Trap, Triathlon, Tug of War, Volleyball (Beach, Indoor), Water Polo, Water Skiing, Weightlifting, Windsurfing/Boardsailing, Wrestling, Wrist Wrestling (seven more)

World Scholar Athlete Games

The Institute for International Sport, the governing body of the World Scholar Athlete Games, was founded in 1986 by Daniel Doyle, an educator and basketball coach. The stated goals of the organization are to:

• Promote understanding, friendship and acceptance among the youth of the world.

• Establish open, nonpolitical, longstanding relationships among tomorrow's world leaders.

• Utilize education, culture and sports as a means of learning and communication, rather than competition among nations.

• Identify and train young people to develop leadership skills and networking strategies as they pursue leading positions in education, government and other professional fields.

The institute's first program involved sending young college athletes to Europe to teach sports to disadvantaged and handicapped students. The institute then embarked on a series of sports seminars relating to media and sports, sports ethics and gender equity.

One of the strengths of the institute is the board of directors that has been created from a pool of some of the most respected educators, coaches and politicians in the United States and throughout the world, including such names as IOC vice-president Anita DeFrantz, Cuban Olympic champion Alberto Juantorena, Penn State football coach Joe Paterno, U.S. senators Bill Bradley and Claiborne Pell, and Dr. James Mangan, Dr. John McAloon, Dr. Richard Lapchick and Dr. John Hoberman, all professors and educators in sports studies.

In 1989, Daniel Doyle proposed the concept of the World Scholar Athlete Games to the board which unanimously supported the idea and set 1993 as the goal for their beginning. The games are meant to be a return to the original idea of Pierre de Coubertin to bring the youth of the world together to learn from one another, not only to compete against one another. After much planning, the idea was introduced to representatives from embassies from 125 countries at a reception in Washington, D.C., in 1991.

In 1993, over 1,600 students and athletes from 109 countries participated in the games in Newport, Rhode Island. The scholar-athletes competed in both sports and the arts. Events included basketball, sailing, soccer, tennis, volleyball, art, choir, poetry and writing. The games are structured so that the teams are randomly made up of athletes from many nations. No medals tables are kept and the emphasis is on participation rather than winning. Along with the sports and cultural activities, theme days with topics such as ethics and sportsmanship, conflict resolution and world hunger bring the students together for discussions in the evenings. At the closing ceremonies, the scholar choir, scholar orchestra and scholar dancers perform works that they have practiced throughout the week. Actors and actresses have the opportunity to display their skills, the musicians produce a recording of their work, and the writers and poets produce works that are published after the games.

The second edition of the games, also in Rhode Island, was held in June 1997, with 2000 scholar–athletes from 147 nations attending.

The eventual goal is to replicate the games on local and national levels in various countries, as well as hold games for each region of the world. A small pilot games in Australia, the Australia Pacific Rim Scholar Athlete Games, was held in 1996. African Scholar Athlete Games and Sri Lanka Scholar Athlete Games were planned for 1999 but postponed. Middle East/Mediterranean Scholar Athlete Games were inaugurated in the summer of the year 2000.

Founder Doyle has stated that one objective for the Institute of International Sport is to see the World Scholar Athlete Games established as one of the most recognized international sporting and cultural events in the world.

Year	Host City	Host Nation	Dates	Nations	Athletes	Sports
1993	Newport, RI	USA	June 20–July 1	109	1600	5
1997	Newport, RI	USA	June 23–July 1	147	2000	8

232

1993   Newport RI   USA   June 20–July 1

Sports: Basketball, Tennis, Soccer, Volleyball, Sailing

1997   Newport RI   USA   June 23–July 1

Sports: Athletics, Baseball, Basketball, Football, Sailing, Swimming, Tennis, Volleyball

Other Events: Art, Choir, Dance, Symphony, Theater, Writing/Poetry

World Transplant Games

The World Transplant Games were conceived in 1978 by Maurice Slapak, a transplant surgeon from Britain, with the intention of publicizing the success of organ donation and transplantation by showing that individuals with organ transplants could return to health and be able to participate in athletic events. The World Transplant Games Federation oversees the games and specifically bans any racial, religious or political restrictions on participation. The games have spawned many national and regional transplant games such as the Euro-Transplant Games, the European Heart/Lung Transplant Games, and the Latin American Transplant Games.

Athletes who have had heart, liver, lung, kidney, pancreas, or bone marrow transplants are eligible to compete, as long as the transplant is stable and at least one year has passed since it was done. Each edition of the games produces numerous inspiring stories of individuals who have overcome life-threatening illnesses and diseases to lead full active lives. Dr. Slapak points out that the transplant athletes do not participate in the Paralympic Games because those with transplanted organs have been rehabilitated to their normal physical state.

The very first games in Portsmouth, England, in 1978 had just ninety-nine participants. Over 1100 athletes took part in the 1997 games in Sydney, Australia. Golf professional Greg Norman served as the patron of the Sydney games, and participants marched around Sydney's Circular Quay to the opening ceremonies at the Sydney Opera House. Competitions for very young transplant recipients were held, the two youngest competitors being three years of age. The oldest competitors in the games were 74 years old.

All the athletes are on steroids and other drugs to fight organ rejection and would not likely pass the traditional drug tests given at other games, so drug testing is not part of the games.

At the Sydney games in 1997, a unique situation occurred when two athletes competed against each other—one had donated his heart to the other. Years before, the first athlete had had a combination lung-heart transplant. His old heart was good, but his lungs were bad. However, due to the nature of the surgery, it was simpler for the doctors to replace both his heart and lungs. His good heart was given to the person he ended up competing against in Sydney.

The French allow for dialysis patients to compete in their national games and have proposed that dialysis patients be allowed to compete in the world games. The rest of the world, however, has yet to agree that this procedure qualifies as a transplant.

The 1999 World Transplant Games were originally scheduled to be held in Tilburg, the Netherlands. Due to organizational difficulties, though, they were moved to Budapest, Hungary.

The Hungarians came through with flying colors. From the opening ceremony in Heroes' Square and throughout the competitions in athletics, badminton, cycling, skittles, squash, chess, golf, volleyball, tennis and swimming, the games were a success.

Tamás Deutsch, Minister of Youth and Sports, welcomed everyone to Hungary at the opening ceremonies. Hungarian boxer István Kovács read the athlete's oath.

The swimming venue for the games was designed many years before by Alfred Hajos, the first Hungarian to ever win a gold medal in the Olympic games, in swimming in 1896. He became an architect and designed the Margit Island Swim Pool which has become known as Hungary's national pool.

The goal of the games is still to promote organ transplantation. Just before the Budapest event, Hungary passed a "presumed consent" law relating to organ transplants. Rather than the next of kin being asked to donate organs, the doctors would only ask whether they objected to donation. This way, the doctors could use more organs.

The 2001 games were awarded to Chiba, Japan, with the hopes of spreading the message of organ transplants to the Japanese who have traditionally had a very low number of organ donors and transplants.

Year	Host City	Host Nation	Dates	Nations	Athletes	Sports
1978	Portsmouth	England		5	99	NA
1979	Portsmouth	England		NA	NA	NA
1980	New York	USA		NA	NA	NA
1982	Athens	Greece		NA	NA	NA
1984	Amsterdam	Netherlands		NA	NA	NA
1987	Innsbruck	Austria	September 17–20	NA	NA	NA
1989	Singapore	Singapore	September 10–14	28	NA	NA
1991	Budapest	Hungary	August 27–31	NA	NA	NA
1993	Vancouver	Canada	July 4–10	30	800	4
1995	Manchester	England	August 14–20	39	600	NA
1997	Sydney	Australia	Sept. 29–Oct. 5	53	1100	12
1999	Budapest	Hungary	Sept. 4–11	47	1500	10

1978   Portsmouth   England

Nations: Germany, Great Britain, Greece, France, United States

1989   Singapore   Singapore   September 10–14

Nations: Australia, Austria, Belgium, Brunei, Canada, Czechoslovakia, Denmark, Finland, France, West Germany, Hungary, Indonesia, Ireland, Italy, Japan, Kenya, Luxembourg, Malaysia, Mauritius, New Zealand, Norway, Portugal, Singapore, Sweden, Thailand, Uganda, United Kingdom, United States

1993   Vancouver   Canada   July 4–10

Nations: Australia, Austria, Belgium, Canada, Czech Republic, Denmark, Finland, France, Germany, Greece, Hong Kong, Hungary, Ireland, Israel, Italy, Japan, Luxembourg, Malaysia, Netherlands, New Zealand, Norway, Philippines, Russia, Singapore, South Africa, Sweden, Switzerland, Thailand, United Kingdom, United States
Sports: Athletics, Swimming, Tennis, Golf

1995   Manchester   England   August 14–20

Nations: Argentina, Australia, Austria, Belgium, Bulgaria, Canada, Cyprus, Czech Republic, Denmark, Finland, France, Germany, Great Britain, Greece, Holland, Hong Kong, Hungary, Iceland, Ireland, Israel, Italy, Japan, Luxembourg, New Zealand, Norway, Malaysia, Philippines, Slovenia, South Africa, Spain, Sweden, Switzerland, Thailand, United States (five more)

1997   Sydney   Australia   September 29–October 5

Nations: Argentina, Australia, Austria, Belgium, Brunei Darussalam, Canada, China (People's Republic of), China (Hong Kong), Cyprus, Czech Republic, Denmark, Egypt, Fiji, Finland, France, Germany, Great Britain, Greece, Hungary, India, Indonesia, Iran, Ireland, Israel, Italy, Japan, Kenya, Kuwait, Luxembourg, Malaysia, Mauritius, Mexico, Netherlands, New Zealand, Norway, Pakistan, Philippines, Poland, Portugal, Romania, Singapore, Slovenia, South Africa, South Korea, Spain, Sri Lanka, Sweden, Switzerland, Thailand, Ukraine, United States, Vietnam
Sports: Athletics, Badminton, Cycling, Golf, Lawn Bowls, Road Race (3 km and 5 km), Squash, Swimming, Table Tennis, Tennis, Ten-pin Bowling, Volleyball
Venues: Sydney Opera House (Opening Ceremony), Whitlam Centre (Badminton, Volleyball, Table Tennis), Cintra Park, Concord (Tennis), Rosehill Bowling Club (Lawn Bowls), Pennant Hills Golf Club (Golf), AMF Bowling Centre (Ten-pin Bowling), Sydney International Aquatics Centre (Swimming), Coolibah Fitness Centre (Squash), Sydney International Athletic Centre (Athletics, Closing Ceremony), Parramatta Civic Centre, Parramatta Park (Road Races), Penrith Course (Cycling)

| | MEDALS | | | |
Nation	Gold	Silver	Bronze	Total
Great Britain	48	51	55	154
Australia	48	50	41	139
USA	32	30	35	97
Netherlands	14	5	11	30
Germany	13	16	16	45
Finland	13	6	8	27
Italy	8	1	4	13

Nation	Gold	Silver	Bronze	Total
Hungary	7	8	14	29
France	5	16	8	29
Canada	5	8	7	20
South Africa	5	2	8	15
Malaysia	4	2	2	8
Spain	3	4	4	11
Argentina	3	0	4	7
Switzerland	2	3	3	8
Sweden	2	0	3	5
Japan	1	3	2	6
Denmark	1	1	1	3
Israel	1	1	1	3
South Korea	1	0	0	1
Singapore	1	0	0	1
Norway	1	0	0	1
Mexico	1	0	0	1
Belgium	0	4	3	7
New Zealand	0	1	4	5
Thailand	0	1	2	3
Cyprus	0	1	1	2
Ireland	0	1	1	2
Austria	0	0	2	2
Czech Republic	0	0	2	2
Hong Kong	0	0	2	2
Slovenia	0	0	1	1

1999   Budapest   Hungary   September 4–11

Nations: (partial list) Argentina, Australia, Austria, Belgium, Brazil, Canada, Denmark, Finland, France, Germany, Great Britain, Greece, Hong Kong, Hungary, Israel, Italy, Japan, Malaysia, Mexico, Netherlands, Singapore, Slovakia, South Africa, South Korea, Spain, Sweden, Switzerland, Thailand, United States, Uruguay

Sports: Athletics, Badminton, Chess, Cycling, Golf, Skittles, Squash, Swimming, Tennis, Volleyball

Venues: Nepstadion (Athletics), Old Lake Golf Club (Golf), Margit Island Swim Pool (Swimming), Csepel Island (Cycling)

MEDALS

Nation	Gold	Silver	Bronze	Total
Great Britain	29	23	27	79
Hungary	12	8	19	39
United States	7	11	11	29
Australia	6	11	12	29
Germany	5	3	3	11
Italy	5	3	3	11
France	5	3	3	11
Belgium	4	0	4	8
Malaysia	3	3	1	7
Greece	3	0	0	3
Thailand	2	2	7	11

Nation	Gold	Silver	Bronze	Total
Argentina	2	2	6	10
South Africa	2	2	2	6
Switzerland	2	1	2	5
Israel	2	1	1	4
Sweden	2	1	0	3
South Korea	2	0	0	2
Spain	1	3	7	11
Austria	1	3	1	5
Japan	1	1	4	6
Finland	1	1	3	5
Netherlands	1	0	1	2
Canada	0	4	0	4
Singapore	0	2	3	5
Denmark	0	2	0	2
Hong Kong	0	2	0	2
Uruguay	0	1	2	3
Slovakia	0	1	0	1
Mexico	0	0	1	1
Brazil	0	0	1	1

World University Games

The World University Games, one of the oldest international multisport events, share the classic organizational struggles, name changes, boycotts and scheduling difficulties of all international games. They have in common with many other games the fact that they have been prohibited by the IOC from using the word "Olympic." Early on, Jean Petitjean was promoting the games as the University Olympic Games and Pierre de Coubertin protested and convinced him to change the name to International University Games to preserve the word Olympic solely for the Olympic Games.

In their earliest days, the games were also called "Student World Championships," "International Collegiate Games" and "International University Championships." Today, this tradition continues with the games being called the Universiade, World Student Games or World University Games by various sources.

The games today are open to university students from all over the world between the ages of 17 and 28, including those who have completed studies in the previous year.

In November 1891, the proposal for competitions between students of separate nations was made at the Universal Peace Congress held in Rome. Hodgson Pratt, the president of the International University Alliance, set before the congress the idea for international student conferences in which university students from Europe and America would gather in capital cities around the world and participate in competitions in poetry, art, the sciences, and sports. The recommendation passed unanimously, but no conferences were organized.[233]

Between 1909 and 1913 the idea resurfaced, this time under the name Academic Olympia. Little is known about the events or participants in these gatherings, but the groundwork was being laid for a full-scale university games to be established.

On July 11, 1909, the first Academic Olympia was held in Leipzig, Germany. German and Austrian universities organized these games to coincide with the celebration of the 500th anniversary of Leipzig University. One year later, July 3, 1910, in commemoration of the 100th anniversary of Friedrich-Wilhelms University (the University of Berlin), the second Academic Olympia was held. These first two events were one-day affairs. From July 8 to 10, 1911, the third Academic Olympia was held in Dresden, Germany, in conjunction with the Hygiebe Fair. Later that summer, August 1–3, Breslau, Germany, hosted the next Olympia, also as part of the 100th anniversary of the university.

A third competition for 1911 had been scheduled for Rome in September, to celebrate the 50th anniversary of the unification of Italy. Nine universities from throughout Europe were invited and eleven sports were on the program, but the competition was canceled because of poor weather.

The fifth and final Olympia was held in Leipzig, Germany, in 1913 in conjunction with ceremonies to dedicate the monument "The Multi-Nation's Fight Against Napoleon."

After the interruption of World War I, the Italian Student Olympic Committee hosted a University Olympia in Rome between April 23 and May 1, 1922.

More importantly for the establishment of permanent university games was the founding of the CIE, or Confédération Internationale d'Étudiants, on November 18, 1919. Belgium, Czechoslovakia, France, Luxembourg, Poland, Romania and Spain were the founding nations.[234] Jean Petitjean of France was elected the first president of the CIE; he would eventually be recognized as the founder of the games now known as the World University Games.

The first edition in Paris in 1923 was an athletic meet only. The 1924 games in Warsaw consisted of five sports: athletics, fencing, football, rowing and tennis. No events were held for women. Curiously, the participating countries were quite different from the nations that had founded the CIE five years previously. England, Estonia, France, Italy, New Zealand, Poland and the United States took part in the 1924 event.

The plan was to hold the games biennially but this quickly fell apart. Rome's 1926 games became the 1927 games. Women participated in swimming events.

The CIE wanted to retain an every-other-year schedule and hold the next games in 1929. France, however, had been awarded the 1928 games at the eighth CIE Congress in Prague in 1926 and insisted on holding the games in 1928 in Paris. Winter World University Games were also begun in 1928 in Cortina d'Ampezzo, Italy.

The 1928 games were held one week after the Amsterdam Olympic Games, and several athletes took the opportunity to participate in both, including Olympic 200 meter bronze medalist Helmuth Körnig from Germany. Athletes from Germany, Japan, Norway, Sweden and Yugoslavia competed for the first time.

An unfortunate brawl between spectators in the stands, after the Italians defeated Hungary in a football match, led to police intervention with the Italians taking the brunt of the punishment. The Italian delegation was called home from the games immediately, and upon arrival in Rome, were welcomed with anti-French demonstrations.[235]

Despite the goal of the games to bring students together in peaceful contests, the organization within the CIE (independent of the incident at the 1928 games but related to left over animosities from World War I) was divided into three factions, the French, Italian and English. France was allied with Belgium, Czechoslovakia, Denmark, Holland, Luxembourg, Poland, Romania and Yugoslavia while the Italians were aligned with Germany, Hungary, Japan, Estonia, Lithuania and Spain. Countries sympathetic to the British Empire were allied with the English, with the exception of the United States. The Scandinavian countries more or less remained unaligned.[236]

The Darmstadt Games in 1930 saw the addition of athletics events for women. The games had grown substantially by then, with 30 nations competing, 17 of which won medals.

The German Student Sports Federation declined to hold the CIE Congress in conjunction with the games and were working hard behind the scenes to try and gain control of the organization. When the German plans were slowed, they resigned from the CIE, hoping other countries would follow and the organization would break up. Hungary, Japan and Italy, however, did not follow Germany's lead. In 1932, the Dutch, Danes, Canadians and Americans all gave their resignations for reasons of their own. The French and English worked hard to repair the damage and made several concessions including changing the language in the constitution of the games which still used the words "conquering" and "conquered" in relation to the nations in World War I.

The CIE, at its congress in August 1932 in Riga, Latvia, established a control committee in Paris and a sports committee in Rome. The office in Paris was to have jurisdiction in matters of international relations, financial affairs, rules and regulations, sports medical issues, and general physical education issues within universities. Rome was assigned the task of overseeing the technical and organizational aspects of the games themselves.[237]

The Dutch, Danes and Americans came back and participated in the Winter Games of 1933 in Bardonecchia. The summer games of 1933 in Turin were assisted in their organization by the Italian Olympic Committee (CONI) which resulted in the IOC bestowing its patronage for the first time.

IOC President Count Henri Baillet-Latour joined in the games in 1935 in Budapest, along with several other dignitaries including Herr Osten, the sports minister of Germany, who made contacts and agreements for the following year's Olympic Games in Berlin.

The 1937 Games were organized alongside the World Exposition in Paris. The games organizers had not learned the lessons of the earliest Olympic Games. The sporting events were overshadowed by the fair and the organizers were disappointed.

At this time, animosities and disagreements between countries in the CIE led to a split. Germany took the lead and held its own German Student Federation Games in occupied Vienna, in August 1939.

The 1939 CIE Games were held in Monaco from August 21 to 29. The imminent start of World War II meant that several delegations could not remain through the duration of the games.

Twenty-four nations attended the 1939 Monaco games. Twenty nations attended the German Student Federation Games in Vienna: Arabia, Bulgaria, Denmark, Estonia, Finland, Germany, Greece, Hungary, Italy, Japan, Latvia, Netherlands, Peru, Portugal, Romania, Slovakia, South Africa, Sweden, Switzerland and Yugoslavia. Seven nations—Denmark, Finland, Latvia, Netherlands, Sweden, Switzerland and Yugoslavia—had participants at both games that year.

Up to this point in time, the games had been primarily a European endeavor. In all, 53 nations had participated across all the editions of the games; 33 nations had won medals, with Germany, Hungary, France, Italy and England having won two thirds of them.[238]

World War II interrupted the games and their revival was discussed at a meeting in London in 1945. In May 1946, the European nations met in Prague and founded the UIE, Union Internationale d'Étudiants, meant to continue the work of the CIE which had dissolved during the war. The UIE organized the games in Paris in 1947, but continuing discontent between the UIE and several western nations led those nations to break away and establish FISU, the Fédération International du Sport Universitaire, with Paul Schleimer of Belgium as the president. At that point separate competitions were scheduled, with both the UIE and FISU organizing summer and winter games of their own.

In 1949, at the Winter Games UIE in Czechoslovakia, Spain was not allowed to compete for political reasons. Belgium, Holland, Luxembourg, Monaco and Switzerland left the UIE to join FISU.

The 1949 FISU games in Merano that summer did not set the best precedent. Only seven nations showed up and police had to be called to quiet disagreements.[239]

The 1949 UIE version of the games in Budapest, Hungary, was the first time that student athletes from the Soviet Union participated.[240]

The 1951 UIE summer games in Berlin were held in conjunction with the World Youth Festival. They were the largest university games yet, with over 2000 athletes from 42 nations. Western sources estimated that at least 1.25 million visitors came to Berlin for the two-week period of the festival which had a distinct political slant. Commemorative medals were imprinted with the dove of peace and image of Stalin on one side, the bird of war and the United States on the reverse. An eight-hour peace march was staged as part of the festivities and the East Berlin organizers attempted to keep all of the Communist youth away from the corruption of West Berlin, but to no avail. An estimated 250,000 strayed into West Berlin despite warnings (that the westerners would beat, starve or poison them) and threats to suspend their credentials and send them home.[241]

The German spectators let their feelings be known about the visiting Russians in the stadiums and arenas as well. When the Russians used team tactics and elbows to disrupt the progress of a Hungarian runner, the crowd resorted to loud boos. When the Hungarian finished fourth, behind the three Russians, the German crowd cheered the Hungarians efforts all the way to the locker room. The Moscow Dynamo soccer team beat a German team 2–0, reportedly with the help of a referee brought in from Moscow.[242]

The 1951 FISU games were held in Luxembourg later in the month, from August 19 to 26, but the UIE games were considered to be far more prestigious at the time.

The next FISU games were held in Dortmund, West Germany, in 1953 and San Sebastián, Spain, in 1955, while the UIE Games were held in Budapest in 1954 and Warsaw in 1955.

During this entire period, discussions were ongoing in both camps and in the Scandinavian student sports federations and a group of "neutral" federations (led by France, which had not joined FISU or the UIE) to try and unify university sport. The two federations were reunited in Paris in 1957, in a games known as the University Unity Games which were under the jurisdiction of neither the UIE or the FISU but were organized by the French with the blessing of both organizations.[243] Several decades after he was elected the first president of the CIE, Jean Petitjean was named to organize these games.

During and after the Paris games of 1957, the UIE and FISU continued to discuss permanent solutions, each suggesting that the nations of the other organizations should join their own. Gradually, questions were answered and issues addressed, with the

FISU group finally convincing the UIE nations that FISU stood for the entire world of university sport.

The term "Universiade" was adopted for the Turin games in 1959. These games were at first scheduled to be held in Rome as a preliminary competition for the 1960 Olympic Games, but the Rome facilities were not ready in time and Turin stepped in. Primo Nebiolo organized these games and would become the president of FISU in 1961, a position he has held since that time. China, not recognized at the time by Italy or the IOC as a nation, was invited. Nebiolo had the Chinese athletes travel to Czechoslovakia and join as members of an international student group there. By convincing the Italian government to recognize these memberships as temporary passports, Nebiolo was able to get the Chinese athletes into Italy in time to compete in Turin. However, the Italians denied visas to North Korean athletes.

In the 1961 games in Sofia, Bulgaria, Soviet star Valeri Brumel broke the world record in the high jump with a leap of 2.25 meters (7 ft. 4½ in.), his third world record jump in three months.[244]

The United States, which had a few participants in the games in the 1930s, finally joined the University Games movement in 1965 and has competed in every games since.

Hungary, Poland, Bulgaria, Romania, Czechoslovakia and Cuba boycotted the 1967 games in Tokyo, Japan, to show solidarity with North Korea in a dispute over the proper name to use when referring to the North Korean delegation.[245] The Soviet Union joined the boycott in a limited fashion, sending a very small team of eleven athletes and officials. American swimmers set eleven world records at these games.

Jean Petitjean died in 1969, having supported the university sports movement his entire life. Portugal was to host the games that year but canceled within a year of the event. FISU attempted to keep the event on schedule for the summer of 1969 and had interest from Beirut, Sofia, San Diego, Great Britain and Turin in picking it up. Eventually, though, it was decided to postpone the games for one year. They were awarded to Turin for 1970, as that city was deemed capable of organizing them in a short amount of time. China, reemerging to compete in certain international competitions, was welcomed again at the Universiade. Two world records in track and field, both set on September 3, highlighted the games. Wolfgang Nordwig from East Germany leapt 5.46 meters (17 ft. 11 in.) in the pole vault, and Heidi Rosendahl from West Germany jumped 6.84 meters (22 ft. 5¼ in.) in the long jump.

At the 1973 games in Moscow, the Soviets wanted to put on a show for the IOC in hopes of being awarded the 1980 Olympic Games. During the games, there was harsh treatment of Israeli athletes and Jewish spectators. The Israeli team was jeered at the opening ceremonies; Israeli fans were barred from attending one Israeli basketball game and attacked at another. Special security measures had to be taken to protect the Israelis, and due to these incidents, Henry Kissinger was quoted as saying that he might have to rethink the issue of détente with the USSR.

The Soviets and Nebiolo had been worried that more terrorist attacks might take place at the 1973 Universiade. To avert this, FISU authorized a Palestinian team for the games and invited Yasser Arafat as a guest of honor. The intention was to placate the Palestinian leader and guarantee there would be no disruptions to the games.

The U.S. and Cuban basketball teams engaged in a brawl in Moscow in a competition that had already seen four players from other teams expelled from the competition for throwing punches. The Cuban team apologized for instigating the incident, and a rules committee of three Soviets, a Hungarian, one Sudanese, one Japanese and one American did not issue any further disqualifications.

At the end of the 1973 Moscow Universiade, Belgrade, Yugoslavia, Mexico City, and Waterloo, Canada, were in the running to host the next games. Belgrade was chosen and the games nearly met their waterloo. Belgrade backed out of its commitment in January 1975. Rome had to take over as host and organized a last-minute games, with the competition limited to track and field.

The highlights of the 1977 Sofia, Bulgaria, and the 1979 Mexico City games were world records in track and field. In 1977, Cuba's Alberto Juantorena ran the 800 meters in 1:43.5. Alejandro Casanas also of Cuba raced the 110 meter hurdles in 13.21. In Mexico City in 1979, Pietro Mennea of Italy took advantage of the high altitude and ran the 200 meters 19.72 seconds.

Between the 1980 and 1984 Olympic boycotts, the Soviets and U.S. competed in the World University Games in 1981 in Bucharest and 1983 in Edmonton. Charles and Diana, Prince and Princess of Wales, opened the 1983 games, the first summer World University Games held in North America. Tragedy struck when Soviet diver Sergei Shilibashvili died after hitting his head on the 10 meter platform. The Soviet Union sent a full delegation to Edmonton in preparation for the 1984 Los Angeles Olympic Games.

After the Olympic boycott of 1984, the nations joined again in Kobe, Japan, in 1985. East Germany was the only notable team not to participate.

The games were a catalyst for a change in policy on the issue of genetic testing, or "femininity control," a practice that had been carried out in various forms since 1966 in several international competitions to ensure that only women were competing against women. Maria Patino, a hurdler from Spain was told just before her race that her test had shown the presence of a Y chromosome and she would be disqualified. She refused to leave and competed anyway. On returning to Spain, however, she was banned from her federation and the sport. She continued to protest and was eventually reinstated having lost several years of eligibility. The arguments that followed concerning femininity control in athletics led to the process being dropped little by little until it was banned entirely in 1999.

Also in Kobe, Igor Paklin of the Soviet Union jumped 2.41 meters (7 ft. 10¾ in.) to defend his games title and set a new world record in the high jump. Swimming world record holder Matt Biondi won the 100 meters and 200 meters freestyle events in Universiade record times.

A very successful games in 1987 in Zagreb, Yugoslavia, brought together 3,904 athletes from 122 countries. One small controversy occurred when Kuwait refused to play Israel in volleyball. Michael Powell won the long jump and would become the man to break Bob Beamon's world record four years later at the World Championships in Tokyo.

In early 1989, São Paulo, Brazil, canceled its commitment to the games. Pyongyang, North Korea, was briefly mentioned as a possible host for the games, but it was the city of Duisburg, Germany, that eventually took up the challenge and organized a competition, though only four sports could be planned: athletics, men's basketball, fencing and rowing. Fittingly, the games' slogan was "All in the Same Boat."

The 1991 edition in Sheffield, England, saw the first ever reported positive drug test at the World University Games when Xinmei Sui of China failed a test after winning the shot put. Princess Anne, an IOC member from Great Britain, opened the games.

British astronaut Helen Sharman was chosen to carry the games torch, but stumbled and fell during the opening ceremonies. The flame went out and had to be relit before the ceremony could continue. Controversy ruled the day in women's gymnastics where twenty-eight competitors were penalized for having uniforms that were considered risqué.[246]

The first summer Universiade in the United States was in Buffalo in 1993, with some events held in southern Ontario, Canada. Security was very tight, with a total of fifty law enforcement agencies from New York and Canada participating in games security operations.

Planning was poor. The food services at the beginning of the event were only open for two hours in the evenings causing many athletes to miss their meals, a disaster for an athlete in training. This was quickly remedied.

U.S. President Bill Clinton rejected the application of the Libyan team to compete and denied them visas. There were also Cuban defections. Baseball player Edilberto Oropesa leapt a fence at Sal Maglie stadium in Niagara Falls, yelling "asylum!" and hopped into a car that sped away. South Africa was welcomed back to the games, having been reinstated as a member of FISU at the same time that the IOC accepted South Africa into membership.

FISU, the IOC and the Buffalo Organizing Committee followed the example set in Sheffield and provided $300,000 for forty different nations to each send two athletes and one official to the games.

The games in Buffalo suffered from numerous organizational difficulties. Organizers were very disappointed with the attendance figures and the event lost a reported $3 million. Nora Lynn Finch, then president of the United States Collegiate Sports Council, remarked that the Buffalo games were so disorganized that the U.S. should not expect to host them again for a long time.

The 1995 Universiade in Fukuoka, Japan, has been called the most extravagant games to date. The team medals race was close between the United States and Japan throughout the games. On the last day, Japan won both marathon events, but the U.S. countered by winning three of four relays on the track and the two nations finished the games tied with twenty-four gold medals apiece. Vitali Scherbo, Olympic champion gymnast from Belarus and South African swimmer Penny Heyns, who won two gold medals, were two stars of the games.

The 1997 Universiade was held on the island of Sicily, Italy, with events and accommodations spread out all across the island. The opening ceremonies were held in Palermo, the closing ceremonies in Catania, and the events were staged in over thirteen cities. A rest day after the opening ceremonies allowed the teams to travel to other venues. The games themselves took much criticism for their lack of organization and the fact that many of the facilities were not ready for use. The Italian Olympic Committee had hoped to use the games to showcase its organizational talents just weeks before the IOC voted to choose a host for the 2004 Olympic Games for which Rome was a candidate. Accusations of Mafia interference in the construction of games venues were so strong that the regional Anti-Mafia Commission set up an investigation into the matter after the event.[247]

The athletic quality of the games was high. Olympic gymnast Shannon Miller carried the U.S. flag in the opening ceremonies, then went on the win the all-around title. World Champion long jumper Ivan Pedroso of Cuba led a strong Cuban contingent, and competed against Jamaica's Olympian James Beckford. Other Olympians included

South African swimmer Penny Heyns and 800 meter runner Hezekiel Sepeng, and Hungary's Olympic champion in the hammer throw, Balazs Kiss, who won his event for the second games in a row. Olympian Yuri Chechi won gold medals for the home team in gymnastics.

The United States lost in the quarterfinal football match to Italy after one American and two Italians were sent off for fighting.

The U.S. finished with 20 gold medals to top the overall medals table for the fourth games in a row. Prior to that, the Soviet Union had won the overall medals race in every games since 1967.

The 1999 Universiade was held in Palma de Mallorca, Spain. Disappointing crowds welcomed the games. The new Son Moix stadium was virtually empty for many of the track and field events, with 1,000 the largest crowd until the final day's events.

Russian gymnast Svetlana Khorkina and U.S. swimmer Mark Warkentin each won four gold medals. Spain upset the defending champion U.S. team in women's basketball and won the gold in water polo and football. The U.S. men won their sixth consecutive basketball gold medal.

Primo Nebiolo, then FISU president, threw his weight behind Moscow to host the 2003 edition of the games. Izmir, Turkey, Daegu, South Korea, and Monterrey, Mexico, were also bidding. The 2001 games had been awarded to Beijing.

On November 7, 1999, Nebiolo died. He had been head of FISU since 1961 and of the IAAF since 1981. On November 26, 1999, American George E. Killian, FISU first vice-president since 1995, took over as president. Killian had formerly served as president of FIBA (Fédération Internationale de Basketball).

Year	Host City	Host Nation	Dates	Nations	Athletes	Sports
1923	Paris	France	May 3–6	10	NA	1
1924	Warsaw	Poland	Sept. 17–20	7	NA	5
1927	Rome	Italy	Aug. 28–Sept. 4	15	269	5
1928	Paris	France	Aug. 9–17	20	300	5
1930	Darmstadt	Germany	Aug. 1–10	30	NA	8
1933	Turin	Italy	Sept. 1–10	27	NA	9
1935	Budapest	Hungary	Aug. 10–18	26	774	10
1937	Paris	France	Aug. 21–29	22	NA	14
1939	Monte Carlo	Monaco	Aug. 21–29	24	NA	9
1949	Merano	Italy	Aug. 28–Sept. 4	7	NA	5 (FISU)*
1951	Luxembourg	Luxembourg	Aug. 19—26	12	NA	9 (FISU)*
1953	Dortmund	W. Germany	Aug. 9–16	22	987	7 (FISU)*
1955	San Sebastián	Spain	Aug. 7—14	26	612	9 (FISU)*
1957	Paris	France	Aug. 31–Sept. 8	32	NA	NA
	(organized by France, not explicitly by FISU or the UIE)					
1959	Turin	Italy	Aug. 26—Sept. 9	45	1407	7
1961	Sofia	Bulgaria	Aug. 25–Sept. 3	33	1627	9
1963	Pôrto Alegre	Brazil	Aug. 30–Sept. 8	27	713	9
1965	Budapest	Hungary	Aug. 20–30	32	2366	9
1967	Tokyo	Japan	Aug. 27–Sept. 4	48	2407	10
1970	Turin	Italy	Aug. 26–Sept. 6	58	2808	9
1973	Moscow	Soviet Union	Aug. 15–25	73	3634	10
1975	Rome	Italy	Sept. 17–21	38	712	1

*these games known as International University Sports Week (FISU)

Year	Host City	Host Nation	Dates	Nations	Athletes	Sports
1977	Sofia	Bulgaria	Aug. 17–28	78	4391	9
1979	Mexico City	Mexico	Sept. 2–13	94	4381	10
1981	Bucharest	Romania	July 19–30	86	4369	10
1983	Edmonton	Canada	July 1–12	73	3471	10
1985	Kobe	Japan	Aug. 24–Sept. 4	106	3946	11
1987	Zagreb	Yugoslavia	July 8–19	122	3904	12
1989	Duisburg	West Germany	Aug. 22–30	79	2916	4
1991	Sheffield	England	July 14–27	101	4622	12
1993	Buffalo	USA	July 8–18	117	5105	12
	Hamilton	Canada[248]				
1995	Fukuoka	Japan	Aug. 23–Sept. 3	162	3949	13
1997	Sicily	Italy	Aug. 18–31	124	3496	10
1999	Palma de Mallorca	Spain	July 2–July 13	125	4076	12

WORLD STUDENT CHAMPIONSHIPS (UIE)

Year	Host City	Host Nation	Dates	Nations	Athletes	Sports
1947	Paris	France	Aug. 24–31	18	789	10
1949	Budapest	Hungary	Aug. 14–21	16	NA	13
1951	Berlin**	West Germany	Aug. 6–15	42	2000	13
1954	Budapest	Hungary	July 31–Aug. 8	34	NA	15
1955	Warsaw	Poland	Aug. 1–14	NA	NA	NA
1957*	Moscow**	Soviet Union	July 29–Aug. 4	NA	NA	NA
1959*	Vienna	Austria	July 29–Aug. 2	NA	NA	NA
1962*	Helsinki	Finland	July 28–Aug. 6	NA	NA	NA

*Kutassi makes no mention of these events in his work.
**Also known as World Youth Festivals.

1924   Warsaw   Poland   September 17–20

Nations: England, Estonia, France, Italy, New Zealand, Poland, United States
Sports: Athletics, Fencing, Football, Rowing, Tennis

MEDALS

Nation	Gold	Silver	Bronze	Total
Poland	10	12	5	27
France	5	7	8	20
Estonia	4	7	7	18
Italy	3	0	0	3
New Zealand	2	0	0	2
England	1	0	0	1
United States	0	0	1	1

1927   Rome   Italy   August 28–September 4

Nations: Austria, Czechoslovakia, Estonia, France, Haiti, Hungary, Italy, Latvia, Poland, Switzerland, United States (four more)
Sports: Athletics, Fencing, Football, Swimming, Tennis
Sports for Women: Swimming

MEDALS

Nation	Gold	Silver	Bronze	Total
Italy	16	9	11.5	36.5
Hungary	10	11	9	30
France	4	10	3	17
Czechoslovakia	2	1	3	6
Austria	2	1	3	6
Switzerland	2	1	0	3
Poland	1	1	4.5	6.5
Estonia	1	0	2	3
Haiti	1	0	0	1
United States	0	1	0	1
Latvia	0	1	0	1

1928   Paris   France   August 9–17

Nations: Austria, Belgium, Czechoslovakia, England, France, Germany, Haiti, Hungary, Italy, Japan, Norway, Poland, Sweden, Switzerland, United States, Yugoslavia
Sports: Athletics, Fencing, Football, Swimming, Tennis (four more)
Sports for Women: Swimming
Venues: Porte Doree (Athletics, Tennis), Stade de Paris, St. Ouen (Football), Tourelles Pool (Swimming), Salle Hoche (Fencing)

MEDALS

Nation	Gold	Silver	Bronze	Total
Germany	10	11	7	28
Hungary	8	8	8	24
Italy	7	3	6	16
France	5	7	7	19
Japan	3	3	0	6
England	2	1	0	3
Austria	1	0	2	3
Norway	1	0	1	2
Sweden	1	0	0	1
Switzerland	1	0	0	1
United States	1	0	0	1
Haiti	1	0	0	1
Czechoslovakia	0	4	6	10
Poland	0	1	1	2

1930   Darmstadt   Germany   August 1–10

Nations: Argentina, Australia, Austria, Belgium, Bulgaria, Czechoslovakia, Denmark, Egypt, England, Estonia, Finland, France, Germany, Haiti, Hungary, India, Ireland, Italy, Japan, Latvia, Luxembourg, Netherlands, New Zealand, Norway, Poland, South Africa, Spain, Sweden, Switzerland, United States
Sports: Athletics, Fencing, Football, Rowing, Rugby, Swimming, Tennis, Water Polo
Sports for Women: Athletics, Swimming

MEDALS

Nation	Gold	Silver	Bronze	Total
Germany	22	18	16	56
Italy	11	12	5.5	28.5
France	5	6	1	12
Hungary	5	4	6	15
Finland	4	2	2	8
Japan	3	3	2	8
England	2	1	2.5	5.5
Estonia	0	2	0	2
United States	0	1	2	3
Czechoslovakia	0	1	1	2
Belgium	0	0	3	3
Norway	0	0	1	1
Poland	0	0	1	1
Spain	0	0	1	1
Sweden	0	0	1	1
Luxembourg	0	0	1	1

1933   Turin   Italy   September 1–10

Nations: Argentina, Canada, Czechoslovakia, Denmark, England, Estonia, Finland, France, Germany, Hungary, Italy, Latvia, New Zealand, Spain, Sweden, Switzerland, United States (ten more)

Sports: Athletics, Basketball, Fencing, Football, Rowing, Rugby, Swimming, Tennis, Water Polo

Sports for Women: Athletics, Fencing, Swimming, Tennis

MEDALS

Nation	Gold	Silver	Bronze	Total
Italy	25	18	19	62
Germany	10	10	8	28
Hungary	10	6	12	28
France	6	5	1	12
Denmark	2	2	0	4
England	1	7	4	12
Estonia	1	4	1	6
Czechoslovakia	1	2	3	6
Finland	1	2	2	5
United States	1	1	0	2
Sweden	1	0	1	2
Canada	1	0	0	1
New Zealand	0	1	1	2
Latvia	0	1	1	2
Switzerland	0	1	0	1
Argentina	0	1	0	1
Spain	0	0	1	1

1935   Budapest   Hungary   August 10–18

Nations: Austria, Belgium, Czechoslovakia, Denmark, England, Estonia, Finland, France, Germany, Hungary, Japan, Latvia, New Zealand, Poland (twelve more)
Sports: Athletics, Basketball, Fencing, Football, Gymnastics, Rowing, Rugby, Swimming, Tennis, Water Polo
Sports for Women: Athletics, Basketball, Fencing, Gymnastics, Swimming, Tennis

MEDALS

Nation	Gold	Silver	Bronze	Total
Hungary	24	13	20	57
Germany	18	24	16	58
England	7	5	7	19
France	6	1	3	10
Poland	4	5	3	12
Japan	3	4	4	11
Austria	1	5	0	6
Czechoslovakia	1	3	2	6
Latvia	1	2	1	4
Estonia	1	0	1	2
New Zealand	1	0	0	1
Finland	0	3	1	4
Denmark	0	1	0	1
Belgium	0	0	2	2

1937   Paris   France   August 21–29

Nations: Austria, Belgium, Brazil, Czechoslovakia, Denmark, Egypt, England, Estonia, France, Germany, Greece, Hungary, Italy, Latvia, Poland, Scotland, Switzerland, Yugoslavia (four more)
Sports: Athletics, Basketball, Boxing, Cycling, Fencing, Field Hockey, Football, Handball, Rowing, Rugby, Shooting, Swimming, Tennis, Water Polo

MEDALS

Nation	Gold	Silver	Bronze	Total
Germany	29	18	25	72
France	14	15	15	44
England	12	11	4	27
Hungary	11	9	7	27
Latvia	3	2	2	7
Poland	3	2	0	5
Austria	2	2	3	7
Italy	2	2	1	5
Estonia	2	1	1	4
Denmark	2	1	0	3
Belgium	1	3	2	6
Egypt	1	1	1	3
Greece	1	1	1	3
Czechoslovakia	0	3	1	4
Scotland	0	2	2	4
Brazil	0	2	0	2

Nation	Gold	Silver	Bronze	Total
Switzerland	0	1	1	2
Yugoslavia	0	1	0	1

1939   Monte Carlo   Monaco   August 21–29

Nations: Belgium, Brazil, Denmark, Egypt, England, Estonia, Finland, France, Latvia, Luxembourg, Monaco, Netherlands, Norway, Poland, Scotland, Sweden, Switzerland, United States, Yugoslavia (five more)

Sports: Athletics, Basketball, Boxing, Fencing, Shooting, Swimming, Tennis, Volleyball, Water Polo

Sports for Women: Athletics, Fencing, Swimming, Tennis

MEDALS

Nation	Gold	Silver	Bronze	Total
France	23	15	13	51
United States	13	3	2	18
England	5	1	7	13
Scotland	3	4	5	12
Poland	3	3	2	8
Switzerland	3	0	2	5
Egypt	2	3	1	6
Finland	2	0	4	6
Netherlands	1	3	1	5
Estonia	1	3	1	5
Latvia	1	2	1	4
Denmark	1	1	1	3
Belgium	1	0	0	1
Sweden	0	3	1	4
Brazil	0	1	2	3
Monaco	0	1	0	1
Yugoslavia	0	1	0	1
Luxembourg	0	1	0	1
Norway	0	0	2	2

1947   Paris   August 24—31   (UIE)

Nations: Austria, Belgium, Bulgaria, Czechoslovakia, Denmark, Egypt, England, Finland, France, Hungary, Italy, Lebanon, Luxembourg, Netherlands, Poland, Scotland, Sweden, Switzerland

Sports: Athletics, Basketball, Cycling, Fencing, Football, Handball, Swimming, Tennis, Volleyball, Water Polo.

Sports for Women: Athletics, Fencing, Swimming, Tennis

MEDALS

Nation	Gold	Silver	Bronze	Total
Hungary	18	6	7	31
France	13	14	11	38
Czechoslovakia	8	10	12	30
Italy	8	8	7	23

Nation	Gold	Silver	Bronze	Total
England	4	2	3	9
Austria	3	5	8	16
Scotland	2	6	1	9
Sweden	2	5	3	10
Netherlands	2	0	1.5	3.5
Luxembourg	1	3	4.5	8.5
Egypt	1	2	5	8
Switzerland	1	2	1	4
Denmark	1	2	1	4
Finland	1	0	0	1
Lebanon	0	1	0	1

1949   Budapest   Hungary   August 14–21   (UIE)

Nations: Austria, Bulgaria, Czechoslovakia, France, Hungary, Korean P.R., Poland, Romania, Scotland, Soviet Union (six more)
Sports: Athletics, Basketball, Boxing, Cycling, Fencing, Football, Gymnastics, Rowing, Swimming, Tennis, Volleyball, Weightlifting, Wrestling
Sports for Women: Athletics, Basketball, Fencing, Gymnastics, Swimming, Tennis, Volleyball

MEDALS

Nation	Gold	Silver	Bronze	Total
Soviet Union	43	23.5	22.5	89
Hungary	41	39.5	22.5	103
France	14	13	9	36
Poland	3	3.5	8.5	15
Czechoslovakia	2	11.5	8	21.5
Romania	1	8	12.5	21.5
Austria	1	3	4	8
Scotland	1	2	3	6
Korean P.R.	0	0	1	1
Bulgaria	0	0	1	1

1949   Merano   Italy   August 28–September 4 (FISU)

Nations: Austria, Egypt, Luxembourg, Olaszorszag, Spain, Switzerland, West Germany
Sports: Athletics, Basketball, Fencing, Football, Tennis
Sports for Women: Athletics

MEDALS

Nation	Gold	Silver	Bronze	Total
Olaszorszag	12	13	5	30
West Germany	12	5	8	25
Spain	2	6	2	10
Austria	2	3	3	8
Luxembourg	2	0	5	7
Switzerland	1	1	1	3
Egypt	0	3	5	8

1951   Berlin   East Germany   August 6–15 (UIE)

Nations: Bulgaria, Czechoslovakia, East Germany, Finland, Hungary, Indonesia, Poland, Romania, Soviet Union (thirty-three more)
Sports: Athletics, Basketball, Boxing, Cycling, Football, Gymnastics, Swimming, Table Tennis, Tennis, Volleyball, Water Polo, Weightlifting, Wrestling
Sports for Women: Athletics, Basketball, Gymnastics, Table Tennis, Tennis, Swimming, Volleyball

MEDALS

Nation	Gold	Silver	Bronze	Total
Soviet Union	62	33	23	118
Hungary	42	39	20.5	101.5
East Germany	9	16	30	55
Czechoslovakia	5	11	14.5	30.5
Poland	3	10	19	32
Romania	3	9	12	24
Bulgaria	0	4	2	6
Indonesia	0	1	1	2
Finland	0	1	0	1

1951   Luxembourg   August 19–26   (FISU)

Nation: Austria, Belgium, Egypt, England, France, Lebanon, Luxembourg, Netherlands, South Africa, Spain, Switzerland, West Germany
Sports: Athletics, Basketball, Diving, Fencing, Field Hockey, Football, Tennis, Swimming, Volleyball
Sports for Women: Athletics, Basketball, Diving, Fencing, Swimming, Tennis

MEDALS

Nation	Gold	Silver	Bronze	Total
West Germany	17.5	13	8	38.5
England	11	12	10	33
Spain	6	3	5	14
Austria	5.5	8	6	19.5
Luxembourg	4	6	4	14
Switzerland	3	1	2	6
Egypt	2	2	4	8
Belgium	1	4	5	10
Netherlands	1	3	5	9
Lebanon	1	1	2	4
France	1	1	1	3
South Africa	1	0	0	1

1953   Dortmund   West Germany   August 9–16   (FISU)

Nations: Argentina, Austria, Belgium, Brazil, Egypt, England, Italy, Japan, Luxembourg, Saarland, Spain, West Germany, Yugoslavia (nine more)
Sports: Athletics, Basketball, Fencing, Football, Lawn Tennis, Swimming, Water Polo
Sports for Women: Athletics, Fencing, Swimming, Tennis

MEDALS

Nation	Gold	Silver	Bronze	Total
West Germany	17	10	12	39
Italy	11	5	4	20
Argentina	7	3	1	11
England	6	17	10	33
Yugoslavia	4	4	2	10
Brazil	3	4	3	10
Japan	3	3	3	9
Spain	2	2	4	8
Belgium	2	0	6	8
Luxembourg	1	0	3	4
Saarland	1	0	0	1
Austria	0	7	2	9
Egypt	0	1	1	2

1954   Budapest   Hungary   July 31–August 8   (UIE)

Nations: Austria, Bulgaria, China, Czechoslovakia, Denmark, East Germany, Egypt, Hungary, Ireland, Lebanon, Poland, Romania, Soviet Union (twenty-one more)

Sports: Athletics, Basketball, Boxing, Cycling, Diving, Fencing, Football, Gymnastics, Swimming, Table Tennis, Tennis, Volleyball, Water Polo, Weightlifting, Wrestling

Sports for Women: Athletics, Basketball, Diving, Fencing, Gymnastics, Swimming, Table Tennis, Tennis, Volleyball

MEDALS

Nation	Gold	Silver	Bronze	Total
Hungary	50	46	30.75	126.75
Soviet Union	38	31	19	88
East Germany	14	7.5	4	25.5
Poland	10	15	19	44
Romania	4	10.5	22.5	37
Bulgaria	3	3	5	11
Czechoslovakia	3	2	7.75	12.75
Austria	1	3	3	7
China	0	2	5	7
Denmark	0	1	2	3
Lebanon	0	1	0	1
Egypt	0	0	3	3
Ireland	0	0	1	1

1955   San Sebastián   Spain   August 7–14 (FISU)

Nations: Austria, Belgium, Brazil, Egypt, England, Israel, Italy, Japan, Luxembourg, Netherlands, Spain, Switzerland, United States, West Germany (twelve more)

Sports: Athletics, Basketball, Diving, Fencing, Field Hockey, Football, Swimming, Tennis, Water Polo

Sports for Women: Athletics Diving, Fencing, Swimming, Tennis

MEDALS

Nation	Gold	Silver	Bronze	Total
Italy	18	5	6	29
West Germany	12	21	13	46
England	7	12	25	44
Brazil	7	2	2	11
Netherlands	6	2	1	9
Austria	4	4	3	11
United States	3	0	0	3
Spain	2	8	7	17
Belgium	2	0	0	2
Switzerland	1	3	1	5
Egypt	1	1	2	4
Japan	0	3	1	4
Luxembourg	0	1	0	1
Israel	0	1	0	1

1959   Turin   Italy   August 26–September 9

Sports: Athletics, Basketball, Fencing, Swimming, Tennis, Volleyball, Water Polo

1961   Sofia   Bulgaria   August 25–September 3

Nations: Brazil, Bulgaria, Ceylon, Cuba, Czechoslovakia, Ghana, Great Britain, Hungary, Indonesia, Iran, Ireland, Israel, Japan, North Korea, Poland, Romania, South Africa, Soviet Union, Switzerland, Togo, West Germany (12 more)
Sports: Athletics, Basketball, Diving, Fencing, Gymnastics, Swimming, Tennis, Volleyball, Water Polo

1963   Pôrto Alegre   Brazil   August 30–September 8

Sports: Athletics, Basketball, Diving, Fencing, Gymnastics, Swimming, Tennis, Volleyball, Water Polo

1965   Budapest   Hungary   August 20–August 30

Nations: Australia, Austria, Canada, Cuba, Czechoslovakia, East Germany, France, Great Britain, Hungary, Israel, Italy, Japan, Netherlands, Poland, Romania, Spain, Soviet Union, Sweden, United States, West Germany, Yugoslavia (11 more)
Sports: Athletics, Basketball, Diving, Fencing, Gymnastics, Swimming, Tennis, Volleyball, Water Polo

MEDALS

Nation	Gold	Silver	Bronze	Total
Hungary	16	8	14	38
United States	14	9	9	32

Nation	Gold	Silver	Bronze	Total
Soviet Union	13	27	14	54
Italy	6	2	1	9
Japan	5	0	2	7
Poland	4	4	4	12
West Germany	4	3	6	13
Romania	3	4	4	11
France	3	2	3	8
Great Britain	1	4	4	9
Yugoslavia	1	1	3	5
Bulgaria	1	1	1	3
Canada	1	0	3	4
Sweden	1	0	1	2
Czechoslovakia	0	3	2	5
Holland	0	3	1	4
Cuba	0	2	0	2
Austria	0	0	2	2

1967   Tokyo   Japan   August 27–September 4

Sports: Athletics, Basketball, Diving, Fencing, Gymnastics, Judo, Swimming, Tennis, Volleyball, Water Polo

MEDALS

Nation	Gold	Silver	Bronze	Total
United States	32	23	6	61
Japan	21	17	26	64
Germany	8	9	5	22
Great Britain	4	11	9	24
France	4	5	13	22
Italy	4	5	9	18
Australia	2	1	3	6
Sweden	2	1	2	5
Korea	1	9	2	12
Finland	1	1	3	5
Netherlands	1	1	1	3
Austria	1	0	4	5
Yugoslavia	1	0	0	1
Ivory Coast	1	0	0	1
Spain	1	0	0	1
Canada	0	2	0	2
Mexico	0	1	0	1
Brazil	0	0	4	4
Indonesia	0	0	1	1
Belgium	0	0	1	1
Portugal	0	0	1	1

1970   Turin   Italy   August 26–September 6

Sports: Athletics, Basketball, Diving, Fencing, Gymnastics, Swimming, Tennis, Volleyball, Water Polo

MEDALS (PARTIAL)

Nation	Gold	Silver	Bronze	Total
Soviet Union	26	18	15	59
United States	22	18	11	51
East Germany	8	3	4	15
Italy	4	4	7	15
Great Britain	4	4	7	15
Japan	3	7	5	15
Hungary	3	6	6	15
Poland	3	1	5	9
West Germany	2	6	3	11
Yugoslavia	2	2	1	5
Netherlands	1	1	2	4
Bulgaria	1	1	1	3
Austria	1	1	1	3
France	1	0	4	5
Romania	0	4	2	6

1973   Moscow   Soviet Union   August 15–25

Nations: Australia, Austria, Algeria, Bangladesh, Belgium, Bolivia, Brazil, Bulgaria, Canada, Central African Republic, Ceylon, Chile, Congo, Costa Rica, Cuba, Czechoslovakia, Dahomey, Denmark, East Germany, Finland, France, Great Britain, Ghana, Greece, Guinea, Holland, Honduras, Hungary, Iceland, India, Indonesia, Israel, Iran, Iraq, Ireland, Italy, Japan, Jordan, Kenya, Republic of Korea, Kuwait, Lebanon, Liechtenstein, Luxembourg, Malta, Mexico, Mongolia, Nigeria, Norway, Pakistan, Panama, Peru, Puerto Rico, Poland, Portugal, Romania, Sierra Leone, Soviet Union, Spain, Sudan, Sweden, Switzerland, Syria, Thailand, Uganda, United Arab Republic, United States, Venezuela, West Germany, Yugoslavia, Zaire (two more)

Sports: Athletics, Basketball, Diving, Fencing, Gymnastics, Swimming, Tennis, Volleyball, Water Polo, Wrestling

Sports for Women: Athletics, Basketball, Diving, Fencing, Gymnastics, Swimming, Tennis, Volleyball

MEDALS

Nation	Gold	Silver	Bronze	Total
Soviet Union	68	36	30	134
United States	19	16	18	53
Romania	4	7	8	19
Japan	3	8	1	12
Poland	2	3	5	10
Cuba	2	3	1	6
Great Britain	2	3	1	6
Czechoslovakia	2	2	1	5
Italy	2	0	6	8
Finland	2	0	0	2
Hungary	1	9	4	14
Bulgaria	1	7	7	15
West Germany	1	4	7	12

Nation	Gold	Silver	Bronze	Total
East Germany	1	3	8	12
France	1	2	1	4
Yugoslavia	1	1	2	4
Mongolia	1	0	1	2
Iran	0	4	0	4
Canada	0	2	5	7
Australia	0	1	3	4
Korea	0	0	2	2
India	0	0	1	1
Kenya	0	0	1	1
Mexico	0	0	1	1

1975   Rome   Italy   September 17–21

Sports: Athletics

MEDALS (PARTIAL)

Nation	Gold	Silver	Bronze	Total
Soviet Union	7	5	11	23
Poland	7	3	1	11
Italy	5	1	1	7
West Germany	3	2	2	7
Finland	3	2	0	5
Romania	2	6	4	12
United States	2	3	1	6
Bulgaria	2	0	4	6
Canada	1	4	2	7
Czechoslovakia	1	1	0	2
France	1	1	0	2
Austria	1	0	0	1
Yugoslavia	0	3	4	7
Hungary	0	2	0	2
Great Britain	0	1	2	3

1977   Sofia   Bulgaria   August 17–28

Sports: Athletics, Basketball, Diving, Fencing, Gymnastics, Swimming, Tennis, Volleyball, Water Polo

MEDALS (PARTIAL)

Nation	Gold	Silver	Bronze	Total
Soviet Union	32	35	29	96
United States	19	10	14	43
Bulgaria	15	10	12	37
Romania	11	10	14	35
Japan	5	5	1	11
Czechoslovakia	5	4	1	10
Canada	4	6	5	15

Nation	Gold	Silver	Bronze	Total
Cuba	4	3	5	12
Poland	3	6	4	13
France	2	1	2	5
Mongolia	2	0	2	4
Italy	1	3	3	7
Yugoslavia	1	3	1	5
Belgium	1	0	0	1
Austria	1	0	0	1

1979   Mexico City   Mexico   September 2–13

Sports: Athletics, Basketball, Diving, Fencing, Football,* Gymnastics, Swimming, Tennis, Volleyball, Water Polo

*Football on the program for the first time.

MEDALS (PARTIAL)

Nation	Gold	Silver	Bronze	Total
Soviet Union	33	26	12	71
United States	22	13	16	51
Romania	12	3	15	30
East Germany	6	4	3	13
West Germany	4	6	8	18
Hungary	4	3	3	10
Italy	3	2	5	10
Netherlands	2	4	3	9
Poland	2	3	3	8
Czechoslovakia	2	0	3	5
Great Britain	1	6	4	11
Japan	1	4	6	11
Mexico	1	1	3	5
France	1	1	3	5
Canada	0	0	3	3

1981   Bucharest   Romania   July 19–30

Nations: Afghanistan, Algeria, Angola, Australia, Austria, Belgium, Benin, Brazil, Bulgaria, Canada, Central African Republic, China, Columbia, Congo, Cuba, Czechoslovakia, Denmark, Dominican Republic, East Germany, Ecuador, Egypt, England, Finland, France, Ghana, Great Britain, Greece, Guinea, Guyana, Holland, Hungary, India, Indonesia, Iraq, Ireland, Israel, Italy, Ivory Coast, Japan, Jordan, Kenya, Lebanon, Liberia, Libya, Luxembourg, Madagascar, Malta, Mauritania, Mexico, Mongolia, Morocco, Mozambique, New Zealand, Nicaragua, Nigeria, North Korea, Norway, Panama, Peru, Pakistan, Poland, Portugal, Puerto Rico, Romania, Senegal, Somalia, South Korea, Soviet Union, Spain, Sudan, Sweden, Switzerland, Syria, Tanzania, Turkey, United States, Upper Volta, Uruguay, Venezuela, Vietnam, West Germany, Yugoslavia, Zaire, Zambia, Zimbabwe (one more)

Sports: Athletics, Basketball, Diving, Fencing, Gymnastics, Swimming, Tennis, Volleyball, Water Polo, Wrestling

Sports for Women: Athletics, Basketball, Diving, Fencing, Gymnastics, Swimming, Tennis, Volleyball

MEDALS

Nation	Gold	Silver	Bronze	Total
Soviet Union	38	38	35	111
Romania	30	17	20	67
United States	29	18	9	56
China	10	6	5	21
Italy	6	4	3	13
East Germany	4	7	1	12
Japan	3	2	2	7
Cuba	2	2	3	7
West Germany	2	1	3	6
Great Britain	2	1	2	5
Czechoslovakia	1	2	2	5
Hungary	1	2	2	5
Yugoslavia	1	2	2	5
Poland	1	0	4	5
Morocco	1	0	0	1
Sweden	1	0	0	1
Bulgaria	0	4	5	9
South Korea	0	3	4	7
Canada	0	3	2	5
France	0	1	4	5
Australia	0	1	0	1
Switzerland	0	1	0	1
Finland	0	1	0	1
Greece	0	1	0	1
Brazil	0	0	10	10
Algeria	0	0	1	1
Austria	0	0	1	1
Ghana	0	0	1	1
Ivory Coast	0	0	1	1
Mongolia	0	0	1	1

1983   Edmonton   Canada   July 1—12

Sports: Athletics, Basketball, Cycling, Diving, Fencing, Gymnastics, Swimming, Tennis, Volleyball, Water Polo

MEDALS (PARTIAL)

Nation	Gold	Silver	Bronze	Total
Soviet Union	59	28	27	114
United States	12	22	18	52
Canada	9	10	19	38
Italy	9	10	6	25
Romania	6	12	9	27
China	5	3	4	12
Nigeria	5	0	0	5

Nation	Gold	Silver	Bronze	Total
Japan	3	3	6	12
West Germany	2	6	2	10
Cuba	2	1	4	7
Australia	2	0	2	4
Poland	1	5	6	12
Great Britain	1	3	3	7
Belgium	1	2	1	4
Brazil	1	1	0	2

1985   Kobe   Japan   August 24–September 4

Sports: Athletics, Basketball, Diving, Fencing, Football, Gymnastics, Judo, Swimming, Tennis, Volleyball, Water Polo

MEDALS (PARTIAL)

Nation	Gold	Silver	Bronze	Total
Soviet Union	44	21	19	84
United States	22	20	23	65
Cuba	9	8	5	22
China	6	7	6	19
Japan	6	3	7	16
Romania	5	10	6	21
Italy	4	6	5	15
Bulgaria	3	5	5	13
North Korea	3	3	2	8
Netherlands	3	2	3	8
Poland	3	1	3	7
South Korea	3	0	5	8
West Germany	2	4	9	15
Australia	2	4	2	8
Nigeria	2	1	2	5

1987   Zagreb   Yugoslavia   July 8–19*

*Football and Fencing competitions began on the 5th and 6th of July.

Sports: Athletics, Basketball, Canoeing, Diving, Gymnastics, Fencing, Rowing Soccer, Swimming, Tennis, Volleyball, Water Polo

Venues: Dinamo Stadium (Opening Ceremonies, Closing Ceremonies, Athletics, Football), Zagreb Sports Center Hall 1 (Basketball, Gymnastics), Zagreb Sports Center Hall 2, Kreso Rakic Sports Hall, Karlovac Sports Hall, Bjelovar Sports Hall, Sisak Sports Hall, V. Bakaric Sports Hall, Sutinska Vrela Sports Hall (Volleyball), Zagreb FC Stadium, Samobor Stadium, Jugokeramika FC Stadium, Varzdin Stadium, Sisak Stadium, Petrinja Stadium, Cakovek Stadium, Karlovak Stadium (Soccer), Faculty of Economics Sports Hall (Fencing), Jarun Rowing Complex (Rowing, Canoeing), Mladost Swimming Pool (Swimming, Water Polo), Salata Sports Center (Water Polo, Tennis, Diving), KTOC Sports Hall, Martinkova Sports Hall, Pescenica Sports Hall, Varazdin Sports Hall, Cakovek Sports Hall, Jastrebarsko Sports Hall, Petrinja Sports Hall, Tresnjvevka Sports Hall, MIOC Sports Hall, Bogumil Toni Sports Hall (Basketball)

MEDALS

Nation	Gold	Silver	Bronze	Total
United States	26	20	25	71
Soviet Union	25	34	21	80
Romania	22	12	9	43
Italy	12	8	10	30
China	11	9	13	33
Yugoslavia	7	7	5	19
Hungary	5	2	5	12
East Germany	5	3	5	13
Great Britain	4	1	4	9
West Germany	3	5	5	13
Bulgaria	3	4	1	8
Japan	3	3	6	12
Holland	3	10	8	21
Poland	2	1	3	6
Belgium	1	1	0	2
Cuba	1	3	2	6
Czechoslovakia	1	2	2	5
New Zealand	1	1	0	2
Spain	1	0	1	2
Morocco	1	0	0	1
Norway	1	0	0	1
Portugal	1	0	0	1
Australia	1	1	0	2
Greece	1	2	1	4
Canada	0	2	5	7
Mexico	0	0	1	1
Jamaica	0	0	1	1
North Korea	0	0	2	2
Switzerland	0	1	0	1
Senegal	0	1	0	1
Brazil	0	1	0	1
France	0	1	4	5
Nigeria	0	3	3	6
Puerto Rico	0	0	1	1
South Korea	0	1	1	2

1989   Duisburg   West Germany   August 22–30

Sports: Athletics, Basketball, Fencing, Rowing
Sports for Women: Athletics, Fencing, Rowing

MEDALS (PARTIAL)

Nation	Gold	Silver	Bronze	Total
Soviet Union	9	11	8	28
United States	9	9	8	26
Cuba	8	7	4	19
Italy	8	3	5	16
Romania	8	2	0	10
Hungary	4	4	1	9

Nation	Gold	Silver	Bronze	Total
China	4	2	5	11
East Germany	3	8	8	19
Kenya	3	2	1	6
France	1	1	3	5
West Germany	1	1	2	4
Poland	1	1	2	4
Great Britain	1	1	2	4
Spain	0	3	4	7
Canada	0	3	2	5

1991   Sheffield   England   July 14–27

Sports: Athletics, Basketball, Diving, Fencing, Field Hockey, Football, Gymnastics, Rhythmic Gymnastics, Swimming, Tennis, Volleyball, Water Polo

MEDALS (PARTIAL)

Nation	Gold	Silver	Bronze	Total
United States	29	23	24	76
China	20	17	11	48
Soviet Union	15	15	21	51
North Korea	11	3	5	19
Italy	6	7	8	21
South Korea	5	1	3	9
Japan	4	15	9	28
Germany	4	8	4	16
Great Britain	4	5	5	14
Canada	3	4	11	18
Poland	3	3	5	11
France	3	2	4	9
Australia	2	2	3	7
Spain	0	0	0	7
Romania	0	0	0	6

1993   Buffalo   USA   July 8–18*

*Soccer tournament began play on the 7th.

Nations: Algeria, Argentina, Armenia, American Samoa, Australia, Austria, Azerbaijan, Bahamas, Bangladesh, Barbados, Belgium, Belarus, Brazil, Bosnia and Herzegovina, Bulgaria, Burkina Faso, Central African Republic, Canada, Chad, Chile, China, Chinese Taipei, Congo, Côte d'Ivoire, Costa Rica, Croatia, Cuba, Cyprus, Czech Republic, Denmark, Dominican Republic, Ecuador, El Salvador, Estonia, Ethiopia, Fiji, Finland, France, Gabon, Great Britain, Germany, Ghana, Greece, Guatemala, Guam, Guyana, Hong Kong, Hungary, Indonesia, India, Ireland, Iceland, Israel, Virgin Islands, Italy, Jamaica, Jordan, Japan, Kenya, Kazakhstan, Latvia, Lesotho, Liberia, Lithuania, Luxembourg, Madagascar, Morocco, Malawi, Mexico, Mongolia, Macedonia, Malta, Mauritania, Namibia, Netherlands, Nepal, Nigeria, Norway, New Zealand, Pakistan, Paraguay, Peru, PIP,* Papua New Guinea, Poland, Portugal, Puerto Rico, Qatar, Romania, Russia, Rwanda, Senegal, Sierra Leone, San Marino, South Africa,

*PIP (Independent Athletes).

South Korea, Spain, Sri Lanka, Sudan, Switzerland, Suriname, Slovakia, Sweden, Swaziland, Tanzania, Thailand, Trinidad, Turkey, Uganda, Ukraine, Uruguay, United States, Venezuela, Vietnam, Zaire, Zambia, Zimbabwe

Sports: Athletics, Baseball, Basketball, Diving, Fencing, Football, Gymnastics, Rowing, Swimming, Tennis, Volleyball, Water Polo

Venues: In U.S.: Rich Stadium (Opening Ceremonies), University of Buffalo Athletics Stadium (Athletics), Memorial Auditorium (Basketball), Niagara Falls Convention Center (Gymnastics), Alumni Arena (Volleyball), Lew Port (Football), Erie County Fairgrounds Agri Center (Fencing), University of Buffalo Sportsplex (Tennis), E.C.C. City Buffalo (Swimming), University of Buffalo Natatorium (Diving), Tonawanda Town Pool (Water Polo), Pilot Field, (Baseball) In Canada: Royal Canadian Regatta Course (Rowing), McMaster University, Brian Timmis Stadium, Sackville Hill Memorial Park, Mohawk Sports Park (Football)

MEDALS (PARTIAL)

Nation	Gold	Silver	Bronze	Total
United States	30	24	21	75
China	17	6	5	28
Canada	12	14	14	40
Ukraine	11	6	9	26
Cuba	8	4	4	16
Romania	7	2	3	12
Germany	6	9	13	28
Japan	5	13	12	30
Italy	5	9	11	25
France	5	8	11	24
Hungary	4	4	6	14
Great Britain	3	6	4	13
South Korea	3	4	4	11
Poland	3	0	4	7
Belgium	2	3	3	8

1995   Fukuoka   Japan   August 23–September 3

Nations: Albania, Algeria, American Samoa, Angola, Antigua and Barbuda, Argentina, Armenia, Australia, Austria, Azerbaijan, Bangladesh, Barbados, Belarus, Belgium, Benin, Bhutan, Bolivia, Botswana, Brazil, British Virgin Islands, Bulgaria, Burkina Faso, Burundi, Cambodia, Cameroon, Canada, Cape Verde, Central African Republic, Chad, Chile, Chinese Taipei, Commonwealth of Dominica, Comoros, Congo, Costa Rica, Côte d'Ivoire, Croatia, Cuba, Cyprus, Czech Republic, Dominican Republic, Ecuador, El Salvador, Equatorial Guinea, Estonia, Fiji, Finland, France, Gambia, Georgia, Germany, Ghana, Great Britain, Greece, Grenada, Guatemala, Guyana, Haiti, Honduras, Hong Kong, Hungary, India, Indonesia, Iraq, Ireland, Islamic Republic of Iran, Israel, Italy, Jamaica, Japan, Jordan, Kazakhstan, Kenya, Korea, Kyrgyzstan, Laos, Latvia, Lebanon, Lesotho, Liberia, Libyan, Lithuania, Luxembourg, Macau, Madagascar, Malawi, Malaysia, Maldives, Mali, Malta, Mauritania, Mauritius, Mexico, Mongolia, Morocco, Mozambique, Myanmar, Namibia, Nauru, Nepal, Netherlands, Netherlands Antilles, New Zealand, Nicaragua, Niger, Nigeria, Norway, Pakistan, Panama, Papua New Guinea, Paraguay, People's Republic of China,

Peru, Philippines, Poland, Portugal, Puerto Rico, Republic of Moldova, Romania, Russian Federation, Saint Lucia, San Marino, Sao Tome and Principe, Senegal, Seychelles, Sierra Leone, Singapore, Slovakia, Slovenia, South Africa, Spain, Sri Lanka, St. Vincent and the Grenadines, Sudan, Suriname, Swaziland, Sweden, Switzerland, Syrian Arab Republic, Tajikistan, Tanzania, Thailand, Togo, Tonga, Trinidad and Tobago, Tunisia, Turkey, Turkmenistan, Uganda, Ukraine, United Arab Emirates, United States of America, Uruguay, Uzbekistan, Vanuatu, Vietnam, Virgin Islands, Western Samoa, Yemen, Yugoslavia, Zambia, Zimbabwe

Sports: Athletics, Baseball, Basketball, Diving, Fencing, Football, Gymnastics, Rhythmic Gymnastics, Judo, Swimming, Tennis, Volleyball, Water Polo (men did not compete in Rhythmic Gymnastics)

Sports for Women: Athletics, Basketball, Diving, Fencing, Gymnastics, Rhythmic Gymnastics, Judo, Swimming, Tennis, Volleyball

Venues: Fukuoka Dome (Opening Ceremony, Closing Ceremony, Baseball), Heiwadai Baseball Stadium (Baseball), Hakata no Mori Track and Field Stadium (Athletics), Fukuoka Kokusai Center (Basketball), Kyuden Memorial Gymnasium (Basketball), Minami Gymnasium (Basketball), Sawara Gymnasium (Basketball), Munakata Yurix (Basketball), Higashi (Basketball), Fukuoka University Memorial Gymnasium 2 (Fencing), Hakata no Mori Football Stadium (Football), Prefecture Kasuga Park Bakk Field (Football), Shirozu Oike Park and Recreation Area (Football), Marine Messe Fukuoka (Gymnastics, Volleyball), Prefectural Pool Complex (Swimming, Diving), Nishi Civic Pool Complex (Water Polo), Hakata no Mori Tennis Stadium (Tennis), Fukuoka Civic Gymnasium (Volleyball), Nishi Gymnasium (Volleyball), Jonan Gymnasium (Volleyball), Accion Fukuoka (Volleyball), Chuo Gymnasium, (Volleyball), Fukuoka Kokusai Center (Judo)

MEDALS

Nation	Gold	Silver	Bronze	Total
United States	24	27	18	69
Japan	24	16	24	64
Russia	14	12	23	49
China	13	10	16	39
South Korea	10	7	10	27
Hungary	8	4	2	14
Germany	6	6	8	20
Bulgaria	5	4	2	11
Ukraine	4	5	6	15
Romania	4	5	2	11
Cuba	4	3	3	10
Italy	3	7	11	21
South Africa	3	1	0	4
France	2	6	7	15
Brazil	2	5	2	9
Belarus	2	3	3	8
Mexico	2	1	2	5
Yugoslavia	2	1	0	3
Australia	1	2	3	6
Netherlands	1	2	2	5
Kenya	1	2	0	3

Nation	Gold	Silver	Bronze	Total
Chinese Taipei	1	1	2	4
Nigeria	1	1	2	4
Slovakia	1	1	1	3
Czech Republic	1	1	1	3
Belgium	1	0	1	2
Madagascar	1	0	0	1
Croatia	1	0	0	1
St. Vincent and Grenadines	1	0	0	1
Great Britain	0	3	7	10
Poland	0	3	4	7
Spain	0	2	1	3
Kazakhstan	0	2	0	2
Canada	0	1	2	3
Greece	0	1	1	2
Morocco	0	1	1	2
Armenia	0	1	0	1
Barbados	0	1	0	1
Austria	0	1	0	1
Algeria	0	0	1	1
Portugal	0	0	1	1
Slovenia	0	0	1	1
Switzerland	0	0	1	1
Finland	0	0	1	1

1997   Sicily   Italy   August 18–31

Sports: Athletics, Basketball, Diving, Fencing, Gymnastics, Soccer, Swimming, Tennis, Volleyball, Water Polo (Baseball canceled)

MEDALS

Nation	Gold	Silver	Bronze	Total
United States	20	19	22	61
Ukraine	17	6	4	27
Japan	14	8	11	33
Russia	10	14	10	34
China	10	9	7	26
Italy	7	14	10	31
Cuba	7	11	4	22
Hungary	7	4	1	12
South Korea	5	2	3	10
Slovakia	4	0	1	5
Romania	3	4	6	13
Belarus	3	2	3	8
Brazil	3	2	1	6
France	2	4	6	12
Australia	2	3	5	10
South Africa	2	2	2	6
Germany	2	1	8	11
Taiwan	2	1	1	4
Great Britain	2	0	3	5

Nation	Gold	Silver	Bronze	Total
Nigeria	2	0	0	2
Czech Republic	1	4	4	9
Mexico	1	2	1	4
Netherlands	1	2	1	4
Poland	1	1	5	7
Greece	1	0	0	1
Canada	0	4	4	8
Jamaica	0	2	1	3
Kenya	0	1	1	2
Portugal	0	1	1	2
Belgium	0	1	0	1
Israel	0	1	0	1
Spain	0	1	0	1
Austria	0	0	3	3
Slovenia	0	0	2	2
Bulgaria	0	0	1	1
Croatia	0	0	1	1
Cyprus	0	0	1	1
Qatar	0	0	1	1

1999   *Palma de Mallorca   Spain   July 2–July 13*

Nations: Albania, Algeria, Angola, Argentina, Armenia, Australia, Austria, Azerbaijan, Bangladesh, Barbados, Belarus, Belgium, Bhutan, Botswana, Brazil, Bulgaria, Burkina Faso, Burundi, Cameroon, Canada, Central African Republic, Chad, Chile, China, Chinese Taipei, Colombia, Costa Rica, Croatia, Cuba, Cyprus, Czech Republic, Denmark, Dominican Republic, El Salvador, Estonia, Finland, France, Gabon, Georgia, Germany, Great Britain, Greece, Guatemala, Guinea, Honduras, Hong Kong, Hungary, Iceland, India, Indonesia, Iran, Iraq, Ireland, Israel, Italy, Ivory Coast, Jamaica, Japan, Jordan, Kazakhstan, Kenya, Kyrgyzstan, Latvia, Lebanon, Liechtenstein, Lithuania, Luxembourg, Macedonia, Madagascar, Malawi, Malaysia, Maldives, Malta, Mexico, Moldova, Mongolia, Morocco, Mozambique, Namibia, Nepal, Netherlands, New Zealand, Nicaragua, Nigeria, Norway, Panama, Papua New Guinea, Paraguay, Peru, Poland, Portugal, Puerto Rico, Qatar, Romania, Russia, Rwanda, Sao Tome and Principe, Saudi Arabia, Senegal, Seychelles, Slovakia, Slovenia, South Africa, South Korea, Spain, Sri Lanka, Sudan, Swaziland, Sweden, Switzerland, Tajikistan, Thailand, Tunisia, Turkey, Uganda, Ukraine, United Arab Emirates, United States, Uruguay, Uzbekistan, Vietnam, Virgin Islands, Yugoslavia, Zimbabwe[249]

Sports: Athletics, Basketball, Fencing, Football, Gymnastics, Swimming, Diving, Water Polo, Tennis, Volleyball, Judo, Sailing

Sports for Women: Athletics, Basketball, Fencing, Gymnastics, Swimming, Diving, Tennis, Volleyball, Judo, Sailing

		MEDALS		
Nation	Gold	Silver	Bronze	Total
United States	30	18	15	63
Russia	14	18	8	40
Cuba	12	3	10	25
Japan	11	13	16	40

Nation	Gold	Silver	Bronze	Total
China	9	5	10	24
Romania	8	4	3	15
Spain	7	7	11	25
Ukraine	7	7	7	21
Italy	6	11	8	25
France	6	3	7	16
Poland	4	7	1	12
Czech Republic	4	5	4	13
Korea	3	4	6	13
Germany	2	4	3	9
Australia	2	3	3	8
Netherlands	2	3	1	6
Belarus	2	3	0	5
Hungary	2	2	1	5
Chinese Taipei	2	2	0	4
South Africa	2	1	3	6
Brazil	2	0	4	6
Canada	1	3	6	10
Great Britain	1	3	5	9
Mexico	1	2	0	3
Belgium	1	1	2	4
Portugal	1	1	1	3
Kenya	1	0	0	1
Latvia	1	0	0	1
Mongolia	1	0	0	1
Austria	0	2	1	3
Slovenia	0	2	0	2
Greece	0	1	2	3
Israel	0	1	2	3
Switzerland	0	1	2	3
Georgia	0	1	1	2
Argentina	0	1	1	2
Qatar	0	1	0	1
Yugoslavia	0	1	0	1
Uzbekistan	0	1	0	1
Jamaica	0	1	0	1
Slovakia	0	0	3	3
Norway	0	0	1	1
Croatia	0	0	1	1
Nigeria	0	0	1	1
Denmark	0	0	1	1
Senegal	0	0	1	1

World Youth Games

The World Youth Games were proposed in 1996 by the city of Moscow and the Russian Olympic Committee. The International Olympic Committee gave its full approval of the event which was created for athletes between the ages of 12 and 17, and held between July 11 and 19, 1998.

A torch relay began in June in Athens, Greece, and traveled throughout Russia before arriving in Moscow. Boris Yeltsin, the Russian president, officially opened the games, with IOC president Juan Antonio Samaranch a guest of honor at the opening ceremonies. Mishutka, the bear cub, served as the games mascot, bringing back memories of Misha, the mascot for the 1980 Olympics.

The mayor of Moscow, Yuri Luzhkov, attempted to hold off rainy weather on the day of the opening ceremony by seeding the clouds to make them drop their rain before reaching Moscow. The weather for the ceremony was cloudy, but the rain stayed away.

Many of the same stadiums and facilities that were used for the 1980 Moscow Olympic Games were refurbished for use in the World Youth Games. The Russian Olympic Committee presented the event with the intention of bidding for the 2012 Olympic Games.

The Arab-Israeli issue reared its ugly head again when Iranian and Syrian wrestlers, one from each country, refused to compete against Israeli wrestlers, choosing disqualification instead.

The Russian team ran away with the overall medal title. The United States sent participants in some events, but had no entries in the athletics or swimming competitions.

Year	Host City	Host Nation	Dates	Nations	Athletes	Sports
1998	Moscow	Russia	July 11–19	130	5000	14

Nations: Afghanistan, Albania, Algeria, Angola, Argentina, Armenia, Australia, Azerbaijan, Bahrain, Bangladesh, Barbados, Belarus, Belgium, Benin, Bolivia, Botswana, Brazil, Bulgaria, Burkina Faso, Burundi, Cambodia, Cameroon, Canada, Cape Verde, Chile, China, Chinese Taipei, Colombia, Congo, Cook Islands, Croatia, Cuba, Cyprus, Czech Republic, Denmark, Djibouti, Egypt, Ecuador, Guinea, Estonia, Ethiopia, Fiji, Finland, France, Gabon, Gambia, Georgia, Ghana, Gibraltar, Great Britain, Guatemala, Guinea, Guinea-Bissau, Honduras, Hong Kong, Hungary, India, Iran, Ireland, Israel, Italy, Ivory Coast, Jordan, Japan, Kazakhstan, Kenya, Korea, Kuwait, Kyrgyzstan, Laos, Latvia, Lebanon, Lesotho, Libya, Lithuania, Luxembourg, Macedonia, Madagascar, Malaysia, Malta, Mexico, Moldova, Mongolia, Mozambique, Namibia, Nauru, Nepal, Netherlands, New Zealand, Nigeria, Norway, Oman, Pakistan, Palestine, Paraguay, Peru, Poland, Portugal, Qatar, Romania, Russia, Rwanda, St. Kitts-Nevis, St. Vincent and the Grenadines, Saudi Arabia, Senegal, Seychelles, Slovakia, Slovenia, South Africa, Spain, Suriname, Sweden, Syria, Tajikistan, Tanzania, Togo, Tonga, Trinidad and Tobago, Turkmenistan, Turkey, Uganda, Ukraine, United States, Uruguay, Uzbekistan, Vietnam, Western Samoa, Yugoslavia, Zimbabwe

Sports: Athletics, Basketball, Fencing, Football, Gymnastics, Judo, Rhythmic Gymnastics, Swimming, Synchronized Swimming, Table Tennis, Tennis, Volleyball, Wrestling (Greco Roman and Freestyle)

Venues: Central Tourist House Bowling Center (Bowling), The Chertanovo Sports Complex (Fencing), Druzhba All-Purpose Sports Hall (Judo, Tennis), Dynamo Sports Palace (Rhythmic Gymnastics), Luzhniki Big Arena (Athletics, Soccer, Ceremonies), Luzhniki Small Arena (Table Tennis), Luzhniki Sports Palace (Team Handball), the "Moskovich" Stadium (Soccer), Olympic Sports Complex (Aquatic Events, Artistic Gymnastics, Volleyball), The "Torpedo" Stadium (Soccer), Trudovye Rezervy Sports Complex (Greco-Roman Wrestling), TsSKA Sports Palace (Basketball)

MEDALS

Nation	Gold	Silver	Bronze	Total
Russia	64	29	31	124
China	21	7	4	32
Ukraine	10	19	23	52
Poland	7	10	9	26
Korea	6	2	5	13
Cuba	6	1	0	7
Belarus	5	8	12	25
Brazil	5	5	6	16
South Africa	4	5	6	15
Greece	3	1	3	7
Kazakhstan	2	5	3	10
Georgia	2	4	11	17
Armenia	2	3	0	5
Romania	2	2	4	8
Lithuania	2	2	1	5
Iran	2	1	2	5
Great Britain	2	1	1	4
Denmark	2	0	0	2
Ireland	2	0	0	2
Italy	1	6	8	15
North Korea	1	6	3	10
Germany	1	4	2	7
Uzbekistan	1	3	6	10
Chinese Taipei	1	2	5	8
Azerbaijan	1	2	1	4
United States	1	1	5	7
Ethiopia	1	1	1	3
Argentina	1	0	3	4
Slovenia	1	0	3	4
Japan	1	0	2	3
Netherlands	1	0	2	3
Finland	1	0	0	1
Syria	1	0	0	1
Uganda	1	0	0	1
Austria	0	3	3	6
Croatia	0	3	2	5
Spain	0	3	2	5
Canada	0	3	0	3
Hungary	0	3	0	3
Israel	0	1	3	4
Czech Republic	0	1	2	3
Australia	0	1	1	2
Chile	0	1	1	2
Kyrgyzstan	0	1	1	2
Moldova	0	1	1	2
Sweden	0	1	1	2
Belgium	0	1	0	1
Bulgaria	0	1	0	1
Hong Kong	0	1	0	1

Nation	Gold	Silver	Bronze	Total
Latvia	0	1	0	1
Mexico	0	1	0	1
Mongolia	0	1	0	1
Namibia	0	1	0	1
Saudi Arabia	0	1	0	1
Turkey	0	1	0	1
France	0	0	3	3
Barbados	0	0	2	2
Egypt	0	0	2	2
Estonia	0	0	2	2
Malaysia	0	0	2	2
Cyprus	0	0	1	1
Kenya	0	0	1	1
Luxembourg	0	0	1	1
Qatar	0	0	1	1
Slovakia	0	0	1	1
Turkmenistan	0	0	1	1
Vietnam	0	0	1	1
Yugoslavia	0	0	1	1

X Games

The X Games, originally named the "Extreme Games," were created by ESPN and bring athletes from around the world together to compete in the "extreme" sports of bungee jumping, in-line downhill skating, mountain biking, skateboarding, street luge, skysurfing, sport climbing, and wakeboarding. Athletes from Russia, Germany, France, South Africa, Brazil, Japan and other corners of the globe have competed in the games, but the international aspect is not the focus of the games as much as getting together and showing off the latest extreme tricks.

The first X Games were held in Newport, Rhode Island, in 1995. The original plan was to hold the second edition in 1997, but the games were so successful, with 130,000 spectators and a large TV audience, that the organizers decided to hold them again in 1996 using the same Rhode Island venues. Some 200,000 spectators showed up the second time around at historic Fort Adams to watch the athletes compete for $300,000 in prize money.

During the 1996 games, skysurfers Joe Jennings and Patrick de Gayardon scattered the ashes of former skysurfer Rob Harris to the wind as part of their final routine. Harris and Jennings had won the skysurfing gold medal in the 1995 games, but Harris had been killed later that year while filming a television commercial.[250]

The 1997 and 1998 games were both held in San Diego, California, with 220,000 and 243,000 spectators in those years. A month before the 1997 games, the Audubon Society brought a lawsuit, charging that holding the games on the San Diego beaches would harm the nesting and breeding areas of two birds, the California least tern and the Western snowy plover. The lawsuit was settled a week before the games when the city of San Diego ensured that no X Games activities would be held within 500 feet of the nesting sites, which were already fenced in to protect them.

The games have been derided by some as not true sports events, a notion refuted by the daring grace of the skateboarders and bicycle stunt riders who show as much skill and athleticism as any gymnast, pole vaulter or ice skater.

Dave Mirra is the X Games' most decorated athlete to date. He has won nine gold and three silver medals in bicycle stunt riding between 1995 and 2000 including three golds in the 1998 edition of the games.

Brazil's Fabiola da Silva became the games' first three time winner in a single event when she won the gold medal in women's in-line vert skating in 1998.

ESPN moved the dates of the 1999 games to the first week in July so as to avoid conflicts with the Women's World Cup soccer tournament held in the U.S. When San Diego declined the invitation to host the event for the third year in a row, because of its already full beaches on the July 4th weekend, San Francisco outbid Seattle, Washington, St. Petersburg, Florida, and Providence for the right to host the 1999 edition.

The phenomenally successful fifth edition of the games held on the pier in San Francisco underneath the stunning backdrop of the Golden Gate Bridge, saw established stars such as bicycle stunt rider Dave Mirra, and skateboarders Andy McDonald and Tony Hawk add to their already massive stash of X Games medals. New stars such as fifteen-year-old motorcyclist Travis Pastrana pushed the games to further extremes.

Pastrana, having already won the Moto X stunt event, exited the stadium with a leap off of the pier into the San Francisco Bay, with a preplanned rescue boat waiting to pick him up. ESPN decided the stunt went too far, and withheld the $10,000 prize money for his winning the competition. Pastrana was allowed to keep the gold medal and the victory, but the prize money was donated to organizations involved in keeping the waters of San Francisco Bay clean. ESPN refused to give the stunt any more publicity by not showing the jump in any of its coverage.

Year	Host City	Host Nation	Dates	Nations	Athletes	Sports
1995	Newport	USA	June 24	NA	NA	9
1996	Newport	USA	June 24–30	NA	NA	8
1997	San Diego	USA	June 23–29	NA	400	11
1998	San Diego	USA	June 19–28	27	400	8
1999	San Francisco	USA	June 25–July 3	NA	NA	9
2000	San Francisco	USA	June 24–July 2	NA	NA	7

1995   Newport   USA   June

Sports: Extreme Marathon, Sky surfing, Sport Climbing, Water Sports (Windsurfing, Kiteskiing, barefoot jumping), Wakeboarding, Skateboarding, In-line skating, Bungee-jumping, Street Luge Mountain Biking
Venues: Fort Adams State Park

1996   Newport   USA   June 24–30

Sports: Extreme Marathon, Sky surfing, Sport Climbing, Water Sports (Barefoot Jumping, Wakeboarding), Skateboarding, In-line Skating, Bungee Jumping, Street Luge
Venues: Fort Adams State Park

1997   San Diego   USA   June 23–29

Nations: (preliminary list from medal lists—not official or complete) Australia, New Zealand, Germany, USA, Mexico, Great Britain, Canada, Russia, Belgium, France, Japan, Brazil, Denmark, Sweden, Switzerland, South Africa, South Korea

Sports: Big-Air Snowboarding, Aggressive In-Line, Barefoot Jumping, Bicycle Stunt, Downhill In-Line, Skateboarding, Skysurfing, Sportclimbing, Street Luge, Wakeboarding, X-Venture Race

1998   San Diego   USA   June 19–28

Sports: Bicycle Stunt Riding, Big-Air Snowboarding, In-Line Skating, Skateboarding, Sportclimbing, Street Luge, Skysurfing, Watersports

1999   San Francisco   USA   June 25–July 3

Sports: Bicycle Stunt Riding, Big-Air Snowboarding, In-Line Skating, Moto X, Skateboarding, Sportclimbing, Street Luge, Skysurfing, Watersports
Venues: Pier 30 and 32

2000   San Francisco   USA   June 24–July 2

Sports: Bicycle Stunt Riding, In-Line Skating, Moto X, Skateboarding, Street Luge, Skysurfing, Wakeboarding

Appendix 1.
Games by Year

The abbreviation G = *Games*

1896

Olympic G, Athens, Greece, April 6–15

1900

Olympic G, Paris, France, May 20–Oct. 28

1901

Nordic G, Stockholm, Sweden, Feb. 9–17

1903

Nordic G, Kristiania (Oslo), Norway, Jan. 31–
Feb. 6

1904

Olympic G, St. Louis, USA, July 1–Nov. 23

1905

Nordic G, Stockholm, Sweden, Feb. 4–12

1906

Olympic G, Athens, Greece, April 22–May 2

1908

Olympic G, London, England, April 27–Oct. 31

1909

Nordic G, Stockholm, Sweden, Feb. 6–14
Academic Olympia, Leipzig, Germany, July 11

1910

Academic Olympia, Berlin, Germany, July 3

1911

Festival of the Empire Sports Meeting, London,
England, June 24–July 1
Academic Olympia, Dresden, Germany, July 8–10
Academic Olympia, Breslau, Germany, Aug. 1–3

1912

Olympic G, Stockholm, Sweden, May 5–July 22

1913

Far East Championships, Manila, Philippines,
Feb. 3–7
Nordic G, Stockholm, Sweden, Feb. 7–16
Academic Olympia, Leipzig, Germany, Oct. 18–
19

1914

Baltic G, Malmö, Sweden, June 7–Aug. 9

1915

Far East Championships, Shanghai, China, May
15–21

1917

Nordic G, Stockholm, Sweden, Feb. 10–18
Far East Championships, Tokyo, Japan, May 8–
12

1919

Far East Championships, Manila, Philippines,
May 12–16
Inter-Allied G, Paris, France, June 22–July 6

1920

Olympic G, Antwerp, Belgium, April 20–Sept. 12

1921

Far East Championships, Shanghai, China, May
30–June 3
Red Sport International Spartakiade, Prague,
Czechoslovakia, June 19–26
Socialist Olympics, Prague, Czechoslovakia, June
24–30

Central American G, Guatemala City, Guatemala, Sept. 11–18

1922

Nordic G, Stockholm, Sweden, Feb. 4–12
University Olympia, Rome, Italy, April 23–May 1
International Women's G, Paris, France, Aug. 20
Latin American G, Rio de Janeiro, Brazil

1923

World University G, Paris, France, May 3–6
Far East Championships, Osaka, Japan, May 21–25
SELL Games (Summer), Tartu, Estonia

1924

Olympic Winter G, Chamonix, France, Jan. 25–Feb. 4
Olympic G, Paris, France, May 4–July 27
Red Sport International Spartakiade, Paris, France, July 13–14
Tailteann G, Dublin, Ireland, Aug. 2–18
World G for the Deaf, Paris, France, Aug. 10–17
World University G, Warsaw, Poland, Sept. 17–20
SELL Games (Summer), Riga, Latvia

1925

Socialist Worker Sports International Winter Worker Olympiad, Schrieberhau (Riesenberge), Germany, Jan. 31–Feb. 2
Far East Championships, Manila, Philippines, May 17–22
Socialist Olympics, Frankfurt, Germany, July 22–25

1926

Nordic G, Stockholm, Sweden, Feb. 6–14
International Women's G, Götenburg, Sweden, Aug. 27–29
Central American and Caribbean G, Mexico City, Mexico, Oct. 12–Nov. 2
SELL Games (Summer), Helsinki, Finland

1927

Far East Championships, Shanghai, China, Aug. 28–31
World University G, Rome, Italy, Aug. 28–Sept. 4
Socialist Olympics, Prague, Czechoslovakia

1928

Winter World University G, Cortina d'Ampezzo, Italy, Jan. 22–29
Olympic Winter G, St. Moritz, Switzerland, Feb. 11–19
Red Sport International Winter Spartakiade, Oslo, Norway, Feb. 17–28
Olympic G, Amsterdam, Netherlands, May 17–Aug. 12
World University G, Paris, France, Aug. 9–17
Tailteann G, Dublin, Ireland, Aug. 11–22

Red Sport International Spartakiade, Moscow, Soviet Union, Aug. 12–28
World G for the Deaf, Amsterdam, Netherlands, Aug. 18–26
Hapoel G, Tel Aviv, Israel, Sept. 29–30
Red Sport International Winter Spartakiade, Moscow, Soviet Union, Dec.

1929

SELL Games (Winter), Riga, Latvia
SELL Games (Summer), Kaunas, Lithuania

1930

Winter World University G, Davos, Switzerland, Jan. 4–12
Central American and Caribbean G, Havana, Cuba, March 15–April 5
Far East Championships, Tokyo, Japan, May 24–27
SELL Games (Summer), Tallin, Estonia
World University G, Darmstadt, Germany, Aug. 1–10
Commonwealth G, Hamilton, Canada, Aug. 16–23
International Women's G, Prague, Czechoslovakia, Sept.
Hapoel G, Tel Aviv, Israel, Oct. 10–12

1931

Socialist Worker Sports International Winter Worker Olympiad, Murzzuschlag, Austria, Feb. 5–8
SELL Games (Winter), Helsinki, Finland
Red Sport International Spartakiade, Moscow, Soviet Union, July 5–19
SELL Games (Summer), Riga, Latvia
Socialist Olympics, Vienna, Austria, July 16–26
World G for the Deaf, Nürnberg, Germany, Aug. 19–25

1932

Olympic Winter G, Lake Placid, USA, Feb. 4–15
Maccabiah G, Tel Aviv, Israel, March 29–April 6
Tailteann G, Dublin, Ireland, June 29–July 10
Counter Olympics, Chicago, USA, July 28–Aug. 1
SELL Games (Summer), Helsinki, Finland
Olympic G, Los Angeles, USA, July 30–Aug. 14
Hapoel G, Tel Aviv, Israel, Oct. 21–25

1933

Winter World University G, Bardonecchia, Italy, Jan. 29–Feb. 5
Maccabiade Winter G, Zakopane, Poland, Feb. 1–5
SELL Games (Summer), Kaunas, Lithuania
World University G, Turin, Italy, Sept. 1–10

1934

Western Asiatic G, Delhi-Patalia, India, February 25–March 3
Far East Championships, Manila, Philippines, May 16–20

Socialist Olympics, Prague, Czechoslovakia, July 4–9

SELL Games (Summer), Tartu, Estonia

Commonwealth G, London, England, Aug. 4–11

International Women's G, London, England, Aug.

1935

Winter World University G, St. Moritz, Switzerland, Feb. 4–10

Maccabiade Winter G, Banská-Bystrica, Czechoslovakia, Feb. 18–25

Central American and Caribbean G, San Salvador, El Salvador, March 16–April 5

SELL Games (Winter), Riga, Sigulda, Latvia

Maccabiah G, Tel Aviv, Israel, April 2–10

Hapoel G, Tel Aviv, Israel, April 18–21

SELL Games (Summer), Riga, Latvia

World University G, Budapest, Hungary, Aug. 10–18

World G for the Deaf, London, England, Aug. 18–24

1936

Olympic Winter G, Garmisch-Partenkirchen, Germany, Feb. 6–16

SELL Games (Summer), Helsinki, Finland

Olympic G, Berlin, Germany, Aug. 1–16

1937

Winter World University G, Zeel am See, Austria, Feb. 2–10

Socialist Worker Sports International Winter Worker Olympiad, Johannesbad, Czechoslovakia, Feb. 18–21

Pan-American Exposition, Dallas, USA, July 13–18

Socialist Olympics, Antwerp, Belgium, July 25–Aug. 1

SELL Games (Summer), Kaunas, Lithuania

World University G, Paris, France, Aug. 21–29

1938

Commonwealth G, Sydney, Australia, Feb. 5–12

Central American and Caribbean G, Panama City, Panama, Feb. 5–24

SELL Games (Winter), Zarasai, Lithuania

Bolivarian G, Bogota, Colombia, Aug. 6–21

SELL Games (Summer), Tartu, Estonia

International Women's G, Vienna, Austria

1939

Winter World University G, Lillehammer, Norway, Feb. 19–23

World University G, Monte Carlo, Monaco, Aug. 21–29

World G for the Deaf, Stockholm, Sweden, Aug. 24–27

German Student Federation G, Vienna, Austria, August

1940

SELL Games (Winter), Otepaa, Estonia, March 2–3

1946

Central American and Caribbean G, Barranquilla, Colombia, Dec. 8–28

Bolivarian G, Lima, Peru, Dec. 26–Jan. 6

1947

Winter World University G, Davos, Switzerland, Jan. 19–26

World Student Championships (UIE) (IUS), Paris, France, Aug. 24–31

1948

Olympic Winter G, St. Moritz, Switzerland, Jan. 30–Feb. 8

Stoke Mandeville Wheelchair G, Buckinghamshire, England, July 28

Olympic G, London, England, July 29–Aug. 14

1949

World Student Championships Winter (UIE), Spindleruv Mlyn, Czechoslovakia, Jan. 29–Feb. 6

Winter World G for the Deaf, Seefeld, Austria, Feb. 26–March 2

Stoke Mandeville Wheelchair G, Buckinghamshire, England, last week of July

World G for the Deaf, Copenhagen, Denmark, Aug. 12–16

World Student Championships (UIE), Budapest, Hungary, Aug. 14–21

International University Sports Week (FISU), Merano, Italy, Aug. 28–Sept. 4

1950

Commonwealth G, Auckland, New Zealand, Feb. 4–11

Central American and Caribbean G, Guatemala City, Guatemala, Feb. 8–March 12

Stoke Mandeville Wheelchair G, Buckinghamshire, England, last week of July

Maccabiah G, Tel Aviv, Israel, Sept. 28–Oct. 9

Canterbury Centennial G, Christchurch, New Zealand, Dec. 25–Jan. 5

1951

University Sports Week Winter (FISU), Gastein, Austria, Jan. 22–28

World Student Championships Winter (UIE), Poiana, Romania, Jan. 28–Feb. 7

Pan-American G, Buenos Aires, Argentina, Feb. 26–March 9

Asian G, New Dehli, India, March 4–15

Britain's Festival of Sport, London, England, May 5–Sept. 8

Stoke Mandeville Wheelchair G, Buckinghamshire, England, last week of July

World Student Championships (UIE), Berlin, East Germany, Aug. 6–15

International University Sports Week (FISU), Luxembourg, Luxembourg, Aug. 19–26

Mediterranean G, Alexandria, Egypt, Oct. 5–20

Bolivarian G, Caracas, Venezuela, Dec. 5–21

1952

Olympic Winter G, Oslo, Norway, Feb. 14–25

Hapoel G, Tel Aviv, Israel, April 14–18

Olympic G, Helsinki, Finland, July 19–Aug. 3

Stoke Mandeville Wheelchair G, Buckinghamshire, England, last week of July

1953

Winter World G for the Deaf, Oslo, Norway, Feb. 20–24

World Student Championships Winter (UIE), Semeringen-Vienna, Austria, Feb. 23– March 1

University Sports Week Winter (FISU), St. Moritz, Switzerland, March 2–8

Stoke Mandeville Wheelchair G, Buckinghamshire, England, last week of July

Arab G, Alexandria, Egypt, July 26–Aug. 10

International University Sports Week (FISU), Dortmund, West Germany, Aug. 9–16

World G for the Deaf, Brussels, Belgium, Aug. 15–19

Maccabiah G, Tel Aviv, Israel, Sept. 20–29

1954

Central American and Caribbean G, Mexico City, Mexico, March 6–20

Asian G, Manila, Philippines, May 1–9

Commonwealth G, Vancouver, Canada, July 30–Aug. 7

World Student Championships (UIE), Budapest, Hungary, July 31–Aug. 8

Stoke Mandeville Wheelchair G, Buckinghamshire, England, last week of July

1955

Winter World G for the Deaf, Oberammergau, West Germany, Feb. 10–13

Pan-American G, Mexico City, Mexico, March 12–26

University Sports Week Winter (FISU), Mt. Jahorina, Yugoslavia, April 1–7

Mediterranean G, Barcelona, Spain, July 16–25

Stoke Mandeville Wheelchair G, Buckinghamshire, England, last week of July

World Student Championships (UIE), Warsaw, Poland, Aug. 1–14

International University Sports Week (FISU), San Sebastián, Spain, Aug. 7–14

1956

Olympic Winter G, Cortina d'Ampezzo, Italy, Jan. 26–Feb. 5

World Student Championships Winter (UIE), Zakopane, Poland, March 7–13

Hapoel G, Tel Aviv, Israel, May 10–17

Olympic G, Stockholm, Sweden, June 10–17

Stoke Mandeville Wheelchair G, Buckinghamshire, England, last week of July

Olympic G, Melbourne, Australia, Nov. 22–Dec. 8

1957

University Sports Week Winter (FISU), Oberammergau, West Germany, Feb. 19–24

World Student Championships (UIE), Moscow, Soviet Union, July 29–Aug. 4

Stoke Mandeville Wheelchair G, Buckinghamshire, England, last week of July

World G for the Deaf, Milan, Italy, Aug. 25–30

World University G, Paris, France, Aug. 31–Sept. 8

Maccabiah G, Tel Aviv, Israel, Sept. 15–24

Arab G, Beirut, Lebanon, Oct. 13–27

1958

University Sports Week Winter (FISU), Zeel am See, Austria, Feb. 16–21

Asian G, Tokyo, Japan, May 24–June 1

Commonwealth G, Cardiff, Wales, July 18–26

Stoke Mandeville Wheelchair G, Buckinghamshire, England, last week of July

SCFA Summer Spartakiade, Leipzig, East Germany

1959

Central American and Caribbean G, Caracas, Venezuela, Jan. 6–18

Winter World G for the Deaf, Montana-Vermala, Switzerland, Jan. 27–30

Stoke Mandeville Wheelchair G, Buckinghamshire, England, last week of July

World Student Championships (UIE), Vienna, Austria, July 29–Aug. 2

European Maccabi G, Copenhagen, Denmark, Aug. 16–19

World University G, Turin, Italy, Aug. 26–Sept. 9

Pan-American G, Chicago, USA, Aug. 27–Sept. 7

Mediterranean G, Beirut, Lebanon, Oct. 11–26

South East Asian G, Bangkok, Thailand, Dec. 12–17

1960

Olympic Winter G, Squaw Valley, USA, Feb. 18–28

Winter World University G, Chamonix, France, Feb. 28–Mar. 6

Community/Friendship G, Antananarivo, Madagascar, April 13–19

Olympic G, Rome, Italy, Aug. 25–Sept. 11

Paralympic G, Rome, Italy, Sept. 17–22

West African G, Lagos, Nigeria

1961

SCFA Winter Spartakiade, Poland

Hapoel G, Tel Aviv, Israel, May 1–6

Stoke Mandeville Wheelchair G, Buckinghamshire, England, last week of July

World G for the Deaf, Helsinki, Finland, Aug. 6–10

Arab G, Casablanca, Morocco, Aug. 24–Sept. 8

World University G, Sofia, Bulgaria, Aug. 25–Sept. 3

Maccabiah G, Tel Aviv, Israel, Aug. 29–Sept. 5

Bolivarian G, Barranquilla, Colombia, Dec. 3–16

Community/Friendship G, Abidjan, Ivory Coast, Dec. 24–30

West African G, Abidjan, Ivory Coast, Dec. 24–31

1962

Winter World University G, Villars, Switzerland, March 6–12

Stoke Mandeville Wheelchair G, Buckinghamshire, England, last week of July

World Student Championships (UIE) (IUS), Helsinki, Finland, July 28–Aug. 6

Central American and Caribbean G, Kingston, Jamaica, Aug. 14–26

Asian G, Jakarta, Indonesia, Aug. 24–Sept. 4

Commonwealth G, Perth, Australia, Nov. 21–Dec. 1

British Commonwealth Paraplegic G, Perth, Australia

South East Asian G, Rangoon, Burma, Dec. 11–16

1963

Winter World G for the Deaf, Are, Sweden, March 11–16

Community/Friendship G, Dakar, Senegal, April 11–21

Pan-American G, São Paulo, Brazil, April 20–May 5

European Maccabi G, Lyon, France, June 1–3

Stoke Mandeville Wheelchair G, Buckinghamshire, England, July 24–28

South Pacific G, Suva, Fiji, Aug. 29–Sept. 7

World University G, Pôrto Alegre, Brazil, Aug. 30–Sept. 8

Mediterranean G, Naples, Italy, Sept. 21–29

Games of the New Emerging Forces (GANEFO), Jakarta, Indonesia, Nov. 10–22

1964

Olympic Winter G, Innsbruck, Austria, Jan. 29–Feb. 9

Winter World University G, Spindleruv Mlyn, Czechoslovakia, Feb. 11–17

Olympic G, Tokyo, Japan, Oct. 10–24

Pan-American Maccabi G, Buenos Aires, Argentina, Oct. 25–Nov. 1

Paralympic G, Tokyo, Japan, Nov. 6–14

1965

World G for the Deaf, Washington DC, USA, June 27–July 3

African G, Brazzaville, Republic of the Congo, July 18–25

Stoke Mandeville Wheelchair G, Buckinghamshire, England, July 27–30

World University G, Budapest, Hungary, Aug. 20–30

Maccabiah G, Tel Aviv, Israel, Aug. 23–Aug. 31

Arab G, Cairo, Egypt, Sept. 2–14

Bolivarian G, Quito, Guayaquil, Ecuador, Nov. 20–Dec. 5

South East Asian G, Kuala Lumpur, Malaysia, Dec. 14–21

West African University G, Ibadan, Nigeria

1966

Winter World University G, Sestriere, Italy, Feb. 5–13

Hapoel G, Tel Aviv, Israel, May 1–7

Central American and Caribbean G, San Juan, Puerto Rico, June 11–25

Stoke Mandeville Wheelchair G, Buckinghamshire, England, last week of July

Commonwealth G, Kingston, Jamaica, Aug. 4–13

British Commonwealth Paraplegic G, Kingston, Jamaica

Dutch Commonwealth G, Paramaribo, Suriname, Aug. 7–

Asian Games of the New Emerging Forces (GANEFO), Phnom Penh, Cambodia, Nov. 25–Dec. 6

South Pacific G, Nouméa, New Caledonia, Dec. 8–18

Asian G, Bangkok, Thailand, Dec. 9–20

1967

Winter World G for the Deaf, Berchtesgaden, West Germany, Feb. 20–25

Pan-American G, Winnipeg, Canada, July 23–Aug. 6

Stoke Mandeville Wheelchair G, Buckinghamshire, England, last week of July

Dutch Commonwealth G, Willemstad, Curaçao, Aug. 13–21

Pan-American Maccabi G, São Paulo, Brazil, Aug. 23–28

Pan-American Wheelchair G, Winnipeg, Canada, Aug.–24–

World University G, Tokyo, Japan, Aug. 27–Sept. 4

Mediterranean G, Tunis, Tunisia, Sept. 8–17

South East Asian G, Bangkok, Thailand, Dec. 9–16

West African University G, Legon, Ghana

1968

Winter World University G, Innsbruck, Austria, Jan. 18–28

Olympic Winter G, Grenoble, France, Feb. 6–18

International School Children's G, Celje, Yugoslavia, June 5

Special Olympics Summer World G, Chicago, USA, July 19–20

Dutch Commonwealth G, Utrecht, Netherlands, Aug. 5–11

Olympic G, Mexico City, Mexico, Oct. 12–27
Paralympic G, Tel Aviv, Israel, Nov. 5–13

1969

SCFA Winter Spartakiade, Spindleruv Mlyn, Czechoslovakia
Pan-American Wheelchair G, Buenos Aires, Argentina, May 25
Micronesian G, Saipan, Northern Marianas, July 4–12
Dutch Commonwealth G, Paramaribo, Suriname, July 25–Aug. 2
Maccabiah G, Tel Aviv, Israel, July 28–Aug. 6
Stoke Mandeville Wheelchair G, Buckinghamshire, England, last week of July
World G for the Deaf, Belgrade, Yugoslavia, Aug. 9–16
South Pacific G, Port Moresby, Papua New Guinea, Aug. 13–23
West African University G, Freetown, Sierra Leone
SCFA Summer Spartakiade, Kiev, Soviet Union
South East Asian G, Rangoon, Burma, Dec. 6–13

1970

Central American and Caribbean G, Panama City, Panama, Feb. 27–March 14
Arctic Winter G, Yellowknife, Canada, March 8–14
Winter World University G, Rovanieme, Finland, April 3–9
International School Children's G, Udine, Italy, June 20–21
Commonwealth G, Edinburgh, Scotland, July 16–25
British Commonwealth Paraplegic G, Edinburgh, Scotland
Stoke Mandeville Wheelchair G, Buckinghamshire, England, last week of July
Dutch Commonwealth G, Oranjestad, Aruba, July 31–Aug. 9
Special Olympics Summer World G, Chicago, USA, Aug. 13–15
Bolivarian G, Maracaibo, Venezuela, Aug. 22–Sept. 6
World University G, Turin, Italy, Aug. 26–Sept. 6
East African University G, Kampala, Uganda, Dec. 7–12
Asian G, Bangkok, Thailand, Dec. 9–20

1971

SCFA Winter Spartakiade, Zakopane, Poland
Winter World G for the Deaf, Adelboden, Switzerland, Jan. 25–29
Hapoel G, Tel Aviv, Israel, April 29–May 5
Stoke Mandeville Wheelchair G, Buckinghamshire, England, last week of July
Dutch Commonwealth G, Utrecht, Netherlands, July 31
Pan-American G, Cali, Colombia, July 30–Aug. 12

South Pacific G, Papeete, Tahiti, Sept. 8–19
Pan-American Wheelchair G, Kingston, Jamaica, Sept.–12–
Mediterranean G, Izmir, Turkey, Oct. 6–17
South East Asian G, Kuala Lumpur, Malaysia, Dec. 11–18
West African University G, Lagos, Nigeria

1972

Olympic Winter G, Sapporo, Japan, Feb. 3–13
Winter World University G, Lake Placid, USA, Feb. 26–March 5
Arctic Winter G, Whitehorse, Canada, March 5–11
International School Children's G, Graz, Austria, June 30–July 1
Dutch Commonwealth G, Willemstad, Curaçao, July 21–30
Central American and Caribbean University G, San Juan, Puerto Rico
Paralympic G, Heidelberg, West Germany, Aug. 2–10
Special Olympics Summer World G, Los Angeles, USA, Aug. 13–18
Olympic G, Munich, West Germany, Aug. 26–Sept. 10

1973

African G, Lagos, Nigeria, Jan. 7–18
SCFA Winter Spartakiade, Pamporovo, Bulgaria
Bolivarian G, Panama City, Panama, Feb. 17–March 3
Maccabiah G, Tel Aviv, Israel, July 9–July 19
World G for the Deaf, Malmö, Sweden, July 21–28
Stoke Mandeville Wheelchair G, Buckinghamshire, England, last week of July
Dutch Commonwealth G, Paramaribo, Suriname, Aug. 8, 1973
World University G, Moscow, Soviet Union, Aug. 15–25
South East Asian G, Singapore, Singapore, Sept. 1–8
SCFA Summer Spartakiade, Prague, Czechoslovakia
Pan-American Wheelchair G, Lima, Peru, Nov. 17–
Arab School G, Beirut, Lebanon
Central American G (orig. 1973), Guatemala City, Guatemala, Nov. 24–Dec. 1
West African University G, Kumasi, Ghana

1974

Commonwealth G, Christchurch, New Zealand, Jan. 24–Feb. 2
British Commonwealth Paraplegic G, Christchurch, New Zealand
Central American and Caribbean G, Santo Domingo, Dominican Republic, Feb. 27–March 13
Arctic Winter G, Anchorage, USA, March 3–9
International School Children's G, Murska Sobota, Yugoslavia, May 19

ISF Gymnasiade, Wiesbaden, West Germany, June 7–8

Stoke Mandeville Wheelchair G, Buckinghamshire, England, last week of July

European Maccabi G, Copenhagen, Denmark, Aug. 8–11

Dutch Commonwealth G, Zandvoort, Netherlands, Aug. 10–17

International School Children's G, Darmstadt, West Germany, Aug. 22–25

All-Africa University G, Accra, Ghana

Asian G, Tehran, Iran, Sept. 1–16

International Law Enforcement G, San Francisco, USA

1975

New Zealand G, Christchurch, New Zealand, Jan. 23–26

Winter World G for the Deaf, Lake Placid, USA, Feb. 11–16

SCFA Winter Spartakiade, Leningrad, Soviet Union, Feb. 21–March 3

Winter World University G, Livigno, Italy, April 6–13

Hapoel G, Tel Aviv, Israel, May 1–9

Far East and South Pacific G for the Disabled, Oita & Beppu, Japan, June 1–3

Stoke Mandeville Wheelchair G, Buckinghamshire, England, last week of July

Dutch Commonwealth G, Paramaribo, Suriname, Aug. 1–6

South Pacific G, Tumon, Guam, Aug. 1–10

Special Olympics Summer World G, Mt. Pleasant, USA, Aug. 7–11

Pan-American Wheelchair G, Mexico City, Mexico, Aug. 9–

Mediterranean G, Algiers, Algeria, Aug. 23–Sept. 6

World University G, Rome, Italy, Sept. 17–21

Pan-American G, Mexico City, Mexico, Oct. 12–26

Pan-American G for the Deaf, Maracaibo, Venezuela, Nov. 15–22

South East Asian G, Bangkok, Thailand, Dec. 9–16

Aalborg Youth G, Aalborg, Denmark

Central American and Caribbean University G, Mexico City, Mexico

West African University G, Ife, Nigeria

1976

Olympic Winter G, Innsbruck, Austria, Feb. 4–15

Winter Paralympic G, Ornskoldsvik, Sweden, Feb. 23–28

Arctic Winter G, Shefferville, Canada, March 21–27

International School Children's G, Murska Sobota, Yugoslavia, May 20–23

International School Children's G, Geneva, Switzerland, June 11–13

Central African G, Libreville, Gabon, June 30–July 10

Olympic G, Montreal, Canada, July 17–Aug. 1

Pan-American Maccabi G, Lima, Peru, July 23–29

Paralympic G, Toronto, Canada, Aug. 3–11

Arab G, Damascus, Syria, Oct. 6–21

International Law Enforcement G, Jacksonville, USA

ISF Gymnasiade, Orléans, France, June 26

1977

Special Olympics Winter World G, Steamboat Springs, USA, Feb. 5–11

SCFA Winter Spartakiade, Spindleruv Mlyn, Czechoslovakia, Feb.

Can-Am Police-Fire G, Spokane, USA, June 20–26

Maccabiah G, Tel Aviv, Israel, July 12–21

World G for the Deaf, Bucharest, Romania, July 17–27

Stoke Mandeville Wheelchair G, Buckinghamshire, England, July 23–31

World University G, Sofia, Bulgaria, Aug. 17–28

West African G, Lagos, Nigeria, Aug. 20–28

SCFA Summer Spartakiade, Havana, Cuba, Sept.

Bolivarian G, La Paz, Bolivia, Oct. 15–29

South East Asian G, Kuala Lumpur, Malaysia, Nov. 19–26

Far East and South Pacific G for the Disabled, Parramatta, Australia, Nov. 20–26

Central American G, San Salvador, El Salvador, Nov. 25–Dec. 4

Central American and Caribbean University G, Santo Domingo, Dominican Republic

West African University G, Yamoussoukro, Ivory Coast

1978

Winter World University G, Spindleruv Mlyn, Czechoslovakia, Feb. 5–12

Arctic Winter G, Hay River/Pine Point, Canada, March 19–25

Can-Am Police-Fire G, Seattle, USA, June 19–25

World Medical G, Cannes, France, June 12–17

Central American and Caribbean G, Medellin, Colombia, July 7–22

African G, Algiers, Algeria, July 13–28

ISF Gymnasiade, Izmir, Turkey, July 22–23

Stoke Mandeville Wheelchair G, Buckinghamshire, England, July 22–30

Commonwealth G, Edmonton, Canada, Aug. 3–12

International School Children's G, Ravne na Koroskem, Yugoslavia, Sept. 22–24

South American G, La Paz, Bolivia, Nov. 3–13

Pan-American Wheelchair G, Rio de Janeiro, Brazil, Nov. 28–

Asian G, Bangkok, Thailand, Dec. 9–20

All-Africa University G, Nairobi, Kenya, Dec. 29–Jan. 7

International Law Enforcement G, San Diego, USA

World Transplant G, Portsmouth, England

1979

Winter World G for the Deaf, Meribel, France, Jan. 21–27

SCFA Winter Spartakiade, Novi-Targ, Poland, Feb. 27–March 2

Hapoel G, Tel Aviv, Israel, May 1–8

Can-Am Police-Fire G, Ellensburg, USA, June 18–24

Pan-American G, San Juan, Puerto Rico, July 1–15

Stoke Mandeville Wheelchair G, Buckinghamshire, England, July 21–29

European Maccabi G, Liecester, England, Aug. 3–10

Special Olympics Summer World G, Brockport, USA, Aug. 8–13

Pan-American Maccabi G, Mexico City, Mexico, Aug. 21–29

Indian Ocean Island G, St. Denis, Réunion, Aug. 25–Sept. 2

South Pacific G, Suva, Fiji, Aug. 27–Sept. 8

World University G, Mexico City, Mexico, Sept. 2–13

Mediterranean G, Split, Yugoslavia, Sept. 15–29

South East Asian G, Jakarta, Indonesia, Sept. 21–30

World Transplant G, Portsmouth, England

Aalborg Youth G, Aalborg, Denmark

West African G, Cotonou, Benin

1980

Olympic Winter G, Lake Placid, USA, Feb. 14–23

Arctic Winter G, Whitehorse, Canada, March 16–22

Paralympic G, Arnhem, Netherlands, June 21–July 5

Can-Am Police-Fire G, Spokane, USA, June 23–29

World Medical G, Cannes, France, June 8–14

Olympic G, Moscow, Soviet Union, July 19–Aug. 3

International School Children's G, Lausanne, Switzerland, Sept. 26–29

Winter Paralympic G, Geilo, Norway

World Transplant G, New York, USA

International Law Enforcement G, Nassau, NY, USA

ISF Gymnasiade, Turin, Italy, June 6–7

1981

Winter World University G, Jaca, Spain, Feb. 23–March 4

Special Olympics Winter World G, Smugglers Cove, USA, March 8–13

European Special Olympics, Brussels, Belgium, May

Can-Am Police-Fire G, Bellevue, USA, June 22–28

Maccabiah G, Tel Aviv, Israel, July 6–16

World University G, Bucharest, Romania, July 19–30

World G for the Deaf, Cologne, West Germany, July 24–Aug. 2

World G, Santa Clara, USA, July 24–Aug. 2

Stoke Mandeville Wheelchair G, Buckinghamshire, England, July 25–Aug. 2

Central African G, Luanda, Angola, Aug. 20–Sept. 2

Bolivarian G, Barquisimeto, Venezuela, Dec. 4–14

South East Asian G, Manila, Philippines, Dec. 6–15

South Pacific Mini G, Honiara, Solomon Islands

SCFA Summer Spartakiade, Budapest, Hungary

SCFA Winter Spartakiade, Borovec, Bulgaria

1982

Arctic Winter G, Fairbanks, USA, March 14–20

Alps-Adriatic Winter Youth G, Auronzo, Italy, March 28–30

Windsor Classic Indoor G, Windsor, Canada

International School Children's G, Darmstadt, West Germany, June 11–13

World Medical G, Cannes, France, June 13–19

Can-Am Police-Fire G, New Westminster, Canada, June 21–27

Pan-American Wheelchair G, Halifax, Canada, July 21–

Stoke Mandeville Wheelchair G, Buckinghamshire, England, July 24–Aug. 1

Central American and Caribbean G, Havana, Cuba, Aug. 7–18

JCC Maccabi G, Memphis, USA, Aug.

Gay G, San Francisco, USA, Aug. 28–Sept. 5

Commonwealth G, Brisbane, Australia, Sept. 30–Oct. 9

East African Military G, Lusaka, Zambia, Oct. 13–18

Far East and South Pacific G for the Disabled, Sha Tin, Hong Kong, Oct. 31–Nov. 7

Asian G, New Delhi, India, Nov. 19–Dec. 4

South American G, Rosario/Santa Fe, Argentina, Nov. 26–Dec. 5

ISF Gymnasiade, Lille, France, June 4–6

Central American and Caribbean University G, Barquisimeto, Venezuela

International Law Enforcement G, Austin, USA

World Transplant G, Athens, Greece

Pacific School G, Brisbane, Australia

Journalists World G, Nice, France

1983

Winter World G for the Deaf, Madonna di Campoglio, Italy, Jan. 16–22

Winter World University G, Sofia, Bulgaria, Feb. 17–27

Windsor Classic Indoor G, Windsor, Canada

Hapoel G, Tel Aviv, Israel, May 1–7

South East Asian G, Singapore, Singapore, May 28–June 6

International School Children's G, Troyes, France, June 17–19

Can-Am Police-Fire G, Edmonton, Canada, June 20–26

World University G, Edmonton, Canada, July 1–12

European Maccabi G, Antwerp, Belgium, July 8–15

Stoke Mandeville Wheelchair G, Buckinghamshire, England, July 23–31

Special Olympics Summer World G, Baton Rouge, USA, July 12–18

Asia Pacific G for the Deaf, Taipei, Taiwan, July

Pan-American G, Caracas, Venezuela, Aug. 15–29

World Medical G, Paris, France, August 28–Sept. 3

Mediterranean G, Casablanca, Morocco, Sept. 3–17

South Pacific G, Apia, Western Samoa, Sept. 5–16

International School Children's G, Murska Sobota, Yugoslavia, Sept. 23

Pan-American Maccabi G, São Paulo, Brazil, Dec. 20–30

Aalborg Youth G, Aalborg, Denmark

SCFA Winter Spartakiade, Strbske Pleso, Czechoslovakia

World Peace G, Bellegarde, France

1984

Winter Paralympic G, Innsbruck, Austria, Jan. 11–20

Olympic Winter G, Sarajevo, Yugoslavia, Feb. 7–19

Arctic Winter G, Yellowknife, Canada, March 18–24

Windsor Classic Indoor G, Windsor, Canada

ISF Gymnasiade, Florence, Italy, June 7–9

International School Children's G, Geneva, Switzerland, June 15–17

Can-Am Police-Fire G, Seattle, USA, June 18–24

World Medical G, Abano Terme, Italy, June 24–30

Olympic G, Los Angeles, USA, July 28–Aug. 12

Friendship G 84, Moscow, Havana, Prague, Warsaw, Katowice, Olomouc, Tallin, Soviet Union, Cuba, Poland

JCC Maccabi G, Detroit, USA, Aug.

Asia Pacific G for the Deaf, Hong Kong, Hong Kong, Sept.

International Law Enforcement G, Phoenix, USA

Pacific School G, Melbourne, Australia

Alps-Adriatic Summer Youth G, Graz, Austria

World Transplant G, Amsterdam, Netherlands

Paralympic G, New York, USA, June 16–30

South Asian Federation G, Kathmandu, Nepal

Paralympic G, Aylesbury, England, July 22–August 1

1985

Winter World University G, Belluno, Italy, Feb. 16–24

SCFA Winter Spartakiade, Minsk, Soviet Union, Feb. 23–March 2

Special Olympics Winter World G, Park City, USA, March 24–29

Windsor Classic Indoor G, Windsor, Canada

CARIFTA Games, Bridgetown, Barbados, April 6–9

Games of the Small Countries of Europe, San Marino, San Marino, May 23–26

Can-Am Police-Fire G, Calgary, Canada, June 24–30

World Medical G, Monte Carlo, Monaco, June 23–29

European Special Olympics, Dublin, Ireland, July 4–7

World G for the Deaf, Los Angeles, USA, July 10–20

Maccabiah G, Tel Aviv, Israel, July 15–25

Island G, Douglas, Isle of Man, July 18–24

Stoke Mandeville Wheelchair G, Buckinghamshire, England, July 20–28

World G, London, England, July 25–Aug. 4

Arab G, Casablanca, Morocco, Aug. 2–16

World Police and Fire G, San Jose, USA, Aug. 4–11

World Masters G, Toronto, Canada, Aug. 7–25

JCC Maccabi G, Columbus OH, USA, Aug.

Indian Ocean Island G, Port Louis, Mauritius, Aug. 24–Sept. 1

World University G, Kobe, Japan, Aug. 24–Sept. 4

International School Children's G, Granollers, Spain, Sept. 7–9

Bolivarian G, Cuenca, Ecuador, Nov. 9–18

South East Asian G, Bangkok, Thailand, Dec. 8–17

South Asian Federation G, Dhaka, Bangladesh, Dec. 20–26

SCFA Summer Spartakiade, Warsaw, Poland

World Peace G, Echiroles, France

Alps-Adriatic Winter Youth G, Villach, Austria

South Pacific Mini G, Rarotonga, Cook Islands

1986

Central American G, Guatemala City, Guatemala, Jan. 4–

Asian Winter G, Sapporo, Japan, March 1–8

International Police Winter G, South Lake Tahoe, USA, March 2–6

Arctic Winter G, Whitehorse, Canada, March 16–21

Windsor Classic Indoor G, Windsor, Canada

CARIFTA Games, Basse-Terre, Guadeloupe, March 29–31

ISF Gymnasiade, Nice, France, June 4–6

International School Children's G, Lausanne, Switzerland, June 5–8

Can-Am Police-Fire G, Ellensburg, USA, June 23–29

World Medical G, Montecatini Terme, Italy, June 22–28

Central American and Caribbean G, Santiago de los Caballeros, Dominican Republic, June 24–July 5

Goodwill G, Moscow, Soviet Union, July 5–20

Stoke Mandeville Wheelchair G, Buckinghamshire, England, July 19–27

Commonwealth G, Edinburgh, Scotland, July 24–Aug. 2

Gay G, San Francisco, USA, Aug. 7–18
JCC Maccabi G, Toronto, Canada, Aug.
Asia Pacific G for the Deaf, Kyoto, Japan, Aug.
Far East and South Pacific G for the Disabled, Surakarta, Indonesia, Aug. 31–Sept. 7
Asian G, Seoul, South Korea, Sept. 20–Oct. 5
Pan-American Wheelchair G, San Juan, Puerto Rico, Oct. 1–11
South American G, Santiago, Chile, Nov. 29–Dec. 7
Alps-Adriatic Summer Youth G, Pula, Yugoslavia
International Law Enforcement G, Columbus, USA
Central American and Caribbean University G, Havana, Cuba
Honda Masters G, Alice Springs, Australia

1987

Winter World G for the Deaf, Oslo, Norway, Feb. 7–14
Winter World University G, Strbske Pleso, Czechoslovakia, Feb. 21–28
SCFA Winter Spartakiade, Bucharest, Romania, Feb. 27–March 4
International Police Winter G, South Lake Tahoe, USA, March 1–5
International Firefighters Winter G, North Lake Tahoe, USA, March 1–5
European Maccabi G, Copenhagen, Denmark, March 10–17
Windsor Classic Indoor G, Windsor, Canada
CARIFTA Games, Port of Spain, Trinidad, April 18–20
Central African G, Brazzaville, Republic of the Congo, April 18–30
Hapoel G, Tel Aviv, Israel, May 4–11
Games of the Small Countries of Europe, Monte Carlo, Monaco, May 14–17
Can-Am Police-Fire G, Salem, USA, June 22–28
International School Children's G, Graz, Austria, June 23
World Medical G, Casablanca, Morocco, July 5–11
Peace Arch G, Bellingham, USA, June 28–July 5
World University G, Zagreb, Yugoslavia, July 8–19
Stoke Mandeville Wheelchair G, Buckinghamshire, England, July 18–26
Pan-American Maccabi G, Caracas, Venezuela, July 19–26
Special Olympics Summer World G, South Bend, USA, July 31–Aug. 8
World Police and Fire G, San Diego, USA, Aug. 1–9
African G, Nairobi, Kenya, Aug. 1–12
JCC Maccabi G, Miami, USA, Aug.
Pan-American G, Indianapolis, USA, Aug. 7–23
FISEC Games, Genk, Belgium
South East Asian G, Jakarta, Indonesia, Sept. 9–20
Island G, St. Peter Port, Guernsey, Sept. 10–17

Mediterranean G, Latakia, Syria, Sept. 11–25
World Transplant G, Innsbruck, Austria, Sept. 17–20
Huntsman World Senior G, St. George, USA, Oct. 10–23
South Asian Federation G, Calcutta, India, Nov. 20–27
Australian Masters G, Hobart, Australia, Nov. 28–Dec. 12
Aalborg Youth G, Aalborg, Denmark
Alps-Adriatic Winter Youth G, Piancavallo
South Pacific G, Nouméa, New Caledonia
World Peace G, Neuchâtel/Marignane, Switzerland/ France

1988

Winter Paralympic G, Innsbruck, Austria, Jan. 17–24
Olympic Winter G, Calgary, Canada, Feb. 13–28
Asia Pacific G for the Deaf, Melbourne, Australia, Feb.
International Firefighters Winter G, North Lake Tahoe, USA, March 6–10
International Police Winter G, South Lake Tahoe, USA, March 6–10
Arctic Winter G, Fairbanks, USA, March 13–19
CARIFTA Games, Kingston, Jamaica, April 7–9
Windsor Classic Indoor G, Windsor, Canada
Défi Sportif, Montreal, Canada, May 3–8
World Medical G, Lyon, France, June 19–25
Can-Am Police-Fire G, Moscow-Pullman, USA, June 20–26
International School Children's G, Szombathely, Hungary, June 24–25
Peace Arch G, Bellingham, USA, June 26–July 5
ISF Gymnasiade, Barcelona, Spain, July 6–8
JCC Maccabi G, Chicago, USA, Aug. 18–25
Olympic G, Seoul, South Korea, Sept. 17–Oct. 2
FISEC Games, Louvain, Belgium
Huntsman World Senior G, St. George, USA, Oct. 8–21
Paralympic G, Seoul, South Korea, Oct. 15–25
Pacific School G, Sydney, Australia
Alps-Adriatic Summer Youth G, Trento, Italy
World Corporate G, San Francisco, USA
Honda Masters G, Alice Springs, Australia
International Law Enforcement G, Sydney, Australia
European Heart/Lung Transplant G, Gorsel, Netherlands

1989

Bolivarian G, Maracaibo, Venezuela, Jan. 15–25
World G for the Deaf, Christchurch, New Zealand, Jan. 17–30
Winter World University G, Sofia, Bulgaria, March 2–12
International Police Winter G, South Lake Tahoe, USA, March 5–9
International Firefighters Winter G, North Lake Tahoe, USA, March 5–9
Windsor Classic Indoor G, Windsor, Canada

Can-Am Police-fire G, Mt. Bachelor, USA
Special Olympics Winter World G, Reno, USA, April 1–8
Défi Sportif, Montreal, Canada, May 2–7
Games of the Small Countries of Europe, Nicosia, Cyprus, May 17–20
International School Children's G, Andorra, Andorra, June 2–4
Peace Arch G, Bellingham, USA, June 24–July 9
World Medical G, Montreal, Canada, July 16–22
Maccabiah G, Tel Aviv, Israel, July 3–13
Island G, Tórshavn, Faroe Islands, July 5–13
Francophone G, Rabat, Casablanca, Morocco, July 8–22
World G, Karlsruhe, West Germany, July 20–30
Stoke Mandeville Wheelchair G, Buckinghamshire, England, July 22–30
World Police and Fire G, Vancouver, Canada, July 29–Aug. 6
CARIFTA Games, Bridgetown, Barbados, Aug. 19–22
South East Asian G, Kuala Lumpur, Malaysia, Aug. 20–31
World University G, Duisburg, West Germany, Aug. 22–30
South Pacific Mini G, Nukualofa, Tonga, Aug. 22–Sept. 1
FISEC Games, Burgos, Spain
JCC Maccabi G, Pittsburgh, USA, Aug.
World Transplant G, Singapore, Singapore, Sept. 10–14
Far East and South Pacific G for the Disabled, Kobe, Japan, Sept. 15–20
Huntsman World Senior G, St. George, USA, Oct. 14–27
South Asian Federation G, Islamabad, Pakistan, Oct. 20–27
West African University G, Ouagadougou, Burkina Faso
Robin Hood G, Nottingham, England
World Corporate Games, Concord, USA
SCFA Winter Spartakiade, Jasna, Osrblie, Strbske Pleso, Czechoslovakia
SCFA Summer Spartakiade, Sofia, Bulgaria
Alps-Adriatic Winter Youth G, Kranjska Gora, Yugoslavia
World Masters G, Henning, Århus, Aalborg, Denmark
Australian Masters G, Adelaide, Australia

1990

Central American G, Tegucigalpa, Honduras, Jan. 5–14
Commonwealth G, Auckland, New Zealand, Jan. 24–Feb. 3
International Firefighters Winter G, North Lake Tahoe, USA, March 4–8
International Police Winter G, Blackcomb/Whistler, Canada, March 4–8
Asian Winter G, Sapporo, Japan, March 9–14
Arctic Winter G, Yellowknife, Canada, March 11–17

CARIFTA Games, Kingston, Jamaica, March 19–21
Windsor Classic Indoor G, Windsor, Canada
Firefighters World G, Auckland, New Zealand, April 22–29
Défi Sportif, Montreal, Canada, May 1–6
Can-Am Police-Fire G, Boise, USA, June 18–25
Alps-Adriatic Summer Youth G, Linz, Austria, June 26–29
International School Children's G, Uzhgorod, Ukraine, June 30–July 3
World Medical G, Perpignan, France, June 17–23
North American Indigenous G, Edmonton, Canada, July 1–7
Peace Arch G, Bellingham, USA, June 20–July 8
World Peace G, Fès/Ifrane/Meknes, Morocco, July 17–22
European Special Olympics, Strathclyde/Glasgow, Scotland, July 20–27
Goodwill G, Seattle, USA, July 20–Aug. 5
Stoke Mandeville Wheelchair G, Buckinghamshire, England, July 21–29
European Heart/Lung Transplant G, Paris, France
World Equestrian G, Stockholm, Sweden, July 24–Aug. 5
Gay G, Vancouver, Canada, Aug. 4–11
FISEC Games, Liverpool, England
JCC Maccabi G, Detroit, USA, Aug. 19–26
Indian Ocean Island G, Antananarivo, Madagascar, Aug. 24–Sept. 2
Pan-American Wheelchair G, Caracas, Venezuela, Sept. 1–9
Winter Pan-American G, Las Lenas, Argentina, Sept. 18–22
Asian G, Beijing, China, Sept. 21–Oct. 5
World Corporate G, Oahu, USA, Oct. 6–13
Huntsman World Senior G, St. George, USA, Oct. 13–26
Central American and Caribbean G, Mexico City, Mexico, Nov. 20–Dec. 4
South American G, Lima, Peru, Dec. 1–10
ISF Gymnasiade, Brugge, Belgium, May 24–27
International Law Enforcement G, Calgary, Canada
Central American and Caribbean University G, Guatemala City, Guatemala
Micronesian G, Saipan, Northern Marianas
Honda Masters G, Alice Springs, Australia

1991

Alps-Adriatic Winter Youth G, Carinthia, Austria, Feb. 25–27
Winter World G for the Deaf, Banff, Canada, March 2–9
Winter World University G, Sapporo, Japan, March 2–10
International Police Winter G, South Lake Tahoe, USA, March 3–7
International Firefighters Winter G, North Lake Tahoe, USA, March 3–7
CARIFTA Games, Port of Spain, Trinidad, March 30–April 1

Windsor Classic Indoor G, Windsor, Canada

Défi Sportif, Montreal, Canada, April 26–May 5

Hapoel G, Tel Aviv, Israel, May 6–13

Arafura G, Darwin, Australia, May 18–25

Games of the Small Countries of Europe, Andorra, Andorra, May 21–25

International School Children's G, Bratislava, Slovakia, May 31–June 2

World Police and Fire G, Memphis, USA, June 22–30

Island G, Mariehamn, Åland, June 23–29

Can-Am Police-Fire G, Tri-Cities (Kennewick), USA, June 24– 30

Mediterranean G, Athens, Greece, June 28–July 12

Peace Arch G, Bellingham, USA, June 29–July 7

World Medical G, Heraklion, Greece, July 6–13

European Maccabi G, Marseille, France, July 10–17

European Youth Olympic Days, Brussels, Belgium, July 12–21

World University G, Sheffield, England, July 14–27

Special Olympics Summer World G, Minneapolis, USA, July 19–27

Stoke Mandeville Wheelchair G, Buckinghamshire, England, July 20–28

Pan-American Maccabi G, Montevideo, Uruguay, July 4–14

Pan-American G, Havana, Cuba, Aug. 2–18

World Transplant G, Budapest, Hungary, Aug. 27–31

JCC Maccabi G, Wayne, USA, Aug.

JCC Maccabi G, Omaha, USA, Aug.

JCC Maccabi G, Cleveland, USA, Aug.

South Pacific G, Port Moresby/Lae, Papua New Guinea, Sept. 2–23

FISEC Games, Maastricht, Netherlands

African G, Cairo, Egypt, Sept. 20–Oct. 1

Australian Masters G, Brisbane, Australia, Oct. 8–20

Huntsman World Senior G, St. George, USA, Oct. 14–25

South East Asian G, Manila, Philippines, Nov. 24–Dec. 5

South Asian Federation G, Colombo, Sri Lanka, Nov. or Dec.

World Corporate Games, Lille, France

Aalborg Youth G, Aalborg, Denmark

European Heart/Lung Transplant Games, London, England

Winter World Corporate G, Steamboat Springs, USA

1992

Olympic Winter G, Albertville, France, Feb. 8–23

International Police Winter G, South Lake Tahoe, USA, March 1–5

International Firefighters Winter G, North Lake Tahoe, USA, March 1–5

Arctic Winter G, Whitehorse, Canada, March 15–21

Winter Paralympic G, Albertville, France, March 25–April 1

Pacific School G, Darwin, Australia, April 3–13

CARIFTA Games, Nassau, Bahamas, April 18–20

Défi Sportif, Montreal, Canada, April 27–May 3

Windsor Classic Indoor G, Windsor, Canada

Firefighters World G, Las Vegas, USA, May 16–22

International School Children's G, Geneva, Switzerland, June 18–21

Can-Am Police-Fire G, Walla Walla, USA, June 22–28

Alps-Adriatic Summer Youth G, Zalaegerszeg, Hungary, June 23–26

World Medical G, Osturi, Italy, June 21–28

Olympic G, Barcelona, Spain, July 25–Aug. 10

Peace Arch G, Bellingham, USA, July

JCC Maccabi G, Baltimore, USA, Aug. 23–29

Asia Pacific G for the Deaf, Seoul, South Korea, August

FISEC Games, Milan, Italy

Paralympic G, Barcelona, Spain, Sept. 3–14

Arab G, Damascus, Syria, Sept. 4–18

European Special Olympics, Barcelona, Spain, Sept. 9–13

Huntsman World Senior G, St. George, USA, Oct. 13–24

Honda Masters G, Alice Springs, Australia, Oct. 17–25

Euro G, The Hague, Netherlands

European Heart/Lung Transplant Games, Enschede, Netherlands

International Law Enforcement G, Washington DC, USA

World Corporate G, London, England

1993

Alps-Adriatic Winter Youth G, Bormio, Italy, Jan. 26–29

Winter World University G, Zakopane, Poland, Feb. 6–14

Winter European Youth Olympic Days, Aosta, Italy, Feb. 7–11

Muslim Women's G, Tehran, Iran, Feb. 13–19

Special Olympics Winter World G, Salzburg/Schladming, Austria, March

International Police Winter G, South Lake Tahoe, USA, March 7–11

International Firefighters Winter G, North Lake Tahoe, USA, March 7–11

CARIFTA Games, Fort de France, Martinique, April 9–11

Windsor Classic Indoor G, Windsor, Canada

Australian Masters G, Perth, Australia, April 20–May 2

Bolivarian G, Cochabamba, Bolivia, April 24–May 2

Arafura G, Darwin, Australia, April 24–May 1

Défi Sportif, Montreal, Canada, April 30–May 9

East Asian G, Shanghai, China, May 9–18

Games of the Small Countries of Europe, Valletta, Malta, May 25–29

South East Asian G, Singapore, Singapore, June 12–20

Mediterranean G, Languedoc-Rousillon, France, June 16–27

World Scholar Athlete G, Newport RI, USA, June 20–July 1

Can-Am Police-Fire G, Calgary, Canada, June 21–27

Baltic Sea G, Tallin, Estonia, June 22–July 3

World Medical G, Saint-Malo, France, June 27–July 3

World Dwarf G, Chicago, USA, July 1–6

European Youth Olympic Days, Valkenswaard, Netherlands, July 3–9

Island G, Sandown, Isle of Wight, July 3–10

World Transplant G, Vancouver, Canada, July 4–10

Maccabiah G, Tel Aviv, Israel, July 5–15

World University G, Buffalo, USA, July 8–18

World Ex-Service Wheelchair and Amputee G, Aylesbury, England, July 10–16

International School Children's G, Darmstadt, Germany, July 17–18

North American Indigenous G, Prince Albert, Canada, July 18–25

World G, The Hague, Netherlands, July 22–Aug. 1

World G for the Deaf, Sofia, Bulgaria, July 24–Aug. 2

Stoke Mandeville Wheelchair G, Buckinghamshire, England, July 24–Aug. 1

World Police and Fire G, Colorado Springs, USA, July 31–Aug. 7

JCC Maccabi G, St. Louis, USA, Aug. 15–19

JCC Maccabi G, Sarasota, USA, Aug. 15–19

Indian Ocean Island G, Victoria, Seychelles, Seychelles, Aug. 21–29

JCC Maccabi G, Boston, USA, Aug. 22–26

JCC Maccabi G, Pittsburgh, USA, Aug. 22–26

Huntsman World Senior G, St. George, USA, Oct. 11–22

Central American and Caribbean G, Ponce, San Juan, Puerto Rico, Nov. 19–30

South Asian Federation G, Dhaka, Bangladesh, Dec. 20–27

Euro G, The Hague, Netherlands

UK & Ireland Corporate G, Milton Keynes, England

South Pacific Mini G, Pont-Vila, Vanuatu

Robin Hood G, Nottingham, England

World Corporate G, Kuala Lumpur, Malaysia

Australian Corporate G, Sydney, Australia

1994

Central American G, San Salvador, El Salvador, Jan. 14–23

Winter International School Children's G, Ravne na Koroskem, Slovakia, Feb. 10–13

Olympic Winter G, Lillehammer, Norway, Feb. 12–25

International Police Winter G, South Lake Tahoe, USA, March 6–10

International Firefighters Winter G, North Lake Tahoe, USA, March 6–10

Arctic Winter G, Slave Lake, Canada, March 6–12

Winter Paralympic G, Lillehammer, Norway, March 10–19

Windsor Classic Indoor G, Windsor, Canada

Firefighters World G, Perth, Australia, March 20–26

Micronesian G, Agana, Guam, March 26–April 2

CARIFTA Games, Bridgetown, Barbados, April 2–4

Défi Sportif, Montreal, Canada, April 27–May 1

ISF Gymnasiade, Nicosia, Cyprus, May 17–20

International School Children's G, Hamilton, Canada, June 15–19

Gay G, New York, USA, June 18–25

Can-Am Police-Fire G, Portland, USA, June 20–26

Alps-Adriatic Summer Youth G, Burghausen, Germany, June 21–24

World Medical G, Evian, France, June 29–July 2

Francophone G, Paris, France, July 5–13

Muslim Student G, Tehran, Iran, July 21–28

Stoke Mandeville Wheelchair G, Buckinghamshire, England, July 23–31

Goodwill G, St. Petersburg, Russia, July 23–Aug. 7

World Equestrian G, The Hague, Netherlands, July 27th–Aug. 7

JCC Maccabi G, Cleveland, USA, Aug. 14–19

Commonwealth G, Victoria, Canada, Aug. 18–28

Far East and South Pacific G for the Disabled, Beijing, China, Sept. 4–10

International School Children's G, Slovenj Gradec, Slovenia, Sept. 24

Australian Universities G, Wollongong, Australia, Sept. 25–30

World Masters G, Brisbane, Australia, Sept. 26–Oct. 8

Asian G, Hiroshima, Japan, Oct. 2–16

Huntsman World Senior G, St. George, USA, Oct. 10–23

World Corporate G, Johannesburg, South Africa, Oct.

South American G, Valencia, Venezuela, Nov. 19–28

UK & Ireland Corporate G, Milton Keynes, England

Australian Corporate G, Sydney, Australia

European Special Olympics, Granollers, Spain

International Law Enforcement G, Birmingham, USA

Winter World Transplant G, Tignes, France

European Heart/Lung Transplant G, Helsinki, Finland

Honda Masters G, Alice Springs, Australia

African Francophone Games for the Handicapped, Ouagadougou, Burkina Faso

1995

Alps-Adriatic Winter Youth G, Biasca/Ticino, Switzerland, Jan. 24–27

Winter International School Children's G, Prakovce-Helcmanovc, Slovenia, Feb. 2–3

Winter European Youth Olympic Days, Andorra, Andorra, Feb. 5–10

Winter World University G, Jaca, Spain, Feb. 18–26

Winter G for the Disabled, Solleftea, Sweden, Feb. 23–26

World Police and Fire G, Melbourne, Australia, Feb. 26–March 4

International Police Winter G, South Lake Tahoe, USA, March 5–9

International Firefighters Winter G, North Lake Tahoe, USA, March 5–9

Pan-American G, Mar del Plata, Argentina, March 14–25

Winter World G for the Deaf, Yllas, Finland, March 14–19

Windsor Classic Indoor G, Windsor, Canada

Euro G, Frankfurt, Germany, April 14–17

CARIFTA Games, George Town, Cayman Islands, April 15–17

Défi Sportif, Montreal, Canada, April 26–30

Arafura G, Darwin, Australia, May 6–13

Games of the Small Countries of Europe, Luxembourg, Luxembourg, May 29–June 3

International School Children's G, Celje, Slovenia, June 11

Hapoel G, Tel Aviv, Israel, June 11–15

Pacific Ocean G, Cali, Colombia, June 23–July 3

X Games, Newport RI, USA, June 24–27

World Medical G, Limerick, Ireland, June 24–July 1

Can-Am Police-Fire G, Bellingham, USA, June 25–29

Special Olympics Summer World G, New Haven, USA, July 1–9

European Maccabi G, Amsterdam, Netherlands, July 7–14

European Youth Olympic Days, Bath, England, July 9–14

Island G, Gibraltar, Gibraltar, July 15–22

Dutch Commonwealth G, Oranjestad, Aruba, July 16–21

Stoke Mandeville Wheelchair G, Buckinghamshire, England, July 22–30

World University G, Fukuoka, Japan, Aug. 23–Sept. 3

North American Indigenous G, Blaine, USA, July 31–Aug. 5

South Pacific G, Papeete, Tahiti, Aug. 12–26

JCC Maccabi G, Columbus OH, USA, Aug. 13–17

JCC Maccabi G, Los Angeles, USA, Aug. 13–17

JCC Maccabi G, Orlando, USA, Aug. 13–17

JCC Maccabi G, Houston, USA, Aug. 13–17

World Transplant G, Manchester, England, Aug. 14–20

JCC Maccabi G, Long Island, USA, Aug. 20–24

Central Asian G, Tashkent, Uzbekistan, Sept. 2–9

World Corporate G, Geneva, Switzerland, Sept. 2–9

Military World G, Rome, Italy, Sept. 6–15

African G, Harare, Zimbabwe, Sept. 13–23

Pan-American Wheelchair G, Buenos Aires, Argentina, Sept. 17–30

Australian Universities G, Darwin, Australia, Sept. 24–30

Huntsman World Senior G, St. George, USA, Oct. 17–29

Ataturk Dam International Sports Festival, Ataturk Dam, Turkey, October 6–7

Australian Masters G, Melbourne, Australia, Oct.

South East Asian G, Chiang Mai, Thailand, Dec. 9–17

South Asian Federation G, Madras, India, Dec. 18–26

West African University G, Benin City, Nigeria

UK & Ireland Corporate G, Peterborough, England

Australian Corporate G, Sydney, Australia

Irelands' Scholar Athlete G, Jordanstown, Northern Ireland

Aalborg Youth G, Aalborg, Denmark

Pan-American Maccabi G, Buenos Aires, Argentina, Dec. 24–Jan. 4

1996

Winter World Transplant G, Pra-Loup, France, Jan. 7–13

Asian Winter G, Harbin, China, Feb. 4–11

International Police Winter G, South Lake Tahoe, USA, March 3–7

International Firefighters Winter G, North Lake Tahoe, USA, March 3–7

Arctic Winter G, Chugiak-Eagle River, USA, March 3–10

Australian Corporate G, Sydney, Australia, March 21–24

Windsor Classic Indoor G, Windsor, Canada

Asia Pacific G for the Deaf, Kuala Lumpur, Malaysia, March

CARIFTA Games, Kingston, Jamaica, April 6–8

Défi Sportif, Montreal, Canada, April 24–28

International Senior G, Hamilton, Bermuda, April

Special Olympics Small Nations G, Monte Carlo, Monaco, May 10–12

Euro G, Berlin, Germany, May 16–19

European Special Olympics, Athens, Greece, May 19–25

UK & Ireland Corporate G, Aberdeen, Scotland, June 14–16

X Games, Newport RI, USA, June 24–30

Alps-Adriatic Summer Youth G, Siofok, Hungary, June 24–27

Can-Am Police-Fire G, Tri-Cities (Kennewick), USA, June 24–30

International School Children's G, Sopron, Hungary, June 26–30

World Medical G, Lisbon, Portugal, June 29–July 6

International Electrical Engineering Students Sports G, Zagreb, Croatia, July 16–18

European Heart/Lung Transplant G, Lausanne, Switzerland, July 18–22

Olympic G, Atlanta, USA, July 19–Aug. 4

Firefighters World G, Edmonton, Canada, July 28–Aug. 3

Gorge G, Hood River, USA, July

International Law Enforcement G, Salt Lake City, USA, Aug. 3–10

Centennial Youth G, Aalborg, Denmark, Aug. 4–11

Eastern European Transplant G, Tiszaujvaros, Hungary, Aug. 5–14

Irelands' Scholar Athlete G, Jordanstown, Northern Ireland, Aug. 10–17

JCC Maccabi G, St. Louis, USA, Aug. 11–16

Paralympic G, Atlanta, USA, Aug. 15–25

JCC Maccabi G, Wayne, USA, Aug. 18–23

World Air G, Ankara, Turkey, Aug. 28–Sept. 22

FISEC Games, Somerset/London, England

World Corporate G, Stuttgart, Germany, Sept. 7–14

CUCSA Games, Zomba, Malawi, Sept. 16–21

Australian Universities G, Canberra, Australia, Sept. 29–Oct. 4

Ataturk Dam International Sports Festival, Ataturk Dam, Turkey, October 4–5

Huntsman World Senior G, St. George, USA, Oct. 12–25

Honda Masters G, Alice Springs, Australia, Oct. 19–27

Muslim Women's G, Islamabad, Pakistan, Nov. 1–5

Special Olympics Gulf G, Abu Dhabi, United Arab Emirates, Nov. 1–10

Special Olympics Asia-Pacific G, Shanghai, China, Nov. 8–11

Pacific School G, Perth, Australia, Dec. 7–13

Winter Australian Corporate G, Thredbo, Australia

Stockholm Summer G, Stockholm, Sweden

World Wheelchair G, Buckinghamshire, England

Special Olympics West African G, Abidjan, Ivory Coast

Winter World Corporate G, Seefeld, Austria

African Francophone Games for the Handicapped, Cotonou, Benin

1997

Winter World University G, Chonju-Moju, South Korea, Jan. 24–Feb. 2

Winter X Games, Big Bear Lake, USA, Jan. 30–Feb. 2

Special Olympics Winter World G, Toronto/Collingwood, Canada, Feb. 7–11

Winter European Youth Olympic Days, Sundsvall, Sweden, Feb. 7–13

International Police Winter G, North Lake Tahoe, USA, March 2–6

International Firefighters Winter G, South Lake Tahoe, USA, March 2–6

Winter World Corporate G, Seefeld, Austria, March 9–14

Winter G for the Disabled, Solleftea, Sweden, March 11–16

Australian Corporate G, Sydney, Australia, March 13–16

Windsor Classic Indoor G, Windsor, Canada

CARIFTA Games, Nassau, Bahamas, March 29–31

Défi Sportif, Montreal, Canada, April 30–May 4

Arafura G, Darwin, Australia, May 10–17

East Asian G, Pusan, South Korea, May 10–19

Games of the Small Countries of Europe, Reykjavik, Iceland, June 3–7

International School Children's G, Sparta, Greece, June 11–15

UK & Ireland Corporate G, Belfast, Northern Ireland, June 13–15

Mediterranean G, Bari, Italy, June 13–27

Euro G, Paris, France, June 20–23

World Scholar Athlete G, Newport, RI, USA, June 23–July 1

X Games, San Diego, USA, June 23–29

Baltic Sea G, Vilnius, Lithuania, June 25–July 6

World Police and Fire G, Calgary, Canada, June 27–July 4

World Medical G, Le Touquet, France, June 28–July 5

Island G, St. Helier, Jersey, June 28–July 5

Stockholm Summer G, Stockholm, Sweden, June 29–July 5

Gorge G, Hood River, USA, July 11–19

Arab G, Beirut, Lebanon, July 13–27

World G for the Deaf, Copenhagen, Denmark, July 13–23

Maccabiah G, Tel Aviv, Israel, July 14–25

World Dwarf G, Peterborough, England, July 18–25

Robin Hood G, Nottingham, England, July 18–28

European Youth Olympic Days, Lisbon, Portugal, July 18–24

Dutch Commonwealth G, Willemstad, Curaçao, July 26–Aug. 1

World Wheelchair G, Buckinghamshire, England, July 27–Aug. 2

Central American and Caribbean University G, Guadalajara, Mexico, July

North American Indigenous G, Victoria, Canada, Aug. 3–10

World G, Lahti, Finland, Aug. 7–17

JCC Maccabi G, Sarasota, USA, Aug. 10–15

JCC Maccabi G, Milwaukee, USA, Aug. 10–15

JCC Maccabi G, Kansas City, USA, Aug. 10–15

South Pacific Mini G, Pago Pago, American Samoa, Aug. 11–21

JCC Maccabi G, Seattle, USA, Aug. 17–22

JCC Maccabi G, Pittsburgh, USA, Aug. 17–22

JCC Maccabi G, Hartford, USA, Aug. 17–22

World University G, Sicily, Italy, Aug. 18–31

FISEC Games, Valletta, Malta

Francophone G, Antananarivo, Madagascar, Aug. 27–Sept. 6

World Air G, Ankara, Turkey, Sept. 3–21

Central Asian G, Alma-Ata, Kazakhstan, Sept. 13–20

World Corporate G, Oranjestad, Aruba, Sept. 13–20

World Ex-Service Wheelchair and Amputee G, Pretoria, South Africa, Sept. 20–28

World Nature G, Foz de Iguazi, Parana, Brazil, Sept. 27–Oct. 5

Australian Universities G, Bundoora, Australia, Sept. 28–Oct. 3

World Transplant G, Sydney, Australia, Sept. 29–Oct. 5

Ataturk Dam International Sports Festival, Ataturk Dam, Turkey, October 3–4

South East Asian G, Jakarta, Indonesia, Oct. 11–19

Huntsman World Senior G, St. George, USA, Oct. 13–24

Bolivarian G, Arequipa, Peru, Oct. 17–26

Australian Masters G, Canberra, Australia, Oct. 23–31

West Asian G, Tehran, Iran, Nov. 19–28

Central American G, San Pedro Sula, Honduras, Dec. 5–14

Muslim Women's G, Tehran, Iran, Dec. 13–22

Winter Australian Corporate G, Thredbo, Australia

Victorian Corporate G, Melbourne, Australia

Alps-Adriatic Winter Youth G, Styria, Austria

CUCSA Games, Harare, Zimbabwe

Pan-American G for the Blind, Buenos Aires, Argentina

1998

Winter X Games, Crested Butte, USA, Jan. 15–18

Olympic Winter G, Nagano, Japan, Feb. 7–22

International Police Winter G, Innsbruck, Austria, March 1–5

International Firefighters Winter G, South Lake Tahoe, USA, March 1–5

Winter Paralympic G, Nagano, Japan, March 5–14

Australian Corporate G, Sydney, Australia, March 11–14

Southern Cross G, Hobart, Australia, March 14–20

Arctic Winter G, Yellowknife, Canada, March 15–22

Winter World Corporate G, Seefeld, Austria, March 15–20

World Peace G, Dubai, United Arab Emirates, March 19–April 18

Pan-American Medical G, Mar. del Plata, Argentina, March 22–29

Windsor Classic Indoor G, Windsor, Canada

Special Olympics Mediterranean G, Athens, Greece, April 6–10

CARIFTA Games, Port of Spain, Trinidad, April 11–13

Australasian Public Sector G, Melbourne, Australia, April 15–19

Renaissance G, Lewiston ME, USA, April 17–19

African Francophone Games for the Handicapped, Dakar, Senegal, April 23–30

Défi Sportif, Montreal, Canada, May 1–3

SELL Games (Summer), Tartu, Estonia, May 1–10

Firefighters World G, Durban, South Africa, May 17–23

International School Children's G, Logroño, Spain, June 10–14

UK & Ireland Corporate G, Bracknell, England, June 12–14

X Games, San Diego, USA, June 19–28

Can-Am Police-Fire G, Regina, Canada, June 22–28

Stockholm Summer G, Stockholm, Sweden, June 28–July 4

World Medical G, Klagenfurt, Austria, June 27–July 4

Gorge G, Hood River, USA, July 11–18

World Youth G, Moscow, Russia, July 12–19

IBSA World Championships for the Blind, Madrid, Spain, July 17–26

Goodwill G, New York, USA, July 19–Aug. 2

FISEC Games, Gran Canaria, Spain, July 22–28

CUCSA Games, Johannesburg, South Africa, July 20–25

Gay G, Amsterdam, Netherlands, Aug. 1–8

Alps-Adriatic Summer Youth G, Venice, Italy

Micronesian G, Koror, Palau, Aug. 1–9

Winter Australian Corporate G, Thredbo, Australia, Aug. 7–9

Central American and Caribbean G, Maracaibo, Venezuela, Aug. 8–22

Indian Ocean Island G, St. Denis, Réunion, Aug. 8–16

JCC Maccabi G, Charlotte, USA, Aug. 9–14

World Masters G, Portland, USA, Aug. 9–22

Journalists World G, Athens, Greece

Irelands' Scholar Athlete G, Jordanstown, Northern Ireland, Aug. 14–22

JCC Maccabi G, Detroit, USA, Aug. 16–23

World Wheelchair G, Buckinghamshire, England, Aug. 20–31

World Corporate G, The Hague, Netherlands, Aug. 29–Sept. 5

Asian Sports Festival, Shenyang, China, Aug. 29–Sept. 6

Arab School G, Casablanca, Morocco, Sept. 5–15

Commonwealth G, Kuala Lumpur, Malaysia, Sept. 11–21

World Equestrian G, Rome, Italy, Sept. 30–Oct. 11

Australian Universities G, Melbourne, Australia, Sept. 28–Oct. 3

Ataturk Dam International Sports Festival, Ataturk Dam, Turkey, October 9–10

ISF Gymnasiade, Shanghai, China, Oct. 12–19

Huntsman World Senior G, St. George, USA, Oct. 12–24

Honda Masters G, Alice Springs, Australia, Oct. 17–24

South American G, Cuenca, Ecuador, Oct. 21–31

Asia Pacific Masters G, Gold Coast, Australia, Oct. 31–Nov. 8

International Law Enforcement G, Dubai, United Arab Emirates, Nov. 6–12

Victorian Corporate G, Melbourne, Australia, Nov. 20–22

Special Olympics Gulf G, Doha, Qatar, Nov. 21–26

Asian G, Bangkok, Thailand, Dec. 6–20

European Heart/Lung Transplant G, Bad Oeynhausen, Germany

1999

Winter World Transplant G, Salt Lake City, USA, Jan. 10–15

Far East and South Pacific G for the Disabled, Bangkok, Thailand, Jan. 10–16

Winter X Games, Crested Butte, USA, Jan. 14–17

Winter World University G, Poprad, Slovakia, Jan. 22–30

Asian Winter G, Kangwon, South Korea, Jan. 30–Feb. 6

Winter International School Children's G, Maribor, Slovenia, Feb. 6–8

International Firefighters Winter G, North Lake Tahoe, USA, Feb. 28–March 4

Winter G for the Disabled, Solleftea, Sweden, March 5–13

Winter European Youth Olympic Days, Poprad-Tatry, Slovakia, March 6–12

International Police Winter G, Blackcomb/Whistler, Canada, March 7–12

Winter World G for the Deaf, Davos, Switzerland, March 8–14

Winter World Corporate G, Gastein, Austria, March 26–28

Australian Corporate G, Sydney, Australia, March

Windsor Classic Indoor G, Windsor, Canada

Défi Sportif, Montreal, Canada, April 29–May 2

SELL Games (Summer), Kaunas, Lithuania, May 11–17

Arafura G, Darwin, Australia, May 22–29

Games of the Small Countries of Europe, Vaduz, Liechtenstein, May 24–29

South Pacific G, Agana, Guam, May 29–June 12

International School Children's G, Medias, Romania, June 9–13

CUCSA Games, Lusaka, Zambia, June 13–20

X Games, San Francisco, USA, June 25–July 3

Island G, Visby, Gotland, June 26–July 2

World Medical G, Saint-Tropez, France, June 26–July 3

Special Olympics Summer World G, Raleigh-Durham, USA, June 26–July 4

World University G, Palma de Mallorca, Spain, July 2–July 13

Stockholm Summer G, Stockholm, Sweden, July 4–10

Pan-American Maccabi G, Mexico City, Mexico, July 8–20

European Youth Olympic Days, Esbjerg, Denmark, July 10–16

World Police and Fire G, Stockholm, Sweden, July 16–24

FISEC Games, Lisbon, Portugal, July 21–27

Pan-American G, Winnipeg, Canada, July 24–Aug. 8

Dutch Commonwealth G, St. Maarten, Netherlands Antilles, July 24–30

European Maccabi G, Glasgow, Scotland, July 25–30

Aalborg Youth G, Aalborg, Denmark, July 26–30

JCC Maccabi G, Houston, USA, Aug. 8–13

JCC Maccabi G, Columbus, USA, Aug. 8–13

South East Asian G, Bandar Seri Bagawan, Brunei, Aug. 8–14

Military World G, Zagreb, Croatia, Aug. 8–17

Arab G, Amman, Jordan, Aug. 12–31

JCC Maccabi G, Rochester, NY, USA, Aug. 15–20

JCC Maccabi G, Cherry Hill, NJ, USA, Aug. 15–20

Pan-American G for the Deaf, Havana, Cuba, Aug. 16–26

Pan-Armenian G, Yerevan, Armenia, Aug. 28–Sept. 4

World Transplant G, Budapest, Hungary, Sept. 4–11

Gravity G, Providence, USA, Sept. 5–12

Arab G for the Handicapped, Amman, Jordan, Sept. 9–20

African G, Johannesburg, South Africa, Sept. 10–19

Ataturk Dam International Sports Festival, Ataturk Dam, Turkey, Sept. 24–25

International School Children's G, Csky Krumlov, Czech Republic, Sept. 24–26

Journalists World G, Estrie, Canada, Sept. 24–Oct. 3

Australian Masters G, Adelaide, Australia, Sept. 25–Oct. 3

South Asian Federation G, Kathmandu, Nepal, Sept. 25–Oct. 4

Australian Universities G, Perth, Australia, Sept. 26–Oct. 1

International School Children's G, Velenje, Slovenia, Sept. 27–29

Islands Corporate G, St. Helier, Jersey, Oct. 8–10

World Wheelchair G, Christchurch, New Zealand, Oct. 8–18

Huntsman World Senior G, St. George, USA, Oct. 11–22

Pan-American Wheelchair G, Mexico City, Mexico, Nov. 1–8

Pan-American Medical G, Punte del Este, Uruguay, Dec. 4–11

World Corporate G, Montevideo, Uruguay, Dec. 13–16

Pan-American G for the Blind, Mexico City, Mexico

East African University G, Njoro, Kenya, Dec.

West African University G, Cotonou, Benin

Central Asian G, Bishkek, Kyrgyzstan, Oct. 2–7

UK & Ireland Corporate G, Limerick, Ireland

Winter Australian Corporate G, Thredbo, Australia

Victorian Corporate G, Melbourne, Australia

CARIFTA Games, Martinique

2000

Winter Gravity G, Mammoth, USA, Jan. 20–23

Winter World Corporate G, Gastein, Austria, Jan. 28–30

Winter X Games, Mount Snow, USA, Feb. 3–6

Winter Goodwill G, Lake Placid, USA, February 16–20

International Firefighters Winter G, North Lake Tahoe, USA, Feb. 27–March 2

Alps-Adriatic Summer Youth G, Friuli-Venezia Giulia, Italy

International Police Winter G, Lake Tahoe, USA, March

Arctic Winter G, Whitehorse, Canada, March 5–11

Australian Corporate G, Sydney, Australia, March 16–19

Windsor Classic Indoor G, Windsor, Canada, March 24–26

CARIFTA Games, St. George, Grenada

African Francophone Games for the Handicapped, Abidjan, Ivory Coast, April 11–15

Défi Sportif, Montreal, Canada, April 26–30

Australasian Public Sector G, Melbourne, Australia, April 26–30

Pacific School G, Sydney, Australia, April 27–May 8

European Special Olympics, Groningen, Netherlands, May 26–June 4

Southern Cross G, Apia, Samoa, May 22–26

Euro G, Zurich, Switzerland, June 2–3

Middle East/Mediterranean Scholar Athlete G, Tel Aviv, Israel, June 24–July 3

European Heart/Lung Transplant G, Sandefjord, Norway, June 25–July 3

Irelands' Scholar Athlete G, Jordanstown, Northern Ireland

Irelands' Scholar Athlete G, Limerick, Ireland, Aug. 11–19

World Medical G, Cannes, France, July 1–8

International School Children's G, Hamilton, Canada, July 1–8

Can-Am Police-Fire G, Milwaukee, USA, July 2–10

Stockholm Summer G, Stockholm, Sweden, July 2–8

Firefighters World G, Mantes-Yvelines, France, July 6–13

SkyG, Cervinia, Italy, July 7–9

SELL Games (Summer), Jelgava, Latvia, May 18–27

Gorge G, Hood River, USA, July 8–15

World Corporate G, Aberdeen, Scotland, July 13–16

Gravity G, Providence, USA, July 15–23

CUCSA Games, Maputo, Mozambique, July 16–23

FISEC Games, Nantes, France, July 19–25

Great Outdoor G, Lake Placid, USA, July 20–23

JCC Maccabi G, Tucson, USA, Aug. 3–9

Asia Pacific Masters G, Gold Coast, Australia, Oct. 25–Nov. 5

Central American and Caribbean University G, San German, Puerto Rico, July 30–Aug. 5

International Law Enforcement G, Cocoa Beach, USA, Aug. 3–13

JCC Maccabi G, Boca Raton, USA, Aug. 6–11

Commonwealth Youth G, Edinburgh, Scotland, Aug. 10–14

JCC Maccabi G, Richmond, USA, Aug. 13–18

JCC Maccabi G, Cincinnati, USA, Aug. 13–18

X Games, San Francisco, USA, Aug. 17–22

JCC Maccabi G, Staten Island, USA, Aug. 20–25

Winter Australian Corporate G, Thredbo, Australia, Aug.

Australian Universities G, Ballarat, Australia, Oct. 2–6

Olympic G, Sydney, Australia, Sept. 15–Oct. 1

Pan-American G for Patients with Asthma, River Plate, Argentina, Sept. 22–23

Ataturk Dam International Sports Festival, Ataturk Dam, Turkey, Sept. or Oct

Huntsman World Senior G, St. George, USA, Oct. 9–21

Paralympic G, Sydney, Australia, Oct. 14–24

Honda Masters G, Alice Springs, Australia, Oct. 21–28

Asia Pacific G for the Deaf, Taipei, Taiwan, Nov. 1–12

Pan-American Medical G, Foz de Iguazi, Brazil, Nov. 18–25

Victorian Corporate G, Melbourne, Australia, Nov. 24–26

Journalists World G, Liège, Belgium

Appendix 2.
Games by Nation

Åland
1991 Mariehamn, Island Games

Algeria
1975 Algiers, Mediterranean Games
1978 Algiers, African Games

American Samoa
1997 Pago Pago, South Pacific Mini Games

Andorra
1989 Andorra, International School Children's Games
1991 Andorra, Games of the Small Countries of Europe
1995 Andorra, Winter European Youth Olympic Days

Angola
1981 Luanda, Central African Games

Argentina
1951 Buenos Aires, Pan-American Games
1964 Buenos Aires, Pan-American Maccabi Games
1969 Buenos Aires, Pan-American Wheelchair Games
1982 Rosario/Santa Fe, South American Games
1990 Las Lenas, Winter Pan-American Games
1995 Buenos Aires, Pan-American Wheelchair Games
1995 Mar del Plata, Pan-American Games
1995 Buenos Aires, Pan-American Maccabi Games
1997 Buenos Aires, Pan-American Games for the Blind

1998 Mar del Plata, Pan-American Medical Games
2000 River Plate, Pan-American Games for Patients with Asthma

Armenia
1999 Yerevan, Pan-Armenian Games

Aruba
1970 Oranjestad, Dutch Commonwealth Games
1995 Oranjestad, Dutch Commonwealth Games
1997 Oranjestad, World Corporate Games

Australia
1938 Sydney, Commonwealth Games
1956 Melbourne, Olympic Games
1962 Perth, British Commonwealth Paraplegic Games
1962 Perth, Commonwealth Games
1977 Parramatta, Far East and South Pacific Games for the Disabled
1982 Brisbane, Pacific School Games
1982 Brisbane, Commonwealth Games
1984 Melbourne, Pacific School Games
1986 Alice Springs, Honda Masters Games
1987 Hobart, Australian Masters Games
1988 Sydney, International Law Enforcement Games
1988 Melbourne, Asia Pacific Games for the Deaf
1988 Alice Springs, Honda Masters Games
1988 Sydney, Pacific School Games
1989 Adelaide, Australian Masters Games
1990 Alice Springs, Honda Masters Games
1991 Darwin, Arafura Games
1991 Brisbane, Australian Masters Games
1992 Darwin, Pacific School Games

1992 Alice Springs, Honda Masters Games
1993 Perth, Australian Masters Games
1993 Darwin, Arafura Games
1993 Sydney, Australian Corporate Games
1994 Brisbane, World Masters Games
1994 Wollongong, Australian Universities Games
1994 Perth, Firefighters World Games
1994 Alice Springs, Honda Masters Games
1994 Sydney, Australian Corporate Games
1995 Darwin, Arafura Games
1995 Sydney, Australian Corporate Games
1995 Melbourne, Australian Masters Games
1995 Melbourne, World Police and Fire Games
1995 Darwin, Australian Universities Games
1996 Alice Springs, Honda Masters Games
1996 Perth, Pacific School Games
1996 Sydney, Australian Corporate Games
1996 Canberra, Australian Universities Games
1996 Thredbo, Winter Australian Corporate Games
1997 Darwin, Arafura Games
1997 Sydney, World Transplant Games
1997 Sydney, Australian Corporate Games
1997 Canberra, Australian Masters Games
1997 Melbourne, Victorian Corporate Games
1997 Bundoora, Australian Universities Games
1997 Thredbo, Winter Australian Corporate Games
1998 Melbourne, Australian Universities Games
1998 Melbourne, Victorian Corporate Games
1998 Hobart, Southern Cross Games
1998 Thredbo, Winter Australian Corporate Games
1998 Sydney, Australian Corporate Games
1998 Alice Springs, Honda Masters Games
1998 Melbourne, Australasian Public Sector Games
1998 Gold Coast, Asia Pacific Masters Games
1999 Darwin, Arafura Games
1999 Sydney, Australian Corporate Games
1999 Perth, Australian Universities Games
1999 Thredbo, Winter Australian Corporate Games
1999 Adelaide, Australian Masters Games
1999 Melbourne, Victorian Corporate Games
2000 Gold Coast, Asia Pacific Masters Games
2000 Thredbo, Winter Australian Corporate Games
2000 Sydney, Australian Corporate Games
2000 Ballarat, Australian Universities Games
2000 Sydney, Paralympic Games
2000 Melbourne, Victorian Corporate Games
2000 Sydney, Pacific School Games
2000 Alice Springs, Honda Masters Games
2000 Sydney, Olympic Games
2000 Melbourne, Australasian Public Sector Games

Austria

1931 Murzzuschlag, Socialist Worker Sports International Winter Worker Olympiad

1931 Vienna, Socialist Olympics
1937 Zeel am See, Winter World University Games
1938 Vienna, International Women's Games
1939 Vienna, German Student Federation Games
1949 Seefeld, Winter World Games for the Deaf
1951 Gastein, University Sports Week Winter (FISU)
1953 Semeringen-Vienna, World Student Championships Winter (UIE)
1958 Zeel am See, University Sports Week Winter (FISU)
1959 Vienna, World Student Championships (UIE)
1964 Innsbruck, Olympic Winter Games
1968 Innsbruck, Winter World University Games
1972 Graz, International School Children's Games
1976 Innsbruck, Olympic Winter Games
1984 Graz, Alps-Adriatic Summer Youth Games
1984 Innsbruck, Winter Paralympic Games
1985 Villach, Alps-Adriatic Winter Youth Games
1987 Innsbruck, World Transplant Games
1987 Graz, International School Children's Games
1988 Innsbruck, Winter Paralympic Games
1990 Linz, Alps-Adriatic Summer Youth Games
1991 Carinthia, Alps-Adriatic Winter Youth Games
1993 Salzburg/Schladming, Special Olympics Winter World Games
1996 Seefeld, Winter World Corporate Games
1997 Seefeld, Winter World Corporate Games
1997 Styria, Alps-Adriatic Winter Youth Games
1998 Innsbruck, International Police Winter Games
1998 Klagenfurt, World Medical Games
1998 Seefeld, Winter World Corporate Games
1999 Gastein, Winter World Corporate Games
2000 Gastein, Winter World Corporate Games

Bahamas

1992 Nassau, CARIFTA Games
1997 Nassau, CARIFTA Games

Bangladesh

1985 Dhaka, South Asian Federation Games
1993 Dhaka, South Asian Federation Games

Barbados

1985 Bridgetown, CARIFTA Games
1989 Bridgetown, CARIFTA Games
1994 Bridgetown, CARIFTA Games

Belgium

1920 Antwerp, Olympic Games
1937 Antwerp, Socialist Olympics
1953 Brussels, World Games for the Deaf
1981 Brussels, European Special Olympics
1983 Antwerp, European Maccabi Games

1987 Genk, FISEC Games
1988 Louvain, FISEC Games
1990 Brugge, ISF Gymnasiade
1991 Brussels, European Youth Olympic Days
2000 Liège, Journalists World Games

Benin

1979 Cotonou, West African Games
1996 Cotonou, African Francophone Games for the Handicapped
1999 Cotonou, West African University Games

Bermuda

1996 Hamilton, International Senior Games

Bolivia

1977 La Paz, Bolivarian Games
1978 La Paz, South American Games
1993 Cochabamba, Bolivarian Games

Brazil

1922 Rio de Janeiro, Latin American Games
1963 Pôrto Alegre, World University Games
1963 São Paulo, Pan-American Games
1967 São Paulo, Pan-American Maccabi Games
1978 Rio de Janeiro, Pan-American Wheelchair Games
1983 São Paulo, Pan-American Maccabi Games
1997 Foz de Iguazi, Parana, World Nature Games
2000 Foz de Iguazi, Pan-American Medical Games

Brunei

1999 Bandar Seri Bagawan, South East Asian Games

Bulgaria

1961 Sofia, World University Games
1973 Pamporovo, SCFA Winter Spartakiade
1977 Sofia, World University Games
1981 Borovec, SCFA Winter Spartakiade
1983 Sofia, Winter World University Games
1989 Sofia, SCFA Summer Spartakiade
1989 Sofia, Winter World University Games
1993 Sofia, World Games for the Deaf

Burkina Faso

1989 Ouagadougou, West African University Games
1994 Ouagadougou, African Francophone Games for the Handicapped

Burma

1962 Rangoon, South East Asian Games
1969 Rangoon, South East Asian Games

Cambodia

1966 Phnom Penh, Asian Games of the New Emerging Forces (GANEFO)

Canada

1930 Hamilton, Commonwealth Games
1954 Vancouver, Commonwealth Games
1967 Winnipeg, Pan-American Wheelchair Games
1967 Winnipeg, Pan-American Games
1970 Yellowknife, Arctic Winter Games
1972 Whitehorse, Arctic Winter Games
1976 Toronto, Paralympic Games
1976 Shefferville, Arctic Winter Games
1976 Montreal, Olympic Games
1978 Hay River/Pine Point, Arctic Winter Games
1978 Edmonton, Commonwealth Games
1980 Whitehorse, Arctic Winter Games
1982 Windsor, Windsor Classic Indoor Games
1982 Halifax, Pan-American Wheelchair Games
1982 New Westminster, Can-Am Police-Fire Games
1983 Windsor, Windsor Classic Indoor Games
1983 Edmonton, World University Games
1983 Edmonton, Can-Am Police-Fire Games
1984 Yellowknife, Arctic Winter Games
1984 Windsor, Windsor Classic Indoor Games
1985 Windsor, Windsor Classic Indoor Games
1985 Toronto, World Masters Games
1985 Calgary, Can-Am Police-Fire Games
1986 Toronto, JCC Maccabi Games
1986 Windsor, Windsor Classic Indoor Games
1986 Whitehorse, Arctic Winter Games
1987 Windsor, Windsor Classic Indoor Games
1988 Windsor, Windsor Classic Indoor Games
1988 Montreal, Défi Sportif
1988 Calgary, Olympic Winter Games
1989 Montreal, World Medical Games
1989 Vancouver, World Police and Fire Games
1989 Windsor, Windsor Classic Indoor Games
1989 Montreal, Défi Sportif
1990 Vancouver, Gay Games
1990 Windsor, Windsor Classic Indoor Games
1990 Montreal, Défi Sportif
1990 Yellowknife, Arctic Winter Games
1990 Blackcomb/Whistler, International Police Winter Games
1990 Calgary, International Law Enforcement Games
1990 Edmonton, North American Indigenous Games
1991 Banff, Winter World Games for the Deaf
1991 Montreal, Défi Sportif
1991 Windsor, Windsor Classic Indoor Games
1992 Windsor, Windsor Classic Indoor Games
1992 Montreal, Défi Sportif
1992 Whitehorse, Arctic Winter Games
1993 Prince Albert, North American Indigenous Games
1993 Vancouver, World Transplant Games
1993 Montreal, Défi Sportif
1993 Calgary, Can-Am Police-Fire Games
1993 Windsor, Windsor Classic Indoor Games
1994 Slave Lake, Arctic Winter Games
1994 Victoria, Commonwealth Games

1994 Windsor, Windsor Classic Indoor Games
1994 Hamilton, International School Children's Games
1994 Montreal, Défi Sportif
1995 Montreal, Défi Sportif
1995 Windsor, Windsor Classic Indoor Games
1996 Windsor, Windsor Classic Indoor Games
1996 Montreal, Défi Sportif
1996 Edmonton, Firefighters World Games
1997 Windsor, Windsor Classic Indoor Games
1997 Montreal, Défi Sportif
1997 Calgary, World Police and Fire Games
1997 Toronto/Collingwood, Special Olympics Winter World Games
1997 Victoria, North American Indigenous Games
1998 Montreal, Défi Sportif
1998 Yellowknife, Arctic Winter Games
1998 Regina, Can-Am Police-Fire Games
1998 Windsor, Windsor Classic Indoor Games
1999 Montreal, Défi Sportif
1999 Estrie, Journalists World Games
1999 Blackcomb/Whistler, International Police Winter Games
1999 Winnipeg, Pan-American Games
1999 Windsor, Windsor Classic Indoor Games
2000 Hamilton, International School Children's Games
2000 Whitehorse, Arctic Winter Games
2000 Windsor, Windsor Classic Indoor Games
2000 Montreal, Défi Sportif

Cayman Islands
1995 George Town, CARIFTA Games

Chile
1986 Santiago, South American Games

China
1915 Shanghai, Far East Championships
1921 Shanghai, Far East Championships
1927 Shanghai, Far East Championships
1990 Beijing, Asian Games
1993 Shanghai, East Asian Games
1994 Beijing, Far East and South Pacific Games for the Disabled
1996 Harbin, Asian Winter Games
1996 Shanghai, Special Olympics Asia-Pacific Games
1998 Shenyang, Asian Sports Festival
1998 Shanghai, ISF Gymnasiade

Colombia
1938 Bogota, Bolivarian Games
1946 Barranquilla, Central American and Caribbean Games
1961 Barranquilla, Bolivarian Games
1971 Cali, Pan-American Games
1978 Medellín, Central American and Caribbean Games
1995 Cali, Pacific Ocean Games

Congo, Republic of the
1965 Brazzaville, African Games
1987 Brazzaville, Central African Games

Cook Islands
1985 Rarotonga, South Pacific Mini Games

Croatia
1996 Zagreb, International Electrical Engineering Students Sports Games
1999 Zabreb, Military World Games

Cuba
1930 Havana, Central American and Caribbean Games
1977 Havana, SCFA Summer Spartakiade
1982 Havana, Central American and Caribbean Games
1986 Havana, Central American and Caribbean University Games
1991 Havana, Pan-American Games
1999 Havana, Pan-American Games for the Deaf

Curacao
1967 Willemstad, Dutch Commonwealth Games
1972 Willemstad, Dutch Commonwealth Games
1997 Willemstad, Dutch Commonwealth Games

Cyprus
1989 Nicosia, Games of the Small Countries of Europe
1994 Nicosia, ISF Gymnasiade

Czech Republic
1999 Csky Krumlov, International School Children's Games

Czechoslovakia
1921 Prague, Red Sport International Spartakiade
1921 Prague, Socialist Olympics
1927 Prague, Socialist Olympics
1930 Prague, International Women's Games
1934 Prague, Socialist Olympics
1935 Banská-Bystrica, Maccabiade Winter Games
1937 Johannesbad, Socialist Worker Sports International Winter Worker
1949 Spindleruv Mlyn, World Student Championships Winter (UIE)
1964 Spindleruv Mlyn, Winter World University Games
1969 Spindleruv Mlyn, SCFA Winter Spartakiade
1973 Prague, SCFA Summer Spartakiade
1977 Spindleruv Mlyn, SCFA Winter Spartakiade
1978 Spindleruv Mlyn, Winter World University Games
1983 Strbske Pleso, SCFA Winter Spartakiade

1987 Strbske Pleso, Winter World University Games
1989 Jasna, Osrblie, Strbske Pleso, SCFA Winter Spartakiade

Denmark

1949 Copenhagen, World Games for the Deaf
1959 Copenhagen, European Maccabi Games
1974 Copenhagen, European Maccabi Games
1975 Aalborg, Aalborg Youth Games
1979 Aalborg, Aalborg Youth Games
1983 Aalborg, Aalborg Youth Games
1987 Copenhagen, European Maccabi Games
1987 Aalborg, Aalborg Youth Games
1989 Henning, Århus, Aalborg, World Masters Games
1991 Aalborg, Aalborg Youth Games
1995 Aalborg, Aalborg Youth Games
1996 Aalborg, Centennial Youth Games
1997 Copenhagen, World Games for the Deaf
1999 Aalborg, Aalborg Youth Games
1999 Esbjerg, European Youth Olympic Days

Dominican Republic

1974 Santo Domingo, Central American and Caribbean Games
1977 Santo Domingo, Central American and Caribbean University Games
1986 Santiago de los Caballeros, Central American and Caribbean Games

East Germany

1951 Berlin, World Student Championships (UIE)
1958 Leipzig, SCFA Summer Spartakiade

Ecuador

1965 Quito, Guayaquil, Bolivarian Games
1985 Cuenca, Bolivarian Games
1998 Cuenca, South American Games

Egypt

1951 Alexandria, Mediterranean Games
1953 Alexandria, Arab Games
1965 Cairo, Arab Games
1991 Cairo, African Games

El Salvador

1935 San Salvador, Central American and Caribbean Games
1977 San Salvador, Central American Games
1994 San Salvador, Central American Games

England

1908 London, Olympic Games
1911 London, Festival of the Empire Sports Meeting
1934 London, Commonwealth Games
1934 London, International Women's Games
1935 London, World Games for the Deaf
1948 Buckinghamshire, Stoke Mandeville Wheelchair Games

1948 London, Olympic Games
1949 Buckinghamshire, Stoke Mandeville Wheelchair Games
1950 Buckinghamshire, Stoke Mandeville Wheelchair Games
1951 Buckinghamshire, Stoke Mandeville Wheelchair Games
1951 London, Britain's Festival of Sport
1952 Buckinghamshire, Stoke Mandeville Wheelchair Games
1953 Buckinghamshire, Stoke Mandeville Wheelchair Games
1954 Buckinghamshire, Stoke Mandeville Wheelchair Games
1955 Buckinghamshire, Stoke Mandeville Wheelchair Games
1956 Buckinghamshire, Stoke Mandeville Wheelchair Games
1957 Buckinghamshire, Stoke Mandeville Wheelchair Games
1958 Buckinghamshire, Stoke Mandeville Wheelchair Games
1959 Buckinghamshire, Stoke Mandeville Wheelchair Games
1961 Buckinghamshire, Stoke Mandeville Wheelchair Games
1962 Buckinghamshire, Stoke Mandeville Wheelchair Games
1963 Buckinghamshire, Stoke Mandeville Wheelchair Games
1965 Buckinghamshire, Stoke Mandeville Wheelchair Games
1966 Buckinghamshire, Stoke Mandeville Wheelchair Games
1967 Buckinghamshire, Stoke Mandeville Wheelchair Games
1969 Buckinghamshire, Stoke Mandeville Wheelchair Games
1970 Buckinghamshire, Stoke Mandeville Wheelchair Games
1971 Buckinghamshire, Stoke Mandeville Wheelchair Games
1973 Buckinghamshire, Stoke Mandeville Wheelchair Games
1974 Buckinghamshire, Stoke Mandeville Wheelchair Games
1975 Buckinghamshire, Stoke Mandeville Wheelchair Games
1977 Buckinghamshire, Stoke Mandeville Wheelchair Games
1978 Portsmouth, World Transplant Games
1978 Buckinghamshire, Stoke Mandeville Wheelchair Games
1979 Buckinghamshire, Stoke Mandeville Wheelchair Games
1979 Portsmouth, World Transplant Games
1979 Leicester, European Maccabi Games
1981 Buckinghamshire, Stoke Mandeville Wheelchair Games
1982 Buckinghamshire, Stoke Mandeville Wheelchair Games

1983 Buckinghamshire, Stoke Mandeville Wheelchair Games
1984 Aylesbury, Paralympic Games
1985 Buckinghamshire, Stoke Mandeville Wheelchair Games
1985 London, World Games
1986 Buckinghamshire, Stoke Mandeville Wheelchair Games
1987 Buckinghamshire, Stoke Mandeville Wheelchair Games
1989 Buckinghamshire, Stoke Mandeville Wheelchair Games
1989 Nottingham, Robin Hood Games
1990 Buckinghamshire, Stoke Mandeville Wheelchair Games
1990 Liverpool, FISEC Games
1991 London, European Heart/Lung Transplant Games
1991 Sheffield, World University Games
1991 Buckinghamshire, Stoke Mandeville Wheelchair Games
1992 London, World Corporate Games
1993 Aylesbury, World Ex-Service Wheelchair and Amputee Games
1993 Milton Keynes, UK & Ireland Corporate Games
1993 Buckinghamshire, Stoke Mandeville Wheelchair Games
1993 Nottingham, Robin Hood Games
1994 Buckinghamshire, Stoke Mandeville Wheelchair Games
1994 Milton Keynes, UK & Ireland Corporate Games
1995 Bath, European Youth Olympic Days
1995 Manchester, World Transplant Games
1995 Peterborough, UK & Ireland Corporate Games
1995 Buckinghamshire, Stoke Mandeville Wheelchair Games
1996 Somerset/London, FISEC Games
1996 Buckinghamshire, World Wheelchair Games
1997 Peterborough, World Dwarf Games
1997 Buckinghamshire, World Wheelchair Games
1997 Nottingham, Robin Hood Games
1998 Buckinghamshire, World Wheelchair Games
1998 Bracknell, UK & Ireland Corporate Games

Estonia
1923 Tartu, SELL Games (Summer)
1930 Tallin, SELL Games (Summer)
1934 Tartu, SELL Games (Summer)
1938 Tartu, SELL Games (Summer)
1940 Otepaa, SELL Games (Winter)
1993 Tallin, Baltic Sea Games
1998 Tartu, SELL Games (Summer)

Faroe Islands
1989 Tórshavn, Island Games

Fiji
1963 Suva, South Pacific Games
1979 Suva, South Pacific Games

Finland
1926 Helsinki, SELL Games (Summer)
1931 Helsinki, SELL Games (Winter)
1932 Helsinki, SELL Games (Summer)
1936 Helsinki, SELL Games (Summer)
1952 Helsinki, Olympic Games
1961 Helsinki, World Games for the Deaf
1962 Helsinki, World Student Championships (UIE) (IUS)
1970 Rovaniemi, Winter World University Games
1994 Helsinki, European Heart/Lung Transplant Games
1995 Yllas, Winter World Games for the Deaf
1997 Lahti, World Games

France
1900 Paris, Olympic Games
1919 Paris, Inter-Allied Games
1922 Paris, International Women's Games
1923 Paris, World University Games
1924 Chamonix, Olympic Winter Games
1924 Paris, Olympic Games
1924 Paris, Red Sport International Spartakiade
1924 Paris, World Games for the Deaf
1928 Paris, World University Games
1937 Paris, World University Games
1947 Paris, World University Games
1957 Paris, World University Games
1960 Chamonix, Winter World University Games
1963 Lyon, European Maccabi Games
1968 Grenoble, Olympic Winter Games
1976 Orléans, ISF Gymnasiade
1978 Cannes, World Medical Games
1979 Meribel, Winter World Games for the Deaf
1980 Cannes, World Medical Games
1982 Cannes, World Medical Games
1982 Nice, Journalists World Games
1982 Lille, ISF Gymnasiade
1983 Paris, World Medical Games
1983 Bellegarde, World Peace Games
1983 Troyes, International School Children's Games
1985 Echiroles, World Peace Games
1986 Nice, ISF Gymnasiade
1988 Paris, European Heart/Lung Transplant Games
1988 Lyon, World Medical Games
1990 Perpignan, World Medical Games
1991 Marseille, European Maccabi Games
1991 Lille, World Corporate Games
1992 Albertville, Winter Paralympic Games
1992 Albertville, Olympic Winter Games
1993 Languedoc-Rousillon, Mediterranean Games
1993 Saint-Malo, World Medical Games
1994 Paris, Francophone Games

1994 Tignes, Winter World Transplant Games
1994 Évian, World Medical Games
1996 Pra-Loup, Winter World Transplant Games
1997 Le Touquet, World Medical Games
1997 Paris, Euro Games
1999 Saint-Tropez, World Medical Games
2000 Cannes, World Medical Games
2000 Mantes-Yvelines, Firefighters World Games
2000 Nantes, FISEC Games

Gabon

1976 Libreville, Central African Games

Germany

1909 Leipzig, Academic Olympia
1910 Berlin, Academic Olympia
1911 Breslau, Academic Olympia
1911 Dresden, Academic Olympia
1913 Leipzig, Academic Olympia
1925 Frankfurt, Socialist Olympics
1925 Schrieberhau (Riesenberge), Socialist Worker Sports International Winter Worker
1930 Darmstadt, World University Games
1931 Nürnberg, World Games for the Deaf
1936 Berlin, Olympic Games
1936 Garmisch-Partenkirchen, Olympic Winter Games
1993 Darmstadt, International School Children's Games
1994 Burghausen, Alps-Adriatic Summer Youth Games
1995 Frankfurt, Euro Games
1996 Berlin, Euro Games
1996 Stuttgart, World Corporate Games
1998 Bad Oeynhausen, European Heart/Lung Transplant Games

Ghana

1967 Legon, West African University Games
1973 Kumasi, West African University Games
1974 Accra, All-Africa University Games

Gibraltar

1995 Gibraltar, Island Games

Gotland

1999 Visby, Island Games

Greece

1896 Athens, Olympic Games
1906 Athens, Olympic Games
1982 Athens, World Transplant Games
1991 Athens, Mediterranean Games
1991 Heraklion, World Medical Games
1996 Athens, European Special Olympics
1997 Sparta, International School Children's Games
1998 Athens, Journalists World Games
1998 Athens, Special Olympics Mediterranean Games

Grenada

2000 St. George, CARIFTA Games

Guadeloupe

1986 Basse-Terre, CARIFTA Games

Guam

1975 Tumon, South Pacific Games
1994 Agana, Micronesian Games
1999 Agana, South Pacific Games

Guatemala

1921 Guatemala City, Central American Games
1950 Guatemala City, Central American and Caribbean Games
1973 Guatemala City, Central American Games
1986 Guatemala City, Central American Games
1990 Guatemala City, Central American and Caribbean University Games

Guernsey

1987 St. Peter Port, Island Games

Honduras

1990 Tegucigalpa, Central American Games
1997 San Pedro Sula, Central American Games

Hong Kong

1982 Sha Tin, Far East and South Pacific Games for the Disabled
1984 Hong Kong, Asia Pacific Games for the Deaf

Hungary

1935 Budapest, World University Games
1949 Budapest, World Student Championships (UIE)
1954 Budapest, World Student Championships (UIE)
1965 Budapest, World University Games
1981 Budapest, SCFA Summer Spartakiade
1988 Szombathely, International School Children's Games
1991 Budapest, World Transplant Games
1992 Zalaegerszeg, Alps-Adriatic Summer Youth Games
1996 Sopron, International School Children's Games
1996 Siofok, Alps-Adriatic Summer Youth Games
1996 Tiszaujvaros, Eastern European Transplant Games
1999 Budapest, World Transplant Games

Iceland

1997 Reykjavik, Games of the Small Countries of Europe

India

1934 Delhi-Patalia, Western Asiatic Games
1951 New Delhi, Asian Games

1982 New Delhi, Asian Games
1987 Calcutta, South Asian Federation Games
1995 Madras, South Asian Federation Games

Indonesia

1962 Jakarta, Asian Games
1963 Jakarta, Games of the New Emerging Forces
  (GANEFO)
1979 Jakarta, South East Asian Games
1986 Surakarta, Far East and South Pacific Games
  for the Disabled
1987 Jakarta, South East Asian Games
1997 Jakarta, South East Asian Games

Iran

1974 Tehran, Asian Games
1993 Tehran, Muslim Women's Games
1994 Tehran, Muslim Student Games
1997 Tehran, Muslim Women's Games
1997 Tehran, West Asian Games

Ireland

1924 Dublin, Tailteann Games
1928 Dublin, Tailteann Games
1932 Dublin, Tailteann Games
1985 Dublin, European Special Olympics
1995 Limerick, World Medical Games
1999 Limerick, UK & Ireland Corporate Games
2000 Limerick, Irelands' Scholar Athlete Games

Isle of Man

1985 Douglas, Island Games

Isle of Wight

1993 Sandown, Island Games

Israel

1928 Tel Aviv, Hapoel Games
1930 Tel Aviv, Hapoel Games
1932 Tel Aviv, Hapoel Games
1932 Tel Aviv, Maccabiah Games
1935 Tel Aviv, Maccabiah Games
1935 Tel Aviv, Hapoel Games
1950 Tel Aviv, Maccabiah Games
1952 Tel Aviv, Hapoel Games
1953 Tel Aviv, Maccabiah Games
1956 Tel Aviv, Hapoel Games
1957 Tel Aviv, Maccabiah Games
1961 Tel Aviv, Maccabiah Games
1961 Tel Aviv, Hapoel Games
1965 Tel Aviv, Maccabiah Games
1966 Tel Aviv, Hapoel Games
1968 Tel Aviv, Paralympic Games
1969 Tel Aviv, Maccabiah Games
1971 Tel Aviv, Hapoel Games
1973 Tel Aviv, Maccabiah Games
1975 Tel Aviv, Hapoel Games
1977 Tel Aviv, Maccabiah Games
1979 Tel Aviv, Hapoel Games
1981 Tel Aviv, Maccabiah Games
1983 Tel Aviv, Hapoel Games

1985 Tel Aviv, Maccabiah Games
1987 Tel Aviv, Hapoel Games
1989 Tel Aviv, Maccabiah Games
1991 Tel Aviv, Hapoel Games
1993 Tel Aviv, Maccabiah Games
1995 Tel Aviv, Hapoel Games
1997 Tel Aviv, Maccabiah Games
2000 Tel Aviv, Middle East/Mediterranean
  Scholar Athlete Games

Italy

1922 Rome, University Olympia
1927 Rome, World University Games
1928 Cortina d'Ampezzo, Winter World University Games
1933 Turin, World University Games
1933 Bardonecchia, Winter World University
  Games
1949 Merano, International University Sports
  Week (FISU)
1956 Cortina d'Ampezzo, Olympic Winter
  Games
1957 Milan, World Games for the Deaf
1959 Turin, World University Games
1960 Rome, Paralympic Games
1960 Rome, Olympic Games
1963 Naples, Mediterranean Games
1966 Sestriere, Winter World University Games
1970 Turin, World University Games
1970 Udine, International School Children's
  Games
1975 Livigno, Winter World University Games
1975 Rome, World University Games
1980 Turin, ISF Gymnasiade
1982 Auronzo, Alps-Adriatic Winter Youth
  Games
1983 Madonna di Campoglio, Winter World
  Games for the Deaf
1984 Abano Terme, World Medical Games
1984 Florence, ISF Gymnasiade
1985 Belluno, Winter World University Games
1986 Montecatini Terme, World Medical
  Games
1987 Piancavallo, Alps-Adriatic Winter Youth
  Games
1988 Trento, Alps-Adriatic Summer Youth
  Games
1992 Milan, FISEC Games
1992 Osturi, World Medical Games
1993 Aosta, Winter European Youth Olympic
  Days
1993 Bormio, Alps-Adriatic Winter Youth Games
1995 Rome, Military World Games
1997 Bari, Mediterranean Games
1997 Sicily, World University Games
1998 Rome, World Equestrian Games
1998 Venice, Alps-Adriatic Summer Youth
  Games
2000 Friuli-Venezia Giulia, Alps-Adriatic Summer Youth Games
2000 Cervinia, SkyGames

Ivory Coast

1961 Abidjan, Community/Friendship Games
1961 Abidjan, West African Games
1977 Yamoussoukro, West African University Games
1996 Abidjan, Special Olympics West African Games
2000 Abidjan, African Francophone Games for the Handicapped

Jamaica

1962 Kingston, Central American and Caribbean Games
1966 Kingston, Commonwealth Games
1966 Kingston, British Commonwealth Paraplegic Games
1971 Kingston, Pan-American Wheelchair Games
1988 Kingston, CARIFTA Games
1990 Kingston, CARIFTA Games
1996 Kingston, CARIFTA Games

Japan

1917 Tokyo, Far East Championships
1923 Osaka, Far East Championships
1930 Tokyo, Far East Championships
1958 Tokyo, Asian Games
1964 Tokyo, Olympic Games
1964 Tokyo, Paralympic Games
1967 Tokyo, World University Games
1972 Sapporo, Olympic Winter Games
1975 Oita & Beppu, Far East and South Pacific Games for the Disabled
1985 Kobe, World University Games
1986 Sapporo, Asian Winter Games
1986 Kyoto, Asia Pacific Games for the Deaf
1989 Kobe, Far East and South Pacific Games for the Disabled
1990 Sapporo, Asian Winter Games
1991 Sapporo, Winter World University Games
1994 Hiroshima, Asian Games
1995 Fukuoka, World University Games
1998 Nagano, Winter Paralympic Games
1998 Nagano, Olympic Winter Games

Jersey

1997 St. Helier, Island Games
1999 St. Helier, Islands Corporate Games

Jordan

1999 Amman, Arab Games for the Handicapped
1999 Amman, Arab Games

Kazakhstan

1997 Alma-Ata, Central Asian Games

Kenya

1978 Nairobi, All-Africa University Games
1987 Nairobi, African Games
1999 Njoro, East African University Games

Kyrgyzstan

1999 Bishkek, Central Asian Games

Latvia

1924 Riga, SELL Games (Summer)
1929 Riga, SELL Games (Winter)
1931 Riga, SELL Games (Summer)
1935 Riga, Sigulda, SELL Games (Winter)
1935 Riga, SELL Games (Summer)
2000 Jelgava, SELL Games (Summer)

Lebanon

1957 Beirut, Arab Games
1959 Beirut, Mediterranean Games
1973 Beirut, Arab School Games
1997 Beirut, Arab Games

Liechtenstein

1999 Vaduz, Games of the Small Countries of Europe

Lithuania

1929 Kaunas, SELL Games (Summer)
1933 Kaunas, SELL Games (Summer)
1937 Kaunas, SELL Games (Summer)
1938 Zarasai, SELL Games (Winter)
1997 Vilnius, Baltic Sea Games
1999 Kaunas, SELL Games (Summer)

Luxembourg

1951 Luxembourg, International University Sports Week (FISU)
1995 Luxembourg, Games of the Small Countries of Europe

Madagascar

1960 Antananarivo, Community/Friendship Games
1990 Antananarivo, Indian Ocean Island Games
1997 Antananarivo, Francophone Games

Malawi

1996 Zomba, CUCSA Games

Malaysia

1965 Kuala Lumpur, South East Asian Games
1971 Kuala Lumpur, South East Asian Games
1977 Kuala Lumpur, South East Asian Games
1989 Kuala Lumpur, South East Asian Games
1993 Kuala Lumpur, World Corporate Games
1996 Kuala Lumpur, Asia Pacific Games for the Deaf
1998 Kuala Lumpur, Commonwealth Games

Malta

1993 Valletta, Games of the Small Countries of Europe
1997 Valletta, FISEC Games

Martinique

1993 Forn-de-France, CARIFTA Games
1999 CARIFTA Games

Mauritius
1985 Port Louis, Indian Ocean Island Games

Mexico
1926 Mexico City, Central American and Caribbean Games
1954 Mexico City, Central American and Caribbean Games
1955 Mexico City, Pan-American Games
1968 Mexico City, Olympic Games
1975 Mexico City, Central American and Caribbean University Games
1975 Mexico City, Pan-American Games
1975 Mexico City, Pan-American Wheelchair Games
1979 Mexico City, World University Games
1979 Mexico City, Pan-American Maccabi Games
1990 Mexico City, Central American and Caribbean Games
1997 Guadalajara, Central American and Caribbean University Games
1999 Mexico City, Pan-American Maccabi Games
1999 Mexico City, Pan-American Wheelchair Games
1999 Mexico City, Pan-American Games for the Blind

Monaco
1939 Monte Carlo, World University Games
1985 Monte Carlo, World Medical Games
1987 Monte Carlo, Games of the Small Countries of Europe
1996 Monte Carlo, Special Olympics Small Nations Games

Morocco
1961 Casablanca, Arab Games
1983 Casablanca, Mediterranean Games
1985 Casablanca, Arab Games
1987 Casablanca, World Medical Games
1989 Rabat, Casablanca, Francophone Games
1990 Fès/Ifrane/Meknes, World Peace Games
1998 Casablanca, Arab School Games

Mozambique
2000 Maputo, CUCSA Games

Nepal
1984 Kathmandu, South Asian Federation Games
1999 Kathmandu, South Asian Federation Games

Netherlands
1928 Amsterdam, Olympic Games
1928 Amsterdam, World Games for the Deaf
1968 Utrecht, Dutch Commonwealth Games
1971 Utrecht, Dutch Commonwealth Games
1974 Zandvoort, Dutch Commonwealth Games
1980 Arnhem, Paralympic Games
1984 Amsterdam, World Transplant Games

1986 Gorsel, European Heart/Lung Transplant Games
1991 Maastricht, FISEC Games
1992 The Hague, Euro Games
1992 Enschede, European Heart/Lung Transplant Games
1993 Valkenswaard, European Youth Olympic Days
1993 The Hague, Euro Games
1993 The Hague, World Games
1994 The Hague, World Equestrian Games
1995 Amsterdam, European Maccabi Games
1998 The Hague, World Corporate Games
1998 Amsterdam, Gay Games
2000 Groningen, European Special Olympics

Netherlands Antilles
1999 St. Maarten, Dutch Commonwealth Games

New Caledonia
1966 Nouméa, South Pacific Games
1987 Nouméa, South Pacific Games

New Zealand
1950 Auckland, Commonwealth Games
1950 Christchurch, Canterbury Centennial Games
1974 Christchurch, British Commonwealth Paraplegic Games
1974 Christchurch, Commonwealth Games
1975 Christchurch, New Zealand Games
1989 Christchurch, World Games for the Deaf
1990 Auckland, Firefighters World Games
1990 Auckland, Commonwealth Games
1999 Christchurch, World Wheelchair Games

Nigeria
1960 Lagos, West African Games
1965 Ibadan, West African University Games
1971 Lagos, West African University Games
1973 Lagos, African Games
1975 Ife, West African University Games
1977 Lagos, West African Games
1995 Benin City, West African University Games

Northern Ireland
1995 Jordanstown, Ireland's Scholar Athlete Games
1996 Jordanstown, Ireland's Scholar Athlete Games
1997 Belfast, UK & Ireland Corporate Games
1998 Jordanstown, Irelands' Scholar Athlete Games
2000 Jordanstown, Irelands' Scholar Athlete Games

Northern Marianas
1969 Saipan, Micronesian Games
1990 Saipan, Micronesian Games

Norway
1903 Kristiania (Oslo), Nordic Games
1928 Oslo, Red Sport International Winter Spartakiade

1939 Lillehammer, Winter World University Games
1952 Oslo, Olympic Winter Games
1953 Oslo, Winter World Games for the Deaf
1980 Geilo, Winter Paralympic Games
1987 Oslo, Winter World Games for the Deaf
1994 Lillehammer, Olympic Winter Games
1994 Lillehammer, Winter Paralympic Games
2000 Sandefjord, European Heart/Lung Transplant Games

Pakistan

1989 Islamabad, South Asian Federation Games
1996 Islamabad, Muslim Women's Games

Palau

1998 Koror, Micronesian Games

Panama

1938 Panama City, Central American and Caribbean Games
1970 Panama City, Central American and Caribbean Games
1973 Panama City, Bolivarian Games

Papua New Guinea

1969 Port Moresby, South Pacific Games
1991 Port Moresby/Lae, South Pacific Games

Peru

1946 Lima, Bolivarian Games
1973 Lima, Pan-American Wheelchair Games
1976 Lima, Pan-American Maccabi Games
1990 Lima, South American Games
1997 Arequipa, Bolivarian Games

Philippines

1913 Manila, Far East Championships
1919 Manila, Far East Championships
1925 Manila, Far East Championships
1934 Manila, Far East Championships
1954 Manila, Asian Games
1981 Manila, South East Asian Games
1991 Manila, South East Asian Games

Poland

1924 Warsaw, World University Games
1933 Zakopane, Maccabiade Winter Games
1955 Warsaw, World Student Championships (UIE)
1956 Zakopane, World Student Championships Winter (UIE)
1961 SCFA Winter Spartakiade
1971 Zakopane, SCFA Winter Spartakiade
1979 Novi-Targ, SCFA Winter Spartakiade
1985 Warsaw, SCFA Summer Spartakiade
1993 Zakopane, Winter World University Games

Portugal

1996 Lisbon, World Medical Games
1997 Lisbon, European Youth Olympic Days
1999 Lisbon, FISEC Games

Puerto Rico

1966 San Juan, Central American and Caribbean Games
1972 San Juan, Central American and Caribbean University Games
1979 San Juan, Pan-American Games
1986 San Juan, Pan-American Wheelchair Games
1993 Ponce, San Juan, Central American and Caribbean Games
2000 San Germán, Central American and Caribbean University Games

Qatar

1998 Doha, Special Olympics Gulf Games

Réunion

1979 St. Denis, Indian Ocean Island Games
1998 St. Denis, Indian Ocean Island Games

Romania

1951 Poiana, World Student Championships Winter (UIE)
1977 Bucharest, World Games for the Deaf
1981 Bucharest, World University Games
1987 Bucharest, SCFA Winter Spartakiade
1999 Medias, International School Children's Games

Russia

1994 St. Petersburg, Goodwill Games
1998 Moscow, World Youth Games

Samoa

2000 Apia, Southern Cross Games

San Marino

1985 San Marino, Games of the Small Countries of Europe

Scotland

1970 Edinburgh, Commonwealth Games
1970 Edinburgh, British Commonwealth Paraplegic Games
1986 Edinburgh, Commonwealth Games
1990 Strathclyde/Glasgow, European Special Olympics
1996 Aberdeen, UK & Ireland Corporate Games
1999 Glasgow, European Maccabi Games
2000 Edinburgh, Commonwealth Youth Games
2000 Aberdeen, World Corporate Games

Senegal

1963 Dakar, Community/Friendship Games
1998 Dakar, African Francophone Games for the Handicapped

Seychelles

1993 Victoria, Indian Ocean Island Games

Sierra Leone

1969 Freetown, West African University Games

Singapore

1973 Singapore, South East Asian Games
1983 Singapore, South East Asian Games
1989 Singapore, World Transplant Games
1993 Singapore, South East Asian Games

Slovakia

1991 Bratislava, International School Children's
Games
1994 Ravne na Koroskem, Winter International
School Children's Games
1999 Poprad, Winter World University Games
1999 Poprad-Tatry, Winter European Youth
Olympic Days

Slovenia

1994 Slovenj Gradec, International School Children's Games
1995 Prakovce-Helcmanovc, Winter International School Children's Games
1995 Celje, International School Children's
Games
1999 Maribor, Winter International School Children's Games
1999 Velenje, International School Children's
Games

Solomon Islands

1981 Honiara, South Pacific Mini Games

South Africa

1994 Johannesburg, World Corporate Games
1997 Pretoria, World Ex-Service Wheelchair and
Amputee Games
1998 Durban, Firefighters World Games
1998 Johannesburg, CUCSA Games
1999 Johannesburg, African Games

South Korea

1986 Seoul, Asian Games
1988 Seoul, Paralympic Games
1988 Seoul, Olympic Games
1992 Seoul, Asia Pacific Games for the Deaf
1997 Pusan, East Asian Games
1997 Chonju-Moju, Winter World University
Games
1999 Kangwon, Asian Winter Games

Soviet Union

1928 Moscow, Red Sport International Winter
Spartakiade
1928 Moscow, Red Sport International Spartakiade
1931 Moscow, Red Sport International Spartakiade
1957 Moscow, World Student Championships
(UIE) (IUS)
1969 Kiev, SCFA Summer Spartakiade
1973 Moscow, World University Games
1975 Leningrad, SCFA Winter Spartakiade
1980 Moscow, Olympic Games
1985 Minsk, SCFA Winter Spartakiade
1986 Moscow, Goodwill Games

Soviet Union, Cuba, Poland

1984 Moscow, Havana, Prague, Warsaw, Friendship Games 84

Spain

1955 San Sebastián, International University
Sports Week (FISU)
1955 Barcelona, Mediterranean Games
1981 Jaca, Winter World University Games
1985 Granollers, International School Children's
Games
1988 Barcelona, ISF Gymnasiade
1989 Burgos, FISEC Games
1992 Barcelona, Olympic Games
1992 Barcelona, European Special Olympics
1992 Barcelona, Paralympic Games
1994 Granollers, European Special Olympics
1995 Jaca, Winter World University Games
1998 Madrid, IBSA World Championships for
the Blind
1998 Logroño, International School Children's
Games
1998 Gran Canaria, FISEC Games
1999 Palma de Mallorca, World University Games

Sri Lanka

1991 Colombo, South Asian Federation Games

Suriname

1966 Parimaribo, Dutch Commonwealth Games
1969 Parimaribo, Dutch Commonwealth Games
1973 Parimaribo, Dutch Commonwealth Games
1975 Parimaribo, Dutch Commonwealth Games

Sweden

1901 Stockholm, Nordic Games
1905 Stockholm, Nordic Games
1909 Stockholm, Nordic Games
1912 Stockholm, Olympic Games
1913 Stockholm, Nordic Games
1914 Malmö, Baltic Games
1917 Stockholm, Nordic Games
1922 Stockholm, Nordic Games
1926 Stockholm, Nordic Games
1926 Götenburg, International Women's Games
1939 Stockholm, World Games for the Deaf
1963 Are, Winter World Games for the Deaf
1973 Malmö, World Games for the Deaf
1976 Ornsköldsvik, Winter Paralympic Games
1990 Stockholm, World Equestrian Games
1995 Sollefteå, Winter Games for the Disabled
1996 Stockholm, Stockholm Summer Games
1997 Stockholm, Stockholm Summer Games
1997 Sollefteå, Winter Games for the Disabled
1997 Sundsvall, Winter European Youth Olympic Days
1998 Stockholm, Stockholm Summer Games
1999 Sollefteå, Winter Games for the Disabled

1999 Stockholm, World Police and Fire Games
1999 Stockholm, Stockholm Summer Games
2000 Stockholm, Stockholm Summer Games

Switzerland

1928 St. Moritz, Olympic Winter Games
1930 Davos, Winter World University Games
1935 St. Moritz, Winter World University Games
1947 Davos, Winter World University Games
1948 St. Moritz, Olympic Winter Games
1953 St. Moritz, University Sports Week Winter (FISU)
1959 Montana-Vermala, Winter World Games for the Deaf
1962 Villars, Winter World University Games
1971 Adelboden, Winter World Games for the Deaf
1976 Geneva, International School Children's Games
1980 Lausanne, International School Children's Games
1984 Geneva, International School Children's Games
1986 Lausanne, International School Children's Games
1992 Geneva, International School Children's Games
1995 Geneva, World Corporate Games
1995 Biasca/Ticino, Alps-Adriatic Winter Youth Games
1996 Lausanne, European Heart/Lung Transplant Games
1999 Davos, Winter World Games for the Deaf
2000 Zurich, Euro Games

Switzerland/France

1987 Neuchâtel/Marignane, World Peace Games

Syria

1976 Damascus, Arab Games
1987 Latakia, Mediterranean Games
1992 Damascus, Arab Games

Tahiti

1971 Papeete, South Pacific Games
1995 Papeete, South Pacific Games

Taiwan

1983 Taipei, Asia Pacific Games for the Deaf
2000 Taipei, Asia Pacific Games for the Deaf

Thailand

1959 Bangkok, South East Asian Games
1966 Bangkok, Asian Games
1967 Bangkok, South East Asian Games
1970 Bangkok, Asian Games
1975 Bangkok, South East Asian Games
1978 Bangkok, Asian Games
1985 Bangkok, South East Asian Games
1995 Chiang Mai, South East Asian Games
1998 Bangkok, Asian Games

1999 Bangkok, Far East and South Pacific Games for the Disabled

Tonga

1989 Nukualofa, South Pacific Mini Games

Trinidad

1987 Port of Spain, CARIFTA Games
1991 Port of Spain, CARIFTA Games
1998 Port of Spain, CARIFTA Games

Tunisia

1967 Tunis, Mediterranean Games

Turkey

1971 Izmir, Mediterranean Games
1978 Izmir, ISF Gymnasiade
1995 Ataturk Dam, Ataturk Dam International Sports Festival
1996 Ankara, World Air Games
1996 Ataturk Dam, Ataturk Dam International Sports Festival
1997 Ataturk Dam, Ataturk Dam International Sports Festival
1997 Ankara, World Air Games
1998 Ataturk Dam, Ataturk Dam International Sports Festival
1999 Ataturk Dam, Ataturk Dam International Sports Festival
2000 Ataturk Dam, Ataturk Dam International Sports Festival

Uganda

1970 Kampala, East African University Games

Ukraine

1990 Uzhgorod, International School Children's Games

United Arab Emirates

1996 Abu Dhabi, Special Olympics Gulf Games
1998 Dubai, International Law Enforcement Games
1998 Dubai, World Peace Games

Uruguay

1991 Montevideo, Pan-American Maccabi Games
1999 Punte del Este, Pan-American Medical Games
1999 Montevideo, World Corporate Games

USA

1904 St. Louis, Olympic Games
1932 Lake Placid, Olympic Winter Games
1932 Los Angeles, Olympic Games
1932 Chicago, Counter Olympics
1937 Dallas, Pan-American Exposition
1959 Chicago, Pan-American Games
1960 Squaw Valley, Olympic Winter Games
1965 Washington DC, World Games for the Deaf
1968 Chicago, Special Olympics Summer World Games

1970 Chicago, Special Olympics Summer World Games

1972 Lake Placid, Winter World University Games

1972 Los Angeles, Special Olympics Summer World Games

1974 San Francisco, International Law Enforcement Games

1974 Anchorage, Arctic Winter Games

1975 Lake Placid, Winter World Games for the Deaf

1975 Mt. Pleasant, Special Olympics Summer World Games

1976 Jacksonville, International Law Enforcement Games

1977 Spokane, Can-Am Police-Fire Games

1977 Steamboat Springs, Special Olympics Winter World Games

1978 San Diego, International Law Enforcement Games

1978 Seattle, Can-Am Police-Fire Games

1979 Brockport, Special Olympics Summer World Games

1979 Ellensburg, Can-Am Police-Fire Games

1980 Lake Placid, Olympic Winter Games

1980 Nassau NY, International Law Enforcement Games

1980 Spokane, Can-Am Police-Fire Games

1980 New York, World Transplant Games

1981 Smugglers Cove, Special Olympics Winter World Games

1981 Bellevue, Can-Am Police-Fire Games

1981 Santa Clara, World Games

1982 San Francisco, Gay Games

1982 Memphis, JCC Maccabi Games

1982 Fairbanks, Arctic Winter Games

1982 Austin, International Law Enforcement Games

1983 Baton Rouge, Special Olympics Summer World Games

1984 Seattle, Can-Am Police-Fire Games

1984 Los Angeles, Olympic Games

1984 New York, Paralympic Games

1984 Phoenix, International Law Enforcement Games

1984 Detroit, JCC Maccabi Games

1985 Columbus OH, JCC Maccabi Games

1985 San Jose, World Police and Fire Games

1985 Los Angeles, World Games for the Deaf

1985 Park City, Special Olympics Winter World Games

1986 Columbus, International Law Enforcement Games

1986 San Francisco, Gay Games

1986 South Lake Tahoe, International Police Winter Games

1986 Ellensburg, Can-Am Police-Fire Games

1987 San Diego, World Police and Fire Games

1987 Miami, JCC Maccabi Games

1987 Salem, Can-Am Police-Fire Games

1987 Indianapolis, Pan-American Games

1987 South Lake Tahoe, International Police Winter Games

1987 Bellingham, Peace Arch Games

1987 North Lake Tahoe, International Firefighters Winter Games

1987 St. George, Huntsman World Senior Games

1987 South Bend, Special Olympics Summer World Games

1988 Moscow-Pullman, Can-Am Police-Fire Games

1988 South Lake Tahoe, International Police Winter Games

1988 Chicago, JCC Maccabi Games

1988 St. George, Huntsman World Senior Games

1988 North Lake Tahoe, International Firefighters Winter Games

1988 Fairbanks, Arctic Winter Games

1988 Bellingham, Peace Arch Games

1988 San Francisco, World Corporate Games

1989 South Lake Tahoe, International Police Winter Games

1989 Bellingham, Peace Arch Games

1989 North Lake Tahoe, International Firefighters Winter Games

1989, Mt. Bachelor, Can-Am Police-Fire Fighters Games

1989 St. George, Huntsman World Senior Games

1989 Concord, World Corporate Games

1989 Reno, Special Olympics Winter World Games

1989 Pittsburgh, JCC Maccabi Games

1990 Bellingham, Peace Arch Games

1990 Oahu, World Corporate Games

1990 Seattle, Goodwill Games

1990 North Lake Tahoe, International Firefighters Winter Games

1990 Boise, Can-Am Police-Fire Games

1990 Detroit, JCC Maccabi Games

1990 St. George, Huntsman World Senior Games

1991 South Lake Tahoe, International Police Winter Games

1991 St. George, Huntsman World Senior Games

1991 Steamboat Springs, Winter World Corporate Games

1991 Cleveland, JCC Maccabi Games

1991 Bellingham, Peace Arch Games

1991 Minneapolis, Special Olympics Summer World Games

1991 Tri-Cities (Kennewick), Can-Am Police-Fire Games

1991 North Lake Tahoe, International Firefighters Winter Games

1991 Omaha, JCC Maccabi Games

1991 Wayne, JCC Maccabi Games

1991 Memphis, World Police and Fire Games

1992 Baltimore, JCC Maccabi Games

1992 St. George, Huntsman World Senior Games

1992 North Lake Tahoe, International Firefighters Winter Games

1992 Washington DC, International Law Enforcement Games

1992 Walla Walla, Can-Am Police-Fire Games
1992 South Lake Tahoe, International Police Winter Games
1992 Las Vegas, Firefighters World Games
1992 Bellingham, Peace Arch Games
1993 Newport RI, World Scholar Athlete Games
1993 South Lake Tahoe, International Police Winter Games
1993 Buffalo, World University Games
1993 North Lake Tahoe, International Firefighters Winter Games
1993 Pittsburgh, JCC Maccabi Games
1993 Boston, JCC Maccabi Games
1993 Colorado Springs, World Police and Fire Games
1993 St. George, Huntsman World Senior Games
1993 Sarasota, JCC Maccabi Games
1993 St. Louis, JCC Maccabi Games
1993 Chicago, World Dwarf Games
1994 Portland, Can-Am Police-Fire Games
1994 New York, Gay Games
1994 North Lake Tahoe, International Firefighters Winter Games
1994 St. George, Huntsman World Senior Games
1994 Cleveland, JCC Maccabi Games
1994 South Lake Tahoe, International Police Winter Games
1994 Birmingham, International Law Enforcement Games
1995 Columbus OH, JCC Maccabi Games
1995 Houston, JCC Maccabi Games
1995 Orlando, JCC Maccabi Games
1995 Long Island, JCC Maccabi Games
1995 Newport RI, X Games
1995 North Lake Tahoe, International Firefighters Winter Games
1995 South Lake Tahoe, International Police Winter Games
1995 Los Angeles, JCC Maccabi Games
1995 Blaine, North American Indigenous Games
1995 New Haven, Special Olympics Summer World Games
1995 Bellingham, Can-Am Police-Fire Games
1995 St. George, Huntsman World Senior Games
1996 Wayne NJ, JCC Maccabi Games
1996 Newport RI, X Games
1996 Atlanta, Olympic Games
1996 Chugiak-Eagle River, Arctic Winter Games
1996 Atlanta, Paralympic Games
1996 St. George, Huntsman World Senior Games
1996 St. Louis, JCC Maccabi Games
1996 Hood River, Gorge Games
1996 Tri-Cities (Kennewick), Can-Am Police-Fire Games
1996 North Lake Tahoe, International Firefighters Winter Games
1996 Salt Lake City, International Law Enforcement Games
1996 South Lake Tahoe, International Police Winter Games

1997 Milwaukee, JCC Maccabi Games
1997 Newport, RI, World Scholar Athlete Games
1997 North Lake Tahoe, International Police Winter Games
1997 St. George, Huntsman World Senior Games
1997 Big Bear Lake, Winter X Games
1997 San Diego, X Games
1997 Pittsburgh, JCC Maccabi Games
1997 South Lake Tahoe, International Firefighters Winter Games
1997 Kansas City, JCC Maccabi Games
1997 Hartford, JCC Maccabi Games
1997 Seattle, JCC Maccabi Games
1997 Hood River, Gorge Games
1997 Sarasota, JCC Maccabi Games
1998 Detroit, JCC Maccabi Games
1998 Lewiston ME, Renaissance Games
1998 Crested Butte, Winter X Games
1998 St. George, Huntsman World Senior Games
1998 Portland, World Masters Games
1998 South Lake Tahoe, International Firefighters Winter Games
1998 Charlotte, JCC Maccabi Games
1998 New York, Goodwill Games
1998 Hood River, Gorge Games
1998 San Diego, X Games
1999 St. George, Huntsman World Senior Games
1999 Salt Lake City, Winter World Transplant Games
1999 Fargo, North American Indigenous Games
1999 Crested Butte, Winter X Games
1999 San Francisco, X Games
1999 Providence, Gravity Games
1999 Rochester NY, JCC Maccabi Games
1999 Cherry Hill NJ, JCC Maccabi Games
1999 Houston, JCC Maccabi Games
1999 Columbus, JCC Maccabi Games
1999 North Lake Tahoe, International Firefighters Winter Games
1999 Raleigh-Durham, Special Olympics Summer World Games
2000 Mammoth, Winter Gravity Games
2000 Lake Placid, Great Outdoor Games
2000 Providence, Gravity Games
2000 Mount Snow, Winter X Games
2000 St. George, Huntsman World Senior Games
2000 San Francisco, X Games
2000 Tucson, JCC Maccabi Games
2000 Cocoa Beach, International Law Enforcement Games
2000 Lake Tahoe, International Police Winter Games
2000 North Lake Tahoe, International Firefighters Winter Games
2000 Hood River, Gorge Games
2000 Boca Raton, JCC Maccabi Games
2000 Milwaukee, Can-Am Police-Fire Games
2000 Lake Placid, Winter Goodwill Games
2000 Staten Island, JCC Maccabi Games
2000 Cincinnati, JCC Maccabi Games
2000 Richmond, JCC Maccabi Games

Uzbekistan

1995 Tashkent, Central Asian Games

Vanuatu

1993 Port Vila, South Pacific Mini Games

Venezuela

1951 Caracas, Bolivarian Games
1959 Caracas, Central American and Caribbean Games
1970 Maracaibo, Bolivarian Games
1975 Maracaibo, Pan-American Games for the Deaf
1981 Barquisimeto, Bolivarian Games
1982 Barquisimeto, Central American and Caribbean University Games
1983 Caracas, Pan-American Games
1987 Caracas, Pan-American Maccabi Games
1989 Maracaibo, Bolivarian Games
1990 Caracas, Pan-American Wheelchair Games
1994 Valencia, South American Games
1998 Maracaibo, Central American and Caribbean Games

Wales

1958 Cardiff, Commonwealth Games

West Germany

1953 Dortmund, World University Games
1955 Oberammergau, Winter World Games for the Deaf
1957 Oberammergau, University Sports Week Winter (FISU)
1967 Berchtesgaden, Winter World Games for the Deaf
1972 Munich, Olympic Games
1972 Heidelberg, Paralympic Games
1974 Wiesbaden, ISF Gymnasiade
1974 Darmstadt, International School Children's Games
1981 Cologne, World Games for the Deaf
1982 Darmstadt, International School Children's Games
1989 Duisburg, World University Games
1989 Karlsruhe, World Games

Western Samoa

1983 Apia, South Pacific Games

Yugoslavia

1955 Mt. Jahorina, University Sports Week Winter (FISU)
1968 Celje, International School Children's Games
1969 Belgrade, World Games for the Deaf
1974 Murska Sobota, International School Children's Games
1976 Murska Sobota, International School Children's Games
1978 Ravne na Koroskem, International School Children's Games
1979 Split, Mediterranean Games
1983 Murska Sobota, International School Children's Games
1984 Sarajevo, Olympic Winter Games
1986 Pula, Alps-Adriatic Summer Youth Games
1987 Zagreb, World University Games
1989 Kranjska Gora, Alps-Adriatic Winter Youth Games

Zambia

1982 Lusaka, East African Military Games
1999 Lusaka, CUCSA Games

Zimbabwe

1995 Harare, African Games
1997 Harare, CUCSA Games

Appendix 3.
Games by Host City

Aalborg, Denmark
1975 Aalborg Youth Games
1979 Aalborg Youth Games
1983 Aalborg Youth Games
1987 Aalborg Youth Games
1991 Aalborg Youth Games
1995 Aalborg Youth Games
1996 Centennial Youth Games, Aug. 4–11
1999 Aalborg Youth Games, July 26–30

Abano Terme, Italy
1984 World Medical Games, June 24–30

Aberdeen, Scotland
1996 UK & Ireland Corporate Games, June 14–16
2000 World Corporate Games, July 13–16

Abidjan, Ivory Coast
1961 West African Games, Dec. 24–31
1961 Community/Friendship Games, Dec. 24–30
1996 Special Olympics West African Games
2000 African Francophone Games for the Handicapped

Abu Dhabi, United Arab Emirates
1996 Special Olympics Gulf Games, Nov. 1–10

Accra, Ghana
1974 All-Africa University Games

Adelaide, Australia
1989 Australian Masters Games
1999 Australian Masters Games, Sept. 25–Oct. 3

Adelboden, Switzerland
1971 Winter World Games for the Deaf, Jan. 25–29

Agana, Guam
1994 Micronesian Games, March 26–April 2
1999 South Pacific Games, May 29–June 12

Albertville, France
1992 Winter Paralympic Games, March 25–April 1
1992 Olympic Winter Games, Feb. 8–23

Alexandria, Egypt
1951 Mediterranean Games, Oct. 5–20
1953 Arab Games, July 26–Aug. 10

Algiers, Algeria
1975 Mediterranean Games, Aug. 23–Sept. 6
1978 African Games, July 13–28

Alice Springs, Australia
1986 Honda Masters Games
1988 Honda Masters Games
1990 Honda Masters Games
1992 Honda Masters Games, Oct. 17–25
1994 Honda Masters Games
1996 Honda Masters Games, Oct. 19–27
1998 Honda Masters Games, Oct. 17–24
2000 Honda Masters Games, Oct. 21–28

Alma-Ata, Kazakhstan
1997 Central Asian Games, Sept. 13–20

Amman, Jordan
1999 Arab Games for the Handicapped, Sept. 9–20
1999 Arab Games, Aug. 12–31

Amsterdam, Netherlands
1928 World Games for the Deaf, Aug. 18–26
1928 Olympic Games, May 17–Aug. 12
1984 World Transplant Games
1995 European Maccabi Games, July 7–14
1998 Gay Games, Aug. 1–8

Anchorage, USA
1974 Arctic Winter Games, March 3–9

Andorra, Andorra
1989 International School Children's Games, June 2–4
1991 Games of the Small Countries of Europe, May 21–25
1995 Winter European Youth Olympic Days, Feb. 5–10

Ankara, Turkey
1996 World Air Games, Aug. 28–Sept. 22
1997 World Air Games, Sept. 3–21

Antananarivo, Madagascar
1960 Community/Friendship Games, April 13–19
1990 Indian Ocean Island Games, Aug. 24–Sept. 2
1997 Francophone Games, Aug. 27–Sept. 6

Antwerp, Belgium
1920 Olympic Games, April 20–Sept. 12
1937 Socialist Olympics, July 25–Aug. 1
1983 European Maccabi Games, July 8–15

Aosta, Italy
1993 Winter European Youth Olympic Days, Feb. 7–11

Apia, Western Samoa (Samoa)
1983 South Pacific Games, Sept. 5–16
2000 Southern Cross Games, May 22–26

Are, Sweden
1963 Winter World Games for the Deaf, March 11–16

Arequipa, Peru
1997 Bolivarian Games, Oct. 17–26

Arnhem, Netherlands
1980 Paralympic Games, June 21–July 5

Ataturk Dam, Turkey
1995 Ataturk Dam International Sports Festival, Oct. 6–7
1996 Ataturk Dam International Sports Festival, Oct. 4–5
1997 Ataturk Dam International Sports Festival, Oct. 3–4
1998 Ataturk Dam International Sports Festival, Oct. 9–10

1999 Ataturk Dam International Sports Festival, Sept. 24–25
2000 Ataturk Dam International Sports Festival, Sept. or Oct

Athens, Greece
1896 Olympic Games, April 6–15
1906 Olympic Games, April 22–May 2
1982 World Transplant Games
1991 Mediterranean Games, June 28–July 12
1996 European Special Olympics, May 19–25
1998 Special Olympics Mediterranean Games, April 6–10
1998 Journalists World Games

Atlanta, USA
1996 Paralympic Games, Aug. 15–25
1996 Olympic Games, July 19–Aug. 4

Auckland, New Zealand
1950 Commonwealth Games, Feb. 4–11
1990 Firefighters World Games, April 22–29
1990 Commonwealth Games, Jan. 24–Feb. 3

Auronzo, Italy
1982 Alps-Adriatic Winter Youth Games, March 28–30

Austin, USA
1982 International Law Enforcement Games

Aylesbury, England (*see also* Buckinghamshire)
1984 Paralympic Games
1993 World Ex-Service Wheelchair and Amputee Games, July 10–16

Bad Oeynhausen, Germany
1998 European Heart/Lung Transplant Games

Ballarat, Australia
2000 Australian Universities Games, Oct. 2–6

Baltimore, USA
1992 JCC Maccabi Games, Aug. 23–29

Bandar Seri Bagawan, Brunei
1999 South East Asian Games, Aug. 8–14

Banff, Canada
1991 Winter World Games for the Deaf, March 2–9

Bangkok, Thailand
1959 South East Asian Games, Dec. 12–17
1966 Asian Games, Dec. 9–20
1967 South East Asian Games, Dec. 9–16
1970 Asian Games, Dec. 9–20
1975 South East Asian Games, Dec. 9–16
1978 Asian Games, Dec. 9–20

1985 South East Asian Games, Dec. 8–17
1998 Asian Games, Dec. 6–20
1999 Far East and South Pacific Games for the Disabled, Jan. 10–16

Banská-Bystrica, Czechoslovakia
1935 Maccabiade Winter Games, Feb. 18–25

Barcelona, Spain
1955 Mediterranean Games, July 16–25
1988 ISF Gymnasiade, July 6–8
1992 Paralympic Games, Sept. 3–14
1992 Olympic Games, July 25–Aug. 10
1992 European Special Olympics, Sept. 9–13

Bardonecchia, Italy
1933 Winter World University Games, Jan. 29– Feb. 5

Bari, Italy
1997 Mediterranean Games, June 13–27

Barquisimeto, Venezuela
1981 Bolivarian Games, Dec. 4–14
1982 Central American and Caribbean University Games

Barranquilla, Colombia
1946 Central American and Caribbean Games, Dec. 8–28
1961 Bolivarian Games, Dec. 3–16

Basse-Terre, Guadeloupe
1986 CARIFTA Games, March 29–31

Bath, England
1995 European Youth Olympic Days, July 9– 14

Baton Rouge, USA
1983 Special Olympics Summer World Games, July 12–18

Beijing, China
1990 Asian Games, Sept. 21–Oct. 5
1994 Far East and South Pacific Games for the Disabled, Sept. 4–10

Beirut, Lebanon
1957 Arab Games, Oct. 13–27
1959 Mediterranean Games, Oct. 11–26
1973 Arab School Games
1997 Arab Games, July 13–27

Belfast, Northern Ireland
1997 UK & Ireland Corporate Games, June 13– 15

Belgrade, Yugoslavia
1969 World Games for the Deaf, Aug. 9–16

Bellegarde, France
1983 World Peace Games

Bellevue, USA
1981 Can-Am Police-Fire Games, June 22–28

Bellingham, USA
1987 Peace Arch Games, June 28–July 5
1988 Peace Arch Games, June 26–July 5
1989 Peace Arch Games, June 24–July 9
1990 Peace Arch Games, June 20–July 8
1991 Peace Arch Games, June 29–July 7
1992 Peace Arch Games, July
1995 Can-Am Police-Fire Games, June 25–29

Belluno, Italy
1985 Winter World University Games, Feb. 16– 24

Benin City, Nigeria
1995 West African University Games

Berchtesgaden, West Germany
1967 Winter World Games for the Deaf, Feb. 20– 25

Berlin, Germany (*also* East Germany)
1910 Academic Olympia, July 3
1936 Olympic Games, Aug. 1–16
1951 World Student Championships (UIE), Aug. 6–15
1996 Euro Games, May 16–19

Biasca/Ticino, Switzerland
1995 Alps-Adriatic Winter Youth Games, Jan. 24–27

Big Bear Lake, USA
1997 Winter X Games, Jan. 30–Feb. 2

Birmingham, USA
1994 International Law Enforcement Games

Bishkek, Kyrgyzstan
1999 Central Asian Games

Blackcomb/Whistler, Canada
1990 International Police Winter Games, March 4–8
1999 International Police Winter Games, March 7–12

Blaine, USA
1995 North American Indigenous Games, July 31–Aug. 5

Boca Raton, USA
2000 JCC Maccabi Games, Aug. 6–11

Bogota, Colombia
1938 Bolivarian Games, Aug. 6–21

Boise, USA
1990 Can-Am Police-Fire Games, June 18–25

Bormio, Italy
1993 Alps-Adriatic Winter Youth Games, Jan. 26–29

Borovec, Bulgaria
1981 SCFA Winter Spartakiade

Boston, USA
1993 JCC Maccabi Games, Aug. 22–26

Bracknell, England
1998 UK & Ireland Corporate Games, June 12–14

Bratislava, Slovakia
1991 International School Children's Games, May 31–June 2

Brazzaville, Republic of the Congo
1965 African Games, July 18–25
1987 Central African Games, April 18–30

Breslau, Germany
1911 Academic Olympia, Aug. 1–3

Bridgetown, Barbados
1985 CARIFTA Games, April 6–9
1989 CARIFTA Games, Aug. 19–22
1994 CARIFTA Games, April 2–4

Brisbane, Australia
1982 Commonwealth Games, Sept. 30–Oct. 9
1982 Pacific School Games
1991 Australian Masters Games, Oct. 8–20
1994 World Masters Games, Sept. 26–Oct. 8

Brockport, USA
1979 Special Olympics Summer World Games, Aug. 8–13

Brugge, Belgium
1990 ISF Gymnasiade, May 24–27

Brussels, Belgium
1953 World Games for the Deaf, Aug. 15–19
1981 European Special Olympics, May
1991 European Youth Olympic Days, July 12–21

Bucharest, Romania
1977 World Games for the Deaf, July 17–27
1981 World University Games, July 19–30
1987 SCFA Winter Spartakiade, Feb. 27–March 4

Buckinghamshire, England (*see also* Aylesbury
1948 Stoke Mandeville Wheelchair Games, July 28

1949 Stoke Mandeville Wheelchair Games, last week of July
1950 Stoke Mandeville Wheelchair Games, last week of July
1951 Stoke Mandeville Wheelchair Games, last week of July
1952 Stoke Mandeville Wheelchair Games, last week of July
1953 Stoke Mandeville Wheelchair Games, last week of July
1954 Stoke Mandeville Wheelchair Games, last week of July
1955 Stoke Mandeville Wheelchair Games, last week of July
1956 Stoke Mandeville Wheelchair Games, last week of July
1957 Stoke Mandeville Wheelchair Games, last week of July
1958 Stoke Mandeville Wheelchair Games, last week of July
1959 Stoke Mandeville Wheelchair Games, last week of July
1961 Stoke Mandeville Wheelchair Games, last week of July
1962 Stoke Mandeville Wheelchair Games, last week of July
1963 Stoke Mandeville Wheelchair Games, July 24–28
1965 Stoke Mandeville Wheelchair Games, July 27–30
1966 Stoke Mandeville Wheelchair Games, last week of July
1967 Stoke Mandeville Wheelchair Games, last week of July
1969 Stoke Mandeville Wheelchair Games, last week of July
1970 Stoke Mandeville Wheelchair Games, last week of July
1971 Stoke Mandeville Wheelchair Games, last week of July
1973 Stoke Mandeville Wheelchair Games, last week of July
1974 Stoke Mandeville Wheelchair Games, last week of July
1975 Stoke Mandeville Wheelchair Games, last week of July
1977 Stoke Mandeville Wheelchair Games, July 23–31
1978 Stoke Mandeville Wheelchair Games, July 22–30
1979 Stoke Mandeville Wheelchair Games, July 21–29
1981 Stoke Mandeville Wheelchair Games, July 25–Aug. 2
1982 Stoke Mandeville Wheelchair Games, July 24–Aug. 1
1983 Stoke Mandeville Wheelchair Games, July 23–31
1985 Stoke Mandeville Wheelchair Games, July 20–28

1986 Stoke Mandeville Wheelchair Games, July 19–27
1987 Stoke Mandeville Wheelchair Games, July 18–26
1989 Stoke Mandeville Wheelchair Games, July 22–30
1990 Stoke Mandeville Wheelchair Games, July 21–29
1991 Stoke Mandeville Wheelchair Games, July 20–28
1993 Stoke Mandeville Wheelchair Games, July 24–Aug. 1
1994 Stoke Mandeville Wheelchair Games, July 23–31
1995 Stoke Mandeville Wheelchair Games, July 22–30
1996 World Wheelchair Games
1997 World Wheelchair Games, July 27–Aug. 2
1998 World Wheelchair Games, Aug. 20–31

Budapest, Hungary

1935 World University Games, Aug. 10–18
1949 World Student Championships (UIE), Aug. 14–21
1954 World Student Championships (UIE), July 31–Aug. 8
1965 World University Games, Aug. 20–30
1981 SCFA Summer Spartakiade
1991 World Transplant Games, Aug. 27–31
1999 World Transplant Games, Sept. 4–11

Buenos Aires, Argentina

1951 Pan-American Games, Feb. 26–March 9
1964 Pan-American Maccabi Games, Oct. 25–Nov. 1
1969 Pan-American Wheelchair Games, May 25
1995 Pan-American Maccabi Games, Dec. 24–Jan. 4
1995 Pan-American Wheelchair Games, Sept. 17–30
1997 Pan-American Games for the Blind

Buffalo, USA

1993 World University Games, July 8–18

Bundoora, Australia

1997 Australian Universities Games, Sept. 28–Oct. 3

Burghausen, Germany

1994 Alps-Adriatic Summer Youth Games, June 21–24

Burgos, Spain

1989 FISEC Games

Cairo, Egypt

1965 Arab Games, Sept. 2–14
1991 African Games, Sept. 20–Oct. 1

Calcutta, India

1987 South Asian Federation Games, Nov. 20–27

Calgary, Canada

1985 Can-Am Police-Fire Games, June 24–30
1988 Olympic Winter Games, Feb. 13–28
1990 International Law Enforcement Games
1993 Can-Am Police-Fire Games, June 21–27
1997 World Police and Fire Games, June 27–July 4

Cali, Colombia

1971 Pan-American Games, July 30–Aug. 12
1995 Pacific Ocean Games, June 23–July 3

Canberra, Australia

1996 Australian Universities Games, Sept. 29–Oct. 4
1997 Australian Masters Games, Oct. 23–31

Cannes, France

1978 World Medical Games, June 12–17
1980 World Medical Games, June 8–14
1982 World Medical Games, June 13–19
2000 World Medical Games, July 1–8

Caracas, Venezuela

1951 Bolivarian Games, Dec. 5–21
1959 Central American and Caribbean Games, Jan. 6–18
1983 Pan-American Games, Aug. 15–29
1987 Pan-American Maccabi Games, July 19–26
1990 Pan-American Wheelchair Games, Sept. 1–Sept. 9

Cardiff, Wales

1958 Commonwealth Games, July 18–26

Carinthia, Austria

1991 Alps-Adriatic Winter Youth Games, Feb. 25–27

Casablanca, Morocco

1961 Arab Games, Aug. 24–Sept. 8
1983 Mediterranean Games, Sept. 3–17
1985 Arab Games, Aug. 2–16
1987 World Medical Games, July 5–11
1989 Francophone Games, July 8–22
1998 Arab School Games, Sept. 5–15

Celje, Yugoslavia (Slovenia)

1968 International School Children's Games, June 5
1995 International School Children's Games, June 11

Cervinia, Italy

2000 SkyGames, July 7–9

Chamonix, France

1924 Olympic Winter Games, Jan. 25–Feb. 4
1960 Winter World University Games, Feb. 28–Mar. 6

Charlotte, USA
1998 JCC Maccabi Games, Aug. 9–14

Cherry Hill NJ, USA
1999 JCC Maccabi Games, Aug. 15–20

Chiang Mai, Thailand
1995 South East Asian Games, Dec. 9–17

Chicago, USA
1932 Counter Olympics, July 28–Aug. 1
1959 Pan-American Games, Aug. 27–Sept. 7
1968 Special Olympics Summer World Games,
    July 19–20
1970 Special Olympics Summer World Games,
    Aug. 13–15
1988 JCC Maccabi Games, Aug. 18–25
1993 World Dwarf Games, July 1–6

Chonju-Moju, South Korea
1997 Winter World University Games, Jan. 24–
    Feb. 2

Christchurch, New Zealand
1950 Canterbury Centennial Games, Dec. 25–
    Jan. 5
1974 British Commonwealth Paraplegic Games
1974 Commonwealth Games, Jan. 24–Feb. 2
1975 New Zealand Games, Jan. 23–26
1989 World Games for the Deaf, Jan. 17–30
1999 World Wheelchair Games, Oct. 8–18

Chugiak–Eagle River, USA
1996 Arctic Winter Games, March 3–10

Cincinnati, USA
2000 JCC Maccabi Games, Aug. 13–18

Cleveland, USA
1991 JCC Maccabi Games, Aug
1994 JCC Maccabi Games, Aug. 14–19

Cochabamba, Bolivia
1993 Bolivarian Games, April 24–May 2

Cocoa Beach, USA
2000 International Law Enforcement Games,
    August 3–13

Cologne, West Germany
1981 World Games for the Deaf, July 24–Aug. 2

Colombo, Sri Lanka
1991 South Asian Federation Games, Nov. or
    Dec

Colorado Springs, USA
1993 World Police and Fire Games, July 31–
    Aug. 7

Columbus, USA
1985 JCC Maccabi Games, Aug
1986 International Law Enforcement Games
1995 JCC Maccabi Games, Aug. 13–17
1999 JCC Maccabi Games, Aug. 8–13

Concord, USA
1989 World Corporate Games

Copenhagen, Denmark
1949 World Games for the Deaf, Aug. 12–16
1959 European Maccabi Games, Aug. 16–19
1974 European Maccabi Games, Aug. 8–11
1987 European Maccabi Games, March 10–17
1997 World Games for the Deaf, July 13–23

Cortina d'Ampezzo, Italy
1928 Winter World University Games, Jan. 22–
    29
1956 Olympic Winter Games, Jan. 26–Feb. 5

Cotonou, Benin
1979 West African Games
1996 African Francophone Games for the Handi-
    capped
1999 West African University Games

Crested Butte, USA
1998 Winter X Games, Jan. 15–18
1999 Winter X Games, Jan. 14–17

Csky Krumlov, Czech Republic
1999 International School Children's Games,
    Sept. 24–26

Cuenca, Ecuador
1985 Bolivarian Games, Nov. 9–18
1998 South American Games, Oct. 21–31

Dakar, Senegal
1963 Community/Friendship Games, April 11–
    21
1998 African Francophone Games for the Handi-
    capped

Dallas, USA
1937 Pan-American Exposition, July 13–18

Damascus, Syria
1976 Arab Games, Oct. 6–21
1992 Arab Games, Sept. 4–18

Darmstadt, Germany (*also* West Germany)
1930 World University Games, Aug. 1–10
1974 International School Children's Games,
    Aug. 22–25
1982 International School Children's Games,
    June 11–13
1993 International School Children's Games, July
    17–18

Darwin, Australia

1991 Arafura Games, May 18–25
1992 Pacific School Games, April 3–13
1993 Arafura Games, April 24–May 1
1995 Australian Universities Games, Sept. 24–30
1995 Arafura Games, May 6–13
1997 Arafura Games, May 10–17
1999 Arafura Games, May 22–29

Davos, Switzerland

1930 Winter World University Games, Jan. 4–12
1947 Winter World University Games, Jan. 19–26
1999 Winter World Games for the Deaf, March 8–14

Delhi-Patalia, India

1934 Western Asiatic Games, Feb. 25–March

Detroit, USA

1984 JCC Maccabi Games, Aug
1990 JCC Maccabi Games, Aug. 19–26
1998 JCC Maccabi Games, Aug. 16–23

Dhaka, Bangladesh

1985 South Asian Federation Games, Dec. 20–26
1993 South Asian Federation Games, Dec. 20–27

Doha, Qatar

1998 Special Olympics Gulf Games, Nov. 21–26

Dortmund, West Germany

1953 World University Games, Aug. 9–16

Douglas, Isle of Man

1985 Island Games, July 18–24

Dresden, Germany

1911 Academic Olympia, July 8–10

Dubai, United Arab Emirates

1998 International Law Enforcement Games, Nov. 6–12
1998 World Peace Games, March 19–April 18

Dublin, Ireland

1924 Tailteann Games, Aug. 2–18
1928 Tailteann Games, Aug. 11–22
1932 Tailteann Games, June 29–July 10
1985 European Special Olympics, July 4–7

Duisburg, Germany

1989 World University Games, Aug. 22–30

Durban, South Africa

1998 Firefighters World Games, May 17–23

Echiroles, France

1985 World Peace Games

Edinburgh, Scotland

1970 Commonwealth Games, July 16–25
1970 British Commonwealth Paraplegic Games
1986 Commonwealth Games, July 24–Aug. 2
2000 Commonwealth Youth Games, Aug. 10–14

Edmonton, Canada

1978 Commonwealth Games, Aug. 3–12
1983 Can-Am Police-Fire Games, June 20–26
1983 World University Games, July 1–12
1990 North American Indigenous Games, July 1–7
1996 Firefighters World Games, July 28–Aug. 3

Ellensburg, USA

1979 Can-Am Police-Fire Games, June 18–24
1986 Can-Am Police-Fire Games, June 23–29

Esbjerg, Denmark

1999 European Youth Olympic Days, July 10–16

Enschede, Netherlands

1992 European Heart/Lung Transplant Games

Estrie, Canada

1999 Journalists World Games, Sept. 24–Oct. 3

Évian, France

1994 World Medical Games, June 29–July 2

Fairbanks, USA

1982 Arctic Winter Games, March 14–20
1988 Arctic Winter Games, March 13–19

Fès/Ifrane/Meknes, Morocco

1990 World Peace Games, July 17–22

Florence, Italy

1984 ISF Gymnasiade, June 7–9

Fort de France, Martinique

1993 CARIFTA Games, April 9–11

Foz de Iguazi, Brazil

1997 World Nature Games, Sept. 27–Oct. 5
2000 Pan-American Medical Games, Nov. 18–25

Frankfurt, Germany

1925 Socialist Olympics, July 22–25
1995 Euro Games, April 14–17

Freetown, Sierra Leone

1969 West African University Games

Friuli-Venezia Giulia, Italy

2000 Alps-Adriatic Summer Youth Games

Fukuoka, Japan

1995 World University Games, Aug. 23–Sept. 3

Garmisch-Partenkirchen, Germany

1936 Olympic Winter Games, Feb. 6–16

Gastein, Austria

1951 University Sports Week Winter (FISU), Jan. 22–28
1999 Winter World Corporate Games, March 26–28
2000 Winter World Corporate Games, Jan. 28–30

Geilo, Norway

1980 Winter Paralympic Games

Geneva, Switzerland

1976 International School Children's Games, June 11–13
1984 International School Children's Games, June 15–17
1992 International School Children's Games, June 18–21
1995 World Corporate Games, Sept. 2–9

Genk, Belgium

1987 FISEC Games

George Town, Cayman Islands

1995 CARIFTA Games, April 15–17

Gibraltar, Gibraltar

1995 Island Games, July 15–22

Glasgow, Scotland

1999 European Maccabi Games, July 25–30

Gold Coast, Australia

1998 Asia Pacific Masters Games, Oct. 31–Nov. 8
2000 Asia Pacific Masters Games, Oct. 25–Nov. 5

Gorsel, Netherlands

1986 European Heart/Lung Transplant Games

Götenburg, Sweden

1926 International Women's Games, Aug. 27–29

Gran Canaria, Spain

1998 FISEC Games, July 22–28

Granollers, Spain

1985 International School Children's Games, Sept. 7–9
1994 European Special Olympics

Graz, Austria

1972 International School Children's Games, June 30–July 1
1984 Alps-Adriatic Summer Youth Games
1987 International School Children's Games, June 23

Grenoble, France

1968 Olympic Winter Games, Feb. 6–18

Groningen, Netherlands

2000 European Special Olympics, May 26–June 4

Guadalajara, Mexico

1997 Central American and Caribbean University Games, July

Guatemala City, Guatemala

1921 Central American Games, Sept. 11–18
1950 Central American and Caribbean Games, Feb. 8–March 12
1973 Central American Games, Nov. 24–Dec. 1
1986 Central American Games, Jan. 4–
1990 Central American and Caribbean University Games

Halifax, Canada

1982 Pan-American Wheelchair Games, July 21

Hamilton, Bermuda

1996 International Senior Games, April

Hamilton, Canada

1930 Commonwealth Games, Aug. 16–23
1994 International School Children's Games, June 15–19
2000 International School Children's Games, July 1–8

Harare, Zimbabwe

1995 African Games, Sept. 13–23
1997 CUCSA Games

Harbin, China

1996 Asian Winter Games, Feb. 4–11

Hartford, USA

1997 JCC Maccabi Games, Aug. 17–22

Havana, Cuba

1930 Central American and Caribbean Games, March 15–April 5
1977 SCFA Summer Spartakiade, Sept.
1982 Central American and Caribbean Games, Aug. 7–18
1986 Central American and Caribbean University Games
1991 Pan-American Games, Aug. 2–18
1999 Pan-American Games for the Deaf, Aug. 16–26

Hay River/Pine Point, Canada

1978 Arctic Winter Games, March 19–25

Heidelberg, West Germany

1972 Paralympic Games, Aug. 2–10

Helsinki, Finland
1926 SELL Games (Summer)
1931 SELL Games (Winter)
1932 SELL Games (Summer)
1936 SELL Games (Summer)
1952 Olympic Games, July 19–Aug. 3
1961 World Games for the Deaf, Aug. 6–10
1962 World Student Championships (UIE), July 28–Aug. 6
1994 European Heart/Lung Transplant Games

Henning, Århus, Aalborg, Denmark
1989 World Masters Games

Heraklion, Greece
1991 World Medical Games, July 6–13

Hiroshima, Japan
1994 Asian Games, Oct. 2–16

Hobart, Australia
1987 Australian Masters Games, Nov. 28–Dec. 12
1998 Southern Cross Games, March 14–20

Hong Kong, Hong Kong
1984 Asia Pacific Games for the Deaf, Sept.

Honiara, Solomon Islands
1981 South Pacific Mini Games

Hood River, USA
1996 Gorge Games, July
1997 Gorge Games, July 11–19
1998 Gorge Games, July 11–18
2000 Gorge Games, July 8–15

Houston, USA
1995 JCC Maccabi Games, Aug. 13–17
1999 JCC Maccabi Games, Aug. 8–13

Ibadan, Nigeria
1965 West African University Games

Ife, Nigeria
1975 West African University Games

Indianapolis, USA
1987 Pan-American Games, Aug. 7–23

Innsbruck, Austria
1964 Olympic Winter Games, Jan. 29–Feb. 9
1968 Winter World University Games, Jan. 18–28
1976 Olympic Winter Games, Feb. 4–15
1984 Winter Paralympic Games, Jan. 11–20
1987 World Transplant Games, Sept. 17–20
1988 Winter Paralympic Games, Jan. 17–24
1998 International Police Winter Games, March 1–5

Islamabad, Pakistan
1989 South Asian Federation Games, Oct. 20–27
1996 Muslim Women's Games, Nov. 1–5

Izmir, Turkey
1971 Mediterranean Games, Oct. 6–17
1978 ISF Gymnasiade, July 22–23

Jaca, Spain
1981 Winter World University Games, Feb. 23–March 4
1995 Winter World University Games, Feb. 18–26

Jacksonville, USA
1976 International Law Enforcement Games

Jakarta, Indonesia
1962 Asian Games, Aug. 24–Sept. 4
1963 Games of the New Emerging Forces (GANEFO), Nov. 10–22
1979 South East Asian Games, Sept. 21–30
1987 South East Asian Games, Sept. 9–20
1997 South East Asian Games, Oct. 11–19

Jasna, Osrblie, Strbske Pleso, Czechoslovakia
1989 SCFA Winter Spartakiade

Jelgava, Latvia
2000 SELL Games (Summer)

Johannesbad, Czechoslovakia
1937 Socialist Worker Sports International Winter Worker Olympiad, Feb. 18–21

Johannesburg, South Africa
1994 World Corporate Games, Oct.
1998 CUCSA Games, July 20–25
1999 African Games, Sept. 10–19

Jordanstown, Northern Ireland
1995 Irelands' Scholar Athlete Games
1996 Irelands' Scholar Athlete Games, Aug. 10–17
1998 Irelands' Scholar Athlete Games, Aug. 14–22
2000 Irelands' Scholar Athlete Games, Aug. 4–14

Kampala, Uganda
1970 East African University Games, Dec. 7–12

Kangwon, South Korea
1999 Asian Winter Games, Jan. 30–Feb. 6

Kansas City, USA
1997 JCC Maccabi Games, Aug. 10–15

Karlsruhe, West Germany
1989 World Games, July 20–30

Kathmandu, Nepal
1984 South Asian Federation Games
1999 South Asian Federation Games, Sept. 25–
Oct. 4

Kaunas, Lithuania
1929 SELL Games (Summer)
1933 SELL Games (Summer)
1937 SELL Games (Summer)
1999 SELL Games (Summer), May 11–17

Kiev, Soviet Union
1969 SCFA Summer Spartakiade

Kingston, Jamaica
1962 Central American and Caribbean Games,
Aug. 14–26
1966 Commonwealth Games, Aug. 4–13
1966 British Commonwealth Paraplegic Games
1971 Pan-American Wheelchair Games, Sept. 12
1988 CARIFTA Games, April 7–9
1990 CARIFTA Games, March 19–21
1996 CARIFTA Games, April 6–8

Klagenfurt, Austria
1998 World Medical Games, June 27–July 4

Kobe, Japan
1985 World University Games, Aug. 24–Sept. 4
1989 Far East and South Pacific Games for the
Disabled, Sept. 15–20

Koror, Palau
1998 Micronesian Games, Aug. 1–9

Kranjska Gora, Yugoslavia
1989 Alps-Adriatic Winter Youth Games

Kristiania (Oslo), Norway
1903 Nordic Games, Jan. 31–Feb. 6

Kuala Lumpur, Malaysia
1965 South East Asian Games, Dec. 14–21
1971 South East Asian Games, Dec. 11–18
1977 South East Asian Games, Nov. 19–26
1989 South East Asian Games, Aug. 20–31
1993 World Corporate Games
1996 Asia Pacific Games for the Deaf, March
1998 Commonwealth Games, Sept. 11–21

Kumasi, Ghana
1973 West African University Games

Kyoto, Japan
1986 Asia Pacific Games for the Deaf, Aug.

La Paz, Bolivia
1977 Bolivarian Games, Oct. 15–29
1978 South American Games, Nov. 3–13

Lagos, Nigeria
1960 West African Games
1971 West African University Games
1973 African Games, Jan. 7–18
1977 West African Games, Aug. 20–28

Lahti, Finland
1997 World Games, Aug. 7–17

Lake Placid, USA (*see also* North Lake Tahoe, South Lake Tahoe)
1932 Olympic Winter Games, Feb. 4–15
1972 Winter World University Games, Feb. 26–
March 5
1975 Winter World Games for the Deaf, Feb. 11–
16
1980 Olympic Winter Games, Feb. 14–23
2000 Great Outdoor Games, July 20–23
2000 Winter Goodwill Games, Feb. 16–20

Lake Tahoe, USA
2000 International Police Winter Games, March

Languedoc-Rousillon, France
1993 Mediterranean Games, June 16–27

Las Lenas, Argentina
1990 Winter Pan-American Games, Sept. 18–
22

Las Vegas, USA
1992 Firefighters World Games, May 16–22

Latakia, Syria
1987 Mediterranean Games, Sept. 11–25

Lausanne, Switzerland
1980 International School Children's Games,
Sept. 26–29
1986 International School Children's Games,
June 5–8
1996 European Heart/Lung Transplant Games,
July 18–22

Le Touquet, France
1997 World Medical Games June 28–July 5

Legon, Ghana
1967 West African University Games

Leicester, England
1979 European Maccabi Games, Aug. 3–10

Leipzig, Germany (*also* East Germany)
1909 Academic Olympia, July 11
1913 Academic Olympia, Oct. 18–19
1958 SCFA Summer Spartakiade

Leningrad, Soviet Union (*see also* St. Petersburg)
1975 SCFA Winter Spartakiade, Feb. 21–March 3

Lewiston ME, USA
1998 Renaissance Games, April 17–19

Libreville, Gabon
1976 Central African Games, June 30–July 10

Liège, Belgium
2000 Journalists World Games

Lille, France
1982 ISF Gymnasiade, June 4–6
1991 World Corporate Games

Lillehammer, Norway
1939 Winter World University Games, Feb. 19–23
1994 Winter Paralympic Games, March 10–19
1994 Olympic Winter Games, Feb. 12–25

Lima, Peru
1946 Bolivarian Games, Dec. 26–Jan. 6
1973 Pan-American Wheelchair Games, Nov. 17
1976 Pan-American Maccabi Games, July 23–29
1990 South American Games, Dec. 1–10

Limerick, Ireland
1995 World Medical Games, June 24–July 1
1999 UK & Ireland Corporate Games
2000 Irelands' Scholar Athlete Games, Aug. 11–19

Linz, Austria
1990 Alps-Adriatic Summer Youth Games, June 26–29

Lisbon, Portugal
1996 World Medical Games, June 29–July 6
1997 European Youth Olympic Days, July 18–24
1999 FISEC Games, July 21–27

Liverpool, England
1990 FISEC Games

Livigno, Italy
1975 Winter World University Games, April 6–13

Logroño, Spain
1998 International School Children's Games, June 10–14

London, England
1908 Olympic Games, April 27–Oct. 31
1911 Festival of the Empire Sports Meeting, June 24–July 1
1934 Commonwealth Games, Aug. 4–11
1934 International Women's Games, Aug.
1935 World Games for the Deaf, Aug. 18–24
1948 Olympic Games, July 29–Aug. 14
1951 Britain's Festival of Sport, May 5–Sept. 8
1985 World Games, July 25–Aug. 4
1990 European Heart/Lung Transplant Games
1992 World Corporate Games

Long Island, USA
1995 JCC Maccabi Games, Aug. 20–24

Los Angeles, USA
1932 Olympic Games, July 30–Aug. 14
1972 Special Olympics Summer World Games, Aug. 13–18
1984 Olympic Games, July 28–Aug. 12
1985 World Games for the Deaf, July 10–20
1995 JCC Maccabi Games, Aug. 13–17

Luanda, Angola
1981 Central African Games, Aug. 20–Sept. 2

Lusaka, Zambia
1982 East African Military Games, Oct. 13–18
1999 CUCSA Games, June 13–20

Luxembourg, Luxembourg
1951 International University Sports Week (FISU), Aug. 19–26
1995 Games of the Small Countries of Europe, May 29–June 3

Lyon, France
1963 European Maccabi Games, June 1–3
1988 World Medical Games, June 19–25

Maastricht, Netherlands
1991 FISEC Games

Madonna di Campoglio, Italy
1983 Winter World Games for the Deaf, Jan. 16–22

Madras, India
1995 South Asian Federation Games, Dec. 18–26

Madrid, Spain
1998 IBSA World Championships for the Blind, July 17–26

Malmö, Sweden
1914 Baltic Games, June 7–Aug. 9
1973 World Games for the Deaf, July 21–28

Mammoth, USA
2000 Winter Gravity Games, Jan. 20–23

Manchester, England
1995 World Transplant Games, Aug. 14–20

Manila, Philippines
1913 Far East Championships, Feb. 3–7
1919 Far East Championships, May 12–16
1925 Far East Championships, May 17–22
1934 Far East Championships, May 16–20
1954 Asian Games, May 1–9
1981 South East Asian Games, Dec. 6–15
1991 South East Asian Games, Nov. 24–Dec. 5

Mantes-Yvelines, France
2000 Firefighters World Games, July 6–13

Maputo, Mozambique
2000 CUCSA Games, July 16–23

Mar del Plata, Argentina
1995 Pan-American Games, March 14–25
1998 Pan-American Medical Games, March 22–29

Maracaibo, Venezuela
1970 Bolivarian Games, Aug. 22–Sept. 6
1975 Pan-American Games for the Deaf, Nov. 15–22
1989 Bolivarian Games, Jan. 15–25
1998 Central American and Caribbean Games, Aug. 8–22

Maribor, Slovenia
1999 Winter International School Children's Games, Feb. 6–8

Mariehamn, Åland
1991 Island Games, June 23–29

Marseille, France
1991 European Maccabi Games, July 10–17

Medellín, Colombia
1978 Central American and Caribbean Games, July 7–22

Medias, Romania
1999 International School Children's Games, June 9–13

Melbourne, Australia
1956 Olympic Games, Nov. 22–Dec. 8
1984 Pacific School Games
1988 Asia Pacific Games for the Deaf, Feb.
1995 Australian Masters Games, Oct.
1995 World Police and Fire Games, Feb. 26–March 4
1997 Victorian Corporate Games
1998 Australasian Public Sector Games, April 15–19
1998 Australian Universities Games, Sept. 28–Oct. 3
1998 Victorian Corporate Games, Nov. 20–22
1999 Victorian Corporate Games
2000 Victorian Corporate Games, Nov. 24–26
2000 Australasian Public Sector Games, April 26–30

Memphis, USA
1982 JCC Maccabi Games, Aug
1991 World Police and Fire Games, June 22–30

Merano, Italy
1949 International University Sports Week (FISU), Aug. 28–Sept. 4

Meribel, France
1979 Winter World Games for the Deaf, Jan. 21–27

Mexico City, Mexico
1926 Central American and Caribbean Games, Oct. 12–Nov. 2
1954 Central American and Caribbean Games, March 6–20
1955 Pan-American Games, March 12–26
1968 Olympic Games, Oct. 12–27
1975 Central American and Caribbean University Games
1975 Pan-American Games, Oct. 12–26
1975 Pan-American Wheelchair Games, Aug. 9–
1979 Pan-American Maccabi Games, Aug. 21–29
1979 World University Games, Sept. 2–13
1990 Central American and Caribbean Games, Nov. 20–Dec. 4
1999 Pan-American Wheelchair Games, Nov. 1–8
1999 Pan-American Maccabi Games, July 8–20
1999 Pan-American Games for the Blind

Miami, USA
1987 JCC Maccabi Games, Aug.

Milan, Italy
1957 World Games for the Deaf, Aug. 25–30
1992 FISEC Games

Milton Keynes, England
1993 UK & Ireland Corporate Games
1994 UK & Ireland Corporate Games

Milwaukee, USA
1997 JCC Maccabi Games, Aug. 10–15
2000 Can-Am Police-Fire Games, July 2–10

Minneapolis, USA
1991 Special Olympics Summer World Games, July 19–27

Minsk, Soviet Union
1985 SCFA Winter Spartakiade, Feb. 23–March 2

Montana-Vermala, Switzerland
1959 Winter World Games for the Deaf, Jan. 27–30

Monte Carlo, Monaco
1939 World University Games, Aug. 21–29
1985 World Medical Games, June 23–29
1987 Games of the Small Countries of Europe, May 14–17
1996 Special Olympics Small Nations Games, May 10–12

Montecatini Terme, Italy
1986 World Medical Games, June 22–28

Montevideo, Uruguay
1991 Pan-American Maccabi Games, July 4–14
1999 World Corporate Games, Dec. 13–16

Montreal, Canada
1976 Olympic Games, July 17–Aug. 1
1988 Défi Sportif, May 3–8
1989 Défi Sportif, May 2–7
1989 World Medical Games, July 16–22
1990 Défi Sportif, May 1–6
1991 Défi Sportif, April 26–May 5
1992 Défi Sportif, April 27–May 3
1993 Défi Sportif, April 30–May 9
1994 Défi Sportif, April 27–May 1
1995 Défi Sportif, April 26–30
1996 Défi Sportif, April 24–28
1997 Défi Sportif, April 30–May 4
1998 Défi Sportif, May 1–3
1999 Défi Sportif, April 29–May 2
2000 Défi Sportif, April 26–30

Moscow, Havana, Prague, Warsaw, Soviet Bloc Countries
1984 Friendship Games 84, Aug. 16–30

Moscow, Soviet Union (*later* Russia)
1928 Red Sport International Spartakiade, Aug. 12–28
1928 Red Sport International Winter Spartakiade, Dec.
1931 Red Sport International Spartakiade, July 5–19
1957 World Student Championships (UIE), July 29–Aug. 4
1973 World University Games, Aug. 15–25
1980 Olympic Games, July 19–Aug. 3
1986 Goodwill Games, July 5–20
1998 World Youth Games, July 12–19

Moscow/Pullman, USA
1988 Can-Am Police-Fire Games, June 20–26

Mt. Bachelor, USA
1989 Can-Am Police-Fire Games

Mt. Jahorina, Yugoslavia
1955 University Sports Week Winter (FISU), April 1–7

Mt. Pleasant, USA
1975 Special Olympics Summer World Games, Aug. 7–11

Mount Snow, USA
2000 Winter X Games, Feb. 3–6

Munich, West Germany
1972 Olympic Games, Aug. 26–Sept. 10

Murska Sobota, Yugoslavia
1974 International School Children's Games, May 19
1976 International School Children's Games, May 20–23
1983 International School Children's Games, Sept. 23

Murzzuschlag, Austria
1931 Socialist Worker Sports International Winter Worker Olympiad, Feb. 5–8

Nagano, Japan
1998 Olympic Winter Games, Feb. 7–22
1998 Winter Paralympic Games, March 5–14

Nairobi, Kenya
1978 All-Africa University Games, Dec. 29–Jan. 7
1987 African Games, Aug. 1–12

Nantes, France
2000 FISEC Games, July 19–25

Naples, Italy
1963 Mediterranean Games, Sept. 21–29

Nassau, Bahamas
1992 CARIFTA Games, April 18–20
1997 CARIFTA Games, March 29–31

Nassau NY, USA
1980 International Law Enforcement Games

Neuchâtel/Marignane, Switzerland/France
1987 World Peace Games

New Delhi, India
1951 Asian Games, March 4–15
1982 Asian Games, Nov. 19–Dec. 4

New Haven, USA
1995 Special Olympics Summer World Games, July 1–9

New Westminster, Canada
1982 Can-Am Police-Fire Games, June 21–27

New York, USA
1980 World Transplant Games
1984 Paralympic Games
1994 Gay Games, June 18–25
1998 Goodwill Games, July 19–Aug. 2

Newport RI, USA
1993 World Scholar Athlete Games, June 20–July 1
1995 X Games, June 24–27
1996 X Games, June 24–30
1997 World Scholar Athlete Games, June 23–July 1

Nice, France
1982 Journalists World Games
1986 ISF Gymnasiade, June 4–6

Nicosia, Cyprus
1989 Games of the Small Countries of Europe, May 17–20
1994 ISF Gymnasiade, May 17–20

Njoro, Kenya
1999 East African University Games, Dec.

North Lake Tahoe, USA
1987 International Firefighters Winter Games, March 1–5
1988 International Firefighters Winter Games, March 6–10
1989 International Firefighters Winter Games, March 5–9
1990 International Firefighters Winter Games, March 4–8
1991 International Firefighters Winter Games, March 3–7
1992 International Firefighters Winter Games, March 1–5
1993 International Firefighters Winter Games, March 7–11
1994 International Firefighters Winter Games, March 6–10
1995 International Firefighters Winter Games, March 5–9
1996 International Firefighters Winter Games, March 3–7
1997 International Police Winter Games, March 2–6
1999 International Firefighters Winter Games, Feb. 28–March 4
2000 International Firefighters Winter Games, Feb. 27–March 2

Nottingham, England
1989 Robin Hood Games
1993 Robin Hood Games
1997 Robin Hood Games, July 18–28

Nouméa, New Caledonia
1966 South Pacific Games, Dec. 8–18
1987 South Pacific Games

Novi-Targ, Poland
1979 SCFA Winter Spartakiade, Feb. 27–March 2

Nukualofa, Tonga
1989 South Pacific Mini Games, Aug. 22–Sept. 1

Nürnberg, Germany
1931 World Games for the Deaf, Aug. 19–25

Oahu, USA
1990 World Corporate Games, Oct. 6–13

Oberammergau, West Germany
1955 Winter World Games for the Deaf, Feb. 10–13
1957 University Sports Week Winter (FISU), Feb. 19–24

Oita & Beppu, Japan
1975 Far East and South Pacific Games for the Disabled, June 1–3

Omaha, USA
1991 JCC Maccabi Games, Aug.

Oranjestad, Aruba
1970 Dutch Commonwealth Games, July 31–Aug. 9
1995 Dutch Commonwealth Games, July 16–21
1997 World Corporate Games, Sept. 13–20

Orlando, USA
1995 JCC Maccabi Games, Aug. 13–17

Orléans, France
1976 ISF Gymnasiade, June 26

Ornskoldsvik, Sweden
1976 Winter Paralympic Games, Feb. 23–28

Osaka, Japan
1923 Far East Championships, May 21–25

Oslo, Norway
1928 Red Sport International Winter Spartakiade, Feb. 17–28
1952 Olympic Winter Games, Feb. 14–25
1953 Winter World Games for the Deaf, Feb. 20–24
1987 Winter World Games for the Deaf, Feb. 7–14

Osturi, Italy
1992 World Medical Games, June 21–28

Otepaa, Estonia
1940 SELL Games (Winter), March 2–3

Ouagadougou, Burkina Faso
1989 West African University Games
1994 African Francophone Games for the Handicapped

Pago Pago, American Samoa
1997 South Pacific Mini Games, Aug. 11–21

Palma de Mallorca, Spain
1999 World University Games, July 2–July 13

Pamporovo, Bulgaria
1973 SCFA Winter Spartakiade

Panama City, Panama
1938 Central American and Caribbean Games, Feb. 5–24

1970 Central American and Caribbean Games, Feb. 27–March 14
1973 Bolivarian Games, Feb. 17–March 3

Papeete, Tahiti
1971 South Pacific Games, Sept. 8–19
1995 South Pacific Games, Aug. 12–26

Parimaribo, Suriname
1966 Dutch Commonwealth Games, Aug. 7
1969 Dutch Commonwealth Games, July 25–Aug. 2
1973 Dutch Commonwealth Games, Aug. 8 1973
1975 Dutch Commonwealth Games, Aug. 1–6

Paris, France
1900 Olympic Games, May 20–Oct. 28
1919 Inter-Allied Games, June 22–July 6
1922 International Women's Games, Aug. 20
1923 World University Games, May 3–6
1924 World Games for the Deaf, Aug. 10–17
1924 Olympic Games, May 4–July 27
1924 Red Sport International Spartakiade, July 13–14
1928 World University Games, Aug. 9–17
1937 World University Games, Aug. 21–29
1947 World University Games, Aug. 24–31
1957 World University Games, Aug. 31–Sept. 8
1983 World Medical Games, Aug. 28–Sept. 3
1988 European Heart/Lung Transplant Games
1994 Francophone Games, July 5–13
1997 Euro Games, June 20–23

Park City, USA
1985 Special Olympics Winter World Games, March 24–29

Parramatta, Australia
1977 Far East and South Pacific Games for the Disabled, Nov. 20–26

Perapignan, France
1990 World Medical Games, June 17–23

Perth, Australia
1962 British Commonwealth Paraplegic Games
1962 Commonwealth Games, Nov. 21–Dec. 1
1993 Australian Masters Games, April 20–May 2
1994 Firefighters World Games, March 20–26
1996 Pacific School Games, Dec. 7–13
1999 Australian Universities Games, Sept. 26–Oct. 1

Peterborough, England
1995 UK & Ireland Corporate Games
1997 World Dwarf Games, July 18–25

Phnom Penh, Cambodia
1966 Asian Games of the New Emerging Forces (GANEFO), Nov. 25–Dec. 6

Phoenix, USA
1984 International Law Enforcement Games

Piancavallo, Italy
1987 Alps-Adriatic Winter Youth Games

Pittsburgh, USA
1989 JCC Maccabi Games, Aug.
1993 JCC Maccabi Games, Aug. 22–26
1997 JCC Maccabi Games, Aug. 17–22

Poiana, Romania
1951 World Student Championships Winter (UIE), Jan. 28–Feb. 7

Ponce, San Juan, Puerto Rico
1993 Central American and Caribbean Games, Nov. 19–30

Poprad, Slovakia
1999 Winter World University Games, Jan. 22–30

Poprad-Tatry, Slovakia
1999 Winter European Youth Olympic Days, March 6–12

Port Louis, Mauritius
1985 Indian Ocean Island Games, Aug. 24–Sept. 1

Port Moresby, Lae, Papua New Guinea
1991 South Pacific Games, Sept. 2–23

Port Moresby, Papua New Guinea
1969 South Pacific Games, Aug. 13–23

Port of Spain, Trinidad
1987 CARIFTA Games, April 18–20
1991 CARIFTA Games, March 30–April 1
1998 CARIFTA Games, April 11–13

Port Vila, Vanuatu
1993 South Pacific Mini Games

Portland, USA
1994 Can-Am Police-Fire Games, June 20–26
1998 World Masters Games, Aug. 9–22

Pôrto Alegre, Brazil
1963 World University Games, Aug. 30–Sept. 8

Portsmouth, England
1978 World Transplant Games
1979 World Transplant Games

Pra-Loup, France
1996 Winter World Transplant Games, Jan. 7–13

Prague, Czechoslovakia
1921 Red Sport International Spartakiade, June
   19–26
1921 Prague Socialist Olympics, June 24–30
1927 Socialist Olympics
1930 International Women's Games, Sept.
1934 Socialist Olympics, July 4–9
1973 SCFA Summer Spartakiade

Prakovce-Helcmanovc, Slovenia
1995 Winter International School Children's
   Games, Feb. 2–3

Pretoria, South Africa
1997 World Ex-Service Wheelchair and Amputee
   Games, Sept. 20–28

Prince Albert, Canada
1993 North American Indigenous Games, July
   18–25

Providence, USA
1999 Gravity Games, Sept. 5–12
2000 Gravity Games, July 15–23

Pula, Yugoslavia
1986 Alps-Adriatic Summer Youth Games

Punte del Este, Uruguay
1999 Pan-American Medical Games, Dec. 4–11

Pusan, South Korea
1997 East Asian Games, May 10–19

Quito, Guayaquil, Ecuador
1965 Bolivarian Games, Nov. 20–Dec. 5

Rabat, Casablanca, Morocco
1989 Francophone Games, July 8–22

Raleigh-Durham, USA
1999 Special Olympics Summer World Games,
   June 26–July 4

Rangoon, Burma
1962 South East Asian Games, Dec. 11–16
1969 South East Asian Games, Dec. 6–13

Rarotonga, Cook Islands
1985 South Pacific Mini Games

Ravne na Koroskem, Yugoslavia (*later* Slovakia)
1978 International School Children's Games,
   Sept. 22–24
1994 Winter International School Children's
   Games, Feb. 10–13

Regina, Canada
1998 Can-Am Police-Fire Games, June 22–28

Reno, USA
1989 Special Olympics Winter World Games,
   April 1–8

Reykjavik, Iceland
1997 Games of the Small Countries of Europe,
   June 3–7

Richmond, USA
2000 JCC Maccabi Games, Aug. 13–18

Riga, Latvia
1924 SELL Games (Summer)
1929 SELL Games (Winter)
1931 SELL Games (Summer)
1935 SELL Games (Summer)

Riga, Sigulda, Latvia
1935 SELL Games (Winter)

Rio de Janeiro, Brazil
1922 Latin American Games
1978 Pan-American Wheelchair Games, Nov.
   28–

River Plate, Argentina
2000 Pan-American Games for Patients with
   Asthma, Sept. 22–23

Rochester NY, USA
1999 JCC Maccabi Games, Aug. 15–20

Rome, Italy
1922 University Olympia
1927 World University Games, Aug. 28–Sept. 4
1960 Olympic Games, Aug. 25–Sept. 11
1960 Paralympic Games, Sept. 17–22
1975 World University Games, Sept. 17–21
1995 Military World Games, Sept. 6–15
1998 World Equestrian Games, Sept. 30–Oct. 11

Rosario/Santa Fe, Argentina
1982 South American Games, Nov. 26–Dec. 5

Rovaniemi, Finland
1970 Winter World University Games, April 3–9

St. Denis, Réunion
1979 Indian Ocean Island Games, Aug. 25–
   Sept. 2
1998 Indian Ocean Island Games, Aug. 8–16

St. George, Grenada
2000 CARIFTA Games

St. George, USA
1987 Huntsman World Senior Games, Oct. 10–23
1988 Huntsman World Senior Games, Oct. 8–21
1989 Huntsman World Senior Games, Oct. 14–27
1990 Huntsman World Senior Games, Oct. 13–26

1991 Huntsman World Senior Games, Oct. 14–25
1992 Huntsman World Senior Games, Oct. 13–24
1993 Huntsman World Senior Games, Oct. 11–22
1994 Huntsman World Senior Games, Oct. 10–23
1995 Huntsman World Senior Games, Oct. 17–29
1996 Huntsman World Senior Games, Oct. 12–25
1997 Huntsman World Senior Games, Oct. 13–24
1998 Huntsman World Senior Games, Oct. 12–24
1999 Huntsman World Senior Games, Oct. 11–22
2000 Huntsman World Senior Games, Oct. 9–21

St. Helier, Jersey

1997 Island Games, June 28–July 5
1999 Islands Corporate Games, Oct. 8–10

St. Louis, USA

1904 Olympic Games, July 1–Nov. 23
1993 JCC Maccabi Games, Aug. 15–19
1996 JCC Maccabi Games, Aug. 11–16

St. Maarten, Netherlands

1999 Dutch Commonwealth Games, July 24–30

St. Moritz, Switzerland

1928 Olympic Winter Games, Feb. 11–19
1935 Winter World University Games, Feb. 4–10
1948 Olympic Winter Games, Jan. 30–Feb. 8
1953 University Sports Week Winter (FISU), March 2–8

St. Peter Port, Guernsey

1987 Island Games, Sept. 10–17

St. Petersburg, Russia (*see also* Leningrad)

1994 Goodwill Games, July 23–Aug. 7

Saint-Malo, France

1993 World Medical Games, June 27–July 3

Saint-Tropez, France

1999 World Medical Games, June 26–July 3

Saipan, Northern Marianas

1969 Micronesian Games, July 4–12
1990 Micronesian Games

Salem, USA

1987 Can-Am Police-Fire Games, June 22–28

Salt Lake City, USA

1996 International Law Enforcement Games, Aug. 3–10
1999 Winter World Transplant Games, Jan. 10–15

Salzburg/Schladming, Austria

1993 Special Olympics Winter World Games, March

San Diego, USA

1978 International Law Enforcement Games
1987 World Police and Fire Games, Aug. 1–9
1997 X Games, June 23–29
1998 X Games, June 19–28

San Francisco, USA

1974 International Law Enforcement Games
1982 Gay Games, Aug. 28–Sept. 5
1986 Gay Games, Aug. 7–18
1988 World Corporate Games
1999 X Games, June 25–July 3
2000 X Games, August 17–22

San Germán, Puerto Rico

2000 Central American and Caribbean University Games, July 30–Aug. 5

San Jose, USA

1985 World Police and Fire Games, Aug. 4–11

San Juan, Puerto Rico

1966 Central American and Caribbean Games, June 11–25
1972 Central American and Caribbean University Games
1979 Pan-American Games, July 1–15
1986 Pan-American Wheelchair Games, Oct. 1–11

San Marino, San Marino

1985 Games of the Small Countries of Europe, May 23–26

San Pedro Sula, Honduras

1997 Central American Games, Dec. 5–14

San Salvador, El Salvador

1935 Central American and Caribbean Games, March 16–April 5
1977 Central American Games, Nov. 25–Dec. 4
1994 Central American Games, Jan. 14–23

San Sebastián, Spain

1955 International University Sports Week (FISU), Aug. 7–14

Sandefjord, Norway

2000 European Heart/Lung Transplant Games, June 25–July 3

Sandown, Isle of Wight

1993 Island Games, July 3–10

Santa Clara, USA

1981 World Games, July 24–Aug. 2

Santiago, Chile

1986 South American Games, Nov. 29–Dec. 7

Santiago de los Caballeros, Dominican Republic

1986 Central American and Caribbean Games, June 24–July 5

Santo Domingo, Dominican Republic

1974 Central American and Caribbean Games, Feb. 27–March 13
1977 Central American and Caribbean University Games

São Paulo, Brazil

1963 Pan-American Games, April 20–May 5
1967 Pan-American Maccabi Games, Aug. 23–28
1983 Pan-American Maccabi Games, Dec. 20–30

Sapporo, Japan

1972 Olympic Winter Games, Feb. 3–13
1986 Asian Winter Games, March 1–8
1990 Asian Winter Games, March 9–14
1991 Winter World University Games, March 2–10

Sarajevo, Yugoslavia

1984 Olympic Winter Games, Feb. 7–19

Sarasota, USA

1993 JCC Maccabi Games, Aug. 15–19
1997 JCC Maccabi Games, Aug. 10–15

Schrieberhau (Riesenberge), Germany

1925 Socialist Worker Sports International Winter Worker, Jan. 31–Feb. 2

Seattle, USA

1978 Can-Am Police-Fire Games, June 19–25
1984 Can-Am Police-Fire Games, June 18–24
1990 Goodwill Games, July 20–Aug. 5
1997 JCC Maccabi Games, Aug. 17–22

Seefeld, Austria

1949 Winter World Games for the Deaf, Feb. 26–March 2
1996 Winter World Corporate Games
1997 Winter World Corporate Games, March 9–14
1998 Winter World Corporate Games, March 15–20

Semeringen-Vienna, Austria

1953 World Student Championships Winter (UIE) (IUS), Feb. 23–March 1

Seoul, South Korea

1986 Asian Games, Sept. 20–Oct. 5
1988 Olympic Games, Sept. 17–Oct. 2
1988 Paralympic Games, Oct. 15–25
1992 Asia Pacific Games for the Deaf, Aug.

Sestriere, Italy

1966 Winter World University Games, Feb. 5–13

Sha Tin, Hong Kong

1982 Far East and South Pacific Games for the Disabled, Oct. 31–Nov. 7

Shanghai, China

1915 Far East Championships, May 15–21
1921 Far East Championships, May 30–June 3
1927 Far East Championships, Aug. 28–31
1993 East Asian Games, May 9–18
1996 Special Olympics Asia-Pacific Games, Nov. 8–11
1998 ISF Gymnasiade, Oct. 12–19

Shefferville, Canada

1976 Arctic Winter Games, March 21–27

Sheffield, England

1991 World University Games, July 14–27

Shenyang, China

1998 Asian Sports Festival, Aug. 29–Sept. 6

Sicily, Italy

1997 World University Games, Aug. 18–31

Singapore, Singapore

1973 South East Asian Games, Sept. 1–8
1983 South East Asian Games, May 28–June 6
1989 World Transplant Games, Sept. 10–14
1993 South East Asian Games, June 12–20

Siofok, Hungary

1996 Alps-Adriatic Summer Youth Games, June 24–27

Slave Lake, Canada

1994 Arctic Winter Games, March 6–12

Slovenj Gradec, Slovenia

1994 International School Children's Games, Sept. 24

Smugglers Cove, USA

1981 Special Olympics Winter World Games, March 8–13

Sofia, Bulgaria

1961 World University Games, Aug. 25–Sept. 3
1977 World University Games, Aug. 17–28
1983 Winter World University Games, Feb. 17–27
1989 SCFA Summer Spartakiade
1989 Winter World University Games, March 2–12
1993 World Games for the Deaf, July 24–Aug. 2

Sollefteå, Sweden

1995 Winter Games for the Disabled, Feb. 23–26

1997 Winter Games for the Disabled, March 11–16

1999 Winter Games for the Disabled, March 5–13

Somerset, London, England

1996 FISEC Games

Sopron, Hungary

1996 International School Children's Games, June 26–30

South Bend, USA

1987 Special Olympics Summer World Games, July 31–Aug. 8

South Lake Tahoe, USA

1986 International Police Winter Games, March 2–6

1987 International Police Winter Games, March 1–5

1988 International Police Winter Games, March 6–10

1989 International Police Winter Games, March 5–9

1991 International Police Winter Games, March 3–7

1992 International Police Winter Games, March 1–5

1993 International Police Winter Games, March 7–11

1994 International Police Winter Games, March 6–10

1995 International Police Winter Games, March 5–9

1996 International Police Winter Games, March 3–7

1997 International Firefighters Winter Games, March 2–6

1998 International Firefighters Winter Games, March 1–5

Sparta, Greece

1997 International School Children's Games, June 11–15

Spindleruv Mlyn, Czechoslovakia

1949 World Student Championships Winter (UIE), Jan. 29–Feb. 6

1964 Winter World University Games, Feb. 11–17

1969 SCFA Winter Spartakiade

1977 SCFA Winter Spartakiade, Feb.

1978 Winter World University Games, Feb. 5–12

Split, Yugoslavia

1979 Mediterranean Games, Sept. 15–29

Spokane, USA

1977 Can-Am Police-Fire Games, June 20–26

1980 Can-Am Police-Fire Games, June 23–29

Squaw Valley, USA

1960 Olympic Winter Games, Feb. 18–28

Staten Island, USA

2000 JCC Maccabi Games, Aug. 20–25

Steamboat Springs, USA

1977 Special Olympics Winter World Games, Feb. 5–11

1991 Winter World Corporate Games

Stockholm, Sweden

1901 Nordic Games, Feb. 9–17

1905 Nordic Games, Feb. 4–12

1909 Nordic Games, Feb. 6–14

1912 Olympic Games, May 5–July 22

1913 Nordic Games, Feb. 7–16

1917 Nordic Games, Feb. 10–18

1922 Nordic Games, Feb. 4–12

1926 Nordic Games, Feb. 6–14

1939 World Games for the Deaf, Aug. 24–27

1990 World Equestrian Games, July 24–Aug. 5

1996 Stockholm Summer Games

1997 Stockholm Summer Games, June 29–July 5

1998 Stockholm Summer Games, June 28–July 4

1999 Stockholm Summer Games, July 4–10

1999 World Police and Fire Games, July 16–24

2000 Stockholm Summer Games, July 2–8

Strathclyde/Glasgow, Scotland

1990 European Special Olympics, July 20–27

Strbske Pleso, Czechoslovakia

1983 SCFA Winter Spartakiade

1987 Winter World University Games, Feb. 21–28

Stuttgart, Germany

1996 World Corporate Games, Sept. 7–14

Styria, Austria

1997 Alps-Adriatic Winter Youth Games

Sundsvall, Sweden

1997 Winter European Youth Olympic Days, Feb. 7–13

Surakarta, Indonesia

1986 Far East and South Pacific Games for the Disabled, Aug. 31–Sept. 7

Suva, Fiji

1963 South Pacific Games, Aug. 29–Sept. 7

1979 South Pacific Games, Aug. 27–Sept. 8

Sydney, Australia

1938 Commonwealth Games, Feb. 5–12

1988 Pacific School Games

1988 International Law Enforcement Games

1993 Australian Corporate Games

1994 Australian Corporate Games

1995 Australian Corporate Games
1996 Australian Corporate Games, March 21–24
1997 World Transplant Games, Sept. 29–Oct. 5
1997 Australian Corporate Games, March 13–16
1998 Australian Corporate Games, March 11–14
1999 Australian Corporate Games, March
2000 Pacific School Games, April 27–May 8
2000 Paralympic Games, Oct. 14–24
2000 Australian Corporate Games, March 16–19
2000 Olympic Games, Sept. 15–Oct. 1

Szombathely, Hungary
1988 International School Children's Games, June 24–25

Taipei, Taiwan
1983 Asia Pacific Games for the Deaf, July
2000 Asia Pacific Games for the Deaf, Nov. 1–12

Tallin, Estonia
1930 SELL Games (Summer)
1993 Baltic Sea Games, June 22–July 3

Tartu, Estonia
1923 SELL Games (Summer)
1934 SELL Games (Summer)
1938 SELL Games (Summer)
1998 SELL Games (Summer), May 1–10

Tashkent, Uzbekistan
1995 Central Asian Games, Sept. 2–9

Tegucigalpa, Honduras
1990 Central American Games, Jan. 5–14

Tehran, Iran
1974 Asian Games, Sept. 1–16
1993 Muslim Women's Games, Feb. 13–19
1994 Muslim Student Games, July 21–28
1997 West Asian Games, Nov. 19–28
1997 Muslim Women's Games, Dec. 13–22

Tel Aviv, Israel
1928 Hapoel Games, Sept. 29–30
1930 Hapoel Games, Oct. 10–12
1932 Hapoel Games, Oct. 21–25
1932 Maccabiah Games, March 29–April 6
1935 Hapoel Games, April 18–21
1935 Maccabiah Games, April 2–10
1950 Maccabiah Games, Sept. 28–Oct. 9
1952 Hapoel Games, April 14–18
1953 Maccabiah Games, Sept. 20–29
1956 Hapoel Games, May 10–17
1957 Maccabiah Games, Sept. 15–24
1961 Hapoel Games, May 1–6
1961 Maccabiah Games, Aug. 29–Sept. 5
1965 Maccabiah Games, Aug. 23–Aug. 31
1966 Hapoel Games, May 1–7
1968 Paralympic Games, Nov. 5–13
1969 Maccabiah Games, July 28–Aug. 6
1971 Hapoel Games, April 29–May 5

1973 Maccabiah Games, July 9–July 19
1975 Hapoel Games, May 1–9
1977 Maccabiah Games, July 12–21
1979 Hapoel Games, May 1–8
1981 Maccabiah Games, July 6–16
1983 Hapoel Games, May 1–7
1985 Maccabiah Games, July 15–25
1987 Hapoel Games, May 4–11
1989 Maccabiah Games, July 3–13
1991 Hapoel Games, May 6–13
1993 Maccabiah Games, July 5–15
1995 Hapoel Games, June 11–15
1997 Maccabiah Games, July 14–25
2000 Middle East/Mediterranean Scholar Athlete Games, June 24–July 3

The Hague, Netherlands
1992 Euro Games
1993 World Games, July 22–Aug. 1
1993 Euro Games
1994 World Equestrian Games, July 27–Aug.
1998 World Corporate Games, Aug. 29–Sept. 5

Thredbo, Australia
1996 Winter Australian Corporate Games
1997 Winter Australian Corporate Games
1998 Winter Australian Corporate Games, Aug. 7–9
1999 Winter Australian Corporate Games
2000 Winter Australian Corporate Games, August?

Tignes, France
1994 Winter World Transplant Games

Tiszaujvaros, Hungary
1996 Eastern European Transplant Games, Aug. 5–14

Tokyo, Japan
1917 Far East Championships, May 8–12
1930 Far East Championships, May 24–27
1958 Asian Games, May 24–June 1
1964 Olympic Games, Oct. 10–24
1964 Paralympic Games, Nov. 6–14
1967 World University Games, Aug. 27–Sept. 4

Toronto, Canada
1976 Paralympic Games, Aug. 3–11
1985 World Masters Games, Aug. 7–25
1986 JCC Maccabi Games, Aug.

Toronto/Collingwood, Canada
1997 Special Olympics Winter World Games, Feb. 7–11

Tórshavn, Faroe Islands
1989 Island Games, July 5–13

Trento, Italy
1988 Alps-Adriatic Summer Youth Games

Tri-Cities (Kennewick), USA
1991 Can-Am Police-Fire Games, June 24–30
1996 Can-Am Police-Fire Games, June 24–30

Troyes, France
1983 International School Children's Games, June 17–19

Tucson, USA
2000 JCC Maccabi Games, Aug. 3–9

Tumon, Guam
1975 South Pacific Games, Aug. 1–10

Tunis, Tunisia
1967 Mediterranean Games, Sept. 8–17

Turin, Italy
1933 World University Games, Sept. 1–10
1959 World University Games, Aug. 26–Sept. 9
1970 World University Games, Aug. 26–Sept. 6
1980 ISF Gymnasiade, June 6–7

Udine, Italy
1970 International School Children's Games, June 20–21

Utrecht, Netherlands
1968 Dutch Commonwealth Games, Aug. 5–11
1971 Dutch Commonwealth Games, July 31

Uzhgorod, Ukraine
1990 International School Children's Games, June 30–July 3

Vaduz, Liechtenstein
1999 Games of the Small Countries of Europe, May 24–29

Valencia, Venezuela
1994 South American Games, Nov. 19–28

Valkenswaard, Netherlands
1993 European Youth Olympic Days, July 3–9

Valletta, Malta
1993 Games of the Small Countries of Europe, May 25–29
1997 FISEC Games

Vancouver, Canada
1954 Commonwealth Games, July 30–Aug. 7
1989 World Police and Fire Games, July 29–Aug. 6
1990 Gay Games, Aug. 4–11
1993 World Transplant Games, July 4–10

Velenje, Slovenia
1999 International School Children's Games, Sept. 27–29

Venice, Italy
1998 Alps-Adriatic Summer Youth Games

Victoria, Canada
1994 Commonwealth Games, Aug. 18–28
1997 North American Indigenous Games, Aug. 3–10

Victoria, Seychelles
1993 Indian Ocean Island Games, Aug. 21–29

Vienna, Austria
1931 Socialist Olympics, July 16–26
1938 International Women's Games
1939 German Student Federation Games
1959 World Student Championships (UIE), July 29–Aug. 2

Villach, Austria
1985 Alps-Adriatic Winter Youth Games

Villars, Switzerland
1962 Winter World University Games, March 6–12

Vilnius, Lithuania
1997 Baltic Sea Games, June 25–July 6

Visby, Gotland
1999 Island Games, June 26–July 2

Walla Walla, USA
1992 Can-Am Police-Fire Games, June 22–28

Warsaw, Poland
1924 World University Games, Sept. 17–20
1955 World Student Championships (UIE), Aug. 1–14
1985 SCFA Summer Spartakiade

Washington DC, USA
1965 World Games for the Deaf, June 27–July 3
1992 International Law Enforcement Games

Wayne NJ, USA
1991 JCC Maccabi Games, Aug.
1996 JCC Maccabi Games, Aug. 18–23

Whitehorse, Canada
1972 Arctic Winter Games, March 5–11
1980 Arctic Winter Games, March 16–22
1986 Arctic Winter Games, March 16–21
1992 Arctic Winter Games, March 15–21
2000 Arctic Winter Games, March 5–11

Wiesbaden, West Germany
1974 ISF Gymnasiade, June 7–8

Willemstad, Curaçao
1967 Dutch Commonwealth Games, Aug. 13–21

1972 Dutch Commonwealth Games, July 21–30

1997 Dutch Commonwealth Games, July 26–Aug. 1

Windsor, Canada

1982 Windsor Classic Indoor Games
1983 Windsor Classic Indoor Games
1984 Windsor Classic Indoor Games
1985 Windsor Classic Indoor Games
1986 Windsor Classic Indoor Games
1987 Windsor Classic Indoor Games
1988 Windsor Classic Indoor Games
1989 Windsor Classic Indoor Games
1990 Windsor Classic Indoor Games
1991 Windsor Classic Indoor Games
1992 Windsor Classic Indoor Games
1993 Windsor Classic Indoor Games
1994 Windsor Classic Indoor Games
1995 Windsor Classic Indoor Games
1996 Windsor Classic Indoor Games
1997 Windsor Classic Indoor Games
1998 Windsor Classic Indoor Games
1999 Windsor Classic Indoor Games
2000 Windsor Classic Indoor Games, March 24–26

Winnipeg, Canada

1967 Pan-American Wheelchair Games, Aug. 24–
1967 Pan-American Games, July 23–Aug. 6
1999 Pan-American Games, July 24–Aug. 8

Wollongong, Australia

1994 Australian Universities Games, Sept. 25–30

Yamossoukro, Ivory Coast

1977 West African University Games

Yellowknife, Canada

1970 Arctic Winter Games, March 8–14
1984 Arctic Winter Games, March 18–24

1990 Arctic Winter Games, March 11–17
1998 Arctic Winter Games, March 15–22

Yerevan, Armenia

1999 Pan-Armenian Games, Aug. 28–Sept. 4

Yllas, Finland

1995 Winter World Games for the Deaf, March 14–19

Zagreb, Yugoslavia (*later* Croatia)

1987 World University Games, July 8–19
1996 International Electrical Engineering Students Sports Games, July 16–18
1999 Military World Games, Aug. 8–17

Zakopane, Poland

1933 Maccabiade Winter Games, Feb. 1–5
1956 World Student Championships Winter (UIE), March 7–13
1971 SCFA Winter Spartakiade
1993 Winter World University Games, Feb. 6–14

Zalaegerszeg, Hungary

1992 Alps-Adriatic Summer Youth Games, June 23–26

Zandvoort, Netherlands

1974 Dutch Commonwealth Games, Aug. 10–17

Zarasai, Lithuania

1938 SELL Games (Winter)

Zeel am See, Austria

1937 Winter World University Games, Feb. 2–10
1958 University Sports Week Winter (FISU), Feb. 16–21

Zomba, Malawi

1996 CUCSA Games, Sept. 16–21

Zurich, Switzerland

2000 Euro Games, June 2–3

Appendix 4.
Largest Games by
Number of Participants
(Top 100)

Games	Host City	Host Nation	Year	Participants
World Peace Games	Dubai	United Arab Emirates	1998	28000
World Masters Games	Brisbane	Australia	1994	24000
World Peace Games	Fès/Ifrane/Meknes	Morocco	1990	22000
World Peace Games	Neuchâtel/ Marignane	Switzerland/ France	1987	18000
World Masters Games	Henning/Århus/Aalborg	Denmark	1989	15000
Gay Games	Amsterdam	Netherlands	1998	14403
Socialist Olympics	Antwerp	Belgium	1937	14000
World Masters Games	Portland	USA	1998	11000
Gay Games	New York	USA	1994	10864
Olympic Games	Sydney	Australia	2000	10651
Olympic Games	Atlanta	USA	1996	10310
World Peace Games	Echiroles	France	1985	10200
Hapoel Games	Tel Aviv	Israel	1935	10000
Asia Pacific Masters Games	Gold Coast	Australia	1998	9500
Olympic Games	Barcelona	Spain	1992	9370
Pan-American Games	Winnipeg	Canada	1999	8949
World Police and Fire Games	Calgary	Canada	1997	8900
Australian Masters Games	Canberra	Australia	1997	8811
Olympic Games	Seoul	South Korea	1988	8465
North American Indigenous Games	Blaine	USA	1995	8000

Games	Host City	Host Nation	Year	Participants
Australian Masters Games	Melbourne	Australia	1995	8000
World Masters Games	Toronto	Canada	1985	7769
Gay Games	Vancouver	Canada	1990	7400
Olympic Games	Munich	West Germany	1972	7173
Special Olympics Summer World Games	New Haven	USA	1995	7000
Special Olympics Summer World Games	Raleigh-Durham	USA	1999	7000
Olympic Games	Los Angeles	USA	1984	6797
Hapoel Games	Tel Aviv	Israel	1983	6700
Hapoel Games	Tel Aviv	Israel	1991	6700
World Police and Fire Games	Melbourne	Australia	1995	6692
Tailteann Games	Dublin	Ireland	1924	6500
Asian Games	Hiroshima	Japan	1994	6078
Olympic Games	Montreal	Canada	1976	6024
Asian Games	Bangkok	Thailand	1998	6000
Special Olympics Summer World Games	Minneapolis	USA	1991	6000
Australian Universities Games	Melbourne	Australia	1998	6000
African Games	Harare	Zimbabwe	1995	6000
Pan-American Games	Indianapolis	USA	1987	6000
International Law Enforcement Games	Cocoa Beach	USA	2000	5600
Australian Universities Games	Canberra	Australia	1996	5500
Maccabiah Games	Tel Aviv	Israel	1997	5500
Olympic Games	Mexico City	Mexico	1968	5423
World Police and Fire Games	Colorado Springs	USA	1993	5375
Olympic Games	Rome	Italy	1960	5348
Central American and Caribbean Games	Maracaibo	Venezuela	1998	5314
Olympic Games	Moscow	Soviet Union	1980	5217
Pan-American Games	Mar del Plata	Argentina	1995	5144
World University Games	Buffalo	USA	1993	5105
Olympic Games	Tokyo	Japan	1964	5081
Maccabiah Games	Tel Aviv	Israel	1993	5061
North American Indigenous Games	Victoria	Canada	1997	5000
World Youth Games	Moscow	Russia	1998	5000
World Police and Fire Games	San Diego	USA	1987	4972
Olympic Games	Helsinki	Finland	1952	4879
World Police and Fire Games	San Jose	USA	1985	4713
Special Olympics Summer World Games	South Bend	USA	1987	4700

Games	Host City	Host Nation	Year	Participants
Asian Games	Beijing	China	1990	4655
World University Games	Sheffield	England	1991	4622
Arab Games	Amman	Jordan	1999	4600
Pan-American Games	Havana	Cuba	1991	4519
Huntsman World Senior Games	St. George	USA	1998	4500
Maccabiah Games	Tel Aviv	Israel	1989	4417
North American Indigenous Games	Prince Albert	Canada	1993	4400
World University Games	Sofia	Bulgaria	1977	4391
World University Games	Mexico City	Mexico	1979	4381
World Police and Fire Games	Vancouver	Canada	1989	4373
South East Asian Games	Jakarta	Indonesia	1997	4300
Central American and Caribbean Games	Mexico City	Mexico	1990	4224
Arafura Games	Darwin	Australia	1997	4200
Commonwealth Games	Kuala Lumpur	Malaysia	1998	4100
World Police and Fire Games	Memphis	USA	1991	4097
World University Games	Palma de Mallorca	Spain	1999	4076
Olympic Games	London	England	1948	4064
Pan-American Games	San Juan	Puerto Rico	1979	4000
Special Olympics Summer World Games	Baton Rouge	USA	1983	4000
Military World Games	Rome	Italy	1995	4000
Centennial Youth Games	Aalborg	Denmark	1996	4000
International Law Enforcement Games	Salt Lake City	USA	1996	4000
Huntsman World Senior Games	St. George	USA	1997	4000
Firefighters World Games	Las Vegas	USA	1992	4000
Red Sport International Spartakiade	Moscow	Soviet Union	1928	4000
African Games	Nairobi	Kenya	1987	4000
South East Asian Games	Bandar Seri Bagawan	Brunei	1999	4000
Olympic Games	Berlin	Germany	1936	3956
World University Games	Fukuoka	Japan	1995	3949
World University Games	Kobe	Japan	1985	3946
World University Games	Zagreb	Yugoslavia	1987	3904
Paralympic Games	Sydney	Australia	2000	3900
Pan-American Games	Caracas	Venezuela	1983	3800
European Special Olympics	Barcelona	Spain	1992	3700
Maccabiah Games	Tel Aviv	Israel	1985	3639
World University Games	Moscow	Soviet Union	1973	3634
Australian Masters Games	Hobart	Australia	1987	3600
Huntsman World Senior Games	St. George	USA	1996	3600

Games	Host City	Host Nation	Year	Participants
Central American and Caribbean Games	Ponce, San Juan	Puerto Rico	1993	3570
Special Olympics Summer World Games	Brockport	USA	1979	3500
Australasian Public Sector Games	Melbourne	Australia	2000	3500
World University Games	Sicily	Italy	1997	3496
World University Games	Edmonton	Canada	1983	3471
Maccabiah Games	Tel Aviv	Israel	1981	3450

Appendix 5.
Largest Games by
Number of Nations
(Top 100)

Games	Host City	Host Nation	Year	Nations
Olympic Games	Sydney	Australia	2000	199
Olympic Games	Atlanta	USA	1996	197
Olympic Games	Barcelona	Spain	1992	172
World University Games	Fukuoka	Japan	1995	162
Olympic Games	Seoul	South Korea	1988	160
Special Olympics Summer World Games	Raleigh-Durham	USA	1999	147
World Scholar Athlete Games	Newport RI	USA	1997	147
Olympic Games	Los Angeles	USA	1984	141
Special Olympics Summer World Games	New Haven	USA	1995	140
World Youth Games	Moscow	Russia	1998	130
World University Games	Palma de Mallorca	Spain	1999	125
World University Games	Sicily	Italy	1997	124
Olympic Games	Munich	West Germany	1972	122
World University Games	Zagreb	Yugoslavia	1987	122
Paralympic Games	Sydney	Australia	2000	122
Paralympic Games	Atlanta	USA	1996	120
World University Games	Buffalo	USA	1993	117
Olympic Games	Mexico City	Mexico	1968	112
World Scholar Athlete Games	Newport RI	USA	1993	109
World University Games	Kobe	Japan	1985	106
World Masters Games	Portland	USA	1998	102

Games	Host City	Host Nation	Year	Nations
World University Games	Sheffield	England	1991	101
Special Olympics Summer World Games	Minneapolis	USA	1991	100
World University Games	Mexico City	Mexico	1979	94
Olympic Games	Tokyo	Japan	1964	93
Olympic Games	Montreal	Canada	1976	92
World University Games	Bucharest	Romania	1981	86
Military World Games	Rome	Italy	1995	86
Olympic Games	Rome	Italy	1960	83
Paralympic Games	Barcelona	Spain	1992	82
Olympic Games	Moscow	Soviet Union	1980	81
Special Olympics Winter World Games	Toronto/ Collingwood	Canada	1997	80
World University Games	Duisburg	Germany	1989	79
Goodwill Games	Moscow	Soviet Union	1986	79
Military World Games	Zagreb	Croatia	1999	78
World University Games	Sofia	Bulgaria	1977	78
World Peace Games	Dubai	United Arab Emirates	1998	75
World Games	The Hague	Netherlands	1993	74
World University Games	Moscow	Soviet Union	1973	73
World University Games	Edmonton	Canada	1983	73
IBSA World Championships for the Blind	Madrid	Spain	1998	72
Olympic Winter Games	Nagano	Japan	1998	72
World Masters Games	Brisbane	Australia	1994	71
World Games	Lahti	Finland	1997	71
Special Olympics Summer World Games	South Bend	USA	1987	70
World Games for the Deaf	Copenhagen	Denmark	1997	70
Commonwealth Games	Kuala Lumpur	Malaysia	1998	70
Olympic Games	Helsinki	Finland	1952	69
Olympic Games	Melbourne	Australia	1956	67
Olympic Winter Games	Lillehammer	Norway	1994	67
Olympic Winter Games	Albertville	France	1992	64
Commonwealth Games	Victoria	Canada	1994	63
Paralympic Games	Seoul	South Korea	1988	61
Gay Games	Amsterdam	Netherlands	1998	61
World Masters Games	Toronto	Canada	1985	60
World Air Games	Ankara	Turkey	1997	60
Goodwill Games	New York	USA	1998	60
Olympic Games	London	England	1948	59
World University Games	Turin	Italy	1970	58
Olympic Winter Games	Calgary	Canada	1988	57
Goodwill Games	St. Petersburg	Russia	1994	56
World Nature Games	Foz de Iguazi	Brazil	1997	55
Commonwealth Games	Auckland	New Zealand	1990	54
Goodwill Games	Seattle	USA	1990	54
World Games	Karlsruhe	West Germany	1989	54
World Transplant Games	Sydney	Australia	1997	53

Games	Host City	Host Nation	Year	Nations
African Games	Johannesburg	South Africa	1999	53
Maccabiah Games	Tel Aviv	Israel	1997	53
World Games for the Deaf	Sofia	Bulgaria	1993	51
Special Olympics Winter World Games	Salzburg/ Schladming	Austria	1993	50
Olympic Winter Games	Sarajevo	Yugoslavia	1984	49
African Games	Harare	Zimbabwe	1995	49
Olympic Games	Berlin	Germany	1936	49
Francophone Games	Antananarivo	Madagascar	1997	49
Games of the New Emerging Forces (GANEFO)	Jakarta	Indonesia	1963	48
European Youth Olympic Days	Esbjerg	Denmark	1999	48
Maccabiah Games	Tel Aviv	Israel	1993	48
World University Games	Tokyo	Japan	1967	48
World Games	London	England	1985	48
Winter World University Games	Chonju-Moju	South Korea	1997	48
European Youth Olympic Days	Lisbon	Portugal	1997	47
European Youth Olympic Days	Bath	England	1995	47
World Transplant Games	Budapest	Hungary	1999	47
Olympic Games	Amsterdam	Netherlands	1928	46
Maccabiah Games	Tel Aviv	Israel	1989	46
Commonwealth Games	Brisbane	Australia	1982	46
World University Games	Turin	Italy	1959	45
World Medical Games	Cannes	France	2000	45
Commonwealth Games	Edmonton	Canada	1978	45
Friendship Games 84	Multiple		1984	45
Paralympic Games	New York	USA	1984	45
African Games	Algiers	Algeria	1978	45
African Games	Nairobi	Kenya	1987	44
Olympic Games	Paris	France	1924	44
Paralympic Games	Heidelberg	West Germany	1972	44
Gay Games	New York	USA	1994	44
World Police and Fire Games	Melbourne	Australia	1995	43
European Youth Olympic Days	Valkenswaard	Netherlands	1993	43
World Equestrian Games	Rome	Italy	1998	43
Asian Games	Bangkok	Thailand	1998	43
Francophone Games	Paris	France	1994	43

Appendix 6.
Largest Games by
Number of Sports
(Top 54)

Games	Host City	Host Nation	Year	Sports
World Police and Fire Games	Stockholm	Sweden	1999	68
World Police and Fire Games	Calgary	Canada	1997	64
Firefighters World Games	Edmonton	Canada	1996	57
World Police and Fire Games	Melbourne	Australia	1995	56
Firefighters World Games	Durban	South Africa	1998	55
Firefighters World Games	Perth	Australia	1994	48
World Police and Fire Games	Colorado Springs	USA	1993	48
Can-Am Police-Fire Games	Regina	Canada	1998	46
Australian Masters Games	Melbourne	Australia	1995	45
Firefighters World Games	Las Vegas	USA	1992	45
Can-Am Police-Fire Games	Milwaukee	USA	2000	44
World Police and Fire Games	Vancouver	Canada	1989	43
World Police and Fire Games	San Diego	USA	1987	43
Can-Am Police-Fire Games	Tri-Cities (Kennewick)	USA	1996	43
Pan-American Games	Winnipeg	Canada	1999	41
World Police and Fire Games	San Jose	USA	1985	41
World Police and Fire Games	Memphis	USA	1991	41
Australian Masters Games	Adelaide	Australia	1989	40
Australian Masters Games	Brisbane	Australia	1991	40
Australian Masters Games	Perth	Australia	1993	40
International Law Enforcement Games	Cocoa Beach	USA	2000	40

Games	Host City	Host Nation	Year	Sports
Australian Masters Games	Hobart	Australia	1987	40
Asian Games	Bangkok	Thailand	1998	36
International Law Enforcement Games	Salt Lake City	USA	1996	35
Asian Games	Hiroshima	Japan	1994	35
Pan-American Games	Mar del Plata	Argentina	1995	34
South East Asian Games	Jakarta	Indonesia	1997	34
Firefighters World Games	Auckland	New Zealand	1990	34
Asia Pacific Masters Games	Gold Coast	Australia	1998	33
Maccabiah Games	Tel Aviv	Israel	1993	32
Maccabiah Games	Tel Aviv	Israel	1981	32
Maccabiah Games	Tel Aviv	Israel	1989	32
Australian Masters Games	Canberra	Australia	1997	32
Central American and Caribbean Games	Maracaibo	Venezuela	1998	32
Olympic Games	Atlanta	USA	1996	31
Pan-American Games	Indianapolis	USA	1987	31
Gay Games	New York	USA	1994	31
Pan-American Games	Havana	Cuba	1991	31
Maccabiah Games	Tel Aviv	Israel	1997	30
Central American and Caribbean Games	Ponce, San Juan	Puerto Rico	1993	30
World Masters Games	Brisbane	Australia	1994	30
Central American and Caribbean Games	Mexico City	Mexico	1990	30
Maccabiah Games	Tel Aviv	Israel	1985	30
Arab Games	Amman	Jordan	1999	29
South East Asian Games	Singapore	Singapore	1993	29
Asian Games	Beijing	China	1990	29
Gay Games	Amsterdam	Netherlands	1998	29
International Law Enforcement Games	Dubai	United Arab Emirates	1998	29
Honda Masters Games	Alice Springs	Australia	1996	29
Gay Games	Vancouver	Canada	1990	29
Olympic Games	Sydney	Australia	2000	28
Olympic Games	Barcelona	Spain	1992	28
Central American Games	San Pedro Sula	Honduras	1997	28
Maccabiah Games	Tel Aviv	Israel	1977	28

Appendix 7.
Other Games

Research for this book occasionally turned up mentions of games about which no information could be located. A list of all such games follows, in the hope that other researchers can begin study of these games or perhaps provide information on them.

African Scholar Athlete Games
Afro-Asian Games
AGBU World Games
Amazon Games
Arab University Games (Maghreb or Maugra-bin University Games)
Arborough Games
Aruba Caribbean Corporate Games
Asian University Games
Australia and New Zealand Police Games
Australia/Pacific Rim Scholar-Athlete Games
Baja Sports Fiesta
Balkan Games
Balkan Olympic Days
Baltic Maccabi Games
BIMP-EAGA Friendship Games
Black Sea Games
Burlington International Games
Canadian Police Alpine Games
Can-Amera International Games
Canandaigua-Midland Friendship Games
Canus International Games
CANUSA Games
Catalan Olympiads
Central African Cup
Central Europe Corporate Games
Central European Games
Children of Asia International Sport Games
China-Japan-Korea Junior Games

East African Games
Euro Transplant Games
EuroAsia Corporate Games
European Cerebral Palsy (European) Games
European Masters Games
European Olympiade of the Minorities
European Police Games
European School Games
European Students Games
Friendship and Peace Games
Friendship Games
Friendship Games Sault Ste.- Saginaw
Friendship Games Thunder Bay—Duluth
FSM Games
GCC Cerebral Palsy Games
GCC Games for the Disabled
Han Ma Dong Games (Hanmadang)
Havalanta Games
Hawaii Pacific Games
HGWSS International Sports Festival
Hindu Games (same as Indian Empire Games?)
Homenetmen World Games
Hunter Festival of Sport
Indian Empire Games
Indianapolis Scarborough Peace Games
International Athletes Jubilee
International Ex-Servicemen Wheelchair Games
International Friendship Games

International Sports Festival For the Blind
International Sports Festival of Paraplegics
International University World Championships
International Womensport Festival
International (World) Cerebral Palsy Games
Israel Special Olympics National Games
Italian Youth Games
Juegos Deportivos Sudamericanos Escolares
Kalev Games
Latin American and Caribbean Games for the Blind
Latin American Transplant Games
Latin American University Games
Maccabi Australia Sports Carnival
MBA Students' Olympics
Mediterranean Corporate Games
Michitario Games
Military Games
Military Olympics
New Zealand Corporate Games
New Zealand Masters Games
New Zealand University Games
Nordic University Games
North American Corporate Games
Northern Games
OhiOntario Games
Olympic Games of the Enslaved Nations
Olympic Hopes Summer
Olympic Hopes Winter Games
Pacific Rim Scholar Athlete Games
Palm Springs International Senior Olympics
Pan-American University Games
Paralympic Games for the Mentally Handicapped
PNG Corporate Games
Prince de Asturias Olympic Youth Rally
Queensland Corporate Games

Queensland Masters Games
Russian Corporate Games
Russian Olympics
Samoa International Games
Scandinavian Transplant Games
Sherwood Forest Games
South Africa Corporate Games
South African Games
South African Masters Games
South American Corporate Games
South East Asian Corporate Games
South Pacific Games for the Disabled
South Pacific Masters Games
Soviet Spartakiade
Special Olympics Tanzania National Games
Sports Festival for Paraplegics CAIIII
Sydney Olympic Youth Festival
Texas Police World Games
University Olympia
Wild 'n' Woolly Games
Winter Can-Am Police-Fire Games
Winter World Masters Games
Women's Global Challenge
World Amputee Games
World Aquatic Games
World Championships and Games for the Disabled
World Culture and Sports Festival
World Eskimo Indian Olympics
World Extreme Games
World Games for Disabled Youth
World Indigenous Games
World Latvian Games
World Lithuanian Games
World Senior Games
World Youth Festival

Appendix 8.
Olympic Games Participants:
Information Sources Compared

The following charts compare five sources of information relating to the numbers of male, female and total participants at each Olympic Games.

The sources are:

Wall92—David Wallechinsky's *Complete book of the Olympics*, 1992 edition.
Wall96—David Wallechinsky's *Complete book of the Olympics*, 1996 edition.
Wall00—David Wallechinsky's *Complete book of the Olympics*, 2000 edition.
Mallon—*Golden Book of the Olympics* (1996).
Lyberg—*Fabulous 100 years of the IOC* (1996).

It is interesting to note that with all the work that these three leading Olympic historians have completed, there is still not 100 percent unanimity on the figures for how many athletes have competed at each games.

One should look at the first three columns to compare how Wallechinsky has refined his numbers from one version of his book to the next. The one should look at the last three columns to compare how the three authors are still not entirely in agreement.

COMPARISON OF MEN'S PARTICIPATION

Year	Wall92M	Wall96M	Wall00M	MallonM	LybergM
1896	311	245	245	245	280
1900	1319	1206	1097	1206	1066
1904	681	681	621	681	673
1906**	877	877	841	820	
1908	1999	1999	1979	1999	1956
1912	2490	2490	2435	2490	2435
1920	2543	2591	2591	2591	2591

Year	Wall92M	Wall96M	Wall00M	MallonM	LybergM
1924	2956	2956	2945	2956	2945
1928	2724	2724	2724	2724	2724
1932	1281	1281	1201	1281	1201
1936	3738	3738	3628	3738	3628
1948	3714	3714	3709	3714	3709
1952	4407	4407	4361	4407	4361
1956*					132
1956	2958	2958	2874	2958	2742
1960	4738	4738	4738	4738	4738
1964	4457	4457	4398	4457	4398
1968	4750	4750	4655	4750	4655
1972	5848	6065	6115	6065	6115
1976	4834	4781	4778	4781	4778
1980	4265	4092	4093	4092	4093
1984	5458	5230	5230	5230	5230
1988	6983	6279	6276	6279	6279
1992		6659	6662	6659	6662

COMPARISON OF WOMEN'S PARTICIPATION

Year	Wall92W	Wall96W	Wall00W	MallonW	LybergW
1896	0	0	0	0	0
1900	11	19	21	19	0
1904	6	6	6	6	8
1906**	7	7	6	6	
1908	36	36	44	36	43
1912	57	57	55	57	55
1920	64	78	77	77	77
1924	136	136	125	136	125
1928	290	290	290	290	290
1932	127	127	127	127	127
1936	328	328	328	328	328
1948	385	385	355	385	355
1952	518	518	518	518	518
1956*					13
1956	384	384	384	384	371
1960	610	610	610	610	610
1964	683	683	683	683	683
1968	781	781	768	781	768
1972	1299	1058	1058	1058	1058
1976	1251	1247	1246	1247	1246
1980	1088	1125	1124	1125	1124
1984	1620	1567	1567	1567	1567
1988	2438	2186	2189	2186	2186
1992		2708	2708	2708	2708

COMPARISON OF MEN'S AND WOMEN'S PARTICIPATION

Year	Wall92Total	Wall96Total	Wall00Total	MallonTotal	LybergTotal
1896	311	245	245	245	280
1900	1330	1225	1118	1225	1066
1904	687	687	627	687	681
1906**	884	884	847	826	
1908	2035	2035	2023	2035	1999
1912	2547	2547	2490	2547	2490

Year	Wall92Total	Wall96Total	Wall00Total	MallonTotal	LybergTotal
1920	2607	2669	2668	2668	2668
1924	3092	3092	3070	3092	3070
1928	3014	3014	3014	3014	3014
1932	1408	1408	1328	1408	1328
1936	4066	4066	3956	4066	3956
1948	4099	4099	4064	4099	4064
1952	4925	4925	4879	4925	4879
1956*				158	145
1956	3342	3342	3258	3184	3113
1960	5348	5348	5348	5346	5348
1964	5140	5140	5081	5140	5081
1968	5531	5531	5423	5530	5423
1972	7147	7123	7173	7123	7173
1976	6085	6028	6024	6028	6024
1980	5353	5217	5217	5217	5217
1984	7078	6797	6797	6797	6797
1988	9421	8465	8465	8465	8465
1992		9367	9370	9367	9370

*Equestrian events held in Sweden. Not included by Wallechinsky.

**Lyberg does not include 1906 figures.

Notes

1. The Huntsman World Senior Games and the Stoke Mandeville Wheelchair Games, held in the same city each year, have not kept this type of historical data on each games.

2. Lyberg, Wolf, "The Athletes of Nagano," *Journal of Sport History*, Vol. 6, No. 2, Summer 1998.

3. Starter in Mr. Lyberg's definition is an athlete who actually plays in the games or participates in the competition. This is distinguished from the American definition of starter, those on the field at the beginning of the game, and substitutes, those who enter the games to give the starters a rest.

4. See Addendum for a treatment of the Lyberg participation numbers.

5. Data received by mail from the Olympic Council of Asia headquarters in Kuwait. Compiled March 27, 1994.

6. From the Website of the USOC: http://www.olympic-usa.org/games/ga_2_3_3.html

7. See Bill Mallon's books on the 1896, 1900, 1904 and 1908 Olympic Games published by McFarland & Co.

8. Harris, H.A., *Greek Athletes and Athletics*, Indiana University Press, Bloomington and London, 1966.

9. Gardiner, E. Norman, *Athletics of the Ancient World*, Ares Publishers, Chicago, Ill., 1978.

10. Research continues on hundreds of other games and gatherings.

11. Golden, Mark, *Sport and Society in Ancient Greece*, Cambridge University Press, 1998, p. 16.

12. Ibid., p. 17.

13. Burns, Francis, "Robert Dover's Cotswold Olympick Games," *Olympic Review*, 1985, No. 210, pp. 230–236.

14. Joachim Ruhl and Anette Keuser, in "Olympic Games in 19th Century England with Special Consideration of the Liverpool Olympics," write that Dovers games only lasted until 1641 (in *Contemporary Studies in the National Olympic Games Movement*, Roland Naul, ed., Peter Lang Publisher, Frankfurt, 1997.

15. Anthony, Don, "Olympic Glory," British Olympic Association.

16. Svahn, Ake, "The Olympic Games at Ramlösa in 1834 and 1836, *Olympic Review*, 1984, No. 204, pp. 752–758.

17. See note 15.

18. Rees, Roy, "The Olympic festivals of mid–Victorian England," *Olympic Review*, 1977, p. 21–23.

19. Joachim Ruhl and Anette Keuser, in "Olympic Games in 19th Century England with Special Consideration of the Liverpool Olympics," write that Dovers games only lasted until 1641 (in *Contemporary Studies in the National Olympic Games Movement*, Roland Naul, ed., Peter Lang Publisher, Frankfurt, 1997).

20. Arvin-Berod, Alain, "In France, the idea of the Olympic Games crosses the centuries," *Olympic Review*, 1994, No. 321, pp. 339–341.

21. Cholley, Patrice, "The Rondeau Olympic Games," *Olympic Review*, May 1996, p. 48. The games evidently were held until 1952, according to the title of the book by Alain, Aarvin Berod, *Et Didon*

Créa la devise des Jeux Olympiques, ou l'histoire oublié des Jeux Olympiques de Rondeau (Grenoble 1832–1952) Editions Sciriolus, Echirolles, 1994.

22. Proposed Rules for Regional Games, *Olympic Bulletin*, June 1951, p. 39.

23. Rules for Regional Games, *Olympic Review*, November 1952, p. 12–13.

24. IOC Bulletin No. 63, August 15, 1958.

25. IOC Bulletin No 76, Nov. 15, 1961, pp. 28–29.

26. Other examples include the prohibition, or attempt to prohibit, the use of the terms: "American Olympic Games," "Olympiade Catalan," "Deaf Olympics," "Workers Olympics," "Chess Olympics," and "Transplant Olympics."

27. With possible games still being researched and verified.

28. The History of the International Student Games. unpublished document (Gary Allison).

29. Deutsch Olympiade Kalendar, Borgers, Walter; Lennartz, Karl; Quanz, Dietrich; Teutenberg, Walter, Agon Sportverlag, Frankfurt.

30. Ukah, Matthias, "Socio-Cultural Forces in the Growth of All-African Games," *Journal of the International Council for Health, Physical education and Recreation*, Winter 1990, pp. 16–20.

31. Ukah, p. 16.

32. *Daily Nation*, Nairobi, Kenya, July 19, 1965 "Soldiers patrol as Games open."

33. *Daily Nation*, July 15, 1965 "Kenya athletes shine in Brazzaville."

34. *Daily Nation*, July 17, 1965 "Single Gov't for Africa."

35. Noronha, Francis, *Kipchoge of Kenya*, Elimu Publishers, Nakuru, Kenya, 1970.

36. *Daily Nation*, January 9, 1973.

37. *Daily Nation*, August 1, 1987.

38. *Egyptian Gazette*, July 26, 1953.

39. Information on participating nations and number of athletes conflicts for these games. Data provided by the Arab Sports Confederation lists seven nations: Egypt, Iraq, Jordan, Kuwait, Lebanon, Syria and Palestine. *The Egyptian Gazette*, July 27, 1953 states that 463 athletes marched in the Opening ceremonies, from nine nations: Egypt, Indonesia, Iraq, Jordan, Kuwait, Lebanon, Libya, Syria and Palestine. The same paper, the following day, while enumerating the number of entries per sport, substitutes Iran for Libya in the above list, and gives a total of 657 participating athletes. Egypt had the largest team by far with 215 athletes. Indonesia had four participants, in shooting and athletics. Iran brought 8 weightlifters.

40. *Egyptian Gazette*, August 11, 1957.

41. *London Times*, October 14, 1957.

42. *Le Jour*, Beirut, Lebanon, October 12, 1957. (Arab Sports Confederation data lists seven nations for these games. Iraq, Jordan, Kuwait, Lebanon, Morocco, Syria, and Tunisia. Le Jour, the Beirut newspaper the day before the Opening Ceremony lists adds Libya and Saudi Arabia to this list.)

43. *London Times*, October 14, 1957.

44. *New York Times*, August 25, 1961.

45. *Le Jour*, Beirut, August 24, 1961.

46. *Le Jour*, Beirut, Sept. 6, 1961.

47. "Maroc Soir," *Maroc Magazine*, Aug 3–4, 1985.

48. *Olympic Review*, No. 210, 1985, p. 284.

49. Arab Sports Confederation data lists 17 nations. *Syria Times*, September 5, 1992 lists 19 nations.

50. *Reuters*, July 3, 1993.

51. Reuters News Service, July 9, 1997.

52. Reuters News Service, July 28, 1997.

53. Arafura Games, Official Rules and Regulations, 1997.

54. Arafura Flyer, Vol. 4, No. 1, July 1996.

55. *Anchorage Daily Times*, March 9, 1972.

56. *Anchorage Daily Times*, March 4, 1974.

57. *Anchorage Daily Times*, March 8, 1974.

58. *The Anchorage Times*, March 15, 1982.

59. *New York Times*, May 20, 1958.

60. *New York Times*, May 20, 1958.

61. *New York Times*, June 3, 1958.

62. *New York Times*, June 4, 1958.

63. "Sport and Politics, The Case of Asian Games and the GANEFO," Sie, Swanpo, in *Sport and International Relations*. Lowe, Kanin, Strenk.

64. More recent sources (the official 1998 Asian Games Web Site) have stricken Israel from the medals tables. The *Asian Games, Asian Championships, Commonwealth Games, Olympic Games, World*

Championships Book of Records, published by the 1982 Asian Games organizing committee includes Israel's medals for 1954, 1958, 1966, 1970 and 1974.

65. *Olympic Review*, July 1990, No. 273, pp. 339–340.

66. The 3rd Asian Winter Games Harbin 1996 Official Report, p. 63.

67. Correspondence with Kenth Sjoblom, Helsinki, Finland, 1998. Information from Allhems *Sportlexicon*.

68. Official Brochure for the second Baltic Sea Games, 1997.

69. *Olympic Review*, 1977, p. 718.

70. *New York Times*, December 5, 1951.

71. *New York Times*, December 19, 1951.

72. The author is still trying to obtain results for these games which would prove this point either in the negative or affirmative.

73. El Comercio, Quito, Ecuador, November 19, 1985.

74. Diario Mayor de Santa Cruz (Bolivia), October 22, 1997.

75. The written history of the Bolivarian Games is incomplete. Numerous inquiries to each of the National Olympic Committees eligible to participate in the games met with no response at all. Very sparse histories have been written in *Factores Intervinientes en el Exito Deportivo: Un Estudio de los Atletas participantes en los VIII Juegos Bolivarianos*. Published January 1979, available in the Library of Congress. Another brief history is available in the 1973 report of the games, "VII Juegos Bolivarianos."

76. No evidence to the contrary has been found that all six of the eligible nations have competed on each occasion, but no confirming sources were found except for the games of 1938, 1951, 1965, 1973, 1985 and 1997.

77. The soccer tournament began on August 6th, the Opening Ceremony was held on August 16, the day of the 400th Anniversary of the founding of Bogota.

78. At 126 days, these were the fifth longest games on record with only the 1900, 1904, 1908 and 1920 Olympics longer.

79. These 23 nations were scheduled to participate.

80. List is from *World Sports*, May 1951, pp. 6–7. These were the events scheduled to be held at that time, with others to be scheduled later.

81. Some have objected to the use of the word paraplegic in this context. The terminology has been retained as this was the term in use, and the official name of the games at the time of the games.

82. "A Brief History of Participation on the Commonwealth Games," Tony Stansbury, February, 1997.

83. "Report of the Sub-Committee on Events for Athletes with a Disability," Tony Stansbury, February 1997.

84. The others were the 1946 Bolivarian Games in Lima, Peru (Dec. 26–Jan 6), 1978 All-African University Games in Nairobi, Kenya (Dec. 29–Jan. 7), and the 1995 Pan-American Maccabi Games in Buenos Aires (Dec. 24–Jan. 4).

85. "The Canterbury Tale," *World Sports*, February 1951, pp. 18–19.

86. Acronym for the Caribbean Free Trade Agreement.

87. *Barbados Advocate*, April 3, 1994.

88. *Barbados Advocate*, coverage from April 5 to April 13, 1993.

89. *La Semaine*, "Du basket au pugilat: La terribel finale masculine," July 25, 1976.

90. *Centroamericanos y del Caribe '93*, Vol. 1, No. 1, Feb. 1993.

91. *Olympic Review*, Dec. 1934, p. 10, and Lyberg (100 years), both indicate that a tornado was the cause of the delay. The book *Los Juegos Regionales mas Antiguos* and the historical record *Centroamericanos y del Caribe* (Vol. 1, Feb. 1993) from the 1993 Organizing Committee attributes the delay to an earthquake.

92. McGehee, Richard, "Los Juegos de las Americas" [Four Inter-American Multisport Competitions (Chapter 26 in *Sport in the Global Village*, Ralph W. Wilcox, editor, Fitness Information Technology, Inc., 1994)].

93. Correspondence with Olympic Committees in the region has turned up no further information.

94. Efforts to discover where the 7th games were held have yet to be successful.

95. See note 92.

96. "Historia de los Juegos Deportivos Centroamericanos, La Prensa, 1997" (part of the 1997 San Pedro Sulas Central American Games web site).

97. IOC Press releases, September 1995 and September 12, 1997.

98. Riordan, James, *Sport in Soviet Society: Development of Sport and Physical Education in Russia and the USSR*, Cambridge, New York, Cambridge University Press, 1980.

99. Dheenshar, Cleve, *The Commonwealth Games: The First Sixty Years, 1930–1990*, Orca Book Publishers, Victoria, Canada, 1994, p. 7.

100. *The Official History of the VIth British Empire and Commonwealth Games, 1958*, p. 169, Cardiff, Wales. Published by the Organising Committee, C.E. Newham, J.D.B. Williams, Eileen M. Richards, editors.

101. These Games are also claimed by the organizers of the West African Games to be the first West African Games.

102. Diack, Lamine, "The Development of African sport: achievements, obstacles and future prospects," *Olympic Review*, June-July 1997, pp. 59–63.

103. July 1, 1999, *The Monitor*, Lusaka Zambia.

104. *The Namibian*, July 26, 2000, "Chaos at CUCSA Games."

105. December 2000, Republic of Namibia Government Web site.

106. O.P. Arya, C.B. Bosa, J.A.F. Lobo, L.J. de Souza, "Injury Experience in the Seventh University Games in Kampala, Uganda," *East African Medical Journal*, August 1971, pp. 411–419.

107. www.africanews.com/monitor/freeissues/25oct99/sports.html. October 25, 1999.

108. While no evidence has been presented for this, it is likely that the change was due to requests by the IOC and de Coubertin to change the name, as they had in a number of other occasions attempted to reserve the use of the word Olympic, for the Olympic Games.

109. Manchukuo was a Chinese province that had been controlled by the Russians from around 1860 until the Japanese-Russian war (1902–1905).

110. John Robinson, *The Atlantic*, 8/27/97.

111. Bonnie Brown, Canadian Member of Parliament, http://web.spinners.on.ca/brown/press.html #francophone.

112. Correspondence from Madagascar Olympic Committee stated in February 1997 that Sydney, Australia was to be the host of the 2001 Francophone Games.

113. 43 countries were scheduled to compete. At least 28 did. No source other than the medals table has yet been found to confirm this.

114. 49 "countries or governments" were originally scheduled to take part in the games. The official Games web site lists entries for only the 30 countries listed. Also invited, Bulgaria, Cambodia, Cote D'Ivoire, Djibouti, Dominica, Egypt, Equatorial Guinea, Guinea Bissau, Laos, Mauritania, Morocco, Niger, St. Lucie, Vanuatu and Zaire.

115. *New York Times*, July 9, 1984.

116. *New York Times*, August 19, 1984.

117. The *New York Times* mentions Budapest as a main venue, but no other events are mentioned specifically associated with Budapest. *New York Times*, July 9, 1984.

118. *New York Times*, August 20, 1984.

119. *New York Times*, August 22, 1984.

120. Newspaper reports in *New York Times* mentioned between nine and forty sports but only these twelve sports were listed in the *New York Times* results during the days of the games.

121. Press Conference, Goodwill Games, New York City, 1998, July 16, 1998 on www.goodwill.com.

122. Reports of the games in 1995 make no mention of the South Africa issue. One would assume with the inclusion of South Africa in the Olympic Movement, Commonwealth Games and African Games the South Africans would once again be invited to the Hapoel Games.

123. Major George Wythe, Captain Joseph Mills Hanson, The Inter-allied games : Paris, 22nd June to 6th July, 1919 / pub. by the Games Committee, Paris : Printed by Société anonyme de publications périodiques, 1919.

124. "Elwood S. Brown, Missionary Extraordinary," Ian Buchanan, *Journal of Olympic History*, Vol. 6, No. 3, Fall 1998.

125. Current figures for nations are derived from nations that are represented on the event results.

126. The games are traditionally held during this time in the month of March, but exact dates were not provided by the games organizers.

127. Dates may be for athletics events only (Raul Leoni list). ISF was not able to provide dates for these games.

128. *The Island Games, 1985–1985*, Geoffrey Corbett (book available from the Isle of Man Tourist Office).

129. The definition of Jewish for the games is if the athlete's mother is Jewish or if the athlete has converted to Judaism. If the father is the only Jewish parent, the athlete is eligible if he or she has been brought up Jewish.

130. Eisen, George, p. 267.

131. Eisen, George, p. 276.

132. *IOC Bulletin*, August 15, 1955, p. 38.

133. *IOC Bulletin*, November 15, 1955, pp. 47–48. "Echoes of the IInd Mediterranean Games," Juan Antonio Samaranch.

134. *IOC Bulletin*, August 15, 1959, p. 68.

135. *IOC Bulletin*, February 15, 1959. "The Mediterranean Games in Danger," p. 54.

136. *IOC Bulletin*, Feb. 15, 1960. The IIIrd Mediterranean Games.

137. *IOC Bulletin*, May 15, 1963. Minutes of the meeting of the Executive Board of the International Olympic Committee with the Representatives of the International Sports Federations. February 8, 1963.

138. *IOC Bulletin*, June 1964. Minutes of the meeting of the Executive Board of the International Olympic Committee with the Representatives of the International Sports Federations, June 6, 1963, pp. 47–53.

139. Reuters, September 18, 1995.

140. Brooks, Geraldine, 1995, *Nine Parts of Desire: The Hidden World of Islamic Women*, New York, Doubleday.

141. *An Illustrated Report of the First Islamic Countries' Women Sports Solidarity Games*, 1993 Tehran.

142. *Nordisk Familjebiks Sportlexikon*, "Upplaslagsverk för Sport, Gymnastik och Friluftsliv," Stockholm, Förlagsaktiebolaget A. Sohlman & Co. 1943.

143. Yttergren, Lief I. "The Nordic Games: Visions of a Winter Olympics or a National Festival?" *The International Journal of the History of Sport*, Vol. 11. No. 3 (Dec. 1994), pp. 495–505.

144. 1997 North American Indigenous Games website.

145. *Edmonton Journal*, July 8, 1990.

146. 1993 Games organizers press release, July 8, 1993.

147. *Minneapolis Star Tribune*, July 28, 1995. The precedent for this was set at the International School Games in 1994 in Hamilton Ontario, which had a team named Aboriginal Team Ontario.

148. See Precursors to the Modern Games section in the introduction for more detailed treatments on the events leading up to 1896.

149. Burns, Francis, "Robert Dover's Cotswold Olympick Games," *Olympic Review*, 1985, No. 210, pp. 230–236.

150. Joachim Ruhl and Anette Keuser, in "Olympic Games in 19th Century England with Special Consideration of the Liverpool Olympics," write that Dover's games only lasted until 1641 (in *Contemporary Studies in the National Olympic Games Movement*, Roland Naul, ed., Peter Lang Publisher, Frankfurt, 1997.

151. Anthony, Don, "Olympic Glory," British Olympic Association.

152. *Ibid.*

153. Pierre de Coubertin, Letter to William May Garland, June 6, 1921.

154. Pierre de Coubertin, Letter to William May Garland, October 10, 1930.

155. "Anthropology Days at the Stadium," *Spalding's Official Athletic Almanac for 1905*, pp. 249–263, James E. Sullivan.

156. Mallon, Bill, *The 1904 Olympic Games: Results for All Competitors in All Events, with Commentary*, McFarland, Jefferson, NC, 1999.

157. Lyberg, p. 139.

158. Kieran, John, and Daley, Arthur, *The Story of the Olympic Games, 776 B.C. to 1972*, J.B. Lippincott Company, Philadelphia–New York, 1973.

159. Pierre de Coubertin, Letter to William May Garland, June 6, 1921.

160. William May Garland, letter to Pierre de Coubertin, Dec, 9, 1924.

161. Cohen, Stan, *The Games of '36*, Pictoral Histories Publishing Company, Missoula, 1996.

162. Borgers, Walter, *Olympic Torch Relays*, Agon Sportverlag, 1996, p. 44.

163. John M. Goshko, "Oberweisenfeld: Site of Olympics, Cameo of German History," *Los Angeles Times*, August 14, 1972.

164. *The 1936 Olympic Oaks: Where are they Now?* Authored and published by James Ross Constandt, Eagle, Michigan. 1994.

165. Lyberg, p. 147.

166. Lyberg, p. 153.

167. Lyberg, p. 125.

168. *Olympic Review*, May, 1971, "The Olympic Villages," Herbert Schmitt, pp. 258–261.

169. *Olympic Review*, April 1971, p. 200.

170. *Washington Post*, May 1, 2000.

171. *Olympic Review*, 1980, No. 149, pp. 109–110.

172. Lyberg, p. 164.

173. *Olympic Review*, 1981, No. 169, pp. 616–617.

174. Lyberg, p. 164.

175. "IOC 2000 Reforms," Supplement of the *Olympic Review XXVI*, 30 December 1999–January 2000.

176. Mallon, Bill, "The Olympic Bribery Scandal," *Journal of Olympic History*, Vol. 8, No 2. May 2000, pp. 11–27.

177. Wallechinsky, Lyberg and Mallon, the three foremost authorities on the issue of the number of athletes and sports at the Olympic Games, all disagree on this issue. Wallechinsky has had the courage to update his numbers twice. See Appendix 8 in this book for tables comparing the 1992, 1996 and 2000 editions of the numbers in Wallechinsky's *Complete Book of the Olympics*, with Mallon and Lyberg. The figures used here are from Wallechinsky's latest edition.

178. Mallon lists Australasia as two separate countries. Australia and New Zealand and Wallechinsky has adopted the same convention in the medals tables for the 1908 and 1912 games.

179. Wallechinsky lists this nation as VIR (Virgin Islands) but in the abbreviations in the back of his work, 2000 edition of *The Complete Book of the Olympics*, lists ISV as the US Virgin Islands and IVB as the British Virgin Islands and no country listed under VIR.

180. Lyberg, p. 142.

181. Lyberg, p. 151.

182. Lyberg, pp. 301–302.

183. "Nagano Keeps Paying," *Deseret News*, deseretnews.com, February 5, 2001.

184. See Olympic Games chapter and footnotes for the full treatment of the IOC bribery scandal.

185. Wallechinsky's 1984 *Complete Book of the Olympics* list Switzerland as winning one bronze medal at the 1928 games. Wallechinsky's 1998 Complete book of the Winter Olympics omits this medal.

186. Wallechinsky's 1984 *Complete Book of the Olympics* list Italy as winning one bronze medal at the 1960 games. Wallechinsky's 1998 *Complete Book of the Winter Olympics* omits this medal.

187. Wallechinsky's 1984 *Complete Book of the Olympics* does not list France or Canada as winning medals at the 1972 games. Wallechinsky's 1998 *Complete Book of the Winter Olympics* includes France and Canada in these medals tables.

188. Sources such as Wallechinsky's *Complete Book of the Winter Olympics* say 64 nations competed, but only 63 show up on the available list.

189. Participation and nations figures from pre-games information.

190. Winnipeg reports list these 29 nations as entered. USOC data says 27 countries entered.

191. Federation Mexicana de Deportes Sobre Silla de Ruedas web site lists just one date for each games rather than a range of dates.

192. Joan Scruton, "Paralympism, Olympism, sport for handicapped people." Unpublished manuscript.

193. Participation figures from "Paralympics, Where Heroes Come," Steadward and Peterson, and IPC website, www.paralympic.org. Both sources agree.

194. This list contains the 128 nations who entered in the games. Official figures stated that only 122 nations eventually participated, but this list does not account for the six-nation discrepancy.

195. "Peace Arch Games set to begin, Games look for focal point," *Bellingham Herald*, June 19, 1989.

196. "Peace Arch Games to play in winter too," *Bellingham Herald*, July 6, 1990.

197. Institute for International Sport website, www.internationalsport.com.

198. NCAA News, March 30, 1998.

199. Information provided from the Bulgarian Pentathlon Union.

200. Kruger, Arnd, Riordan, James, *The Story of Worker Sport, Human Kinetics*, Champaign, IL, 1996, pp. 62, 170.

201. The SWSI timeline in *Worker Sport* (Kruger, Riordan, 1996) mentions the Czechoslovak Worker Olympiads, held in 1921, the First "Worker Olympiad" held in 1927, the Second Worker Olympiad in Vienna in 1931, and the Third Czechoslovak Olympiad in Prague in 1934. It is unclear whether there were games titled Worker Olympiads, and another competition titled Czechoslovak Worker Olympiads. Wagner in Prague's Socialist Olympics of 1934 (*Canadian Journal of the History of Sport*, May 1992) mentions Socialist games of 1920 (p. 6), though the SWSI (specifically the Lucerne Sports International, LSI, which would become the SWSI) was not founded until September 1921. Furthermore the timeline in worker sport mentions the Czechoslovak Worker Olympiad in Prague June 24–30 (p. 167), and the first Spartakiad of Red Sport International, June 19–26, 1921 also in Prague (p. 168).

202. Riordan, James, "Worker Sport within a Worker State" (in *The Story of Worker Sport*, Human Kinetics, Champaign, IL, 1996), p. 61.

203. These games are treated in depth in Baker, James, "Muscular Marxism and the Chicago Counter-Olympics," pp. 285–299, in *The New American Sport History: Recent Approaches and Perspectives*, University of Illinois Press, 1997, S.W. Pope.

204. Wagner, p. 16.

205. *Olympic Review*, 1988, p. 190.

206. Pre-games discussions (*Pakistani Times*, Dec. 19, 1993) mentions that the women's events may be restricted to a female only audience, but no other mention or indication of this occurring in the rest of the games coverage.

207. *The Hindu & The India Information, Inc.*, Dec 16, 1995.

208. *The Hindu & The India Information, Inc.*, Jan 30, 1996, and August 27, 1996.

209. Dillon, Kathryn, "The Historical Development of the South Pacific Games," Masters Thesis, California State University, Sacramento, 1975, p. 56.

210. "Bumps in road paved with good intentions," Batsell, Jake, *Seattle Times*, May 31, 1997.

211. The Stoke Mandeville games dates are traditionally in the last week of July.

212. The book *The Aonach Tailteann and the Tailteann Games, their Origin, History and Ancient Associations*, page 61, claims the Tailteann games predate the Olympic Games by 400 years, and were in fact the inspiration for the games of Greece, the idea having been brought back from Ireland by Grecian traders.

213. Other famous assemblies or Aonach were the Aonach Carman, Aonach Cruchuan, and Aonach Colmain.

214. The modern phrase "Teltown marriage" comes from this tradition. No mention is made in *The Aonach Tailteann and the Tailteann Games: Their Origin, History and Ancient Associations* as to why the Aonach Tailteann ended in 1169 A.D.

215. *New York Times*, August 19, 1924.

216. *New York Times*, Sunday, August 26, 1928.

217. "The Third Tailteann Games," Dublin, June 29–July 10, 1932 Syllabus, p. 15.

218. Mohamed Amin from the University of Ghana provided the full list of games.

219. *Tehran Times*, November 20, 1997.

220. Lebanese web site lists these 21 sports. Other sources mention fourteen sports with no list. Water Polo is on the venue list but not the sports list, which brings the number to 22.

221. *First Western Asiatic Games*, New Delhi, 1934, Official Report.

222. Data has not yet been made available for the later years.

223. "ACOG hit by more flak," Grania Willis, *Irish Times*, July 25, 1996.

224. FEI, *World Equestrian Games Report*, 1994.

225. Figures provided by the FEI list the number of nations per discipline. The largest list is jumping with 27 nations, but the nations are not listed. The nations are listed in the dressage, driving and endurance disciplines and this list is derived from the combination of those three lists, which happens coincidentally to equal 27, the number in the first discipline. As the nations are not known for the jumping discipline, it is not known if these two lists overlap perfectly.

226. Same as above note. The lists are incomplete but the jumping report indicates that 27 nations were part of the competition.

227. Other than the Olympic Games, the World Games for the Deaf are the second oldest ongoing international games. The World University Games are the oldest, having begun one year before in 1923.

228. History of the International Committee of Sports for the Deaf (CISS) based on extracts from articles by Mr. Antoine Dresse, Founding General Secretary, CISS and from CISS bulletins. On the web at www.gallaudet.edu/history.html

229. Jordan, Jerald, "World Games for the Deaf and Paralympic Games" (CISS website).

230. *Toronto Globe and Mail*, August 21, 1985.

231. There is only one missing, as 40 was reported as the number.

232. Continuing the regionalization of the Scholar Athlete Games, a pilot program for the Pacific Rim Scholar Athlete Games was held in Cairns in 1996 with 150 Australian students. A full fledged games were planned for 1998, but subsequently postponed one year to 1999.

233. "The History of International Student Games," unpublished document, 1st Century Project.

234. "The History of FISU," Lazlo Kutassi, unpublished thesis.

235. "Recall of Italian delegation," *London Times*, August 23, 1928.

236. Kutassi, p. 20.

237. Kutassi, p. 30.

238. Kutassi, p. 42.

239. Kutassi, p. 63.

240. Riordan, James. *Sport, Politics and Communism*. Manchester Univ. Press 1991, p. 128. Riordan

mentions that the 1949 and 1951 games were held in conjunction with the Communist World Youth Festivals.

241. Background, U.S. Dept. of State, "Two weeks in August. East German Youth Strays West" September 1951.

242. "East German fans bolt party line with boos for Russia's Athletes," *New York Times*, August 16, 1951.

243. Documents provided by the Olympic Century Project mention that UIE games continued to be held (despite the assertion in Kutassi that both the UIE and FISU would forego their own games in 1957) in Moscow in 1957, Vienna in 1959, and Helsinki in 1962. Kutassi (p. 99) mentions Summer International Competitions held in Krakow, Poland July 8–13, 1958, with no additional mention of sanctioning body, events or participants. A second source has not been found that mentions these games.

244. A letter from the games founder Jean Petitjean in the 1961 games official report congratulates Sofia on a successful games and asks the organizers for a medal "just like the athletes, so I may complete my archive."

245. World University Games Buffalo 93, Guide to the Games for the FISU family, guests and Observers, p. 94.

246. *Sports Illustrated*, "Scorecard," July 29, 1991.

247. "Sicily to probe alleged Mafia involvement in Games," Reuters News Service, August 22, 1997.

248. Some football and rowing competitions were held in Hamilton, Ontario, Canada.

249. The Official participants list, *FISU Magazine*, September 1999, lists 125 nations, one abbreviated MAC which is not an official IOC abbreviation. This may be an error? Macedonia or the Former Yugoslavian Republic of Macedonia, a logical guess, is known as MKD in its abbreviated form.

250. Broker, Kevin, "Way inside ESPN's X Games," p. 7.

Bibliography

African Games

Africans to Hold Games, New York Times, May 30, 1927, pg. 13

1ers jeux Africains et XXVIe session annuelle du Comité International Olympique. 1929, Alexandria, Egypt.

United we stand Moi tells Africa, Daily Nation–Nairobi, July 21, 1978

Kenya to host 1982 All-Africa Games, Jerusalem Post, April 30, 1979

Penman, Kenneth A.; Spechalske, Frank H., The Feasibility of Kenya Hosting the 1983 All-African Games:A preliminary Report to the Kenya National Sports Council, United States International Communication Agency, United States Sports Academy, August 1980

Diack, Lamine, The Development of African Sport: achievements, obstacles and future prospects., Olympic Review, June–July 1997, pg. 59–63

Nigeria named as host of 2003 All-Africa Games, Reuter Information Service, January 14, 1997

1965

Brazzaville: Capitale Africaine du sport; Reunion du comite d'organisation des premiers jeux africains, Dipanda-Brazzaville, May 15, 1965

Le Congo-Brazzaville Prepare les Premiers Jeux Africains, Dipanda; Hebdomidaire del la Revolution Congolaise, June 5, 1965

Message du Frere Secretaire d'Etat a La Jeunesse et Sports, Dipanda; Hebdomidaire del la Revolution Congolaise, July 10, 1965

Kenya athletes shine in Brazzaville, Daily Nation–Nairobi, July 15, 1965

Vivent Les Jeux Africains, Dipanda; Hebdomidaire del la Revolution Congolaise, July 17, 1965

Single Gov't for Africa, Daily Nation–Nairobi, July 17, 1965

Soldiers Patrol as Games Open, Daily Nation–Nairobi, July 19, 1965

Kipchoge Wins as he likes, Daily Nation–Nairobi, July 22, 1965

Les Premiers Jeux Africains se Deroulent bien a Brazzaville, Dipanda; Hebdomidaire del la Revolution Cngolaise, July 24, 1965

Cloture des Jeux Africans, Dipanda; Hebdomidaire de la Revolution Congolaise, July 31, 1965

Noronha, Francis, Kipchoge of Kenya, Elimu Publishers, 1970

1973

Africa seeks unity with Games, London Times, January 5, 1973

Trente neuf pays a Lagos, La Semaine–Brazzaville Congo, January 7, 1973

Gen. Gowon opens Africa's Greatest Sports Showpiece, Daily Nation–Nairobi, January 9, 1973

Les deuxiemes jeux panafricains de Lagos, La Semaine–Brazzaville Congo, January 14, 1973

Unknown Tanzanian keeps Kenyan at bay, Daily Nation–Nairobi, January 15, 1973

When a record is not a record, London Times, January 16, 1973

Egypt keep up medal count, Daily Nation–Nairobi, January 17, 1973

Whitfield Predicts Africa will top in Sport, Daily Nation–Nairobi, January 18, 1973

Games prove a Triumph for Eastern Africa, Daily Nation–Nairobi, January 19, 1973

1978

Les 3eme Jeux Africains et les 11eme Jeux du Commonwealth se derouleron a dix semaines

551

d'intervalle, La Semaine Africaine, May 14, 1978

Jeux africains d'Alger: 350 sportifs en France, La Semaine Africaine, July 8, 1978

Running to school was early training for the world beater. How Rono won through—against all odds, Daily Nation–Nairobi, July 13, 1978

Battle for African honours is on, Daily Nation–Nairobi, July 14, 1978

6000 athletes au rendez-vous d'Alger 78, La Semaine Africaine, July 18, 1978

Yifter fails to match Rono's pace, London Times, July 21, 1978

Les Jeux d'Alger, un motif de fierte pour le sport africain, La Semaine Africaine, July 23, 1978

Football fight angers Egypt, London Times, July 24, 1978

No Venue for boxing, Daily Nation–Nairobi, July 27, 1978

Tunisia and Mali's penalties shortened, Daily Nation–Nairobi, July 27, 1978

Apres les Troisiemes Jeux Africains d'Alger, La Semaine Africaine, Sept. 3, 1978

Les "gazelles noirs" de L;afrique et les JO 80, La Semaine Africaine, Sept. 17, 1978

1987

Zimbabwe: Sports for all in Chitungwiza, Africa-news, September 1986

Kick-start for Africa Games, New African, December 1986, pgs. 53–54

Preparation of the 4th African Games, Nairobi 1st to 16th August 1987, Olympic Review, 1986, pg 192

The 4th All-Africa Games, New African, July 1987, pgs. 39–43

IVth African Games, 1st to 12th August 1987, Olympic Review, 1987, pg. 344

4th All-Africa Games Official Program, 1987

The 4th African Games A Demonstration of International Solidarity, Olympic Review, 1987 pg. 135

Now Let's make the games a great hit, Daily Nation–Nairobi, July 7, 1987

Sh 125,000 boost for Games, Daily Nation–Nairobi, July 15, 1987

2000 more join city clean-up team, Daily Nation–Nairobi, July 18, 1987

Games officials hold rehearsal, Daily Nation–Nairobi, July 18, 1987

Tickets sale starts, Daily Nation–Nairobi, July 23, 1987

Relay torch now in city, Daily Nation–Nairobi, July 23, 1987

Sunguh, George, Games: It's a boon for hotels, Daily Nation–Nairobi, July 30, 1987

Ochieng, Angela, Moi to watch the Games every day, Daily Nation–Nairobi, July 30, 1987

Games stalls: Duo may lose millions, Daily Nation–Nairobi, July 30, 1987

Ouko, Charles, Countdown: 23 countries are already in, Daily Nation–Nairobi, July 30, 1987

de Souza, Anton, A Win: Ticket to the Olympics, Daily Nation–Nairobi, August 1, 1987

Wandera, Hector, A continental meet is born, Daily Nation–Nairobi, August 1, 1987

Nduati,Samuel, Open air market for Games venue, Daily Nation–Nairobi, August 1, 1987

Pewa, Johhny, Transport hitches hit arriving teams, Daily Nation–Nairobi, August 1, 1987

Ochieng, Angela, Kenya does not expect profits from games, Daily Nation–Nairobi, August 1, 1987

Agudah, Dick, It's all systems go, Daily Nation–Nairobi, August 1, 1987

President to open Games, Daily Nation–Nairobi, August 1, 1987

Let's all have a ball the next 12 days, Daily Nation–Nairobi, August 1, 1987

Agudah, Dick, A golden start caps spectacle to behold, Daily Nation–Nairobi, August 3, 1987

Nduati, Samuel, Games venue shift hurts kiosk trade, Daily Nation–Nairobi, August 4, 1987

Ivory Coast supporters weave magic spells on opponents, Daily Nation–Nairobi, August 8, 1987

Agudah, Dick; Ongaro, Stephen, President Moi visits venues, Daily Nation–Nairobi, August 5, 1987

Kurgat, Japser, Tempers flare up as Kenya dispute loss, Daily Nation–Nairobi, August 8, 1987

Otieno, Barrack; Ochieng, Angela, Victory ends in protection for ref, Daily Nation–Nairobi, August 8, 1987

Ongaro, Stephen; Olita, Reuben; Pewa, Johhny, Power failure curtails long awaited thriller, Daily Nation–Nairobi, August 10, 1987

Odindo, Joseph, The Good, the bad and the ugly in games coverage, Daily Nation–Nairobi, August 10, 1987

Olita, Reuben, Fight Breaks out as Egypt lose, Daily Nation–Nairobi, August 11, 1987

Ongaro, Stephen, New continental body formed to help boxers, Daily Nation–Nairobi, August 11, 1987

Pewa, Johhny, Harambee stars into historic final, Daily Nation–Nairobi, August 11, 1987

Machua, Wilfred, Nairobi becomes Tower of Babel, Daily Nation–Nairobi, August 12, 1987

Pewa, Johhny, The curtain falls on games today, Daily Nation–Nairobi, August 12, 1987

Wandera, Hector; Angwenyi, Peter, Ngugi returns to track, Daily Nation–Nairobi, August 12, 1987

President Moi presents golds, Daily Nation–Nairobi, August 12, 1987

Moi set to close games, Daily Nation–Nairobi, August 12, 1987

Muhong, Paul, Moi invites games contingents to tea, Daily Nation–Nairobi, August 13, 1987

1991

Cairo Hosts the 5th African Games, Olympic Review, 1991, pgs. 465–6

Officials reluctant to name contingent, Daily Nation–Nairobi, Sept. 7, 1991

King'Dri, Marianne, NGOs on Africa's recovery plan, Daily Nation–Nairobi, Sept. 17, 1991

Africa Games to open today, Daily Nation–Nairobi, Sept. 20, 1991

Davies order "silly" bickering to cease, Daily Nation–Nairobi, Sept. 20, 1991

Musonye, Nicholas, Sport remains the only symbol of African Unity, Daily Nation–Nairobi, Sept. 21, 1991

Games won't help Egypt's Olympic hopes, Daily Nation–Nairobi, Sept. 28, 1991

Nigeria, Egypt in ring-side brawl, Daily Nation–Nairobi, Oct. 2, 1991

Diving medals cancelled, Daily Nation–Nairobi, Oct. 2, 1991

Africa Games doors close: Egypt wins medals but irks IOC bosses, Daily Nation–Nairobi, Oct. 2, 1991

Minshull, Phil, Cairo Games Fiasco, New African, November 1991, pgs 50–52

1995

Egypt Threatens Boycott, West Africa, January 10–16, 1994, pg 57

South Africa will use games to develop team, Seattle Times, July 27, 1995

Makori, Elius, Games start tomorrow, Daily Nation–Nairobi, Sept. 12, 1995

Kenya's steeplechase trio expected in Harare, Daily Nation–Nairobi, Sept. 13, 1995

Zimbabwe scrambles to make venues ready, Daily Nation–Nairobi, Sept. 13, 1995

Games organizers told not to copy Olympics, Daily Nation–Nairobi, Sept. 14, 1995

Start marked by confusion, Daily Nation–Nairobi, Sept. 14, 1995

Brits asked for event switch after losing poles, Reuter Information Service, Sept. 14, 1995

South Africa Leads gold rush at African Games, Reuter Information Service, Sept. 14, 1995

Zimbabwe says Africa Games too big, Reuter Information Service, Sept. 15, 1995

Fresh problems plague Games, Daily Nation–Nairobi, Sept. 15, 1995

Manguti, Kennedy, Track standards low—Keino, Daily Nation–Nairobi, Sept. 16, 1995

Onyali says drug officials harass Nigerians, Reuter Information Service, Sept. 18, 1995

Africans see no changes in games format, Reuter Information Service, Sept. 18, 1995

Nigeria urges Afircan businesses to back athletics, Reuter Information Service, Sept. 19, 1995

Nigerian fails dope test at All Africa Games, Reuter Information Service, Sept. 19, 1995

Contestants complain at shooting cancellation, Reuter Information Service, Sept. 19, 1995

South African kicked out of Games over citizenship, Reuter Information Service, Sept. 19, 1995

African Games come to life on last night of track, Reuter Information Service, Sept. 19, 1995

Africans doubt patriotism of athletics stars, Reuter Information Service, Sept. 19, 1995

Games official accuses woman of being a man, Daily Nation–Nairobi, Sept. 20, 1995

Controversial doctor dismissed as announcer after insulting Games official, Reuter Information Service, Sept. 20, 1995

Kenyan upset by bias at games, Daily Nation–Nairobi, Sept. 20, 1995

Egypt beats Nigeria 1-0 as referee escorted off, Reuter Information Service, Sept. 21, 1995

Fresh drug scandal hits Africa Games, Reuter Information Service, Sept. 21, 1995

'Unity' Games polarize Africans, Reuter Information Service, Sept. 22, 1995

Curtain comes down on troubled African Games, Reuter Information Service, Sept. 23, 1995

Manguti, Kennedy, Lukewarm reception for Kenya's Games squad, Daily Nation–Nairobi, Sept. 25, 1995

Africa meets in Cairo, Olympic Review, 1991 pgs. 520–522

Whitfield, Mal, Africa becomes a major sports power, Los Angeles Sentinel, November 22, 1995

Afro-Asian Games

Afro-Asian Games, Olympic Review, 1985, pg. 284

Afro-Asian Games, Olympic Review, 1989, pg. 344

All-African University Games

Njoroge, Gishinga, University Games teams arrive, Daily Nation–Nairobi, Dec. 27, 1978

All systems go, Daily Nation–Nairobi, Dec. 28, 1978

Njoroge, Gishinga, Second All Africa University Games—Teams bubbling with confidence, Daily Nation–Nairobi, Dec. 28, 1978

President Moi to open Games, Daily Nation–Nairobi, Dec. 29, 1978

Getting all set for the big event, Daily Nation–Nairobi, Dec. 29, 1978

Superstar Rono in action today, Daily Nation–Nairobi, Dec. 29, 1978

Kenyan Musyoki wins first Games gold medal, Daily Nation–Nairobi, Dec. 30, 1978

Games of to rather shaky start, Daily Nation–Nairobi, Dec. 30, 1978

Moi opens FASU games, Daily Nation–Nairobi, Dec. 30, 1978

Problems hit games, Daily Nation–Nairobi, Jan. 2, 1979

Disputes hit matches, Daily Nation–Nairobi, Jan. 2, 1979

Refs down tools!, Daily Nation–Nairobi, Jan. 4, 1979

Teams accused of fielding 'mercenaries', Daily Nation–Nairobi, Jan. 5, 1979

Egyptians top FASU Games, Daily Nation–Nairobi, Jan. 8, 1979

Njoroge, Gishinga, FASU Games: It's time to go home, Daily Nation–Nairobi, Jan. 9, 1979

Alps-Adriatic Youth Games

Sport u radnoj zajednici Alpe-Jadran, 1998

Ancient Games

Crowther, Nigel B., Athlete and State: Qualifying for the Olympic Games in Ancient Greece, Journal of Sport History, Spring 1996, pgs. 34–43

Gibson, Rex, Sport Alone for Sam at Last, The Star International Weekly, September 8–14, 1994

Howell, Maxwell, L; Howell, Reet A; Thornton, C.A., Nemea Revisited, North American Society for Sport History Proceedings, 1978

Slowikowski, Synthia, S, Games and Cult; The Festivals of Fourth and Third Century B.C. Alexandria, North American Society for Sport History Proceedings and Newsletter, 1990, pgs. 8–9

Mandell, Richard D, Sport: A Cultural History, Columbus University Press, New York, 1984

Harris, H.A., Sport in Greece and Rome, Cornell University Press, Ithaca N.Y., 1972

Rees, Roy, The Olympic Festivals of mid–Victorian England, Olympic Review, January 1977, pgs. 21–23

Burns, Francis, Robert Dover's Cotswold Olimpick Games:, Olympic Review, 1985, pgs. 231–236

Lapchick, Richard, The Politics of Race and International Sport, 1975

Goulstone, John, The Northern Origins of the Olympic Games, Olympic Review, 1980, pgs. 336–339

Durantez, Conrado, The Games of Antiquity Face Up to History—Olympia Under Roman Law, Olympic Review, February 1989

Durantez, Conrado, The Games of Antiquity Face Up to History—Lucius Miniculus Natalis First Spanish Olympic Champion, Olympic Review, March 1989

Boutros, Labib, Details on the origin of the

Ancient Games, Olympic Review, 1981, pgs. 243–244

Burgener, Louis, Games and Physical Exercises in Switzerland in the 15th and 16th centuries, Olympic Review, 1981, pgs. 237–240

Greece and the Olympic Games, Olympic Review, 1978, pg 256–257

The "Saxon Olympic Games" in 1738, Olympic Review, 1985, pg. 560

Archer, Robert; Bouillon, Antoine, The South African Games: Sport and Apartheid (chapter), Zed Press, London, 1982

Svahn, Ake, The Olympic Games at Ramlosa in 1834 and 1836, Olympic Review, 1984, pgs. 753–756

Borgers, Walter; Lennartz, Karl; Quanz, Dietrich; Teutenberg, Walter, Deutsch Olympiade Kalendar, Agon Sportverlag

Arab Games

1953

President opens Pan-Arab Games, Egyptian Gazette–Cairo, July 27, 1953

Egyptian athletes shine in First Day's Arab Games, Egyptian Gazette–Cairo, July 28, 1953

Analytical table of the nine in the Pan-Arab Games, Egyptian Gazette–Cairo, July 28, 1953

Pan-Arab Games attract larger crowds yesterday, Egyptian Gazette–Cairo, July 29, 1953

Pan-Arab Games on E.S.B, Egyptian Gazette–Cairo, July 29, 1953

Alexandria fete for Arab Games, Egyptian Gazette–Cairo, July 30, 1953

More records tumble at Pan-Arab Games, Egyptian Gazette–Cairo, August 1, 1953

Pan-Arab Games at Stadium, Egyptian Gazette–Cairo, August 2, 1953

Libya outclassed at Pan-Arab Soccer—Egypt wins 10-2, Egyptian Gazette–Cairo, August 7, 1953

Egypt carry off soccer honours, Egyptian Gazette–Cairo, August 11, 1953

Naguib closes 1st Arab Games, Egyptian Gazette–Cairo, August 11, 1953

1957

Officiel: La Libye participe aux Jeux, Le Jour–Beirut, Sept. 24, 1957

Les Jeux Panarabes, Le Jour–Beirut, Oct. 10, 1957

La Mission seoudite est arrive hier, Le Jour–Beirut, Oct. 12, 1957

En presence du Roi Seoud et du President Chamoun, Ceremonie D'Ouverture, Le Jour–Beirut, Oct. 12, 1957

100.000 spectateurs ont assiste heir a la grandiose ceremonie d'ouverture, Le Jour–Beirut, Oct. 13, 1957

Arab Display of Sporting Prowess, London Times, Oct. 14, 1957

Deux Nouveaux records etablis au cours de le premiere journee, Le Jour–Beirut, Oct. 14, 1957

Mohamed El-Goureh trouve les cotes libanaises tres dures, et les descentes dangereuses Le Jour–Beirut, Oct. 17, 1957

Modification des programmes, Le Jour–Beirut, Oct. 20, 1957

Propos a batons rompus avec le directeur du volley et du basket, Le Jour–Beirut, Oct. 23, 1957

Le Maroc confirme sa pretention au titre, Le Jour–Beirut, Oct. 26, 1957

Imposante Ceremonie de Cloture, Le Jour–Beirut, Oct. 28, 1957

Coup d'oeil retrospectif sur les Iiemes Jeux Panarabes, Le Jour–Beirut, Oct. 31, 1957

1961

Officiel: 8 Nations a Casablanca a partir demain aux IIIemes J.P., Le Jour–Beirut, Aug. 24, 1961Politics is hurdled by Arab Olympics, New York Times, August 25, 1961

United Arab Republic wins Pan Arab Games, New York Times, September 10, 1961

1965

Jeux Panarabes, Le Jour–Beirut, Sept. 3, 1965

1985

Sous la presidence de moulay Ahmed Alaoui; Ouverture de la 2eme assemblee generale de l'union Arabe des sports, Maroc Soir, July 30, 1985

Une Participation Record, Maroc Soir, Aug. 1, 1985

Les Jeux Panarabes: Histoire, une evolution, Maroc Magazine (Maroc Soir), Aug. 3–4, 1985

La Ceremonie D'ouverture du Grand Spectacle, Maroc Magazine (Maroc Soir), Aug. 3–4, 1985

Des 9 mes Jeux Mediterraneens aux 6 mes Jeux Panarabes; Le Maroc Pays de la Fraternite de la concord, de L'amitie et de la Paix., Maroc Magazine (Maroc Soir), Aug. 3–4, 1985

1400 Journalistes couviriront les Viemes Jeux Panarabes, Maroc Magazine (Maroc Soir), Aug. 3–4, 1985

Une belle soiree, un beau spectacle sous le signe d 'lunite et de la fraternite, Maroc Soir, Aug. 3–4, 1985

Les Jeux Panarabes seront un succes, Maroc Soir, Aug. 3–4, 1985

Historique des Jeux, Maroc Soir, Aug. 3–4, 1985

La Septieme edition en Irak en 1989, Maroc Soir, Aug. 7, 1985

De la liberation a l'Emancipation de la femme Arabes, Maroc Soir, Aug. 14, 1985

Les Casablancais ont reserve un accueil grandios a Sa Saintete le Pape Jean-Paul II, Maroc Soir, Aug. 17, 1985

Pan Arab Games, Olympic Review, 1985, pg 284

1992

Under President Assad's patronage 7th Arab Games opens: Sports champions are heroes of peace and war, for Arab unity, Syria Times, Sept. 5, 1992

Arab media lauds Syria's initiative of hosting Games, Syria Times, Sept. 5, 1992

Proud of meeting in Syria, hopeful of more success, Syria Times, Sept. 7, 1992

Syria's hosting Arab Games boosts solidarity, Syria Times, Sept. 7, 1992

Syria tops participants with gold, Syria Times, Sept. 13, 1992

Pan-Arab Games conclude with Syria ahead, Syria Times, Sept. 19, 1992

President receives cable of appreciation from Arab athletes, Syria Times, Sept. 19, 1992

1997

1997 Pan Arab Games web site, 1997

Folding their tents, The Gazette–Montreal, July 6, 1993

Rebuilding Beirut Stadium to cost $120 million, Reuter Library Report, July 6, 1993

Lebanon seeks symbolic Iraqi presence, Reuters News Service, July 9, 1997

Iraqi sportsmen try to beat Arab Games ban, Agence France Presse, July 10, 1997

Maghreb states dominate Pan Arab Games, Reuters News Service, July 13, 1997

Moroccan women dominate Arab Games, Associated Press, July 16, 1997

Drug scandal rocks Games while Egypt wins ten more golds, Agence France Presse, July 20, 1997

Iraq condems Lebanon's decision to bar athletes, Reuters News Service, July 9, 1997

Two women athletes fail drug tests at Arab Games, Agence France Presse, July 23, 1997

Fans riot after seeing Syria lose Arab Games final, Reuters News Service, July 28, 1997

1999

Pan-Arab Games gets Mascot, Sept. 1998

Arafura Games

Arafura Flyer, July 1996

Arafura Games: Sporting Neighbours, Northern Territory Government, 1996

1999 Arafura Games Web site, 1996–1999

Arctic Winter Games

Paraschak, V; Scott, H, Ganes Northerners Play The Arctic Winter Games and the Northern Games—Reflections of one or several Canada Norths?, NAASH Proceedings, 1980

History of the Arctic Winter Games, Arctic Winter Games Society, 1989

Northwest Territories wrap up winter games, Anchorage Daily Times, March 14, 1970

Athletes set for Arctic Games, Anchorage Daily Times, March 2, 1972

Anchorage, Fairbanks bid for 1974 Games, Anchorage Daily Times, March 4, 1972

Winter Games to start today, Anchorage Daily Times, March 5, 1972

Egan bids warmth at start of Winter Games, Anchorage Daily Times, March 7, 1972

Expedition Names Peak 'Mt. Ulu', Anchorage Daily Times, March 11, 1972

Yukon wins 2nd Arctic Winter Games, Anchorage Daily Times, March 13, 1972

Arctic Friendship, Anchorage Daily Times, March 5, 1974

Godwin, Mark, Barrow dancers give Games ancient touch, Anchorage Daily Times, March 5, 1974

Scottish bagpipes and kilts Spark Evening's Festivities, Anchorage Daily Times, March 6, 1974

Souvenir Snatchers Create New Sport, Anchorage Daily Times, March 6, 1974

Schmidt, Margaret, Olympic organizer studies Arctic Games, Anchorage Daily Times, March 7, 1974

Godwin, Mark, Editor Pans 'City' Games, Anchorage Daily Times, March 8, 1974

Arctic Winter Games are colorful, but costly, Anchorage Daily Times, March 8, 1974

Festivities End Games, Anchorage Daily Times, March 9, 1974

Arctic Winter Games Exhausting Extravaganza, Anchorage Daily Times, March 9, 1974

Games flavor touches all, Anchorage Daily Times, March 9, 1974

Fans Excite Games, Anchorage Daily Times, March 9, 1974

Streakers spark closing ceremony, Anchorage Daily Times, March 11, 1974

Hay River and Pine Point Poised to Host Winter Games, Anchorage Times, March 19, 1978

McDiffett, Tim, Arctic Winter Games Open with Procession of Athletes, Anchorage Times, March 20, 1978

McDiffett, Tim, Traditional Sports take over Games, Anchorage Times, March 24, 1978

McDiffett, Tim, Arctic Winter Games wind down with finals today, Anchorage Times, March 25, 1978

McDiffett, Tim, Alaska takes top honors as Arctic Winter Games End, Anchorage Times, March 26, 1978

Hansen, Steve, Arctic Games Open, Anchorage Times, March 7, 1980

Yellowknife to host 84 Games, Anchorage Times, March 20, 1980

Hansen, Steve, Games village lifestyle spirited, Anchorage Times, March 18, 1980

Hansen, Steve, Unknown illness strikes athletes, Anchorage Times, March 19, 1980

Hansen, Steve, Winter Games' illness vanishes, Anchorage Times, March 20, 1980

Hansen, Steve, Bantams, Midgets add golds as Games close, Anchorage Times, March 22, 1980

Hansen, Steve, Alaskan gold rush, hospitality highlight Games, Anchorage Times, March 23, 1980

Arctic's stars meet, Anchorage Times, March 14, 1982

Cole, Dermot, Canada selects 600 to take on Alaska's best, Anchorage Times, March 15, 1982

Turcotte, Steve, This Whitehorse is different … this time around, Anchorage Times, March 16, 1986

Fidelman, Nell, Arctic Games return to birthplace, Anchorage Times, March 17, 1984

Fidelman, Nell, Pomp gives way to 84 competition, Anchorage Times, March 19, 1984

Fidelman, Nell, A warm 747 welcome, Anchorage Times, March 19, 1984

Fidelman, Nell, 86 Games move to Whitehorse, Anchorage Times, March 23, 1984

Fidelman, Nell, Up close and personal, it's the CBC, Anchorage Times, March 21, 1984

Turcotte, Steve, Arctic Games spectacle rivals Olympics, Anchorage Times, March 17, 1986

Turcotte, Steve, Arctic games mix tradition, hard work, Anchorage Times, March 21, 1986

Whitehorse: Arctic Games brighten long Yukon winter, Anchorage Times, March 23, 1986

Freedman, Lew, Winter Games a celebration for the human spirit, Anchorage Daily News, March 11, 1990

Freedman, Lew, The North competes; Winter Games begin, Anchorage Daily News, March 12, 1990

Freedman, Lew, No question about it: Native athlete still the best, Anchorage Daily News, March 14,

1990

Bingham, Charles, Whitehorse puts on impressive display, Anchorage Times, March 16, 1992

Woodbury, John, Alaskans put best foot forward, Anchorage Times, March 17, 1992

Freedman, Lew, Knuckle hopper pays a price, Anchorage Daily News, March 18, 1990

Alaska's lead is 18 medals if you count the dogs, Anchorage Times, March 19, 1992

Theft victim gets proper payback, Anchorage Times, March 21, 1992

Woodbury, John, Randazzo knuckles to gold ulu, Anchorage Times, March 22, 1992

Woodbury, John, The Winners: northern heritage, Whitehorse hospitality, Anchorage Times, March 22, 1992

Winter Weather stalls Arctic Games, Anchorage Times, March 22, 1992

Killoran, John, Arctic Winter Games Press Release # 1, Oct. 6, 1995

New appointees for YRAC sub-committee, Whitehorse Star Daily News, April 30, 1997

Heath, Brad, Arctic Winter Games 98; It's not winning that counts, Above & Beyond, Winter 1998, pgs. 54–60

O'Hara hired to manage 2000 AWG hosting effort, Whitehorse Star, Feb. 6, 1998

Asia Pacific Masters Games

Asia Pacific Masters Games web site, 1998, 2000

Asian Games

Trevithick, Alan, Asian Games, Encyclopedia of World Sport, David Levinson and Karen Christensen, editors. ABC-CLIO, 1996. pgs. 56–59

Asian Games, Olympic Games, Commonwealth Games Book of Records, Special Organising Committee of the IX Asian Games Delhi 1982, 1983

1951

Japan widens Asian Games Lead; Philippines gains basketball title, New York Times, March 11, 1951

Japan finishes first, India second as Asian Games end in New Delhi, New York Times, March 12, 1951

1954

Japan Far Ahead in Manila Games, New York Times, May 5, 1954

Trumpets, 5-Gun salute mark end of Asian Games, New York Times, May 10, 1954

1958

Red China out of Games, New York Times, March 16, 1958

Tokyo stadium built with eye on 64 Olympics, New York Times, May 20, 1958

70,000 fans watch Asian Games open, New York Times, May 25, 1958

Japan takes Nine Asian Games events; Deyro of Philippines scores in Tennis, New York Times, May 31, 1958

New Goodwill for Japan balances deficit, New York Times, June 3, 1958

1962

Official Program Asian Games 1962, Asian Games Organizing Committee, 1962

1974

Official report of the Seventh Asian Games, Tehran, September 1–16, 74. Tehran: Editeam, Ltd., 1974.

Asia Games: IOC backs China entry, New York Times, Feb. 11, 1974

South Africa ban continued (China's Asian Games participation approved), New York Times, Aug 31, 1974

Asian Games, New York Times, Sept. 2, 1974

Japan Dominates Asian Games, New York Times, Sept. 4, 1974

Games fencer stabbed accidentally, New York Times, Sept. 6, 1974

Israel Wins Medal in swim, New York Times, Sept. 7, 1974

Israel protests attitudes in Asian Games, New York Times, Sept. 15, 1974

Iran gets Kick out of soccer and Shah, New York Times, Sept. 17, 1974

(Letters) No peace in Sports world (re: Israel and Asian Games), New York Times, Oct. 13, 1974

1978

Asian Games Threat, Daily Nation–Nairobi, July 14, 1978

1982

Asian Games, Olympic Review, 1982, pg. 521

Asian Games, Olympic Review, 1983, pgs. 17–19

700 Sikhs seized as Asian Games are due, New York Times, Nov. 16, 1982

Asian Games fever adds zip to autumn in India, New York Times, Nov. 18, 1982

Under Threat, New Delhi braces for Sikh protests, New York Times, Nov. 19, 1982

Asian Games 82, sportsmen Souvenir Delhi: Asian Games' Sportsmen Souvenir Publishers, 1982

1986

Regional Games, Olympic Review, 1984, pg. 852

Strandberg, Keith, The Spirit of Competition, The China Business Review, Nov.–Dec. 1985, pgs. 51–53

The Xth Asian Games in Seoul: A successful venture, Olympic Review, 1986, pgs. 700–702

1990

Beijing, Showcase for Asian Sport, Olympic Review, 1990, pgs. 290–292

Billing, Christen, Sponsoring the Asian Games, The China Business Review, Nov.–Dec. 1990, pgs. 52–54

1994

Liu Yi, All Roads Lead to the Olympics, China Today, June 1993, pgs. 14–16

Zou, Sicheng, Ma's army creates miracles, Beijing Review, Oct. 25–31, 1993, pgs. 14–17

Hiroshima Asian Games Website, 1994 http://www.hiroshima-cu.ac.jp/C/ASIA/

North Korea shuns 94 Asian Games, New York Times, June 28, 1994

May, William, Sayonara and on to Bangkok, Olympic Review, 1994, pgs. 487–490

1998

Kuala Lumpur Asian Games Website, http://www.sadec.com/Asiad98/Pages/Index.htm

Thailand Confident of keeping 1998 Asian Games, Reuter Information Service, Jan 3, 1995

Bangkok to still host 1998 Asian Games, Reuters News Service, August 23, 1997

Thais scramble to keep Asiad, Reuters News Service, August 27, 1997

Thais vow Asiad will go on, Reuters News Service, Oct. 17, 1997

Thailand schools to close for Games, Agence France Press, Aug. 4, 1998

Asian crisis may cut Asian Games numbers, Agence France Press, Sept. 3, 1998

New checks on Bangkok's work on Asian Games, Agence France Press, Oct. 7, 1997

Thai preparations get thumbs up, Agence France Press, March 6, 1998

Three South Koreans fail drug tests, Agence France Press, Nov. 4, 1998

Afghanistan pulls out of Games, Agence France Press, Nov. 10, 1998

North Korea cuts Asian Games team, Agence France Press, Nov 11, 1998

Thai official says Afghanistan should replace sports head, Reuters News Service, Nov 11, 1998

More than 8,000 confirmed for Asian Games, The Associated Press, Nov 16, 1998

Saudi Arabia withdraws from Asian Games, Reuters News Service, Nov. 26, 1998

North Korea must march after South at Asian Games, Reuters News Service, Nov. 30, 1998

Hong Kong, China seek separate identities, Agence France Press, Dec. 3, 1998

Taiwanese flags pulled at Asia Games, BBC World Service, Dec. 5, 1998

Thangarajah, Edward, Taiwan flags quickly replaced. Mixup was "purely an accident," Bangkok Post, Dec 5, 1998

Saudis escape punishment for last minute pull-out, Agence France Press, Dec. 5, 1998

Pathan, Don, Thai king opens Asian Games, The Associated Press, Dec. 6, 1998

Harper, Tony, China's bid gets Samaranch's support, The Associated Press, Dec. 7, 1998

North Korean gymnasts may compete, The Associated Press, Dec. 9, 1998

North Korea trick take center stage at Asian Games, Agence France Press, Dec. 9, 1998

Leicester, John, Weightlifter booted out of Asian Games, The Associated Press, Dec. 9, 1998

Four suspected bombers arrested ahead of Asian Games, Agence France Press, Dec. 12, 1998

Asian Games MVP to be paid, The Associated Press, Dec. 12, 1998

Japan chief shocked with country's results, Reuters News Service, Dec 19, 1998

Asian Games close in Thailand, The Associated Press, Dec. 20, 1998

Thai media praise Asian Games, Agence France Press, Dec. 21, 1998

India bids for 2006 Asian Games, Agence France Press, Dec. 21, 1998

OCA in quandary over karate medals, The Associated Press, Dec. 22, 1998

Uzbekistan coach dies in Bangkok, Agence France Press, Dec. 22, 1998

Harper, Tony, Hosts caught in boycott row, The Associated Press, Dec. 13, 1998

Pusan Asian Games Website, http://www.pusan asiad.org/

Asian Winter Games

Asian Winter Games, Olympic Review, 1986

Winter Games for the Whole of Asia in Sapporo, Olympic Review, 1990, pgs.

The 3rd Asian Winter Games Harbin Official Report, 3rd Asian Winter Games Organizing Committee, 1996

Kangwon 99 Newsletter, 99 Asian Winter Games Organizing Committee, Sept. 1998

Australian Masters Games

First Australian Masters Games, Sports Economics, Feb 1991, pgs 5–6

Melbourne Countdown to Masters Games, Office of the Minister for Sports, Recreation and Racing, October 21,1993

Kennett Government Secures Masters Games for Melbourne, Office of the Minister for Sports, Recreation and Racing, May 2, 1993

Australian Universities Games

Australian Universities Sports Federation Web Site http://www.unisport.com.au/

Balkan Games

Balkan Olympics Open Tomorrow, New York Times, Oct. 5, 1940

Balkan Meet is Hailed; Central Europe Games called better than Olympics, New York Times, Aug. 2, 1948

Baltic Sea Games

Lithuania 97 The Second Baltic Sea Games, Organizing Committee of the 2nd Baltic Sea Games, 1997

Keire, Paul, 3rd Baltic Sea Games, (correspondence) Sept. 2, 1998

Bolivarian Games

Erecting Olympic Stadium in Venezuela, New York Times, Dec. 2, 1951

Games at Caracas will start today, New York Times, Dec. 5, 1951

Bolivarian Games begin in Caracas, New York Times, Dec. 6, 1951

20,000 see finish of Caracas Games, Colorful ceremony completes Bolivarian meet—Honors taken by Venezuela, New York Times, Dec. 22, 1951

Manana comienzan los V Juegos Bolivarian, El Comercio–Quito, Nov. 19, 1965

Junta militar recibra hoy a delegaciones a Bolivarianos, El Comercio–Quito, Nov. 19, 1965

Conoce usted la historia del futbol en los J.D.B., El Comercio–Quito, Nov. 20, 1965

Espero Hacerme Merecedor a la honra de defender a mi Pais en los Quintos Juegos, El Comercio–Quito, Nov. 20, 1965

Los fouls cometidos en torneo de Futbol" Venzuela tiene 82, El Comercio–Quito, Nov. 29, 1965

Seran solomnente clausurados Juegos Bolivarianos en Guayaquil, El Comercio–Quito, Dec 5, 1965

Sencilla ceremonia al clausurar Juegos Bolivarianos en Guayacil, El Comercio–Quito, Dec. 6, 1965

Bolivarianos realizadas en Guayacil, El Comercio–Quito, Dec. 6, 1965

Colombia en los VII Juegos Bolivarianos, Panamá, febrero 17 a marzo de 1973 / Editors, Carlos Alberto Rueda, José Clopatofsky Londoño ; Bogotá: Oficina de Divulgación y Relaciones Públicas del Instituto Colombiano de la Juventud y el Deporte, 1973.

Factores Intervinientes en el Exito Deportivo; Un estudio de los atletas participantes en los VIII Juegos Bolivarianos, January 1979

Escenarios de los X Juegos Bolivarianos, El Comercio–Quito, Nov. 3, 1985

1938: Ecuador brillante, El Comercio–Quito, Nov. 3, 1985

Venezuela, 102 de oro, Ecuador tercero, El Comercio–Quito, Nov 19, 1985

Clasurados Juegos de Arequipa, Diario Mayor de Santa Cruz de la Sierra, Oct. 27, 1997

Una Medalla para la desorganizacion, Diario Mayor de Santa Cruz de la Sierra, Oct. 22, 1997

British Commonwealth Paraplegic Games

Victoria 94 website, 1994, http://www.tbc.gov.bc.ca/cwgames/cwghome.html

Report of the Sub-Committee on Events for Athletes with a disability, Feb. 1997

Sainsbury, Tony, A Brief History of Participation in Commonwealth Games, Feb. 1997

CARIFTA Games

New athletics track is officially opened, Barbados Advocate, April 7, 1985

Colourful CARIFTA, Barbados Advocate, Aug. 20, 1989

Teams refuse medals, Barbados Advocate, Aug. 23, 1989

Games are here once again, Barbados Advocate, Aug. 19, 1989

CARIFTA swimming to start Thursday, Barbados Advocate, April 5, 1993

Hall to address opening of CARIFTA swim meet, Barbados Advocate, April 8, 1993

Athletic Success; Bajans bring home 22 CARIFTA medals, Barbados Advocate, April 13, 1993

CARIFTA Games opens, Barbados Advocate, April 3, 1994

Mohammed, Zaid, NAAA want 1.5M, Trinidad Guardian, Sept. 15, 1997

Mohammed, Zaid, All Sport to run CARIFTA, Trinidad Guardian, Oct.14, 1997

CARIFTA Games 98 Web Site, 1998

Centennial Youth Games

Welcome to the Danish Sports Confederation's Youth Games, 1996

Geisnes, Dorthe, Private correspondence, August 25, 1998 Materials from Organizing Committee

Central African Games

Une Reunion inter-etats tenue a Abidjan le 7 avril a arrete les grandes lignes de l'organisation des Jeux de l'Amitie 1961, Abidjan Matin, Dec. 23, 1961

Abidjan 1961 Date historique du sport en Afrique, Abidjan Matin, Dec. 23, 1961

Tout le peuple d'Abidjan sera demain a Geo Andre pour l'ouverture des "Jeux," Abidjan Matin, Dec. 23, 1961

Palmares des Jeux de Tananarive, Abidjan Matin, Dec. 26, 1961

Les Jeux de l'Amitie sont nes a Tananarive, Abidjan Matin, Dec. 26, 1961

Parade des Couleurs: Les "Jeux" sont ouverts dans un atmosphere de Kermesse fraternelle, Abidjan Matin, Dec. 26, 1961

Les medailles d'Or d'Athletisme font entrer les "Jeux" dans leur phase glorieuse, Abidjan Matin, Dec. 27, 1961

Les Joueurs Arrivent. Gabonais, Nigeriens, Comoriens, Malgaches, Camerounais, Senegalais atteriront demain, Abidjan Matin, Dec. 20, 1961

Les Jeux sont ouverts, Abidjan Matin, April 12, 1963

Debordement d'enthousiasme pour les 2500 athletes concentres a Dakar, Abidjan Matin, April 12, 1963

Les Jeux sont finis, Abidjan Matin, April 22, 1963

Les Jeux de dakar sont finis. Il convient de tirer les lecons de ce que nous avons fait, Abidjan Matin, April 23, 1963

A Luanda, les 2emes Jeux d'Afrique Centrale, La Semaine Africaine–Brazzaville, Aug 20–26, 1981

Ces Jeunes preparent "Libreville 76" et l'avenir, La Semaine Africaine–Brazzaville, June 13, 1976

Comite d'Organisation des 3emes Jeux d'Afrique Centrale, La Semaine Africaine–Brazzaville, April 16–22, 1987

Before Nairobi, Brazzaville; The 3rd Central African Games, Olympic Review, 1987, pg 174

Libreville: 45000 personnes enthousiastes assisten a l'ouverture solonnelle das "Premiers Jeux d'Afrique Centrale" au Stade President Bongo, La Semaine–Brazzaville, July 11, 1976

Jean-Claude Ganga Secretaire General de la CSSA declare a notre envoye special, La Semaine–Brazzaville, July 11, 1976

Jean-Claude Ganga parle des Premiers Jeux d'Afrique Centrale 76 de Libreville et de Montreal, La Semaine–Brazzaville, July 18, 1976

Voici les "Jeux d'Afrique Centrale 76" de Libreville, La Semaine–Brazzaville, June 27, 1976

Les premiers Jeux d'Afrique Centrale a Libreville, La Semaine Africaine–Brazzaville, Feb. 29, 1976

Onze pays membres de la zone V prets pour les "Jeux d'Afrique Centrale" de Libreville (29 Juin–11 Juillet 1976), La Semaine–Brazzaville, May 30, 1976

2nd Central African Games, Olympic Review, 1981

3es Jeux d'Afrique Centrale; Le Cameroun et l'Angola en Finale de Football, La Semaine Africaine–Brazzaville, April 30–May 6, 1987

Afrique Centrale. Enfin Les Jeux, La Semaine Africaine–Brazzaville, April 16–22, 1987

Sous la pluie, la flamme brulait, La Semaine Africaine–Brazzaville, April 23–29, 1987

3emes Jeux d'Afrique Centrale Le Volley-ball, une affaire camerounaise, La Semaine Africaine–Brazzaville, May 14–20, 1987

Elles sont venues, elles ont vu, elles on vaincu, La Semaine Africaine–Brazzaville, May 14–20, 1987

Les 3emes Jeux d'Afrique Centrale cote cour, La Semaine Africaine–Brazzaville, May 14–20, 1987

Les Jeux sont finis, La Semaine Africaine–Brazzaville, May 7–13, 1987

3es Jeux d'Afrique Centrale; Des yeux pour pleurer, La Semaine Africaine–Brazzaville, April 30–May 6, 1987

Central American and Caribbean Games

180 Mexican athletes to sail for Olympic Games at Havana, New York Times, March 1, 1930

Baseball will open Olympics in Havana, New York Times, March 11, 1930

Four Porto Rican athletes off by airplane for Havana Games, New York Times, March 13, 1930

800 athletes of nine nations in review before 50,000 as Havana Olympics start, New York Times, March 16, 1930

50,000 see Cuba win in Olympic Baseball, New York Times, March 20, 1930

Panama recalls team, New York Times, April 2, 1930

Central Olympics are won by Cuba, New York Times, April 5, 1930

Juantorena: 44:27 & 1:47.2, Track and Field News, September 1978

Puerto Rico and the Olympic Games, Olympic Review, 1979

XIVth Central American and Caribbean Games, Olympic Review, 1982

Roukhadze, Marie-Helene, Don German Rieckehoff, Man of Principle, Olympic Review, 1987 pgs. 645–649

Days of glory in Santiago (DOM) and Mexico, Olympic Review, 1986, pgs 441–442

XVI Central American and Caribbean Sports Games (cancelled), Olympic Review, 1990

Games of Solidarity in Mexico, Olympic Review, 1991

Castro, Elliot, The oldest regional competition on the planet, Centroamericanos y del Caribe Vol 1, Feb. 1993

Castro, Elliot, History 1935, 1938 and 1946, Centroamericanos y del Caribe Year 1. no 4, June 1993

Castro, Elliot, 1950 and 1954, Centroamericanos y del Caribe Year 1. no 5, July 1993

Castro, Elliot, 1959, 1962, Centroamericanos y del Caribe Year 1. no 6, Aug. 1993

Castro, Elliot, 1974, 1978, Centroamericanos y del Caribe Year 1. no 8, Oct. 1993

Castro, Elliot, 1966, 1970, Centroamericanos y del Caribe Year 1. no 7, Sept. 1993

Cuban athlete, official flee, Miami Herald, Nov. 22, 1993

Cuba's two records at Games: The most medals, defectors, Miami Herald, Dec 1, 1993

What will Castro do when Athletes are gone?, Miami Herald, Dec. 6, 1993

Montesinos, Enrique; Uriarte Gonzalez, Carlos Editor, Los Juegos Regionales mas Antiguos, 1993

McGehee, Richard, Mexico 1926: The Regional

Olympics birth of the oldest child, NAASH Proceedings 1992 (check), 1992, pg. 86

McGehee, Richard, Los Juegos de las Americas, Four Inter-American Multisport Competitions, in *Sport and the Global Village*, Morgantown WV 1994pg 378

McGehee, Richard, Revolution, Democracy and Sport. The Guatemalan Olympics of 1950, Olympika—The International Journal of Olympic Studies, 1994, pgs. 49–81

Maracaibo 98 XVIII Central American and the Caribbean Games No. 1, December 1995

Maracaibo 98 XVIII Central American and the Caribbean Games No. 2, March 1996

Historia de los Juegos Deportivos Centroamericanos, La Prensa, 1997

Nunez, Eric, Drug scandal jolts another event, Associated Press, Aug. 20, 1998

XVI Central American and Caribbean Games, Olympic Review, 1998

Official Website 1998 Central American and Caribbean Games, 1998, http://www.jcac98.com/

Central American Games

McGehee, Richard, The Rise of Modern Sport in Guatemala and the First Central American Games, NAASH Proceedings 1991, 1991, pg. 35–36

Central Asian Games

II Central Asian Games, IOC Press Release, Sept. 12, 1997

Commonwealth Games

British Empire Games planned to take place every 4 years, New York Times, Aug. 16, 1928

Summaries of British Games, New York Times, Aug. 8, 1934

50,000 at Cardiff see official start of Empire Games, New York Times, July 19, 1958

Dawn Fraser of Australia sets World Swim Record in Cardiff, New York Times, July 22, 1958

Queen Elizabeth Gives Charles the Title of Prince of Wales, New York Times, July 27, 1958

Elliott Triumphs in 3:59 mile run, New York Times, July 27, 1958

Brown. Gwilym, Fierce fight in the family, Sports Illustrated, August 27, 1966, pgs. 56–59

Kenyans relive African Games feat in Edmonton, Daily Nation–Nairobi, Aug 9, 1978

Commonwealth Games Edmonton 1978, Track and Field News, Oct. 1978, pg. 12

The XIIth Commonwealth Games, Olympic Review, 1982, pg 763

Commonwealth Games Brisbane 1982, Track and Field News, Dec. 1982

1994 Commonwealth Games Official Web Site, 1994, http://www.tbc.gov.bc.ca/cwgames/cwg home.html

Khan, Asif, Difficult Challenges ahead for Commonwealth Sport, Commonwealth Features Syndicate, Sept. 27, 1996

Competitive Unity in Auckland, Olympic Review, 1990, pgs 156–157

Maori Festival for the Commonwealth Games, Olympic Review, 1990

Commonwealth Games Edinburgh, Track and Field News, Oct. 1986, pg 9

Versi, Anver, Why Africa must go to Auckland, New African, Sept. 1989, pg 43–44

India withdraw from Commonwealth Games bid, The Pakistan Times, Sept. 10, 1991

The Auckland Commonwealth Games: Africa Triumphs, New African, March 1990, pgs. 46, 49–50

Dheenshaw, Cleve, The Commonwealth Games; The first 60 years 1930–1960, Orca Book Publishers, 1994

Freeman can carry aboriginal flag at KL Games, Agence France Presse, Aug. 5, 1998

Planners defend games against smog attacks, Agence France Presse, Sept. 18, 1997

Start 'club' Games preps, urges Matete, The Times of Zambia, Oct. 13, 1997

The continuing relevance of the Commonwealth Games, The Sports Factor, Oct. 24, 1997

Malaysia slashes Games budget, Agence France Presse, Dec. 10, 1997

New Zealand gets a Commonwealth preview, Agence France Press, March 11, 1998

Commonwealth Games: Planning stays on target, Agence France Presse, March 12, 1998

Official warns Commonwealth organizers, Agence France Presse, April 15, 1998

Malaysia won't change Commonwealth site, Agence France Presse, April 29, 1998

Commonwealth games battling weather, Associated Press, Sept. 7, 1998

Officials will help athletes who test positive, Agence France Presse, Sept. 7, 1998

Foreign athletes warned on Malaysian drug laws, Reuters News Service, Sept. 8, 1998

Commonwealth Games chiefs fear sun could set, Reuters News Service, Sept. 8, 1998

'Friendly Games' tangled in turmoil, Reuters News Service, Sept. 8, 1998

Cash incentives rejected at Commonwealth Games, Agence France Presse, Sept. 9, 1998

Les Jeux du Commonwealth a Edmonton, La Semaine Africaine, Sept. 10, 1978

Transportation getting better at Commonwealth Games, Reuters News Service, Sept. 10, 1998

Angry officials blame Nebiolo, Agence France Presse, Sept. 10, 1998

On your marks, get set, enjoy!, Asia Week, Sept. 11, 1998

English told not to eat out at Commonwealth Games, Agence France Presse, Sept. 11, 1998
Organizers reject rigging allegations, Agence France Presse, Sept. 14, 1998
Commonwealth Games, The Sports Factor (transcript), Sept. 18, 1998
Violence flares in India–South Africa clash, Agence France Presse, Sept. 12, 1998
Malaysians cheer queen, Associated Press, Sept. 21, 1998
Volunteers protest at Games, Reuters News Service, Sept. 21, 1998
Two Games participants test positive for drugs, Reuters News Service, Oct. 6, 1998

Defi Sportif

Defi Sportif Website, http://www.defisportif.com/
Gliserman, Michael, Defi Sportif, a sports challenge since 1984, Abilities, Spring 1987
Defi Sportif, Ca c'est du sport, Press Packet 1997 Defi Sportif, 1997

East African Military Games

K.K to Open Games, Zambia Daily Mail, Oct. 13, 1982
Mwamba, Jay, Zambians march on, Zambia Daily Mail, Oct. 15, 1982
Mwamba, Jay, Hosts Sweep Board, Zambia Daily Mail, Oct. 18, 1982

East African University Games

Injury Experience in the Seventh University Games, Kampala, Uganda, The East African Medical Journal, August 1971

East Asian Games

(Julio Iglesias at East Asian Games), Seattle Times, May 18, 1993
Australia Welcomed by Asia, Australian Olympic Committee Media Release, May 8, 1997
Magnay, Jacquelin, Australia set for Asian Games, The Age Melbourne Online, May 9, 1997
Yong Kim, Un, The East Asian Games in Pusan Korea, GAISF Newsletter, May 15, 1997
East Asian Games 1997 Web Site, 1997

Eastern European Transplant Games

Eastern European Transplant Games 5–10 August 1996, Transweb http://www.transweb.org/reference/journals/wtgf/march97/text/page20.html

Euro Games

1997 Euro Games Web Site, 1997
EGLSF withdraws EuroGames99 from Manchester, EGLSF Press Release, July 20. 1998,
EGLSF elects Zurich to host the EuroGames in 2000, EGLSF Press Release, July 20. 1998

European Heart and Lung Transplant Games

Finnigan, Geoff, The Sixth European Heart and Lung Transplant Games, World Transplant Games Website, January 1997

European Maccabi Games

Dror, Rony, (European Maccabiah Games statistics), March 25, 1997

European Youth Olympic Days

European Youth Olympic Days, Olympic Review, 1991, pgs. 527
European Youth Olympics Update, 1995
1997 EYOD Winter web site, 1997
Winter Days for European Youth, Olympic Review, 1993
European Youth Olympic Days opens in Portugal, Xinhua English Newswire, July 19, 1997

Far East and South Pacific Games for the Disabled

FESPIC 99 Bangkok, http://www.coara.or.jp/~fespic/wel.htm

Far East Championships

IX Asian Games 82, sportsmen Souvenir Delhi: Asian Games' Sportsmen Souvenir Publishers, [1982]
Dispute over Olympics, New York Times, April 10, 1934
Olympic Cause Dispute; Chinese say they will not go to Manila Games if New State is represented, New York Times, April 11, 1934
Japanese ultimatum is expected in Manchukuoan Issue—Manila Firm in Olympics Row, New York Times, April 15, 1934
Records fall in Orient. Japanese swimmers start in Far Eastern Olympic Games, New York Times, May 20, 1934

Festival of the Empire Sports Meeting

Festival of the Empire Sports, London Times, April 22, 1911

Overseas Athletes, London Times, June 22, 1911

Festival of the Empire Sports Tomorrows meeting, London Times, June 23, 1911

Festival of the Empire Sports Victory of Canada, London Times, June 26, 1911

Firefighters World Games

World Firefighters Games Web Site, 1998

Edmonton. What the world is coming to. Official Program Firefighters World Games 1996

Francophone Games

La delegation canadienne sera la plus importante, L'Opinion-Rabat, July 7, 1989

Hommage aux dix mille acteurs, L'Opinion-Rabat, July 10, 1989

Responsibilite de la presse devant l'ethique du sport, L'Opinion-Rabat, July 20, 1989

Le Medecin charge du dopage moleste par le staff technique egyptien, L'Opinion-Rabat, July, 14, 1989

Fiasco Francophone, L'Opinion-Rabat, July, 14, 1989

Une deuxieme journee profitable a la France et au Canada, L'Opinion-Rabat, July 15, 1989

Le departement francais de L'Essonne, candidat A la deuxieme edition des Jeux, L'Opinion-Rabat, July 19, 1989

Une Bonne Lecon, Le Canada difficilement, L'Opinion-Rabat, July 22, 1989

Retour des Jeux en Essone, Le Monde–Paris, Sept. 26–27, 1993

Jeux de la Francophonie, Sport et Culture, Le Monde–Paris, July 1, 1994

Quarante-cinq drapeaux, Le Monde–Paris, July 1, 1994

Sept disciplines sportives: Du tennis de table a la lutte, Le Monde–Paris, July 1, 1994

La tete et les jambes de la jeunesse francophone, Le Monde–Paris, July 1, 1994

1997 Francophone Games website, 1997

Delisle, Norman, Quebec may skip Francophone Games, montrealgazette.com, March 20, 1998

Friendship and Peace Games

Kidane, Fekrou, A Sporting Victory in Kuwait, Olympic Review, December 1989, pgs. 548–550

Friendship Games 84

Turner gets offer to cover Alternative Olympics, New York Times, July 9, 1984

Soviet Bloc set for it's Games, New York Times, Aug. 16, 1984

Games Begin for Glory of Socialism, New York Times, Aug. 19, 1984

The Showdown that never was, New York Times, Aug. 20, 1984

Cycling records are set, New York Times, Aug. 20, 1984

Soviet Bloc games begin Olympic-style, Pakistan Times, Aug 20, 1984

Swimmers beat Olympic Times, New York Times, Aug. 21, 1984

Swim marks set at Soviet-Bloc Games, New York Times, Aug. 22, 1984

Games of the New Emerging Forces (GANEFO)

China dominates Jakarta Games, New York Times, Nov. 19, 1963

Chinese increase lead at Jakarta, New York Times, Nov. 20, 1963

Pauker, E.T., GANEFO I; Sport and politics in Jakarta, Rand Corp. Santa Monica, CA, July 1964

Lowe, B, et al, Sport and politics; the case of the Asian Games and GANEFO, Sport and International Relations, Stipes, Champaign, Ill., 1978, pgs. 279–296

Games of the Small Countries of Europe

1st Games for Small European Countries: A Harvest of Medals, Olympic Review, 1985, No. 213, p. 396.

Panorama Sport: Edizione Speciale Dedicata AI l"Giuochi Dei Piccoli Stati d"europa, 1985

Success in Monaco, the Second Games of the Small European States, Olympic Review, 1987, No. 238, p. 408

The IIIrd Games of the Small Countries of Europe; Cyprus gets ready, Olympic Review, 1988, No. 249, p. 393.

Nicosia: The 3rd Games of the Small States of Europe: Consecration, Olympic Review, June 1989, Vol. 260, p. 284–286

Resultats Finals IV Jocs Dels Petits Estats d'Europa Andorra 91 (atletisme, Judo, Voleibol, Tir), 1991

Andorra Welcomes the Small Countires of Europe, Olympic Review, May 1991, pgs. 220–221

IV Jocs dels Petits Estats d'Europa Andorra 91 Butlleti Oficial del Comite Organitzador, Oct. 1990

Programa oficial dels IV Jocs dels Petits Estats D' Europa, May 1991

Vth Games of the Small States of Europe Malta 93, SportEurope, June 1993

Portelli, Lewis, The Games of the Small States of Europe: From San Marino to Malta, Guttenburg Press, Zabbar, 1993

6th Games of the Small European States, Official Web Site, 1995

7th Games of the Small Countries of Europe Newsletter No. 1, Newsletter of the Organizing Committee 7th Games of the Small Countries of Europe, August 1996

7th Games of the Small Countries of Europe Newsletter No. 2, Newsletter of the Organizing Committee 7th Games of the Small Countries of Europe, Sept. 1996

7th Games of the Small Countries of Europe Newsletter No. 3, Newsletter of the Organizing Committee th Games of the Small Countries of Europe, Nov. 1996

7th Games of the Small Countries of Europe Newsletter No. 4, Newsletter of the Organizing Committee 7th Games of the Small Countries of Europe, October 1996

Small Nations Games begin, Iceland Daily News, June 3, 1997

Small island nation joins world's largest family, Iceland Daily News, June 3, 1997

Cyprus threatens walk-out after publication of wrong flag, Iceland Daily News, June 5, 1997

Official Website Liechtenstein Games 1999, 1998

Gay Games

Int. Olympic Committee v. San Francisco Arts & Athletics, 781 F 2d 733 (9th Cir. 1986), 1986, pgs. 733–739

Adams, Edward, Legal team signs on for Gay Games: Visa, Asylum, Protest Issues to Predominate, New York Law Review, June 13, 1994

Clines, Francis, Let the Games, and the lobbying begin, New York Times, June 17, 1994

Mitchell, Allison, At the Gay Games, Giuliani takes step to forge new ties, New York Times, June 18, 1994

A Gay Festival Banishes Silence, New York Times, June 17, 1994

Gay Games celebrate athletic acceptance, Seattle Times, June 21, 1994

Gay Games Official Web Site 1998

Goodwill Games

Newnham, Blaine, Does Turner want peace or piece of the networks, Seattle Times, June 17, 1986

How Seattle played for Games and won, Seattle Post Intelligencer, June 18, 1986

Bob Walsh sells Seattle to the world, Seattle Post Intelligencer, June 18, 1986

Games seen as possible fortune, "egg on face," Seattle Post Intelligencer, June 19, 1986

Will peace be Turner's Goodwill donation?, Seattle Post Intelligencer, June 19, 1986

Seattle has insurance if Games prove to be a bust, Seattle Post Intelligencer, June 18, 1986

Newnham, Blaine, World may give Goodwill Games cold shoulder in 1990, Seattle Times, July 8, 1986

Smith, Jack, "Communication" breakdowns draw Americans anger, Seattle Times, July 8, 1986

Cosell, Howard, Who made Ted Turner Ambassador to USSR?, Seattle Post Intelligencer, July 9, 1986

Smith, Jack, Israel expected in 1990 Seattle Games, Seattle Post Intelligencer, July 14, 1986

One man's Goodwill is another mans' nightmare, Seattle Post Intelligencer, July 21, 1986

Newnham, Blaine, Can Seattle afford the Goodwill Games?, Seattle Times, Sept. 27, 1986

Sherwin, Bob, UW has yet to get Games proposal, Seattle Times, Dec. 6, 1986

Wilson, Duff, Size of Goodwill Games halved to give them non-olympic identity, Seattle Post Intelligencer, Dec. 17, 1986

Soviet sports officials to tour Goodwill sites, Seattle Post Intelligencer, Jan. 24, 1987

Drosendahl, Glenn, Visit by Soviets seen as turning point for games, Seattle Post Intelligencer, Feb. 16, 1987

$1 million sliced from Goodwill Games budget, Bremerton Sun, June 12, 1987

Good News for Goodwill Games, Tacoma News Tribune, Sept. 18, 1987

Official Newsletter of the Goodwill Games Vol 1. No. 1, Countdown, January 1988

Smith, Jack, Thaw evident in Soviets' Cold War attitude to sports, Seattle Post Intelligencer, Aug. 15, 1988

Smith, Jack, Soviets will see America through Goodwill focus, Seattle Post Intelligencer, Feb. 3, 1988

Organizer says Seattle afraid to back Games, Seattle Times, Dec. 11, 1988

Nelson, Glenn, Goodwill Games prelude to Seattle Olympics?, Seattle Times, July 2, 1989

94 Goodwill Games spark ill will in Russia, Seattle Times, June 10, 1994

Big loss no deterrent, say Goodwill Games exec, Seattle Times, Aug. 11, 1994

Siddons, Larry, 2002 Goodwill Games may move, Associated Press, Jan. 15, 1998

Brisbane hopes to host 2001 Goodwill Games, Reuters News Service, July 17, 1998

Iran to wrestle at Goodwill Games, Associated Press, July 19, 1998

May has his day at Goodwill Games, Associated Press, July 20, 1998

Araton, Harvey, A Great Time and a Better Friendship, New York Times, July 21, 1998

Longman, Jere, Paralyzed gymnast is unlikely to walk again, surgeon says, New York Times, July 23, 1998

Political protest ousts goodwill in wrestling, Seattle Times, July 26, 1998

Siddons, Larry, Cuban cyclist reported missing, Associated Press, July 27, 1998

Eltman, Frank, New Yorkers skipping Goodwill games, Associated Press, July 30, 1998

Bock, Hal, Red ink won't slow Goodwill Games, Associated Press, Aug. 2, 1998

Bock, Hal, Goodwill Games close in the red, Associated Press, Aug 3, 1998

Goodwill Games 98 Official Web Site, 1998

Hapoel Games

16,000 Sportsmen parade at Hapoel Festival conclusion, Jerusalem Post, May 18, 1956

Sports dominate May Day events, Jerusalem Post, May 2, 1961

Pageant opens Hapoel meet, Jerusalem Post, May 2, 1961

Moser, Shlomo, Hapoel 'Olympics' end, Jerusalem Post, May 7, 1961

Israel Runaway Hapoel Winner, Jerusalem Post, May 8, 1961

Raphael, Avi, World athletes here for games, Jerusalem Post, April 29, 1966

Hapoel Games Open, Jerusalem Post, May 2, 1966

Hod, Gideon, 9th Hapoel Games opening tomorrow, Jerusalem Post, April 28, 1971

Keino loses third race, Jerusalem Post, May 5, 1971

Games end tonight, Jerusalem Post, May 5, 1971

800 Athletes to compete in Hapoel Games, Jerusalem Post, April 29, 1975

Kohn, Paul; Leon, Jack, President to open 10th Hapoel Games, Jerusalem Post, April 30, 1975

Kohn, Paul; Leon, Jack, Hapoel Games end tonight with Calisthenics displays, Jerusalem Post, May 8, 1975

Leon, Jack, 1st African sportsmen here since 1973, Jerusalem Post, April 30, 1979

Segal, Mark, Colourful Pageant opens 11th Hapoel Games, Jerusalem Post, May 3, 1979

Begin invited to closing of Hapoel Games, Jerusalem Post, May 8, 1979

Jerusalem ceremony ends Hapoel Games, Jerusalem Post, May 9, 1979

Leon, Jack, Let the Games begin, Jerusalem Post, May 5, 1985

Gordin, Joel, Hapoel Games Called off, Jerusalem Post, Aug. 29, 1990

Gordin, Joel, Hapoel Games athletics meet tonight, Jerusalem Post, May 8, 1991

Gordin, Joel, 14th Hapoel Games wound up in Netanya, Jerusalem Post, May 14, 1991

Chait, Heather, 3000 Athletes gather for Hapoel Games, Jerusalem Post, June 11, 1995

Gordin, Joel, Hapoel Games end on sour note, Jerusalem Post, June 18, 1995

Kalman, Josh; Chait, Heather, Gordin, Joel, Ross, cast of thousands open Hapoel Games, Jerusalem Post, June 13, 1995

15th Hapoel Games, Hapoel Games Organizing Committee, 1995

Hawaii Pacific Games

Hawaii International Sports Federation, Hawaii Pacific Games, 1988

Reardon, Dave, Honolulu is seen as host city, Honolulu Advertiser, March 2, 1988

Reardon, Dave, Pacific Games in 1992, says official, Honolulu Advertiser, March 4, 1988

Reardon, Dave, Hawaii Games gain IOC support, Honolulu Advertiser, July 30, 1988

Borsch, Ferd, Finazzo will be president of Games, Honolulu Advertiser, July 25, 1989

Smith, Kit, Hawaii Pacific Games may be economic windfall, Honolulu Advertiser, Nov. 20, 1989

Honda Masters Games

Honda Masters Games Web Site 1996

Honda Masters Games Web Site 1998

Honda Masters Games Web Site 2000 http://www.hondamastersgames.nt.gov.au/

Huntsman World Senior Games

Huntsman World Senior Games Official Web Site 1995–2000 http://www.senior games.net/

1,000 athletes competing in Senior Games, Salt Lake Tribune, Oct. 18, 1990

Man dies during Senior Games race, Salt Lake Tribune, Oct. 22, 1993

Huntsman World Senior Games 1994 Results Book, 1994

Rosetta, Dick, Japanese athletes shine at Senior Games, Salt Lake Tribune, Oct. 18, 1994

3,000 expected for Huntsman Senior Games, Salt Lake Tribune, Oct. 15, 1995

Celebrities will join athletes for opening of Senior Games, Salt Lake Tribune, Sept. 24, 1996

The Huntsman Senior Games keep growing, Salt Lake Tribune, Oct. 12, 1997

Malone to help kick off World Senior Games, Salt Lake Tribune, Oct. 14, 1997

Webb, Loren, World Senior Games Ceremonies draw huge crown in St. George, Salt Lake Tribune, Oct. 15, 1997

Challis, Paul, A 'Fantastic' First Half for Senior Olympics, Salt Lake Tribune, Oct. 17, 1987

Munsterman, Pamela, Hoops replay looms as grudge match; Russians Salute caliber of competition, Salt Lake Tribune, Oct. 24, 1997

Meyer, Hans, Senior Games coming to St. George again, St. George Spectrum, Oct. 5, 1998

Rosetta, Dick, St. George stages World Senior Games; New Venues promise as many thrills as Games participants, Salt Lake Tribune, Oct. 12, 1998

Rosetta, Dick, Senior Games loaded with real heroes, Salt Lake Tribune, Oct. 15. 1998

Meyer, Hans, Senior Games opens second week with blueprint for future, St. George Spectrum, Oct. 21, 1998

Meyer, Hans, Women from around the planet find common ground at Senior Games, St. George Spectrum, Oct. 23, 1998

IBSA World Championships for the Blind

Official Web Site 1998 IBSA World Championships, 1998

Indian Ocean Island Games

Islands of the Indian Ocean Games, Olympic Review, 1985, pg. 175

Games of the Islands of the Indian Ocean, Olympic Review, 1986

Indian Ocean Games, IOC Weekly Highlights, Aug 21, 1998

Inter-Allied Games

The Inter-allied games: Paris, 22nd June to 6th July, 1919, Inter-Allied Games (1919: Paris, France)

Lewis, Guy, Military Olympics at Paris, France, 1919, Physical Educator, Dec. 1974, pgs. 172–175

Findling, John, Around the World, The Interallied Games, 1919, NASSH Proceedings, 1981, pg. 42

International Firefighters Winter Games

International Firefighters Winter Games official Web Site, 1998–2000

International Law Enforcement Games

Pratt, Sandy, History International Law Enforcement Games, June 10, 1997

Bigold, Pat, Hawaii sending 70 to Law Enforcement Games, Honolulu Star Bulletin, July 28, 1992

International Police Winter Games

International Police Winter Games Web Site 1997–2000

International School Children's Games

Official Website International School Children's Games, 1997–2000

Byl, J., 19th International School Games, Journal of the International Council for Health, Physical Education and Recreation, Fall 1990

International Senior Games

Burgess, Don, 'Huge potential' of senior games, Bermuda Sun, April 1996

Track and Field (International Senior Games), Salt Lake Tribune, Aug. 20, 1995

International Women's Games

Guttmann, Allen, Federation Sportive Feminine Internationale, in Encyclopedia of World Sport, David Levinson and Karen Christensen, editors. ABC-CLIO, 1996

ISF Gymnasiade

Official Web Site 1998 ISF Gymnasiade, 1998

ISF Web Site, 1998

Island Games

Corlett, Geoffrey, The Island Games 1985–1995, May 1997

1999 Island Games Official website, http://www.gotlandweb.com/islandgames/engelska-ig/frigeng_index.htm

1997 Island Games Official website, 1997 http://www.itl.net/sport/islandgames/index.html

JCC Maccabi Games

Maccabi Games kick off, Associated Press, Aug. 17, 1988

Games for Jewish teens to begin, Seattle Times, Aug. 15, 1997

Program: Seattle JCC Maccabi Youth Games 1997, Aug. 1997

JCC Maccabi Games Web Site, 1998

Maccabiah Games

Maccabi World Union (MWU) http://www.mac
cabiworld.org/

Eisen, George, Maccabiah Games: A history of
the Jewish Olympics, University of Maryland
Thesis, 1979

Sasson Moshe, Schrodt, Barbara, The Maccabi
Sport Movement and the Establishment of the
First Maccabiah Games, Canadian Journal of
History of Sport Vol 16, 1, May 1985, pgs. 67–90

Levy, Joseph, The modern Jewish Olympics,
Journal of Physical Ed., Recreation and Dance
(JOPERD), April 1989, pgs. 42–43

Jewish Olympics planned. First World-wide meet
set for Palestine in 1932, New York Times,
Feb. 3, 1931

Palestine will permit unlimited quota of athletes
to enter for Jewish Games, New York Times,
Jan 7. 1932

Ban by Rumania shifts Jewish Games to Prague,
New York Times, July 23, 1933

Prenn in Maccabiade. To play for England in
Jewish Meet. Nazis bar German entry, New
York Times, Aug. 26, 1933

Maccabiade ends as athletes march. Lord Melchett
reviews parade of 1,000 in Prague. Dr. Prenn
defeated., New York Times, Aug. 28, 1933

To compete in Palestine: U.S. to be represented
by 25 Jewish athletes in Games, New York
Times, Oct 24, 1934

Ban Parade at Tel Aviv. Palestine police bar procession of athletes at World Contest, New
York Times, April 1, 1935

U.S. team is favored. Picked to keep title in Jewish Games opening today, New York Times,
April 2, 1935

Jewish Olympics won by U.S. team, New York
Times, April 9, 1935

Jewish Olympics Opened, New York Times, Feb.
19, 1936

30,000 in Israel see Games open. U.S. athletes
cheered at Maccabiah ceremonies, New York
Times, Aug. 30, 1961

U.S. Squad victor in 16 more finals. Gubner and
Savitt triumph as Maccabiah Games end, New
York Times, Sept. 5, 1961

Herman Honored at Ceremonies Closing Sixth
Maccabiah Games, New York Times, Sept. 6,
1961

Overture a Tel Aviv de la Septieme Maccabiade,
Le Monde–Paris, Aug. 25, 1965

U.S wins 4 tests in Israeli Games. Spitz stars as
Maccabiah squad dominates swim., New York
Times, Aug. 25, 1965

South Africans Protest, Jerusalem Post, July 20, 1989

Fattal, Derek, The Opening Ceremony goes on,
Jerusalem Post, July 15, 1997

Linzer, Dafna, Temporary Span collapses at
Games. Tel Aviv official sees no sign it was
sabotage, Seattle Times, July 15, 1997

Poor welding reportedly caused Maccabiah
Games Bridge collapse, Associated Press, July
22, 1997

Maccabiah Games resume amid grief, accusations, Associated Press, July 16, 1997

Chait, Heather, Olympic Bidders coming to see
how Maccabiah does it, Jerusalem Post, July 11,
1997

Hoffman, Joseph, Maccabiah Games: The history
of the games—part 1, Jerusalem Post, July 15,
1997

Gordin, Joel, Maccabiah Games: Who needs it?,
Jerusalem Post, July 15, 1997

A sense of shame, Jerusalem Post, July 16, 1997

Gordin, Joel, Aussies decide not to miss 'dream
of a lifetime', Jerusalem Post, July 16, 1997

Australian team head asks Israel to compen-
sate bridge collapse, Associated Press, July 23,
1997

Ben-Tal, Daniel, Engineer testifies at Maccabiah
Trial, Associated Press, June 22, 1998

Mediterranean Games

King will open the Mediterranean Games today,
Egyptian Gazette, Oct. 5, 1951

Message for Taher Pasha, Egyptian Gazette, Oct. 5,
195

Mimoun turns in Med. Games Best Result: Wins
10,000m, Egyptian Gazette, Oct. 7, 19511

1st Med. Games Close, Egyptian Gazette, Oct.
21, 1951

Lord Killanin: Les installations pour les Jeux d'Alger sont parfaites, Maroc Soir, Aug. 27, 1975

Alger Capitale du sport pendant quinze jours,
Maroc Soir, Aug. 19, 1975

Des Medailles en vue, Maroc Soir, Aug. 21, 1975

Nos athletes sont partis avec beacoup de courage, Maroc Soir, Aug. 23, 1975

Casablanca en concurrence avec Split pour les
Jeux Mediterraneens de 1979, Maroc Soir,
Aug. 24, 1975

Football: France-Algerie en finale; Maroc-
Tunisie pour la medaille de bronze, Maroc
Soir, Sept. 5, 1975

8th Mediterranean Games, Olympic Review,
1979, pg.110

Mediterranean Games, Olympic Review, 1985,
pg. 284

Efforts exerted to ensure best transport services
during Mediterranean Games, Syria Times,
Sept. 9, 1987

Ourabi, Emad, Success of games will reflect
Syria's outstanding culture and civilization:
Lattakia goes big and joyful to host the 10th
Med-Games, Syria Times, Sept. 10, 1987

Syria completed preparations for Med-Games,
guests arrive, new projects inaugurated, Syria
Times, Sept. 10, 1987

Athens to host 11th Med-Games, rules amended;

Syria's efforts appreciated, Syria Times, Sept. 10, 1987

President Assad addresses world at Med-Games opening: Our people waging struggle in defence of values and peace, Syria Times, Sept. 13, 1987

Opening Ceremony of 10th Mediterranean Games. Spell-bound audience and marvelous performances by school children, armed forces, Syria Times, Sept. 13, 1987

Most significant event of weekend. President Assad attends closing ceremony of Med-Games, Syria Times, Sept. 27, 1987

Xth Mediterranean Games Latakia (SYR) 11th to 25th September 1987, Olympic Review, 1987, pg. 407

Mediterranean Feast, Olympic Review, 1987, pg. 543

All the Mediterranean in Athens, Olympic Review, 1991, No. 285, p. 348.

Mazot, Jean-Paul; Laget, Serge, Les Jeux Mediterraneens, Presses du Languedoc, 1993

Official Website 1997 Mediterranean Games, 1997

Micronesian Games

Oceania National Olympic Committees Web site

Second Micronesian Games, Olympic Review, Jan. 1991, pg. 48–51

Micronesian Games 1994 March 26–April 2, 1994, 1994

Branigin, William, Island Hopping for Medals, Washington Post, April 4, 1994

Micronesian Games, Olympic Highlights, Aug. 21, 1998

Information Bulletin, Vol. 2 1998 Micronesian Games, Micronesian Games Organizing Committee, 1998

Johnson, Giff, Nauru prediction—we will dominate Commonwealth lifting in four years, Pacific Islands Monthly, Sept. 1998, pg. 46

Johnson, Giff, Palau shows off as host of Micronesian Games, Pacific Islands Monthly, Sept. 1998, pg. 47–48

Military World Games

Army's Plan for Post-War Olympic Games at Battlefront Approved by Congress, New York Times, March 18, 1944

Manila Olympics planned by army. Athletic program Dec. 21–31 will be patterned after Games staged in ETO, New York Times, Oct. 5, 1945

5,000 in Army Olympics, New York Times, Jan 5, 1946

Libya warned over Military Games shirts, Reuter Information Service, Sept. 4, 1995

Official web Site 1995 World Military Games, 1995

Military Games: competition has drawn some 5,000 athletes, Associated Press, Sept. 5, 1995

World Military Games: Libya takes the novel approach, Reuter Information Service, Sept. 18, 1995

Miles, Donna, Friendship through Sports, Dec. 1995

Muslim Student Games

Iran to host first ever World Muslim Students Games next year, Iran News Agency, May 19, 1993

Sports Olympiad for College students to be held in Tehran, Iran News Agency, July 14, 1993

Tehran to host 1st International students games next year, Iran News Agency, Nov. 11, 1993

Muslim students to hold solidarity games in Tehran, Iran News Agency, July 14, 1994

Azeri athletes come to Iran for student Games, Iran News Agency, July 20, 1994

Iranian athletes rank first at Students Solidarity Games, Iran News Agency, July 24, 1994

Tehran hosts solidarity Games, Iran News News, Feb. 6, 1995

International Sports Federation for Muslim Students, Iran News Agency, March 14, 1995

Muslim Women's Games

Islamic countries sports congress approves by-law, Iran News Agency, April 25, 1994

IOC Chief lauds Iran's efforts to improve women's sports, Iran News Agency, July 13, 1994

The First Meeting; An Illustrated Report of the First Islamic Countrie's Women Sports Solidarity Games Feburary 1993—Tehran, Organizing Committee First Islamic Countrie's Women Sports Solidarity Games, 1993

Hargreaves, Jennifer, Sports for all women, Sporting females; Critical issues in the History of Sociology and Women's Sports, Routledge, Pub. 1994

Brooks, Geraldine, Nine parts of Desire, Doubleday, 1995

Zaman, Hasina, Islam, Well-being and Physical Activity: Perceptions of Muslim Young Women, Researching women and sport, MacMillan Press Ltd., 1997, pgs. 50–67

Presidential advisor on women's affairs commends women athletes, Iran News Agency, Feb. 22, 1993

Pakistan to hold 2nd Islamic Countries Women's Games, Iran News Agency, Nov. 14, 1994

Ms. Hashemi: Main objective, sports for all, Iran News Agency, Nov. 24, 1994

Brunei calls for exchange of female sports teams with Iran, Iran News Agency, Nov. 1, 1995

Muslim women's Sports Solidarity Council

Assembly concludes, Tehran Times, Nov. 28, 1995

Khan, A. Majid, New chapter in our sports history, Dawn Wire Service, Nov. 7, 1996

Siddiqui, Rashid, Women swimmers to represent Pakistan in Solidarity Games, The International News–Pakistan, Oct. 19, 1997

Muslim Women Solidarity Games to Strengthen Islamic Civilization, Tehran Times, Nov. 19, 1997

2nd Islamic Women's Games, IOC Newsletter, Dec. 12, 1997

Faezeh Hashem: Sports, best means for Solidarity among Nations, Iran News Agency, Dec. 14, 1997

Rafsanjani opens Second Islamic Women's Games in Tehran, Tehran Times, Dec. 15, 1997

Islamic Women Games open in Tehran, Pakistan–The News International, Dec. 15, 1997

Iran dominates women's games, Reuters News Service, Dec. 19, 1997

Nordic Games

Nordiska Spelen, Norsk Familjeboks Sportlexicon, Forlagsaktiebolaget A. Sohlman & Co., 1943, pgs. 669–676

Yttergren, Leif, The Nordic Games: Visions of a winter Olympics or a National Festival?, The International Journal of the History of Sport, Frank Cass, London, Dec. 1994, pgs. 495–505

Idrott:Den nordiska Idrottsveckan I Kristiana, Aftonbladet–Stockhom, Jan. 31, 1903

Den nordiska Idrottsveckan I Kristiana, Aftonbladet–Stockhom, Feb. 2, 1903

Den nordiska Idrottsveckan I Kristiana. Holmenkollentaflingarna, Aftonbladet–Stockhom, Feb. 3, 1903

Den nordiska Idrottsveckan I Kristiana. Afsluiniugfesten, Aftonbladet–Stockhom, Feb. 10, 1903

North American Indigenous Games

Warburton, Steve, Indigenous Games 'will make us strong', Edmonton Journal, July 3, 1990

Brownlee, Robin, Dreams live, dreams die at Games, Edmonton Journal, July 3, 1990

Warburton, Steve, Canoeing develops from way of life into top sport, Edmonton Journal, July 3, 1990

Warburton, Steve, Culture an integral part of all events, Edmonton Journal, July 3, 1990

Schuler, Corinna, Natives pray for their culture as Games end, Edmonton Journal, July 8, 1990

Brownlee, Robin, Friends Take home Gold, Edmonton Journal, July 8, 1990

Miller, Kay, Indigenous Games spark pride among athletes, Minneapolis Star Tribune, July 28, 1995

Bachman, Rachel, Chaos, Color are the rule, Minneapolis Star Tribune, Aug. 1, 1995

1997 North American Indigenous Games Web Site http://www.firstnations.com/naig97/main.htm

Winnipeg will host Indigenous games, CFRA 580 News Talk Radio Web Site, Aug. 10, 1998

Olympic Games

Wallechinsky, David The complete book of the Winter Olympics, Woodstock, N.Y.: Overlook Press, 1998.

Wallechinsky, David The complete book of the summer Olympics, Woodstock, N.Y.: Overlook Press, 2000.

Kamper, Erich; Mallon, Bill The golden book of the Olympic games Erich Kamper, Bill Mallon. Milan: Vallardi & Associati, 1992.

Lyberg, Wolf, Fabulous 100 years of the IOC: facts-figures-and much, much more. Lausanne, Switzerland: IOC, 1996.

Mallon, Bill, with Ture Widlund, The 1896 Olympic Games: results for all competitors in all events, with commentary. Jefferson, N.C.: McFarland & Co., 1997.

Mallon, Bill, The 1900 Olympic Games: results for all competitors in all events, with commentary. Jefferson, N.C.: McFarland & Co., 1997.

Mallon, Bill, The 1904 Olympic Games: results for all competitors in all events, with commentary. Jefferson, N.C.: McFarland & Co., 1999.

Mallon Bill, The 1908 Olympic Games: results for all competitors in all events, with commentary. Jefferson, N.C.: McFarland & Co., 2000.

Pouret, Henri, The contribution made by Olympism to the development of human relations, Olympic Review, 1979 Vol. 145, pgs. 638–641

Cholley, Patrice, The Rondeau Olympic Games, Olympic Review, May 1996, Vol. XXV, No. 8, pgs. 48–49

de Lange, Pieter, The Games Cities Play, C.P. de Lange Inc., 1998

McGeoch, Rod; Korporaal, Glenda, The Bid, How Australia won the 2000 Games, William Heinemann Australia, 1994

Cook, Theodore, The Olympic Games, A question of withdrawal (letter), London Times, Aug. 14, 1920

The official report of the Organising Committee for the games of the XV Olympiad, Helsinki, 1952. Helsinki: Organizing Committee, 1955, Porvoo, Finland: Werner Söderström Osakeyhtiö

The official report of the Organizing Committee for the games of the XVI Olympiad, Melbourne, 1956. Melbourne: W.M. Houston, c1958.

The Games of the XVIII Olympiad, Tokyo 1964: the official report of the Organizing Committee. Tokyo, The Committee, 1966. Atlanta, Ga.: Atlanta Committee for the Olympic Games, 1992.

Die Spiele: the official report of the Organizing Committee for the Games of the XXth Olympiad Munich 1972. München: proSport, 1972.

Games of the XXI Olympiad, Montreal 1976: Official Report, Rousseau, C. O. Roger et al. ; Editor in Chief. Montreal, COJO, 1978.

Official report of the Games of the XXIIIrd Olympiad, Los Angeles, 1984. Los Angeles, Los Angeles Olympic Organizing Committee, 1985.

Official report of the Atlanta Committee for the Olympic Games Atlanta, Ga.: Atlanta Committee for the Olympic Games, 1992.

Pacific Ocean Games

Website 1995 Pacific Ocean Games, 1995

Forgacs, Stephen, UBC reviews Pacific Games proposal, Vancouver Sun, April 2, 1998

Morris, Jim, Vancouver to host Pacific Games, CFRA News Talk Radio Transcripts, April 17, 1998

UBC to provide Pacific Games Venues, Vancouver Sun, June 11, 1998

Pacific School Games

Pacific School Games News, Website 1996 Pacific School Games, Oct. 19, 1996

Pacific School Games website 2000

Pan-American Games

Plans New Olympiad (Latin-American Olympiad), New York Times, Nov. 25, 1933

Big Fair Takes on color with Games nearing, Dallas Morning News, July 14, 1937

Ten US Athletes arrive to compete in Pan-Americas, Dallas Morning News, July 6, 1937

Pan-American Games to start Thursday, Dallas Morning News, July 11, 1937

Peru's Jose Rios, Four Cuban stars arrive for Games, Dallas Morning News, July 12, 1937

Cunningham enters Games; Sefton, Towns out. World's Greatest miler will battle San Romani in Cotton Bowl, Dallas Morning News, July 13, 1937

Cunningham is to get plenty of competition, Dallas Morning News, July 14, 1937

Postmaster sending Wife to pinch hit at Pan-American Games, Dallas Morning News, July 14, 1937

All eyes turn to Exposition as Games start, Dallas Morning News, July 15, 1937

Pat Dengis wins marathon: Veteran Baltimore runner celebrates 37th Birthday with victory, Ribas trails, Dallas Morning News, July 19, 1937

Pan-American Games open in Cotton Bowl tonight, Dallas Morning News, July 15, 1937

Olympics open with earnest note of amity, Dallas Morning News, July 16, 1937

Brazil wants Pan-American Games in 1938, Dallas Morning News, July 18, 1937

Woodruff Shatters World Record, Dallas Morning News, July 18, 1937

Athletic Games draw attention at Exposition, Dallas Morning News, July 13, 1937

Sao Paulo looms as 63 Games site. Brazilian city is favored in Pan-American delegates vote today at Chicago., New York Times, Aug. 25, 1959

Latins at Games criticize set-up. Athletes complain of food, lack of training sites. Colombia withdraws, New York Times, Aug. 24, 1959

Eisley, Matthew, Raleigh wants Triangle to be venue for Pan Am games, Raleigh News and Observer, Jan. 8,1998

Sheehan, Joseph, 2,200 will compete in Pan-American Games. 408 to represent US at carnival, New York Times, Aug. 16, 1959

Wehrwein, Austin, Chicago's Olympic Show. Sports Spectacle will be summer seasons main event, New York Times, July 19, 1959

Buenos Aires meet termed a success. Brundage hails Pan-American showing of Latin Nations—Athletes start home, New York Times, March 11, 1951

Picks Buenos Aires site. City favored by Brundage for Post war Pan-American Games, New York Times, May 4, 1945

Pan-America meet held sure to go on. Head of AAU says work is well under way for games this summer in US, New York Times, Jan. 23, 1940

Castro, Fidel, Letter from Fidel Castro to International Olympic Committee President Juan Antonio Samaranch, Havana International Service, Nov. 29, 1984

Finnish Officials Cancel Olympics; Make formal announcement it will be impossible to hold games this year, New York Times, April 24, 1940

Zamorano, Juan, Santo Domingo wins 2003 Pan American Games, Associated Press, Dec 6, 1998

Sheehan, Joseph, Althea Gibson wins Pan-American Games Tennis, New York Times, Sept. 4, 1959

Evolution of the Pan-American Games, Olympic Review, 1977, pg. 121

Brazil to hold games: Intermediate Olympics Awarded to South America for 1922, New York Times, Aug. 25, 1920

Pan-American meet will be held in US. New York among cities bidding for Games this year, New York Times, Jan. 20, 1940

Rhoden, William, The secret of Cuba's Sports Success? Spot the children who are athletes, New York Times, Aug. 19. 1991

Sheehan, Joseph, Third Pan-American Games open. contests to begin today in nine sports. 2162 athletes representing 24 nations in ceremony—symbolic torch lighted, New York Times, Aug. 28, 1959

Chris Von Saltza wins fourth and fifth swimming golds, New York Times, Sept. 7, 1959

Miss Gibson faces rebuke on pro talk, New York Times, Sept. 6, 1959

Cubans pressed to enter Games, New York Times, April 13, 1963

Castro charges U.S. Schemes to keep Cubans out of Games, New York Times, April 16, 1963

Cuban participation in Games approved, New York Times, April 18, 1963

Many taken ill on way to games. Pan-American competitors suffer food poisoning, New York Times, April 19, 1963

De Onis, Juan, Colorful ceremonies Open 4th Pan-American Games, New York Times, April 21, 1963

Winnipeg gets 67 Games, New York Times, April 23, 1963

Underwood, John, The winning ways of Winnipeg, Sports Illustrated, Aug. 7, 1967, pgs. 20, 23–25

Amdur, Neil, Castro hails upsets over U.S. athletes, New York Times, Aug. 16, 1971

VI Juegos Panamericanos, Cali, Colombia, 1971, Organizing Committee VI Pan-American Games, 1971

Hildesheim, Norman, Little fun for U.S. at Games, New York Times, Oct. 17, 1975

Whistling at Games irks U.S., New York Times, Oct. 19, 1975

Moore, Kenny, Not on the up and up, Sports Illustrated, Oct. 27, 1975

Moore, Kenny, A kind of Mexican standoff, Sports Illustrated, Nov. 4, 1975

Papanek, John, Triumph and turmoil in the Pan-Am Games, Sports Illustrated, July 23, 1979

Marshall, Joe, Juantorena gets ambushed, Sports Illustrated, July 23, 1979

Mermel, Marcy, 24 security volunteers walk off job. Worked at Pan Am Athletes village, Indianapolis News, Aug. 6, 1987

Let the Games begin, Indianapolis News, Aug. 6, 1987

Hastings, Janet, Some Pan-Am teams have cleaned house of drugs, Indianapolis News, Aug. 8, 1987

Mermel/Marcy, Pax/I problems multiply as time is speeding past, Indianapolis News, Aug. 7, 1987

U.S. women at loss: Pan Am basketball cut, Seattle Times, March 4, 1995

Muello, Peter, Pan Am Games were staged with Argentine Panache, Associated Press, March 26, 1995

Can the D.R. afford to host the Pan-am Games, DR One News, May 22–29, 1997

Cuba expected to participate fully in 1999 Pan Am Games, Reuters, July 25, 1997

Rubin, Richard, Raleigh-Durham area makes bid for 2007 Pan-Am Games, Duke Chronicle, April 16, 1998

Pan Am Games bar male synchronized swimmer, Reuters, Oct. 1, 1998

Santo Domingo to host Pan Am Games, www.dr! /com, Dec. 7, 1998

Pan Am Proud. A Tribute to Champions, DT Publishing Group Inc., Grimsby ON, 1999

Paralympic Games

Steadward, Robert; Peterson, Cynthia, Paralympics, Where Heroes Come, Alberta Northern Lights Wheelchair Basketball Society, 1997

The Triumph of the Human Spirit. The Atlanta Paralympic Experience, Disability Today Publishing Group Inc., Grimsby ON, 1997

Games for the mentally handicapped in Madrid, Olympic Review, Nov. 1992, pg. 599

The X Paralympic Games, Olympic Review, 1992, pg. 23

Olympiad asked to expel South Africa, Toronto Globe and Mail, Aug. 4, 1976

McCabe, Nora, Hungarian defects—with a little help, Toronto Globe and Mail, Aug. 9, 1976

Atlanta balking to stage 96 Paralympics, Pakistani Times, Sept. 8, 1991

South Africa makes bid for Games, Toronto Globe and Mail, Aug. 9, 1976

Poland drops out of Games when South Africa not expelled, Toronto Globe and Mail, Aug. 9, 1976

'We won't be intimidated by boycott' ISOD head says, Toronto Globe and Mail, Aug. 7, 1976

McCabe, Nora, Hungarian Paraplegic defects, asks for asylum, Toronto Globe and Mail, Aug. 7, 1976

Language, not race separates squad, S.A. manager says, Toronto Globe and Mail, Aug. 6, 1976

Canada collects seven medals in opening of Disabled Games, Toronto Globe and Mail, Aug. 5, 1976

Egyptian, Israeli raise arms together, Toronto Globe and Mail, Aug. 10, 1976

McCabe, Nora, Olympiad for Physically Disabled opens amid state of utter chaos, Toronto Globe and Mail, Aug. 5, 1976

Touche, Amanda, Calgary swimmer admits he misled MDs to gain advantage, Toronto Globe and Mail, Aug. 10, 1976

McCabe, Nora, Cheers, fanfare open Olympiad for disabled, Toronto Globe and Mail, Aug. 4, 1976

McCabe, Nora, Ontario to aid disabled athletes, but how much?, Toronto Globe and Mail, Aug. 3, 1976

International Paralympic Committee Web Site

Heydon, Pat, Paralympic Games History, Canadian Paralympic Committee Web Site, 1996

Britain is leading wheelchair games, New York Times, Nov. 8, 1968

Official 1996 Paralympic Games website, 1996

Allen Beasley, Kim, The Paralympic Village: a Barrier Free City, International Symposium on Olympic Villages, 1996

Wheelchair Olympics, New York Times, Sept. 22, 1960

Cortesi, Arnaldo, Wheelchair stars from 23 Nations to open Rome Games, New York Times, Sept. 19, 1960,

Healthy Russians may lose Disabled Games, Toronto Globe and Mail, Aug. 5, 1976

McCabe, Nora, No action planned in boycott, Toronto Globe and Mail, Aug. 10, 1976

McCabe, Nora, Athletes ignored in confused ceremony as 1976 Olympiad for disabled winds up, Toronto Globe and Mail, Aug. 12, 1976

The Success of the 9th Paralympics, Olympic Review, Nov. 1992, pgs. 596–599

Bad weather fails to curb enthusiasm of athletes, fans, Toronto Globe and Mail, Aug. 9, 1976

Peace Arch Games

Full slate of events set near Peace Arch, Seattle Times, July 2, 1987

Prince de Asturias Olympic Youth Rally

First Prince de Asturias Olympic Youth rally, Olympic Review, 1991, No. 281/ 282, p. 141.

Renaissance Games

Doyle, Daniel, Renaissance Games seek a proper mix, NCAA News, Apr. 27, 1998

Robin Hood Games

Robin Hood Games Web Site, 1997.

Socialist Olympics

Kisses and tears dot Olympic Games, New York Times, Aug 12, 1936

1,100 French flee Barcelona revolt. Athletes and fans home after fighting curtails visit for Workers' Olympics, New York Times, July 24, 1936

Kruger, Arnd; Riordan, James, The Story of Worker Sport, Human Kinetics, Champaign Ill., 1996

Worker Olympics to be held in Europe, New York Times, May 17, 1936

Nine athletes selected. Will compete for U.S. in People's Olympics in Barcelona, New York Times, July 2, 1936

Paine, Ralph, The Gospel of the Turn Verein, Outing Magazine, May 1905

Steinberg, David, Workers' Sport and the United Front, Arena Review 4(1), Feb. 1980, pgs. 1–6

Americans took part in Barcelona fight. Athletes in Spain for Popular Olympics tell at Paris of Urging Solidarity, New York Times, July 28, 1936

Wagner, Jonathan, Prague's socialist Olympics of 1934, Canadian Journal of the History of Sport. Vol XXIII No 1, May 1992, pgs. 1–18

Foreign left athletes cheer fight on rebels, New York Times, July 24, 1936

South African Games

Lapchick, Richard, Militant International opposition to Apartheid Sport and the Resulting Isolation of South Africa: 1969–May 1970, The Politics of Race and International Sport, Greenwood Press, Westport CT, 1975

South American Games

South American Games postponed, IOC Newsletter, March 6, 1998

The First Sports Games of the Southern Cross, Olympic Review, Mar–Apr 1979, pg. 111

1998 South American Games Web Site, 1998

South Asian Federation Games

SAF games get off to a colourful start tomorrow, Pakistan Times, Dec. 19, 1993

SAF Games close in colourful ceremony, Pakistan Times, Dec. 29, 1993

Self-Immolation in Support of Eelam Tamils, The Hindu & The India Information Inc., Dec. 16, 1995

VII SAF Games Inauguration today, The Hindu & The India Information Inc., Dec. 18, 1995

India predict gold rush at SAF Games, Pakistan Times, Dec. 20, 1995

High time for PHF to ponder over follies after SAF Games debacle, Pakistan Times, Dec. 28, 1995

Irregularities alleged in SAF Games village construction, The Hindu & The India Information Inc., Aug. 27, 1996

Nepal to host 1999 South Asian Games, Reuters News Service, Oct. 12, 1998

Kapadia, Novy, India leads in South Asian Games, India Abroad, Dec 29, 1995

Biswas, Chittaranjan, Fourth South Asian Federation Games 20th to 27th October 1989, Olympic Review, 1989, pg. 398

Biswas, Chittaranjan, Islamabad welcomes South Asia, Olympic Review, Jan 1990, pgs. 50–51

South East Asian Games

Extravaganza closes 18th SEA Games, Pakistan Times, Dec. 19, 1995

Southeast Asian Games: Civil strife takes toll on Cambodian athletes, Agence France Press, Oct. 19, 1997

Regional Games and International events 10th South East Asian Games, Olympic Review, 1979, pg. 471

Four medalists fail drug tests, Associated Press, Oct. 28, 1997

Crowds intimidate at Asian Games, Reuters News Service, Oct. 17, 1997

Soccer stampede feared, Agence France Press, Oct. 15, 1997

Talmadge, Eric, Rowdy fans stop soccer final, Associated Press, Oct. 18, 1997

Indonesia increases security, Agence France Press, Oct. 18, 1997

South East Asian Games, Olympic Review, 1989, pg. 264

Athletics: SEA Games kicks off in Military Precision, Agence France Press, Oct. 11, 1997

South Pacific Games

Brooks, Terry, Athletes complaints dying down, Pacific Daily News, Aug. 6, 1975

Dillon, Kathryn Therese, The Historical Development of the South Pacific Games, California State University, Sacramento, December 1975

New Hebrides in '78, Pacific Daily News, Aug. 8, 1975

Guffey, Susan, Games $15,000 mistake, Pacific Daily News, Aug. 2, 1975

Diaz, Tony, SPG opening ceremonies lavish, Pacific Daily News, Aug. 29, 1979

A little politics at the SPG, Pacific Daily News, Sept. 4, 1979

Suva to stage South Pacific Games in 2003, Australian Broadcasting Corporation, Aug. 18, 1997

Ysrael, Catherine, The way it was: Remembering the Fiji Games, The Sunday News–Guam (Pacific daily News), Sept. 4, 1983

Diaz, Tony, Laughter, gaiety herald SPG opening, Pacific Daily News, Sept. 7, 1983

Ige, Ron, Opening ceremony kicks off SPG, Pacific Daily News, Sept. 8, 1991

Greenpeace Rainbow Warrior update, Aug. 24, 1995

Official Report 7th South Pacific Games 5th—16th September 1983, 1983 South Pacific Games organizing committee, 1983

South Pacific Mini Games

Third South Pacific Mini Games, Olympic Review, 1990, No. 268, p. 112.

1997 South Pacific Games Web Site, http://www.samoanet.com/spmg/spmg97.htm

Special Olympics Asia-Pacific Games

First-Ever Special Olympics Asia-Pacific Games to take place in Shanghai, China, Special Olympics International, Nov. 4, 1996

Special Olympics Mediterranean Games

Athens, Greece to host First-Ever Special Olympics Mediterranean Games, Special Olympics International, March 30, 1998

Organization will announce Opening of Europe-Eurasia office, Plans for 2000 European Games, Special Olympics International, Sept. 4, 1997

Special Olympics Summer World Games

1995 Special Olympics World Games Fact Sheet, Special Olympics International, 1995

Kelley, Steve, An event too special for anyone to ignore, Seattle Times, June 2, 1991

O'Connor, Debra, Celebrities draw strength and inspiration from athletes, St. Paul Pioneer Press, July 22, 1991

Klobuchar, Jim, Worthwhile gift is a way to keep

alive spirit of Special Olympics, Minneapolis Star Tribune, Dec 12, 1991

Twyman Bessone, Lisa, Little big man, Sports Illustrated, Nov. 11, 1991

Name dispute benches Taiwan, USA Today, July 13, 1983

Kenya prepares for Special Olympics, Daily Nation–Nairobi, July 24, 1987

Special Olympics celebrates 30ths Anniversary, Special Olympics International, July 20, 1998

Mosher, John, Special Olympics Universal Games for the Disabled, Olympic Review, 1991, pgs. 380–383

Jordanian athletes to join Israelis at Special Olympics National Games, Special Olympics International, April 25, 1996

Lister, Harry, Torchbearer carries flame that his father helped light, USA Today, July 31, 1987

Special Olympics Tanzania to host Regional Games, Athlete Congress, April 1, 1997

Special Olympics Winter World Games

Rinehart, Steve, City wins Winter Special Olympics, Anchorage Daily News, Nov. 21, 1997

DePalma, Anthony, Special Winter Games warm hearts in Toronto, New York Times, Feb. 10, 1997

Stockholm Summer Games Web Site, 1997–1998

Stoke Mandeville Wheelchair Games

Scruton, Joan, Forty Years' History in the Development of Sport for the Disabled as founded at Stoke Mandeville Hospital, Aylesbury, England, Dec. 1991

Tailteann Games

Banquet will open Tailteann Games, New York Times, July 15, 1928

Tailteann Games: An Irish Festival, London Times, Aug. 7, 1928

Stanaland, Peggy, The Fair of Carman: A further Reflection of Ancient Ireland's Affinity to Sport, NAASH Proceedings 1982, 1982, pgs. 6–7

Stanaland, Peggy, The Tailteann Games of Ancient Ireland: Their origin, growth and continuity through centuries of Unwritten history, NAASH Proceedings 1977, 1977, pgs. 7–8

Stanaland, Peggy, Some Commonalities of Two Ancient Fairs: Aenoch Tailteann and the Olympic Games, NAASH Proceedings 1979, 1979, pg. 10

Third Tailteann Games Dublin, New York Times, Wood Printing Works, Dublin, 1932

U.S. Wins 4 events in Tailteann Games, New York Times, Aug. 17, 1928

Politics divide Irish on Tailteann Games; Free state is seeking 1936 Olympic Contest, New York Times, Aug. 26, 1928

Queen Tailte returns to Dublin. Tailteann Games opened with Pageantry. Cardinal MacRory welcomes world competitors., Irish Times, June 30, 1932

Athletic Carnival at Croke Park. Many well known runners competing., Irish Times, Aug. 15, 1928

Tailteann Games competitions. Dramatic Art and Dancing, Irish Times, July 7, 1932

Dublin Prepares for Tunney's Visit, New York Times, July 1, 1928

The Tailteann Games. Keen competition anticipated in boxing section., Irish Times, June 28, 1932

Tailteann Games will begin today, New York Times, Aug. 11, 1928

West African University Games

Amin, Mohamed, West African University Games statistics

West Asian Games

Tehran hosts West Asian Games, Tehran Times, June 22, 1997

Lebanon Olympic Committee Web Site, 1998

West Asian Games swimming results, Tehran Times, Nov. 24, 1997

Turkmenistan to Actively participate in West Asian Games, Tehran Times, Nov 13, 1997

Sports inseperable from Economic, cultural and political issues, Tehran Times, Nov. 20, 1997

Western Asiatic Games

First Western Asiatic Games, New Delhi 1934, Official Report. Lahore, India: Western Asiatic Foundation, 1934.

Winter Pan-American Games

Robbins, Paul, Pan American Winter Games, Olympian, Dec. 1990, pg. 45

1st Pan-American Winter Games, Olympic Review, 1990, pg. 390

Winter Sports (Pan American Winter Games), Seattle Times, Aug. 4, 1993

Winter Paralympic Games

Innsbruck once again site of Winter World Games for Disabled, Olympic Review, 1988, pgs. 53–55

First Asian Winter Paralympics ends, Agence France Press, March 15, 1998

Skier battles monkey in dorm, Agence France Press, March 3, 1998

In Lillehammer, the show goes on with the Paralympics, Olympic Review, 1994, pgs. 218–221

Winter Games for the disabled, Olympic Review, 1983

Winter World University Games

Muju-Chonju Winter Universiade ends; Japan 1st in Medal Tally after winning Ski jump, Women's Slalom, Korea Herald, Feb. 3, 1997

Winter X Games

Gold sponsorships for Inaugural Winter X Games sold out, ESPN.com, Aug. 6, 1996

Crested Butte selected to host Winter X, ESPN.com, Sept. 10, 1997

ESPN Winter X Games to return to Crested Butte, ESPN.com, Oct. 28, 1998

Winter X Games Website 1997–2000 www.espn.com

Women's Global Challenge

Donatelli, Joe, Women's athletics rising to the challenge, Scripps Howard News Service, Aug. 13, 1998

Washington to host Women's sport event, Associated Press, Oct. 14, 1997

Women's Sports Foundation Website

World Air Games

King Juan Carlos backs World Air Games, July 1998, 2001 World Air Games Organizing Committee press release

World Air Games News, February 1997

First World Air Games, Air Sports International, Jan. 1998

World Corporate Games

Wyatt, Jack, Weekend warriors get down to business, Honolulu Star Bulletin, Sept. 26, 1990

World Culture and Sports Festival

World Culture and Sports Festival III, prnews wire, Nov.12, 1997

World Dwarf Games

Dummer, Gail, 1993 World Dwarf Games, March 13, 1997

Babwin, Don, Dwarfs standing tall at tailor-made games, Chicago Tribune, July 6, 1993

Brown, Janet, 1997 World Dwarf Games statistics, Oct. 7, 1997

Brown, Janet, World Dwarf Games Update, SportsSource Vol. 10, pg. 6

World Equestrian Games

New Zealand Golden at Games, Associated Press, Oct. 4, 1998

The Equestrian Times Web Site, 1998

Willis, Grania, ACOG hit by more flak, Irish Times, July 26, 1996

Federation Equestre Internationale, Federation Equestre Internationale

World Equestrian Games, 1994, Federation Equestre Internationale

World Equestrian Games, Stockholm, Federation Equestre Internationale, 1990

World Equestrian Games, IOC Olympic News, Oct. 2, 1998

World Games

Parachuting and Skydiving at the World Games: Lahti 1997, Air Sports International, Jan 1998

World Games, Olympic Review, 1989, pg. 344

Meuret, Jean-Louis, The World Games gain momentum, Olympic Review, 1989, pgs. 474–476

Litsky, Frank, Something New in Sports: World Games, New York Times, May 3, 1981

Anderson, Dave, Next Year—The World Games, New York Times, July 20, 1981

Barnes, Simon, Game for more than a laugh, London Times, July 20, 1985

Pryce, Robert, Nobody died except for the laughter, London Times, Aug. 6, 1985

Pryce, Robert, Benefactor faces costly bill, London Times, July 30, 1985

Meuret, Jean-Louis, Intense Competition in the Hague, Olympic Review, 1993, pgs. 456–459

World Games for the Deaf

Tweede Int. Sportspelen voor Dooven, Nieuwe Amsterdamsche Courant, Aug. 19, 1928

Tweede Int. Sportspelen voor Dooven, Nieuwe Amsterdamsche Courant, Aug. 18, 1928

Burns, S. Robey, International Games Revival, Silent Worker, Nov. 1948, pgs. 26–28

Tenth Deaf Olympic Games open with Parade at Maryland Today, Washington Post, June 27, 1965

Russia Ties US in Deaf Games, with 53 medals, but leads in gold, Washington Post, July 4, 1965

Deaf Olympics start here today, Washington Post, June 28, 1965

International Committee for sports for the Deaf (CISS), Olympic Review, 1983

Official Results from the 15th World Games for the Deaf, Los Angeles 1985, 1985

Stewart, David, Deaf Sport, Gallaudet University, 1991

History of the CISS, www.gallaudet.edu

World Games for the Deaf (Summer) Honour Roll of Medal Winners 1924–1981, www.gallaudet.edu

1997 World Games for the Deaf Web Site, 1997

Samaranch snub angers deaf sportsmen, Agence France Presse, July 8, 1997

14th Winter World Games for the Deaf Web Site, 1998

World Masters Games

Christie, James, Powerlifting not a Games sport, Toronto Globe and Mail, Aug. 22, 1985

Australia's largest international sporting event still to come, June 6, 1994, University of Queensland website

Masters athletes cycling around licence problem, Toronto Globe and Mail, Aug. 15, 1985

Eggers, Kerry, Fosbury will compete with no fear of flop, The Oregonian, Aug. 12, 1998

Christie, James, Boring Masters lack thrilling Olympic decadence, Toronto Globe and Mail, Aug. 16, 1985

Christie, James, Powerlifters upset over medal ruling, Toronto Globe and Mail, Aug. 23, 1985

Christie, James, 8,500 athletes set for Masters Games, Toronto Globe and Mail, Aug. 7, 1985

Christie, James, Glittery show opens Games, Toronto Globe and Mail, Aug. 8, 1985

Masters Games underway, Associated Press, Aug. 10, 1998

Samuelson enjoys life Olympics, Associated Press, Aug. 10, 1998

International Masters Games Association Web Site

1998 Nike World Masters Games projected to produce in excess of $100 million revenue for State of Oregon, World Masters Games organizing committee Press Release, Aug. 9, 1996

Bachman, Rachel, Games will begin today, but open on Sunday, The Oregonian, Aug. 9, 1998

Games grants begrudged, Toronto Globe and Mail, Aug. 15, 1985

World Medical Games

17th World Medical Games Web Site

Going for the Gold, American Medical News, Sept. 1, 1997

Green, Michael, Doctor, my pulse is racing, London Times, June, 18, 1978

18th World Medical Games Brochure, World Medical Games Federation, 1997

Contact, World Medical Games Federation, Nov. 1998

Contact, World Medical Games Federation, 1997

Ryan, Allan, World Medical Games held at Cannes, The Physician and Sportsmedicine, Aug 1978

World Nature Games

World Nature Games, IOC Newsletter, Sept. 26, 1997

World Nature Games 1997 Website, 1997

World Peace Games

5th World Peace Games Website Dubai 1998, 1995

C'est Open!, L'Opinion-Rabat, July 22, 1989

World Police and Fire Games

Results World Police and Fire Games Melbourne 1995

1995 World Police and Fire Games Website, 1995

1987 World Police and Fire Games Statistics, 1987

1989 World Police and Fire Games Statistics, 1989

1991 World Police and Fire Games Statistics, 1991

1993 World Police and Fire Games Statistics, 1993

1995 World Police and Fire Games Statistics, 1995

Results World Police and Fire Games Colorado Springs 1993, 1993

Results World Police and Fire Games Calgary 1997, 1997

These are your games. (Official registration book), 1998

World Police and Fire Games 16–24 July 1999, 1998

1999 World Police and Fire Games Website, 1998

1997 World Police and Fire Games Statistics, 1997

Toneguzzi, Mario, Regina investigator's experience shows police always on duty, Calgary Herald, June 28, 1997

1997 World Police and Fire Games Website, 1997

World Scholar Athlete Games

White, Carolyn, Scholar-athlete Games foster good will, USA Today, July 3, 1997

World Transplant Games

1997 World Transplant Games Web Site http://www.transweb.org/people/recips/lifepost/athletics/world_games/97/index.htm

World Transplant Games Federation Website http://www.wtgf.org/

XI World Transplant Games program, Sydney World Transplant Games Organizers, 1997

World University Games

University Games in Paris, London Times, Aug. 7, 1928

Les Jeux Universitaires, Le Matin–Paris, Aug. 12, 1928

La Derniere Journee des Jeux Olympiques, Le Matin–Paris, Aug. 12, 1928

Au Meeting d'Athletisme de Colombes. Ben Johnson le sprinter noir americain bat le records du monde des

Les Jeux Universitaires, Le Matin–Paris, Aug. 13, 1928

University Games in Paris: Great Britain represented strongly, London Times, Aug. 13, 1928

University Games in Paris: The British Athletic Team, London Times, Aug. 14, 1928

Les Jeux Sportifs Universitaires, Le Matin–Paris, Aug. 14, 1928

La manifestation d'ouverture des Jeux Universitaires de Paris, Le Matin–Paris, Aug. 15, 1928

University Games in Paris: The Athletic Contests, London Times, Aug. 15, 1928

Les Jeux Universitaires, Le Matin–Paris, Aug. 16, 1928

University Games in Paris: British Victories in Track Events, London Times, Aug. 16, 1928

University Games in Paris: French and British Successes, London Times, Aug. 17, 1928

Les Jeux Universitaires de Paris. L'italie remporte le tournoi de football, Le Matin–Paris, Aug. 19, 1928

French Explanation: Recall of Italian Delegation, London Times, Aug. 23, 1928

Fascist Athletes Abroad: "The Sacred Flame of Passion," London Times, Aug. 23, 1928

Fascist Athletes Incident: French Feeling, London Times, Aug. 25, 1928

Ban on Foreign Wines, London Times, Aug. 27, 1928

International Universities Games, London Times, July 24, 1930

University Games in Germany, London Times, Aug. 11, 1930

University Games in Germany, London Times, Aug. 12, 1930

100 metres plats, Le Matin–Paris, Aug. 23, 1937

Les Jeux Universitaires Internationaux, Le Matin–Paris, Aug. 23, 1937

Les championnars universitaires internationaux, Le Matin–Paris, Aug. 25, 1937

Les Jeux Universitaires Internationaux, Le Matin–Paris, Aug. 29, 1937

La dernier journee d'Athletisme aux Jeux Universitaires Internationaux, Le Matin–Paris, Aug. 30, 1937

East German fans bolt party line with boos for Russia's Athletes, New York Times, Aug. 16, 1951

Third University games open next Sunday, Egyptian Gazette–Cairo, August 7, 1953

World University Games; Record attempt fails, London Times, Sept. 6, 1957

Student fencers do well; Hungary take five of eight events, London Times, Sept. 10, 1957

2,000 athletes due at Games in Turin, New York Times, Aug. 7, 1959

Red athletes barred. Italy won't give Chinese and Korean Students Visas, New York Times, Aug. 19, 1959

Kuznetsov tops his world mark, New York Times, Sept. 4, 1959

Lebanese forfeit game, New York Times, Sept. 5, 1959

Universiade 1961 Sofia, Editions D'Etat Meditsina I Fiskoultoura—Sofia, 1961

Les Jeux Universitaires Mondiaux se sont ouverts, hier, a Sofia, Le Jour–Beirut, Aug. 26, 1961

Eliott, Berutti et les Francais, grands absents des jeux universitaires de Sofia, Le Monde–Paris, Aug. 26, 1961

Valeri Brumel veut tenter 2m 27 aujourd'hui A Sofia, Le Jour–Beirut, Aug. 31, 1961

La cloture des Jeux Universitaires de Budapest. Ter-Ovanesian (8 m. 19 en longeur), Le Monde–Paris, Aug. 31, 1965

Profitant du forfait de Bob Schul le Japonais Sawaki remporte le 5,000 metres, Le Monde–Paris, Aug. 29, 1965

Probable: Au Bresil l"universiade 1963, Le Jour–Beirut, Aug. 30, 1961

L'American Wall a pris sa revanche sur Belits-Gueiman dans le 1500 metres nage libre, Le Monde–Paris, Aug. 26, 1965

Il ne faut pas tomber dans le travers des Jeux Olympiques declare la fondateur des Universiades, Le Monde–Paris, Aug. 29, 1965

WUGs (Olga Korbut), New York Times, Aug. 10, 1973

Reception is hostile to Israel, New York Times, Aug. 16, 1973

Soviet Athletes dominate: Jewish fans are barred, New York Times, Aug. 19, 1973

20 Jews in clash at Moscow Games; Russian fans of the Israeli team are set upon after basketball contest, New York Times, Aug. 22, 1973

Shabad, Theodore, US and Cuban fives in brawl in Moscow, New York Times, Aug. 23, 1973

Jewish Congress hits Soviet on Games, New York Times, Aug. 23, 1973

Cuba: We we're at fault—We're sorry, New York Times, Aug. 24, 1973

Soviet terms Attacks at Games the doing of overzealous fans, New York Times, Aug. 27, 1973

Stoytchev, Vladimir, Universiad 77, Olympic Review, 1977, pgs. 552–553

Stelele Universiadei, 1981

Soviets dominating medals race, USA Today, July 5, 1983

Campana, Roch, 13th Universiad Kobe, Olympic Review, 1985, pgs. 720–721

Mecanovic, Ivan, Zagreb welcomes the XIVth Summer Universiade, Olympic Review, pg. 274–277

Students of the World at Zagreb, Olympic Review, 1987 pg. 544

Campana, Roch, Universiade in Duisburg: Positive Balance, Olympic Review, 1989, pgs. 46–47

Universiade in Duisburg, Olympic Review, 1989, pgs. 48–50

World University Games could become top event for Amateurs, NCAA News, April 12, 1989

The Reconversion Universiade, Olympic Review, 1991, pgs. 557–560

Demak, Richard, Run Aground: Lebanese swimmers were hung out to dry, Sports Illustrated, July 29,1991

Positive Test from Student Games, Pakistani Times, Sept. 5, 1991

World University Games Buffalo 93, Guide to the Games for the FISU family, guests and Observers.

Buffalo's World Games looking like financial bust, Vancouver Sun, July 5, 1993

Games have tight security, Seattle Times, July 6, 1993

Dream comes true for women soccer players, Vancouver Sun, July 8, 1993

70,000 fill Buffalo stadium to watch opening ceremonies, Vancouver Sun, July 9, 1993

Pitcher yells 'Asylum' and leaps fence, Seattle Times, July 11, 1993

Brady, Erik, University Games drop Gender test, USA Today, July 15, 1993

University Games owes $3 Million, Seattle Times, June 9, 1994

University Games: Japan shines, but Games fail to excite, Associated Press, Sept. 3, 1995

1995 World University Games official website, 1995 http://universiade.fjct.fit.ac.jp/en/global/index.html

Global Village No. 1,2,3,4, 5, 1995 World University Games online Newsletter, 1995

Summer Universiade 1997 in Sicily, FISU Press Release, June, 11, 1996

Ormezzano, Gian Paolo, Universiade; Round and About, FISU, 1996

Sicily scolds Greek minister over mafia comments, Reuters News Service, Aug. 13, 1997

Fendrich, Howard, University Games could affect Rome's 2004 hopes, Associated Press, Aug. 18, 1997

Fendrich, Howard, Organizational flaws mar start of University Games, Associated Press, Aug. 19, 1997

US Squad ready for World University Games, NCAA News, June 30, 1993

Pickle, P. David, Finch: World U. Games likely to cool on U.S. as host, NCAA News, Sept. 27, 1993

University Games in Trouble, Agence France Presse, July 30, 1997

Sicily to probe alleged Mafia involvement in Games, Reuters News Service, Aug. 22, 1997

Problems hit World Student Games, Reuters News Service, Aug. 22, 1997

Fendrich, Howard, Cuba brings best to University Games, Associated Press, Aug. 25, 1997

1997 World University Games Web Site, 1997 http://www.sicily.cres.it/universiade/indice.html

FISU Website http://www.ulb.ac.be//assoc/fisu/index.html and http://www.fisu.net

World Wheelchair Games

In my view; World Wheelchair Games, Korea Herald, Aug. 30, 1997

Rosen, Norman, The Role of Sports in Rehabilitation of the Handicapped Part 1B, Maryland State Medical Journal, March 1973, pgs. 11–12

Rosen, Norman, The Role of Sports in Rehabilitation of the Handicapped Part 2B, Maryland State Medical Journal, June 1973, pgs. 78–80

Guttman, Sir Ludwig, Development of Sport for the Spinal Paralysed, part II, Olympic Review, 1977, pgs. 179–182

Guttman, Sir Ludwig, The value of sport for the physically handicapped, Olympic Review, 1977, pgs. 16–20, 45

Rosen, Norman, The Role of Sports in Rehabilitation of the Handicapped Part 2A, Maryland State Medical Journal, May 1973, pgs. 63–66

World Wheelchair Games Program, International Stoke Mandeville Wheelchair Sports Federation, 1997

World Youth Games

Riordan, James, Sport, politics and communism, Sport and foreign policy, Manchester University Press, Manchester, 1991, 128–130

Two Weeks in August. East German youth strays West, Background, Office of Public Affairs, Department of State, Sept. 1951

Zatopek, toujours plus fort sur 5,000m, Paris Le Monde, Aug. 7, 1953

Vass, Nathan, Youth Games may not get off starting blocks, Sydney Morning Herald, Jan. 7, 1997

Official Moscow World Youth Games Web Site, 1998

Samaranch satisfied with Moscow's facilities, Agence France Presse, January 17, 1998

Moscow Mayor opens Youth Games, Associated Press, July 13, 1998

Youth Games close in Moscow, Agence France Press, July 20, 1998

X Games

Brooker, Kevin Way inside ESPN's X Games, 1998, Hyperion/ESPN Books

Stein, Jeannine, Extremists Extraordinaire, Los Angeles Times, July 24, 1995

Sandomir, Richard, Restraining Order is sought against ESPN's X Games, New York Times, May 29, 1997

Norcross, Don, X Gamers risk life and limb, Copley News Service, June 19, 1998

Fifth annual X Games set for June, ESPN .com, Sept. 30, 1998

Brazil to host first X Games qualifiers in Latin America, ESPN.com, Oct. 1, 1998

X Games Website 1996–2000 www.espn .com

Index

581